MICHELIN®
ROAD ATLAS
Europe

First published in Great Britain 1988 by
Paul Hamlyn, an imprint of Reed Consumer Books Limited
Michelin House, 81 Fulham Road, London SW3 6RB
and Auckland, Melbourne, Singapore and Toronto

Fourth edition 1993
First impression 1993

A catalogue record for this book is available from the
British Library.

ISBN Hardback 0 600 57750 3
ISBN Softback 0 600 57749 X

Printed in Great Britain

MICHELIN®
ROAD ATLAS
Europe

MICHELIN®
Touring Services

PAUL HAMLYN

Michelin

MICHELIN tyres and road maps have a reputation unsurpassed throughout Europe for quality and technical excellence in their respective fields.

It is appropriate that, at a time when the twelve member states of the European Economic Community are preparing for a single European market in 1993, Michelin should provide a new Road Atlas of Europe, compiled from their authoritative cartography, designed to meet the needs of the professional driver and holidaymaker alike.

There are over a hundred pages of mapping in this Atlas, showing the road network from North Cape to Gibraltar and from the Atlantic to the Black Sea. A full range of symbols show road categories and widths, towns and cities and places of interest as well as numerous other details, in keeping with Michelin's reputation for accuracy, legibility and up-to-date information.

Seventy town plans are included to help the driver negotiate built-up areas and the 'Driving in Europe' section provides details of national motoring regulations which are useful to know when crossing national frontiers. The comprehensive index locates about 30 000 towns and features.

The map showing 'Climates in Europe' will assist travellers in deciding which is the best season to visit a particular country.

The indispensable road mapping can be used in conjunction with other Michelin publications which provide complementary information on accommodation and sightseeing. The Red Guides, in particular the 'Europe' volume which contains a selection of hotels and restaurants in major European cities, and the Green Guides to the various countries of Europe are ideal companions for this Atlas.

Michelin are always happy to receive suggestions and comments from readers of their publications; taking these into account when preparing new editions can only improve their service to the public.

Thank you in advance and have a good journey!

MICHELIN maps and guides complement one another: use them together!

Contents

Inside front cover

Key to symbols

IV Michelin

VI **Route Planning**

X **Distances in Europe**

XII **Driving in Europe**

1 **Key to symbols**

2 **Western Europe** at a scale of 1: 1 000 000

78 **Greece** at a scale of 1: 700 000

94 **Scandinavia** at a scale of 1: 1 500 000

110 **Eastern Europe** at a scale of 1: 3 000 000

116 **Index of place names**

Channel Tunnel

133 Calais Terminal

142 Folkestone Terminal

Inside back cover

Climates in Europe

Plans of cities and principal towns

118 Amsterdam	**136** Dijon	**156** Lausanne	**175** Oslo
120 Antwerpen	**138** Dublin	**157** Liège	**69** Palermo
86 Athina	**138** Düsseldorf	**158** Lille	**178** Paris
122 Barcelona	**139** Edinburgh	**159** Lisboa	**182** Porto
123 Basel	**140** Essen	**162** Liverpool	**183** Praha
124 Belfast	**141** Firenze	**160** London	**62** Roma
125 Berlin	**143** Frankfurt a. M.	**164** Luxembourg	**186** Rotterdam
126 Bern	**145** Genève	**163** Lyon	**190** Salzburg
127 Birmingham	**145** Genova	**165** Madrid	**193** Sevilla
126 Bologna	**144** Gent	**166** Manchester	**194** Stockholm
128 Bonn	**146** Glasgow	**33** Marseille	**195** Strasbourg
129 Bordeaux	**147** Göteborg	**167** Milano	**196** Stuttgart
46 Bremen	**46** Hamburg	**168** Monaco	**198** Torino
130 Brugge	**149** Hannover	**169** München	**199** Toulouse
131 Bruxelles-Brussel	**107** Helsinki	**172** Nantes	**201** Valencia
	151 Istanbul	**65** Napoli	**202** Venezia
130 Budapest	**153** København	**173** Nice	**205** Wien
137 Den Haag	**154** Köln	**174** Nürnberg	**207** Zürich

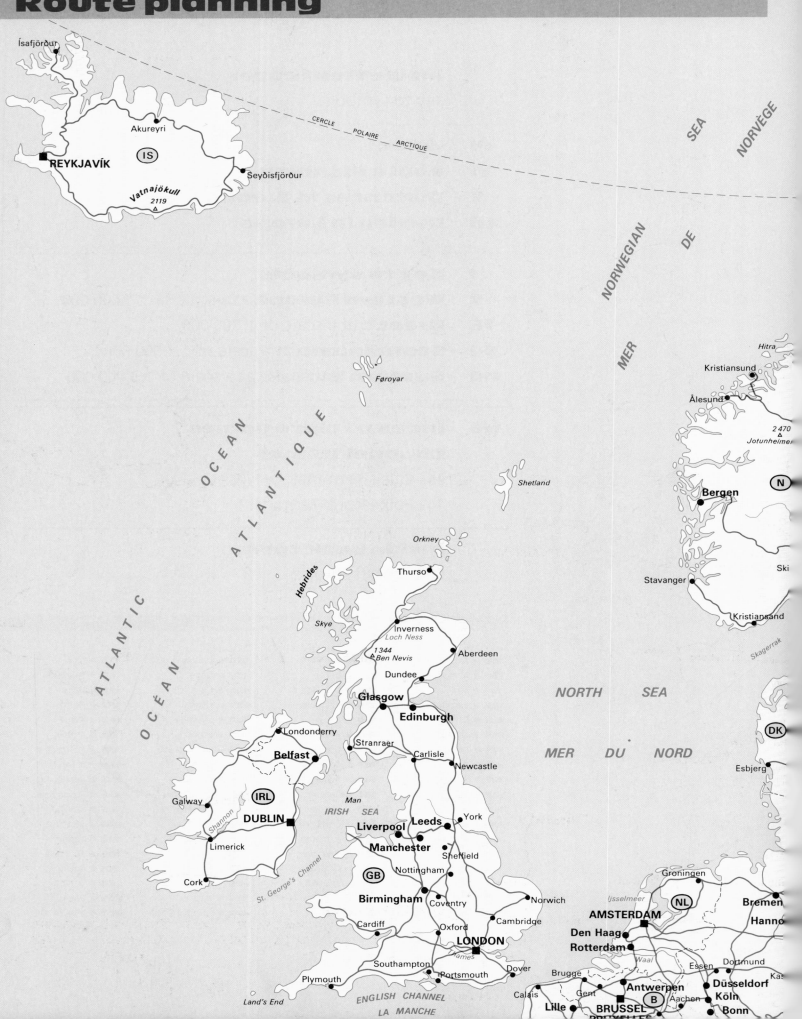

Nordkapp

MER DE BARENTS
BARENTS SEA

Kanin Poluostrov

Hammerfest

Kirkenes

Murmansk

Tromsø

Ivalo

Inarijärvi

L A P L A N D

Kol'skij Poluostrov

ARCTIC CIRCLE

Mezen

Narvik

Kiruna

△ 2111
Kebnekaise

Lofoten

Vesterålen

Kousomen'

WHITE
MER BLANCHE
SEA

Bodø

Malmberget

Kuusamo

Kem'

Archangel'sk

Mo i Rana

Rovaniemi

Tornionjoki

Kemi

Dønna

Luleå

Oulu

Oulujärvi

Severnaja Dvina

BOTHNIA
BOTNIE

Pielinen

S

Umeå

SF

Kuopio

Joensuu

Petrozavodsk

Oneżskoje Oz.

Trondheim

Östersund

Vaasa

Jyväskylä

Saimaa

Ładozskoje oz.

Vologda

Sundsvall

GULF
DE
GOLFE

Tampere

Päijänne

Čerepovec

Mora

Pori

Lahti

St Peterburg

Lillehammer

Gävle

Turku

HELSINKI

FINLAND
DE
FINLANDE

Rybinskoje Vdchr.

Rybinsk

OSLO

Uppsala

Dalälven

Åland

GULF
GOLFE DE

Tver'

Moss

Västerås

STOCKHOLM

Saaremaa

TALLINN

EW

Čudskoje Oz.

Novgorod

Sergiev
Posad

Örebro

BALTIC SEA

Pskov

Norrköping

Linköping

Vättern

Gotland

*Rižskij
Zaliv*

MOSKVA

jerikshavn

Göteborg

Jönköping

RĪGA

LR

Daugava

ROS

Kalmar

Öland

Vitebsk

borg

Kattegat

Smolensk

BENHAVN

Malmö

LT

Klaipéda

Mogil'ov

Br'ansk

Or'ol

ense

Sjælland

Bornholm

ROS

Kaunas

VILNIUS

MINSK

Lolland

Rügen

Kaliningrad

Nemunas

RB

Gomel'

Rostock

Gdańsk

Lübeck

mburg

Szczecin

Toruń

Wisła

Prip'at

Černigov

Desna

Dnepr

BERLIN

Poznań

WARSZAWA

Brest

COMMUNAUTÉ DES ÉTATS INDÉPENDANTS
COMMONWEALTH OF INDEPENDENT STATES

Magdeburg

Odra

PL

Łódź

Lublin

KIJEV

Erfurt

Leipzig

Dresden

Wrocław

Częstochowa

UKR

Žitomir

Poltava

*Kremenčugskoje
Vdchr.*

MER BALTIQUE

MER
BLANCHE

Volga

Elbe

Oder

Glomma

Vänern

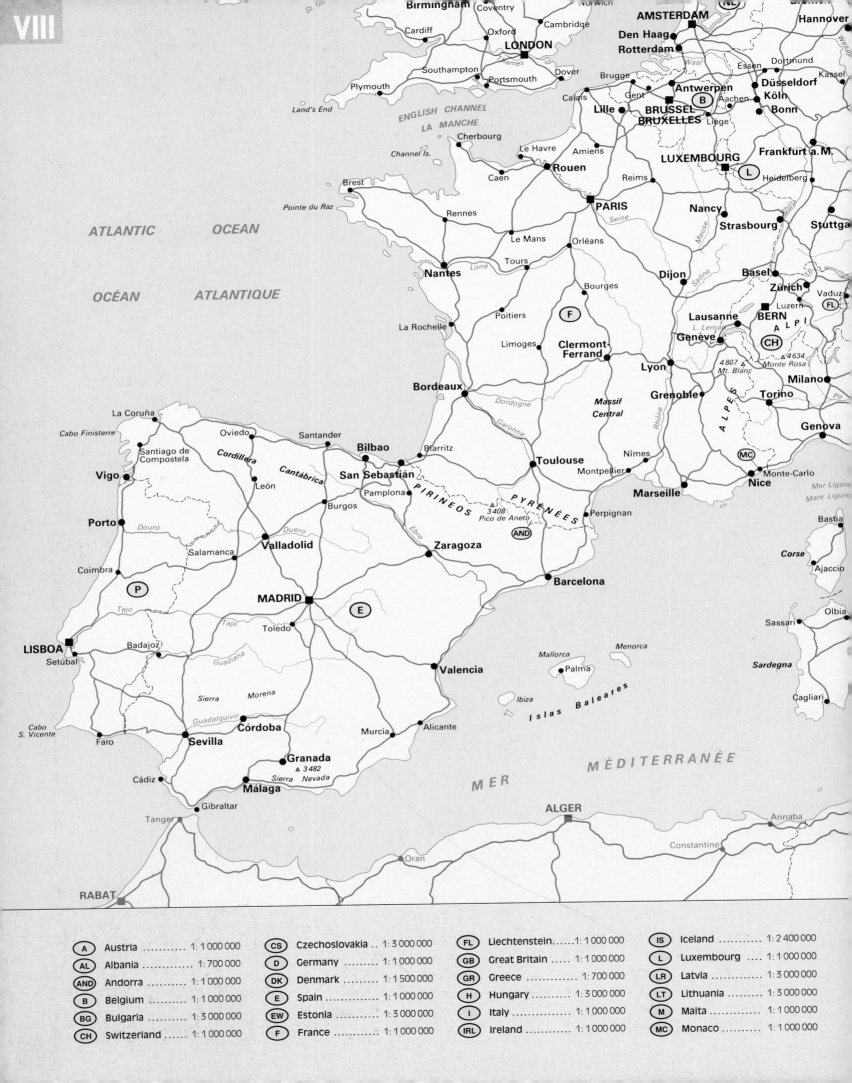

Birmingham Coventry Norwich AMSTERDAM (NL) Hannover

Cardiff Oxford Cambridge Den Haag Essen Dortmund

Southampton LONDON Rotterdam Düsseldorf Kassel

Plymouth Portsmouth Dover Brugge Antwerpen Köln

Land's End Cherbourg ENGLISH CHANNEL Calais Gent (B) Aachen Bonn

LA MANCHE Le Havre Amiens Lille BRUSSEL Liège

Channel Is. Rouen BRUXELLES LUXEMBOURG Frankfurt a. M.

Brest Caen Reims (L) Heidelberg

Pointe du Raz Rennes PARIS Nancy Strasbourg Stuttga

ATLANTIC OCEAN Le Mans Orléans Seine Dijon Basel

Tours Saône Zürich Vaduz

Nantes Loire Bourges (FL)

OCÉAN ATLANTIQUE Poitiers (F) Lausanne BERN ALPI

La Rochelle Limoges Clermont- Genève (CH) △4634 Monte Rosa

Ferrand Lyon 4807 △ Milano

Bordeaux Dordogne Massif Mt. Blanc

La Coruña Santander Central Rhône Grenoble Torino

Cabo Finisterre Oviedo Bilbao Biarritz Nîmes Genova

Santiago de Cordillera Cantábrica San Sebastián PIRINEOS Toulouse (MC)

Compostela León Pamplona PYRÉNÉES Montpellier Monte-Carlo

Vigo Burgos Marseille Nice

Porto Douro Duero Ebro Zaragoza 3408 △ Perpignan Mer Ligure

Valladolid Pico de Aneto (AND) Mare Ligure

Salamanca Barcelona Corse

Coimbra Ajaccio

(P) MADRID Tejo Toledo (E) Mallorca Menorca Olbia

LISBOA Tajo Palma Sassari Sardegna

Setúbal Badajoz Valencia

Guadiana Ibiza Islas Baleares Cagliari

Sierra Morena

Guadalquivir Córdoba Murcia Alicante

Cabo Sevilla MÉDITERRANÉE

S. Vicente Faro Granada △3482

Cádiz Sierra Nevada MER

Málaga

Gibraltar ALGER Annaba

Tanger Oran Constantine

RABAT

(A) Austria 1:1 000 000	(CS) Czechoslovakia .. 1:3 000 000	(FL) Liechtenstein......1:1 000 000	(IS) Iceland 1:2 400 000
(AL) Albania 1:700 000	(D) Germany 1:1 000 000	(GB) Great Britain 1:1 000 000	(L) Luxembourg 1:1 000 000
(AND) Andorra 1:1 000 000	(DK) Denmark 1:1 500 000	(GR) Greece 1:700 000	(LR) Latvia 1:3 000 000
(B) Belgium 1:1 000 000	(E) Spain 1:1 000 000	(H) Hungary 1:3 000 000	(LT) Lithuania 1:3 000 000
(BG) Bulgaria 1:3 000 000	(EW) Estonia 1:3 000 000	(I) Italy 1:1 000 000	(M) Malta 1:1 000 000
(CH) Switzerland 1:1 000 000	(F) France 1:1 000 000	(IRL) Ireland 1:1 000 000	(MC) Monaco 1:1 000 000

Distance chart — European cities (km)

Amsterdam	
Athina	2836
Barcelona	1547 3090
Bari	1971 2621 1792
Basel	745 2466 1029 1226
Belfast	1341 3874 2046 2690 1508
Beograd	1718 1118 1972 1503 1348 2756
Bergen	1817 4017 3178 3244 2187 3112 2899
Berlin	669 2584 1853 1811 862 1906 1466 1463
Bilbao	1424 3422 607 2124 1174 1755 2304 3196 1990
Birmingham	782 3316 1487 2131 950 535 2198 2554 1348 1196
Bordeaux	1081 3240 633 1942 831 1412 2122 2853 1647 334 853
Brest	1098 3501 1242 2278 1096 1244 2383 2870 1664 965 686 627
Brussel/Bruxelles	204 2792 1365 1777 551 1150 1674 1969 781 1229 591 886 903
Bucuresti	2221 1238 2611 2142 1987 3259 639 3200 1711 2943 2701 2761 2886 2177
Budapest	1393 1510 1952 1482 1073 2431 392 2372 883 2283 1873 2041 2058 1349 828
Clermont-Ferrand	902 2752 648 1485 477 1337 1634 2636 1311 706 779 365 808 706 2273 1614
Dublin	1053 3586 1758 2402 1220 165 2468 2824 1618 1467 247 1124 956 862 2971 2143 1049
Dubrovnik	2024 1265 2049 1580 1425 2892 525 3204 1771 2381 2333 2199 2480 1970 1164 787 1711 2604
Edinburgh	1289 3823 1994 2638 1457 251 2705 3061 1855 1703 484 1360 1193 1098 3208 2380 1286 416 2840
Firenze	1391 2115 1075 720 646 2098 997 2664 1231 1407 1539 1225 1686 1197 1636 976 883 1810 1074 2046
Frankfurt A. M.	446 2396 1318 1553 327 1549 1278 1864 566 1502 991 1159 1176 402 1781 953 776 1261 1583 1498 973
Genève	885 2446 770 1203 259 1492 1328 2446 1121 1102 934 682 1081 703 1967 1307 310 1204 1405 1441 611 586
Göteborg	1005 3205 2366 2432 1375 2300 2087 812 651 2384 1742 2041 2058 1157 2388 1560 1824 2012 2392 2249 1852 1052 1634
Hamburg	441 2780 1802 2007 811 1736 1662 1384 289 1820 1178 1477 1494 593 2026 1198 1260 1448 1967 1685 1427 488 1070 572
Hannover	386 2637 1659 1864 668 1623 1519 1527 288 1707 1065 1364 1381 498 2022 1194 1117 1335 1824 1572 1284 345 927 715 151
Helsinki	1204 2540 2388 2346 1397 2441 1422 1186 505 2525 1883 2182 2199 1316 1858 1030 1846 2153 1893 2390 1706 1101 1656 662 776 823
Istanbul	2665 1171 2919 2450 2295 3703 947 3846 2413 3251 3145 3069 3330 2621 692 1339 2581 3415 1326 3652 1944 2225 2275 3034 2609 2466 2369
Kijev	2017 2311 3114 2644 2187 3254 1336 2844 1383 3338 2696 2995 3012 2129 1073 1162 2636 2966 1861 3203 2138 1914 2339 2032 1670 1636 1146 489
København	738 2938 2099 2165 1108 2033 1820 1079 384 2117 1475 1774 1791 890 2121 1293 1557 1745 2125 1982 1585 785 1367 267 305 448 795 2767 1765
Köln	264 2579 1342 1714 488 1361 1461 1802 575 1440 803 1097 1114 211 1964 1136 802 1073 1766 1310 1134 189 747 990 426 292 1110 2408 1923 723
Leningrad	1637 2973 2821 2779 1830 2874 1855 1619 938 2958 2316 2615 2632 1749 2625 1463 2279 2586 2326 2823 2199 1534 2089 1095 1209 1256 433 2041 1552 1228 1543
Lille	283 2910 1308 1836 610 1046 1792 2055 849 1139 487 799 716 116 2295 1467 645 758 2088 994 1256 520 669 1243 679 566 1384 2739 2197 976 329 1817
Lisboa	2322 4320 1285 3022 2072 2653 3202 4094 2888 907 2094 1232 1863 2127 3841 3181 1604 2365 3279 2601 2305 2400 2000 3282 2718 2605 3423 4149 4236 3015 2338 3856 2037
Liverpool	971 3504 1676 2320 1138 416 2386 2742 1536 1385 165 1042 874 780 2889 2061 967 167 2522 365 1728 1179 1122 1930 1366 1253 2071 3333 2884 1663 991 2504 676 2283
London	719 3252 1424 2068 886 722 2134 2490 1284 1133 196 790 622 528 2637 1809 715 434 2270 612 1476 927 870 1678 1114 1001 1819 3081 2632 1411 739 2252 424 2031
Luxembourg	391 2637 1148 1560 334 1338 1519 1994 767 1290 779 947 964 218 1993 1165 608 1050 1758 1286 980 248 486 1182 618 484 1302 2466 2115 915 193 1735 334 2188
Lyon	917 2559 630 1292 400 1415 1441 2548 1223 962 857 538 1018 735 2080 1421 172 1127 1518 1364 690 688 151 1736 1172 1029 1758 2388 2548 1469 711 2191 682 1860
Madrid	1812 3760 686 2462 1562 2143 2642 3584 2378 397 1584 722 1353 1617 3281 2622 1094 1855 2719 2091 1745 1890 1440 2772 2208 2095 2913 3589 3726 2505 1828 3346 1527 658
Málaga	2360 4086 1012 2788 2025 2691 2968 4132 2849 945 2132 1270 1901 2165 3607 2948 1644 2403 3045 2639 2071 2314 1766 3320 2756 2643 3384 3915 4110 3053 2376 3817 2075 634
Marseille	1228 2621 493 1323 710 1727 1503 2593 1534 825 1168 648 1218 1046 2142 1483 417 1439 1580 1675 606 999 452 2047 1483 1340 2069 2450 2645 1780 1023 2502 992 1723
Milano	1088 2128 973 878 343 1810 1010 2493 1040 1305 1251 1123 1398 894 1649 989 629 1522 1087 1758 298 670 323 1681 1117 974 1575 1957 2151 1414 831 2008 953 2203
Moskva	2463 3169 3630 3306 2639 3700 2194 2313 1829 3784 3142 3441 3458 2575 1931 1918 3088 3412 2705 3649 2800 2360 2898 1789 2116 2082 1127 1347 858 2211 2369 694 2643 4682
München	837 2063 1370 1224 399 1794 945 2018 585 1615 1236 1272 1421 769 1506 678 918 1506 1184 1743 644 397 599 1206 781 638 1120 1892 1744 939 580 1553 887 2513
Nantes	887 3290 945 1923 847 1168 2172 2659 1453 669 609 325 302 692 2675 1847 465 880 2125 1116 1331 965 726 1847 1283 1170 1988 3119 2801 1580 903 2421 604 1567
Napoli	1878 2602 1562 261 1133 2585 1484 3151 1718 1894 2026 1712 2173 1684 2123 1463 1370 2297 1561 2533 490 1460 1098 2339 1914 1771 2253 2431 2625 2072 1621 2686 1743 2792
Nice	1387 2434 656 1136 658 1886 1316 2808 1355 988 1327 808 1377 1205 1955 1295 577 1598 1393 1834 419 985 478 1996 1432 1289 1890 2263 2457 1729 1146 2323 1152 1886
Nürnberg	666 2171 1427 1391 436 1715 1053 1867 434 1668 1157 1325 1342 622 1556 728 885 1427 1351 1664 811 226 695 1055 610 467 969 2000 1759 788 409 1402 740 2566
Oslo	1321 3521 2682 2748 1691 2616 2403 496 967 2700 2058 2357 2374 1473 2704 1876 2140 2328 2708 2565 2168 1368 1950 316 888 1031 690 3350 2348 583 1306 1123 1559 3598
Palermo	2599 3322 2283 691 1853 3305 2204 3872 2439 2614 2747 2432 2893 2404 2843 2184 2091 3017 2281 3254 1210 2180 1818 3060 2635 2492 2974 3151 3346 2793 2341 3407 2464 3512
Paris	504 2912 1091 1735 553 965 1794 2275 1069 922 407 579 597 308 2297 1469 426 677 1937 914 1143 587 538 1463 899 786 1604 2741 2417 1196 520 2037 221 1820
Porto	2143 4141 1167 2843 1893 2474 3023 3915 2709 728 1915 1053 1684 1948 3662 3002 1425 2186 3100 2422 2126 2221 1821 3103 2539 2426 3244 3970 4057 2836 2159 3677 1858 314
Praha	950 2154 1711 1596 720 1999 1036 1839 350 1952 1441 1609 1626 906 1361 533 1169 1711 1261 1948 1016 510 979 1027 665 603 859 1983 1389 760 693 1292 1024 2850
Roma	1665 2389 1349 449 920 2372 1271 2938 1505 1681 1813 1499 1960 1471 1910 1250 1157 2084 1348 2320 277 1247 885 2126 1701 1558 2040 2218 2412 1859 1408 2473 1530 2579
Rovaniemi	2483 4683 3844 3910 2853 3778 3565 2824 2129 3862 3220 3519 3536 2635 3866 3038 3302 3490 3870 3727 3330 2530 3112 1528 2050 2193 837 4512 2557 1745 3288 1005 2721 4760
Salzburg	980 1932 1539 1172 586 1912 814 2161 535 1952 816 2161 728 1773 1393 1429 1589 535 1076 1586 1052 1900 660 540 924 781 1263 1761 1601 1082 723 1696 1045 2670
Sevilla	2295 4117 1043 2819 2056 2626 2999 4067 2849 880 2067 1205 1836 2100 3638 2979 1577 2338 3076 2574 2102 2345 1797 3255 2691 2578 3415 3946 4141 2988 2311 3848 2010 417
Sofia	2104 818 2358 1889 1734 3142 386 3285 1852 2690 2584 2508 2769 2060 420 778 2020 2854 765 3091 1383 1664 1714 2473 2048 1905 1808 561 1493 2206 1847 2241 2178 3588
Stockholm	1368 3568 2729 2795 1738 2663 2450 1021 1014 2747 2105 2404 2421 1520 2751 1923 2187 2375 2755 2612 2215 1415 1997 497 935 1078 165 3397 2395 630 1353 598 1606 3645
Strasbourg	634 2438 1110 1371 145 1450 1320 2076 751 1264 892 918 1080 429 1881 1053 563 1162 1559 1399 791 216 404 1264 700 557 1286 2267 2076 997 377 1719 549 2162
Stuttgart	622 2302 1258 1404 267 1592 1184 2046 631 1413 1034 1070 1219 558 1745 917 716 1304 1423 1541 824 204 526 1234 670 527 1166 2131 1956 967 365 1599 676 2311
Thessaloníki	2350 511 2604 2135 1980 3388 632 3531 2098 2936 2830 2754 3015 2306 727 1024 2266 3100 779 3337 1629 1910 1960 2719 2294 2151 2054 660 1800 2452 2093 2487 2424 3834
Torino	1154 2263 779 997 409 1699 1145 2596 1157 1110 1140 864 1287 905 1784 1124 492 1411 1222 1647 395 736 252 1784 1220 1077 1692 2092 2286 1517 897 2125 961 2008
Toulouse	1199 2994 388 1696 933 1611 1876 3082 1757 447 1053 244 870 1003 2515 1856 384 1323 1563 1706 979 1222 675 2270 1706 1563 2292 2823 3018 2003 1414 2745 923 1345
Tromsø	3041 5241 4402 4468 3411 4336 4123 1893 2687 4420 3778 4077 4094 3193 4424 3596 3860 4048 4428 4285 3888 3088 3670 2570 2608 2751 1367 5070 3087 2303 3026 1535 3279 5318
Trondheim	1865 4065 3226 3292 2235 3160 2947 717 1511 3244 2602 2901 2918 2017 3248 2420 2684 2872 3252 3109 2712 1912 2494 1394 1432 1575 949 3894 2892 1127 1850 1382 2103 4142
Valencia	1892 3435 361 2137 1374 2391 2317 3523 2198 606 1832 771 1402 1710 2956 2297 993 2103 2394 2339 1420 1663 1115 2711 2147 2004 2733 3264 3459 2444 1687 3166 1653 924
Venezia	1283 1878 1229 760 605 2072 760 2512 1079 1561 1513 1379 1660 1156 1399 739 891 1784 837 2020 254 891 585 1700 1275 1132 1614 1707 1901 1433 1026 2047 1215 2459
Warszawa	1223 2188 2390 2066 1399 2460 1070 2050 589 2544 1902 2201 2218 1335 1506 678 1848 2172 1465 2409 1560 1120 1658 1238 876 842 352 2017 794 971 1129 785 1403 3442
Wien	1150 1862 1833 1341 830 2188 744 2131 642 2141 1630 1798 1815 1106 1071 243 1370 1900 969 2137 835 710 1030 1319 957 951 924 1691 1309 1052 893 1357 1224 3039
Zagreb	1337 1499 1591 1122 967 2375 381 2518 1085 1923 1817 1741 2002 1293 1020 350 1253 2087 618 2324 616 897 947 1706 1281 1138 1287 1328 1512 1439 1080 1720 1411 2821
Zürich	831 2416 1058 1176 86 1594 1298 2267 852 1260 1036 917 1182 637 1816 988 597 1306 1375 1543 596 412 287 1455 891 748 1387 2245 2054 1188 573 1820 696 2158

Distances in Europe

Distances are calculated from centres and along the best roads from a motoring point of view - not necessarily the shortest

Example: **Luxembourg – Warszawa** 1321 km

1321

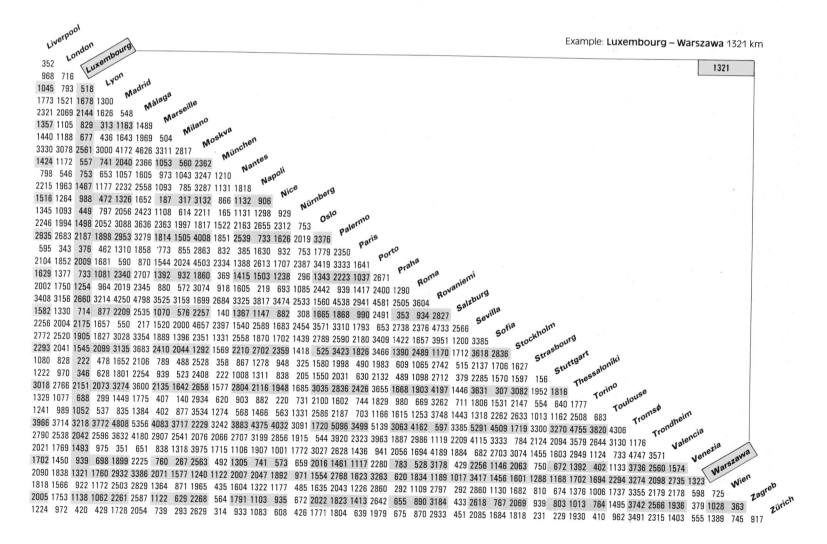

Liverpool
London
352
968 716 — Luxembourg
1045 793 518 — Lyon
1773 1521 1678 1300 — Madrid
2321 2069 2144 1626 548 — Málaga
1357 1105 829 313 1163 1489 — Marseille
1440 1188 677 436 1643 1969 504 — Milano
3330 3078 2561 3000 4172 4626 3311 2817 — Moskva
1424 1172 557 741 2040 2366 1053 560 2362 — München
798 546 753 653 1057 1605 973 1043 3247 1210 — Nantes
2215 1963 1467 1177 2232 2558 1093 785 3287 1131 1818 — Napoli
1516 1264 988 472 1326 1652 187 317 3132 866 1132 906 — Nice
1345 1093 449 797 2056 2423 1108 614 2211 165 1131 1298 929 — Nürnberg
2246 1994 1498 2052 3088 3636 2363 1997 1817 1522 2163 2655 2312 753 — Oslo
2935 2683 2187 1898 2953 3279 1814 1505 4008 1851 2539 733 1626 2019 3376 — Palermo
595 343 376 462 1310 1858 773 855 2863 832 385 1630 932 753 1779 2350 — Paris
2104 1852 2009 1681 590 870 1544 2024 4503 2334 1388 2613 1707 2387 3419 3333 1641 — Porto
1629 1377 733 1081 2340 2707 1392 932 1860 369 1415 1503 1238 296 1343 2223 1037 2671 — Praha
2002 1750 1254 964 2019 2345 880 572 3074 918 1605 219 693 1085 2442 939 1417 2400 1290 — Roma
3408 3156 2660 3214 4250 4798 3525 3159 1699 2684 3325 3817 3474 2533 1560 4538 2941 4581 2505 3604 — Rovaniemi
1582 1330 714 877 2209 2535 1070 576 2257 140 1367 1147 882 308 1665 1868 990 2491 353 934 2827 — Salzburg
2256 2004 2175 1657 550 217 1520 2000 4657 2397 1540 2589 1683 2454 3571 3310 1793 653 2738 2376 4733 2566 — Sevilla
2772 2520 1905 1827 3028 3354 1889 1396 2351 1331 2558 1870 1702 1439 2789 2590 2180 3409 1422 1657 3951 1200 3385 — Sofia
2293 2041 1545 2099 3135 3683 2410 2044 1292 1569 2210 2702 2359 1418 525 3423 1826 3466 1390 2489 1170 1712 3618 2836 — Stockholm
1080 828 222 478 1652 2106 789 488 2528 358 867 1278 948 325 1580 1998 490 1983 609 1065 2742 515 2137 1706 1627 — Strasbourg
1222 970 346 628 1801 2254 939 523 2408 222 1008 1311 838 205 1550 2031 630 2132 489 1098 2712 379 2285 1570 1597 156 — Stuttgart
3018 2766 2151 2073 3274 3600 2135 1642 2658 1577 2804 2116 1948 1685 3035 2836 2426 3655 1668 1903 4197 1446 3631 307 3082 1952 1816 — Thessaloníki
1329 1077 688 299 1449 1775 407 140 2934 620 903 882 220 731 2100 1602 744 1829 980 669 3262 711 1806 1531 2147 554 640 1777 — Torino
1241 989 1052 537 835 1384 402 877 3534 1274 568 1466 563 1331 2586 2187 703 1166 1615 1253 3748 1443 1318 2262 2633 1013 1162 2508 683 — Toulouse
3966 3714 3218 3772 4808 5356 4083 3717 2229 3242 3883 4375 4032 3091 1720 5096 3499 5139 3063 4162 597 3385 5291 4509 1719 3300 3270 4755 3820 4306 — Tromsø
2790 2538 2042 2596 3632 4180 2907 2541 2076 2066 2707 3199 2856 1915 544 3920 2323 3963 1887 2986 1119 2209 4115 3333 784 2124 2094 3579 2644 3130 1176 — Trondheim
2021 1769 1493 975 351 651 838 1318 3975 1715 1106 1907 1001 1772 3027 2628 1436 941 2056 1694 4189 1884 682 2703 3074 1455 1603 2949 1124 733 4747 3571 — Valencia
1702 1450 939 698 1899 2225 760 267 2563 492 1305 741 573 659 2016 1461 1117 2280 783 528 3178 429 2256 1146 2063 750 672 1392 402 1133 3736 2560 1574 — Venezia
2090 1838 1321 1760 2932 3386 2071 1577 1240 1122 2007 2047 1892 971 1554 2768 1623 3263 620 1834 1189 1017 3417 1456 1601 1288 1168 1702 1694 2294 3274 2098 2735 1323 — Warszawa
1818 1566 922 1172 2503 2829 1364 871 1965 435 1604 1322 1177 485 1635 2043 1226 2860 292 1109 2797 292 2860 1130 1682 810 674 1376 1006 1737 3355 2179 2178 598 725 — Wien
2005 1753 1138 1062 2261 2587 1122 629 2268 564 1791 1103 935 672 2022 1823 1413 2642 655 890 3184 433 2618 767 2069 939 803 1013 764 1495 3742 2566 1936 379 1028 363 — Zagreb
1224 972 420 429 1728 2054 739 293 2629 314 933 1083 608 426 1771 1804 639 1979 675 870 2933 451 2085 1684 1818 231 229 1930 410 962 3491 2315 1403 555 1389 745 917 — Zürich

Driving in Europe

Introduction

The information panels which follow give the principal motoring regulations in force when this atlas was prepared for press (1.7.92); an explanation of the symbols is given below, together with some additional notes.

🔧 The name, address and telephone number of the national motoring organisation or organisations; the initials FIA and AIT indicate membership of the international touring associations, the Fédération Internationale de l'Automobile and the Alliance Internationale de Tourisme

⊙ Speed restrictions in kilometres per hour applying to:

🏛 motorways
🏛 dual carriageways
🅰 single carriageways
🏭 urban areas

Where restrictions for 'trailers' or 'towing' are given, it may be assumed that these apply to both trailers and caravans

🍷 The maximum permitted level of alcohol in the bloodstream. This should not be taken as an acceptable level; it is NEVER sensible to drink and drive

🚫 Whether the wearing of seat belts is compulsory

👶 Restrictions applying to children

△ Whether a warning triangle must be carried

🔲 Whether a first aid kit must be carried

💡 Whether a spare bulb kit must be carried

🪖 Whether crash helmets are compulsory for motorcyclists

🏛 Whether tolls are payable on motorways and/or other parts of the road network

⛽ Whether petrol concessions or restrictions apply

⊖ The minimum age for drivers

📄 Documentation required; note that while insurance for driving at home usually provides the legally required minimum third party cover abroad, it will not provide cover against damage, fire, theft or personal accident; for this reason, an International Motoring Certificate (Green Card) is recommended for all countries and essential where 'Green Card required' is given

★ In this section are given any other regulations not falling into the categories above

Andorra

🔧 **Automobil Club d'Andorra FIA,** Babot Camp 13, Andorra-la-Vella Tel: 20-8-90

	🏛	🅰	🏭
⊙	70	70	40 km/h

🍷 0.08%

🚫

👶 Children under 10 years of age not allowed in front seats

△ Recommended (compulsory if vehicle exceeds 3000 kg)

🔲 Recommended

💡 Compulsory

🪖 Compulsory for motorcyclists and passengers

🏛

⛽

⊖ 18

📄 Valid driving licence; Vehicle registration document or Vehicle on hire certificate; Green Card recommended; National vehicle identification plate

Austria

🔧 **Österreicher Automobil-, Motorrad- und Touring Club (ÖAMTC),** FIA & AIT, Schubertring 1-3, 1010 Wien 1 Tel: (01) 711990

	🏛	🏛	🅰	🏭
⊙	100-130		100	50 km/h

If towing trailer over 14.5 cwt:
100   80   50 km/h

If towing trailer under 14.5 cwt:
100   100   100   50 km/h

🍷 0.08%

🚫 Compulsory if fitted for driver and front and rear seat passengers

👶 Children under 12 years of age not allowed in front seats

△ Compulsory

🔲 Compulsory

💡

🪖 Compulsory for motorcyclists and passengers

🏛 Tolls payable on motorways for Brenner (A13), Tauern (part of the A10), and a section of the A9 north of Graz, as well as on certain roads (especially trans-alpine routes) and tunnels

⛽

⊖ 18

📄 Valid driving licence; Vehicle registration document or Vehicle on hire certificate; Green Card recommended; National vehicle identification plate

★ Towing is forbidden on certain alpine routes

Belgium

🔧 **Royal Automobile Club de Belgique (RACB),** FIA, 53 rue d'Arlon, 1040 Bruxelles Tel: (02) 287 09 11

Touring Club Royal de Belgique (TCB), AIT, 128 av. Carton de Wiart 1090 Bruxelles Tel: (02) 233 26 11

Vlaamse Automobilistenbond (VTB-VAB) Sint-Jacobs Markt 45, 2000 Antwerpen Tel: (03) 220 32 11

	🏛	🏛	🅰	🏭
⊙	120	90-120	90	50 km/h

🍷 0.05%

🚫 Compulsory if fitted for driver and front and rear seat passengers

👶 Children under 12 years of age not allowed in front seats unless they are using an approved child's safety seat

△ Compulsory

🔲 Recommended

💡

🪖 Compulsory for motorcyclists

🏛

⛽

⊖ 18

📄 Valid driving licence; Vehicle registration document or Vehicle on hire certificate; Green Card recommended; National vehicle identification plate

Bulgaria

🔧 **Union of Bulgarian Motorists (SBA),** FIA & AIT, 3 Place Pozitano, Sofia 1090 B.P.257 Tel: (02) 86151

	🏛	🏛	🅰	🏭
⊙	120	80	80	60 km/h

🍷 0.0%

🚫 Compulsory if fitted for driver and front seat passengers

👶 Children under 10 years of age not allowed in front seats

△ Compulsory

🔲 Compulsory

💡

🪖 Compulsory for motorcyclists

🏛

⛽ Foreign motorists must buy fuel with coupons available in unlimited quantities at border posts and within Bulgaria

⊖ 18

📄 Valid driving licence or International Driving Permit; Vehicle registration document or Vehicle on hire certificate; Green Card required; National vehicle identification plate

CIS
Belorussia, Moldavia, Russia, Ukraine

🔧 In the event of breakdown or accident contact officer of State Automobile Inspection or nearest office of Intourist (obliged to give tourists assistance)

🏛	🛣	A	🏭
⌚ 90	90	90	60 km/h

🍷 0.0%

🔖 Compulsory if fitted for driver and front seat passengers

👶 Children under 12 years of age not allowed in front seats

△ Compulsory

⊡ Compulsory

💡 Recommended

🧰 Compulsory

🏛 Road tax payable on entry to CIS though some foreign cars exempt

⛽ Petrol coupons recommended; obtainable at border posts

⊖ 18

🪪 Valid driving licence meeting requirements of International Convention on Road Traffic; Vehicle registration document or Vehicle on hire certificate; Car insurance obtainable on entry to CIS at Ingosstrakh offices or at Intourist offices; Itinerary card, service coupons and motor routes map issued by Intourist; Customs obligation to take the car out of the country on departure; National vehicle identification plate

★ Fire extinguisher compulsory

Czechoslovakia

🔧 Ústředni Automotoklub ČSFR, AIT & FIA, Černomořská 9, 101 50 Praha 10
Tel: (02) 746 000

🏛	🛣	A	🏭
⌚ 110	90	90	60 km/h

🍷 0.0%   any alcohol found in the bloodstream may result in prosecution

🔖 Compulsory if fitted for driver and front and back seat passengers

👶 Children under 12 years of age not allowed in front seats

△ Compulsory

⊡ Compulsory

💡 Compulsory

🧰 Crash helmets and goggles compulsory for drivers of motorcycles over 50cc; crash helmets only for passengers

🏛

⛽

⊖ 18

🪪 Valid driving licence; Vehicle registration document or Vehicle on hire certificate; Green Card valid for Czechoslovakia recommended; National vehicle identification plate

Estonia

🔧 Automobile Club: AUTOM Pikk, 41 EE001 Tallinn   Tel: 601-215

🏛	🛣	A	🏭
⌚ 90	90	50	50 km/h

🍷 0.5%

🔖 Compulsory

👶 Children under 16 years of age not allowed in front seats

△ Compulsory

⊡ Compulsory

💡 Recommended

🧰 Compulsory

🏛

⛽

⊖ 18

🪪 Driving licence; Vehicle registration document or Vehicle on hire certificate; assurance

France

🔧 Automobile Club de France, FIA, 6-8 Place de la Concorde, 75008 Paris
Tel: (01) 42 65 34 70

Association Francaise des Automobiles-Clubs (AFA), FIA & AIT, 9 rue Anatole de la Forge, 75017 Paris
Tel: (01) 42 27 82 00

🏛	🛣	A	🏭
⌚ 110-130	110	90	50 km/h
If wet: 100-110	100	80	50 km/h

🍷 0.08% or 0.40 mg per litre of air exhaled

🔖 Compulsory if fitted for driver and front and rear seat passengers

👶 Children under 10 years of age not allowed in front seats

△ Compulsory unless hazard warning lights are fitted; triangle and lights compulsory for cars pulling caravans or trailers and for vehicles greater than 3.5 tons

⊡ Recommended

💡 Recommended

🧰 Compulsory for motorcyclists and passengers

🏛 Tolls payable on most motorways although short urban sections of motorway around Paris and some other major cities are free; tolls also payable on some major bridges and in some tunnels

⛽

⊖ 18

🪪 Valid driving licence; Vehicle registration document or Vehicle on hire certificate; Green Card recommended; National vehicle identification plate

Croatia

🔧 Hrvatski Auto Klub (HAK), AIT & FIA Draskoviceva 25, 41000 Zagreb
Tel: (041) 454433

🏛	🛣	A	🏭
⌚ 120	100	80	60 km/h
If towing: 80	80	80	60 km/h

🍷 0.05%

🔖 Compulsory in the front and back

👶 Children under 12 years of age not allowed in front seats

△ Compulsory

⊡ Compulsory

💡 Compulsory

🧰 Compulsory for motorcyclists and passengers

🏛 Tolls payable on several major roads, Krk Island Bridge and Ucka Tunnel

⛽ Price reduction if payment with convertible currency

⊖ 18

🪪 Valid driving licence; Vehicle registration document or Vehicle on hire certificate; Green Card required; National vehicle identification plate

Denmark

🔧 Forenede Danske Motorejere (FDM), AIT, Firskovvej 32, 2800 Lyngby
Tel: (45) 93 08 00

🏛	🛣	A	🏭
⌚ 110	80	80	50 km/h
If towing: 70	70	70	50 km/h

🍷 0.08%

🔖 Compulsory in front and in back

👶 Children under 3 need not use seat belt. Between 3 and 7 they may use a child's safety seat or booster cushion and seat belt

△ Compulsory

⊡ Recommended

💡

🧰 Compulsory for motorcyclists and passengers

🏛

⛽

⊖ 18

🪪 Valid driving licence; Vehicle registration document or Vehicle on hire certificate; Green Card recommended; National vehicle identification plate

★ Fire extinguisher recommended

Finland

🔧 Autoliitto (Automobile and Touring Club of Finland) (ATCF), FIA & AIT, Kansakoulukatu 10, 00101 Helsinki 10
Tel: (90) 6940022

🏛	🛣	A	🏭
⌚ 100-120		80-100	50 km/h
Towing if trailer has brakes: 80		80	50 km/h
Towing if trailer unbraked: 60		60	50 km/h

🍷 0.05%

🔖 Compulsory if fitted for driver and front and rear seat passengers

👶 Approved safety seats compulsory

△ Compulsory

⊡ Recommended

💡 Recommended

🧰 Compulsory for motorcyclists and passengers

🏛

⛽

⊖ 18

🪪 Valid driving licence; Vehicle registration document or Vehicle on hire certificate; Green Card recommended; National vehicle identification plate

★ Compulsory use of headlights at all times outside built-up areas

Germany

🔧 ADAC - Allgemeiner Deutscher Automobil-Club, FIA & AIT, Am Westpark 8, 8000 München 70
Tel: (089) 76760

Automobil-Club von Deutschland (AvD), FIA, Lyonerstraße 16, 6000 Frankfurt am Main 71
Tel: (069) 66060

🏛	🛣	A	🏭
⌚ 130*	130*	100	50 km/h
If towing: 80	80	80	50 km/h
*recommended			

🍷 0.08%

🔖 Compulsory if fitted for driver and front and rear seat passengers

👶 Children under 12 years of age not allowed in front seats

△ Compulsory

⊡ Compulsory

💡

🧰 Compulsory for motorcyclists and passengers

🏛

⛽

⊖ 18

🪪 Valid driving licence; Vehicle registration document or Vehicle on hire certificate; Green Card recommended; National vehicle identification plate

Great Britain

🔧 **Automobile Association (AA)**, FIA & AIT, Fanum House, Basingstoke, Hampshire RG21 2EA   Tel: (0256) 20123
Royal Automobile Club (RAC), FIA & AIT, RAC House, Bartlett Street, South Croydon CR9 6XW   Tel: (081) 686 0088

🏛	🛣	🅰	🏭
🕐 112	112	96	48 km/h

If towing:
| 96 | 96 | 80 | 48 km/h |

🍷 0.08%

📛 Compulsory if fitted for driver and front and rear seat passengers

🧒 Children under 1 year of age travelling in front seat must be strapped in or placed in an approved child's safety seat

△

⊡ Recommended

⚲

🅒 Compulsory for motorcyclists and passengers

🏛 Tolls payable on certain major bridges and tunnels

⛽

⊖ 17

🪪 Valid driving licence; Vehicle registration document or Vehicle on hire certificate; Green Card recommended; National vehicle identification plate

★ Drive on the left!

Hungary

🔧 **Magyar Autóklub (MAK)**, FIA & AIT, Rómer Flóris utca 4a, Budapest 11
Tel: (01) 115 2040

🏛	🛣	🅰	🏭
🕐 120	100	80	50-60 km/h

If towing:
| 80 | 70 | 70 | 50 km/h |

🍷 0.0%   if the alcohol test changes colour, the driver is taken to a hospital for a blood test and his driving licence confiscated

📛 Compulsory if fitted for driver and front seat passengers

🧒 Children under 6 years of age not allowed in front seats

△ Compulsory

⊡ Compulsory

⚲ Compulsory

🅒 Compulsory for motorcyclists and passengers

🏛

⛽

⊖ 18

🪪 Valid driving licence; Vehicle registration document or Vehicle on hire certificate; Green Card strongly recommended; National vehicle identification plate

Ireland

🔧 **Automobile Association (AA)**, FIA & AIT, 23 Suffolk Street, Dublin 2
Tel: (01) 779481
Royal Automobile Club (RAC), FIA & AIT, 34 Dawson Street, Dublin 2
Tel: (01) 775141

🏛	🛣	🅰	🏭
🕐 88	88	64-88	48 km/h

If towing:
| 56 | 56 | 56 | 48 km/h |

🍷 0.10%

📛 Compulsory if fitted for driver and front seat passengers

🧒 Children under 12 years of age not allowed in front seats unless strapped in or placed in a child's safety seat

△ Recommended

⊡ Recommended

⚲ Recommended

🅒 Compulsory for motorcyclists and passengers

🏛 Toll payable on two bridges over River Liffey in Dublin

⛽

⊖ 17

🪪 Valid driving licence; Vehicle registration document or Vehicle on hire certificate; Green Card recommended; National vehicle identification plate

★ Drive on the left!

Latvia

🔧 **Transporta Ministrija** Brivibas iela 58, Riga   Tel: 226 922

🏛	🛣	🅰	🏭
🕐	100	100	60 km/h

🍷 0.05%

📛 Compulsory if fitted for driver and front seat passengers

🧒 Children under 12 years of age not allowed in front seats

△ Compulsory

⚲

🅒

🏛

⛽

⊖ 18

🪪 Driving licence; Vehicle registration document

Greece

🔧 **The Automobile and Touring Club of Greece (ELPA)**, FIA & AIT, 2-4 Messogion, 115 27 Athina   Tel: (01) 779 1615
Hellenic Touring Club, AIT, 12 Politehniou, 104 33 Athina
Tel: (01) 524 0854

🏛	🛣	🅰	🏭
🕐 100	80	80	50 km/h

🍷 0.05%

📛 Compulsory for driver and front seat passengers

🧒 Children under 10 years of age not allowed in front seats

△ Compulsory

⊡ Compulsory

⚲

🅒 Compulsory for motorcyclists

🏛 Tolls payable on most 'national' roads

⛽

⊖ 18

🪪 Valid international driving licence; Vehicle registration document or Vehicle on hire certificate; Green Card required; National vehicle identification plate

★ Fire extinguisher compulsory

Iceland

🔧 **Felag Islenskra Bifreidaeigenda (FIB)**, FIA & AIT, Borgatun 33, 105 Reykjavik
Tel: (01) 62 99 99

🏛	🛣	🅰	🏭
🕐 80	80-90	80-90	50 km/h

🍷 0.05%

📛 Compulsory for driver and front seat passengers; rear seat belts recommended

🧒 Children in rear seats must be strapped in or placed in a child's safety seat

△ Compulsory

⊡ Recommended

⚲ Recommended

🅒 Compulsory for motorcyclists and passengers

🏛

⛽

⊖ 17

🪪 Driver's passport; Valid driving licence; Vehicle registration document or Vehicle on hire certificate; Green Card, valid for Iceland, required; Temporary importation permit; National vehicle identification plate

★ Vehicle mud flaps compulsory; headlights compulsory at all times; vehicles with diesel engines are subject to a special charge on entry to Iceland

Italy

🔧 **Automobile Club d'Italia (ACI)**, FIA & AIT, Via Marsala 8, 00185 Roma
Tel: (06) 49981
Touring Club Italiano (TCI), AIT, Corso Italia 10, 20122 Milano   Tel: (02) 85261

🏛	🛣	🅰	🏭
🕐 110*-130	110*-130	90	50 km/h

If towing:
| 110*-130 | 110*-130 | 90 | 50 km/h |
* for vehicles up to 1100 cc

🍷 Severe penalties for drinking and driving

📛 Compulsory in front (and in back if installed)

🧒 Children under 12 not allowed in front unless seat is fitted with child restraint system

△ Compulsory

⊡ Recommended

⚲ Compulsory

🅒 Compulsory for motorcyclists and passengers

🏛 Tolls payable on most motorways

⛽ Coupons at a discount available at RAC, AA, and Port Offices and frontier Automobile Clubs to personal callers; must be paid for in foreign currency

⊖ 18

🪪 Valid driving licence (translation in Italian recommended); Vehicle registration document or Vehicle on hire certificate; Green Card recommended; Temporary importation document; National vehicle identification plate

Lithuania

🔧 **Automobilininku Klubas**, 2001 Gynéju 8   Tel: 614602

🏛	🛣	🅰	🏭
🕐 130	130	110	50-70 km/h

🍷 0.00%

📛 Compulsory if fitted for driver and front and rear seat passengers

🧒 Children under 12 years of age not allowed in front seats

△ Compulsory

⊡ Compulsory

⚲ Recommended

🅒 Compulsory

🏛

⛽ Petrol coupons recommended; obtainable at border posts

⊖ 18

🪪 Valid driving licence; Visa; Passport; Green Card (insurance must be taken out at frontier if no Green Card); National identification plate

Luxembourg

Automobile Club du Grand Duché de Luxembourg (ACL), FIA & AIT, 54 route de Longwy, 8007 Bertrange Tel: (012) 45 00 45

🏛	🛣	A	🏭
120	90	90	60 km/h

If towing:
| 90 | 75 | 75 | 60km/h |

🍷 0.08%

Compulsory if fitted for driver and front and rear seat passengers

Children under 10 years of age allowed in front seats if vehicle is equipped with child's safety seat

△ Compulsory

[ ] Recommended

Compulsory

The purchasing, selling and transporting of petrol in drums or jerrycans is prohibited

⊖ 18

Valid driving licence; Vehicle registration document or Vehicle on hire certificate; Green Card recommended; National vehicle identification plate

Norway

Kongelig Norsk Automobilklub (KNA), FIA, Drammensveien 20c, 0201 Oslo 2 Tel: (02) 56 19 00

Norges Automobil-Forbund (NAF), AIT, Storgata 2, 0155 Oslo 1 Tel: (02) 34 15 00

🏛	🛣	A	🏭
80-90	80-90	80-90	50 km/h

If towing trailer with braking system:
| 80 | 80 | 80 | 50 km/h |

If towing trailer without braking system:
| 60 | 60 | 60 | 50 km/h |

🍷 0.05%

Compulsory if fitted for driver and front and rear seat passengers

Children are allowed in front if seat is fitted with child restraint system and seat and belt can be adapted to their size

△ Compulsory

[ ] Recommended

Recommended

Compulsory for motorcyclists and passengers

Tolls payable on some new major roads

⊖ 18 or 20 depending on the type of vehicle

Valid driving licence; Vehicle registration document or Vehicle on hire certificate; Green Card recommended; National vehicle identification plate

★ Dipped headlights compulsory at all times

Portugal

Automóvel Club de Portugal (ACP), FIA & AIT, Rua Rosa Araújo 24, 1200 Lisboa Tel: (01) 3563931

🏛	🛣	A	🏭
120	90	90	60 km/h

If towing:
| 100 | 70 | 70 | 50 km/h |

🍷 0.05%

Compulsory if fitted for driver and front seat passengers outside built-up areas

Children under 12 years of age not allowed in front seat

△ Compulsory

[ ] Recommended

Recommended

Compulsory for motorcyclists

Tolls payable on some motorways and bridges

⊖ 18

Valid driving licence; Vehicle registration document or Vehicle on hire certificate; Green Card required; National vehicle identification plate

★ Vehicle mud flaps are compulsory

Slovenia

Zveza Slovenije (AMZS) Dunajska 128 Ljubljana   Tel: 3861/181111

🏛	🛣	A	🏭
80-120	80-100	80	60 km/h

If towing:
| 80 | 80 | 80 | 60 km/h |

🍷 0.05%

Compulsory if fitted for driver and front and rear seat passengers

Children under 12 years of age not allowed in front seats

△ Compulsory

[ ] Compulsory

Compulsory

Compulsory for motorcyclists and passengers

Tolls on major motorways and the Karavanke tunnel

⊖ 18

Valid driving licence; Vehicle registration document or Vehicle on hire certificate; Green Card required; National vehicle identification plate

Netherlands

Koninklijke Nederlandsche Automobiel Club (KNAC), FIA, Westvlietweg 118, Leidschendam Tel: (070) 399 74 51

Koninklijke Nederlandsche Toeristenbond (ANWB), AIT, Wassenaarseweg 220, Den Haag Tel: (070) 314 71 47

🏛	🛣	A	🏭
100-120	100	80	50 km/h

If towing:
| 80 | 80 | 80 | 50 km/h |

🍷 0.05%

Compulsory if fitted for driver and front and rear seat passengers

Children under 12 years of age allowed in front if seat is fitted with child restraint system; in the back children under 3 years must use child's safety seat

△

[ ] Recommended

Compulsory for motorcyclists and passengers

Tolls payable on: Zeeland Brug, Kiltunnel (from Dordrecht to Hoekse Waard) and Prins Willem Alexander Brug

⊖ 18

Valid driving licence; Vehicle registration document; Green Card recommended; National vehicle identification plate

Poland

Polski Zwiazek Motorowy (PZM), FIA & AIT, Kazimierzowska 52, 02-514 Warszawa 12   Tel: (022) 492067/492751

Auto Assistance, 63 Allée Jerozolimskie 00-950 Warszawa Tel: (022) 628-6254/ 628-6255/ 210-789

🏛	🛣	A	🏭
110	90	90	60 km/h

If towing:
| 70 | 70 | 70 | 60 km/h |

🍷 0.02%

Compulsory for driver and front seat passengers; compulsory if fitted in the back

Children under 10 years of age not allowed in front seats

△ Compulsory

[ ] Recommended

Recommended

Compulsory for motorcyclists and passengers

In exchange for zlotys (PLZ) in currency

⊖ 17

Valid driving licence or International Driving Permit; Vehicle registration document or Vehicle on hire certificate; Green Card, valid for Poland, required; National vehicle identification plate

★ Between 1/11 and 1/3 dipped headlights compulsory at all times

Romania

In the event of breakdown or accident contact **Automobile-Club roumain**, FIA & AIT Strada Tache Ionescu 27, Bucureşti Tel: (400) 155510

🏛	🛣	A	🏭
70-90*	60-90*	60-90*	60 km/h

*according to cylinder capacity

🍷 0.0%   any alcohol found in the bloodstream may result in immediate imprisonment

Compulsory if fitted

Children under 14 years of age not allowed in front seats

△ Compulsory

[ ] Compulsory

Recommended

Compulsory for motorcyclists and passengers

Tolls payable on some major routes (Bucharest-Constanta)

⊖ 18

Valid driving licence; Vehicle registration document or Vehicle on hire certificate; Green Card, valid for Romania, required; National vehicle identification plate

Spain

Real Automóvil Club de España (RACE), FIA & AIT, José Abascal 10, 28003 Madrid   Tel: (91) 447 3200

🏛	🛣	A	🏭
120	120	90-100	50 km/h

If towing:
| 80 | 80 | 70-80 | 50 km/h |

these limits are increased by 20 km/h for overtaking

🍷 0.08%

Compulsory for driver and passengers

Children under 12 years of age not allowed in front seats

△ Compulsory

[ ] Recommended

Compulsory

Compulsory for motorcyclists

Tolls payable on motorways and Cadi tunnel

⊖ 18

International Driving Permit required if 'pink' EC licence not held; Vehicle registration document or Vehicle on hire certificate; Green Card required; Bail Bond strongly recommended; National vehicle identification plate

Sweden

🔧 Motormännens Riksförbund (M), AIT, Sturegatan 32, Stockholm
Tel: (08) 7 82 38 00

🚋	🛣	🅰	🏭
90-110	70-110	70-110	50 km/h

If towing with braking device:
70 70 70 50 km/h
If towing with no braking device:
40 40 40 40 km/h

🍷 0.02%

💺 Compulsory if fitted for driver and front and rear seat passengers

🛆 Special safety seats compulsory for children under 8 years of age

△ Compulsory

⊡ Recommended

💡

🏍 Compulsory for motorcyclists and passengers

🚋

💡

⊖ 18

🗐 Valid driving licence; Vehicle registration document or Vehicle on hire certificate; Green Card required; National vehicle identification plate

★ Dipped headlights compulsory at all times

Switzerland

🔧 Automobile Club de Suisse (ACS), FIA, Wasserwerkgasse 39, 3000 Bern 13
Tel: (031) 22 47 22

Touring Club Suisse (TCS), AIT, 9 rue Pierre-Fatio, 1211 Genève 3
Tel: (022) 737 12 12

🚋	🛣	🅰	🏭
120	80	80	50 km/h

If towing – up to 20 cwt trailer:
80 80 80 50 km/h
If towing – over 20 cwt trailer:
60 60 60 50 km/h

🍷 0.08%

💺 Compulsory if fitted for driver and front seat passengers

🛆 Children under 7 years of age not allowed in front seats

△ Compulsory

⊡

💡

🏍 Compulsory for motorcyclists and passengers

🚋 Vignette compulsory: obtainable from frontier posts, post offices or garages; separate vignette required for trailer or caravan

💡

⊖ 18

🗐 Valid driving licence; Vehicle registration document or Vehicle on hire certificate; Green Card; National vehicle identification plate

Turkey

🔧 Turkiye Turing ve Otomobil Kurumu (TTOK), FIA & AIT, Halaskargasi Cad. 364, 80222 Sisli, Istanbul   Tel: (01) 1314631/6

🚋	🛣	🅰	🏭
	90	90	50 km/h

If towing:
70 70 40 km/h

🍷 0.05%

💺 Compulsory if fitted for driver and front seat passengers

🛆 Children under 12 years of age not allowed in front seats

△ Two must be carried – one to place in front of the vehicle, one behind

⊡ Compulsory

💡

🏍 Compulsory for motorcyclists

🚋 Tolls payable on some roads

💡

⊖ 18

🗐 Passport; Valid driving licence; International Driving Permit advised, compulsory if driving Turkish vehicle (obtainable at frontier with 2 photos and 54 000 Turkish Lire); Vehicle registration document or Vehicle on hire certificate; Green Card required – must cover European and Asian regions; National vehicle identification plate

★ Fire extinguisher, chock and towrope compulsory

Yugoslavia

🔧 Auto-Moto Savez Jugoslavija (AMSJ), FIA & AIT, Ruzveltova 18, 11001 Beograd
Tel: (011) 401699

🚋	🛣	🅰	🏭
120	100	80	60 km/h

If towing:
80 80 80 60 km/h

🍷 0.05%

💺 Compulsory if fitted for driver and rear seat passengers

🛆 Children under 12 years of age not allowed in front seats

△ Compulsory – two are necessary if towing trailer or caravan

⊡ Compulsory

💡 Compulsory

🏍 Compulsory for motorcyclists and passengers

🚋 Tolls payable on several major roads

💡 Concessionary petrol coupons available at frontier posts for purchase with convertible currency; unused coupons refundable at place of purchase

⊖ 18

🗐 Valid driving licence; Vehicle registration document or Vehicle on hire certificate; Green Card required; National vehicle identification plate

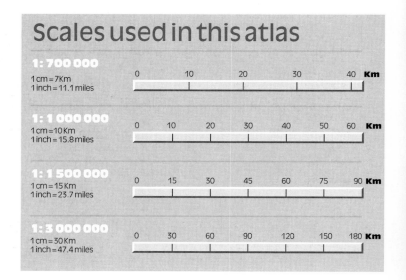

Scales used in this atlas

1: 700 000
1 cm = 7 Km
1 inch = 11.1 miles

0 10 20 30 40 **Km**

1: 1 000 000
1 cm = 10 Km
1 inch = 15.8 miles

0 10 20 30 40 50 60 **Km**

1: 1 500 000
1 cm = 15 Km
1 inch = 23.7 miles

0 15 30 45 60 75 90 **Km**

1: 3 000 000
1 cm = 30 Km
1 inch = 47.4 miles

0 30 60 90 120 150 180 **Km**

Signos convencionales

Para más información ver el interior de la cubierta anterior

Importancia de los itinerarios

Autopista con calzadas separadas
con calzada única
Autovía con calzadas separadas
Número de acceso
Accesos: completo – medio acceso
parcial – sin precisión
Carretera de comunicación internacional o nacional asfaltada:
calzadas separadas
4 carriles – 3 carriles
2 carriles anchos – 2 carriles
Carretera de comunicación interregional asfaltada:
calzadas separadas
2 carriles o más – 2 carriles estrechos
Sin asfaltar: transitable, con macadán
Otra carretera asfaltada – sin asfaltar
Autopista, carretera en construcción
(en su caso: fecha de entrada en servicio)

Distancias en kilómetros (totales o parciales)

en autopista:
tramo de peaje
tramo libre
en carretera
GB e IRL: en millas
en kilómetres

Transporte

Línea férrea – Tren-coche
Barcaza – Barcaza (DK, N, S, SF)
Enlace marítimo: permanente – de temporada
Aeropuerto

Zeichenerklärung

Vollständige Zeichenerklärung siehe Umschlaginnenseite

Verkehrsbedeutung der Straßen

Autobahn mit getrennten Fahrbahnen
mit nur einer Fahrbahn
Schnellstraße mit getrennten Fahrbahnen
Nummer der Anschlußstelle
Anschlußstellen: Autobahnein- und/oder
-ausfahrt – ohne Angabe
Internationale bzw. nationale Hauptverkehrsstraße mit Belag:
getrennte Fahrbahnen
4 Fahrspuren – 3 Fahrspuren
2 breite Fahrspuren – 2 Fahrspuren
Überregionale Verbindungsstraße mit Belag:
getrennte Fahrbahnen
2 u. mehr Fahrspuren – 2 schmale Fahrspuren
Ohne Belag: befahrbar, mit Makadam
Sonstige Straßen: mit Belag, ohne Belag
Autobahn, Straße im Bau
(ggf. Datum der Verkehrsfreigabe)

Entfernungsangaben in Kilometern (Gesamt- und Teilentfernungen)

auf der Autobahn:
gebührenpflichtiger Abschnitt
gebührenfreier Abschnitt
auf anderen Straßen
in GB und IRL: in Meilen
in Kilometern

Transport

Bahnlinie – Autoreisezug
Fähre – Fähre (DK, N, S, SF)
Schiffsverbindung: ganzjährig – während der Saison
Flughafen

Légende

Voir la légende complète à l'intérieur de la couverture

Importance des itinéraires

Autoroute à chaussées séparées
à une seule chaussée
Double chaussée de type autoroutier
Numéro d'échangeur
Echangeurs: complet – demi-échangeur
partiel – sans precision
Route de liaison internationale ou nationale revêtue:
chaussées séparées
4 voies – 3 voies
2 voies larges – 2 voies
Route de liaison interrégionale revêtue:
chaussées séparées
2 voies et plus – 2 voies étroites
Non revêtue: carrossable, en macadam
Autre route revêtue – non revêtue
Autoroute, route en construction
(le cas échéant: date de mise en service)

Distances en kilomètres (totalisées et partielles)

sur autoroute:
section à péage
section libre
sur route
GB et IRL: en miles
en kilomètres

Transport

Voie ferrée –Train-auto
Bac – Bac (DK, N, S, SF)
Liaison maritime: permanente – saisonnière
Aéroport

Segni convenzionali

Vedere la legenda completa all'interno della copertina

Importanza degli itinerari

Autostrada a carreggiate separate
a carreggiata unica
Doppia carreggiata di tipo autostradale
Numero dello svincolo
Svincoli: completo – semi-svincolo
parziale – non precisato
Strada di comunicazione internazionale o nazionale rivestita:
a carreggiate separate
a 4 corsie – a 3 corsie
a 2 corsie larghe – a 2 corsie
Strada di comunicazione interregionale rivestita:
a carreggiate separate
a 2 corsie e più – a 2 corsie strette
Non rivestita: carrozzabile, in macadam
Altre strade con rivestimento – senza rivestimento
Autostrada, strada in costruzione
(se del caso: data di apertura prevista)

Distanze in chilometri (totali e parziali)

su autostrada:
tratto a pedaggio
tratto esente da pedaggio
su strada
GB e IRL: in miglia
in chilometri

Trasporti

Ferrovia – trasporto automobili per ferrovia
Su chiatta – su chiatta (DK, N, S, SF)
Collegamento via-traghetto: tutto l'anno – stagionale
Aeroporto

Verklaring der tekens

Zie voor de volledige verklaring der tekens de binnenzijde van het omslag

Belang van het wegennet

Autosnelweg met gescheiden rijbanen
met één rijbaan
Dubbele rijbaan van het type autosnelweg
Nummer knooppunt/aansluiting
Knooppunten/aansluitingen: volledig – half
gedeeltelijk – niet nader aangegeven
Internationale of nationale verharde verbindingsweg:
gescheiden rijbanen
4 rijstroken – 3 rijstroken
2 brede rijstroken – 2 rijstroken
Regionale verharde verbindingsweg:
gescheiden rijbanen
2 of meer rijstroken – 2 smalle rijstroken
Onverhard: berijdbaar, macadamweg
Andere weg: verhard – onverhard
Autosnelweg, weg in aanleg
(indien van toepassing: datum openstelling)

Afstanden in kilometers (totaal en gedeeltelijk)

op de autosnelweg:
gedeelte met tol
tolvrij gedeelte
op de weg
GB en IRL: in mijlen
in kilometers

Vervoer

Spoorweg – Autotrein
Veerpont – Veerpont (DK, N, S, SF)
Scheepvaartverbinding : permanent – alleen in het seizoen
Luchthaven

Key to symbols

A full key to symbols appears inside the front cover

Road classification

Motorway: dual carriageway
single carriageway
Dual carriageway with motorway characteristics
Interchange number
Interchange: complete – half
limited – unspecified
International and national surfaced road network:
dual carriageway
four lanes – three lanes
two wide lanes – two lanes
Interregional surfaced road network:
dual carriageway
two lanes or more – two narrow lanes
Unsurfaced: suitable for vehicles, macadam
Other surfaced road – unsurfaced
Motorway, road under construction
(where available: with scheduled opening date)

Distances in kilometres (total and intermediate)

on motorway:
toll section
free section
on other roads
GB and IRL: in miles
kilometres

Transportation

Railway – Motorail
Ferry – Ferry (DK, N, S, SF)
Car ferry: all the year – seasonal
Airport

3

D · E · F

ORKNEY ISLANDS

Westray
Pierowall
The North Sound
North Ronaldsay
Westray Firth
Kettletoft
Sanday
Rousay
Brough Head
38
A 987   A 986
Eday
Stronsay Firth
Mainland
Shapinsay
Stronsay
15
A 965   A 966
Stromness   Stenness   Kirkwall
20   A 964   A 960   10
A 961
Skaill
Rora Head   479
Lyness
Scapa Flow
Skaill
St Margaret's Hope
Hoy   21
South Ronaldsay
Burwick
Pentland Firth
Aberdeen

SHETLAND ISLANDS

Herma Ness
Haroldswick   11
A 968   Unst
Gutcher   Belmont
Isbister   Fetlar
450
Mid Yell
18   A 968
Hillswick   A 970   Ulsta   Yell
Toft   17
A 968
St. Magnus Bay   A 970   10
Muckle Roe   Laxo
Papa Stour   Voe   Whalsay
Sandness   A 970
Walls   31   A 971   Mainland
Whiteness
Foula   418
Scalloway   Bressay
Lerwick
293   Tørshavn [Færøerne]
Seydisfjördur
Bergen
Aberdeen
27
Sumburgh
Sumburgh Head
217   Fair I.

Strathy Point   Dunnet Head
Scrabster   Duncansby Head
Bettyhill   Melvich   Thurso   Dunnet   A 836   John o' Groats
27   A 836   16   A 882   Castletown   17
B 876
Roadside   A 9
Reiss
290   Noss Head
A 897   A 885   21   A 882   Wick
39   24   17
A 9
B 871
Kinbrace   706
Morven   20
A 897
206   Helmsdale
128
A 9
21   Brora
Golspie
Dornoch
Dornoch Firth
Tarbat Ness
Tain
Moray Firth
Cromarty
gordon
Lossiemouth
Nairn   A 941   Elgin   Buckie   Cullen   Kinnairds Head
10   13   A 96   A 98   61   Banff   Macduff   Fraserburgh
Forres   Fochabers   23   98   12   B 9031
39   A 940   13   A 941   17   21   A 95   26   A 98   Rattray Head
63   A 839   Rothes   12   Keith   B 9025   A 947   A 950   18
22   R. Spey   Craigellachie   Deveron   A 981   A 952
Dava   Dufftown   Turriff   26   13
A 95   A 920   B 9029   Mintlaw
Findhorn   840   Huntly   New Deer   A 950   Peterhead
549   Grantown-on-Spey   15   A 97   66   A 920   42   14   Buchan Ness
112   A 938   25   28   109   23   Oldmeldrum   67   Cruden Bay
180   Carrbridge   Dulnain   Tomintoul   Rhynie   Ellon   A 975
Bridge   A 939   GRAMPIAN   Inverurie   A 920   Newburgh
Aviemore   A 944   Mossat   Kintore   15   Stromness
Glen More   39   A 97   Alford   15   A 96   Lerwick
Forest Park   871   Craigievar   A 980   34   A 944
Cairn Gorm   1245   Colnabaichin   A 939   Castle   ABERDEEN
Cairngorm Mountains   27   Aboyne   A 93   Crathes   17   A 95
Ben Macdui   1309   Ballater   25   Banchory   Castle   Dee   18   A 957
Braemar   Balmoral Castle   Dee
1155   N. Esk
MOUNTAINS   Stonehaven
Beinn a' Ghlò   Devil's Elbow   1068   Glas Maol   89   A 94
1120   665   55   A 92   22
Blair Atholl   LAND   S. Esk   52   Inverbervie
B 8019   TAYSIDE   Laurencekirk
Pitlochry   Marikirk   A 937   10
Kirriemuir   Brechin   A 935   Montrose

1

2

3

4

5

A B C

12

Blacksod Bay
Achill Island
Keel
Corraun
Mulrany
Clare Island
Clew Bay
Newport
Inishturk
Louisburgh
Croagh Patrick
Westport / Cathair na Mart
Mweelrea Mts.
Inishbofin
Inishshark
Rinvyle Pt.
Killary Harbour
Letterfrack
Leenane
The Twelve Pins
Clifden / An Clochán
Connemara
Maumturk Mts.
Slyne Head
Roundstone
Maam Cross
Gortmore
Carna
Lettermullan
Gorumna Island
Spiddal
Galway / Gaillimh
Barna
Galway Bay
Aran Islands
Inishmore
Kilronan
Black Head
Inishmaan
Inisheer
Ballyvaughan
Lisdoonvarna
Kilfenora
Cliffs of Moher
Lahinch
Ennistimon
Milltown Malbay
Spanish Point
Corrofin
Ennis / Inis
Creegh
Kilkee
Killimer
Kilrush
Labasheeda
Killadysert
Newmarket on Fergus
Shannon
Bunratty Castle
Knappogue Castle
Loop Head
Kilbaha
Mouth of the Shannon
Ballybunnion
Tarbert
Askeaton
Adare
Ballyduff
Listowel
Kerry Head
Ballyheige
Newcastle West
Abbeyfeale
Rathkeale
Croom
Brandon Head
Tralee Bay
Tralee / Trá Lí
Dromcolliher
Sybil Head
Brandon Mountain
Clogher Head
Dingle
Anascaul
Slieve Mish Mts.
Castleisland
Newmarket
Great Blasket I.
Slea Head
Castlemaine
Dingle Bay
Killorglin
Kerry
Boherboy
Kanturk
Glenbeigh
Killarney / Cill Airne
Rathmore
Millstreet
Doulus Head
Ring of Kerry
Muckross House
Carrantuohill
Macgillycuddy's Reeks
Knight's Town
Valencia Island
Waterville
L. Currane
Kilgarvan
Derrynasaggart Mts.
St. Finan's Bay
Iveragh
Ring of Kerry
Sneem
Kenmare
Macroom
Coachford
Blarney
Cork / Corcaigh
Bolus Head
Skellig
Kenmare River
Lauragh
Glengarriff
Pass of Keimaneigh
Bantry / Beanntraí
Beara
Castletownbere
Bantry Bay
Dunmanway
Bandon
Dursey Island
Bere I.
Sheep's Head
Dunmanus Bay
Skull
Roaringwater Bay
Skibbereen
Clonakilty
Timoleague
Rosscarbery
Mizen Head
Galley Head
Old Head of Kinsale
Kinsale

Bangor
Ballycroy
Crossmolina
Ballina / Béal an Átha
Inishcrone
Nephin Beg Range
Nephin
Pontoon
Foxford
Castlebar / Caisleán an Bharraigh
Swinford
Connaught
Kiltamagh
Ballintober
Ballinrobe
Kilmaine
Claremorris
Ballyhaunis
Cong
Dunmore
Tuam / Tuaim
Headford
Oughterard
Mount Bellew
Athenry
Oranmore
Craughwell
Loughrea
Ardrahan
Kinvarra
Gort
Scarriff
Tulla
Broadford
Kilmurry
Killaloe
Nenagh / An tAonach
Limerick / Luimneach
Milestone
Newport
Dolla
Templemore
Thurles / Durlas
Holy Cross Abbey
Rock of Cashel
Cashel / Caiseal
Fethard
Tipperary / Tiobraid Árann
Kilmallock
Caher
Clonmel / Cluain Meala
Galty Mountains
Slievenamon
Kilfinane
Rath Luirc (Charleville)
Kildorrery
Cloheen
Knockmealdown Mts.
Comeragh Mts.
Mitchelstown
Fermoy
Lismore
Cappoquin
Buttevant
Kilworth
Mallow / Mala
Blackwater
Tallow
Dungarvan / Dún Garbhán
Midleton
Youghal / Eochaill
Youghal Bay
Ardmore
Cobh / An Cóbh
Ringaskiddy
Crosshaven
Ballycotton

Sligeach
Ballysadare
Dowra
Drumkeeran
Lough Allen
The Ox Mountains
Tobercurry
Ballymote
L. Arrow
Keadew
Drumshanbo
Boyle / Mainistir na Búille
Gorteen
Charlestown
Carrick-on-Shannon / Cora Droma Rúisc
Frenchpark
Elphin
Ballaghaderreen
Castlerea
Tulsk
Strokestown
Roscommon / Ros Comáin
Glennamaddy
Ballyforan
Lanesborough
Ballinasloe / Béal Átha na Sluaighe
Athlone / Baile Átha Luain
Lough Ree
Clonmacnoise
Ferbane
Clonfert
Portumna
Birr
Kinnitty
Cloghan
Kilcormac
Banagher
Slieve Bloom
Borrisokane
Roscrea
Moneygall
Templemore
Lough Derg
Urlin
River Shannon
Grand Canal
R. Suir
R. Blackwater

D   E   F

Holwerd   Anjum   Zoutkamp   Winsum   Bedum   Appingedam   Delfzijl   Emden   Jade   Brake   Hagen

Dokkum   GRONINGEN   Neermoor   Hesel   Wiefelstede   Rastede   Elsfleth   Schwanewede   Osterholz-Scharmbeck   Ottersberg

Burgum   Eelde   Haren   Hoogezand   Nieuweschans   Leer   Bad Zwischenahn   Apen   Oldenburg   Berne   Vegesack   BREMEN

Drachten   Roden   Veendam   Winschoten   Weener   Papenburg   Edewecht   Wardenburg   Delmenhorst   Ganderkesee   Stuhr-Brinkum   Achim   Oyten

Heerenveen   Norg   Assen   Oude-Pekela   Rhede   Friesoythe   Garrel   Großenkneten   Ahlhorn   Wildeshausen   Bassum   Syke   Hoya

Gorredijk   Smilde   Stadskanaal   Musselkanaal   Börger   Werlte   Cloppenburg   Goldenstedt   Barnstorf   Twistringen   Sulingen

Wolvega   Beilen   Borger   Ter Apel   Lathen   Sögel   Lindern   Lastrup   Vechta   Lohne   Rehden   Diepholz

DRENTHE   Steenwijk   Giethoorn   Hoogeveen   Emmen   Klazienaveen   Meppen   Haselünne   Löningen   Essen   Dinklage   Wagenfeld   Uchte   Stolzenau

Meppel   Coevorden   Twist   Quakenbrück   Steinfeld   Holdorf   Damme   Lemförde   Rahden   Lavelsloh

Steenwijk   OVERIJSSEL   Dedemsvaart   Emlichheim   Neuenhaus   Lingen   Fürstenau   Bersenbrück   Ankum   Bohmte   Lübbecke   Minden   Espelkamp   Petershagen

Hardenberg   Freren   Beesten   Bramsche   Mittelland-Kanal

Zwolle   Ommen   Hellendoorn   Nordhorn   Recke   Mettingen   Bad Essen   Porta Westfal.

Hattem   Wijhe   Raalte   Almelo   Oldenzaal   Bad Bentheim   Rheine   Ibbenbüren   Osnabrück   Melle   Kirchlengern   Bad Oeynhausen

Heerde   Nijverdal   Rijssen   Goor   Denekamp   Gronau   Ochtrup   Wettringen   Emsdetten   Tecklenburg   Lengerich   Bad Iburg   Dissen   Enger   Herford   Bad Salzuflen

Deventer   Hengelo   Delden   Enschede   Steinfurt   Borghorst   Ladbergen   Bad Rothenfelde   Borgholzhausen   Werther   Vlotho   Exter

Apeldoorn   Zutphen   Neede   Haaksbergen   Greven   Halle   Glandorf   Versmold   Bielefeld   Lemgo

GELDERLAND   Lochem   Horstmar   Sassenberg   Brackwede   Lage   Detmold

Ruurlo   Groenlo   Vreden   Altenberge   Telgte   Warendorf   Gütersloh   Sennestadt   Heiligenkirchen

ARNHEM   Doetinchem   Lichtenvoorde   Winterswijk   Stadtlohn   Coesfeld   Billerbeck   Münster   Freckenhorst   Rheda   Wiedenbrück   Berlebeck

Zevenaar   's-Heerenberg   Aalten   Gescher   Ahaus   NORDRHEIN   Oelde   Neubeckum   Rietberg   Bad Driburg

RHEIN   Emmerich   Bocholt   Borken   Groß Reken   Dülmen   Ascheberg   Beckum   Lippstadt   WESTF   Paderborn

Kranenburg   Rees   Rhede   Raesfeld   Haltern   Lüdinghausen   Ahlen   Geseke   Salzkotten

Kleve   Kalkar   Wulfen   Schermbeck   Selm   Bockum-Hövel   Erwitte   Bad Lippspringe

Gennep   Goch   Xanten   Wesel   Dorsten   Werne   Hamm   Rhynern   Soest   Büren

Boxmeer   Kevelaer   Dinslaken   Marl   Herten   Recklinghsn   Waltrop   Lünen   Werl   Rüthen   Wünnenberg

Sonsbeck   Rheinberg   Gladbeck   Castrop-Rauxel   Kamen   Unna   Marsberg   Belecke   Bredelar

Gelderen   Kamp-Lintfort   Walsum   Bottrop   Gelsenkirchen   Herne   DORTMUND   Neheim-Hüsten   Warstein   Brilon

Moers   Homberg   Oberhsn   Bochum   Witten   Schwerte   Menden   Arnsberg   Nuttlar   Olsberg

Venlo   Straelen   Kerken   Rheinhsn   Mülheim   ESSEN   Hattingen   Wetter   Hemer   Sundern   Meschede

DUISBURG   Kettwig   Velbert   Iserlohn   Hohenlimburg   Altena   Eslohe   Winterberg

Krefeld   Kempen   Ratingen   Hagen   Letmathe   Werdohl   Westernbödefeld   Medebach

Mönchengladbach   Viersen   WUPPERTAL   Schwelm   Ennepetal   Gevelsberg   Plettenberg   Oberkirchen   Neuastenberg

Roermond   Neuss   DÜSSELDORF   Mettmann   Lüdenscheid   Finnentrop   Grevenbrück   Schmallenberg   Hallenberg

LIMBURG   Rheydt   Radevormwald   Brügge   Attendorn   Lennestadt   SAUERLAND

Swalmen   Erkelenz   Grevenbroich   Dormagen   Remscheid   Solingen   Hückeswagen   Wipperfürth   Meinerzhagen   Kirchhundem   Bad Berleburg

Mönchengladbach   Leverkusen   Opladen   Odenthal   Gummersbach   Bergneustadt   Hilchenbach   Erndtebrück

Heinsberg   Baal   Bergheim   Berg. Gladbach   Bensberg   Engelskirchen   Freudenberg   Siegen   Marburg

Geilenkirchen   KÖLN   Overath   Much   Waldbröl   Wilnsdorf   Gladenbach

Sittard   Geleen   Brunssum   Jülich   Elsdorf   Kerpen   Frechen   Hürth   Troisdorf   Siegburg   Windeck   Betzdorf   Burbach   Münchhausen

Heerlen   AACHEN   Eschweiler   Düren   Brühl   Hennef   Eitorf   Wissen   Altenkirchen   Biedenkopf

Maastricht   Valkenburg   Erftstadt   Bonn   Königswinter   Marburg

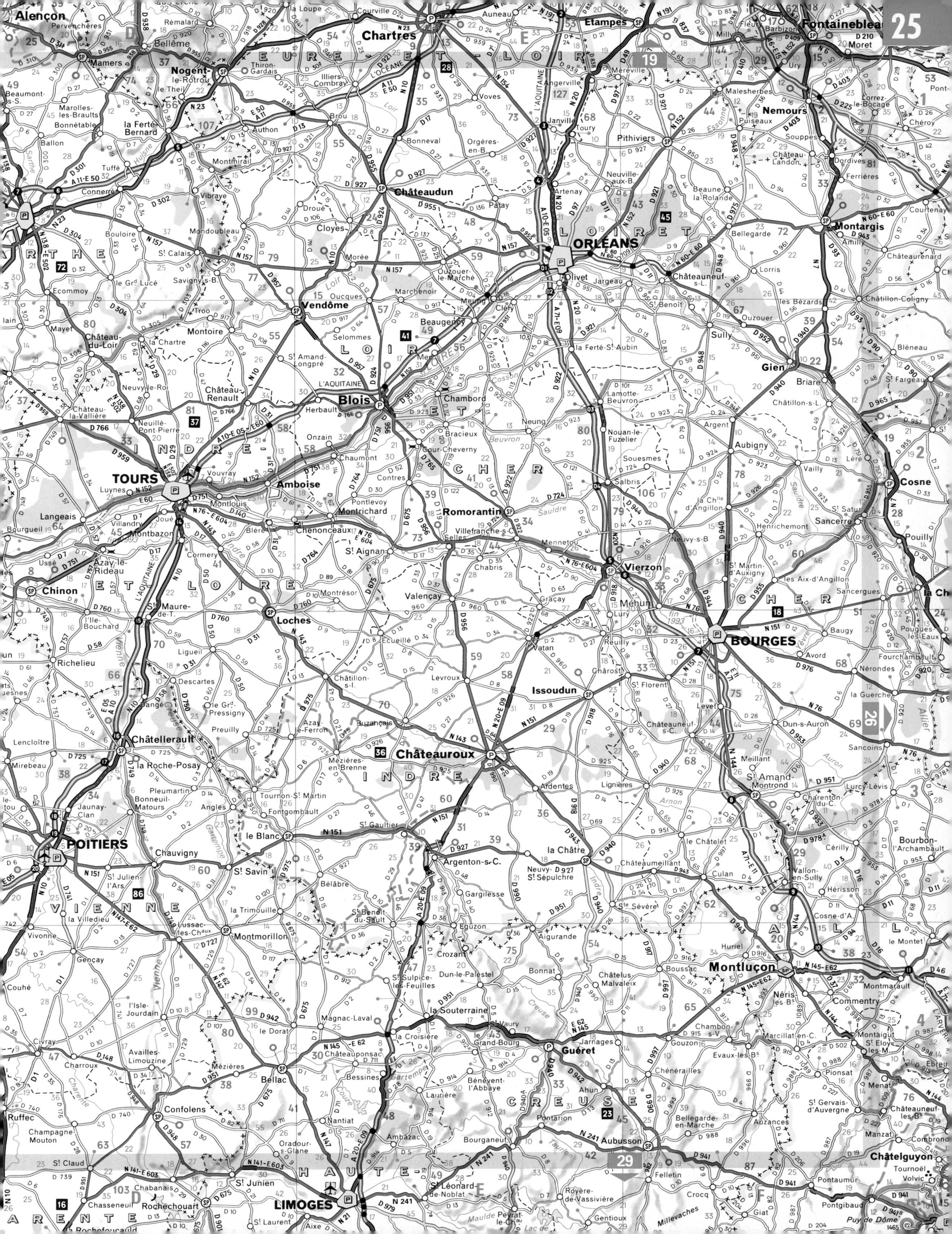

Alençon
Chartres
Étampes
Fontainebleau
19
Nogent-le-Rotrou
Châteaudun
Pithiviers
Nemours
Montargis
ORLÉANS
Vendôme
Blois
Gien
TOURS
Amboise
Romorantin
Vierzon
BOURGES
Chinon
Loches
Issoudun
Châteauroux
Châtellerault
POITIERS
Montluçon
Guéret
LIMOGES
Aubusson
Sancerre
Cosne
26
29
EURE-ET-LOIR
LOIRET
LOIR-ET-CHER
INDRE-ET-LOIRE
CHER
INDRE
VIENNE
CREUSE
HAUTE-VIENNE
ALLIER
L'AQUITAINE
L'OCÉANE

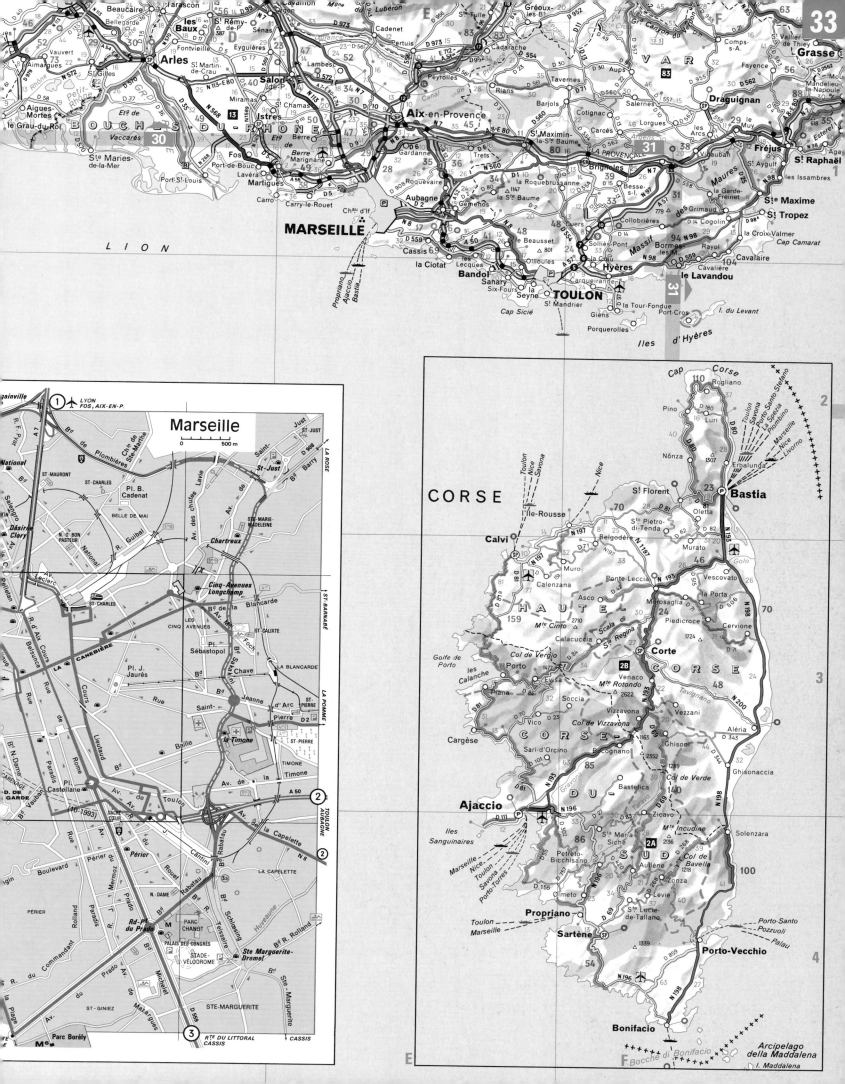

A CORUÑA/LA CORUÑA · SANTIAGO DE COMPOSTELA · Ferrol · Betanzos · Villalba · Lugo · Sarriá · Monforte de Lemos · Ourense/Orense · Chantada · Ribadeo · Mondoñedo · Viveiro · Pontevedra · VIGO · Redondela · Tui · Ribadavia · A Caniza · Verin · Chaves · Bragança · Mirandela · Vila Real · Braga · Guimarães · Póvoa de Varzim · Vila do Conde · PORTO · Viana do Castelo · Ponte de Lima · Amarante · Penafiel · Lamego · Puebla de Sanabria · Ponferrada · Villafranca del Bierzo · Castropol · Ribadeo

GALICIA · MINHO · TRAS-OS-MONTES · DOURO

Cabo Fisterra · Cabo Vilán · Muxía · Camariñas · Corcubión · Carnota · Muros · Noia · Cambados · O Grove · Sanxenxo · Marín · Cangas · Baiona · Cabo Silleiro · Matosinhos · Espinho · Esposende · Ofir · Barcelos

Modifications en cours dans la numérotation des routes
The numbering of roads is subject to modification
Se está cambiando la numeración de las carreteras

Verde

Costa Verde

Cabo Vidio · Cudillero · S. Esteban de Pravia · Salinas · Luanco · Candas · Cabo de Peñas
Canero · N 632 · Soto de Luiña · Soto del Barco · **Gijón** · Tazones · Lastres · Colunga
La Espina · Cornellana · **Avilés** · Valdediós · Villaviciosa · Ribadesella · Llanes · La Franca
Tineo · Salas · Grado · Lugones · Pola de Siero · Nava · Arriondas · Nueva · S. Vicente de la Barquera · Comillas · **SANTANDER**
OVIEDO · El Berrón · Infiesto · Cangas de Onís · Colombres · Santillana del Mar · Suances · Torrelavega
Trubia · La Felguera · Baños de Fuensanta · Covadonga · Carreña de Cabrales · Panes · Unquera · Cuevas de Altamira · El Astillero
Belmonte · **Mieres** · Carbayo · Pola de Laviana · Sierra de Cueva · Arenas de Cabrales · La Hermida · Cabezón de la Sal · Las Caldas de Besaya · Sarón
La Plaza · Desfiladero del Teverga · Campo de Caso · **PICOS DE EUROPA** · Desfiladero de la Hermida · Los Corrales de Buelna · Puente Viesgo
Pola de Lena · Sta Cristina de Lena · Desfiladero de los Beyos · Soto de Sajambre · Fuente Dé · Camaleño · Puentenansa · Corvera de Toranzo
Pto de Ventana · Campomanes · Oseja de Sajambre · Potes · Peña Sagra · Ontaneda · Villacarriedo
Pto de Somiedo · Peña Ubiña · Puente de los Fierros · Pto de Tarna · Sta Marina · Espinama · Arenas de Iguña · Alceda
Peña Prieta · Cervera de Pisuerga · **CANTABRIA** · Reinosa · Aguilar de Campóo
LEÓN · Astorga · La Bañeza · Benavente · Zamora · **VALLADOLID** · Palencia · **BURGOS** · Aranda de Duero

ARQUIPÉLAGO DA MADEIRA

ILHA DE PORTO SANTO
Porto Santo

Porto Moniz · Santana
Pico Ruivo · Funchal · Desertas
ILHA DA MADEIRA · 1/2750000

1/2750000

OCEANO ATLANTICO

ISLAS CANARIAS

LANZAROTE
Haria · Teguise · Parque Nacional de Timanfaya · Arrecife · Playa Blanca
Corralejo · La Oliva

FUERTEVENTURA
Betancuria · Pájara · Puerto del Rosario · Tuineje · Gran Tarajal

Punta de Jandía

TENERIFE
La Laguna · Puerto de la Cruz · Sta Cruz de Tenerife
Icod de los Vinos · La Orotava · Güimar
Teide · Parque Nacional del Teide
Guía de Isora · Granadilla de Abona
Los Cristianos

LA PALMA
Barlovento · Los Sauces · Puntagorda
Parque Nacional de la Caldera de Taburiente
Sta Cruz de la Palma · Los Llanos de Aridane · Fuencaliente

GOMERA
Vallehermoso · Hermigua · S. Sebastián
Garajonay (Parque Nacional)

HIERRO
Valverde · Frontera · Puerto de la Estaca

GRAN CANARIA
Gáldar · Arucas · LAS PALMAS DE GRAN CANARIA
Cruz de Tejeda · Telde
S. Nicolás de Tolentino · Maspalomas

Cádiz · AFRIQUE · Tarfaya · Cap Juby

Sines · Santiago do Cacém · Grândola · Alcácer do Sal · Beja · Serpa · Mértola · Ourique · Castro Verde · Almodôvar
Lagos · Portimão · Albufeira · Faro · Olhão · Tavira · Vila Real de Sto António · Huelva · Ayamonte · Isla Cristina
Monchique · Silves · Loulé · S. Brás de Alportel

GOLFO DE CADIZ

OCEANO ATLANTICO

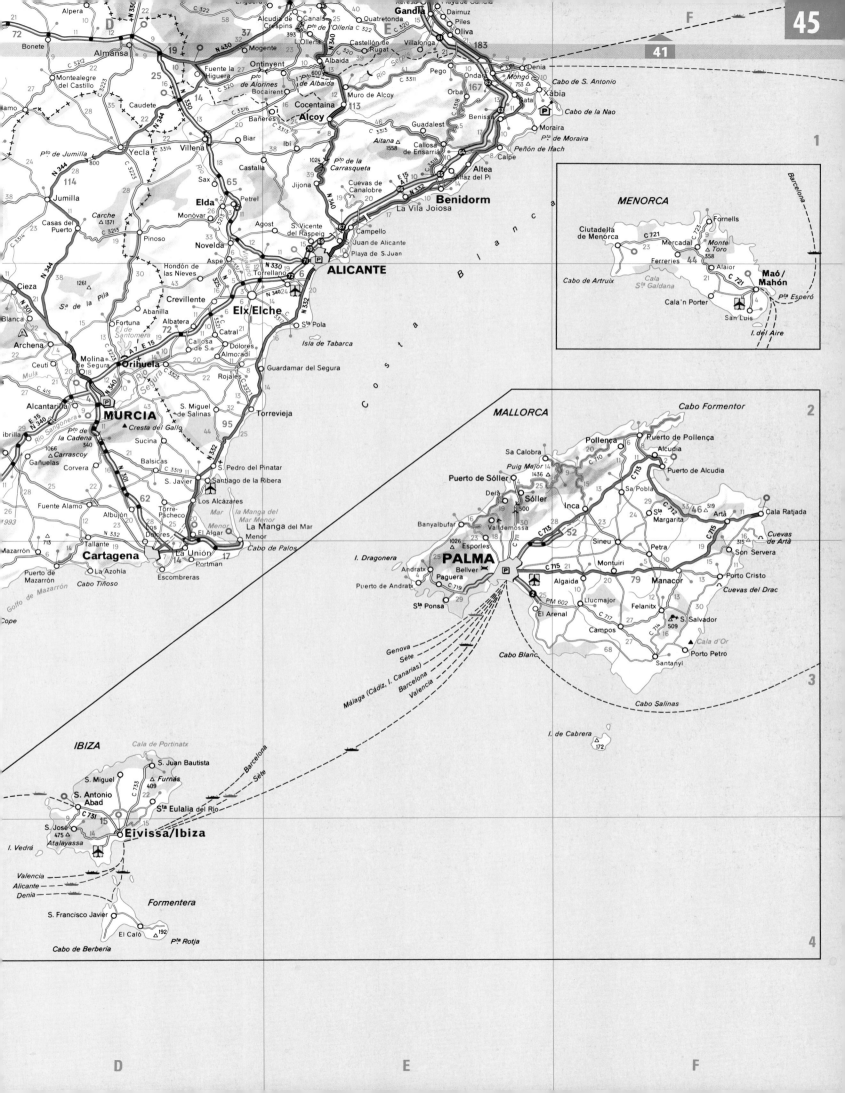

HANNOVER

BRAUNSCHWEIG

MAGDEBURG

Wolfsburg

Minden

Hildesheim

Hameln

Salzgitter

Wolfenbüttel

Halberstadt

Quedlinburg

Aschersleben

Detmold

Goslar

Bad Harzburg

Wernigerode

Blankenburg

Thale

Paderborn

Brocken

HARZ

Braunlage

Nordhausen

Sangerhausen

Göttingen

KASSEL

Mühlhausen

ERFURT

Weimar

Hann.-Münden

Eschwege

Gotha

Bad Hersfeld

Eisenach

Suhl

Marburg

Fulda

Meiningen

Gießen

Bad Kissingen

Coburg

Bad Nauheim

Schweinfurt

FRANKFURT A.M.

Offenbach

Aschaffenburg

Bamberg

Darmstadt

THÜRINGEN

HESSEN

WESTFALEN

SACHSEN-ANHALT

Dessau · Köthen · Wittenberg · Zerbst · Roßlau · Bitterfeld · Wolfen · Delitzsch · Eilenburg · Schkeuditz · **LEIPZIG** · Markkleeberg · Borna · Zeitz · Altenburg · **Gera** · Zwickau · Greiz · Reichenbach · Plauen · Hof · Zeulenroda · Auerbach · Klingenthal · Adorf

Beelitz · Treuenbrietzen · Luckenwalde · Jüterbog · Belzig · Brück · Niemegk · Wiesenburg · Coswig · Wörlitz · Oranienbaum · Gräfenhainichen · Kemberg · Pretzsch · Prettin · Annaburg · Herzberg · Schönewalde · Falkenberg · Torgau · Belgern · Mühlberg · Oschatz · Riesa · Großenhain · Strehla · Wurzen · Grimma · Döbeln · Meißen

Zossen · Trebbin · Baruth · Golßen · Luckau · Dahme · Schlieben · Finsterwalde · Doberlug-Kirchhain · Bad Liebenwerda · Elsterwerda · Sonnewalde · Lauchhammer · Schwarzheide · Ruhland · Ortrand · Königsbrück · Kamenz · Radeberg · Moritzburg · Radebeul · **DRESDEN** · Freital · Pirna · Heidenau

Teupitz · Halbe · Märkisch Buchholz · Neu Lübbenau · Lübben · Lübbenau · Boblitz · Calau · **Cottbus** · Vetschau · Altdöbern · Drebkau · Senftenberg · Spremberg · Weißwasser · Bad Muskau · **Hoyerswerda** · Lauta · Bernsdorf · Wittichenau · Klitten · Weißenberg · Burk · **Bautzen** · Bischofswerda · Stolpen · Neustadt · Sebnitz · Bad Schandau · Königstein · Hřensko · Děčín

W. Pieck-Stadt Guben · Gubin · Lieberose · Peitz · Forst · Zasieki · Döbern · **Görlitz** · Reichenbach · Löbau · Herrnhut · Ostritz · Zittau · Oybin · Neugersdorf · Varnsdorf · Grossschönau · Česká Kamenice · Nový Bor · Benešov · Česká Lípa · Mělník

CHEMNITZ · Augustusburg · Zschopau · Marienberg · Annaberg-Buchholz · Schwarzenberg · Aue · Schneeberg · Eibenstock · Johanngeorgenstadt · Oberwiesenthal · Jáchymov · Klínovec · Boží Dar · Kraslice · Nejdek · Ostrov · **Karlovy Vary** · Loket · Sokolov · Chodov · Kyselka

Freiberg · Frankenberg · Flöha · Oederan · Frauenstein · Altenberg · Zinnwald · Cínovec · Dubí · Krupka · **Teplice** · Duchcov · Bílina · Litvínov · **Most** · Jirkov · **Chomutov** · Klášterec · Kadaň · Žatec · Louny · Litoměřice · Lovosice · Roudnice

Olbernhau · Reitzenhain · Hora Svatého Šebestiána · Havraň · Podbořany · Kralovice · Manětín · Plasy · Úněšov · Lestkov · Pernarec · Planá · Stříbro · Tachov · Bor

Praha · Kladno · Rakovník · Unhošť · Beroun · Karlštejn · Zdice · Hořovice · Dobříš · Příbram · Rožmitál · **Plzeň** · Rokycany · Nýřany · Blovice · Přeštice · Stod

Hof · Rehau · Selb · Münchberg · Kirchenlamitz · Wunsiedel · Marktredwitz · Arzberg · Cheb · Františkovy Lázně · Aš · Bad Brambach · Bad Elster · Markneukirchen · Schönberg · Mähring · Mariánské Lázně · Konstantinovy Lázně · Mittelteich · Tirschenreuth · Waldsassen · Bärnau · **Weiden** · Neustadt an der Waldnaab · Grafenwöhr · Eschenbach · Kemnath · Erbendorf

49 · 56 · 112

Aschaffenburg Bamberg Weiden

52

DEUTSCHLAND

Würzburg Erlangen Fürth NÜRNBERG Amberg

Wertheim Miltenberg Tauberbischofsheim Kitzingen Neustadt an der Aisch Herzogenaurach Schwabach Neumarkt

Walldürn Bad Mergentheim Rothenburg ob der Tauber Ansbach Roth Hilpoltstein

Mosbach Künzelsau Crailsheim Dinkelsbühl Feuchtwangen Gunzenhausen Weißenburg Eichstätt

Heilbronn Schwäbisch Hall Ellwangen Nördlingen Donauwörth Neuburg Ingolstadt

Ludwigsburg Schwäbisch Gmünd Aalen Heidenheim Dillingen Wertingen Schrobenhausen

STUTTGART Esslingen Göppingen Geislingen Günzburg Augsburg Dachau MÜNCHEN

Tübingen Reutlingen Nürtingen Ulm Neu-Ulm Landsberg Fürstenfeldbruck Starnberg

Sigmaringen Ehingen Laupheim Memmingen Kaufbeuren Schongau Weilheim

WÜRTTEMBERG Biberach a.d. Riß Bad Waldsee Bad Wörishofen Marktoberdorf Bad Tölz

Tuttlingen Saulgau Ravensburg Kempten Füssen Garmisch-Partenkirchen

Konstanz Friedrichshafen Lindau Bregenz Oberstdorf Seefeld INNSBRUCK

St. Gallen Dornbirn Herisau Appenzell

Mladá Vožice
Pacov
Tábor
Pelhřimov
Jihlava
Velké Meziříčí
Křižanov
Tišnov
Blansko
Vyškov
Velká Bíteš
Kuřim
BRNO
Bučovice
Slavkov u Brna
Šlapanice
Sezimovo-Ústí
Třešť
Kamenice
Třebíč
Náměšť
Rosice
Ivančice
Židlochovice
Kyjov
Bernartice
Javořice
Telč
Soběslav
Jindřichuv Hradec
Jaroměřice
Moravský Krumlov
Pohořelice
Hustopeče
Čejč
Dubňany
Tyn
Veselí
Dačice
Moravské Budějovice
Hodonín
Jemnice
Jevišovice
Nová Bystřice
Slavonice
Grametten
Vranovská přehr. n.
Drnholec
Mikulov
Břeclav
Poštorná
Holíč
Hluboká
Třeboň
Litschau
Dobersberg
Drosendorf Stadt
Znojmo
Hrusovany
Hrádek
Hevlín
Drasenhofen
České Budějovice
Chlum u Třeboně
Raabs
Hardegg
Šatov
Laa an der Thaya
Bernhardsthal
Heidenreichstein
Haté
Kleinhaugsdorf
Poysdorf
Hohenau
Kúty
Halámky
Neunagelberg
Waidhofen
Gr.-Siegharts
Geras
Retz
Pulkau
Jetzelsdorf
Wilfersdorf
Zistersdorf
Trhové Sviny
Schrems
České Velenice
Gmünd
Allentsteig
Horn
Eggenburg
Mistelbach
Neupölla
Ernstbrunn
Dürnkrut
Kaplice
Weitra
Gars
Maissau
Hollabrunn
Malacky
Dolní Dvořiště
Zwettl
Rastenfeld
Langenlois
Ziersdorf
Göllersdorf
Wullowitz
Karlstift
Groß Gerungs
Angern
Vyšší Brod
Gföhl
Kirchberg
Stockerau
Korneuburg
Wolkersdorf
Gänserndorf
Marchegg
Stupava
Krems
Hadersdorf
Freistadt
Arbesbach
Weißenkirchen
Stein
Dürnstein
Traismauer
Tulln
Klosterneuburg
Deutsch-Wagram
Bad Leonfelden
Ottenschlag
Spitz
Leopoldsdorf
BRATISLAVA
Unterweißenbach
Königswiesen
Judenau
WIEN
Großenzersdorf
Orth
Hainburg
Berg
Herzogenburg
Pöggstall
Aggsbach-Markt
Aggsbach-Dorf
Mönchdorf
Laimbach
Bad Deutsch Altenburg
Gallneukirchen
Pregarten
Purkersdorf
Pressbaum
Schönbrunn
Schwechat
Fischamend Markt
Kittsee
Neulengbach
LINZ
Maria Taferl
Pöchlarn
Melk
St. Pölten
St. Christophen
Perg
Grein
Persenbeug
Loosdorf
Mödling
Wiener-Neudorf
Bruck
Parndorf
Hegyeshalom
Asten
Mauthausen
Ybbs
St. Leonhard
Obergrafendorf
Altlengbach
Nickelsdorf
Neusiedl
Enns
Strengberg
Wilhelmsburg
Alland
Mayerling
Traiskirchen
Mannersdorf
Markt St Florian
St Valentin
Amstetten
Wieselburg
Mank
Baden
Bad Vöslau
Ebreichsdorf
Purbach
Neuhofen an der Krems
Haag
Aschbach Markt
Euratsfeld
Purgstall
Lilienfeld
Traisen
Hainfeld
Pottenstein
Leobersdorf
Frauenkirchen
St. Peter in der Au
Kirchberg a.d. Pielach
Berndorf
Sollenau
Eisenstadt
Podersdorf
Steyr
Seitenstetten
Scheibbs
Pernitz
Wöllersdorf
Ebenfurth
Rust
Gresten
Türnitz
Hohenberg
Gutenstein
Wiener Neustadt
Illmitz
Sierninghofen
Waidhofen
Gaming
Rohrer Sattel
Mattersburg
Klingenbach
Mörbisch
Bad Hall
St. Aegyd
Puchberg
Pamhagen
Gr. Ötscher
Annaberg
Schneeberg
Neunkirchen
Sopron
Losenstein
Lunz
Fertőszentmiklós
Kirchdorf
Weyer-Markt
Mariazell
Ternitz
Deutschkreutz
Micheldorf
Großraming
Göstling
Zellerrain
Heukuppe
Reichenau
Nagycenk
Preiner Gscheid
Gloggnitz
Wiesmath
Mürzsteg
Semmering
Altenmarkt
Aflenzer Seeberg
Mürzzuschlag
Semmering-P.
Aspang
Kirchschlag
Oberpullendorf
Lövő
Windischgarsten
Wildalpen
Seewiesen
Krieglach
Langenwang
Wechsel
Lutzmannsburg
St. Gallen
Hengstpaß
Mönichkirchen
Hinterstoder
Spital
Hieflau
Leopoldsteinersee
Hochschwab
Aflenz Kurort
Ratten
Friedberg
Bernstein
Rattersdorf
Köszeg
Bük
Pyhrnpaß
Gesäuse
Eisenerz
Prabichl
Kindberg
Lockenhaus
Liezen
Admont
Hochtor
Erzberg
Kapfenberg
Vorau
Pinkafeld
Bad Tatzmannsdorf
Rottenmann
Eisenerzer Alpen
Vordernberg
Trofaiach
Birkfeld
Oberwart
Rechnitz
Bucsu
Vát
Irdning
Leoben
Bruck an der Mur
Schachendorf
Szombathely
Gr. Bösenstein
Trieben
Schoberpaß
Hohentauern
Mautern
Donawitz
Pöllau
Hartberg
Großpetersdorf
Rottenmanner Tauern
Hochreichart
St. Michael
Anger
Donnersbachwald
Katerloch
Kaindorf
Stegersbach
Frohnleiten
Gleinalmtunnel
Speikkogel
Seckau
Schöckl
Weiz
BURGENLAND
Moschendorf
Gaaldorf
Oberzeiring
Knittelfeld
Güssing
Körmend
Fohnsdorf
Zeltweg
Gratkorn
Gleisdorf
Fürstenfeld
Hegyhátsál
Sölkerpaß
Oberwölz
Gaberl-Sattel
Piber
GRAZ
Riegersburg
Heiligenkreuz
Rábafüzes
Gasztony
Scheifling
Weißkirchen
Judenburg
Voitsberg
Köflach
Jennersdorf
Szentgotthárd
Murau
Zirbitzkogel
Obdach
Obdacher Sattel
Kalsdorf
Feldbach
Kirchbach
Fehring
Felsőszölnök
Zalalövő
Neumarkt
St. Lambrecht
Packsattel
Wildon
Bad Gleichenberg
Kuzma
Hodoš
Őriszentpéter
Bad St. Leonhard
Klippitztörl
Stainz
Gornji Petrovci
Mačkovci
Bajánsenye
Szilvágy
Metnitz
Friesach
Hüttenberg
Twimberg
Deutschlandsberg
Leibnitz
Pertoča
Cseszteg
Zalabaksa
Flattnitz
Straßburg
Mariani
NIEDERÖSTERREICH
STEIERMARK
MORAVA
DONAU
Thaya
Dyje
Enns
Mur
Raab
Leitha
Neusiedler See
Wienerwald
Salza
Kamp
Jihlava
Oslava
Wachau
Kosice
Budapest 203
Wien-Budapest 254
Győr 87
Sárvár 58
Győr 105
Budapest 228
Nagykanizsa 79
112
70

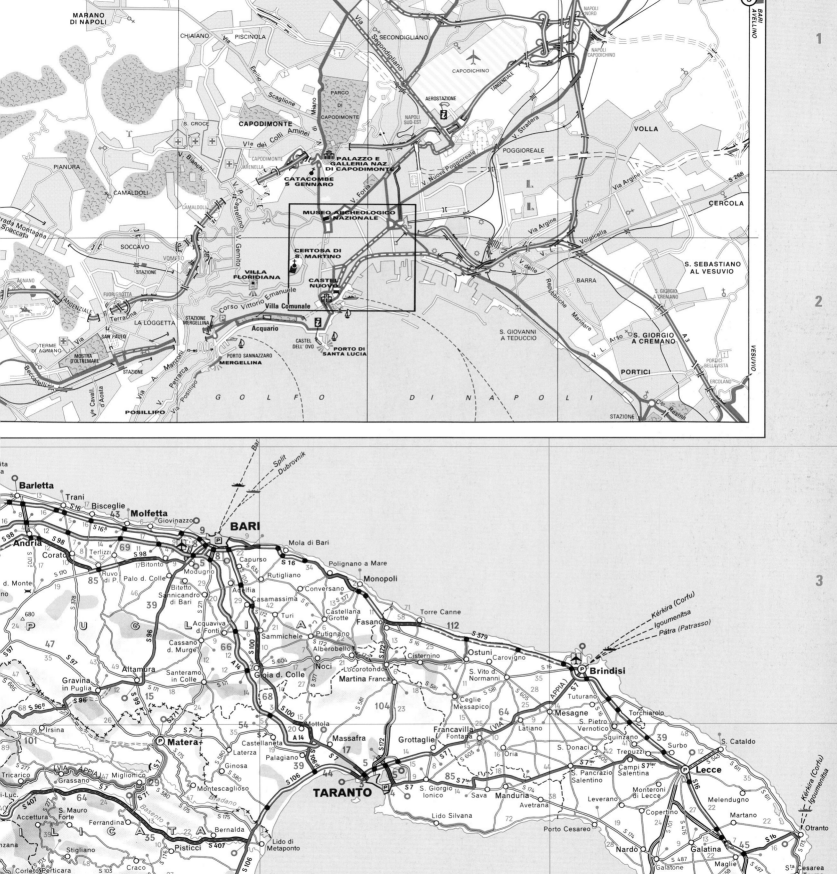

Napoli

2 km

ROMA P1, S7 qu. ⑩ · ① ROMA S7bis · CASERTA S87 ② · ROMA CASERTA ③ · AVELLINO · ⑤ BARI AVELLINO

CALVIZZANO
MARANO DI NAPOLI
MUGNANO DI NAPOLI
PISCINOLA
CHIAIANO
S. CROCE
CAPODIMONTE
PIANURA
CAMALDOLI
SOCCAVO
VOMERO
VILLA FLORIDIANA
FUORIGROTTA
AGNANO
TERME DI AGNANO
MOSTRA D'OLTREMARE
SAN PAULO
LA LOGGETTA
STAZIONE MERGELLINA
Acquario
MERGELLINA
PORTO SANNAZZARO
POSILLIPO

ARZANO
CASORIA
AFRAGOLA
CASALNUOVO DI NAPOLI
SECONDIGLIANO
CAPODICHINO
AEROSTAZIONE
NAPOLI NORD
NAPOLI CAPODICHINO
NAPOLI SUD-EST
VOLLA
POGGIOREALE
CERCOLA
S. SEBASTIANO AL VESUVIO
S. GIORGIO A CREMANO
BARRA
S. GIOVANNI A TEDUCCIO
PORTICI
ERCOLANO
PORTICI-BELLAVISTA
VESUVIO

PALAZZO E GALLERIA NAZ. DI CAPODIMONTE
CATACOMBE S. GENNARO
MUSEO ARCHEOLOGICO NAZIONALE
CERTOSA DI S. MARTINO
CASTEL NUOVO
Villa Comunale
Corso Vittorio Emanuele
CASTEL DELL'OVO
PORTO DI SANTA LUCIA

GOLFO DI NAPOLI

STAZIONE

Barletta
Trani
Bisceglie
Molfetta
Giovinazzo
Andria
Corato
Terlizzi
Ruvo di P.
Palo d. Colle
Modugno
BARI
Mola di Bari
Bitonto
Bitetto
Sannicandro di Bari
Capurso
Rutigliano
Polignano a Mare
Monopoli
Conversano
Adelfia
Casamassima
Turi
Castellana Grotte
Acquaviva d. Fonti
Sammichele
Putignano
Alberobello
Fasano
Torre Canne
Cassano d. Murge
Gravina in Puglia
Altamura
Santeramo in Colle
Gioia d. Colle
Noci
Locorotondo
Martina Franca
Cisternino
Ostuni
Carovigno
S. Vito d. Normanni
Ceglie Messapico
BRINDISI
Tuturano
Mesagne
Torchiarolo
S. Pietro Vernotico
Irsina
Mottola
Massafra
Grottaglie
Francavilla Fontana
Latiano
Squinzano
Surbo
S. Donaci
Oria
S. Pietro
Trepuzzi
Matera
Castellaneta
Laterza
Palagiano
Ginosa
Montescaglioso
TARANTO
Manduria
Sava
S. Giorgio Ionico
S. Pancrazio Salentino
Campi Salentina
Lecce
Leverano
Monteroni di Lecce
Melendugno
Martano
Otranto
Tricarico
Grassano
Miglionico
Bernalda
Avetrana
Porto Cesareo
Copertino
Nardò
Galatina
Galatone
Maglie
S. Cataldo
Sta Cesarea Terme
Accettura
S. Mauro Forte
Ferrandina
Pisticci
Lido di Metaponto
Lido Silvana
Parabita
Gallipoli
Casarano
Tricase
Stigliano
Craco
Colobraro
Scanzano
Tursi
Policoro
Nova Siri
Ugento
Gagliano d. Capo
Leuca
Oriolo
Rotondella
Corleto Perticara
Senise

PUGLIA
LUCANIA

GOLFO DI TARANTO

Split Dubrovnik
Kérkira (Corfu)
Igoumenitsa
Pátra (Patrasso)

67

Capo S. Maria di Leuca

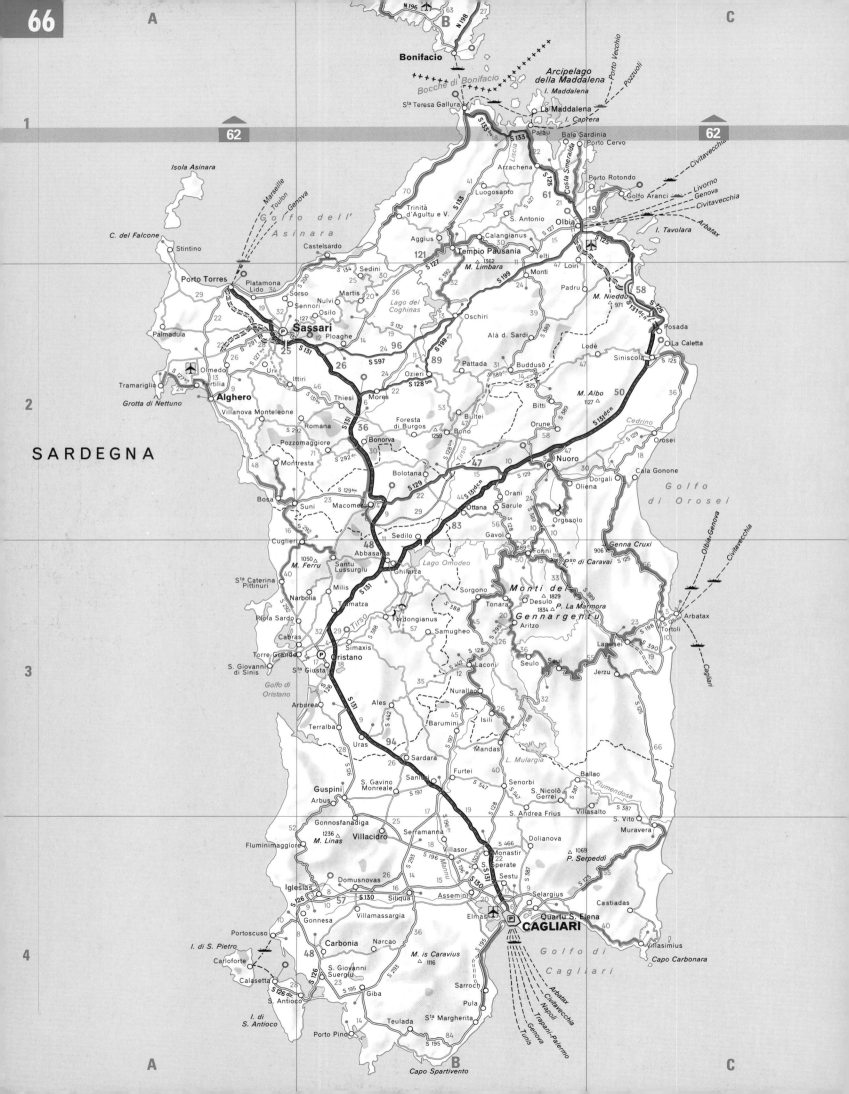

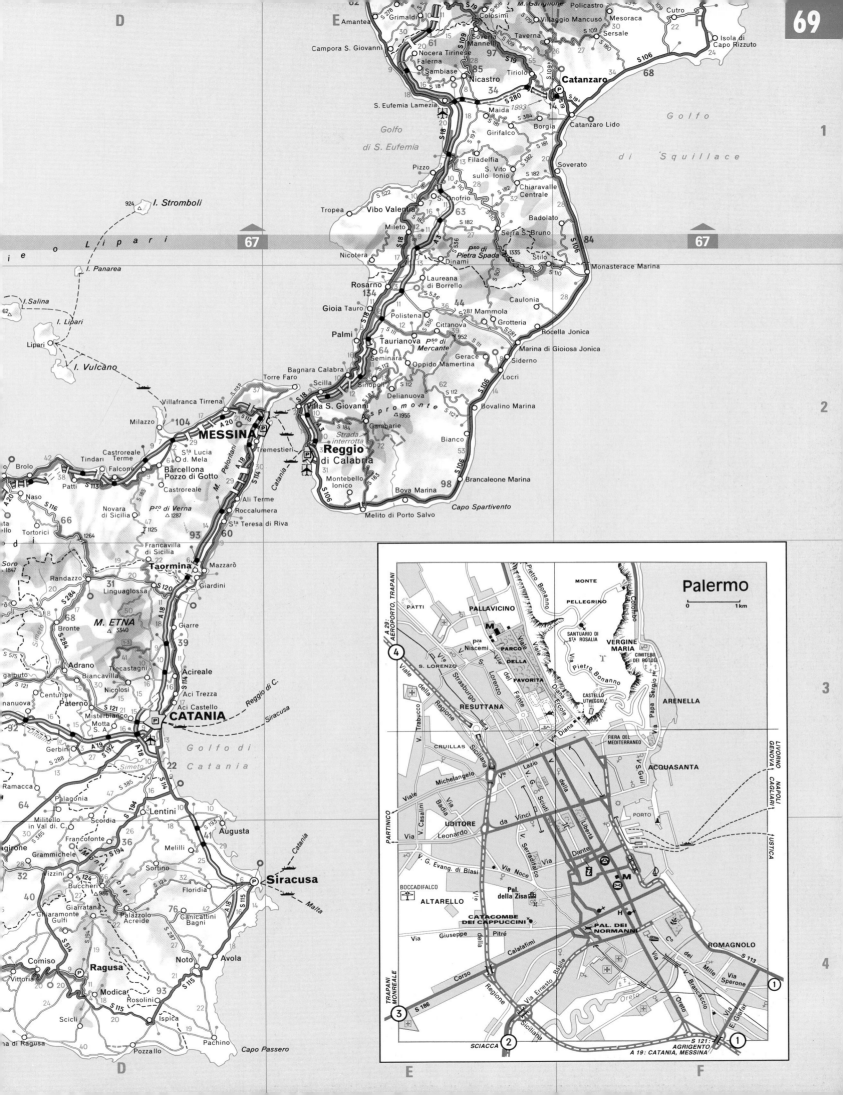

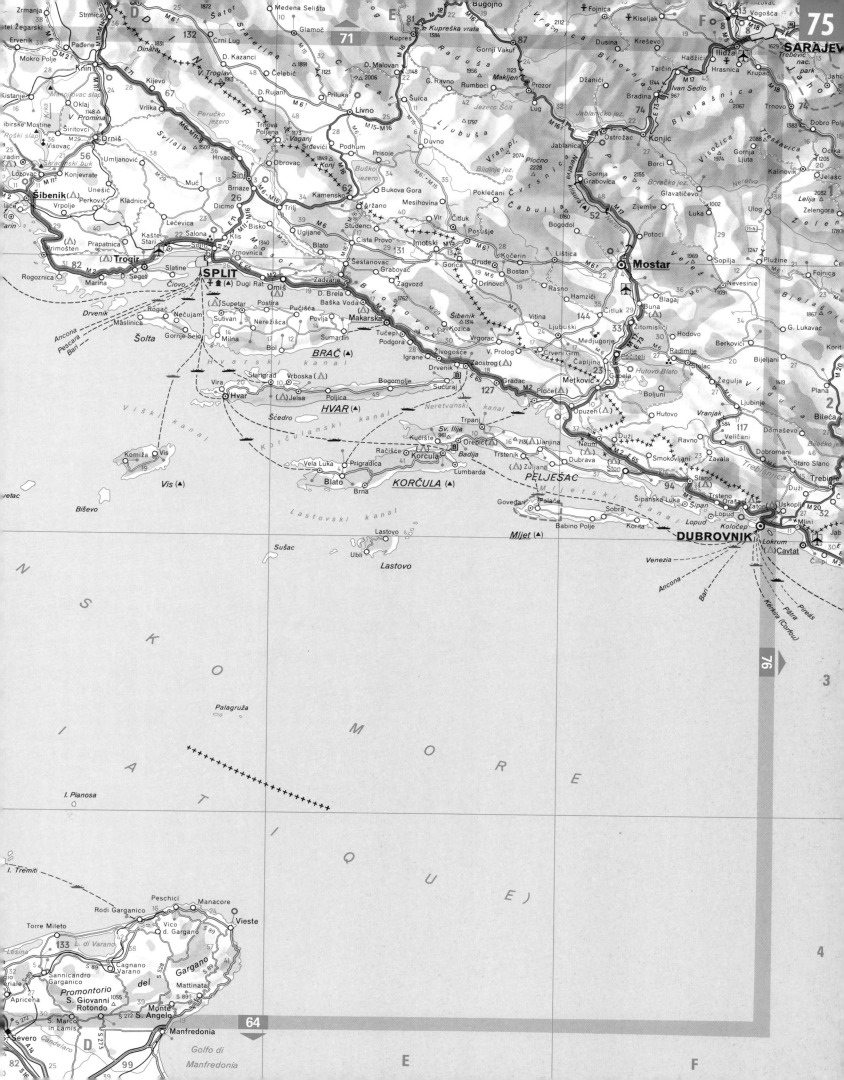

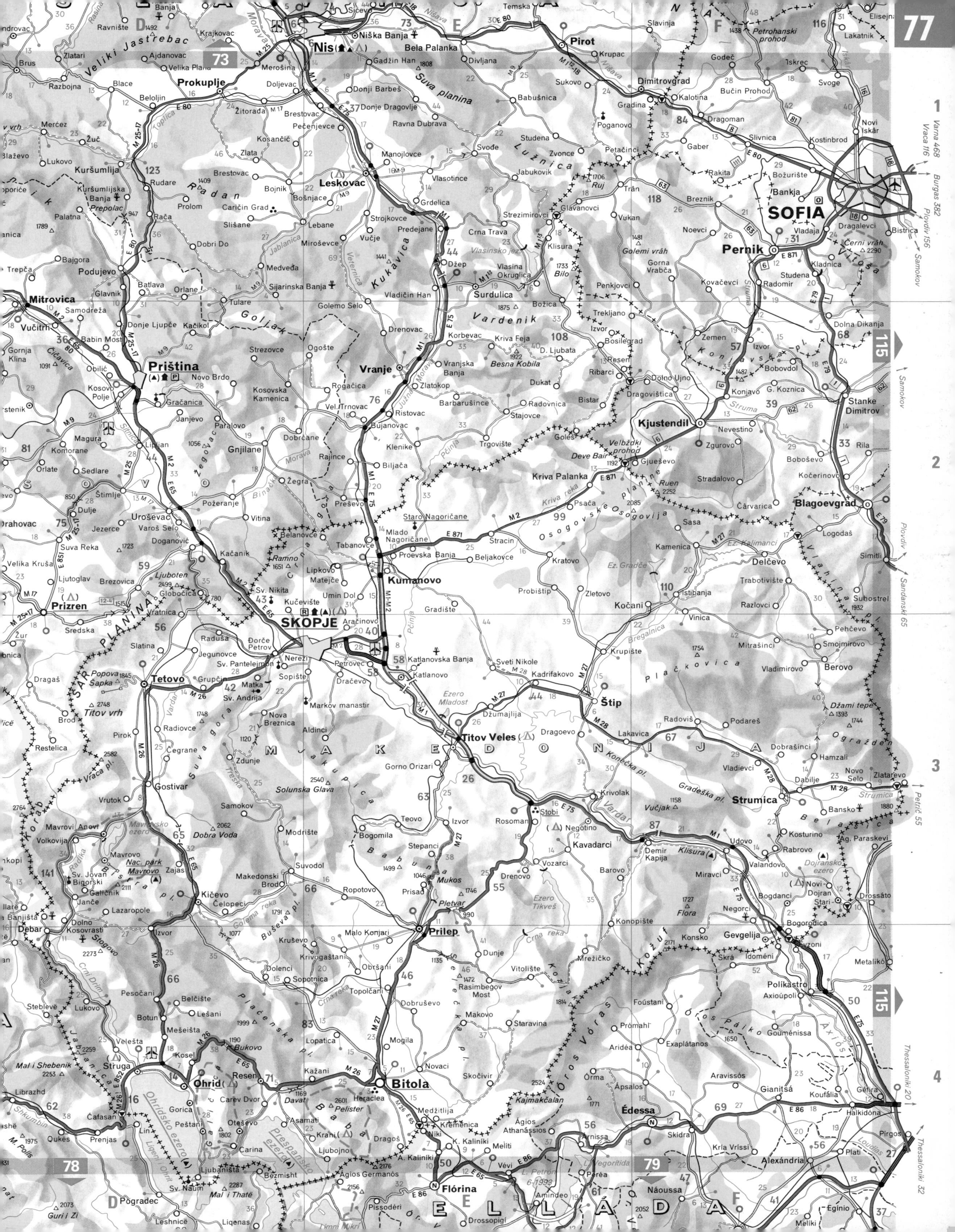

SOFIA

Niš
Pirot
Dimitrovgrad
Pernik
Leskovac
Prokuplje
Mitrovica
Priština
Vranje
Kjustendil
Blagoevgrad
Kriva Palanka
Kumanovo
Skopje
Tetovo
Štip
Strumica
Gostivar
Kičevo
Titov Veles
Prilep
Kavadarci
Gevgelija
Ohrid
Struga
Bitola
Débar
Prizren
Uroševac
Édessa
Náoussa
Flórina
Alexándria
Políkastro

MAKEDONIJA
ELLÁDA

KALA... D · Panagía · Díporo · Olympiáda · E · Pandeleímonas Platamónas · F
Ag. Theódori · Kraniá Elassónas · Κρανιά Ελασσόνας · Platamónas
Karperó · Eláti · Ákri · Skotína · Pandeleímonas Παντελεήμονας
Aníxi · Paliouriá · Mikr. Eleftherohóri · Kalipéfki · N. Messángala · Μ. Μεσάγκαλα
Deskáti · Elassóna Ελασσόνα (300) · Kalithéa · Akr. Platamónas

Hássia · Óros Óssa · Akr. Dermatás · Ακρ. Δερματάς
Meteora · Kastráki · Metéora · Kefalóvrisso · Tsarítsani · Góni Γόννοι · Rapsáni · Stómio Στόμιο
Kalambáka Καλαμπάκα · Stefanóvouno · Argiropoúlio · Makrihóri · Evangelismós · Kókino Neró
Tríkala Τρίκαλα · Doméniko · Tírnavos Τίρναβος · Deléria · Ambelákia · Anatolí
Neohóri · Mavréli · Messohóri · Diásselo · Damássi · Ambelónas · Agiá Αγιά
LÁRISSA ΛΑΡΙΣΑ · Omorfohóri · Dímitra · Agiókambos
Megalohóri · Farkadóna · Koutsóhero · Platíkambos · Kastrí
Sikoúrio · Skíti · A. Polidéndri

THESSALÍA · LÁRISSA
Agnanderó · Maráthea · Mavrovoúni · Ág. Anárgiri · Nikea Νίκαια · Melía · Ahílio · Kalamáki
Mouzáki · Fanári · Rizovoúni · Palamás Παλαμάς · Kiparissos · Zápio · Sofó · N. Perivóli · Kanália
Kardítsa Καρδίτσα · Sofádes Σοφάδες · Vassilis · Vamvakoú · Velestíno Βελεστίνο · VÓLOS ΒΟΛΟΣ
Artessianó · Pashalítsa · Fársala Φάρσαλα · Rígeo · N. Pagassés · Agriá Αγριά · Zagorá Ζαγορά

KARDÍTSA · Gefíria · Ambelía · Aerinó · Portariá · Tsangaráda
Loutrá Smokóvou · Gramatikó · Nartháki · Mikrothíves · N. Anhíalos · Milíes · Kalamáki
Rendína · Dómokos Δομοκός · Óros Nartháki · Skopiá · Almirós Αλμυρός · Argalastí
Makriráhi · Metállio · Kariés · Anávra · Plátanos · Soúrpi · Metóhi · Milína

RITANÍA · Loutrá Kaítsas · Xiniáda · Moshokariá · MAGNISSÍA · Pagassitikós Kólpos · Láfkos
Frangísta · Paleókastro · Kastrí · Lianokládi · FTHIÓTIDA · Ág. Ioánnis · Tríkeri · Plataniá
Karpeníssi Καρπενήσι · Makrakómi Μακρακώμη · Lamía Λαμία · Pelasgía · Ag. Theódori · Kanatádika
Timfristós Τυμφρηστός · Sperhiáda · Loutrá Ipátis · Karavómilos · Oreí · Istiéa

Proussós · Ág. Dimítrios · Aráhova · Iráklia · Thermópiles Θερμοπύλες · Kaména Voúrla Καμένα-Βούρλα · Loutrá Edipsoú Λουτρά Αιδηψού
Kaliakoúda · Oxiá Óxia · Neohóri · Mólos Μόλος · Skárfia · Gregolímano · Roviés
Domnísta · Pávliani · Óros Kalídromo · Ág. Nikólaos · Arkitsa Αρκίτσα · Límni

STEREÁ ELLÁDA
Artotína · Kaloskopí · Mendenítsa · Karyá · Livanátes Λιβανάτες · Skála
Thérmo Θέρμο · Lefkadíti · Óros Gióna · Gravia · Polidróssos · Megaplátanos · Akr. Kérata
FOKIDA · Drossohóri · Eptálofos · Amfíklia · Atalándi Αταλάντη · Malesína
Amfissa Άμφισσα · Óros Parnassós Παρνασσός · K. Tithoréa · Dávlia · Proskinás · Kolláka

Náfpaktos Ναύπακτος · Lidóri · Delfí Δελφοί · Aráhova Αράχοβα · Orhomenós Ορχομενός · Pávlos · Kástro
Eupálio · Itéa Ιτέα · Dístomo · Herónia · VIOTÍA · Gla
Paleópirgos · Galaxídi · Ossios Loukás Όσιος Λουκάς · Livadiá Λειβαδειά · Alíartos · Thíva Θήβα

PÁTRA ΠΑΤΡΑ · Égio Αίγιο · Diakoftó · Akráta · Kópais Κωπαΐδα · Thespiés · Pláties
Paralía · Óros Panahaïkó · Paralía Akrátas · Korinthiakós Kólpos · Koróni · Elópia · Léfktra · Vágia

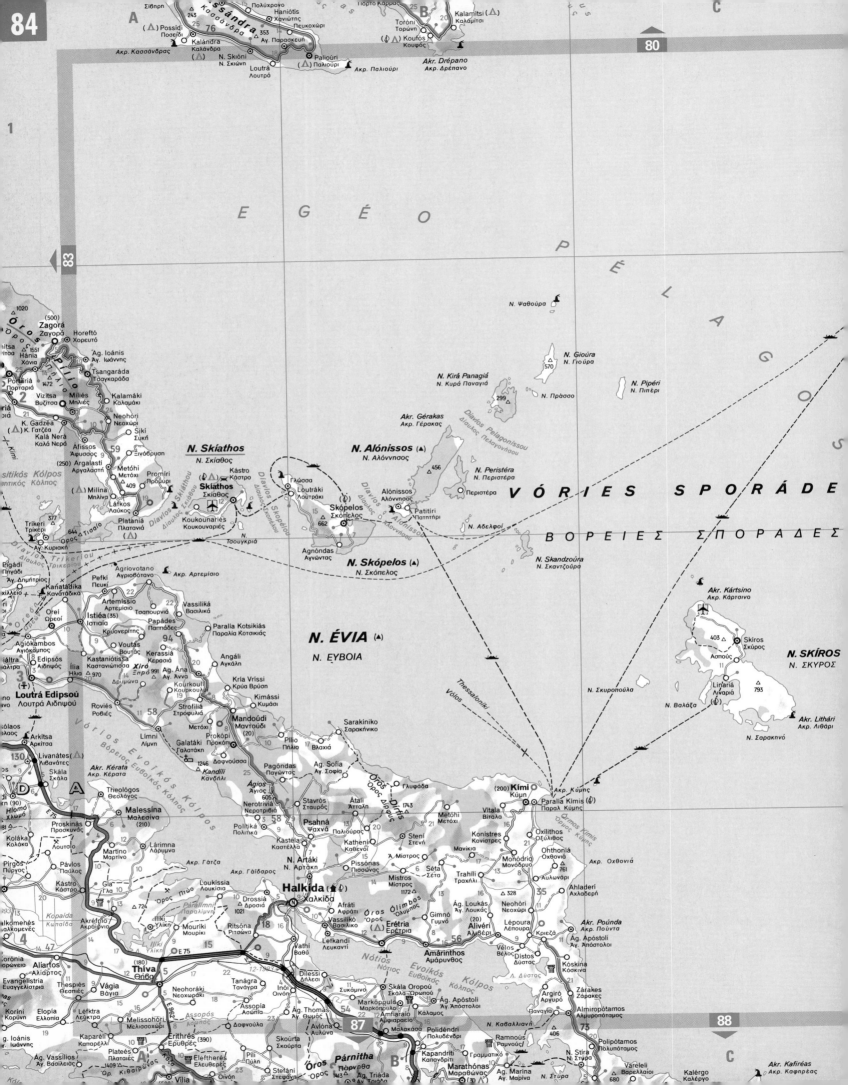

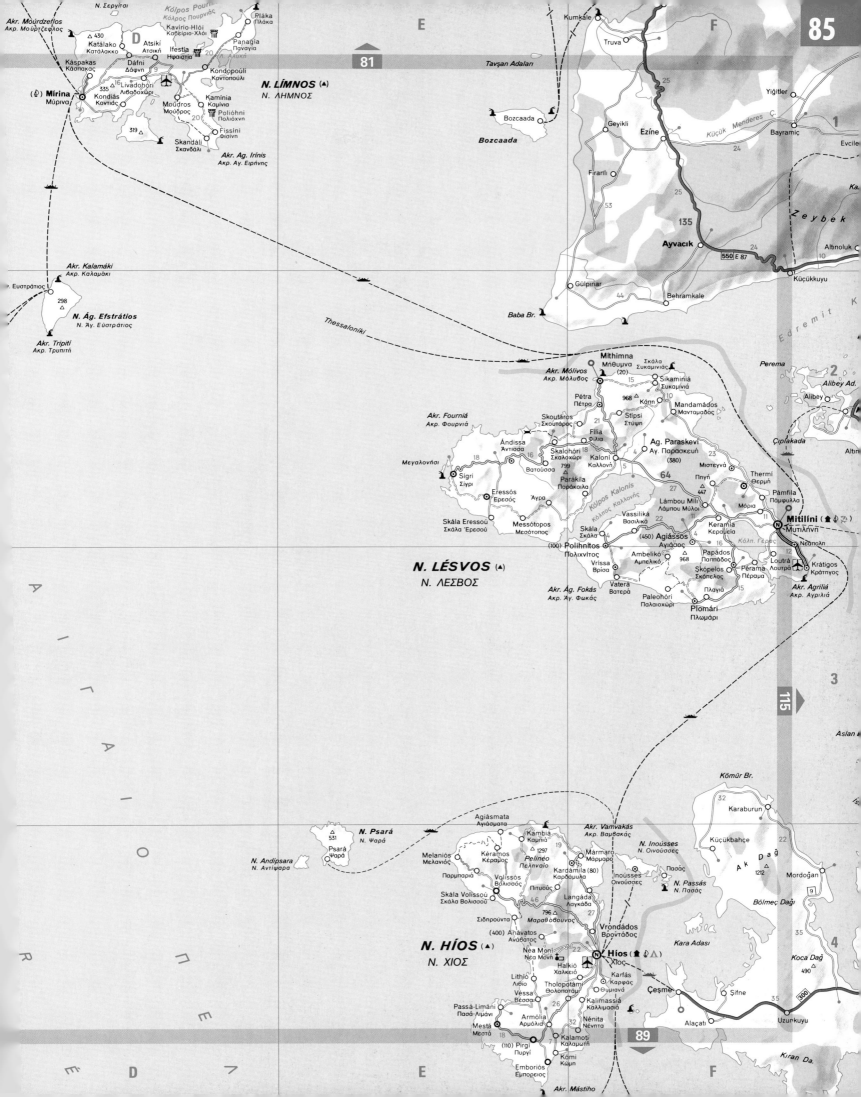

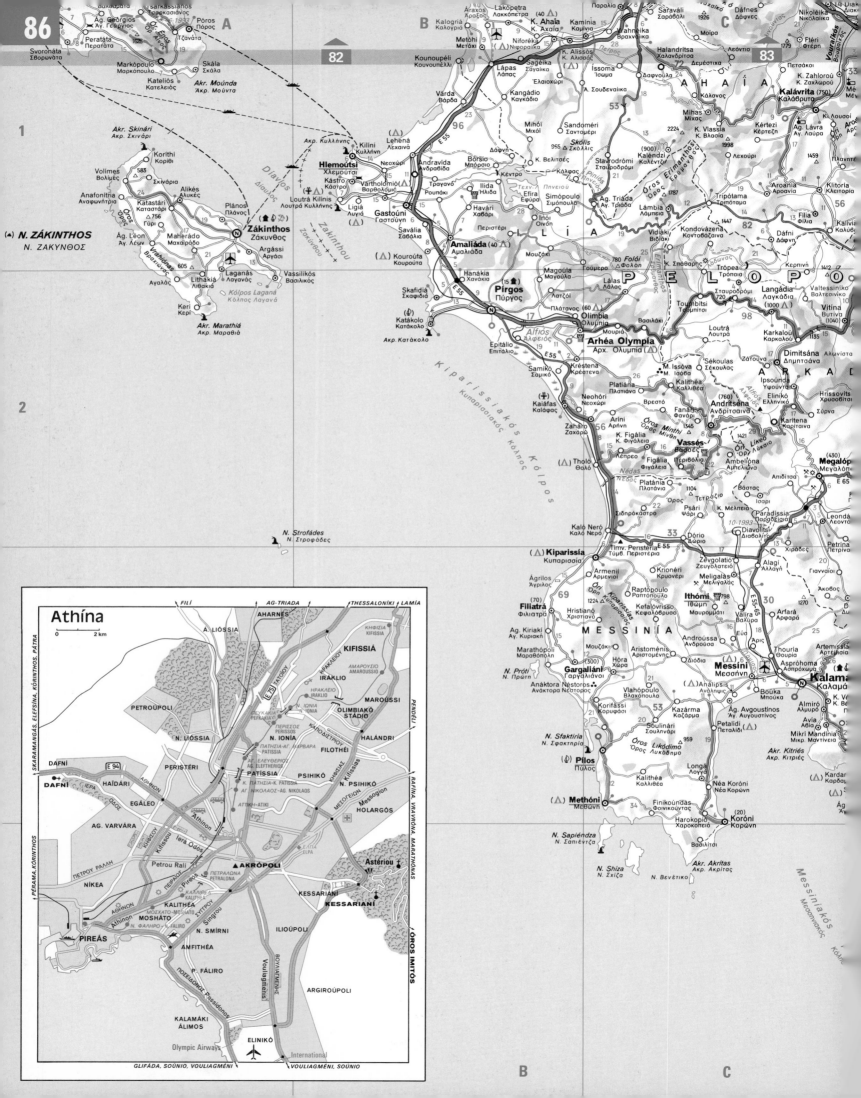

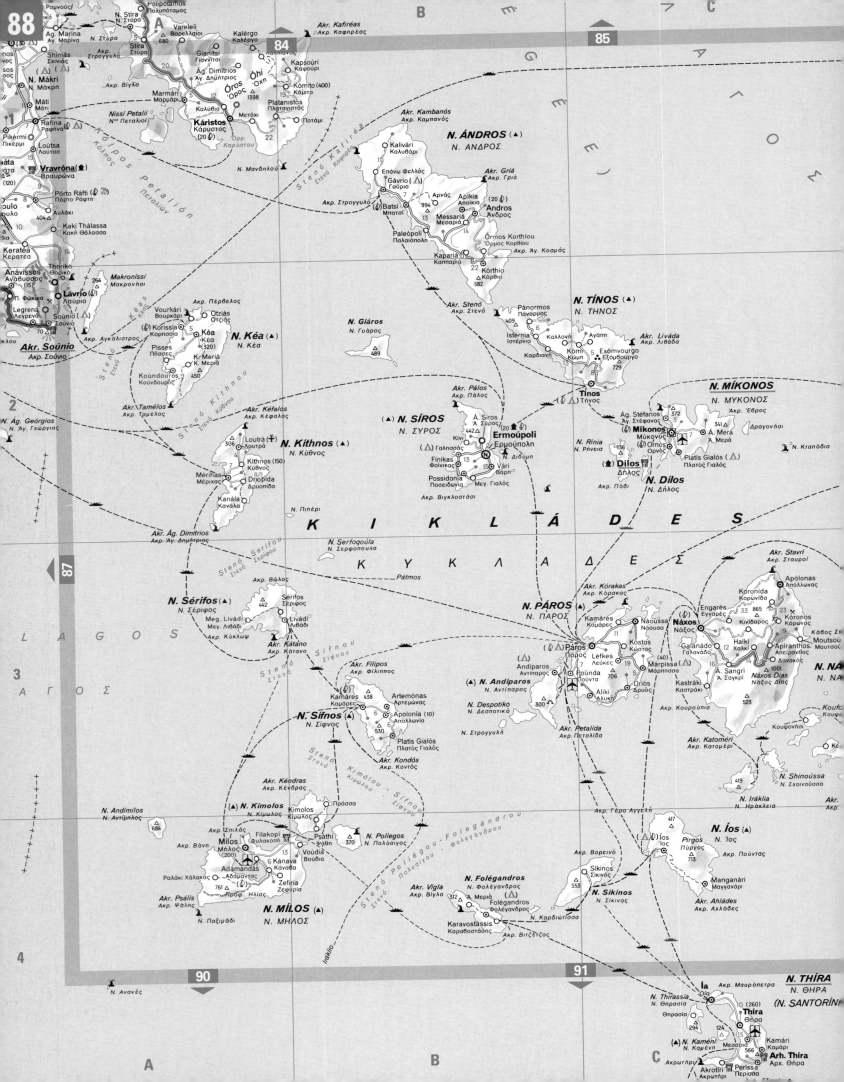

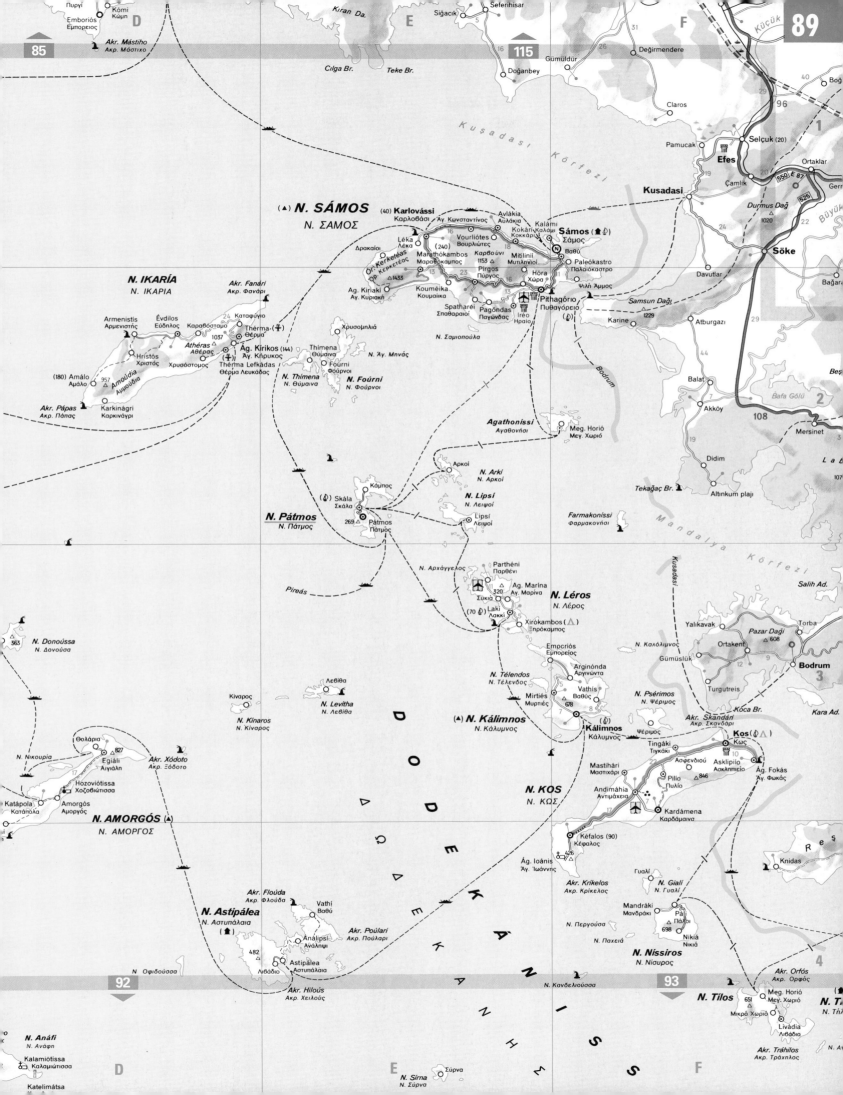

Tálanda
Τάλαντα

Nómia
Νόμια

Pandánassa
Πανδάνασσα

716

Ág. Apóstoli
Άγ. Απόστολοι

Viglafía
Βιγλαφία

Elafónissos
Ελαφόνησος

Elafoníssi
Ελαφόνησοι

34

Neápoli
Νεάπολη

772

Kólpos Epidávrou Limirás
Κόλπος Επιδαύρου Λιμηράς

Όρος Κράθιον

Ά. Kastaniá
Ά. Καστανιά

Ág. Andréas
Άγ. Ανδρέας

Velanídia
Βελανίδια

Akr. Maléas
Ακρ. Μαλέας

N. Ananés
Ν. Ανανές

Akr. Psális
Ακρ. Ψάλις

761

Προφ. Ηλίας

Ζεφυρία

N. MÍLOS
Ν. ΜΗΛΟΣ

Ν. Παξιμάδι

Akr. Spathí
Ακρ. Σπαθί

Karavás
Καραβάς

Ag. Pelagía
Αγ. Πελαγία

Potamós
Ποταμός

Aroniádika
Αρωνιάδικα

Diakófti
Διακόφτι

Milopótamos
Μυλοπόταμος

Frilingiánika
Φριλιγκιάνικα

389

Avlémonas
Αβλέμονας

507

Livádi
Λιβάδι

Kíthira
Κύθηρα

Kapsáli
Καψάλι

N. KÍTHIRA
Ν. ΚΥΘΗΡΑ

Akr. Kapélo
Ακρ. Καπέλλο

K R I T I K O   P E L A

Akr. Kefáli
Ακρ. Κεφάλι

Potamós
Ποταμός

Galanianá
Γαλανιανά

378

N. Andikíthira
Ν. Αντικύθηρα

Akr. Apolitáres
Ακρ. Απολυτάρες

Kastéli

Potamós
Ποταμός

(M
E

Akr. Spánda
Ακρ. Σπάντα

Diktíneon
Δικτιναίον

748

Akr. Voúxa
Ακρ. Βούξα

Kólpos Kissámou
Κόλπος Κισσάμου

Kólpos Haníon
Κόλπος Χανίων

Stavrós
Σταυρός

Pireás Thessaloníki

Rodopós
Ροδοπός

Kolimvári
Κολυμβάρι

Goniá
Γωνιά

Hers. Akrotíri
Χερσ. Ακρωτήρι

762

Kastéli
Καστέλλι

Tavronítis
Ταυρωνίτης

Haniá
Χανιά

Kounoupidianá
Κουνουπιδιανά

Perivolítsa
Περβολίτσα

Falássarna
Φαλάσαρνα

E 65   13

Plataniás
Πλατανιάς

Máleme
Μάλεμε

39

Ag. Marína
Αγ. Μαρίνα

Soúda
Σούδα

Stérnes
Στέρνες

Plátanos
Πλάτανος

Kaloudianá
Καλουδιανά

Manoliópoulo
Μανολιόπουλο

14

Mournés
Μουρνιές

Maláxa
Μαλάξα

Kallíves
Καλύβες

Akr. Drápano
Ακρ. Δράπανο

Órmos Soúdas
Όρμος Σούδας

Órmos Almírou
Όρμος Αλμύρου

Polirínia
Πολυρρηνία

Topólia
Τοπόλια

37

Voukoliés
Βουκολιές

Alikianós
Αλικιανός

Fournés
Φουρνές

Áptera
Άπτερα

32

Kefalás
Κεφαλάς

Kámbos
Κάμπος

Kakópetros
Κακόπετρος

Láki
Λάκκοι

Ramní
Ραμνή

Vríses
Βρύσες

Réthimno
Ρέθυμνο

1071

N. Roúmata
Ν. Ρούματα

19

36

Thérisa
Θέρισα

HANIÁ
ΧΑΝΙΑ

13

Vámos
Βάμος

Georgioúpoli
Γεωργιούπολη

23

Perivólia
Περιβόλια

Plata
Πλατ

Strovlés
Στροβλές

1331

Omalós
Ομαλός

22

12

2133

Óri
Όρη

Emprósneros
Εμπρόσνερος

Kournás
Κουρνάς

20

E 75

Prinés
Πρινές

21

Prassiés
Πρασιές

Élos
Έλος

Kándanos
Κάνδανος

Xilóskalo
Ξυλόσκαλο

Lefká
Λευκά

Farángi
Φαράγγι

2453

40

Askífou
Ασκύφου

Argiroúpoli
Αργυρούπολη

Episkopí
Επισκοπή

19

Arméni
Αρμένοι

RÉTHIM
ΡΕΘΥΜ

Íboutás
Ιβουτάς

16

Rodováni
Ροδοβάνι

Sanariás
Σαμαριάς

Pахnes
Πάχνες

2218

1512

Myriokéfala
Μυριοκέφαλα

Agkouseliána
Αγκουσελιανά

Sélia
Σελλιά

Sklavopoúla
Σκλαβοπούλα

18

Soúgia
Σούγια

Anópoli
Ανώπολη

Ásfendos
Άσφενδος

Á. Rodákino
Α. Ροδάκινο

38

984

Aó,motos
Αόματος

Akr. Kriós
Ακρ. Κριός

Paleohóra
Παλαιοχώρα

Ag. Rouméli
Αγ. Ρουμέλη

Sfakiá
Σφακιά
(80)

Frangokástelo
Φραγκοκάστελλο

Patsianós
Πατσιανός

Plakiás
Πλακιάς

27

Kissoú K
Κισσού Κ

Préveli
Πρέβελη

N. Gavdopoúla
Ν. Γαυδοπούλα

N. Paxim
Ν. Παξιμ

368

N. Gávdos
Ν. Γαύδος

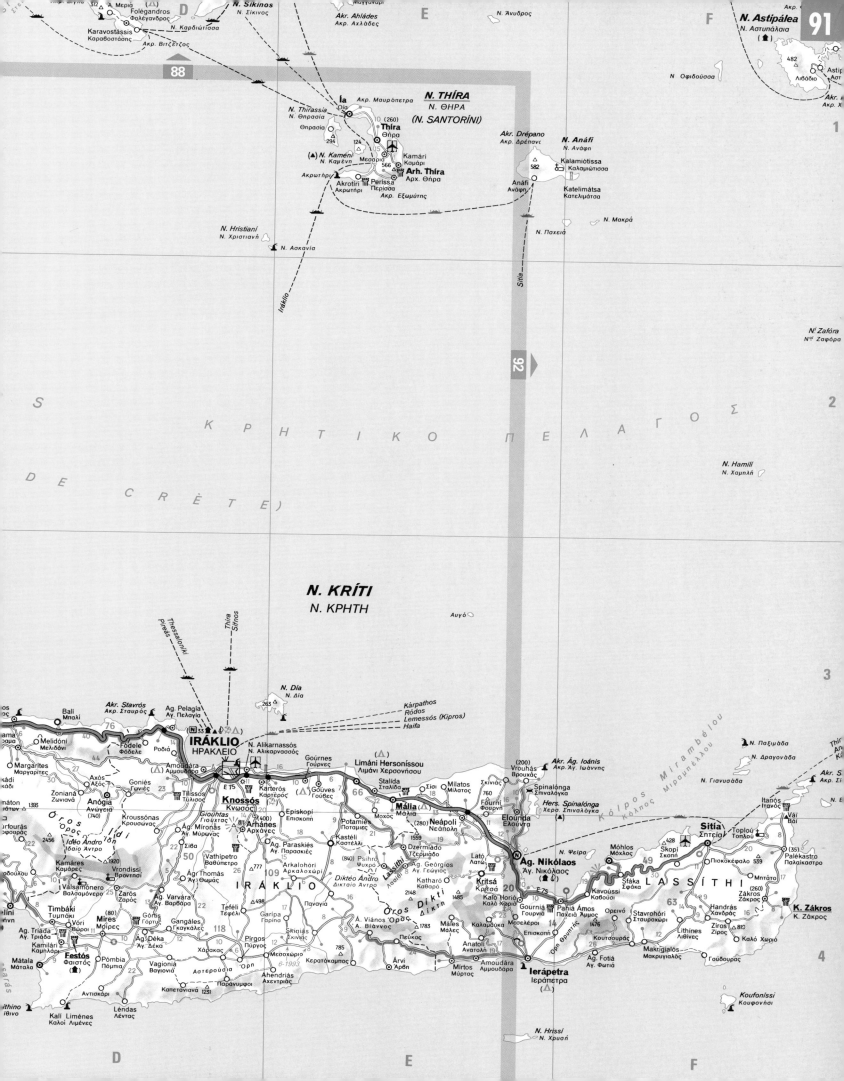

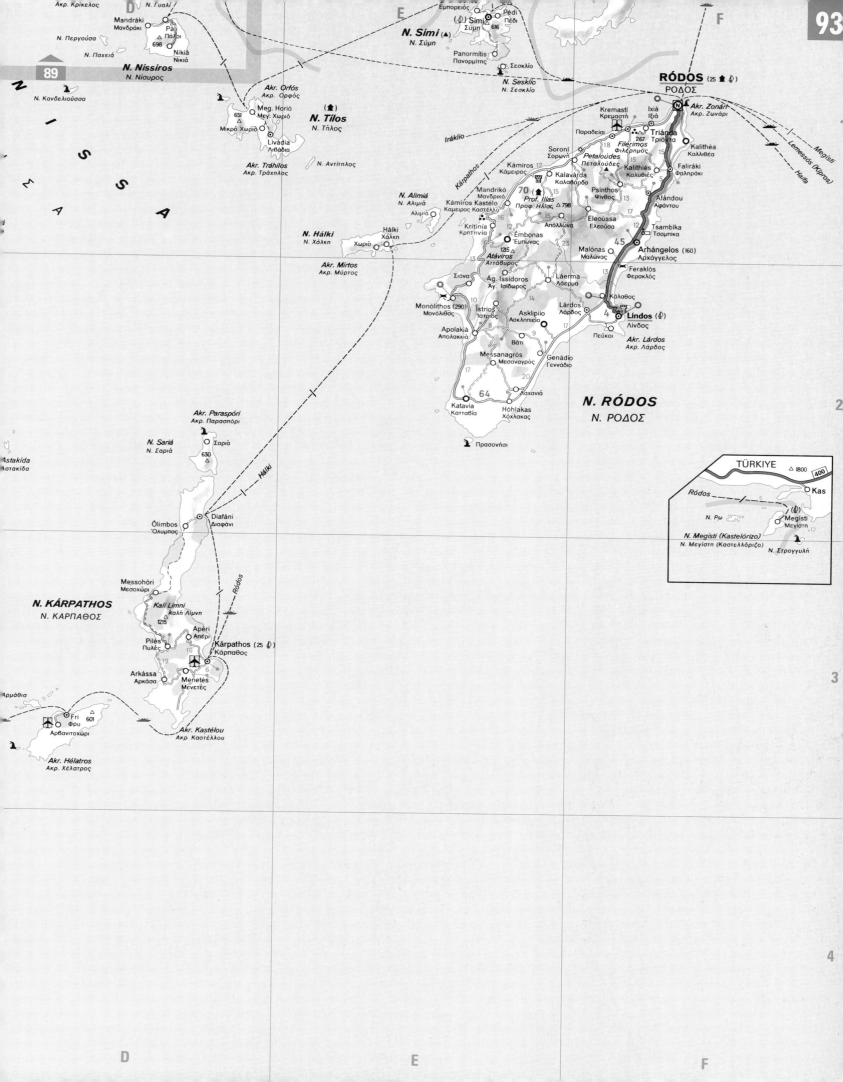

Akr. Krikelos
Ακρ. Κρίκελος

N. Gialí
N. Γυαλί

Emboreiós
Εμπορειός

Simi
(🏛) Simí
Σύμη

Pédi
Πέδι

N. Simí (🏔)
N. Σύμη

616

Mandráki
Μανδράκι

Ráli
Ράλι

698

Nikiá
Νικιά

Panormítis
Πανορμίτης

Seskli
Σεσκλίο

N. Pergoúsa
N. Περγούσα

N. Pacheiá
N. Παχειά

N. Níssiros
N. Νίσυρος

N. Sesklío
N. Σεσκλίο

RÓDOS (25 🏛 ⚓)
ΡΟΔΟΣ

N. Kandelioússa
N. Κανδελιούσσα

Akr. Orfós
Ακρ. Ορφός

Meg. Horió
Μεγ. Χωριό

N. Tílos
N. Τήλος

Kremasti
Κρεμαστή

Ixiá
Ιξιά

Akr. Zonári
Ακρ. Ζωνάρι

651

Mikró Chorió
Μικρό Χωριό

Paradeísi
Παραδείσι

267

Filérimos
Φιλέρημος

Triánda
Τριάντα

Iráklio

Livádia
Λιβάδια

Soroní
Σορωνή

Petaloúdes
Πεταλούδες

Kalithiés
Καλυθιές

Kalithéa
Καλλιθέα

Lemessós (Kípros)

Akr. Tráhilos
Ακρ. Τράχηλος

N. Antítplos
N. Αντίτηλος

Kámiros
Κάμιρος

12

Kalavárda
Καλαβάρδα

15

Psinthos
Ψίνθος

Faliráki
Φαλιράκι

Háifa

Mandrikó
Μανδρικό

70 (🏛)

15

Prof. Ilías
Προφ. Ηλίας △798

Afándou
Αφάντου

N. Alimiá
N. Αλιμιά

Kámiros Kastéllo
Καμειρος Καστέλλο

16

Eleoússa
Ελεούσσα

13

Kritinía
Κρητινία

Émbonas
Έμπωνας

Apóllona
Απόλλωνα

Tsambíka
Τσαμπίκα

N. Hálki
N. Χάλκη

Hálki
Χάλκη

125

Atáviros
Ατάβυρος

45

Arhángelos (160)
Αρχάγγελος

Chorió
Χωριό

13

23

Malónas
Μαλώνας

Akr. Mírtos
Ακρ. Μύρτος

Sióna
Σιόνα

Ág. Issídoros
Άγ. Ισίδωρος

Láerma
Λάερμα

Feraklós
Φεράκλος

10

14

Kálathos
Κάλαθος

Monólithos (290)
Μονόλιθος

Ístrios
Ίστριος

Asklipiío
Ασκληπιείο

Lárdos
Λάρδος

17

4

Líndos (⚓)
Λίνδος

8

9

Apolakiá
Απολακκιά

Báti
Βάτι

Peúkoi
Πεύκοι

Akr. Lárdos
Ακρ. Λάρδος

Messanagrós
Μεσαναγρός

Genádio
Γεννάδιο

N. RÓDOS
N. ΡΟΔΟΣ

17

20

Katavia
Κατταβία

64

Chachaniá
Χάχανιά

Hóhlakas
Χόχλακας

Prasonísi
Πρασονήσι

Akr. Paraspóri
Ακρ. Παρασπόρι

N. Sariá
N. Σαριά

Sariá
Σαριά

TÜRKIYE
△1800
400

630

Rödos

Kas

Hálki

N. Rö
N. Ρω

Megísti
Μεγίστη

Ólimbos
Όλυμπος

Diafáni
Διαφάνι

N. Megísti (Kastelórizo)
N. Μεγίστη (Καστελλόριζο)

N. Stroggylí
N. Στρογγυλή

Astakída
Ασтακίδα

Rödos

N. KÁRPATHOS
N. ΚΑΡΠΑΘΟΣ

Messohóri
Μεσοχώρι

Kali Limni
Καλή Λίμνη

1215

Apéri
Απέρι

Pilés
Πυλές

16

Kárpathos (25 ⚓)
Κάρπαθος

Arkássa
Αρκάσα

19

6

Ménetes
Μένετες

Armáthia
Αρμάθια

Fri
Φρυ

601

Akr. Kastélou
Ακρ. Καστέλλου

Arvanitochóri
Αρβανιτοχώρι

Akr. Hélatros
Ακρ. Χέλατρος

A　　　　　　　　　　B　　　　　　　　　　C

66°33

Cercle polaire arctique　　　Norðurheimskautsbaugur　　　Grímsey

1

Hornbjarg

Jökulfirðir　　Reykjafjörður

Bolungarvík
(△) Ísafjörður
18
Drangajökull
925
Norðurfjörður
Raufarhöfn
85
Kópasker　78　29
Þórshöfn
867　36
Húsavík　38
Bakkafjörður
Bakkaflói

Ísafjarðardjúp
62　60
40
835
96
Siglufjörður
Ólafsfjörður
80
Hrísey
Dalvík　82
Árskógssandur
76
Húnaflói
122
Skagafjörður
Skagaströnd
715
Saúðárkrókur
115
Blönduós
Vopnafjörður
70
Borgarfjörð

þingeyri
184
Gláma
68
643
71
76
54
Krafla 818
Reykjahlíð
62
Dettifoss

Bíldudalur
120
37
Hólmavík
Hvammstangi
Akureyri
(△) Akureyri
89
82
Goðafoss
Mývatn
274
107
Egilsstaðir
(△)　93
Eiðar　25
Seyðisfjörð

Patreksfjörður
62　48
Brjánslækur
50
123
Reykhólar
Flatey
45
7
Laugarbakki
24
93
F 82
F 95
Skjálfandafljót
Jökulsá á Fjöllum
27
F 98
Laggarfljót
31
Neskau
40
Eskifjörð

Látrabjarg
Breiðafjörður
99
Laugar
590
59
425
33
86
F 74
123
Askja
Dreki
190
Reyðarfjörður
96　102
Fáskrúðsfjörður
Breiðdalsvík

Stykkishólmur
Grundarfjörður
Ólafsvík
20
1448
Snæfellsnes
Búðir
37
Búðardalur
57
76
43
48
Í S L A N D
Laugafell
F 26
Hofsjökull
△1765
45
Sprengisandur
Óðáðahraun
68
241
Djúpivogur

2

Faxaflói
Reykholt
1675
Hveravellir
Hvítárnes
F 37
Nýidalur
2000
1570

Borgarnes
Húsafell (△)
102
Hvítá
Pjórsá
105
Kaldakvísl
V A T N A J Ö K U L L

Akranes
(△)
þingvellir
914
(△)
365
Laugarvatn (△)
26
130
Höfn

REYKJAVÍK
Garður
36
þingvallavatn
46
Flúðir
63
110
Hekla
△1491
95
Eldgjá
Skaftá
(△) Skaftafell
△ 2219
461

Sandgerði
47
50
Hveragerði
30
Landmannalaugar
F 22
96

Keflavík
25　41　42　35
Selfoss
Hella (△)
Pjórsá
Kirkjubæjarklaustur
Skeiðarársandur
Fagurhólsmýri

Grindavík
þórlákshöfn
44
Hvolsvöllur
Myrdals-
249
Þórsmörk
jökull
204

135
Seljalandsfoss
Skógafoss
(△)
Vík
50

ATLANTSHAF

Vestmannaeyjar

1 / 2 400 000

0 ———— 50

ATLANTSHAF

3

100

FØROYAR
FÆRØERNE
(**DK**)

NORÐOYAR

Seyðisfjörður

Viðareiði
Gjógv
882
Kunoy Viðoy
Eiði
Oyndarfjörður
Svínoy
Tjørnuvík
790
Borðoy
Hvalvík
Eysturoy
Leirvík
Klaksvík
Streymoy

Mykines
Vestmanna
722 Vágar
18
58
Sørvágur
Toftir

Tórshavn (A ▲)

Kirkjubøur

Skopun
Sandoy
479
Sandur
Skálavík

4

Hvalba
10
Tvøroyri
618
Fámjin
Suðuroy
Vágur
Sumba

0 ———— 30 km

A　　　　　　　　　　B　　　　　　　　　　C

N O R S K E H A V E T

(△) Sør-Flatang

Osen

Roan

Harsvík

66

(F) Lorsqu'un nom figure plusieurs fois dans l'index, une précision est ajoutée entre parenthèses pour permettre de l'identifier plus facilement: pays, région ou ville la plus proche, élément géographique d'après les abréviations ci-dessous.

(GB) Where there are two or more identical place names, the name of the distinguishing country or region or nearest large town is given in brackets; geographical features are indicated by the abbreviations below.

(D) Tritt ein Name mehrfach im Register auf, wird er durch eine in Klammern gesetzte nähere Bestimmung genauer definiert. Sie finden folgende Zusätze: Land, Region oder nächstgelegene Stadt, geographische Gegebenheiten, ggf. abgekürzt

(NL) Bij namen die meermalen in het register voorkomen, staat tussen haakjes een aanduiding ter verklaring: het land, de streek, de dichtstbijgelegen stad of een geografisch gegeven (zie de afkortingen hieronder).

(E) Para poder localizar más fácilmente un nombre que figura varias veces en el índice, se añade entre paréntesis el país, la región o ciudad más cercana, o un elemento geográfico, con las abreviaturas siguientes.

(I) Quando un nome figura più volte nell'indice, una precisazione viene aggiunta tra parentesi per permettere d'identificarlo più facilmente: nazione, regione o città la più vicina, elemento geografico come da abbreviazioni qui di seguito.

Akr	Akra, Akrotírion	Liq	Liquen	Pk	Park
B	Bay, Baie, Bucht, Bahía, Baia, Bukt(en), Bugt, Bukhta	Meg	Méga, Megál, -a, -i, -o	Pl	Planina
		Mikr.	Mikr-í, -ón	Pque	Parque
		Mgne(s)	Montagne(s)	Prov	Province
Bgem	Barragem	M, Mte(s)	Maj, Maj'e, Monte(s)	Pso	Passo
C	Cape, Cap, Cabo, Capo			Pt(e)	Point(e)
Co	County	Mt(s), *Mt(s)*	Mount(s), Mountain(s), Mont(s)	Rib	Ribeirão
Ch	Chaîne			R, *R*	River, Rivière, Rio, Ria, Rijeka
Chan	Channel	Mti	Monti, Muntii		
Dépt	Département	Nac	Nacional(e)	Reg	Region, Région
Emb	Embalse	Nat	National	Res	Reservoir, Reservoire
Ez	Ezero	Naz	Nazionale	Sa	Sierra, Serra
G	Gulf, Golfe, Golfo	N	Nissi, Nissos	Sd	Sound, Sund
Gges	Gorges	Ni	Nissiá, Nissi	St	Saint, Sankt, Sint
I(s), *I(s)*	Isles(s), Island(s), Ile(s), Ilha(s), Isla(s), Isola(e)	Os	Ostrov(a)	Ste(s)	Sainte(s)
		Ot	Otok(i), Otoci	Teh L	Tehniti Límni
Jez	Jezoro, Jezioro	Oz	Ozero(a)	V	Valley, Vale, Vallée, Val, Valle, Vall
K	Kanal, Kanaal	P	Pass		
L, *L*	Lake, Loch, Lough, Llyn, Lac, Laguna, Lago, Límni	Pal	Paleós, á, ó		
		Pen	Peninsula, Penisola		

A

Aachen	51 D3	A Baiuca	34 A1
Aalen	55 E2	Abanilla	45 D2
Aalsmeer	16 C2	Abano Terme	61 D1
Aalst	50 B3	Abbadia	
Aalten	17 D3	San Salvatore	63 D1
Aalter	50 B3	Abbasanta	66 B3
Äänekoski	103 D2	Abbazia di	
Aapajärvi	95 F4	Casamari	63 F3
Aarau	27 F2	Abbazia di	
Aarberg	27 E2	Fossanova	63 F3
Aarburg	27 F2	Abbazia di	
Aare	58 A3	Montecassino	64 A3
Aargau	27 F2	Abbazia San Clemente	
Aarlen	21 D2	a Casauria	64 A2
Aarschot	50 C3	Abbeville	19 E2
Aavasaksa	98 C2	Abbeyfeale	14 B3
Abades	40 A1	Abbeyleix	12 C4
Abadiño	36 B1	Abbey Town	5 D4
		Abbiategrasso	60 A1
		Abborrträsk	98 B3
		Abbots Bromley	6 C3

Abbotsbury	9 D3	Abergwaun	8 B1
Abcoude	16 C2	Aberhonddu	8 C1
Abejar	36 B3	Aberlady	5 D2
Abejuela	41 E3	Aberpennar	8 C2
Abela	42 A1	Aberporth	8 B1
Abelvær	97 D4	Abersoch	6 A3
Abenberg	55 E2	Abertawe	8 C2
Abenójar	39 F4	Aberteifi	8 B1
Åbenrå	108 A4	Abertillery	9 D2
Abensberg	55 F2	Aber-Wrac'h, l'	22 A2
Aberaeron	8 C1	Aberystwyth	8 C1
Aberdâr	8 C2	Abetone	60 C3
Aberdare	8 C2	Abiego	37 E3
Aberdaron	6 A3	Abingdon	9 E2
Aberdeen	3 E4	Abington	5 D3
Aberdovey	6 A3	Abisko	94 B3
Aberfeldy	4 C1	Abisko (Nat park)	94 B4
Aberfoyle	4 C2	Abla	44 B3
Abergavenny	9 D2	Ablis	19 E4
Abergele	6 B2	Åbo	107 D2
		Abondance	27 E3

Abony	112 B4	Acedo	36 B2
Aboyne	3 E4	Acehuche	39 D3
Abrantes	38 B3	Acerno	64 B4
Abreschviller	21 E4	Acerra	64 B4
Abrets, les	30 C1	Aceuchal	39 D4
Abriès	31 E2	Ache	59 E1
Abruzzo	63 F2	Achenkirch	59 D1
Abruzzo, Parco		Achenpaß	56 A4
Nazionale d'	64 A2	Achensee	59 D1
Abstadt-		Achern	54 C3
Tailfingen	55 D3	Acheux	19 F2
Abtenau	59 E1	Achill I	12 A2
Åby	105 F4	Achim	17 F1
Åbybro	108 B2	Achnacroish	4 B1
A Caniza	34 A3	Achnasheen	2 C3
Acceglio	31 E2	A'Chràlaig	2 C4
Accettura	65 D4	Aci Castello	69 D3
Acciaroli	67 D1	Acipayam	115 F4
Accous	37 D1	Acireale	69 D3
Accrington	6 C2	Aci Trezza	69 D3
Acebo	39 D2	Acle	7 F3
		A Coruña	34 B1

Acqualagna	61 E4
Acquapendente	63 D1
Acquasanta	
Terme	63 F1
Acquasparta	63 E1
Acquaviva delle	
Fonti	65 D3
Acqui-Terme	60 A2
Acri	67 E2
Ada	72 C1
Adaja, R	39 F2
Adak	98 A3
Ådalsel	104 C2
Adamandás	88 A4
Adamclisi	115 E1
Adamello	58 C3
Adamello Brenta,	
Parco Naturale	58 C3
Adamello, Mont'	58 C3
Adamuz	43 F2
Adanero	39 F1
Adapazari	115 F3
Adare	14 B3
Adaševci	72 B3
Adda	60 B2
Adelboden	27 E3
Adelfia	65 D3
Adelsheim	55 D1
Ademuz	41 D3
Adenau	51 E4
Ádendro	79 F3
Adéres, Óros	87 E2
Adiça, Sa da	42 C1
Adige	61 D1
Adjud	113 E4
Admont	57 D3
Adolfström	97 F3
Adorf	53 D3
Adour	28 B4
Adra	44 B4
Adradas	36 B4
Adrall	32 A3
Adrano	69 D3
Adria	61 D2
Adriatic Sea	114 A3
Adzaneta	41 E3
Aegean Sea	115 E4
Aenona	74 C1
Aerinó	83 F2
Ærø	108 B4
Ærøskøbing	108 B4
A Estrada	34 A2
Aetópetra	82 B1
Aetós (Kefaloniá)	82 B4
Aetós	
(Makedonía)	79 D3
Aetós	
(Stereá Eláda)	82 C3
Äetsä	107 D2
Afándou	93 F1
Åfarnes	100 B2
Aféa	87 F2
Affi	60 C1
Afiónas	82 A1
Áfissos	83 F2

Áfitos	80 B4
Åfjord	100 C1
Åfjorden	104 A1
Aflenzer Seeberg	57 E3
Aflenz Kurort	57 E3
Afráti	84 B4
Afsluitdijk	16 C1
A Garda	34 A3
Agathoníssi	89 E2
Agay	31 E4
Agazzano	60 B2
Agde	30 A4
Agdenes	100 C1
Agen	28 C3
Ager	37 F3
Åger	56 C3
Ageranós	87 D4
Agerbæk	108 A3
Agger	17 E4
Aggius	66 B1
Aggsbach-Dorf	57 E2
Aggsbach-Markt	57 E2
Agiá	83 F1
Agiá, Akr	83 F4
Agía Ana (Évia)	84 A3
Agía Ana	
(Viotía)	83 F4
Agía Efimía	82 B4
Agía Efthimía	83 E4
Agía Ekateríni, Akr	82 A1
Agía Fotiá	91 F4
Agía Galíni	91 D4
Agía Kiriakí	
(Makedonía)	78 C3
Agía Kiriakí	
(Pelopónissos)	86 B4
Agía Kiriakí	
(Sámos)	89 E2
Agía Lávra	86 C1
Agía Marína	
(Égina)	87 F2
Agía Marína (Kríti)	90 B3
Agía Marína (Léros)	89 E3
Agía Marína	
(Stereá Eláda)	83 E2
Agía Marína	
(Stereá Eláda)	88 A1
Agía Paraskeví	
(Lésvos)	85 E2
Agía Paraskeví	
(Makedonía)	80 C2
Agía Paraskiés	91 E4
Agía Pelagía	
(Kíthira)	90 A1
Agía Pelagía (Kríti)	91 D3
Agía Pelagía	90 B4
Agía Rouméli	90 B4
Agiásma	80 C2
Agiásmata	85 E4
Agía Sofía (Évia)	84 B3
Agía Sofía	
(Pelopónissos)	87 D2
Agía Sotíra	87 E1
Agiássos	85 F2
Agía Triáda (Kríti)	91 D4
Agía Triáda	
(Makedonía)	79 F3
Agía Triáda	
(Pelopónissos)	86 C1
Agía Triáda	
(Stereá Eláda)	87 F1
Agía Varvára	91 D4
Agiófilo	83 D1
Agiókambos	
(Évia)	83 F3
Agiókambos	
(Thessalía)	83 F1
Agionóri	87 E2
Ágio Óros	80 C4
Agiopigí	83 D2
Ágios	84 A3
Ágios Anárgiri	
(Pelopónissos)	87 D3
Ágios Anárgiri	
(Thessalía)	83 E2
Ágios Andónios	80 A3
Ágios Andréas	
(Arkadía)	87 D3

Ágios Andréas (Lakonía) 87 E4
Ágios Apóstoli (Évia) 84 B4
Ágios Apóstoli (Pelopónnissos) 87 E4
Ágios Apóstoli (Stereá Eláda) 84 B4
Ágios Athanássios (Dráma) 80 C2
Ágios Athanássios (Péla) 79 D2
Ágios Avgoustínos 86 C3
Ágios Déka 91 D4
Ágios Dimítrios, Akr 88 A3
Ágios Dimítrios (Évia) 88 A1
Ágios Dimítrios (Lakonía) 87 D3
Ágios Dimítrios (Makedonía) 79 E4
Ágios Dimítrios (Messinía) 87 D4
Ágios Dimítrios (Stereá Eláda) 83 D3
Ágios Dioníssios 79 E4
Ágios Efstrátios, N 85 D2
Ágios Fokás 89 F3
Ágios Fokás, Akr 85 F3
Ágios Geórgios (Évia) 83 F3
Ágios Geórgios, N 87 F2
Ágios Geórgios (Lassíthi) 91 E4
Ágios Geórgios (Stereá Eláda) 83 D3
Ágios Geórgios (Zákinthos) 86 A1
Ágios Georgíou, Órmos 87 E3
Ágios Germanós 79 D2
Ágios Górdis 82 A1
Ágios Harálambos 81 E2
Ágios Ioánis, Akr 91 F3
Ágios Ioánis (Dodekánissa) 89 F4
Ágios Ioánis (Pelopónnissos) 87 E2
Ágios Ioánis (Stereá Eláda) 83 F4
Ágios Ioánis (Thessalía) 83 F3
Ágios Ioánis (Thessalía) 83 F2
Ágios Irínis, Akr 85 D1
Ágios Issídoros 93 E2
Ágios Kirikos 89 D2
Ágios Konstandínos (Stereá Eláda) 83 F3
Ágios Konstandínos (Thessalía) 83 E2
Ágios Kosmás (Grevená) 79 D3
Ágios Kosmás (Kavála) 80 C2
Ágios Léon 86 A1
Ágios Loukás 84 B4
Ágios Mámas 80 A4
Ágios Márkos 80 A2
Ágios Mathéos 82 A2
Ágios Mironas 91 D4
Ágios Nikítas 82 B3
Ágios Nikólaos (Etolía-Akarnanía) 82 B3
Ágios Nikólaos (Fokída) 83 E4
Ágios Nikólaos (Fthiótida) 83 E3
Ágios Nikólaos (Hers.Methánon) 87 E2
Ágios Nikólaos (Ípiros) 82 B1
Ágios Nikólaos (Kríti) 91 E4
Ágios Nikólaos (Lakonía) 87 D3
Ágios Nikólaos (Makedonía) 80 B4
Ágios Nikólaos (Messinía) 86 C3
Ágios Pandeleímonos 79 D3

Ágios Pángalos, Akr 83 E4
Ágios Paraskeví (Ípiros) 78 C4
Ágios Paraskeví (Makedonía) 79 F2
Ágios Pávlos 80 A3
Ágios Pétros 87 D2
Ágios Pnévma 80 B2
Ágios Pródromos 80 A3
Ágios Sóstis 83 E3
Ágios Stéfanos (Kikládes) 88 C2
Ágios Stéfanos (Stereá Eláda) 87 F1
Ágios Theódori (Makedonía) 79 D4
Ágios Theódori (Pelopónnissos) 87 E1
Ágios Theódori (Thessalía) 83 F3
Ágios Thomás (Kríti) 91 D4
Ágios Thomás (Stereá Eláda) 84 B4
Ágios Vassílios (Makedonía) 80 A3
Ágios Vassílios (Stereá Eláda) 84 A4
Ágios Vissários 83 E2
Agíou Órous, Kólpos 80 C4
Agira 68 C3
Agly 32 B2
Ágnanda 82 C2
Agnanderó 83 D2
Ágnandi 83 F3
Agnóndas 84 B3
Agnone 64 B2
Agnoúnda 87 E2
Agon-Coutainville 18 B3
Agorá 80 C2
Agordo 59 D3
Agost 45 E1
Agout 29 D4
Agrafiótis 83 D2
Agramunt 37 F3
Agrate Br. 60 A1
Agreda 36 C3
Agreliá 83 D1
Agri 65 D4
Agrigento 68 B4
Agriliá 82 C4
Agriliá, Akr 85 F3
Ágrilos 86 B3
Agrínio 82 C3
Agriovótano 83 F3
Agrópoli 64 B4
Agskaret 97 D2
Aguadulce (Almería) 44 B4
Aguadulce (Sevilla) 43 E3
Aguas Vivas, R 37 D4
Aguaviva 41 E2
A Gudiña 34 C3
Agudo 39 F4
Agueda 38 B1
Agueda, R 39 D2
Aguiar 42 B1
Aguiar da Beira 38 C1
Aguilafuente 40 A1
Aguilar 43 F2
Aguilar de Campóo 35 F2
Aguilar del Alfambra 41 E2
Aguilar, Emb de 35 F2
Águilas 44 C3
Ahala 86 C1
Aharnés 87 F1
Ahaus 17 E3
Åheim 100 A3
Aheloós 82 C4
Ahendriás 91 E4
Ahérondas 82 B2
Ahigal 39 D2
Ahilio (Kérkira) 82 A1
Ahilio (Thessalía) 83 E2
Ahinós 80 B2
Ahjärvi 103 F3
Ahladerí 84 B4
Ahládes, Akr 88 C4

Ahladohóri 80 B1
Ahlainen 102 B3
Ahlbeck 49 E2
Ahlen 17 E3
Ahlhorn 17 F1
Ahrensbök 48 B1
Ahrensburg 48 B2
Ahrweiler 51 E4
Ähtäri 102 C2
Ähtärinjärvi 102 C2
Ahtävänjoki 102 C2
Ahtopol 115 E2
Ahun 25 E4
Åhus 109 D3
Ahvenanmaa 106 C3
Ahvenselkä 99 E1
Aichach 55 F3
Aidenbach 56 B2
Aidone 68 C3
Aigen 56 C2
Aigle 27 E3
Aigle, Bge de l' 29 E1
Aigle, l' 19 D4
Aignan 28 C4
Aignay-le-Duc 26 C2
Aigoual, Mt 29 F3
Aigre 24 C4
Aigrefeuille-d'Aunis 24 B4
Aigrefeuille-sur-Maine 24 B3
Aiguablava 32 C3
Aiguebelette 30 C1
Aiguebelle 31 D1
Aigueperse 26 A4
Aigues 30 C3
Aigues-Mortes 30 B4
Aigües Tortes, Parque Nac de 37 F2
Aiguilles 31 E2
Aiguillon 28 C3
Aiguillon, l' 24 B4
Aigurande 25 E4
Ailefroide 31 D2
Aillant 26 A1
Ailly-le-Haut-locher 19 E2
Ailly-sur-Noye 19 F2
Ailsa Craig 4 B3
Aimargues 30 B4
Aime 31 D1
Ain 27 D3
Ain (Dépt) 26 C4
Ainhoa 28 A4
Ainsa 37 E2
Ainsdale 6 B2
Ainzón 36 C3
Airaines 19 E2
Airasca 31 D2
Airdrie 4 C2
Aire R 7 D2
Aire 19 F1
Aire, I del 45 F2
Aire, Sa de 38 B3
Aire-sur-l'Adour 28 B4
Airisto 107 D2
Airolo 58 A3
Airvault 24 C3
Aisne 20 A3
Aisne (Dépt) 20 A2
Aitana 45 E1
Aiterhofen 56 B2
Aitrach 55 E3
Aitzgorri 36 B1
Aiud 112 C4
Aix-d'Angillon, les 26 A2
Aixe 29 D1
Aix-en-Othe 26 B1
Aix-en-Provence 30 C4
Aix, I d' 24 B4
Aix-les-Bains 27 D4
Aizenay 24 B3
Aizkraukle 110 C3
Ajaccio 33 E4
Ajdanovac 77 D1
Ajdovščina 70 A2
Ajka 112 A4
Ajo 35 F1
Ajo, C de 36 A1
Ajos 99 D3
Ajtos 115 E2
Akarnaniká, Óri 82 C3
Äkäsjokisuu 95 D4

Äkäskero 95 D4
Äkäslompolo 95 D4
Akçakoca 115 F3
Aken 53 D1
Åkersberga 106 B3
Akershus 105 D3
Åkers styckebruk 106 B4
Akhisar 115 F4
Åkirkeby 109 D4
Akkajaure 94 B4
Akkerhaugen 104 C3
Akku 95 D3
Akranes 96 A2
Akráta 87 D1
Akrathos, Akr 80 C4
Akréfnio 83 F4
Åkrehamn 104 A3
Akrestrømmen 100 C3
Akrítas 79 D2
Akrítas, Akr 86 C4
Akrogiáli 80 B3
Akropótamos 80 B3
Akrotíri 91 E1
Akrovoúni 80 C2
Aktí Apólona 87 F2
Akujärvi 95 F3
Akureyrí 96 B1
Ål 104 C2
Ala 60 C1
Ala di Stura 31 E1
Alà dei Sardi 66 B2
Alaejos 35 E4
Alagí 86 C3
Alagna Valsesia 27 F4
Alagnon 29 F2
Alagón 37 D3
Alagón, R 39 D2
Alagonía 86 C3
Alahärmä 102 C2
Ala-Honkajoki 102 B3
Alaior 45 F2
Alajärvi 102 C2
Alakylä 99 D1
Alalkomenés 83 F4
Alameda 43 F3
Alamillo 43 F1
Alanäs 101 F1
Aland 48 C3
Åland 106 C3
Alandroal 38 C4
Alange 39 D4
Alange, Emb de 39 D4
Alanís 43 E2
Alapitkä 103 E2
Alaraz 39 E1
Alarcón 40 C3
Alarcón, Emb de 40 C3
Alar del Rey 35 F3
Alaşehir 115 F4
Alassio 31 F3
Alastaro 107 D2
Alatoz 41 D4
Alatri 63 F3
Alavieska 102 C1
Ala-Vuokki 99 F4
Alavus 102 C2
Alba 31 F2
Alba Adriatica 64 A1
Albacete 40 C4
Albacken 101 F2
Alba de Tormes 39 E1
Albæk 108 B1
Albaida 45 E1
Albaida, Pto de 45 E1
Alba Iulia 114 C1
Albaladejo 44 B1
Albalate de Cinca 37 E3
Albalate del Arzobispo 37 D4
Albalate de las Nogueras 40 C2
Alban 29 E3
Albánchez 44 C3
Albano di Lucania 65 D4
Albano Laziale 63 E3
Albarca 37 F4
Albarella, I 61 D1
Albares 35 D2
Albarracín 41 D2
Albarracín, Sa de 41 D2
Albatera 45 D1
Albena 115 E2

Albenga 31 F3
Albens 27 D4
Alberche, R 39 F2
Alberga 105 F4
Albergaria-a-Velha 38 B1
Alberique 41 E4
Albernoa 42 B1
Alberobello 65 E3
Albersdorf 48 A2
Albert 19 F2
Albert Kanaal 50 C3
Albertville 27 D4
Albestroff 21 E3
Albi 29 E3
Albiano 31 F1
Albinia 63 D2
Albino 58 B4
Albisola Marina 60 A3
Albo, M 66 C2
Albocácer 41 F2
Albolodúy 44 B3
Albolote 44 A3
Alborea 41 D4
Ålborg 108 B2
Ålborg Bugt 108 B2
Albox 44 C3
Albstadt-Ebingen 55 D3
Albufeira 42 A3
Albujón 45 D2
Albulapass 58 B3
Albuñol 44 A4
Alburno, Mte 64 C4
Alburquerque 38 C3
Alby (F) 27 D4
Alby (S) 101 E2
Alcácer do Sál 42 A1
Alcáçovas 42 B1
Alcadozo 44 C1
Alcafozes 38 C2
Alcains 38 C2
Alcalá de Chivert 41 F2
Alcalá de Guadaira 43 D3
Alcalá de Henares 40 B2
Alcalá de la Selva 41 E2
Alcalá del Júcar 41 D4
Alcalá de los Gazules 43 D4
Alcalá del Río 43 D2
Alcalá la Real 44 A3
Alcamo 68 B3
Alcampel 37 E3
Alcanadre, R 37 E3
Alcanar 41 F2
Alcanede 38 A3
Alcanena 38 B3
Alcanhões 38 B3
Alcañices 34 C4
Alcañiz 37 E4
Alcántara 39 D3
Alcántara, Emb de 39 D3
Alcantarilha 42 A2
Alcantarilla 45 D2
Alcaracejos 43 E1
Alcaraz 44 B1
Alcaraz, Sa de 44 C1
Alcaria do Cume 42 B2
Alcaria Ruiva 42 B2
Alcarrache, R 42 C1
Alcarràs 37 E4
Alcaudete 43 F3
Alcaudete de la Jara 39 F3
Alcázar de San Juan 40 B4
Alcester 9 E1
Alcoba 39 F3
Alcobaça 38 A3
Alcoba de los Montes 39 F4
Alcobendas 40 B2
Alcoceber 41 F3
Alcochete 38 A4
Alcolea 43 F2
Alcolea de Cinca 37 E3
Alcolea del Pinar 36 B4
Alcolea del Río 43 E2
Alconchel 42 C1
Alcora 41 E3
Alcorisa 41 E2
Alcorlo, Emb de 40 B1
Alcoutim 42 B2

Alcover 37 F4
Alcoy 45 E1
Alcubierre 37 D3
Alcubierre, Sa de 37 D3
Alcubilla de Avellaneda 36 A3
Alcublas 41 E3
Alcudia 45 F2
Alcudia de Crespins 41 E4
Alcudia de Guadix 44 B3
Alcuéscar 39 D4
Aldeacentenera 39 E3
Aldeadávila, Emb de 34 C4
Aldea del Cano 39 D3
Aldea del Fresno 40 A2
Aldea del Rey 44 A1
Aldeanueva de Ebro 36 C3
Aldeanueva de la Vera 39 E2
Aldeanueva del Camino 39 E2
Aldeburgh 11 E1
Aldeia da Ponte 39 D2
Aldeia Nova de São Bento 42 C1
Alderney 18 A2
Aldershot 9 F3
Aldinci 77 E3
Aldocer 40 C2
Aledo 44 C2
Aleksandrija 113 F2
Aleksandrovac (Srbija) 73 D3
Aleksandrovac (Srbija) 77 D1
Aleksa Šantić 72 B1
Aleksinac 73 E4
Alençon 23 F3
Alenquer 38 A3
Alentejo 42 B1
Alepohóri (Pelopónnissos) 87 D2
Alepohóri (Stereá Eláda) 87 E1
Aléria 33 F3
Alès 30 B3
Ales 66 B3
Aleşd 112 C4
Alessandria 60 A2
Alessandria d. Rocca 68 B3
Alestrup 108 A2
Ålesund 100 A2
Aletschhorn 27 F3
Alexandria (GB) 4 C2
Alexándria (GR) 79 E3
Alexandria (RO) 115 D2
Alexandroúpoli 81 E2
Alf 51 E4
Alfajarín 37 D3
Alfambra (E) 41 D2
Alfambra (P) 42 A2
Alfândega da Fé 34 C4
Alfaro 36 C3
Alfarrás 37 E3
Alfaz del Pi 45 E1
Alfedena 64 A2
Alfeizerão 38 A3
Alfeld (Bayern) 55 F1
Alfeld (Niedersachsen) 52 B1
Alfiós 86 B2
Alfonso XIII, Emb de 44 C2
Alford (Grampian) 3 E4
Alford (Lincs) 7 E3
Alfreton 7 D3
Alfta 101 F4
Algaida 45 F3
Algar 43 F3
Ålgård 104 A4
Algar de Palancia 41 E3
Algarinejo 43 F3
Algarrobo 43 F3
Algarve 42 B2
Algatocín 43 E4
Algeciras 43 D4
Algemesi 41 E4
Alghero 66 A2

Alginet 41 E4
Algodonales 43 E3
Algodor, R 40 A3
Algora 40 C1
Algorta 36 B1
Algoz 42 A2
Alhama de Almería 44 B3
Alhama de Aragón 36 C4
Alhama de Granada 43 F3
Alhama de Murcia 45 D2
Alhambra 40 B4
Alhamilla, Sa 44 B3
Alhaurín el Grande 43 E4
Alhóndiga 40 C2
Alia (E) 39 E3
Alia (I) 68 C3
Aliaga 41 E2
Aliaguilla 41 D3
Aliákmona, L 79 E4
Aliákmonas 79 D4
Alíartos 83 F4
Alibunar 73 D2
Alicante 45 E2
Alicudi, I 68 C2
Alicún de Ortega 44 B2
Alife 64 B3
Alijó 34 B4
Alikés 86 A1
Alikianós 90 B3
Alikí (Kikládes) 88 C3
Alikí (Thássos) 81 D3
Alimiá, N 93 E1
Alingsås 108 C1
Alinyà 32 A3
Aliseda 39 D3
Alise-Ste-Reine 26 B2
Aliste, R 35 D4
Alistráti 80 B2
Ali Terme 69 D2
Alivéri 84 B4
Aljezur 42 A2
Aljibe 43 D4
Aljucén 39 D4
Aljustrel 42 B1
Alkionídon, Kólpos 87 E1
Alkmaar 16 C2
Allaire 22 C4
Allaman, M 76 C4
Allanche 29 E2
Alland 57 E3
Allariz 34 B3
Alleen 104 B4
Alleghe 59 D3
Allègre 29 F2
Allen, L 12 C2
Allensbach 55 D4
Allentsteig 57 E2
Allepuz 41 E2
Aller 48 A4
Allersberg 55 F1
Allershausen 55 F3
Alleuze 29 F2
Allevard 31 D1
Allier (Dépt) 26 A3
Allier R 26 A3
Allinge-Sandvig 109 D4
Allo 36 C2
Alloa 5 D2
Allonnes 23 F4
Allos 31 D3
Allos, Col d' 31 D3
Allstedt 52 C2
Almacelles 37 E3
Almáchar 43 F3
Almada 38 A4
Almadén 39 F4
Almadén de la Plata 43 D2
Almadenejos 43 F1
Almagro 40 A4
Almajano 36 B3
Almansa 45 D1
Almansil 42 B2
Almanza 35 E2
Almanzora, R 44 C3
Almanzor, Pico 39 E2
Almaraz 39 E3
Almargen 43 E3
Almarza 36 B3
Almazán 36 B4
Almazora 41 E3

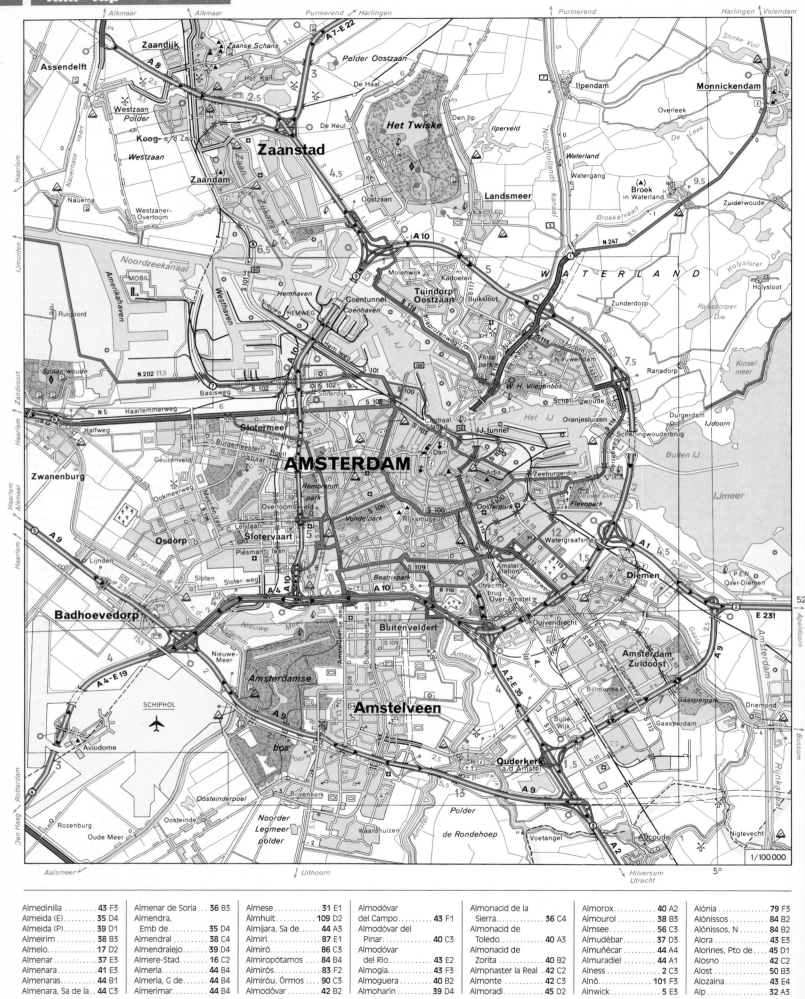

Almedinilla 43 F3	Almenar de Soria . . . 36 B3	Almese 31 E1	Almodóvar del Campo 43 F1	Almonacid de la Sierra 36 C4	Almorox 40 A2	Alónia 79 F3
Almeida (E) 35 D4	Almendra, Emb de . . 35 D4	Älmhult 109 D2	Almodóvar del Pinar 40 C3	Almonacid de Toledo 40 A3	Almourol 38 B3	Alónissos 84 B2
Almeida (P) 39 D1	Almendral 38 C4	Almijara, Sa de 44 A3			Almsee 56 C3	Alónissos, N 84 B2
Almeirim 38 B3	Almendralejo 39 D4	Almiró 86 C3	Almodóvar del Río 43 E2	Almonacid de Zorita 40 B2	Almudébar 37 D3	Alora 43 E3
Almelo 17 D2	Almere-Stad 16 C2	Almiró 87 E1			Almuñécar 44 A4	Alorines, Pto de . . . 45 D1
Almenar 37 E3	Almería 44 B4	Almiropótamos 84 B4	Almogía 43 F3	Almpnaster la Real . 42 C2	Almuradiel 44 A1	Alosno 42 C2
Almenara 41 E3	Almería, G de 44 B4	Almirós 83 F2	Almoguera 40 B2	Almonte 42 C3	Alness 2 C2	Alost 50 B3
Almenaras 44 B1	Almerimar 44 B4	Almiróu, Órmos . . . 90 C3	Almoharín 39 D4	Almoradí 45 D2	Alnö 101 F3	Alozaina 43 E4
Almenara, Sa de la . 44 C3	Almodôvar 42 B2				Alnwick 5 E3	Alp 32 A3

Alpalhão . . . 38 C3
Alpbach . . . 59 D1
Alpe-d'Huez, l' . . . 31 D1
Alpedrinha . . . 38 C2
Alpera . . . 41 D4
Alpes-de-Haute-
  Provence . . . 31 D3
Alpes-Maritimes . . . 31 E3
Alpe Veglia . . . 58 A3
Alphen aan den
  Rijn . . . 16 C3
Alpi Apuane . . . 60 B3
Alpiarça . . . 38 B3
Alpignano . . . 31 E1
Alpi Orobie . . . 58 B3
Alpirsbach . . . 54 C3
Alpua . . . 99 D4
Alqueva . . . 42 B1
Alqueva,
  Bgem de . . . 42 B1
Alquézar . . . 37 E3
Als . . . 108 B2
Als (Reg) . . . 108 B4
Alsasua . . . 36 B2
Alsdorf . . . 17 D4
Alsen . . . 101 E2
Alsfeld . . . 52 A3
Alstahaug . . . 97 D3
Alston . . . 5 E4
Alta . . . 95 D2
Altaelva . . . 95 D2
Altafjorden . . . 95 D2
Altamura . . . 65 D3
Alta, Sa . . . 41 D2
Altastenberg . . . 17 F4
Altaussee . . . 56 C3
Altavilla . . . 68 B3
Altdöbern . . . 53 E1
Altdorf (CH) . . . 58 A2
Altdorf (D) . . . 55 F1
Altea . . . 45 E1
Altedo . . . 61 D2
Altena . . . 17 E4
Altenahr . . . 51 E4
Altenau . . . 52 B2
Altenberg . . . 53 E3
Altenberge . . . 17 E3
Altenburg . . . 53 D3
Altenholz . . . 48 A1
Altenhundem . . . 17 F4
Altenkirchen
  (Mecklenburg-
  Vorpommern) . . . 49 D1
Altenkirchen
  (Rheinland-
  Pfalz) . . . 51 E3
Altenmarkt (D) . . . 56 B3
Altenmarkt
  (Salzburg) . . . 59 F1
Altenmarkt
  (Steiermark) . . . 57 D3
Altenstadt . . . 55 E3
Altensteig . . . 54 C3
Altentreptow . . . 49 D2
Altenwalde . . . 47 F2
Alte Oder . . . 49 D2
Alter do Chão . . . 38 C3
Altglashütten . . . 54 C4
Altheim . . . 56 C3
Althofen . . . 70 B1
Altkirch . . . 27 E1
Altlandsberg . . . 49 E4
Altlengbach . . . 57 E2
Altmühl . . . 55 F2
Altmühlsee . . . 55 E2
Altmünster . . . 56 C3
Altnaharra . . . 2 C2
Alto Campó . . . 35 F2
Alto Cruz . . . 36 C4
Alto de Allariz . . . 34 B3
Alto de Barazar . . . 36 B1
Alto de
  Covelo . . . 34 C3
Alto de Estividas . . . 34 B3
Alto de Fumaces . . . 34 B3
Alto del Couso . . . 34 B3
Alto del Portalé . . . 37 E4
Alto del Rodicio . . . 34 B3
Alto de
  Santo Domingo . . . 34 B2
Alto do Cañizo . . . 34 C3
Alto Laza . . . 37 D2
Alto Lindoso,
  Bgem do . . . 34 B3

Altomira . . . 40 B2
Alton . . . 9 F3
Altopascio . . . 60 C3
Alto Rabagão,
  Bgem do . . . 34 B3
Altorricon . . . 37 E3
Altotero . . . 36 A2
Altötting . . . 56 B3
Altrincham . . . 6 C2
Alt Ruppin . . . 49 D3
Altshausen . . . 55 D4
Altstätten . . . 58 B2
Altura . . . 41 E3
Altweilnau . . . 51 F4
Alustante . . . 41 D2
Alva . . . 4 C2
Alvaiázere . . . 38 B2
Alvalade . . . 42 A1
Alvão, Sa de . . . 34 B4
Alva, R. . . . 38 B2
Alvdal . . . 100 C3
Älvdalen . . . 101 E4
Alvelos, Sa de . . . 38 B2
Alverca do
  Ribatejo . . . 38 A4
Alvesta . . . 109 D2
Alvignac . . . 29 D2
Ålvik . . . 104 B2
Alvito . . . 42 B1
Alvito, Bgem do . . . 42 B1
Älvkarleby . . . 106 B2
Alvor . . . 42 A2
Älvros . . . 101 E3
Älvsborgs Län . . . 108 C1
Älvsbyn . . . 98 B3
Alyth . . . 5 D1
Alytus . . . 110 C4
Alz . . . 56 B3
Alzenau . . . 52 A4
Alzey . . . 54 C1
Alzira . . . 41 E4
Alzola . . . 36 B1
Alzon . . . 29 F3
Alzonne . . . 32 B1
Amadora . . . 38 A4
Åmål . . . 105 E4
Amalfi . . . 64 B4
Amaliáda . . . 86 B1
Amaliápoli . . . 83 F2
Amálo . . . 89 D2
Amance . . . 27 D1
Amancey . . . 27 D2
Amandola . . . 61 F4
Amantea . . . 67 E3
Amárandos
  (Ípiros) . . . 78 C4
Amárandos
  (Thessalía) . . . 83 D2
Amarante . . . 34 B4
Amareleja . . . 42 C1
Amares . . . 34 A4
Amárinthos . . . 84 B4
Amatrice . . . 63 F1
Amay . . . 50 C4
Amaya . . . 35 F3
Ambarès-et-
  Lagrave . . . 28 B2
Ambasaguas . . . 35 E2
Ambazac . . . 25 E4
Ambelákia
  (Thessalía) . . . 83 E1
Ambelákia (Thráki) . . . 81 F1
Ambelia . . . 83 E2
Ambelikó . . . 85 F3
Ambelióna . . . 86 C2
Ambelónas . . . 83 E1
Amberg . . . 55 F1
Ambérieu-en-
  Bugey . . . 26 C4
Ambert . . . 29 F1
Ambès . . . 28 B2
Ambierle . . . 26 B4
Amble . . . 5 E3
Ambleside . . . 5 D4
Amblève . . . 51 D4
Amboise . . . 25 D2
Ambra . . . 61 D4
Ambrières-les-
  Vallées . . . 18 C4
Ameixial . . . 42 B2
Ameland . . . 16 C1
Amelia . . . 63 E2
Amélie-les-Bains-
  Palalda . . . 32 B3

Amelinghausen . . . 48 B3
Amer . . . 32 B3
A Merca . . . 34 B3
Amerongen . . . 16 C3
Amersfoort . . . 16 C3
Amersham . . . 9 F2
Amesbury . . . 9 E3
A Mezquita . . . 34 C3
Amfiaraio . . . 84 B4
Amfiklia . . . 83 E3
Amfilohía . . . 82 C3
Amfípoli . . . 80 B2
Åmfissa . . . 83 E4
Amiata, Mont' . . . 63 D1
Amiens . . . 19 F2
Amigdaleónas . . . 80 C2
Amigdaliá . . . 83 E4
Amíndeo . . . 79 D3
Åmli . . . 104 B4
Amlwch . . . 6 A2
Ammanford . . . 8 C2
Ämmänsaari . . . 99 E3
Ammarfjället . . . 97 F3
Ammarnäs . . . 97 F3
Ammel . . . 56 A4
Ammersattel . . . 55 F4
Ammersee . . . 56 A3
Amohóri . . . 79 D3
Amoliani . . . 80 B4
Amorbach . . . 55 D1
Amorebieta . . . 36 B1
Amorgós . . . 89 D3
Amorgós, N . . . 89 D3
Amório . . . 81 F1
Åmot (Buskerud) . . . 104 C3
Åmot (S) . . . 105 F2
Åmot (Telemark) . . . 104 B3
Åmotfors . . . 105 D3
Amótopos . . . 82 C2
Amou . . . 28 B4
Amoudára . . . 91 D3
Amoudára . . . 91 E4
Amoúdia . . . 89 D2
Ampezzo . . . 59 E3
Ampfing . . . 56 B3
Amphion . . . 27 D3
Amplepuis . . . 26 B4
Amposta . . . 41 F2
Ampthill . . . 9 F2
Ampudia . . . 35 E4
Ampuero . . . 36 A1
Amriswil . . . 58 B1
Amrum . . . 47 F1
Amsele . . . 98 B4
Amstelveen . . . 16 C2
Amsterdam . . . 16 C2
Amstetten . . . 57 D3
Amungen . . . 101 E4
Amurrio . . . 36 B1
Amusco . . . 35 F3
Amvrakía, L. . . . 82 C3
Amvrakikós
  Kólpos . . . 82 C3
Anadia . . . 38 B1
Anáfi . . . 91 E1
Anafí, N . . . 91 F1
Anafonítria . . . 86 A1
Anagni . . . 63 F3
Anáktora
  Néstoros . . . 86 B3
Análipsi . . . 83 F4
Análipsi . . . 92 C1
Análipsis . . . 86 C3
Ananjev . . . 113 E3
Anáráhi . . . 79 D3
Anárgiri . . . 79 D3
Änarjohka . . . 95 E2
Anascaul . . . 14 A3
Ånaset . . . 102 B1
Åna Sira . . . 104 A4
Anatolí (Ípiros) . . . 82 C1
Anatolí (Kríti) . . . 91 E4
Anatolí (Thessalía) . . . 83 F1
Anatolikí Rodópi . . . 81 D2
Anatolikó . . . 79 D3
Änättijärvi . . . 99 F4
Anávatos . . . 85 E4
Anávissos . . . 87 F2
Anávra (Kardítsa) . . . 83 E2
Anávra (Magnisía) . . . 83 E3

Anchuras . . . 39 F3
An Clochán . . . 12 A3
An Cóbh . . . 14 C4
Ancona . . . 61 F3
Ancy-le-Franc . . . 26 B1
Anda . . . 100 A3
Andalo . . . 58 C3
Andalucía . . . 43 E2
Andarax, R. . . . 44 B3
Andartikó . . . 79 D2
Andebu . . . 104 C3
Andelot . . . 26 C1
Andelys, les . . . 19 E3
Andenes . . . 94 A3
Andenne . . . 50 C4
Anderlues . . . 50 B4
Andermatt . . . 58 A3
Andernach . . . 51 E4
Andernos . . . 28 A2
Anderstorp . . . 109 D2
Andfjorden . . . 94 B3
Andigonos . . . 79 D3
Andikíra . . . 83 E4
Andikíras, Kólpos . . . 83 E4
Andikíthira, N. . . . 90 A2
Andimáhia . . . 89 F3
Andímilos, N . . . 88 A4
Andinítsa . . . 83 E3
Andíparos . . . 88 B3
Andíparos, N . . . 88 B3
Andipaxi, N. . . . 82 B2
Andipsara, N . . . 85 E4
Andírio . . . 83 D4
Andíssa . . . 85 E2
Andoain . . . 36 C1
Andorno Micca . . . 31 F1
Andorra . . . 41 E1
Andorra la Vella . . . 32 A2
Andosilla . . . 36 C2
Andover . . . 9 E3
Andøya . . . 94 A3
Andratx . . . 45 E3
Andravida . . . 86 B1
Andretta . . . 64 C3
Andrézieux-
  Bouthéon . . . 30 B1
Andria . . . 65 D3
Andrijevica . . . 76 C2
Andrítsena . . . 86 C2
Andros . . . 88 B1
Ándros, N . . . 88 B1
Androússa . . . 86 C3
Andselv . . . 94 B3
Andújar . . . 43 F2
Anduze . . . 30 B3
Aneby . . . 109 D1
Ånes . . . 100 C1
Anet . . . 19 E4
Aneto, Pico de . . . 37 E2
Ånge (Jämtlands
  Län) . . . 101 E2
Ånge (Västernorrlands
  Län) . . . 101 E3
Ängelholm . . . 108 C3
Angeja . . . 38 B1
Angeli . . . 95 E3
Angelohóri . . . 79 E3
Angelókastro
  (Pelopónissos) . . . 87 E2
Angelókastro
  (Stereá Eláda) . . . 82 C4
Anger . . . 57 E4
Angera . . . 58 A4
Ångermanälven . . . 101 F2
Angermünde . . . 49 E3
Angern . . . 57 F2
Angers . . . 23 E4
Angerville . . . 25 E1
Ängesån . . . 98 C2
Anghiari . . . 61 D4
Angístis,
  Stathmós . . . 80 B2
Angístri . . . 87 E2
Angístri, N . . . 87 E2
Ångistro . . . 80 B1
Angitís . . . 80 B2
Angles . . . 25 D3
Anglès (E) . . . 32 B3
Anglès (F) . . . 32 B1
Anglesey, I of . . . 6 A2
Anglesola . . . 37 F3
Anglet . . . 28 A4

Anglure . . . 20 B4
Angoulême . . . 28 C1
Angri . . . 64 B4
Ängsö . . . 106 C3
Angüés . . . 37 E3
Anguiano . . . 36 B2
Anguillara Veneta . . . 61 D1
Angvik . . . 100 B2
Anholt . . . 108 C2
Aniane . . . 30 A4
Aniche . . . 20 A1
Aniene . . . 63 F2
Ánixi . . . 79 D4
Anizy-le-Château . . . 20 A3
Anjalankoski . . . 107 F2
Anjum . . . 47 D3
Ankaran . . . 70 A3
Ankarsrum . . . 109 E1
Anklam . . . 49 E2
Ankogel . . . 59 E2
An Longfort . . . 12 C3
An Muileann
  gCearr . . . 13 D3
Ånn L. . . . 101 D2
Ånn L. . . . 101 D2
Annaberg . . . 57 E3
Annaberg-
  Buchholz . . . 53 E3
Annaburg . . . 53 E1
Annan . . . 5 D3
Annan R. . . . 5 D3
Anndalsvågen . . . 97 D3
Annecy . . . 27 D4
Annemasse . . . 27 D4
Annevoie-
  Rouillon . . . 50 C4
Annonay . . . 30 B1
Annone Veneto . . . 59 E4
Annot . . . 31 D3
Annweiler . . . 54 C2
Áno Drossiní . . . 81 E2
Anógia . . . 87 D3
Anógia . . . 91 D3
Áno Hóra . . . 83 D4
Áno Kalendíni . . . 82 C2
Áno Kaliníki . . . 79 D2
Áno Kómi . . . 79 D4
Áno Lefkími . . . 82 A2
Áno Melás . . . 79 D3
Áno Merá . . . 88 C2
Anópoli . . . 90 C4
Áno Polidéndri . . . 83 F1
Áno Poróia . . . 80 A2
Áno Rodákino . . . 90 C4
Áno Sangrí . . . 88 C3
Áno Síros . . . 88 B2
Añover de Tajo . . . 40 A3
Áno Viános . . . 91 E4
Áno Vrondoú . . . 80 B1
Áno Zervohóri . . . 79 E3
Ansbach . . . 55 E1
Anse . . . 26 C4
Ansedonia . . . 63 D2
Ansião . . . 38 B2
Ansnes . . . 100 C1
Ansó . . . 37 D2
Anstruther . . . 5 D2
An tAonach . . . 12 C4
Antas . . . 44 C3
Antegnate . . . 60 B1
Antemil . . . 34 A1
Antequera . . . 43 F3
Anterselva . . . 59 D2
Ánthia . . . 81 E2
Anthili . . . 83 E3
Ánthis . . . 80 B2
Antholz . . . 59 D2
Anthótopos . . . 83 E2
Antibes . . . 31 E4
Antifer, Cap d' . . . 19 D3
An tInbhear Mór . . . 15 E3
Antnäs . . . 98 C3
Antraigues . . . 30 B2
Antrain . . . 18 B4
Antrim . . . 13 E2
Antrim (Co) . . . 13 E2
Antrim Coast . . . 13 E1
Antrim Mts . . . 13 E1
Antrodoco . . . 63 F2
Anttola . . . 103 E3
Antwerpen . . . 50 B3
Antwerpen (Prov) . . . 50 C3
An Uaimh . . . 13 D3

Anvers . . . 50 B3
Anzano di Puglia . . . 64 C3
Anzio . . . 63 E3
Anzola d'Ossola . . . 58 A4
Anzy-le-Duc . . . 26 B4
Aoiz . . . 36 C2
Aóos . . . 78 C4
Aosta . . . 27 E4
Aoste . . . 27 E4
Apatin . . . 72 B2
Apatovac . . . 71 D2
Apecchio . . . 61 E4
Apeldoorn . . . 17 D2
Apen . . . 47 E3
Apéri . . . 93 D3
Aphrodisias . . . 115 F4
Apidiá . . . 87 D3
Apikia . . . 88 B1
Apíranthos . . . 88 C3
Apolakiá . . . 93 E2
Apolda . . . 52 C3
Apolitáres, Akr. . . . 90 A2
Apólonas . . . 88 C3
Apolonía
  (Kikládes) . . . 88 B3
Apolonía
  (Makedonía) . . . 80 B3
A Pontenova
  Villaodriz . . . 34 C1
Apóstoli . . . 90 C4
Äppelbo . . . 105 E2
Appenweier . . . 54 C3
Appenzell . . . 58 B2
Appiano . . . 59 D3
Appingedam . . . 47 D3
Appleby . . . 5 D4
Aprica . . . 58 C3
Apricena . . . 64 C2
Aprília . . . 63 E3
Äpsalos . . . 79 E2
Apt . . . 30 C3
Áptera . . . 90 C4
Aquileia . . . 59 F3
Aquitaine, L' . . . 25 E2
Arabba . . . 59 D3
Aracena . . . 42 C2
Aracena, Emb de . . . 43 D2
Aracena, Sa de . . . 42 C2
Aračinovo . . . 77 E3
Arad . . . 112 C4
Åradalsfjorden . . . 104 B1
Arada, Sa de . . . 38 B1
Aragón . . . 37 D3
Aragona . . . 68 B4
Aragón, R . . . 36 C2
Arahnéo, Óros . . . 87 E2
Aráhova (Etolía-
  Akarnanía) . . . 83 D3
Aráhova (Viotía) . . . 83 E4
Arákinthos, Óros . . . 83 D4
A Ramallosa . . . 34 A3
Aramits . . . 37 D1
Aranda de Duero . . . 36 A3
Aranda, Sa de . . . 38 B1
Aranđelovac . . . 73 D3
Aran I . . . 12 C1
Aran Is . . . 12 A4
Aranjuez . . . 40 B3
Arantzazu . . . 36 B1
Aran, Vall d' . . . 37 F2
Aras de Alpuente . . . 41 D3
Aras, R . . . 36 C2
Ara, R . . . 37 E2
Arazede . . . 38 B2
Arba, R . . . 36 C3
Arbatax . . . 66 C3
Arbeca . . . 37 F4
Arbesbach . . . 57 D2
Arboga . . . 105 F3
Arbois . . . 27 D3
Arbon . . . 58 B1
Arbón, Emb de . . . 34 C1
Arborea . . . 66 B3
Arborio . . . 31 F1
Arbrå . . . 101 F4
Arbresle, l' . . . 26 B4

Arbúcies . . . 32 B4
Arbus . . . 66 B3
Arc. . . . 31 D1
Arcachon . . . 28 A2
Arce . . . 64 A3
Arcen . . . 17 D3
Arc-en-Barrois . . . 26 C1
Arceniega . . . 36 A1
Arcevia . . . 61 E4
Archena . . . 45 D2
Arches . . . 27 D1
Archiac . . . 28 B1
Archidona . . . 43 F3
Arcidosso . . . 63 D1
Arcipelago
  Toscano . . . 62 B1
Arcis . . . 20 B4
Arciz . . . 113 E4
Arco . . . 58 C4
Arco de Baúlhe . . . 34 B4
Arcos . . . 35 F3
Arcos de Jalón . . . 36 B4
Arcos de la
  Frontera . . . 43 D3
Arcos de
  Valdevez . . . 34 A3
Arcouest, Pte de l' . . . 22 C2
Arcs, les (Savoie) . . . 31 D1
Arcs, les (Var) . . . 31 D4
Arcusa . . . 37 E2
Arda . . . 115 E3
Ardales . . . 43 E3
Årdalstangen . . . 104 B1
Ardánio . . . 81 F2
Ardara . . . 12 C1
Árdas . . . 81 F1
Ardbeg . . . 4 B2
Ardèche (Dépt) . . . 30 B2
Ardèche R. . . . 30 B2
Ardèche,
  Gges de l' . . . 30 B3
Ardee . . . 13 D3
Ardennes (Dépt) . . . 20 B3
Ardennes,
  Canal des . . . 20 C3
Ardentes . . . 25 E3
Ardentinny . . . 4 C2
Ardes . . . 29 F1
Ardez . . . 58 B2
Ardglass . . . 13 E2
Ardila, R . . . 42 C1
Ardila, Rib de . . . 42 C1
Ardisa . . . 37 D3
Ardlussa . . . 4 B2
Ardmore . . . 14 C4
Ardrahan . . . 12 B4
Ardres . . . 19 E1
Ardrishaig . . . 4 B2
Ardrossan . . . 4 C2
Ards Pen . . . 13 E2
Arduaine . . . 4 B1
Ardvasar . . . 2 B4
Åre . . . 101 D2
Arenas de
  Cabrales . . . 35 E2
Arenas de Iguña . . . 35 F2
Arenas de San
  Juan . . . 40 B4
Arenas de San
  Pedro . . . 39 F2
Arendal . . . 104 C4
Arendonk . . . 50 C3
Arendsee . . . 48 C3
Arenos, Emb de . . . 41 E3
Arenys de Mar . . . 32 B4
Arenzano . . . 60 A3
Areópoli . . . 87 D4
Ares (Galicia) . . . 34 B1
Ares (Valencia) . . . 41 E2
Ares, Col des . . . 37 F2
Ares, Pte de . . . 32 B3
Åreskutan . . . 101 D2
Aréthoussa . . . 80 B3
Aretí . . . 80 A3
Arévalo . . . 39 F1
Arez . . . 38 C3
Arezzo . . . 61 D4
Arfará . . . 86 C3
Argalastí . . . 83 F2
Argamasilla de
  Alba . . . 40 B4
Argamasilla de
  Calatrava . . . 44 A1

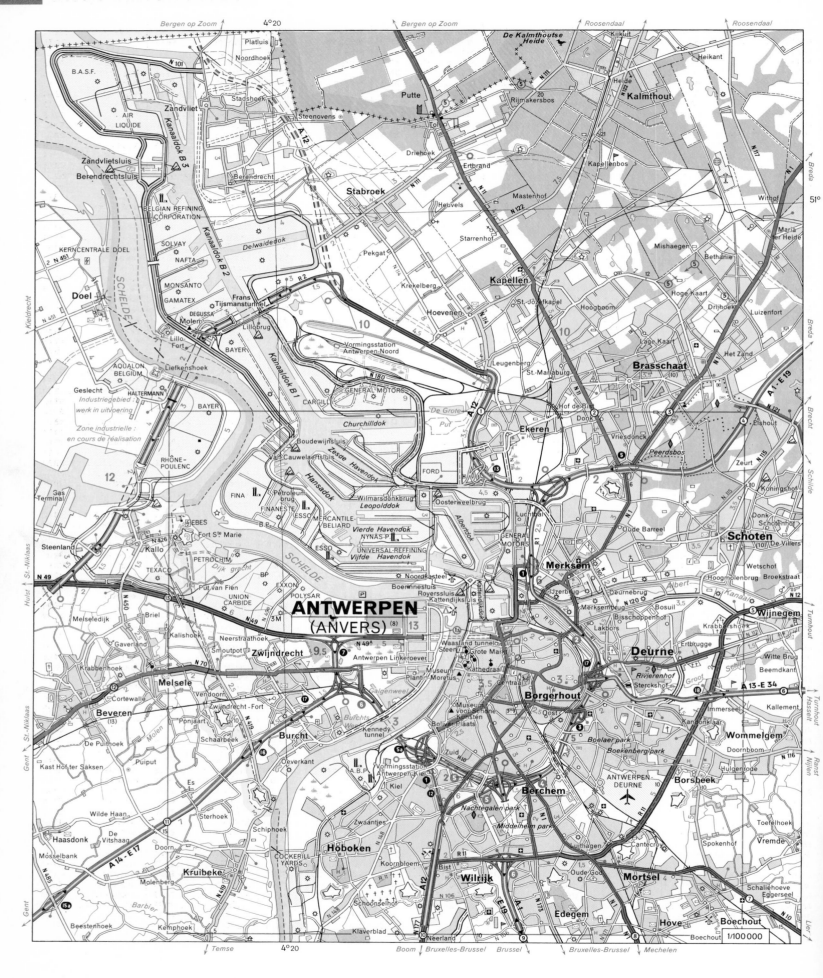

Arganda 40 B2
Arganil 38 B2
Arga, R 36 C2
Argássi 86 A2
Argelès 32 B2
Argelès-Gazost 37 E1
Argens 31 D4
Argent 25 F2
Argenta 61 D2
Argentan 19 D4
Argentario, Mte 63 D2
Argentat 29 D2
Argente 41 D2
Argentera 31 E3
Argentière 27 E4
Argentière-la-
  Bessée, l' 31 D2
Argentona 32 B4
Argenton-
  Château 24 C3
Argenton-sur-
  Creuse 25 E3
Argentré-du-
  Plessis 23 E3
Arginónda 89 F3
Argirádes 82 A2
Argiró 84 B4
Argiropoúlio 83 E1
Argiroúpoli 90 C3
Argithéa 83 D2
Argolída 87 E2
Argolikós Kólpos . . . 87 E2
Árgos 87 D2
Árgos Orestikó 79 D3
Argos, R 44 C2
Argostóli 82 B4
Arguedas 36 C3
Argueil 19 E3
Arguellite 44 B1
Arguis 37 D2
Argyll 4 B1
Argyll Forest Park . . 4 C2
Arhánes 91 D4
Arhángelos
  (Makedonía) 79 E2
Arhángelos
  (Ródos) 93 F1
Arhéa Epídavros . . . 87 E2
Arhéa Kleonés 87 D1
Arhéa Kórinthos . . . 87 E1
Arhéa Neméa 87 D1
Arhéa Olympía 86 C2
Arhéa Thíra 91 E1
Árhus 108 B3
Arianá 81 E2
Ariano Irpino 64 B3
Ariano nel
  Polesine 61 D2
Aridéa 79 E2
Ariège (Dépt) 32 A2
Ariège R 32 A2
Arija 35 F2
Arild 108 C3
Arilje 72 C4
Arinagour 2 B4
Aríni 86 C2
Ariño 37 D4
Arinthod 27 D3
Arisaig 2 B4
Arisaig, Sd of 2 B4
Aristi 78 C4
Aristoménis 86 C3
Arisví 81 E2
Aritzo 66 B3
Arive 36 C2
Ariza 36 B4
Årjäng 105 D3
Arjeplog 98 A3
Arjona 44 A2
Arkádi 91 D3
Arkadía 86 C2
Arkaig, L 2 C4
Arkalohóri 91 E4
Arkássa 93 D3
Arkessíni 89 D3
Arki, N 89 E2
Arkítsa 83 F3
Arklow 15 E3

Arkona, Kap 49 D1
Arkoúdi, N 82 B4
Arlaban, Pto de 36 B1
Arlanc 29 F1
Arlanda 106 B3
Arlanza, R 36 A3
Arlanzón 36 A2
Arlanzón, R 35 F3
Arlbergpaß 58 B2
Arlberg-
  Straßentunnel 58 B2
Arlempdes 30 A2
Arles (Bouches-du-
  Rhône) 30 B4
Arles (Pyrénées-
  Orientales) 32 B3
Arlesheim 27 E2
Arlon 21 D2
Arlsleben 52 C2
Armação
  de Pêra 42 A3
Armadale 5 D2
Arma di Taggia 31 F3
Armagh 13 D2
Armagh (Co) 13 D2
Armamar 34 B4
Arméni 90 C3
Armenii 86 C3
Armenistís 89 D2
Armentières 19 F1
Armilla 44 A3
Armólia 85 E4
Armunia 35 D3
Árna 87 D3
Arnac-
  Pompadour 29 D1
Arnay-le-Duc 26 B2
Arnéa 80 B3
Arneburg 48 C4
Arnedillo 36 B3
Arnedo 36 C3
Arnes 41 F2
Årnes 105 D3
Arnhem 17 D3
Arni 60 B3
Árnissa 79 E2
Arno 60 C4
Arnoldstein 59 F2
Arnon 25 F3
Arnøy 94 C2
Arnsberg 17 F3
Arnstadt 52 C3
Arnstein 52 B4
Aroania, Óri 86 C1
Aroche 42 C2
Aroche Mt 42 C1
Arogí 81 D2
Arolsen 52 A2
Arona 58 A4
Aroniádika 90 A1
Aronkylä 102 B3
Åros 104 C3
Arosa 58 B2
Arouca 38 B1
Arousa, I de 34 A2
Årøysund 104 C3
Arpajon 19 F4
Arpela 99 D3
Arquata del
  Tronto 63 F1
Arques (Pas-de-
  Calais) 19 F1
Arques (Seine-
  Maritime) 19 E2
Arquillos 44 A2
Arrabal 34 A3
Arrábida, Sa da 38 A4
Arracourt 21 D4
Arraiolos 38 B4
Arran 4 B2
Arras 19 F2
Arrasate-
  Mondragon 36 B1
Arreau 37 E2
Arrecife 42 C4
Arredondo 36 A1
Arrée, Mts d' 22 B2
Arrens 37 E2

Arrifana 38 C1
Arrigorriaga 36 B1
Arriondas 35 E1
Arrochar 4 C2
Arromanches 18 C3
Arronches 38 C4
Arroux 26 B3
Arrow, L 12 C2
Arroyo de la Luz . . . 39 D3
Arroyo del Ojanco . . 44 B1
Arroyo de San
  Serván 39 D4
Arroyomolinos de
  León 43 D1
Arroyomolinos de
  Montánchez 39 D4
Arruda dos Vinhos . 38 A3
Ars (Charente-
  Maritime) 24 B4
Ars (Moselle) 21 D3
Arsiè 59 D3
Arsiero 59 D4
Árs Kógssanður 96 B1
Arsunda 106 B2
Arsy 19 F3
Artà 45 F2
Árta 82 C2
Árta (Nomos) 82 C2
Arta Terme 59 E3
Arteaga, G de 36 B1
Artemissía 86 C3
Artemíssio (Évia) . . 83 F3
Artemíssio
  (Pelopónnissos) . . . 87 D2
Artemónas 88 B3
Artena 63 F3
Artenay 25 E1
Artern 52 C2
Artesa de Segre . . . 37 F3
Artessianó 83 D2
Artfjället 97 E3
Arth (CH) 58 A2
Arth (D) 56 B2
Arthurstown 15 D4
Arties 37 F2
Artjärvi 107 F2
Artotína 83 D3
Artruix, C de 45 F2
A Rúa 34 C3
Arucas 42 B4
Arudy 37 D1
Arundel 9 F3
Arve 27 E4
Árvi 91 E4
Arvidsjaur 98 A3
Årvik 100 A2
Arvika 105 E3
Årviksand 94 C2
Arzachena 66 B1
Arzacq-Arraziguet . 28 B4
Arzano 22 B3
Aržano 75 E1
Arzberg 53 D4
Arzignano 60 C1
Árzos 81 F1
Arzúa 34 B2

Asco 33 F3
Ascó 37 E4
Ascoli Piceno 63 F1
Ascoli Satriano 64 C3
Ascona 58 A3
Åse 94 A3
Åseda 109 E2
Åsele 101 F1
Åsen 101 D1
Asenovgrad 115 D3
Ashbourne (GB) 6 C2
Ashbourne (IRL) . . . 13 D3
Ashburton 8 C4
Ashby de la Zouch . . 6 C3
Ashford 11 D3
Ashington 5 E3
Ashton-under-
  Lyne 6 C2
Asiago 59 D4
Asikkala 107 F2
Asín 37 D3
Asinara, G dell' 66 B1
Asinara, I 66 A1
Ask 105 D3
Askainen 107 D2
Askeaton 14 B3
Askersund 105 F4
Askífou 90 C3
Askim 105 D3
Áskio, Óros 79 D3
Askja 96 C2
Asklipío
  (Dodekánissa) 89 F3
Asklipío (Ródos) . . . 93 E2
Askola 107 F2
Askós 80 A3
Askøy 104 A2
Askvoll 104 A1
Asmunti 99 D3
Asnæs 108 B3
Asnen 109 D2
As Neves 34 A3
Asola 60 B1
Asolo 59 D4
Aspang 57 F3
Aspatria 5 D4
Aspe 45 D2
Aspe, Gave d' 37 D1
Asperg 55 D2
Aspet 37 F2
Aspin, Col d' 37 E2
As Ponte de Garcia
  Rodriguez 34 B1
Áspra Spítia 83 E4
Aspres 30 C2
Áspro 79 E3
Aspróhoma 86 C3
Asprókavos, Akr . . . 82 A2
Aspromonte 67 E4
Asprópirgos 87 F1
Asproválta 80 B3
Asse 50 B4
Assemini 66 B4
Assen 17 D1
Assens 108 B3
Assergi 63 F2
Assini 87 E2
Assisi 63 E1
Assomáton 91 D3
Assopía 84 A4
Assopós
  (Korinthía) 87 D1
Assopós
  (Lakonía) 87 E4
Assopós R 87 E1
Ássos (Ípiros) 82 B2
Ássos (Kefaloniá) . . 82 B4
Astaffort 28 C3
Astakída, N 93 D2
Astakós 82 C4
Asten 57 D4
Asti 31 F2

Astipálea 92 C1
Astipálea, N 92 C1
Astorga 35 D3
Åstorp 108 C3
Ástros 87 D2
Astudillo 35 F3
Asturias 34 C2
Asvestádes 81 F1
Asvestohóri 82 B1
Asvestópetra 79 D3
Atalaia 38 A3
Atalándi 83 F3
Atalaya de la
  Calzada 44 A1
Atalayassa 45 D4
Átali 84 B3
Ataquines 39 F1
Atarfe 44 A3
Atáviros 93 E2
Ateca 36 C4
Atella 64 C3
Atessa 64 B2
Ath 50 B4
Athamánon, Óri . . . 82 C2
Athánio 82 B3
Athboy 13 D3
Athenry 12 B3
Athéras 89 D2
Athéras, Akr 82 B4
Athína 87 F1
Áthira 79 F2
Athlone 12 C3
Áthos 80 C4
Athy 13 D4
Atienza 36 B4
Atiki-Piréas 87 F1
Atina 64 A3
Átokos, N 82 C4
Atouguia da Baleia . 38 A3
Ätran 108 C2
Ätran R 108 C2
Atri 64 A1
Atsiki 85 D1
Attendorn 17 F4
Attersee 56 C3
Attersee L 56 C3
Attigliano 63 E2
Attigny 20 B3
Attleborough 11 D1
Attnang 56 C3
Åtvidaberg 109 E1
Au 55 F2
Aub 55 E1
Aubagne 30 C4
Aubange 21 D2
Aube 20 B4
Aube (Dépt) 20 B4
Aubenas 30 B2
Aubenton 20 B2
Auberive 26 C1
Aubeterre 28 C1
Aubigny (Cher) 25 F2
Aubigny (Pas-de-
  Calais) 19 F2
Aubin 29 E3
Aubisque, Col d' . . . 37 E1
Aubonne 27 D3
Aubrac 29 F2
Aubrac, Mts d' 29 F2
Aubusson 25 F4
Auch 28 C4
Auchencairn 4 C3
Auchterarder 5 D1
Auchtermuchty 5 D1
Aude (Dépt) 32 B2
Aude R 32 B1
Audenge 28 A2
Audeux 27 D2
Audierne 22 A3
Audincourt 27 E2
Audlem 6 C3
Audruicq 19 F1
Audun-le-Roman . . 21 D3
Audun-le-Tiche 21 D3
Aue R 48 A4
Aue 53 D3
Auer 59 D3

Auerbach
  (Bayern) 55 F1
Auerbach
  (Sachsen) 53 D3
Auffach 59 D1
Aughnacloy 13 D2
Aughrim 13 D4
Augsburg 55 F3
Augusta 69 D4
Augustenborg 108 B4
Augustów 110 C4
Augustusburg 53 E3
Aukan 100 B2
Aukra 100 B2
Aulanko 107 E2
Auletta 64 C4
Aulla 60 B3
Aullène 33 F4
Aulnay 24 C4
Aulne 22 B3
Aulnoye-Aymeries . 20 B2
Ault 19 E2
Aulus-les-Bains . . . 37 F2
Auma 53 D3
Aumale 19 E2
Aumetz 21 D3
Aumont-Aubrac . . . 29 F2
Aunay-sur-Odon . . . 18 C3
Auneau 19 E4
Auneuil 19 E3
Auning 108 B2
Aups 31 D4
Aura 107 D2
Aurajoki 107 D2
Aurich 47 E3
Aurignac 37 F1
Aurillac 29 E2
Aurland 104 B2
Auron 31 E3
Auron R 25 F3
Auronzo di
  Cadore 59 E2
Auros 28 B3
Aursjøen 100 B3
Aursunden 101 D2
Ausonia 64 A3
Außernbrünst 56 C2
Ausso Corno 59 F3
Aust-Agder 104 B4
Austbygd 104 C3
Austvågøy 94 A3
Auterive 37 F1
Authie 19 F2
Autol 36 C3
Autrans 30 C1
Autrey 26 C2
Auttoinen 107 E1
Autun 26 B3
Auvézère 28 C2
Auvillar 28 C3
Auxerre 26 A1
Auxi-le-Château . . . 19 E2
Auxonne 26 C2
Auzances 25 F4
Auzon 29 F1
Availles-
  Limouzine 25 D4
Avala 73 D3
Avaldsnes 104 A3
Avallon 26 B2
Avaloirs, Mt des . . . 23 E3
Avas 81 E2
Avaviken 98 A3
A Veiga 34 C3
Aveiras de Cima . . . 38 A3
Aveiro 38 B1
Aveiro, R de 38 B1
Avellino 64 B4
Aven Armand 29 F3
Aven d'Orgnac 30 B3
Averøya 100 B2
Aversa 64 B4
Avesnes 20 B2

Avesnes-le-Comte . 19 F2
Avesta 105 F3
Avetrana 65 E4
Aveyron 29 D3
Aveyron (Dépt) 29 E3
Avezzano 63 F2
Avgerinós 79 D4
Avgó 82 C2
Avía 86 C3
Aviano 59 E3
Aviémonas 90 A2
Aviemore 3 D4
Aviés 79 E4
Avigliana 31 E1
Avigliano 64 C4
Avignon 30 B3
Ávila 39 F2
Ávila, Sa de 39 F2
Avilés 35 D1
Aviño 34 B1
Avintes 34 A4
Avión 34 B2
Avioth 20 C3
Avis 38 B4
Avisio 59 D3
Avize 20 B3
Avlákia 89 E1
Avlí 80 C2
Avlíótes 82 A1
Avlóna 84 B4
Avlum 108 A2
Avola 69 D4
Avon (Co) 9 D2
Avon R (Hants) 9 E1
Avon R (Warw) 9 E3
Avonmouth 9 D2
Avord 25 F3
Avoriaz 27 E4
Avranches 18 B4
Avre 19 D4
Avtovac 76 A2
Awe, L 4 B1
Axams 59 D2
Axat 32 B2
Axiohóri 79 F2
Axiós 79 F3
Axioúpoli 79 F2
Ax-les-Thermes . . . 32 A2
Axminster 9 D3
Axós 91 D3
Ay 20 B3
Ayamonte 42 B2
Aydın 115 F4
Ayedo 36 B3
Ayerbe 37 D3
Ayllón 36 A4
Ayllón, Sa de 36 A4
Aylesbury 9 F2
Aylsham 7 F3
Ayna 44 C1
Ayora 41 D4
Ayr 4 C3
Ayre, Pt of 6 A1
Ayvacık 115 E4
Ayvalik 115 E4
Aywaille 51 D4
Azáceta, Pto de . . . 36 B2
Azaila 37 D4
Azambuja 38 A3
Azanja 73 D3
Azaruja 38 B4
Azay-le-Ferron 25 E3
Azay-le-Rideau 25 D2
Azinheira dos
  Barros 42 A1
Azkoitia 36 B1
Aznalcázar 43 D3
Aznalcóllar 43 D2
Azpeitia 36 B1
Azuaga 43 E1
Azuara 37 D4
Azuer, R 40 A4
Azuqueca de
  Henares 40 B2
Azután, Emb de . . . 39 F3
Azzano Decimo . . . 59 E3

B

Baad 58 B2
Baal 17 D4
Baamonde 34 B1
Baarle-Nassau . . 16 C4
Baarn 16 C2
Baba 77 E4
Babadag 113 E4
Babajevo 111 E1
Babelsberg 49 D4
Babenhausen
  (Bayern) 55 E3
Babenhausen
  (Hessen) 52 A4
Babina Greda . . 71 F3
Babin Kal 73 F4
Babin Most 77 D2
Babino Polje . . . 75 F2
Babin Potok . . . 70 C4
Babljak 76 B2
Babuna 77 E3
Babušnica 77 E1
Bač 72 B2
Bački Breg 72 B1
Bacau 113 D4
Baccarat 21 E4
Bæccegæhal'di . 94 C2
Baceno 58 A3
Bacharach 51 E4
Bächistock 58 A2
Bachmač 113 F1
Bačina 73 E4
Bačka Palanka . 72 B2
Bäckaskog . . . 109 D3
Bačka Topola . . 72 B1
Backe 101 F1
Bäckebo 109 E2
Bäckefors 105 D4
Bački Breg 71 F1

Bački Brestovac 72 B2
Bački Monoštor 72 B2
Bački Petrovac 72 B2
Backnang 55 D2
Bačko Gradište 72 C2
Bačko Novo Selo . . 72 B2
Bačko Petrovo
  Selo 72 C1
Bačkovo 115 D3
Bacoli 64 A4
Bacqueville 19 D2
Baczyna 49 F3
Bad Aibling 56 B3
Badajoz 38 C4
Badalona 32 B4
Bad Aussee 56 C3
Bad Bentheim 17 E2
Bad Bergzabern . . 54 C2
Bad Berka 52 C3
Bad Berleburg 17 F4
Bad Berneck 53 D4
Bad Bertrich 51 E4
Bad Bevensen . . . 48 B3
Bad Bibra 52 C2
Bad Blankenburg . . 52 C3
Bad Brambach . . . 53 D4
Bad Bramstedt . . . 48 A2
Bad Brückenau . . . 52 B4
Bad Buchau 55 D3
Bad Camberg 51 F4
Bad Deutsch
  Altenburg 57 F2
Bad Doberan 48 C2
Bad Driburg 52 A2
Bad Düben 53 D2
Bad Dürkheim 54 C1
Bad Dürrenberg . . 53 D2
Bad Durrheim 54 C3
Bad Elster 53 D4
Bad Ems 51 E4
Baden (A) 57 F3

Baden (CH) 27 F2
Baden-Baden . . . 54 C2
Bad Endorf 56 B3
Badenweiler 54 C4
Baden-
  Württemberg . . . 55 D3
Baderna 70 A3
Bad Essen 17 F2
Bad Frankenhausen 52 C2
Bad Freienwalde . . 49 E3
Bad Friedrichshall . . 55 D2
Bad Gandersheim . . 52 B1
Badgastein 59 E2
Bad Gleichenberg . . 57 F4
Bad Godesberg . . 51 E3
Bad Goisern 56 C3
Bad Gottleuba . . . 53 E3
Bad Griesbach . . . 56 C2
Bad Grund 52 B2
Bad Hall 57 D3
Bad Harzburg 52 B1
Bad Herrenalb . . . 54 C2
Bad Hersfeld 52 B3
Bad Hofgastein . . 56 C3
Bad Homburg 51 F4
Bad Honnef 51 E3
Bad Honnigen 51 E4
Badia Polesine . . . 61 D2
Badia Tedalda 61 D3
Bad Iburg 17 F2
Badia 75 D2
Bad Ischl 56 C3
Bad Karlshafen . . . 52 A2
Bad Kissingen . . . 52 B4
Bad Kleinen 48 C2
Bad
  Kleinkirchheim . . . 59 F2
Bad König 55 D1
Bad Königshofen . 52 B4
Bad Kösen 52 C2
Bad Kreuznach . . . 54 B1

Bad Krozingen 54 C4
Bad Laasphe 17 F4
Bad Langensalza . . 52 B3
Bad Lauchstädt . . . 53 D2
Bad Lausick 53 D2
Bad Lauterberg . . . 52 B2
Bad Leonfelden . . . 57 D2
Bad Liebenstein . . . 52 B3
Bad Liebenwerda . . 53 E2
Bad Liebenzell 54 C2
Bad Lippspringe . . . 17 F3
Badljevina 71 D2
Bad Meinberg 52 A2
Bad Mergentheim . . 55 D1
Bad Mitterndorf 56 C3
Bad Münder 52 A1
Bad Münster am Stein-
  Ebernburg 54 B1
Bad Münstereifel . . . 51 E4
Bad Muskau 53 F1
Bad Nauheim 52 A4
Bad Nenndorf 52 A1
Bad Neuenahr-
  Ahrweiler 51 E4

Bad Neustadt 52 B4
Bad Oeynhausen . . 17 F2
Badolato 67 F3
Badolatosa 43 F3
Bad Oldesloe 48 B2
Badonviller 21 E4
Bad Orb 52 A4
Badovinci 72 B3
Bad Peterstal-
  Griesbach 54 C3
Bad Pyrmont 52 A1
Bad Radkersburg . . 70 C1
Bad Ragaz 58 B2
Bad Rappenau 55 D2
Bad Reichenhall . . . 56 B3
Bad Rippoldsau-
  Schapbach 54 C3
Bad Rothenfelde . . 17 F2
Bad Saarow-
  Pieskow 49 E4
Bad Sachsa 52 B2
Bad Säckingen 54 C4
Bad St Leonhard . . . 57 D4
Bad Salzdetfurth . . . 52 B1

Bad Salzschlirf 52 B3
Bad Salzuflen 17 F2
Bad Salzungen 52 B3
Bad Schallerbach . . 56 C3
Bad Schandau 53 F2
Bad
  Schmiedeberg . . . 53 D1
Bad Schönborn . . . 54 C2
Badl
  Schussenried 55 D3
Bad Schwalbach . . 51 F4
Bad Schwartau . . . 48 B2
Bad Segeberg 48 B2
Bad Soden 51 F4
Bad Soden-
  Salmünster 52 A4
Bad Sooden-
  Allendorf 52 B2
Bad Sulza 52 C2
Bad Sülze 49 D2
Bad Tatzmannsdorf . 57 F4
Bad Tennstedt 52 C2
Bad Tölz 56 A4
Badules 36 C4

Bad Urach 55 D3
Bad Vibel 52 A4
Bad Vöslau 57 F3
Bad Waldsee 55 D4
Bad Wiessee 56 A4
Bad Wildungen . . . 52 A3
Bad Wilsnack 48 C3
Bad Wimpfen 55 D2
Bad Windsheim . . . 55 E1
Bad Wörishofen . . . 55 E3
Bad Wurzach 55 E4
Bad Zwischenahn . . 47 E3
Bae Colwyn 6 B2
Baena 43 F3
Baeza 44 A2
Bagà 32 A3
Bâgé-le-Châtel 26 C3
Bagenalstown 15 D3
Bagenkop 108 B4
Bagheria 68 B3
Bagnacavallo 61 D2
Bagnara Calabra . . 67 E4
Bagnères-
  de-Bigorre 37 E1

Barcelona

Bagnères-
de-Luchon 37 E2
Bagni del Masino . . . 58 B3
Bagni di Lucca 60 C3
Bagno a Ripoli 61 D3
Bagno di
Romagna 61 D3
Bagnoles-
de-l'Orne 18 C4
Bagnoli
del Trigno 64 B2
Bagnolo Mella 60 B1
Bagnols-les-Bains . . . 29 F3
Bagnols-sur-Cèze . . . 30 B3
Bagnoregio 63 E1
Bagolino 58 C4
Bagrationovsk 110 B4
Bagrdan 73 E4
Baia Mare 112 C3
Baiano 64 B4
Baião 34 B4
Baiersbronn 54 C3
Baignes-Ste-
Radegonde 28 B1
Baigneux-
les-Juifs 26 C2
Baile Átha Cliath . . . 13 E4
Baile Átha Luain . . . 12 C3
Băile Herculane . . . 114 C1
Bailén 44 A2
Băile Tuşnad 113 D4
Baillieborough 13 D3
Bailleul 19 F1
Bain-de-Bretagne . . . 23 D3
Bains-les-Bains 27 D1
Baio 34 A1
Baiono 34 A3
Bais 23 E3
Baïse 28 C3
Baïse-Darré 37 E1
Baja 114 B1
Baja Sardinia 66 B1
Bajgora 77 D1
Bajina Bašta 72 C4
Bajmok 72 B1
Bajram Curri 76 C2
Bajša 72 B1
Bajzë 76 B3
Bakar 70 B3
Bakarac 70 B3
Bakewell 6 C3
Bakio 36 B1
Bakkaflói 96 C1
Bakony 112 A4
Bakvattnet 101 E1
Bala 6 B3
Balaguer 37 F3
Balanegra 44 B4
Balaruc 30 A4
Balassagyarmat . . . 112 B3
Balaton 112 A4
Balatonfüred 112 B4
Balatonkeresztúr . . . 112 A4
Balazote 40 C4
Balbigny 26 B4
Balbriggan 13 E3
Balčik 115 E2
Balderschwang 55 E4
Baldock 9 F2
Baldo, Mte 58 C4
Bale 70 A4
Baleal 38 A3
Baleizão 42 B1
Balerma 44 B4
Balestrand 100 A3
Bali 91 D3
Balıkesir 115 E4
Bälinge 106 B3
Balingen 55 D3
Balivanich 2 A3
Ballachulish 2 C4
Ballaghaderreen 12 C3
Ballangen 94 B3
Ballantrae 4 B3
Ballao 66 B3
Ballater 3 D4
Ballaugh 6 A1
Ballenstedt 52 C2
Balleroy 18 C3
Ballerup 108 C3
Ballina 12 B2
Ballinamore 12 C3
Ballinasloe 12 C3
Ballingarry 14 C3

Ballinrobe 12 B3
Ballintober 12 B3
Ballobar 37 E4
Ballon 23 F3
Ballon d'Alsace 27 E1
Ballstad 97 E1
Ballybay 13 D2
Ballybofey 12 C1
Ballybunnion 12 A4
Ballycastle (IRL) 12 B2
Ballycastle (N Ire) . . . 13 E1
Ballyclare 13 E2
Ballyconnell 12 C2
Ballycotton 14 C4
Ballycroy 12 B2
Ballyduff 14 B3
Ballyforan 12 C3
Ballygawley 13 D2
Ballyhaunis 12 B3
Ballyheige 14 A3
Ballyjamesduff 13 D3
Ballymahon 12 C3
Ballymena 13 E2
Ballymoe 12 C3
Ballymoney 13 E1
Ballymore 12 C3
Ballymote 12 C2
Ballynahinch 13 E2
Ballysadare 12 C2
Ballyshannon 12 C2
Ballyvaughan 12 B4
Balmaseda 36 A1
Balme 31 E1
Balmoral Castle 3 D4
Balneario de
Panticosa 37 E2
Balsareny 32 A3
Balsfjorden 94 B2
Balsicas 45 D2
Balsorano 63 F2
Bålsta 106 B3
Balsthal 27 E2
Balta 113 E3
Baltanás 35 F4
Baltar 34 B3
Baltic Sea 110 B2
Baltijsk 110 B4
Baltinglass 13 D4
Baltrum 47 E3
Bambalió 82 C3
Bamberg 52 C4
Bambíni 82 C3
Bamburgh 5 E3
Bampton 8 C3
Banagher 12 C4
Banat 114 C1
Banatska Palanka . . . 73 D2
Banatska Topola 72 C1
Banatski
Brestovac 73 D3
Banatski Dvor 72 C2
Banatski Karlovac . . . 73 D2
Banatsko
Aranđelovo 72 C1
Banatsko
Karadđorđevo 72 C2
Banatsko Novo
Selo 73 D2
Banbridge 13 E2
Banbury 9 E1
Banchory 3 E4
Bande 34 B3
Bandak 104 B2
Bandırma 115 E3
Bandol 30 C4
Bandon 14 B4
Bandon R. 14 B4
Bañeres 45 E1
Banff 3 E3
Bangor (IRL) 12 B2
Bangor (N Ire) 13 E2
Bangor (Wales) 6 A2
Bangsund 97 D4
Banie 49 E3
Banja (Srbija) 73 D3
Banja (Srbija) 76 B1
Banja Koviljača 72 B3
Banja Luka 71 E3
Banjani 72 C3
Banja Vrućica 71 F3
Banjska 76 C1
Bankeryd 109 D1
Bann (N Ire) 13 D1
Bann (Wexford) 15 D3
Barbadillo del
Mercado 36 A3

Bannalec 22 B3
Banon 30 C3
Bañón 41 D2
Barbarano
Vicentino 61 D1
Baños de Cerrato . . . 35 F4
Baños de la Encina . . 44 A2
Baños de
la Fuensanta 44 C2
Baños de Molgas . . . 34 B3
Baños de
Montemayor 39 E2
Baños de
Fuensanta 35 E1
Banova Jaruga 71 D2
Banović 71 F4
Banque de
Fraiture 51 D4
Banque Michel 51 D4
Bansin 49 E2
Banská-Bystrica . . . 112 B3
Banská-Štiavnica . . 112 B3
Bansko 77 F3
Bantry 14 B4
Bantry B 14 A4
Bañuela 43 F1
Banyalbufar 45 E2
Banyoles 32 B3
Banyuls 32 C3
Bao, Emb de 34 C3
Bapaume 19 F2
Bar (UKR) 113 D3
Bar (Crna Gora) 76 B3
Baracaldo 36 B1
Barači 71 E4
Baradla 112 B3
Barahona 36 B4
Barajas 40 B2
Barajas de Melo 40 B3
Barajevo 73 D3
Baralla 34 C2
Barane 76 C2
Baranovici 111 D4
Baraqueville 29 E3
Barasona, Emb de . . 37 E3
Barban 70 A3
Barbarano
Vicentino 61 D1
Bari 65 D3
Barić Draga 70 C4
Barisciano 63 F2
Barbastro 37 E3
Barbat 70 B4
Barbate de Franco . . 43 D4
Barbate, Emb de . . . 43 D4
Barbazan 37 F2
Barberino
di Mugello 60 C3
Barbezieux 28 B1
Barbizon 19 F4
Barbotan 28 B3
Barby 52 C1
Barca de Alva 39 D1
Barca, Emb de la . . . 35 D1
Barcarrota 42 C1
Barcelona 32 B4
Barcelona Pozzo di
Gotto 69 D2
Barcelonnette 31 D2
Barcelos 34 A4
Barcena, Emb de . . . 34 C2
Barchfeld 52 B3
Barcis 59 E3
Barcones 36 B4
Barcs 114 A1
Bardal 101 D1
Bardejov 112 B3
Bardi 60 B2
Bardineto 31 F3
Bardolino 60 C1
Bardonecchia 31 D1
Bardu 94 B3
Bardufoss 94 B3
Bare 76 B1
Barèges 37 E2
Barentin 19 D3
Barenton 18 C4
Bares, Estaca de . . . 34 B1
Barfleur 18 B2
Barfleur, Pte de 18 B2
Bargas 40 A3
Bargoed 9 D2

Bargteheide 48 B2
Bari 65 D3
Barić Draga 70 C4
Barisciano 63 F2
Barjac 30 B3
Barjols 31 D4
Barlby 7 D2
Bar-le-Duc 20 C4
Barletta 65 D3
Barlinek 49 F3
Barlovento 42 A4
Barmouth 6 A3
Barmstedt 48 A2
Barna 12 B3
Barnard Castle 5 E4
Bärnau 53 D4
Barneveld 16 C3
Barneville 18 B3
Barnsley 7 D2
Barnstaple 8 C3
Barnstorf 17 F1
Barntrup 52 A1
Barovo 77 E3
Barqueiro 38 B2
Barr 21 E4
Barra 2 A4
Barracas 41 E3
Barrachina 41 D2
Barraco 39 F2
Barrafranca 68 C4
Barra Head 2 A4
Barrancos 42 C1
Barranco Velho 42 B2
Barranda 44 C2
Barra, Sd of 2 A4
Barrax 40 C4
Barrea 64 A2
Barre-des-
Cévennes 29 F3
Barreiro 38 A4
Barrême 31 D3
Barrhead 4 C2
Barrhill 4 C3
Barri 9 D2

Barrow 13 D4
Barrow-
in-Furness 6 B1
Barrow, R 15 D3
Barruecopardo 39 D1
Barruelo de
Santullán 35 F2
Barry 9 D2
Barsinghausen 52 A1
Bar-sur-Aube 26 B1
Bar-sur-Seine 26 B1
Barth 49 D1
Barthe-de-Neste,
la 37 E1
Barton-upon-
Humber 7 D2
Barumini 66 B3
Baruth 53 E1
Barvas 2 B2
Barycz 112 A2
Barzio 58 B4
Bašaid 72 C1
Baschi 63 E1
Basconcillos
del Tozo 35 F2
Basel 27 E2
Baselga di Pinè 59 D3
Bas-en-Basset 30 B1
Basento 65 D4
Basildon 11 D2
Basilicata 65 D4
Basingstoke 9 E3
Baška 70 B3
Baška Voda 75 E2
Baške Oštarije 70 C4
Baslow 6 C3
Basovizza 59 F4
Bas-Rhin 21 E4
Bassano del
Grappa 59 D4
Bassée, la 19 F1
Bassella 37 F3
Bassens 28 B2

Bassum 17 F1
Båstad 108 C3
Bastasi 71 D4
Bastelica 33 F3
Bas'tevarri 95 D3
Bastia 33 F2
Bastide-de-
Sérou, la 37 F2
Bastogne 20 C2
Bastunäsfjället 97 E4
Bastuträsk 98 B4
Bataille, Col de la . . 30 C2
Batajnica 72 C3
Batak 115 D3
Batalha 38 B3
Batea 41 F1
Bath 9 D2
Bathgate 5 D2
Bâtie-Neuve, la 31 D2
Batina 72 B1
Batlava 77 D1
Batočina 73 D3
Båtsfjord 95 F1
Batsí 88 B1
Battaglia Terme 61 D1
Battenberg 17 F4
Battice 51 D3
Battipaglia 64 B4
Battle 11 D3
Batz (Finistère) 22 B2
Batz (Loire-
Atlantique) 24 A2
Baud 22 C3
Baugé 23 E4
Baugy 26 A2
Baule, la 24 A2
Baume, Cirque de . . 27 D3
Baume-les-
Dames 27 D2
Baumholder 54 B1
Bauska 110 C3
Bautzen 53 F2
Baux, les 30 B3
Bavanište 73 D3
Bavay 20 B1

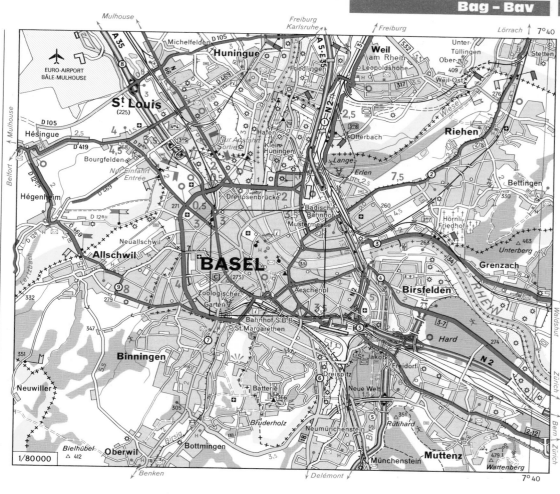

1/80000

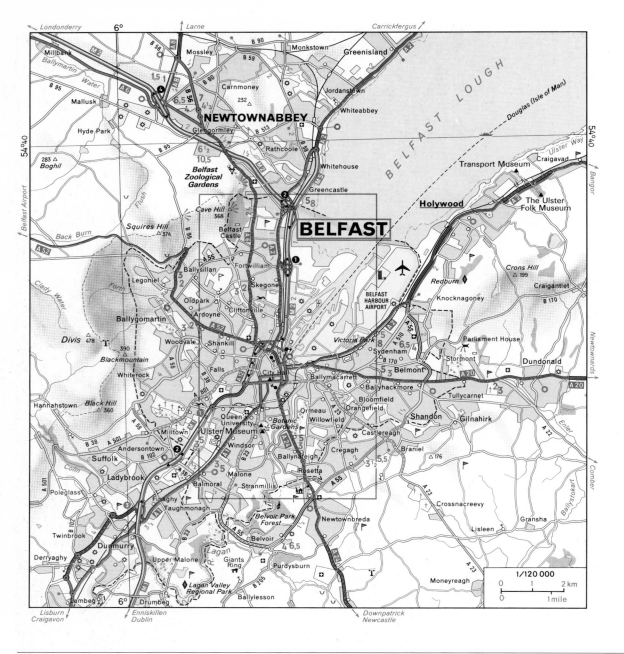

België	16	B3
Belgique	50	B3
Belgodère	33	F3
Belgorod-Dnes-		
trovskij	113	F4
Belianes	37	F3
Belice	68	B3
Beli Drim	76	C2
Beli Manastir	71	F2
Beli Potok	73	F4
Belišće	71	F2
Beli Timok	73	F4
Beljakovce	77	E3
Beljanica	73	E3
Beljina	73	D3
Bellac	25	D4
Bellagio	58	B4
Bellano	58	B4
Bellaria	61	E3
Bellcaire d'Urgell	37	F3
Belledonne,		
Chaîne de	31	D1
Belleek	12	C2
Bellegarde (Ain)	27	D4
Bellegarde (Gard)	30	B3
Bellegarde (Loiret)	25	F1
Bellegarde-en-		
Marche	25	F4
Belle-Ile	22	B4
Belle-Isle-en-Terre	22	B2
Bellême	23	F3
Bellencombre	19	E3
Bellerive	26	A4
Belleville	26	C4
Belley	27	D4
Bellinzona	58	A3
Bell-lloc d'Urgell	37	F3
Bello	41	E3
Bellpuig	37	F3
Belluno	59	E3
Bellver	45	E3
Bellver de		
Cerdanya	32	A3
Bélmez	43	E1
Belmont (F)	26	B4
Belmont (GB)	3	F1
Belmonte		
(Asturias)	35	D1
Belmonte (Castilla-la-		
Mancha)	40	C3
Belmonte (P)	38	C2
Belmont-sur-		
Rance	32	B1
Belmullet	12	A2
Belo Brdo	76	C1
Belogradčik	114	C2
Belo jez	72	C2
Beloljin	77	D1
Belœil	50	B4
Belo Polje	76	C2
Belopolje	113	F1
Belorado	36	A2
Belpech	32	A2
Belper	6	C3
Belsay	5	E1
Belsh	76	C4
Beltinci	70	C1
Belturbet	13	D2
Belušić	73	E4
Belvedere		
Marittimo	67	E2
Belver	37	E3
Belvès	28	C2
Belvis de la Jara	39	F3
Belyj	111	E2
Belz	22	C4
Bembézar, Emb de	43	E2
Bembézar, R.	43	E2
Bembibre	35	D2
Bemposta	38	B3
Bemposta,		
Bgem da	34	C4
Benabarre	37	E3
Benaguacil	41	E3
Benahadux	44	B3
Ben Alder	2	C4
Benalmádena	43	F4
Benalúa		
de las Villas	44	A3
Benamargosa	43	F3
Benamaurel	44	B2
Benameji	43	F3

Bavella, Col de	33	F4	Beariz	34	B2	Beaumont-le-			Becilla de			Bégude-de-Mazenc,		
Båven	106	B4	Beas	42	C2	Roger	19	D3	Valderaduey	35	E3	la	30	C2
Baveno	58	A4	Beasain	36	C1	Beaumont-sur-			Beckenried	58	A2	Begues	32	A4
Bawtry	7	D2	Beas de Segura	44	B2	Sarthe	23	F3	Beckington	9	D3	Begur	32	C3
Bayard, Col	31	D2	Beattock	5	D3	Beaune	26	C2	Beckum	17	F3	Behalúa de Guadix	44	B3
Bayerisch			Beaucaire	30	B3	Beaune-la-			Bečov	53	E4	Behobia	28	A4
Eisenstein	56	C1	Beaufort (Jura)	26	C3	Rolande	25	F1	Bedale	6	C1	Behringersmühle	52	C4
Bayerischer Wald	56	B2	Beaufort (Savoie)	27	E4	Beaupréau	24	C2	Bédarieux	30	A4	Beiarn	97	E2
Bayern	55	F2	Beaufort-en-			Beauraing	50	C4	Beddgelert	6	A3	Beilen	17	D1
Bayeux	18	C3	Vallée	23	E4	Beaurepaire	30	C1	Bedford	9	F1	Beilingries	55	F2
Bayhirivagh	2	A4	Beaugency	25	E2	Beaurepaire-en-			Bedfordshire	9	F1	Beinn a'Ghlò	3	D4
Bayındır	115	F4	Beaujeu	26	C4	Bresse	26	C3	Bedlington	5	E3	Beinn an Oir	4	B2
Bayon	21	D4	Beaulieu (Alpes-			Beausset, le	31	D4	Bedmar	44	A2	Beinn Bheigeir	4	B2
Bayonne	28	A4	Maritime)	31	E3	Beauvais	19	E3	Bednja	70	C1	Beinn Dearg	2	C3
Bayreuth	52	C4	Beaulieu			Beauvoir (Deux-			Bedonia	60	B3	Beira Alta	38	C1
Bayrischzell	56	B4	(Corrèze)	29	D2	Sèvres)	24	C4	Bedum	47	D3	Beira Baixa	38	C2
Baza	44	B3	Beaulieu (GB)	9	E3	Beauvoir			Bedwas	9	D2	Beira Litoral	38	B1
Bazas	28	B3	Beaumaris	6	A2	(Vendée)	24	A3	Bedworth	9	E1	Beisfjord	94	B3
Baza, Sa de	44	B3	Beaumesnil	19	D3	Bebington	6	B2	Beeth	4	C2	Beitostølen	104	C1
Bazoches-sur-			Beaumetz-lès-			Bebra	52	B3	Beeford	7	E2	Beitstadfjorden	101	D1
Hoëne	19	D4	Loges	19	F2	Beccles	11	E1	Beelitz	49	D4	Beiuş	112	C4
Bazzano	60	C2	Beaumont (B)	50	B4	Becedas	39	E2	Beerfelden	55	D1	Beja	42	B1
Beachy Head	10	C3	Beaumont			Beceite	41	F2	Beeskow	49	E4	Béjar	39	E2
Beaconsfield	9	F2	(Dordogne)	28	C2	Bečej	72	C2	Beetzendorf	48	B4	Béjar, Pto de	39	E2
Béal an Átha	12	B2	Beaumont			Becerreá	34	C2	Bégard	22	C2	Békés	112	C4
Béal Átha			(Manche)	18	B3	Bec-Hellouin, le	19	D3	Begejci	72	C2	Bek Begejski kanal	72	C2	Békéscsaba	112	C4
na Sluaighe	12	C3	Beaumont			Bécherel	23	D3	Beg-Meil	22	B3	Belford	5	E2
Beaminster	9	D3	(Val d'Oise)	19	F3	Bechet	115	D2	Begna	104	C2	Belfort	27	E2
Beanntraí	14	B4	Beaumont-de-			Bechhofen	55	E2	Begov Han	71	F4	Belforte all'Isauro	61	E3
Beara	14	A4	Lomagne	28	C3	Bečići	76	B3	Bégude-de-Mazenc,			Belgern	53	E2

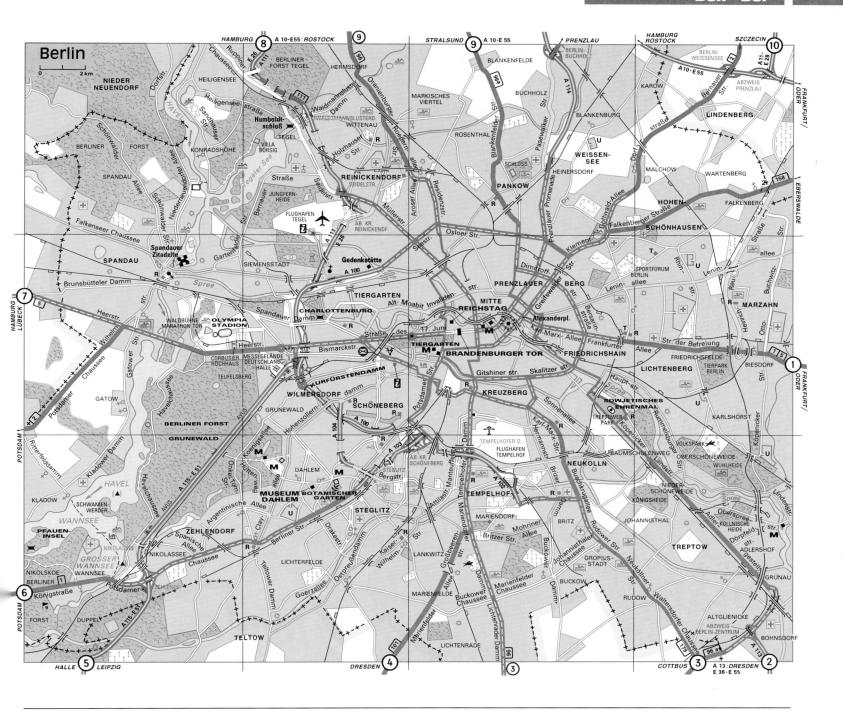

Berlin

Benamocarra	43 F4	Beničanci	71 E2	Bentley	7 D2
Benaoján	43 E4	Benicarló	41 F2	Ben Vorlich	4 C1
Ben Armine	3 D2	Benicasim	41 F3	Ben Wyvis	2 C3
Benasal	41 E2	Benidorm	45 E1	Bény-Bocage, le	18 C3
Benasque	37 E2	Benifaió	41 E4	Beočin	72 C2
Benavente (E)	35 D3	Beninar, Emb de	44 B3	Beograd	73 D3
Benavente (P)	38 A4	Benissa	45 E1	Berane	76 C2
Benavides	35 D3	Benítses	82 A1	Bérarde, la	31 D2
Benbecula	2 A3	Ben Klibreck	2 C2	Berat	114 C3
Ben Chonzie	4 C1	Benkovac	74 C1	Berbegal	37 E3
Ben Cruachan	4 B1	Ben Lawers	4 C1	Berberana	36 B1
Bender	113 E4	Ben Lomond	4 C1	Berbería, C de	45 D4
Bendorf	51 E4	Ben Macdui	3 D4	Berceto	60 B3
Benediktbeuern	56 A4	Ben More		Berching	55 F2
Benešov		(Grampian)	4 C1	Berchtesgaden	56 C4
(Severočeský)	53 F3	Ben More (Mull)	4 B1	Berck-Plage	19 E1
Benešov		Ben More Assynt	2 C2	Berdičev	113 E4
(Středočeský)	53 F4	Benneckenstein	52 B2	Beregovo	112 C3
Bénévent-		Ben Nevis	2 C4	Bereguardo	60 A2
l'Abbaye	25 E4	Bénodet	22 B3	Bere I	14 A4
Benevento	64 B3	Benquerencia		Berek	71 D2
Benfeld	21 E4	de la Serena	43 E1	Bere Regis	9 D3
Benfleet	11 D2	Bensberg	17 E4	Beret	37 F2
Bengtsfors	105 D4	Bensersiel	47 E3	Berettyóújfalu	112 C4
Ben Hope	2 C2	Bensheim	54 C1	Berezina	111 E4

Berezino	111 D4	Berghamn		Berkshire	9 E2
Berg (A)	57 F2	fjärden	107 D3	Berlaimont	20 A2
Berg		Bergheim	17 D4	Berlanga	43 D1
(Nordland)	97 D3	Bergisch Gladbach	17 E4	Berlanga de	
Berg (S)	101 E2	Bergnäset	98 C3	Duero	36 B4
Berg (Troms)	94 B2	Bergneustadt	17 E4	Berlebeck	17 F3
Berga (D)	52 C2	Bergö	102 B2	Berlenga, I	38 A3
Berga (E)	32 A3	Berg-		Berlevåg	95 F1
Bergama	115 E4	Rudolphstein	53 D3	Berlin	49 E4
Bergamo	60 B1	Bergsjö	101 E3	Bermejales, Emb	43 F3
Bergara	36 B1	Bergsviken	98 B3	Bermeja, Sa	43 E4
Bergby	106 B2	Bergues	19 F1	Bermeo	36 B1
Bergedorf	48 B3	Bergum	47 D3	Bermillo	35 D4
Bergen (B)	50 B4	Bergün	58 B3	Bern	27 E2
Bergen (D)	49 D1	Beringel	42 B1	Bernalda	65 D4
Bergen (N)	104 A2	Beringen	50 C3	Bernardsthal	57 F1
Bergen		Berja	44 B4	Bernartice	57 D1
(Niedersachsen)	48 A4	Berka	52 C3	Bernau (Baden-	
Bergen		Berkåk	100 C2	Württemberg)	54 C4
(Niedersachsen)	48 B3	Berkel	17 D2	Bernau (Bayern)	56 B3
Bergen (NL)	16 C2	Berkhamsted	9 F2	Bernau	
Bergen aan Zee	16 C2	Berkheim	55 E3	(Brandenburg)	49 E4
Bergen op Zoom	16 B4	Berkhof	48 A4	Bernaville	19 F2
Bergerac	28 C2	Berkovica	114 C2	Bernay	19 D3
Berggießhübel	53 F2	Berkovići	75 F2	Bernburg	52 C1

Berndorf	57 E3
Berne	47 F3
Bernesga, R	35 D2
Bernina, Piz	58 B3
Bernina, Pso del	58 B3
Bernkastel-Kues	54 B1
Bernsdorf	53 F2
Bernstein	57 F3
Beroun	53 F4
Berounka	53 F4
Berovo	77 F3
Ber'oza	112 C1
Ber'ozovka	113 F3
Berra	61 D2
Berre	30 C4
Berre, Etang de	30 C4
Beršad'	113 E3
Bertincourt	17 E2
Bertamirans	34 A2
Bertinoro	61 D3
Bertrix	20 C2
Berwang	58 C1
Berwick-upon-	
Tweed	5 E2
Berwyn	6 B3

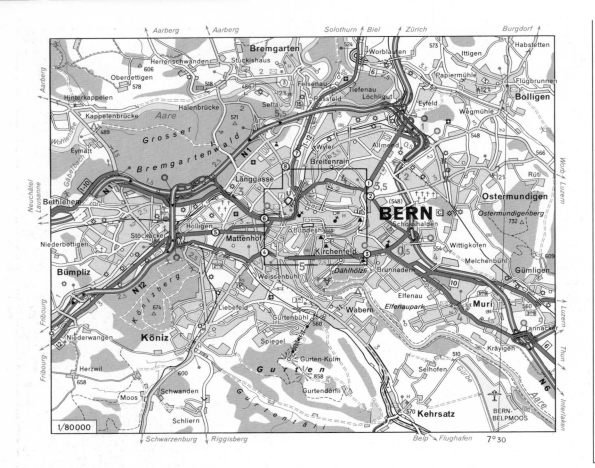

Berzocana	39 E3	Beverungen	52 A2
Berzosa	39 D1	Beverwijk	16 C2
Besalú	32 B3	Bewdley	9 D1
Besançon	27 D2	Bex	27 E3
Besande	35 E2	Bexhill	11 D3
Besaya, R	35 F2	Beynac	29 D2
Besbre	26 B3	Beynat	29 D2
Besigheim	55 D2	Bezards, les	72 C3
Beška	72 C2	Bezas	26 A1
Besna Kobila	77 E2	Bezas	41 E3
Besse	29 E1	Bezdan	72 B1
Bessèges	30 B3	Bezdrep	57 D1
Besse-sur-Issole	31 D4	Bežeck	111 F1
Bessines	25 E4	Béziers	30 A4
Betancuria	42 C4	Bezmisht	77 D4
Betanzos	34 B1	Béznar	44 A3
Betelu	36 C1	Biała Podlaska	112 C1
Bétera	41 E3	Białowieska	112 C1
Beteta	40 C2	Białystok	112 C1
Bétharram,		Biancavilla	69 D3
Grottes de	37 E1	Bianco	67 E4
Bethesda	6 A2	Bianco, M	27 E4
Béthune	19 F1	Biandrate	31 F1
Béthune R	19 E2	Biar	45 D1
Bettna	106 A4	Biarritz	28 A4
Bettola	60 B2	Biasca	58 A3
Bettolle	61 D4	Bibbiena	61 D4
Bettyhill	3 D2	Biberach	54 C3
Betws-y-Coed	6 A3	Biberach an der Ri.	55 E8
Betz	19 F3	Bibinje	74 C1
Betzdorf	51 F3	Bibione	59 F4
Beuil	31 E3	Bibury	9 E2
Beura	58 A4	Bicaj	76 C3
Beuron	55 D3	Bicaz	113 D4
Beuvray, Mont	26 B3	Bicester	9 E2
Beuvron	25 E2	Bichl	56 A4
Beuzeville	19 D3	Bidache	28 A4
Bevagna	63 E1	Bidart	28 A4
Beveren-Waas	50 B3	Bidasoa, R	36 C1
Beverley	7 D2	Biddendon	11 D3
Beverstedt	47 F3	Bidean nam Bian	4 C1

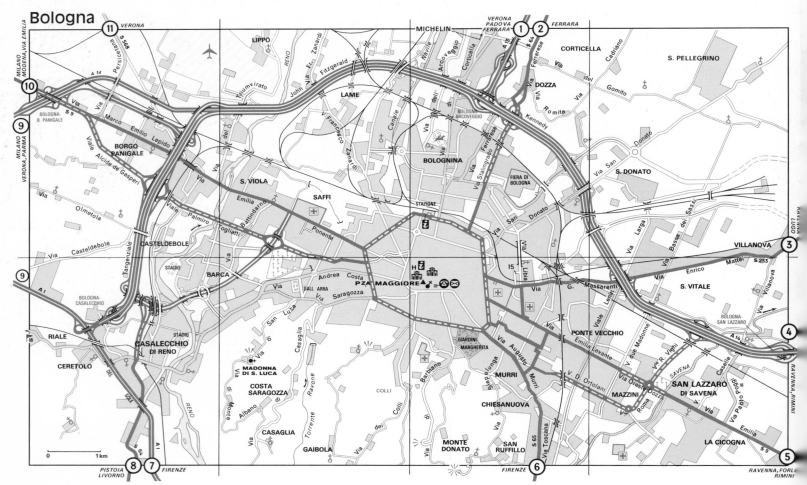

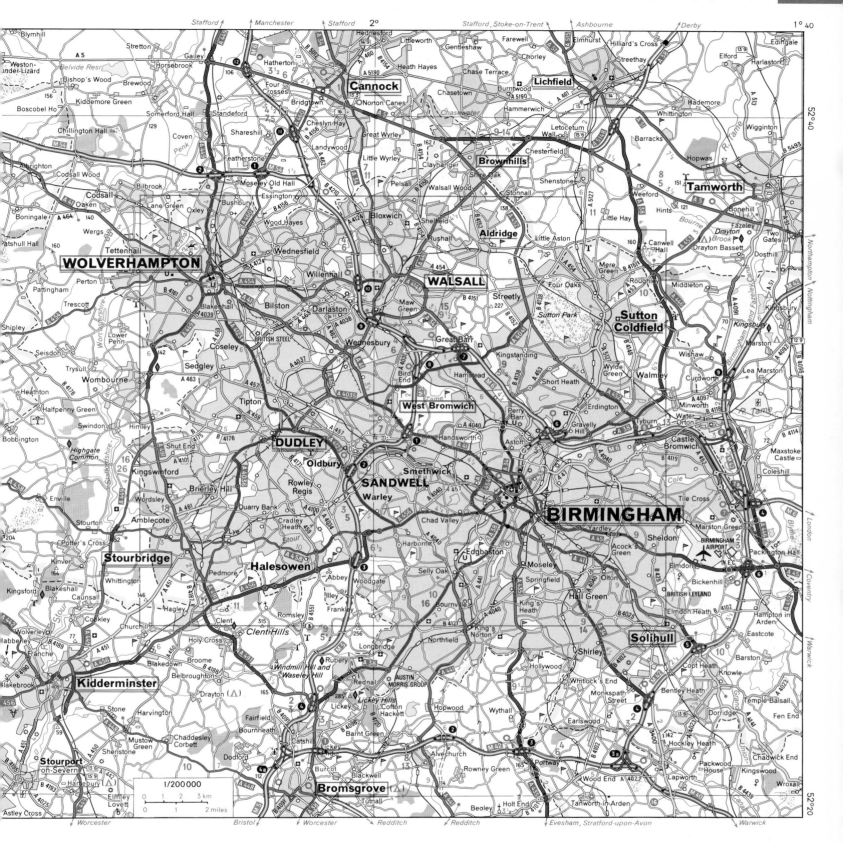

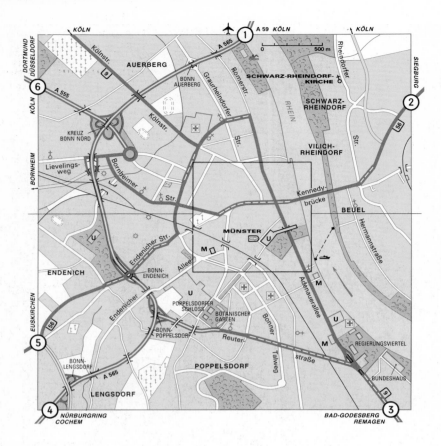

Bonn

Bideford 8 C3
Biebelried 55 E1
Biedenkopf 17 F4
Biel 27 E2
Bielefeld 17 F2
Bielerhöhe 58 B2
Biella 31 F1
Bielsa 37 E2
Bielsa, Tunnel de 37 E2
Bielsko-Biała 112 B3
Bielsk Podlaski 112 C1
Bienne 27 D3
Bienne 27 E2
Bientina 60 C4
Bienvenida 43 D1
Bierné 23 E4
Bierre 26 B2
Biesbosch 16 C3
Biescas 37 D2
Biese 48 C4
Biesenthal 49 E3
Bietigheim-Bissingen 55 D2
Biferno 64 B2
Biga 115 E3
Biggar 5 D2
Biggleswade 9 F1
Bignasco 58 A3
Bihać 70 C3
Bihorului, M 112 C4
Bijele Poljane 76 B2
Bijeljani 75 F2
Bijeljina 72 B3
Bijelo Brdo 71 F2
Bijelolasica 70 B3
Bijelo Polje 76 B2
Bilbao 36 B1
Bileća 76 A2
Bilecik 115 F3
Bilećko jez 76 A2
Biłgoraj 112 C2
Bilina 53 E3
Biljača 77 E2
Biljanovac 76 C1
Bilje 71 F2
Billerbeck 17 E3

Billericay 11 D2
Billingham 5 E4
Billingshurst 10 C3
Billom 29 F1
Billund 108 A3
Bilo 77 E1
Bilogora 71 D2
Bilto 94 C2
Bilzen 50 C3
Binaced 37 E3
Binačka Morava 77 D2
Binasco 60 A1
Binche 50 B4
Binéfar 37 E3
Bingen 51 F4
Bingham 7 D3
Bingley 6 C2
Bingsjö 101 E4
Binic 22 C2
Binz 49 D1
Bioča 76 C2
Bioče 76 B2
Biograd 74 C1
Biogradsko, nac park 76 B2
Biokovo 75 E2
Bionaz 27 E4
Biot, le 27 E3
Birchington 11 D2
Birgi 68 A3
Biri 105 D2
Birkebeiner veien 104 C1
Birkeland 104 B4
Birkenfeld 54 B1
Birkenhead 6 B2
Birkenwerder 49 D4
Birkerød 108 C3
Birkfeld 57 E4
Bîrlad 113 E4
Birmingham 9 E1
Birnau 55 D4
Birr 12 C4
Biržai 110 C3
Birzebugga 68 B4
Biscarrosse 28 A3

Biscarrosse-Plage 28 A3
Bisceglie 65 D3
Bischofsgrün 53 D4
Bischofsheim 52 B4
Bischofshofen 59 E1
Bischofswerde 53 F2
Bischofswiesen 56 C4
Bischofszell 58 A1
Bischwiller 21 F4
Bisenti 63 F1
Biševo 75 D2
Bishop Auckland 5 E4
Bishop's Castle 9 D1
Bishop's Stortford 10 C2
Bisignano 67 E2
Bisko 75 D1
Bismark 48 C4
Bismo 100 B3
Bispgården 101 F2
Bispingen 48 A3
Bistar 77 E2
Bistra pl 77 D3
Bistrica (Crna Gora) 76 B2
Bistrica (Srbija) 76 B1
Bistrica ob S. 70 C2
Bistričak 71 E4
Bistrița 113 D4
Bistrița R. 113 D4
Bitburg 54 A1
Bitche 21 E3
Bitetto 65 D3
Bitola 77 E4
Bitonto 65 D3
Bitovnja 75 F1
Bitterfeld 53 D2
Bitti 66 B2
Bizákos 82 C3
Bizau 58 B2
Bizovac 71 F2
Bjala 115 D2
Bjärky 94 B3
Bjåsta 102 A2
Bjelašnica 75 F1
Bjelašnica 76 A2
Bjelovar 71 D2
Bjerkreim 104 A4

Bjerkvik 94 B3
Bjerringbro 108 B2
Bjrkelangen 105 D3
Björketorp 109 E3
Bjorkfjället 97 F3
Björkliden 94 B3
Björksele 98 A4
Bjørli 100 B3
Björna 102 A2
Bjørnafjorden 104 A2
Bjørneborg 107 D1
Bjørnevatn 95 F2
Bjørntoppen 97 F1
Björsäter 109 E1
Bjurholm 102 A1
Bjursås 101 E4
Bjuv 108 C3
Blace 77 D1
Blackburn 6 C2
Black Head 12 B4
Black Isle 2 C3
Black Mt. 8 C2
Black Mts. 9 D2
Blackpool 6 B2
Black Sea 115 F2
Blacksod B 12 A2
Blackstairs Mts 15 D3
Blackwater 15 D3
Blackwaterfoot 4 B2
Blackwater, R. 14 C4
Blackwater Res 2 C4
Blaenau Ffestiniog 6 A3
Blaenavon 9 D2
Blåfjellhatten 101 E1
Blagaj 75 F2
Blagnac 29 D4
Blagoevgrad 115 D3
Blåhammaren 101 D2
Blåhø 100 C2
Blain 23 D4
Blainville 21 D4
Blair Atholl 3 D4
Blairgowrie 5 D1
Blå Jungfrun 109 E2
Blakeney 7 F3

Blakstad 104 B4
Blåmannsisen 97 F2
Blåmont 21 E4
Blanca 45 D2
Blanc, C 45 E3
Blanc, le 25 D3
Blanc, Mont. 27 E4
Blanco, R 43 E3
Blandford Forum 9 D3
Blanes 32 B4
Blangy 19 E2
Blangy-le-Château 19 D3
Blankenberge 50 A3
Blankenburg 52 C2
Blankenheim 51 D4
Blankernhain 52 C3
Blanquefort 28 B2
Blanquilla 44 B2
Blansko 57 D1
Blanzac 28 C1
Blanzy 26 B3
Blåøret 100 C2
Blarney 14 B4
Blatná 56 C1
Blatnica 71 E4
Blato 75 E1
Blattniksele 98 A3
Blaubeuren 55 D3
Blauen 54 C4
Blaufelden 55 E2
Blaustein 55 E3
Blavet 22 C3
Blaye 28 B2
Blaževo 77 D1
Bleckede 48 B3
Bled 70 A2
Blefjell 104 C3
Bleiburg 70 B1
Bleicherode 52 B2
Bleik 94 A3
Bleiloch-Talsperre 53 D3
Blekinge Län 109 D3
Blendija 73 E4
Bléneau 26 A2
Blenheim Palace 9 D2
Blénod 21 D3
Bléone 31 D3
Blérancourt 19 F3
Bléré 25 D2
Blesle 29 F1
Bletchley 9 F2
Bletterans 26 C3
Blexen 47 F3
Bleymard, le 29 F3
Blidinje jez. 75 E1
Bligny 26 C2
Blinisht 76 C3
Blinja 71 D3
Bloemendaal 16 B2
Blois 25 E2
Blokhus 108 B2
Blomberg 52 A1
Blönduós 96 B1
Blonville 19 D3
Bloody Foreland Head 12 C1
Blosenberg 53 D3
Bloška Polica 70 B2
Blovice 56 C1
Bludenz 58 B2
Blue Stack Mts. 12 C2
Blumberg (Baden-Württemberg) 54 C4
Blumberg (Brandenburg) 49 E4
Blyth 5 E3
Bø (Telemark) 104 C3
Bø (Vesterålen) 94 A3
Boadella, Emb de. 32 B3
Boal 34 C1
Boan 76 B2
Boara Pisani 61 D1
Bobbio 60 A2
Bobigny 19 F4
Bobingen 55 E2
Böblingen 55 D2
Boblitz 53 E1
Boborás 34 B2
Bobova 72 C4
Bóbr 113 F3
Bobrinec 113 F3
Bobrovica 113 E2
Bobrujsk 111 E4

Bočac 71 E4
Bocairent 45 E1
Bocca Trabaria 61 E4
Bocche di Bonifacio 33 F4
Bocco, Pso del 60 B3
Boceguillas 36 A4
Bocholt 17 D3
Bochov 53 E4
Bochum 17 E3
Bockel 48 A3
Bockenem 52 B1
Böckstein 59 E2
Bockum-Hövel 17 E3
Bocognano 33 F3
Boda 101 E4
Böda 109 F2
Bodafors 109 D2
Boddani 72 B2
Bode 52 C1
Bodegraven 16 C3
Boden 98 B3
Bodenmais 56 B1
Bodensee 58 B1
Bodenteich 48 B4
Bodenwerder 52 A1
Bodenwöhr 56 B1
Bodman-Radolfzell 55 D4
Bodmin 8 B4
Bodø 97 E1
Boecillo 35 E4
Boëge 27 D4
Boën 26 B4
Boeza 35 D2
Boffalora 60 A1
Bogarra 44 C1
Bogatić 72 C3
Bogdanci 77 F3
Bogdaniec 49 F3
Bogë 76 C2
Bogen (D) 56 B2
Bogen (N) 94 B3
Bogense 108 B3
Bogetići 76 B2
Boglárlelle 112 B4
Bognanco 27 F4
Bognes 94 A4
Bognor Regis 9 F3
Bogodol 75 F1
Bogojevo 72 B2
Bogomila 77 E3
Bogomolje 75 E2
Bogorodika 77 F4
Bogovina 73 E4
Bogøy 97 E1
Boguslav 113 E2
Bogutovac 73 D4
Bohain-en-Vermandois 20 A2
Boherboy 14 B3
Bohinjska Bistrica 70 A2
Bohinjsko jez 70 A2
Böhlen 53 D2
Böhme 48 A4
Böhmenkirch 55 E2
Böhmer Wald. 56 B1
Bohmte 17 F2
Böhönye 114 A1
Boiano 64 B3
Boiro 34 A2
Bois-d'Amont 27 D3
Boitzenburg 49 E3
Bóixols 37 F3
Boizenburg 48 B3
Bojana 76 B3
Bøjden 108 B4
Bojnik 77 D1
Boka Kotorska 76 A3
Bøkfjorden 95 F2
Bokn 104 A3
Boknafjorden 104 A3
Bol 75 E2
Bøla 101 D1
Bolbec 19 D3
Bolchov 111 F3
Bolera, Emb de la 44 B2
Bolesławiec 112 A2
Boleszkowice 49 E3
Bolgrad 113 E4
Boliden 98 B4
Boliqueime 42 B2
Boljanići 76 B1

Boljevac 73 E4
Boljevci 72 C3
Boljkovci 73 D4
Boljuni 75 F2
Bolkesjø 104 C3
Bollebygd 108 C1
Bollène 30 B3
Bollnäs 101 F4
Bollstabruk 101 F2
Bollullos de la Mitación 43 D2
Bollullos par del Condado 42 C2
Bolmen 109 D2
Bolñãos de Calatrava 40 A4
Bologna 60 C2
Bologne 26 C3
Bologoje 111 E1
Bolos 40 B4
Bolotana 66 B2
Bolsena 63 D1
Bolsena, L di 63 D2
Bolsward 16 C1
Boltaña 37 E2
Boltenhagen 48 B2
Bolton 6 C2
Bolungarvik 96 A1
Bolus Head 14 A4
Bolzano 59 D3
Bombarral 38 A3
Bomenzien 48 C3
Bom Jesus 34 B4
Bømlo 104 A3
Bonaigua, Pto de la 37 F2
Bonar 35 E2
Bonar Bridge 2 C3
Bonares 42 C2
Bonassola 60 B3
Bondeno 60 C2
Bondone, Mte. 58 C3
Bonefro 64 B2
Bo'-Ness 5 D2
Bonete 45 D1
Bonette, Col de la 31 D3
Bonhomme, Col du 27 E1
Bonifacio 33 F4
Bonn 51 D2
Bonnåsjøen 97 F1
Bonnat 25 E4
Bonndorf 54 C4
Bonnétable 23 F3
Bonneuil-Matours 25 D2
Bonneval (Eure-et-Loir) 25 E1
Bonneval (Savoie) 31 E1
Bonneville 27 D4
Bonneville, la 19 E4
Bonnières 19 E3
Bonnieux 30 C3
Bono 66 B2
Bonorva 66 B2
Bønsnes 104 C3
Boo 106 B4
Boom 50 B3
Boos 19 E3
Bootle 6 B2
Bopfingen 55 E2
Boppard 51 E4
Bor (CS) 53 E4
Bor (Srbija) 73 E3
Boračko jez. 75 F1
Borås 108 C1
Borba 38 C4
Borbollón, Emb de 39 D2
Borbona 63 F1
Borča 72 C3
Borci 75 F1
Bordeaux 28 B2
Bordeira 42 A2
Bordères-Louron 37 E2
Border Forest Park, The 5 D3
Borders Region 5 D3
Bordesholm 48 A2
Bordighera 31 E3
Borðoy 96 A3
Bore 60 B2
Borello 61 D3
Borensberg 105 F4

Boréon, le 31 E3
Borga 107 F2
Borgafjäll 97 E4
Borga-fjällen 97 E4
Borgarnes 96 A2
Børgefjell 97 E3
Børgefjellet 97 E3
Borger 17 E1
Börger 17 E1
Borghetto 63 E2
Borghetto S.S. 31 F3
Borgholm 109 E2
Borgholzhausen ... 17 F2
Borghorst 17 E2
Borgia 67 F3
Borgomanero 58 A4
Borgone 31 E1
Borgonovo Val
  Tidone 60 B2
Borgorose 63 F2
Borgo San
  Dalmazzo 31 E2
Borgo
  San Lorenzo 61 D3
Borgosesia 58 A4
Borgo Tufico 61 E4
Borgo Val di Taro .. 60 B3
Borgo Valsugana .. 59 D3
Borgsjö 101 F3
Borgund 104 B1
Borgvattnet 101 F2
Boričje 76 B2
Borisov 111 D4
Borispol' 113 E2
Borja (E) 36 C3
Borja (BH) 71 E4
Borken 17 E3
Borkenes 94 A3
Børkop 108 B3
Borkum 47 D3
Borlänge 105 F2
Bormes-les-
  Mimosas 31 D4
Bormida 60 A2
Bormio 58 C3
Born 48 C1
Borna 53 D2
Bornes 34 C4
Bornes, Sa de 34 C4
Bornholm 109 D4
Bornhöved 48 B2
Börnicke 49 D4
Bornos 43 D3
Bornos, Emb de 43 D3
Boroughbridge 7 D1
Borovec 115 D3
Boroviči 111 E1
Borovnica 70 B2
Borovo 72 B2
Borovsk 111 F2
Borre 104 C3
Borriol 41 E3
Borris 15 D3
Borrisokane 12 C4
Borşa 113 D3
Børselv 95 E1
Børselva 95 E2
Børselvfjellet 95 E2
Bórsio 86 B1
Bort-les-Orgues ... 29 E1
Börtnan 101 E2
Borzna 113 F1
Borzonasca 60 A3
Bosa 66 A2
Bosanci 70 C3
Bosanska Dubica ... 71 D1
Bosanska Gradiška .. 71 E3
Bosanska
  Kostajnica 71 D3
Bosanska Krupa ... 71 D3
Bosanska Rača ... 72 B3
Bosanski Brod 71 E3
Bosanski Kobaš ... 71 E3
Bosanski Novi 71 D3
Bosanski
  Petrovac 71 D4
Bosanski Šamac ... 71 F3
Bosansko
  Grahovo 71 D4
Bosansko Petrovo
  Selo 71 F3
Bosco 61 E4
Bosco
  Chiesanuova 59 D4

Bosilegrad 77 E2
Bosiljevo 70 C3
Bosjökloster 109 D3
Boskoop 16 C3
Bosna 71 F4
Bosna
  i Hercegovina ... 71 E4
Bošnjace 77 E1
Bošnjaci 72 B3
Bossòst 37 F2
Bostan 75 E2
Boštanj 70 B2
Boston 7 E3
Bosut 72 B2
Botev 115 D2
Botevgrad 115 D2
Bothel 5 D4
Boticas 34 B4
Botley 9 E3
Botngård 100 C1
Botnie, G de 102 A3
Botoš 72 C2
Botoşani 113 D3
Botrange 51 D4
Botsmark 102 A1
Botte Donato,
  Mte 67 E3
Bottenhavet 102 A3
Bottniska Viken
  Pohjanlahti 102 A3
Bottrop 17 E3
Botun 77 D4
Bouaye 24 B2
Boucau 28 A4
Bouchain 20 A2
Bouches-
  du-Rhône 30 B4
Boudry 27 E2
Bouillon 20 C2
Bouilly 26 B1
Boúka 86 C3
Boulay-Moselle ... 21 D3
Boulogne
  (Haute-Garonne) . 37 F1
Boulogne
  (Pas-de-Calais) 19 E1
Boulogne R 24 B3
Bouloire 23 F3
Boulou, le 32 B2
Boumort 37 F3
Bourbon-
  Lancy 26 B3
Bourbon-
  l'Archambault 26 A3
Bourbonne-
  les-Bains 27 D1
Bourboule, la 29 E1
Bourbourg 19 F1
Bourbriac 22 C2
Bourdeaux 30 C2
Bourdeilles 28 C1
Bourg 28 B2
Bourg-Achard 19 D3
Bourganeuf 25 E4
Bourg-Argental .. 30 B1
Bourg-de-Péage .. 30 C2
Bourg-de-Visa ... 28 C3
Bourg-d'Oisans, le . 31 D2
Bourg-en-Bresse .. 26 C4
Bourges 25 F3
Bourget, le 30 C1
Bourg-Lastic 29 E1
Bourg-Madame ... 32 A3
Bourgneuf
  -en-Retz 24 B3
Bourgogne 26 C2
Bourgoin-Jallieu .. 30 C1
Bourgtheroulde .. 19 D3
Bourgueil 25 D2
Bourmont 26 C1
Bourne 7 D3
Bourne,
  Gges de la 30 C2
Bournemouth ... 9 E3
Bourniá, Akr 87 E3
Bousquet-d'Orb,
  le 30 A4
Boussac 25 F4
Boussens 37 F1
Boutonne 24 C4
Bouxwiller 21 E3
Bouzonville 21 D3

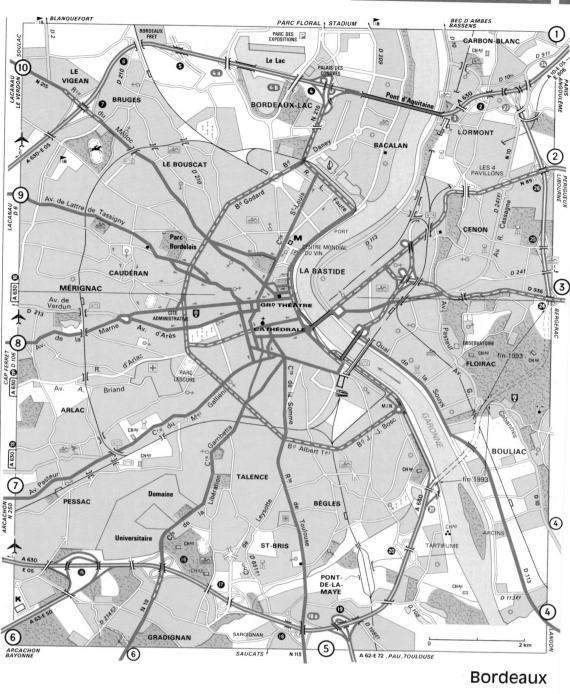

Bordeaux

Bovalino Marina ... 67 F4
Bova Marina 67 E4
Bovan 73 E4
Bovec 70 A2
Bóveda 34 B2
Bøverdal 100 B3
Boves 19 F2
Boves 31 E3
Bovey Tracy 8 C3
Bovolone 60 C1
Bowes 5 E4
Bowness 6 B1
Bowness-
  on-Solway 5 D3
Boxholm 109 E1
Boxmeer 17 D3
Boxtel 16 C3
Boyle 12 C2
Boyne 13 D3
Božaj 76 B3
Božava 74 C1
Bozdoğan 115 F4
Bozel 31 D1
Bozen 59 D3
Božica 77 E2

Boži Dar 53 E3
Bozouls 29 E3
Bozüyük 115 F3
Bozzolo 60 C2
Bra 31 F2
Brabant 50 B3
Brač 75 E2
Bracadale 2 B3
Bracadale, L ... 2 B3
Bracciano 63 E2
Bracciano, L di 63 E2
Bracco, Pso del ... 60 B3
Bračevci 71 F2
Bracieux 25 E2
Bräcke 101 E2
Brackenheim ... 55 D2
Brackley 9 E2
Bracknell 9 F2
Brackwede 17 F3
Brad 112 C4
Bradano 65 D4
Bradashesh ... 76 C4
Bradford 6 C2
Bradford-on-Avon . 9 D2
Bradina 75 F1

Brading 9 E3
Bradwell-on-Sea 11 D2
Braemar 3 D4
Braga 34 A4
Bragança 34 C3
Braguia, Pto de ... 35 F2
Braies, L di 59 D2
Braine 20 A3
Braine-le-Comte 50 B4
Braintree 11 D2
Brake 47 F3
Brakel 52 A2
Bräkne-Hoby 109 D3
Brallo
  di Pregola ... 60 A2
Brálos 83 E3
Bramming ... 108 A3
Brampton ... 5 D3
Bramsche 17 E2
Brancaleone Marina . 67 E4
Brancion 26 C3
Brand 58 B2
Brandbu ... 105 D2
Brande 108 A3

Brandenburg 49 D4
Brandenburg
  (Land) 49 D3
Brand-Erbisdorf ... 53 E3
Brander, Pass of .. 4 B1
Brandis 53 D2
Brändo 107 D2
Brandon 11 D1
Brandon Head .. 14 A3
Brandon Mt ... 14 A3
Brandýs Stará
  Boleslav 53 F3
Braničevo ... 73 E3
Braniewo ... 110 B4
Branne 28 B2
Braño Caballo .. 35 D2
Brañosera .. 35 F2
Br'ansk 111 E4
Brantôme ... 28 C1
Braskereidfoss .. 105 D2
Braslav 111 D3
Braşov 113 D4

Brattvåg 100 A2
Bratunac 72 B4
Braubach 51 E4
Braunau 56 C3
Braunfels 51 F4
Braunlage 52 B2
Braunsbedra 53 D2
Braunschweig ... 52 B1
Braunton 8 C3
Braus, Col de .. 31 E3
Bravães 34 A3
Bravuogn ... 58 B3
Bray (IRL) 13 E4
Bray
  (Seine-et-Marne) .. 20 A4
Bray (Somme) .. 19 F2
Bray-Dunes ... 19 F1
Brazatortas .. 43 F1
Brbinj 74 C1
Brčko 72 B3
Brda 110 A3
Brdđani ... 73 D4
Brea 36 C4
Brécey ... 18 B4
Brechin ... 3 E4

Brecht 50 C3
Břeclav 57 F1
Brecon 8 C1
Brecon Beacons
  Nat Pk 8 C2
Breda (E) 32 B4
Breda (NL) 16 C3
Bredbyn 102 A2
Bredelar 17 F3
Bredstedt 47 F1
Bree 50 C3
Bregalnica 77 F3
Breganze 59 D4
Bregenz 58 B1
Bréhal 18 B4
Bréhat, I de 22 C2
Breiðafjörður 96 A2
Breil-sur-Roya 31 E3
Breisach 54 B4
Breitengüßbach . . . 52 C4
Breitungen 52 B3
Breivikbotn 95 D1
Breivikeidet 94 C2
Brekke 104 A1
Brekken 101 D2
Brekkvasselv 97 D4
Brekstad 100 C1
Bremanger
  Landet 100 A3
Bremen 47 F3
Bremerhaven 47 F3
Bremervörde 47 F3
Bremsnes 100 B2
Breña, Emb de la . . 43 E2
Brenes 43 D2
Brenna 53 D2
Brenner 59 D2
Brennilis 22 B3
Breno 58 C4
Brénod 26 C4
Brentwood 10 C2
Brescia 60 B1
Breskens 16 B4
Bresle 19 E2
Bresles 19 F3
Bressanone 59 D2
Bressay 3 F2
Bresse, la 27 E1
Bressuire 24 C3
Brest (F) 22 A2
Brest (UKR) 112 C1
Brest R. 23 D4
Brestanica 70 C2
Brestova 70 B3
Brestovac (HR) . . . 71 E2
Brestovac (Srbija) . 73 E3
Brestovac (Srbija) . 77 D1
Brestovac (Srbija) . 77 E1
Brestovačka
  Banja 73 E3
Bretenoux 29 D2
Breteuil (Eure) . . . 19 D4
Breteuil (Oise) . . . 19 F3
Bretten 54 C2
Breuil-Cervinia . . . 27 F4
Brevik 104 C4
Breza 71 F4
Brežđđe 72 C4
Brežice 70 C2
Breznica 70 C2
Breznica
  Đakovačka . . . 71 F2
Březnice 56 C1
Brezno 112 B3
Brezolles 19 E4
Brezovica 77 D2
Brezovo Polje (BH) 72 B3
Brezovo Polje (HR) 71 E2
Briançon 31 D2
Briare 26 A2
Bribirske Mostine . 75 D1
Bricquebec 18 B3
Brides 31 D1
Bridgend
  (Scotland) 4 A2
Bridgend (Wales) . . 8 C2
Bridge of Allan 4 C2
Bridgnorth 9 D1
Bridgwater 9 D3
Bridlington 7 E1
Bridport 9 D3
Briec 22 B3
Brie-Comte-
  Robert 19 F4

Brielle 16 B3
Brienne-
  le-Château . . . 20 B4
Brienon 26 A1
Brienz 27 F3
Brienza 64 C4
Briey 21 D3
Brig 27 F3
Brigg 7 D2
Brighouse 6 C2
Brightlingsea 11 D2
Brighton 10 C3
Brignogan 22 A2
Brignoles 31 D4
Brihuega 40 B2
Briksdal 100 A3
Brilon 17 F3
Brimnes 104 B2
Brinches 42 B1
Brindisi 65 F3
Brinon 26 A2
Brioni 70 A4
Brionne 19 D3
Brioude 29 F1
Brioux 24 C4
Briouze 18 C4
Brisighella 61 D3
Brissac-Quincé . . . 24 C2
Brissago 58 A3
Bristol 9 D2
Bristol Chan. 8 C2
Brive-la-Gaillarde . 29 D2
Briviesca 36 A2
Brixen 59 D2
Brixham 8 C4
Brixlegg 59 D1
Brjánslækur 96 A1
Brka 72 B3
Brna 75 E2
Brnaze 75 D1
Brno 57 F1
Bro (Gotlands
  Län) 109 F4
Bro (Stockholms
  Län) 106 B3
Broad B 2 B2
Broadford (GB) . . . 2 B3
Broadford (IRL) . . 12 B4
Broad Haven 12 B1
Broad Law 5 D3
Broadstairs 11 D3
Broadway 9 E1
Broager 108 A4
Broby 109 D3
Brocken 52 B2
Brod (BH) 71 D1
Brod (Makedonija) 77 D3
Brodarevo 76 B1
Brodica 73 E3
Brodick 4 B2
Brod na Kupi 70 B3
Brodnica 112 B1
Brody (PL) 53 F1
Brody (UKR) 113 D2
Broglie 19 D3
Brohl-Lützing 51 E4
Brolo 69 D2
Bromarv 107 D3
Brombachsee 55 E2
Brome 48 B2
Bromölla 109 D3
Bromsgrove 9 E1
Bromyard 9 D1
Bronchales 41 D2
Brønderslev 108 B2
Broni 60 A2
Brønnøysund 97 D3
Brøns 108 A3
Bronte 69 D3
Bronzani Majdan . 71 D3
Broom, L 2 C2
Broons 22 C3
Brora 3 D3
Brösarp 109 D3
Brossac 28 B1
Brøstadbotn 94 B3
Brotas 38 B4
Broto 37 E2
Brotton 5 F4
Brøttum 105 D2
Brou (Ain) 26 C4
Brou
  (Eure-et-Loir) . . 25 E1
Brouage 24 B4

Brough 5 E4
Brough Head 3 D1
Broughshane 13 E1
Broughton-
  in-Furness 6 B1
Brouis, Col de . . . 31 E3
Brovst 108 B2
Brownhills 9 E1
Brozas 39 D3
Bruay-en-Artois . . 19 F1
Bruay-sur-l'Escaut . 20 A1
Bruchsal 54 C2
Brück 53 D1
Bruck (D) 56 B1
Bruck
  (Niederösterreich) 57 F2
Bruck (Salzburg) . . 59 E1
Bruck an der Mur . 57 E4
Brückl 70 B1
Bruckmühl 56 B3
Brüel 48 C2
Brués 34 B2
Bruges 50 A3
Brugg 27 F2
Brügge 17 E4
Brugge 50 A3
Brühl 17 E4
Brújula, Pto de la . 36 A2
Bruksvallarna . . . 101 D2
Brûlon 23 E3
Brumath 21 E4
Brummen 17 D3
Brumunddal 105 D2
Bruneck 59 D2
Brunete 40 A2
Brunico 59 D2
Brünigpass 27 F3
Bruniquel 29 D3
Brunkeberg 104 B3
Brunnen 58 A2
Brunsbüttel 47 F2
Brunssum 17 D4
Bruntál 112 A3
Bruravik 104 B2
Brus 77 D1
Brusand 104 A4
Brušane 70 C4
Brusasco 31 F1
Brusnik 73 F3
Brussel 50 B3
Brusson 27 F4
Brüssow 49 E2
Bruton 9 D3
Bruvno 70 C4
Bruxelles 50 B3
Bruyères 27 D1
Brvenik 76 C1
Bryne 104 A4
Brynmawr 9 D2
Brzan 73 D3
Brza Palanka 73 F3
Brzeće 77 D1
Brzeg 112 A2
Buarcos 38 B2
Buavåg 104 A3
Bubry 22 C3
Bučač 113 D3
Buçaco 38 B2
Buccheri 69 D4
Bucchianico 64 A2
Bucelas 38 A4
Buchan Ness 3 E3
Büchen 48 B3
Buchen 55 D1
Buchenwald 52 C3
Buchholz 48 A3
Buchloe 55 E3
Buchs 58 B2
Buchy 19 E3
Bucine 61 D4
Bučje 73 F4
Bückeburg 52 A1
Buckfastleigh 8 C4
Buckhaven 5 D2
Buckie 3 D3
Buckingham 9 F2
Buckinghamshire . . 9 F2
Buckovička
  Banja 73 D3
Buckow 49 E4
Bückwitz 49 D3
Bučovice 57 F1
Bucovina 113 D3

Bucureşti 115 D1
Bud 100 B2
Budapest 112 B4
Búðardalur 96 A2
Buddon Ness 5 D1
Buddusò 66 B2
Bude 8 B3
Büdelsdorf 48 A2
Budimlić Japra . . . 71 D3
Büdingen 52 A4
Budinščina 70 C2
Budleigh
  Salterton 8 C3
Budrio 61 D2
Budva 76 B3
Budyně nad
  Ohře 53 F3
Buenache
  de Alarcón 40 C3
Buen Amor 39 E1
Buenavista
  de Valdavia . . . 35 E3
Buendia 40 C2
Buendia, Emb de . 40 C2
Buet, Mt. 27 E4
Bueu 34 A2
Bug 112 C1
Bugeat 29 D1
Bugojno 71 E4
Bugøynes 95 F2
Bugue, le 28 C2
Bühl 54 C3
Builth Wells 9 D1
Buin, Piz 58 B2
Buis-les-Baronnies 30 C3
Buitrago
  del Lozoya 40 B1
Bujalance 43 F2
Bujanovac 77 E2
Bujaraloz 37 E4

Brugge

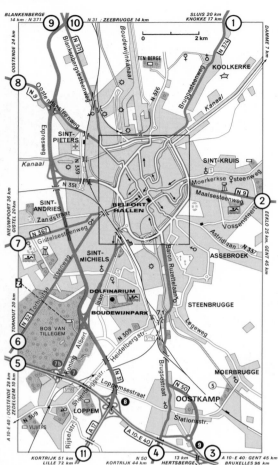

Budapest

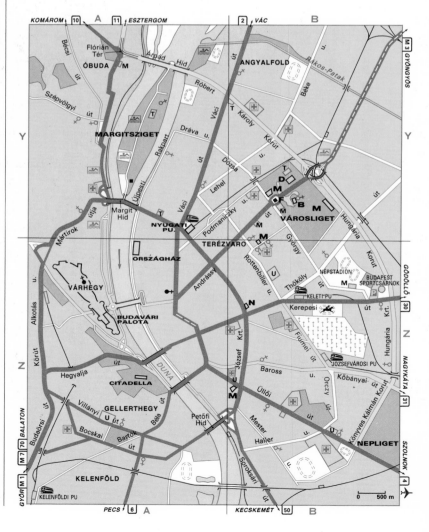

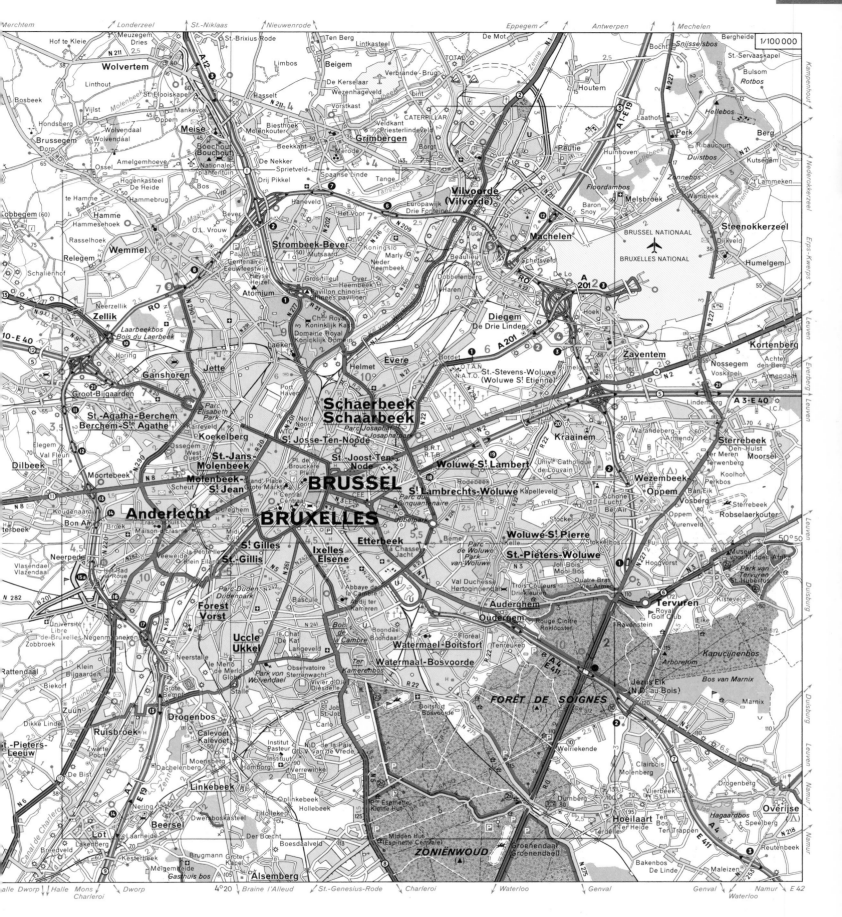

132 **Bud - Cap**

Budinščina 70 C2
Budleigh
  Salterton 8 C3
Budrio 61 D2
Budva 76 B3
Budyně nad
  Ohře 53 F3
Buenache
  de Alarcón 40 C3
Buen Amor 39 E1
Buenavista
  de Valdavia 35 E3
Buendia 40 C2
Buendia, Emb de . . 40 C2
Buet, Mt. 27 E4
Bueu 34 A2
Bug 112 C1
Bugeat 29 D1
Bugojno 71 E4
Bugøynes 95 F2
Bugue, le 28 C2
Bühl 54 C3
Builth Wells 9 D1
Buin, Piz 58 B2
Buis-les-Baronnies . 30 C3
Buitrago
  del Lozoya 40 B1
Bujalance 43 F2

Bujanovac 77 E2
Bujaraloz 37 E4
Buje 70 A3
Bujeo, Pto del 43 D4
Bukinje 71 F3
Bukova Gora 75 E1
Bukovi 72 C4
Bukovo 77 D4
Bülach 58 A1
Buldan 115 F4
Bulgnéville 27 D1
Bullas 44 C2
Bulle 27 E3
Büllingen 51 D4
Bully 19 F1
Bultei 66 B2
Buna 75 E1
Bunclody 15 D3
Buncrana 13 D1
Bünde 17 F2
Bunde 47 E3
Bun Dobhráin 12 C2
Bundoran 12 C2
Bunë 76 B3
Bungay 11 D1
Bunič 70 C4
Bunmahon 14 C4

Buñol 41 E4
Bunratty Castle . . . 12 B4
Buntingford 9 F2
Buñuel 36 C3
Buonabitacolo 67 D1
Buonalbergo 64 B3
Buonconvento 61 D4
Buonfornello 68 C3
Burbach 51 F3
Burbáguena 41 D1
Búrdalo, R. 39 E4
Bure 7 F3
Bureå 98 B4
Burela 34 C1
Büren 17 F3
Buren 47 D3
Burfjord 95 D2
Burford 9 E2
Burg (Sachsen-
  Anhalt) 48 C4
Burg (Schleswig-
  Holstein) 48 B1
Burgas 115 E2
Burgau 55 E3
Burgbernheim 55 E1
Burgdorf (CH) 27 E2
Burgdorf (D) 48 B4
Bürgel 52 C3

Burgenland 57 F4
Burgess Hill 10 C3
Burggrub 52 C4
Burghasungen 52 A2
Burghausen 56 B3
Burgjoß 52 B4
Burgkunstadt 52 C4
Burglengenfeld 55 F1
Burgohondo 39 F2
Burgos 35 F3
Burgsinn 52 B4
Burgstädt 53 E3
Burg Stargard 49 D2
Burgsvik 109 F4
Burgsviken 109 F4
Burguete 36 C1
Burgui 37 D2
Burguillo,
  Emb de 39 F2
Burguillos
  del Cerro 43 D1
Burhaniye 115 E4
Burhave 47 F3
Burie 28 B1
Burjassot 41 E4
Burk 53 F2
Burkau 53 F2
Burnham 9 D3

Burnham-
  on-Crouch 11 D2
Burnley 6 C2
Burntisland 5 D2
Buronzo 31 F1
Burrel 76 C3
Burriana 41 E3
Burrow Head 4 C3
Burry Port 8 C2
Bursa 115 F3
Burscheid 17 E4
Bürstadt 54 C1
Burton-upon-Trent . 6 C3
Burträsk 98 B4
Burwick 3 E1
Bury 6 C2
Buryn' 113 F1
Bury St Edmunds . . 11 D1
Busalla 60 A3
Busambra, Rca 68 B3
Busca 31 E2
Buševa pl 77 D3
Buševec 70 C2
Bushat 76 C3
Bushmills 13 E1
Buskerud 104 C2
Buško Blato 75 E1
Busko-Zdrój 112 B2

Busovača 71 F4
Bussang 27 E1
Busseto 60 B2
Bussière-Badil 28 C1
Bussolengo 60 C1
Bussum 16 C2
Busto Arsizio 60 A1
Busto de Bureba . . 36 A2
Büsum 47 F2
Butera 68 C4
Buthrotum 114 C4
Bute 4 B2
Butera 68 C4
Buttermere 5 D4
Buttevant 14 B3
Butt of Lewis 2 B2
Buttstädt 52 C2
Butxon 6 C3
Buxy 26 C3
Buzançais 25 E3
Buzancy 20 C3
Buzău 113 E4
Buzău, R. 113 E4
Buzet 70 A3
Bužim 70 C3
Bychov 111 E4

Bydgoszcz 112 A1
Bygdeå 102 B1
Bygdin 100 B3
Bygdin L 100 B3
Bygdsiljum 102 B1
Bygland 104 B4
Byglandsfjord 104 B4
Byglandsfjord L . . . 104 B4
Bykle 104 B3
Bykleheiene 104 B3
Bylderup-Bov 108 A4
Byrkjelo 100 A3
Byske 98 B4
Byskeälven 98 B4
Bytom 112 B2
Bytów 110 A4
Byxelkrok 109 E2

C

Cabañaquinta 35 D2
Cabañas 44 B2
Cabanes 41 F3
Cabannes, les 32 A2
Čabar 70 B3
Cabeceiras 34 B4
Cabeço de Vide . . . 38 C3
Cabella Ligure 60 A2
Cabeza del Buey . . 39 E4
Cabezas Rubias . . . 42 C2
Cabezo Gordo 42 C2
Cabezón 35 E4
Cabezón de la Sal . . 35 F2
Cabezuela del
  Valle 39 E2
Cabo de Gata 44 C4
Cabourg 18 C3
Cabra 43 F2
Cabra del
  Santo Cristo 44 A2
Cabras 66 A3
Cabre, Col de 30 C2
Cabreira, Sa da . . . 34 B4
Cabreiros 34 B1
Cabrejas, Pto de . . 40 C3
Cabrejas, Sa de . . . 36 A3
Cabréra 36 C4
Cabrera, I de 45 F3
Cabrera, Sa de la . . 34 C3
Cabrerets 29 D3
Cabril, R 41 D3
Cabril, Bgem do . . 38 B2
Cabrillas 39 E1
Cabrito, Pto del . . . 43 D4
Cabuérniga 35 F2
Čabulja 75 E1
Cacabelos 34 C2
Čačak 73 D4
Caccamo 68 B3
Cacela 42 B3
Cáceres 39 D3
Cachafeiro 34 A2
Cachopo 42 B2
Čačinci 71 E2
Cadabo 34 C2
Cadalso de
  los Vidrios 40 A2
Cadaqués 32 C3
Cadarache 30 C3
Cadaval 38 A3
Čađavica 71 E4
Čadca 112 B3
Cadelbosco di
  Sopra 60 C2
Cadenabbia 58 B4
Cadena, Pto de la . . 45 D2

Cadenberge 47 F2
Cadenet 30 C3
Cader Idris 6 A3
Cádiar 44 A3
Cadillac 28 B2
Cadipietra 59 D2
Cadi, Serra del . . . 32 A3
Cádiz 43 D4
Cádiz, B de 43 D4
Cádiz, G de 42 C3
Cadouin 28 C2
Čadyr-Lunga 113 E4
Caen 18 C3
Caerdydd 9 D2
Caerfyrddin 8 C2
Caergybi 6 A2
Caernarfon 6 A3
Caernarfon B 6 A3
Caerphilly 9 D2
Caersws 9 D1
Cafasan 77 D4
Cagli 61 E4
Cagliari 66 B4
Cagliari, G di 66 B4
Čaglin 71 E2
Cagnano Varano . . 64 C2
Cagnes 31 E3
Caha Mts 14 A4
Caher 14 C3
Cahersiveen 14 A4
Cahors 29 D3
Cahore Pt 15 E3
Caia, Bgem do . . . 38 C4
Caianello 64 A3
Caión 34 A1
Cairn Gorm 3 D4
Cairngorm Mts . . . 3 D4
Cairnryan 4 B3
Cairo Montenotte . . 31 F2
Caiseal 14 C3
Caisléan an
  Bharraigh 12 B3
Caistor 7 D2
Caivano 64 B4
Cajarc 29 D3
Čajetina 72 C4
Čajniče 76 B1
Čakor 76 C2
Cakovice 53 F3
Čakovec 70 C1
Çal 115 F4
Calabor 34 C3
Calabria 67 E2
Calaceite 41 F1
Calacuccia 33 F3
Cala d'Or 45 F3
Cala, Emb de la . . . 43 D2
Calaf 37 F3
Calafat 114 C2

Calafell 37 F4
Calafort Ros Láir . . 15 D4
Cala Gonone 66 C2
Calahonda 44 A4
Calahorra 36 C2
Calais 19 E1
Calamocha 41 D1
Calañas 42 C2
Calanche, les 33 E3
Calanda 41 E1
Calanda, Emb de . . 41 E1
Calangianus 66 B1
Cala'n Porter 45 F2
Calar Alto 44 B3
Cala Ratjada 45 F2
Calasetta 66 A4
Calasparra 44 C2
Calatafimi 68 B3
Calatañazor 36 B3
Calatayud 36 C4
Calatorao 36 C4
Calau 53 E1
Calazzo 64 B3
Calbe 52 C1
Calcena 36 C3
Caldaro 59 D3
Caldarola 61 F4
Caldas da Rainha . . 38 A3
Caldas das Taipas . 34 A4
Caldas de Reis 34 A2
Caldas de Vizela . . 34 A4
Caldeirão, Sa do . . 42 B2
Caldelas 34 A3
Caldera de Taburiente,
  Pque Nac de la . . 42 A4
Calderina 40 A4
Caldes de Boí 37 F2
Caldes de
  Malavella 32 B3
Caldes de
  Montbui 32 A4
Caldirola 60 A2
Caledonian Canal . . 2 C4
Calella
  (Palamós) 32 C3
Calella
  (Pinedo de Mar) . 32 B4
Calenzana 33 F3
Calera de León . . . 43 D1
Calera y Chozas . . 39 F3
Caleruega 36 A3
Caletta, la 66 C2
Cálig 41 F2
Călimăneşti 115 D1
Călimani, M. 113 D4
Calitri 64 C3
Calizzano 31 F3
Callac 22 B3

Callan 15 D3
Callander 4 C1
Calla, Pso della . . . 61 D3
Callington 8 C4
Callosa de
  Ensarriá 45 E1
Callosa de
  Segura 45 D2
Calmazzo 61 E3
Calmbach 54 C2
Calne 9 E2
Calolziocorte 58 B4
Calonge 32 B3
Calpe 45 E1
Caltabellotta 68 B3
Caltagirone 69 D4
Caltanissetta 68 C3
Caltavuturo 68 C3
Caluso 31 E1
Calvados 18 C3
Calvi 33 E3
Calvitero 39 E2
Calvörde 48 C4
Calw 54 C2
Calzada de
  Calatrava 44 A1
Calzada de
  Valdunciel 39 E1
Cam 9 F1
Camacho, Pto 44 A3
Camaiore 60 C3
Camaldoli 61 D3
Camaleño 35 E2
Camarasa 37 F3
Camarasa,
  Emb de 37 F3
Camarat, Cap 31 D4
Camarena 40 A2
Camarès 32 B1
Camaret 22 A3
Camarillas 41 E2
Camarillas,
  Emb de 44 C1
Camariñas 34 A1
Camarzana 35 D3
Camas 43 D2
Cambados 34 A2
Cambas 38 C2
Camberley 9 F2
Cambil 44 A2
Cambo-les-Bains . . 28 A4
Camborne 8 B4
Cambrai 20 A2
Cambre 34 B1
Cambremer 19 D3
Cambrian Mts 8 C1
Cambridge 10 C1
Cambridgeshire . . . 10 C1
Cambrils de Mar . . 37 F4

Camburg 52 C3
Camelford 8 B3
Camerino 61 E4
Camigliatello
  Silano 67 E2
Caminha 34 A3
Caminomorisco . . . 39 D2
Caminreal 41 D2
Camogli 60 A3
Campagna 64 C4
Campagne-lès-
  Hesdin 19 E2
Campan 37 E1
Campana 67 F2
Campanario 39 E4
Campania 64 B4
Campaspero 35 F4
Campbeltown 4 B3
Campello 45 E1
Campi Bisenzio . . . 60 C3
Campiglia
  Marittima 62 C1
Campilhas,
  Bgem de 42 A1
Campillo de
  Altobuey 41 D3
Campillo de
  Aragón 36 C4
Campillo de
  Arenas 44 A2
Campillo de
  Llerena 43 D1
Campillos 43 E3
Campione 58 A4
Campitello M 64 B3
Campli 63 F1
Campo 37 E2
Campobasso 64 B3
Campobello di
  Licata 68 C4
Campobello di
  Mazara 68 A3
Campo Carlo
  Magno 58 C3
Campo de
  Beisteros 38 B1
Campo de Caso . . . 35 E2
Campo de
  Criptana 40 B4
Campo di Fiori . . . 58 A4
Campo di Giove . . 64 A2
Campodonico 61 E4
Campoformido 59 F3
Campogalliano . . . 60 C2
Campo
  Imperatore 63 F1
Campo Ligure 60 A3
Campo Maior 38 C4

Campomanes 35 D2
Campomarino 64 B2
Campora
  San Giovanni . . . 67 E3
Camporredondo,
  Emb de 35 E2
Camporrobles 41 D3
Campos 45 F3
Camposampiero . . . 59 D4
Campos, Canal de . . 35 E4
Campotosto, L di . . 63 F1
Campo Tures 59 D2
Camprodon 32 B3
Camucia 61 D4
Camuñas 40 B4
Cañada de
  Benatanduz 41 E2
Cañadas, Pto 43 D1
Çanakkale 115 E3
Çanakkale Boğazı . . 115 E3
Canal du Nord 19 F2
Canal du Rhône au
  Rhin 27 E2
Canales de la
  Sierra 36 A3
Canals 41 E4
Canal San Bovo . . 59 D3
Cañamero 39 E3
Canarias, Is 42 B4
Canas de
  Senhorim 38 C1
Cañaveral 39 D3
Cañaveral de León . 43 D1
Cañaveras 40 C2
Canazei 59 D3
Cancale 18 B4
Cancárix 45 D1
Canche 19 E1
Cancon 28 C2
Candanchu 37 D2
Candas 35 D1
Candasnos 37 E4
Candé 23 E4
Candeeiros,
  Sa dos 38 A3
Candela 64 C3
Candelaria, Sa 39 E2
Candelario 39 E2
Candelaro 64 C2
Candeleda 39 E2
Candes 25 D2
Canelles, Emb de . . 37 F3
Canelli 31 F2
Canero 35 D1
Cañete 41 D2
Cañete de las
  Torres 43 F2
Cañete la Real 43 E3

Canet-Plage 32 B2
Canfranc-
  Estación 37 D2
Cangas 34 A3
Cangas de Narcea . 34 C2
Cangas de Onís . . . 35 E1
Canha 38 B4
Canicattì 68 C4
Canicattini Bagni . . 69 D4
Canigou, Pic du . . . 32 B2
Cañigral 41 D3
Caniles 44 B3
Canin, M 59 F3
Canino 63 D2
Canis 18 B3
Cañizál 39 E1
Canjáyar 44 B3
Canna 2 B4
Cannero Riviera . . . 58 A4
Cannes 31 E4
Canneto 60 C4
Cannich 2 C3
Cannobio 58 A4
Cannock 9 E1
Canonbie 5 D3
Canosa di Puglia . . 64 C3
Canourgue, la 29 F3
Cansano 64 A2
Cansiglio 59 E3
Cantabria 35 F2
Cantal (Dépt) 29 E2
Cantal, Mts du . . . 29 E2
Cantalapiedra 39 F1
Cantalejo 40 A1
Cantalpino 39 E1
Cantanhede 38 B2
Cantavieja 41 E2
Čantavir 72 B1
Canterbury 11 D3
Cantillana 43 D2
Cantoira 31 E1
Cantoral 35 E2
Cantoria 44 C3
Cantù 60 A1
Canvey I 11 D2
Cany-Barville 19 D2
Caorle 59 E4
Caorso 60 B2
Capaccio 64 C4
Capaci 68 B3
Capalbio 63 D2
Capannelle,
  Pso delle 63 F1
Caparde 72 B4
Caparroso 36 C2
Capbreton 28 A4
Cap Corse 33 F2
Cap-d'Agde, le . . . 30 A4
Cap d'Antibes 31 E4

Terminal de Calais

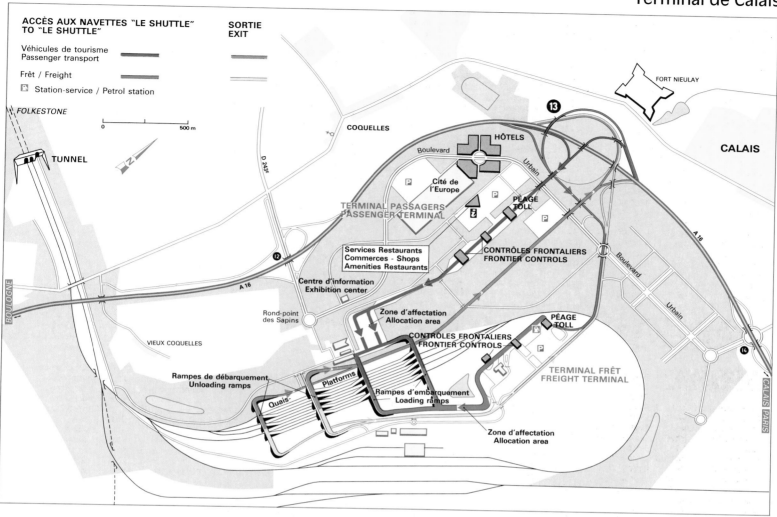

ACCÈS AUX NAVETTES "LE SHUTTLE"
TO "LE SHUTTLE"

SORTIE
EXIT

Véhicules de tourisme
Passenger transport

Frêt / Freight

Station-service / Petrol station

FOLKESTONE

0   500 m

TUNNEL

BOULOGNE

COQUELLES

D 243E

A 16

VIEUX COQUELLES

Rond-point
des Sapins

Centre d'information
Exhibition center

Services Restaurants
Commerces - Shops
Amenities Restaurants

TERMINAL PASSAGERS
PASSENGER TERMINAL

Cité de
l'Europe

Boulevard

Urbain

HÔTELS

PÉAGE
TOLL

CONTRÔLES FRONTALIERS
FRONTIER CONTROLS

Zone d'affectation
Allocation area

Rampes de débarquement
Unloading ramps

Platforms

Quais

Rampes d'embarquement
Loading ramps

CONTRÔLES FRONTALIERS
FRONTIER CONTROLS

PÉAGE
TOLL

Zone d'affectation
Allocation area

TERMINAL FRÊT
FREIGHT TERMINAL

FORT NIEULAY

CALAIS

A 16

Boulevard

Urbain

CALAIS PARIS

Capdenac-Gare **29** E2	Carbonara, Pzo **68** C3	Carignan............ **20** C2	Carnsore Pt........ **15** D4	Carrickmacross **13** D3	Casale Monferrato . **31** F1	Cas-gwent.......... **9** D2
Capel Curig **6** A3	Carbon-Blanc **28** B2	Carignano.......... **31** E2	Carnwath **5** D2	Carrick-on-	Casale sul Sile **59** E4	Cashel **14** C3
Capelle, la **20** B2	Carboneras........ **44** C3	Carina **77** D4	Caroch **41** D4	Shannon **12** C3	Casalmaggiore **60** B2	Casicas del Río
Capendu **32** B2	Carboneras de	Cariñena **36** C4	Carolles........... **18** B4	Carrick-on-Suir ... **14** C3	Casalpusterlengo .. **60** B2	Segura **44** B2
Capestang **30** A4	Guadazaón... **41** D3	Carini **68** B3	Carovigno **65** E3	Carrigart........... **12** C1	Casamassima **65** D3	Casillas **39** D2
Capestrano **64** A2	Carbonero	Cariño **34** B1	Carpaneto	Carrio............. **34** B1	Casamicciola	Casina **60** C2
Capileira **44** A3	el Mayor....... **40** A1	Carinola **64** A3	Piacentino **60** B2	Carrión de	Terme........ **64** A4	Casinos **41** E3
Capistrello **63** F2	Carbonia........... **66** B4	Carisio **31** F1	Carpaţii	Calatrava **40** A4	Casa Nuevas **44** C2	Casnewydd **9** D2
Čapljina **75** F2	Carbonin **59** E2	Carlet **41** E4	Meridionali ... **114** C1	Carrión de	Casarabonela **43** E3	Casoio **34** C3
Capmany **32** B3	Carbonne.......... **37** F1	Carling **21** D3	Carpenedolo **60** B1	los Condes ... **35** E3	Casarano **65** F4	Casola in Lunigiana **60** B3
Cappelle sul Tavo . **64** A1	Carcaboso **39** D2	Carlingford........ **13** E3	Carpentras **30** C3	Carrión, R.......... **35** E3	Casar de Cáceres . **39** D3	Casoli **64** A2
Cappoquin **14** C4	Carcabuey **43** F3	Carlingford L....... **13** E3	Carpi **60** C2	Carrizo de la	Casares **43** E4	Casoria **64** B4
Capracotta **64** A2	Carcaixent **41** E4	Carlisle **5** D3	Carpignano Sesia . **58** A4	Ribera........ **35** D2	Casares de las	Caspe **37** E4
Capraia, I di **62** B1	Carcans **28** A2	Carlit, Pic **32** A2	Carpineti.......... **60** C3	Carro **30** C4	Hurdes........ **39** D2	Cassà de la Selva . **32** B3
Caprera, I **66** B1	Carcans-Plage **28** A2	Carloforte......... **66** A4	Carpineto	Carrouges **18** C4	Casariche **43** E3	Cassagnes-
Capri **64** B4	Carcare **31** F2	Carlow **13** D4	Romano........ **63** F3	Carrù **31** F2	Casarsa **59** E3	Begonhès **29** E3
Capriati a	Carcassonne....... **32** B1	Carlow (Co) **13** D4	Carpinone **64** A3	Carry-le-Rouet ... **30** C4	Casas de	Cassano allo Ionio . **67** E2
Volturno **64** A3	Carcastillo **36** C2	Carloway **2** B2	Carquefou......... **24** B2	Carsoli **63** F2	Don Pedro **39** E4	Cassano delle
Capri,I di **64** B4	Carcès **31** D4	Carluke **4** C2	Carqueiranne...... **31** D4	Cartagena **45** D3	Casas de Fernando	Murge.......... **65** D3
Captieux **28** B3	Carche **45** D1	Carmagnola **31** E2	Carracedelo **34** C2	Cártama **43** F4	Alonso **40** C4	Cassel............ **19** F1
Capua **64** B3	Čardak **71** F4	Carmarthen **8** C2	Carradale **4** B2	Cartaxo **38** A3	Casas de Juan	Cassino **64** A3
Capurso **65** D3	Çardak **115** F4	Carmarthen B **8** B2	Carraig na Siúire .. **14** C3	Cartaya **42** C2	Núñez **41** D4	Cassis **30** C4
Capvern **37** E1	Cardedeu **32** B4	Carmaux **29** E3	Carral **34** B1	Carter Bar **5** D3	Casas del Puerto .. **45** D1	Castalla **45** D1
Caracal **115** D2	Cardeña **43** F1	Carmona **43** E2	Carrantuohill...... **14** A4	Carteret **18** B3	Casas de Luján **40** B3	Castanet-Tolosan . **29** D4
Caracuel **40** A4	Cardener, R........ **32** A4	Carna **12** A3	Carranza **36** A1	Carvajal **43** F4	Casas de Miravete . **39** E3	Castanheira de
Caragh, L **14** A4	Cardenete **41** D3	Carnac **22** C4	Carrara **60** B3	Carviçais **39** D1	Casas Ibáñez **41** D4	Pêra **38** B2
Caraman **29** D4	Cardiff **9** D2	Carnaio, Pso del .. **61** D3	Carrascal **41** E2	Carvin **19** F1	Casasimarro **40** C4	Castaños,
Caramanico Terme. **64** A2	Cardigan **8** B1	Carn Ban.......... **2** C4	Carrascosa del	Carvoeira **42** A3	Casatejada **39** E3	Pto de los....... **39** D3
Caramulo.......... **38** B1	Cardigan B **8** B1	Carndonagh **13** D1	Campo **40** C3	Carvoeiro, C **38** A4	Casavieja **39** F2	Castasegna **58** B3
Caramulo, Sa do .. **38** B1	Cardona **32** A3	Carnedd Llewelyn . **6** A3	Carrascoy **45** D2	Casabermeja **43** F3	Cascais **38** A4	Casteggio **60** A2
Caransebes........ **114** C1	Carei **112** C1	Carn Eige.......... **2** C3	Carrasqueta,	Casa Branca	Cascante **36** C3	Castejón **36** C3
Carantec **22** B3	Carentan **18** B3	Carneros,	Pto de los **45** E1	(Alentejo) **42** A1	Cascia............ **63** E1	Castejón de
Caravaca de la	Cares, R. **35** E2	Pto de los **39** F4	Carrazeda de	Casa Branca	Casciana Terme ... **60** C4	Monègros **37** E4
Cruz......... **44** C2	Carevdar **71** D2	Carnew............ **15** D3	Ansiães......... **34** B4	(Ribatejo)..... **38** B4	Cascina **60** C4	Castejón de Sos ... **37** E4
Caravai, Pso di.... **66** B3	Carev Dvor **77** D4	Carnforth **6** B1	Carrazedo de	Casacalenda **64** B2	Casei Gerola **60** A2	Castejón de
Caravius, M. is **66** B4	Carevo **115** E2	Carnia **59** F3	Montenegro **34** B4	Casalarreina **36** B2	Caselle in Pittari .. **67** D1	Valdejasa **37** D3
Carbajales de Alba . **35** D4	Cargèse............ **33** E3	Carnia (Reg) **59** E3	Carrbridge **3** D4	Casalbordino **64** B2	Caselle Torinese ... **31** E1	Castelbuono **68** C3
Carballiño......... **34** B2	Carhaix-Plouguer . **22** B3	Carnlough **13** E1	Carregado **38** A3	Casalbuttano **60** B1	Caserío	Casteldaccia **68** B3
Carballo **34** B1	Caria............. **38** C2	Carnon **30** B4	Carregal do Sal.... **38** B2	Casal di Principe .. **64** A4	del Puente **35** D3	Casteldelfino **31** E2
Carbayo **35** D2	Cariati **67** F2	Carnota **34** A1	Carreña de Cabrales **35** E1	Casalecchio	Caserta **64** B3	Castel del Monte
Carbonara, C...... **66** C4	Caričin Grad....... **77** D1	Carnoustie **5** D1	Carrickfergus **13** E2	di Reno **60** C2	Casetas **37** D3	(Abruzzo) **63** F2

Castel del Monte (Puglia) 65 D3
Castel del Rio 61 D3
Castel di Sangro . . . 64 C4
Castelfidardo 61 F4
Castelfiorentino . . . 60 C4
Castelfranco Emilia 60 C2
Castelfranco in Miscano 64 B3
Castelfranco Veneto 59 D4
Castel Gandolfo . . . 63 E3
Casteljaloux 28 B3
Castellabate 67 D1
Castellamare di Stabbia 64 B4
Castellammare d. Golfo 48 B3
Castellammare, G di 68 B3
Castellamonte 31 E1
Castellana Grotte . . 65 E3
Castellane 31 D3
Castellaneta 65 E4
Castellar de la Muela 41 D2
Castellar del Vallès 32 A4
Castellar de Santiago 44 B1
Castellar de Santisteban 44 B2
Castelldans 37 F4
Castelldefels 32 A4
Castell de Ferro . . . 44 A4
Castelleone 60 B1
Castellfollit de la Roca 32 B3
Castellina in Chianti. 61 D4
Castell-nedd 8 C2
Castelló de la Plana 41 F3
Castello del Lago . . 64 B3
Castelló d'Empúries 32 B3
Castellolí 32 A4
Castellón de la Plana 41 F3
Castellón de Rugat 45 E1
Castellote 41 E2
Castello Tesino . . . 59 D3
Castelltercol 32 A4
Castelluccia 63 F1
Castel Madama . . . 63 F2
Castelmassa 60 C2
Castelmauro 64 B2
Castelmoron 28 C3
Castelnaudary 32 A1
Castelnau-de-Médoc 28 B2
Castelnau-de-Montmiral 29 D3
Castelnau-Magnoac 37 E1
Castelnau-Montratier 29 D3
Castelnau-Rivière-Basse 28 B4
Castelnovo ne' Monti 60 B3
Castelnuovo Berardenga 61 D4
Castelnuovo Bocca d'Adda 60 B2
Castelnuovo della Daunia 64 B3
Castelnuovo di Garfagnana . . . 60 C3
Castelnuovo di Porto 63 E2
Castelnuovo Scrivia 60 A2
Castelo Branco . . . 38 C2
Castelo de Bode, Bgem do 38 B3
Castelo de Paiva . . 34 A4
Castelo de Vide . . . 38 C3
Castelraimondo . . . 61 E4
Castelrotto 59 D3
Castel San Giovanni 60 A2

Castel San Lorenzo 64 C4
Castel San Pietro Terme 61 D3
Castelsardo 66 B1
Castelsarrasin 29 D3
Castelserás 41 E1
Casteltermini 68 B3
Castelvecchio Subequo 63 F2
Castelvetrano 68 A3
Castel Volturno . . . 64 A4
Castets 28 A3
Castiadas 66 C4
Castiglioncello 60 C4
Castiglione d'Adda 60 B2
Castiglione dei Pepoli 60 C3
Castiglione del Lago 61 D4
Castiglione della Pescaia 62 C3
Castiglione delle Stiviere 60 C1
Castiglione in Teverina 63 E1
Castiglione Messer Marino 64 B2
Castiglione Olona . . 60 A1
Castiglion Fiorentino 61 D4
Castilblanco 39 F4
Castilblanco de los Arroyos 43 D2
Castilla, Canal de . . 35 E4
Castilla-La Mancha . 40 A4
Castilla-León 35 F4
Castilla, Mar de . . . 40 C2
Castilleja del Campo 43 D2
Castilléjar 44 B2
Castillejo 39 E1
Castillejo de Martin Viejo 39 D1
Castillo de Loarre . . 37 D2
Castillo de Locubín . 43 F2
Castillon, Bge de . . 31 D3
Castillon-en-Couserans 37 F2
Castillon-la-Bataille 28 B2
Castillonnès 28 C2
Castillo, Pto del . . . 44 A3
Castillo y Elejabeitia 36 B1
Castilruiz 36 C3
Castions di Strada . 59 F3
Castlebar 12 B3
Castlebay 2 A4
Castlebellingham . . 13 D3
Castleblayney 13 D3
Castlecomer 13 D4
Castledawson 13 D2
Castlederg 13 D2
Castledermot 13 D4
Castle Douglas 4 C3
Castleford 7 D2
Castleisland 14 B3
Castlemaine 14 A3
Castlepollard 13 D3
Castlerea 12 C3
Castlerock 13 D1
Castleton 6 C2
Castletownbere . . . 14 A4
Castletown (I of Man) 6 A1
Castletown (Scotland) 3 D2
Castlewellan 13 E2
Castocalbón 35 D3
Castrejón 39 F1
Castrejón, Emb de . 40 A3
Castres 32 B1
Castries 30 B4
Castril 44 B2
Castrillo de la Reina 36 A3
Castrillo de Villavega 35 F3
Castro 34 B2
Castro Caldelas . . . 34 B3
Castrocaro Terme . . 61 D3
Castrocontrigo 35 D3

Castro Daire 38 C1
Castro del Rio 43 F2
Castrogeriz 35 F3
Castro Laboreiro . . . 34 B3
Castro Marim 42 B2
Castromonte 35 E4
Castronuevo 35 D4
Castronuño 35 E4
Castropol 34 C1
Castrop-Rauxel . . . 17 E3
Castroreale 69 D2
Castroreale Terme 69 D2
Castrotierra 35 E3
Castro Urdiales . . . 36 A1
Castroverde 34 C2
Castro Verde 42 B2
Castroverde de Campos 35 E3
Castrovillari 67 E2
Castuera 39 E4
Cataluña 32 A3
Catalunya 37 F3
Catania 69 D3
Catania, G di 69 D3
Catanzaro 67 F3
Catanzaro Lido 67 F3
Catarroja 41 E4
Cateau, le 20 A2
Catelet, le 20 A2
Catenanuova 69 D3
Catež 70 C2
Cathair na Mart . . . 12 B3
Čatići 71 F4
Catignano 64 A2
Catoira 34 A2
Catoute 35 D2
Catral 45 D2
Catria, Mte 61 E4
Cattenom 21 D3
Cattolica 61 E3
Catus 29 D2
Caudebec 19 D3
Caudete 45 D1
Caudiel 41 E3
Caudry 20 A2
Caulnes 23 D3
Caulonia 67 F4
Caumont-l'Eventé . . 18 C3
Caunes 32 B1
Caussade 29 D3
Čausy 111 E4
Cauterets 37 E2
Cava de' Tirreni . . . 64 B4
Cávado, R. 34 A4
Cavaglià 31 F1
Cavaillon 30 C3
Cavalaire 31 D4
Cavalerie, la 29 F3
Cavalese 59 D3
Cavalière 31 D4
Cavan 13 D3
Cavan (Co) 13 D3
Cavarzere 61 D1
Cavazzo 59 E3
Cavero, Pto de 36 C4
Cavezzo 60 C2
Cavo 62 C1
Cavo, Mte 63 E3
Cavour 31 E2
Cavtat 76 A3
Caya 38 C4
Cayeux 19 E2
Caylar, le 29 F3
Caylus 29 D3
Cayolle, Col de la . . 31 E3
Cayres 29 F2
Cazalla de la Sierra . 43 D2
Cazals 29 D2
Cazaubon 28 B3
Cazaux 28 A2
Cazères 37 F1
Cazin 70 C3
Čazma 71 D2
Cazorla 44 B2
Cazorla, Sa de 44 B2
Cea 34 B2
Ceanannus Mor . . . 13 D3
Cea, R. 35 E3
Ceatharlach 13 D4
Cebolla 39 F3
Cebollera 36 B3
Cebreros 40 A2

Ceccano 63 F3
Cece 112 B4
Cechy 53 F4
Cecina 60 C4
Cecina R 60 C4
Cecita, L di 67 F2
Ceclavín 39 D3
Cedeira 34 B1
Cedillo, Bgem de . . 38 C3
Cedrillas 41 E2
Cedrino 66 C2
Cedynia 49 E3
Cefalù 68 C3
Cega, R 40 A1
Cegléd 112 B4
Ceglie Messapico . . 65 E3
Cehegín 44 C2
Čehotina 76 A1
Ceira, R 38 C2
Čejč 57 F1
Celákovice 53 F3
Celano 63 F2
Celanova 34 B3
Celavevo 72 B2
Čelebić 75 D1
Čelebići 76 B1
Celemín, Emb de . . 43 D4
Čelić 72 B3
Celinac Donji 71 E3
Celje 70 B2
Cella 41 D2
Celle 48 B4
Celle Ligure 60 A3
Celles 24 C4
Čelopeci 77 D3
Celorico 34 B4
Celorico da Beira . . 38 C1
Čemerna pl. 73 D4
Čemernica 71 E4
Čemerno 76 A2
Cenajo, Emb del . . . 44 C1
Cencenighe 59 D3
Cenicero 36 B2
Čenta 72 C2
Centelles 32 B4
Cento 60 C2
Cento Croci, Pso . . . 60 B3
Central Region 4 C1
Centre, Canal du . . . 26 B3
Centuripe 69 D3
Cepagatti 64 A2
Čepin 71 F2
Ceppo 63 F1
Ceprano 63 F3
Cer 72 C3
Čeralije 71 E2
Cerbère 32 C3
Cercal (Alentejo) . . . 42 A1
Cercal (Estremadura) 38 A3
Cercedilla 40 A2
Cerchiara di Calabria 67 E2
Cerchov 56 B1
Cerdedo 34 A2
Cerdeira 39 D2
Cère 29 E2
Cerea 60 C1
Cereda, Pso di 59 D3
Čerepovec 111 F1
Ceres 31 E1
Ceresole Reale 31 E1
Céret 32 B3
Cerezo de Abajo . . . 36 A3
Cerezo de Riotirón . 36 A2
Cerignola 64 C3
Cérilly 26 A3
Cerisiers 26 A1
Cerisy-la-Salle 18 B3
Cerizay 24 C3
Čerkassy 113 F2
Cerknica 70 B2
Cerkniško jez 70 B2
Cerkno 70 A2
Cerkwica 37 E2
Černá 56 C1
Cerna 71 F2
Cernache de Bonjardim 38 B2
Čern'achovsk 110 B4
Cernadilla, Emb de . 34 C3
Cernavodă 115 E1

Cernay 27 E1
Černigov 113 E1
Cernik 71 E3
Cernobbio 58 B4
Černobyl' 113 E1
Cernomorskoje . . . 113 F4
Černovcy 113 D3
Cerreto, Pso del . . . 60 B3
Cerreto Sannita . . . 64 B3
Cerrigydrudion 6 B3
Cërrik 76 C4
Certaldo 60 C4
Certosa di Pavia . . . 60 A2
Cervales 39 E3
Cervaro 64 C3
Cervati, Mte 67 D1
Cervatos 35 F2
Cervatos de la Cueza 35 E3
Červen' 111 D4
Cervera 37 F3
Cervera de la Cañada 36 C4
Cervera del Río Alhama 36 C3
Cervera de Pisuerga 35 F2
Cerveteri 63 E2
Cervia 61 E3
Cervialto, Mte 64 C4
Cervignano del Friuli 59 F3
Cervinara 64 B3
Cervino 27 E4
Cervione 33 F3
Cervo 34 C1
Červonograd 112 C2
Červonograd 112 C2
Cesana Torinese . . . 31 D2
Cesarica 70 C4
Cesarò 69 D3
Cesena 61 D3
Cesenatico 61 E3
Cēsis 110 C2
Česka Kamenice . . 53 F2
Česká Lípa 53 F3
České Budějovice . . 57 D1
České Velenice . . . 57 D2
Český Krumlov 57 D2
Česma 71 D2
Çeşme 115 E4
Cespedosa 39 E2
Cessalto 59 E4
Cetina (E) 36 C4
Cetina R (Hrvatska) 75 D1
Cetinje 76 B3
Cetraro 67 E2
Ceutí 45 D2
Ceva 31 F2
Cevedale, Mte 58 C3
Cévennes, Parc Nat des 29 F3
Cevico de la Torre . . 35 F4
Čevo 76 B2
Ceyrat 29 F1
Ceyzériat 26 C4
Cèze 30 B3
Chabanais 25 D4
Chablis 26 B1
Chabreuil 30 C2
Chabris 25 E2
Chagny 26 C3
Chailland 23 E3
Chaillé 24 B3
Chaise-Dieu, la 29 F1
Chalabre 32 A2
Chalais 28 C1
Chalamont 26 C4
Chalampé 27 E1
Chalindrey 26 C1
Challans 24 A3
Challes 31 D1
Chalonnes 24 C2
Châlons-sur-Marne 20 B3
Chalon-sur-Saône . . 26 C3
Châlus 28 C1
Cham 56 B1
Chambéry 31 D1
Chambley 21 D3
Chambly 19 F3
Chambon, Bge du . . 31 D2
Chambon-Feugerolles, le 30 B1

Chambon-sur-Lac. . 29 E1
Chambon-sur-Lignon, le 30 B2
Chambon-sur-Voueize 25 F4
Chambord 25 E2
Chambre, la 31 D1
Chamonix 27 E4
Champagnac-de-Belair 28 C1
Champagne-Mouton 25 D4
Champagnole 27 D3
Champdeniers 24 C3
Champeaux 23 D3
Champéry 27 E4
Champex 27 E4
Champlitte 26 C2
Champlon, Bre.de . . 50 C4
Champoluc 27 F4
Champorcher 31 E1
Champs-sur-Tarentaine 29 E1
Champtoceaux 24 B2
Chamrousse 31 D1
Chamusca 38 B3
Chanac 29 F3
Chanas 30 B1
Chança, R. 42 C2
Chantada 34 B2
Chantelle 26 A4
Chantemerle 31 D2
Chantilly 19 F3
Chantonnay 24 B3
Chanza, Emb del. . . 42 B2
Chaource 26 B1
Chapel-en-le-Frith . . 6 C2
Chapelle-d'Angillon, la 25 F2
Chapelle-de-Guinchay, la 26 C4
Chapelle-en-Valgaudemar, la . . 31 D2
Chapelle-en-Vercors, la 30 C2
Chapinería 40 A2
Charbonnières 26 C4
Charco Redondo, Emb de 43 D4
Chard 9 D3
Charente 28 B1
Charente (Dépt) . . . 28 C1
Charente-Maritime 24 B4
Charenton-du-Cher 25 F3
Charleroi 50 B4
Charlestown 12 B3
Charleville 14 B3
Charleville-Mézières 20 C2
Charlieu 26 B4
Charlottenberg . . . 105 D3
Charly 20 A3
Charmes 21 D4
Charmes 21 D4
Charny (Meuse) . . . 20 C3
Charny (Yonne) . . . 26 A1
Charolles 26 B3
Chârost 25 E3
Charquemont 27 E2
Charroux 25 D4
Chartre, la 23 F4
Chartres 19 E4
Chas 38 B1
Chasseneuil 28 C1
Chasseral la Neuveville 27 E2
Chasseron, le 27 D3
Châtaigneraie, la . . 24 C3
Château-Arnoux . . . 31 D3
Châteaubourg 23 D3
Châteaubriant 23 D4
Château-Chinon . . . 26 B2
Château-de-Bonaguil 29 D2
Château de Ventadour 29 E1
Château d'Oex 27 E3
Château-du-Loir . . . 23 F4
Châteaudun 25 E1
Châteaugiron 23 D3
Château-Gontier . . . 23 E4
Château-Landon . . . 25 F1

Château-la-Vallière 25 D2
Château, le 24 B4
Châteaulin 22 B3
Châteaumeillant . . . 25 F3
Châteauneuf (Charente) 28 B1
Châteauneuf (Ille-et-Vilaine) . . . 18 B4
Châteauneuf-de-Randon 29 F2
Châteauneuf-du-Faou 22 B3
Châteauneuf-du-Pape 30 B3
Châteauneuf-en-Thymerais 19 E4
Châteauneuf-la-Forêt 29 D1
Châteauneuf-les-Bains 26 A4
Châteauneuf-sur-Cher 25 F3
Châteauneuf-sur-Loire 25 F1
Châteauneuf-sur-Sarthe 23 E4
Châteauponsac . . . 25 E4
Château-Porcien . . . 20 B3
Château-Queyras . . 31 E2
Château-Regnault . . 20 C2
Châteaurenard (Loiret) 25 F1
Châteaurenard (Vaucluse) 30 B3
Château-Renault . . . 25 D2
Châteauroux 25 E3
Château-Salins 21 D4
Château-Thierry . . . 20 A3
Châteauvillain 26 C1
Châtel 27 E3
Châtelaillon-Plage . . 24 B4
Châtelard, le 27 D4
Châtelaudren 22 C2
Châteldon 26 A4
Châtelet 50 C4
Châtelet, le (Cher) . . 25 F3
Châtelet, le (Seine-et-Marne) . 19 F4
Châtelguyon 26 A4
Châtellerault 25 D3
Châtel-Montagne . . 26 B4
Châtel-St-Denis . . . 27 E3
Châtel-sur-Moselle 21 D4
Châtelus-Malvaleix 25 E4
Châtenois 27 D1
Chatham 11 D2
Châtillon 27 F4
Châtillon-Coligny . . 26 A1
Châtillon-en-Bazois 26 B2
Châtillon-en-Diois . . 30 C2
Châtillon-sur-Chalaronne 26 C4
Châtillon-sur-Indre 25 E3
Châtillon-sur-Loire 26 A2
Châtillon-sur-Marne 20 B3
Châtillon-sur-Seine 26 B1
Châtre, la 25 E3
Chatsworth House . . 6 C3
Chatteris 9 F1
Chaudes-Aigues . . . 29 F2
Chauffailles 26 B4
Chaufour 19 E4
Chaulnes 19 F2
Chaumergy 26 C3
Chaumont-en-Vexin 19 E3
Chaumont (Haute-Marne) . . . 26 C1
Chaumont (Loir-et-Cher) 25 E2
Chauny 20 A2
Chausey, I 18 B4
Chaussin 26 C3
Chauvigny 25 D3
Chaux-de-Fonds, la 27 E2

Chaves 34 B3
Chazelles 30 B1
Cheb 53 D4
Cheddar Gorge ... 9 D3
Chef-Boutonne ... 24 C4
Cheles 42 C1
Chełm 112 C2
Chełmno 112 A1
Chelmsford 11 D2
Cheltenham 9 E2
Chelva 41 D3
Chemillé 24 C2
Chemin 26 C3
Chemnitz 53 E3
Chénérailles ... 25 E4
Chenonceaux ... 25 E2
Chepstow 9 D2
Cher 25 F3
Cher (Dépt) ... 25 F2
Chera 41 D3
Cherbourg 18 B2
Chéroy 26 A1
Cherson 113 F3
Chert 41 F2
Cheshire 6 C2
Cheshunt 9 F2
Cheste 41 E4
Chester 6 B3
Chesterfield 7 D3
Chester-le-Street ... 5 E4
Chevagnes 26 A3
Chevillon 20 C4
Cheviot Hills, The ... 5 E3
Cheviot, The ... 5 E3
Chèvre, Cap de la ... 22 A3
Chevreuse 19 E4
Cheylard, le 30 B2
Chèze, la 22 C3
Chiampo 59 D4
Chianciano Terme ... 63 D1
Chianti 61 D4
Chiaramonte Gulfi ... 69 D4
Chiaravalle 61 F3
Chiaravalle Centrale ... 67 F3
Chiari 60 B1
Chiasso 58 A4
Chiavari 60 A3
Chiavenna 58 B3
Chichester 9 F3
Chiclana de la Frontera ... 43 D4
Chieming 56 B3
Chiemsee 56 B3
Chieri 31 E1
Chiers 20 C3
Chiesa in Valmalenco ... 58 B3
Chiesina Uzz. ... 60 C3
Chieti 64 A2
Chiltern Hills ... 9 F2
Chimay 50 B4
Chimorra 43 E1
Chinchilla de Monte Aragón ... 41 D4
Chinchón 40 B2
Chinon 25 D2
Chioggia 61 D1
Chioula, Col de ... 32 A2
Chipiona 42 C3
Chippenham ... 9 E2
Chipping Campden ... 9 E1
Chipping Norton 9 E2
Chipping Sodbury ... 9 D2
Chirivel 44 C2
Chişineu-Criş ... 112 C4
Chisone 31 E2
Chiusa 59 D2
Chiusa di Pesio ... 31 E2
Chiusa Sclafani ... 68 B3
Chiusaforte 59 F3
Chiusi 63 D1
Chiva 41 E4
Chivasso 31 F1
Chlum u Třeboně ... 57 D1
Chmel'nickij ... 113 D2
Chmel'nik ... 113 E2
Chociwel 49 F2
Chodov 53 E4
Chojna 49 E3
Chojnice 110 A4
Chojniki 113 E1
Cholet 24 C3

Chollerford 5 E3
Cholm 111 E2
Chomutov 53 E3
Chorges 31 D2
Chorley 6 C2
Chorol 113 F2
Choszczno 49 F3
Chotin 113 D3
Chouto 38 B3
Chrastava 53 F2
Christchurch 9 E3
Christiansfeld ... 108 A3
Christiansø ... 109 D4
Chur 58 B2
Church Stretton ... 9 D1
Chust 112 C3
Chynčešt 113 E4
Ciamarella 31 E1
Cians, Gorges du ... 31 E3
Čičarija 70 A3
Čičavica 77 D2
Cicciano 64 B4
Čičevac 73 E4
Čičevo 76 A2
Cidacos, R 36 B3
Cidade Nova de Santo André ... 42 A1
Cidones 36 B3
Ciechanów 112 B1
Ciechocinek 112 B1
Ciempozuelos ... 40 B2
Cíes, Is 34 A3
Cieszyn 112 B3
Cieza 45 D2
Cifuentes 40 C2
Cigliano 31 F1
Cigüela R 40 B3
Cijara, Emb de ... 39 F4
Cijevna 76 B3
Cilavegna 60 A1
Čilipi 76 A3
Cill Airne 14 B4
Cillas 36 C4
Cill Chainnigh ... 15 D3
Cilleros 39 D2
Cilleruelo de Bezana ... 35 F2
Cill Mhantáin ... 13 E4
Cima Brenta ... 58 C3
Cima d'Asta ... 59 D3
Cimadolmo ... 59 E3
Cima Presanella ... 58 C3
Čimišlija ... 113 E4
Cimone, Mte ... 60 C4
Cîmpeni ... 112 C4
Cîmpina ... 115 D1
Cîmpulung ... 115 D1
Cîmpulung Moldovenesc ... 113 D3
Cinca, R ... 37 E3
Cincar ... 75 E1
Cinctorres ... 41 E2
Ciney ... 50 C4
Cinfães ... 34 A4
Cingoli ... 61 F4
Cinigiano ... 63 D1
Cinisi ... 68 B3
Cinovec ... 53 E3
Cinque Terre ... 60 B3
Cinto, M ... 33 F3
Cintruénigo ... 36 C3
Ciórraga ... 36 B1
Ciotat, la ... 30 C4
Čiovo ... 75 D2
Cirencester ... 9 E2
Cirey ... 21 E4
Ciria ... 36 C3
Ciriè ... 31 E1
Cirò ... 67 F2
Cirò Marina ... 67 F2
Čirpan ... 115 D2
Cisa, Pso della ... 60 B3
Cisneros ... 35 E3
Čista ... 74 C1
Cista Provo ... 75 E1
Cisterna di Latina ... 63 F3
Cisternino ... 65 E3
Cistierna ... 35 E2
Čitluk (Mostar) ... 75 F2
Čitluk (Posušje) ... 75 E1
Cittadella ... 59 D4
Città del Pieve ... 63 D1
Città di Castello ... 61 E4

Cittaducale ... 63 F2
Cittanova ... 67 E4
Cittareale ... 63 F1
Città Sant' Angelo ... 64 A1
Ciudad Encantada ... 40 C3
Ciudad Real ... 40 A4
Ciudad Rodrigo ... 39 D1
Ciutadella de Menorca ... 45 F1
Cividale del Friuli ... 59 F3
Civita Castellana ... 63 E2
Civitanova Marche ... 61 F4
Civitavecchia ... 63 D2
Civitella del Tronto ... 63 F1
Civitella Roveto ... 63 F2
Civray ... 25 D4
Čivril ... 115 F4
Clacton-on-Sea ... 11 D2
Clain ... 25 D4
Clairvaux-les-Lacs .. 27 D1
Clamecy ... 26 A2
Claonaig ... 4 B2
Clapham ... 6 C1
Clara ... 12 C4
Clare ... 11 D1
Clare ... 12 B3
Clare (Co) ... 12 B4
Clare I ... 12 A3
Claremorris ... 12 B3
Claudy ... 13 D1
Clausthal-Zellerfeld ... 52 B2
Claut ... 59 E3
Claviere ... 31 D2
Clavin, Pto de ... 39 D3
Clay Cross ... 6 C3
Claye-Souilly ... 19 F4
Clayette, la ... 26 B4
Clear I ... 14 A4
Clécy ... 18 C4
Clefmont ... 26 C1
Cléguérec ... 22 C3
Clelles ... 30 C2
Clères ... 19 E3
Clermont ... 19 F3
Clermont-en-Argonne ... 20 C3
Clermont-Ferrand . 29 F1
Clermont-l'Hérault ... 30 A4
Clervaux ... 21 D2
Cléry ... 25 E2
Cles ... 58 C3
Clevedon ... 9 D2
Cleveland Hills ... 7 D1
Cleveleys ... 6 B2
Clew B. ... 12 B3
Clifden ... 12 A3
Clisham ... 2 B2
Clisson ... 24 B2
Clitheroe ... 6 C2
Cloghan ... 12 C4
Clogheen ... 14 C4
Clogherhead ... 13 E3
Clogher Head ... 14 A3
Clogh Mills ... 13 E1
Clonakilty ... 14 B4
Clonbur ... 12 B3
Clondalkin ... 13 D4
Clones ... 13 D2
Clonfert ... 12 C4
Clonmacnoise ... 12 C4
Clonmel ... 14 C3
Cloppenburg ... 17 E1
Clovelly ... 8 B3
Cloyes ... 25 E1
Cloyne ... 14 C4
Cluain Meala ... 14 C3
Cluj-Napoca ... 112 C4
Clun ... 9 D1
Cluny ... 26 C3
Clusaz, la ... 27 D4
Cluse de Pontarlier ... 27 D3
Cluses ... 27 E4
Clusone ... 58 B4
Clwyd ... 6 B3
Clyde ... 4 C2
Clydebank ... 4 C2
Clyde, Firth of ... 4 B2
Coachford ... 14 B4
Coalisland ... 13 D2
Coalville ... 9 E1
Coaña ... 34 C1
Côa, R ... 39 D2

Coatbridge ... 4 C2
Cobeña ... 40 B2
Cobh ... 14 C4
Coburg ... 52 C4
Coca ... 40 A1
Coca, Pso di ... 58 B3
Cocentaina ... 45 E1
Cochem ... 51 E4
Cockburnspath ... 5 E2
Cockermouth ... 5 D4
Codevigo ... 61 D1
Codigoro ... 61 D2
Codogno ... 60 B2
Codos ... 36 C4
Codroipo ... 59 E3
Coesfeld ... 17 E3
Coevorden ... 17 D2
Cofrentes ... 41 D4
Coghinas, L del ... 66 B2
Cognac ... 28 B3
Cogne ... 31 E1
Cogolin ... 31 D4
Cogolludo ... 40 B1
Coigach ... 2 C2
Coimbra ... 38 B2
Coín ... 43 E4
Coina ... 38 A4
Čoka ... 72 C1
Col ... 70 A2
Colares ... 38 A4
Cölbe ... 17 F4
Colchester ... 11 D2
Coldbackie ... 2 C2
Colditz ... 53 D2
Coldstream ... 5 E2
Coleford ... 9 D2
Coleraine ... 13 D1
Colfiorito ... 63 E1
Colico ... 58 B3
Coligny ... 26 C3
Colindres ... 36 A1
Colintraive ... 4 B2
Coll ... 2 A4
Collado Bajo ... 41 D2
Collado Villalba ... 40 A2
Coll de Nargó ... 37 F3
Collecchio ... 60 B2
Colle di Val d'Elsa ... 60 C4
Colleferro ... 63 F3
Colle Isarco ... 59 D2
Collesalvetti ... 60 C4
Colle Sannita ... 64 B3
Collesano ... 68 C3
Colli a Volturno ... 64 A3
Collina, Pso della ... 60 C3
Collinée ... 22 C3
Colline Metallifere ... 60 C4
Collio ... 58 C4
Collioure ... 32 B2
Collobrières ... 31 D4
Collodi ... 60 C3
Collonges ... 27 D4
Collonges-la-Rouge ... 29 D2
Colmar ... 27 E1
Colmars ... 31 D3
Colmenar ... 43 F3
Colmenar de Oreja ... 40 B3
Colmenar Viejo ... 40 A2
Colnabaichin ... 3 D4
Colne ... 6 C2
Colobraro ... 65 D4
Cologna Veneta ... 60 C1
Cologne ... 28 C4
Colombey-les-Belles ... 21 D4
Colombey-les-Deux-Eglises ... 26 C1
Colombière, Col de la ... 27 D4
Colombres ... 35 F1
Colomera ... 44 A3
Colonsay ... 4 A2
Colorno ... 60 B2
Colosimi ... 67 F3
Colunga ... 35 E1
Colwyn Bay ... 6 B2
Comacchio ... 61 D2
Comănești ... 113 D4
Coma-ruga ... 37 F4
Combarro ... 34 A2
Combeaufontaine ... 27 D1
Combe Laval ... 30 C2

Combe Martin 8 C3
Comber 13 E2
Combloux 27 E4
Combourg 18 B4
Combronde 26 A4
Comeglians 59 E2
Comeragh Mts. 14 C3
Comillas 35 F1
Comines 19 F1
Comino 68 B4
Comiso 69 D4
Commentry 26 A4
Commercy 20 C4
Como 58 B4
Como, L di 58 B3
Cómpeta 43 F3
Comunanza 63 F1
Concarneau 22 B3
Conches 19 D4
Concordia sulla Secchia 60 C2
Condat 29 E1
Condé 20 A1
Conde, Emb del ... 43 E3
Condé-en-Brie ... 20 A3
Condeixa-a-Nova ... 38 B2
Condé-sur-Noireau 18 C4
Condom 28 C3
Condrieu 30 B1
Conegliano 59 E3
Conejeros, Pto de los ... 38 C4
Conflans 21 D3
Confolens 25 D4
Cong 12 B3
Congleton 6 C3
Congost de Tresponts 32 A3
Congosto de Valdavia 35 E2
Congresbury 9 D2
Conil de la Frontera 43 D4
Conisbrough 7 D2
Coniston 5 D4
Conlie 23 F3
Conliège 26 C3
Connel 4 B1
Connaught 12 B3
Connemara 12 A3
Connerré 23 F3
Conn, L 12 B2
Čonoplja 72 B1
Conques 29 E2
Conquet, le 22 A2
Conquista 43 F1
Conselice 61 D2
Conselve 61 D1
Consett 5 E4
Constância 38 B3
Constanta 115 E1
Constantina 43 E2
Consuegra 40 A3
Consuma 61 D3
Contamines, les ... 27 E4
Contarina 61 D2
Conthey 27 E3
Contigliano 63 E2
Contin 2 C3
Contrasto, C del ... 68 C3
Contraviesa, Sa de la 44 B4
Contreras, Emb de 41 D3
Contres 25 E2
Contrexéville 27 D1
Contursi 64 C4
Conty 19 F2
Convento de Calatrava 44 A1
Conversano 65 E3
Conwy 6 A2
Cookstown 13 D2
Cootehill 13 D3
Cope 45 D3
Cope, C. 45 D3
Copertino 65 F4
Copparo 61 D2

Corabia 115 D2
Cora Droma Rúisc ... 12 C3
Corato 65 D3
Coray 22 B3
Corbeil-Essonnes ... 19 F4
Corbigny 26 B2
Corbie 19 F2
Corbola 61 D2
Corbones, R 43 E2
Corbridge 5 E3
Corby 9 F1
Corcaigh 14 B4
Corcieux 27 E1
Córcoles, R 40 C4
Corconte 35 F2
Corcubión 34 A1
Cordes 29 D3
Córdoba 43 F2
Cordobilla de Lácara 39 D4
Cordobilla, Emb de 43 F3
Corduente 40 C2
Corella 36 C3
Coreses 35 D4
Corfe Castle 9 E3
Corgo 34 B2
Cori 63 F3
Coria 39 D2
Coria del Río 43 D3
Corias 34 C2
Corigliano Calabro . 67 F2
Corinaldo 61 E3
Coripe 43 E3
Cork 14 B4
Cork (Co) 14 B4
Corlay 22 C3
Corleone 68 B3
Corleto Perticara ... 65 D4
Çorlu 115 E3
Cormatin 26 C3
Cormeilles 19 D3
Cormery 25 D2
Cormons 59 F3
Cornago 36 C3
Cornellana 35 D1
Corniglio 60 B3
Cornimont 27 E1
Cornuda 59 D4
Cornus 29 F3
Cornwall 8 B4
Corps 31 D2
Corral de Almaguer 40 B3
Corral de Cantos ... 39 F3
Corralejo 42 C4
Corrales 35 D4
Corran 2 C4
Corraun 12 B2
Corredoiras 34 B2
Correggio 60 C2
Corrèze 29 D1
Corrèze (Dépt) ... 29 D1
Corrèze R 29 D2
Corrib, L 12 B3
Corridonia 61 F4
Corrofin 12 B4
Corse 33 E2
Corse-du-Sud 33 F3
Corsham 9 D2
Čortanovci 72 C2
Corte 33 F3
Corte de Peleas ... 39 D4
Cortegada 34 B3
Cortegana 42 C2
Cortemaggiore ... 60 B2
Cortemilia 31 F2
Corteolona 60 A2
Cortes de Aragón . 41 E1
Cortes de Baza ... 44 B2
Cortes de la Frontera 43 E4
Cortijos Nuevos ... 44 B2
Cortina d'Ampezzo 59 E3
Čortkov 113 D3
Cortona 61 D4
Coruche 38 B4
Corvara in Badia ... 59 D3
Corvera 45 D2
Corvera Toranzo ... 35 F2

Corwen 6 B3
Cosenza 67 E2
Cosham 9 E3
Cosne 26 A2
Cosne-d'Allier 26 A3
Cossato 31 F1
Cossé-le-Vivien ... 23 E3
Cosson 25 E2
Cossonay 27 D3
Costa Blanca 45 E2
Costa Brava 32 C3
Costa da Caparica ... 38 A4
Costa del Sol 44 A4
Costa de Santo André 42 A1
Costalunga, Pso di . 59 D3
Costa Smeralda 66 B1
Costa Vasca 36 B1
Costa Verde 35 D1
Costigliole d'Asti ... 31 F2
Coswig (Sachsen) . 53 E2
Coswig (Sachsen-Anhalt) 53 D1
Côte-d'Or (Dépt) ... 26 C2
Côtes-d'Armor 22 C3
Côte-St-André, la . 30 C1
Cotignac 31 D4
Cottbus 53 F1
Coubet, Collado de . 32 B3
Coubre, Pointe de la . 28 A1
Couches 26 B3
Couço 38 B4
Coucy-le-Château-Auffrique 20 A3
Couesnon 23 D3
Couhé 25 D4
Couilly 19 F4
Couiza 32 B2
Coulanges 26 A2
Coulanges-la-Vineuse 26 A2
Coulommiers 19 F4
Coulon 24 C4
Coulonges 24 C3
Coupar Angus 5 D1
Couptrain 18 C4
Courchevel 31 D1
Cour-Cheverny 25 E2
Courçon 24 C4
Courmayeur 27 E4
Couronne, la 28 C1
Courpière 29 F1
Cours 26 B4
Coursan 32 B1
Coursegoules 31 E3
Courseulles 18 C3
Courson-les-Carrières 26 A2
Courtenay 26 A1
Courthézon 30 C3
Courtine, la 29 D1
Courtomer 19 D4
Courtown 15 E3
Courtrai 50 A3
Courville 19 E4
Cousin 26 B2
Coussey 20 C4
Coutances 18 B3
Coutras 28 B2
Couvertoirade, la . 29 F3
Couvin 50 C4
Couze 25 E4
Cova da Iria 38 B3
Covadonga 35 E1
Covadonga, Pque Nac de la Sa de ...35 E2
Covarrubias 36 A3
Coventry 9 E1
Covilhã 38 C2
Cowbridge 8 C2
Cowdenbeath 5 D2
Cowes 9 E3
Cowfold 10 C3
Cozes 28 B1
Craco 65 D4
Craigavon 13 E2
Craigellachie 3 D3
Craighouse 4 B2
Craigievar Castle ... 3 E4
Craignure 4 B1
Crail 5 D2
Crailsheim 55 E2

Craiova 115 D2
Cranborne 9 E3
Crans 27 E3
Craon 23 E3
Craonne 20 B3
Craponne 29 F1
Crathes Castle 3 E4
Crati 67 E2
Crato 38 C3
Craughwell 12 B4
Crau, la 31 D4
Craven Arms 9 D1
Crawinkel 52 C3
Crawley 10 C3
Creag Meagaidh 2 C4
Creagorry 2 A3
Crécy 20 A2
Crécy-en-Ponthieu 19 E2
Crécy-la-Chapelle 19 F4
Crediton 8 C3
Creegh 12 B4
Creeslough 12 C1
Creglingen 55 E1
Creil 19 F3
Crema 60 B1
Crémieu 26 C4
Cremona 60 B2
Créon 28 B2
Crepaja 73 D2
Crépy-en-Valois 19 F3
Cres 70 B4
Cres I. 70 B4
Crescentino 31 F1
Crespino 61 D2
Crest 30 C2
Cresta 58 B3
Cresta del Gallo 45 D2
Créteil 19 F4
Crêtes, Route des 27 E1
Creully 18 C3
Creuse 25 E4
Creuse (Dépt) 25 E4
Creusot, le 26 B3
Creußen 53 D4
Creutzwald 21 D3
Creuzburg 52 B3
Crevacuore 58 A4
Crevalcore 60 C2
Crèvecœur-le-Grand 19 E3
Crevillente 45 D2
Crewe 6 C3
Crewkerne 9 D3
Crianlarich 4 C1
Criccieth 6 A3
Crickhowell 9 D2
Cricklade 9 E2
Crieff 4 C1
Criel 19 E2
Crikvenica 70 B3
Crimmitschau 53 D3
Crinan 4 B2
Criquetot-l'Esneval 19 D3
Crissolo 31 E2
Crișu Alb 112 C4
Crișu Negru 112 C4
Crișu Repede 112 C4
Crivitz 48 C2
Crkvice 76 A2
Crmljan 76 C2
Črmošnjice 70 B2
Črna 70 B1
Crna Bara (Srbija) 72 B3
Crna Bara (Vojvodina) 72 C1
Crnac (Hrvatska) 71 E2
Crnac (Srbija) 76 C1
Crna Gora 76 B2
Crna gora 77 E2
Crna reka 77 E4
Crna Trava 77 E1
Crnča 72 B4
Crni Drim 77 D4
Crni Guber 72 C4
Crni Lug (BH) 75 D1
Crni Lug (HR) 70 B3
Crni Timok 73 E4
Crni vrh *Mt* (BH) 71 D4
Črni vrh *Mt* (SLO) 70 B1
Crni vrh *Mt* (Srbija) 76 B1
Črni vrh (SLO) 70 A2
Crnivec 70 B2
Crnjelovo Donje 72 B3
Črnkovci 71 F2
Crno jez 76 B2
Črnomelj 70 B3
Croagh Patrick 12 B3
Croce dello Scrivano, Pso 64 C4
Croce Domini, Pso di 58 C4
Crocello, Pso di 64 C4
Crocq 25 F4
Croisic, le 24 A2
Croisière, la 25 E4
Croix de Fer, Col de la 31 D1
Croix Haute, Col de la 30 C2
Croix-Valmer, la 31 D4
Crolly 12 C1
Cromarty 3 D3
Cromer 7 F3
Crook 5 E4
Croom 14 B3
Cross Fell 5 D4
Cross Hands 8 C2
Crosshaven 14 C4
Crossmaglen 13 D3
Crossmolina 12 B2
Crotone 67 F3
Crotoy, le 19 E2
Crowborough 10 C3
Crowland 9 F1
Crowle 7 D2
Croyde 8 C3
Croydon 9 F2
Crozant 25 E4
Crozon 22 A3
Cruden Bay 3 E3
Crudgington 6 C3
Crumlin 13 E2
Cruseilles 27 D4
Crussol 30 B2
Cruz 40 B3
Cruzamento de Pegões 38 A4
Cruz da Légua 38 A3
Cruz de Tejeda 42 B4
Crven Grm 75 E2
Crvenka 72 B2
Crymmych 8 B1
Csongrád 112 B4
Csorna 112 A4
Cuacos 39 E2
Cualedro 34 B3
Cuba 42 B1
Cubel 36 C4
Cucalón, Sa de 41 D1
Cuckfield 10 C3
Cudillero 35 D1
Čudovo 111 D1
Čudskoje Ozero 110 C1
Cuéllar 35 F4
Cuenca 40 C3
Cuenca, Serr de 40 C2
Cuerda 41 D3
Cuerda del Pozo, Emb de la 36 B3
Cuers 31 D4
Cuerva 40 A3
Cueva de la Pileta 43 E4
Cueva de la Vieja 41 D4
Cueva de Nerja 44 A4
Cueva Foradada, Emb de 41 E1
Cueva, Sa do 35 E1
Cuevas de Altamira 35 F1
Cuevas de Artà 45 F3
Cuevas de Canalobre 45 E1
Cuevas del Aguila 39 F2
Cuevas del Amanzora 44 C3
Cuevas del Becerro 43 E3
Cuevas del Campo 44 B2
Cuevas del Drac 45 F3
Cuevas del Valle 39 F2
Cuevas de San Clemente 35 F3
Cuevas de San Marcos 43 F3
Cuevas de Valporquero 35 D2
Cuevas de Vinromá 41 F2
Cuglieri 66 A3
Cuijk 17 D3
Cuillin Sd 2 B4
Cuillins, The 2 B3
Cuiseaux 26 C3
Cuisery 26 C3
Culan 25 F3
Culdaff 13 D1
Culebra, Sa de la 34 C3
Culemborg 16 C3
Cúllar Baza 44 B2
Cullen 3 E3
Cullera 41 E4
Cullompton 8 C3
Culoz 27 D4
Culross 5 D2
Cumbernauld 4 C2
Cumbre Alta 39 F3
Cumbres Mayores 42 C1
Cumbria 5 D4
Cumbrian Mts 5 D4
Cumiana 31 E2
Čumić 73 D3
Cumnock 4 C3
Cunault 24 C2
Cuneo 31 E2
Cunlhat 29 F1
Čunski 70 B4
Cuorgné 31 E1
Cupar 5 D1
Cupello 64 B2
Cupramontana 61 E4
Ćuprija 73 E4
Cure 26 B2
Cure, la 27 D3
Curia 38 B1
Currane, L 14 A4
Curtea de Argeș 115 D1
Curtis 34 B1
Čurug 72 C2
C'urupinsk 113 F3
Cusano Mutri 64 B3
Cushendall 13 E1
Cushendun 13 E1
Cusna, Mte 60 C3
Cusset 26 A4
Cutro 67 F3
Cuxhaven 47 F2
Cvikov 53 F3
Čvrsnica 75 E1
Čvrstec 71 D2
Cwmbrân 9 D2
Cybinka 49 F4
Cysoing 20 A1
Czarnków 112 A1
Czersk 110 A4
Częstochowa 112 B2
Człuchów 112 A1

D

Dabar 70 C3
Dąbie 49 E2
Dabie, Jez 49 E2
Dabilje 77 F3
Dabo 21 E4
Dachau 55 F3
Dachsteingruppe 59 F1
Dačice 57 E1
Dadiá 81 F2
Dáfnes 86 C1
Dáfni (Límnos) 85 D1
Dáfni (Makedonía) 80 C4
Dáfni (Pelopónissos) 86 C1
Dáfni (Stereá Eláda) 83 D4
Dáfni (Stereá Eláda) 87 F1
Dáfnio 87 D3
Dafnónas (Stereá Eláda) 83 D3
Dafnónas (Thráki) 80 C2
Dafnotí 82 C2
Dafnoúdi, Akr 82 B4
Dagali 104 C2
Dagebüll 47 F1
Dagenham 10 C2
Dahlen 53 E2
Dahlenburg 48 B3
Dahme (Brandenburg) 53 E1
Dahme (Schleswig-Holstein) 48 B2
Dahme *R.* 53 E1
Dahn 54 B2
Daimiel 40 A4

Dijon

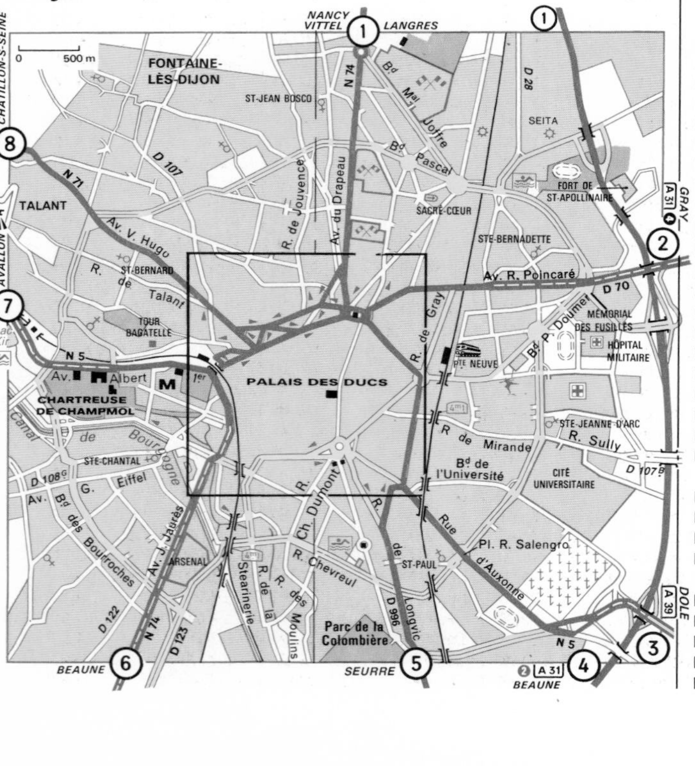
NANCY
VITTEL
LANGRES
TROYES
CHÂTILLON-S-SEINE
0 500 m
FONTAINE-LÈS-DIJON
ST-JEAN BOSCO
SEITA
TALANT
MOULINS
AVALLON
A 38
FORT DE ST-APOLLINAIRE
SACRÉ-CŒUR
STE-BERNADETTE
GRAY
A 31
Av. R. Poincaré
D 70
MÉMORIAL DES FUSILLÉS
HÔPITAL MILITAIRE
TOUR BAGATELLE
N 5
Av. Albert 1er
CHARTREUSE DE CHAMPMOL
PALAIS DES DUCS
STE-JEANNE-D'ARC
R. Sully
R. de Mirande
Bd de l'Université
CITÉ UNIVERSITAIRE
D 107
STE-CHANTAL
ARSENAL
R. Chevreul
Pl. R. Salengro
ST-PAUL
Parc de la Colombière
DOLE
A 39
BEAUNE
SEURRE
N 74
D 122
D 996

Daimuz 41 E4
Dajt, Mal i 76 C4
Đakovica 76 C2
Đakovo 71 F2
Đala 72 C1
Dalälven 106 A3
Dalane 104 A4
Dalbeattie 4 C3
Dalbosjön 105 E4
Dalby 109 D3
Dale (Hordaland) 104 A2
Dale (Sogn og Fjordane) 104 A1
Dalen 104 B3
Dalhem 109 F4
Dalías 44 B4
Daliburgh 2 A3
Dalj 72 B2
Dalkeith 5 D2
Dalkey 13 E4
Dalmally 4 C1
Dalmellington 4 C3
Dalmine 60 B1
Dalry 4 C2
Dalsbruk 107 D3
Dalsfjorden 104 A1
Dalsjöfors 109 D1
Dals Långed 105 D4
Dalton 6 B1
Daluis, Gorges de 31 E3
Dalvik 96 B1
Dalwhinnie 2 C4
Damaskiniá 79 D3
Damássi 83 E1
Damazan 28 C3
Damelevières 21 D4
Damgan 22 C4
Damianó 79 F2
Dammartin-en-Goële 19 F3
Damme 17 F2
Damnjane 76 C2
Dampierre 27 D2
Dampierre-sur-Salon 27 D2
Damville 19 E4
Damvillers 20 C3
Dangé 25 D3
Danilovgrad 76 B2
Dannemarie 27 E2
Dannenberg 48 B3
Dão, R. 38 C1
Daoulas 22 B3
Darda 71 F2
Dardesheim 52 C1
Darfo Boario Terme 58 C4
Dargilan, Grotte de 29 F3
Dargun 49 D2
Darlington 5 E4
Darłowo 110 A4
Darmstadt 54 C1
Darney 27 D1
Daroca 36 C4
Darque 34 A3
Darß 48 C1
Dartford 10 C2
Dartmoor Nat Pk 8 C3
Dartmouth 8 C4
Daruvar 71 E2
Darwen 6 C2
Dasburg 51 D4
Dasing 55 F3
Dassel 52 B2
Dassohóri 81 D2
Dassow 48 B2
D'at'kovo 111 F3
Datteln 17 E3
Daugava 110 C3
Daugavpils 110 C3
Daun 51 E4
Dava 3 D3
Davat 77 D4
Daventry 9 E1
Davia 87 D2
Davidovac 73 F2
Dávlia 83 F4
Davor 71 E3
Davos 58 B2
Dawlish 8 C3
Dax 28 A4
Deădnu 95 E2
Deal 11 D3
Deauville 19 D3
Deba 36 B1
Debar 77 D3
Debarska Banja Banjišta 77 D3
Debeli Lug 73 E3
Debeli vrh 70 B2
Debeljača 72 C2
Dębica 112 B2
De Bilt 16 C3
Dęblin 112 C2
Dębno 49 F3
Debrc 72 C3
Debrecen 112 C4
Dečani 76 C2
Decazeville 29 E2
Děčín 53 F3
Decize 26 A3
Dedemsvaart 17 D2
Dee (Scotland) 3 D4
Dee (Wales/Eng) 6 B3
Degaña 34 C2
Degebe, R 38 B4
Degerfjärden 102 A2
Degerfors 105 E4
Degerndorf 56 B4
Deggendorf 56 B2
Dego 31 F2
Degracias 38 B2
De Haan 50 A3
Dehesa de Montejo 35 F2
Deià 45 E2
Deidesheim 54 C1
Deinze 50 B3
Deiva Marina 60 B3
Dej 112 C4
Deje 105 E3
Dejë, Mal 76 C3
De Koog 16 C1
Delčevo 77 F2
Delden 17 D2
Deleitosa 39 E3
Delémont 27 E2
Deléria 83 E1
Delet Teili 106 C3
Delfí 83 E4
Delft 16 B3
Delfzijl 47 D3
Delia 68 C4
Delianuova 67 E4
Deliblato 73 D2
Deliblatska Peščara 73 D2
Deliceto 64 C3
Delimeđe 76 C1
Delitzsch 53 D2
Delle 27 E2
Dellen, N 101 F3
Dellen, S 101 F3
Delme 21 D3
Delmenhorst 47 F3
Delnice 70 B3
Delsbo 101 F3
Delta Dunării 113 E4
Delvin 13 D3
Delvináki 82 B1
Demanda, Sa de la 36 B2
Demer 50 C3
Demidov 111 E3
Demirci 115 F4
Demir Kapija 77 F3
Demmin 49 D2
Demoiselles, Grotte des 29 F3
Demonía 87 E4
Denain 20 A1
Denbigh 6 B3
Den Burg 16 C1
Dendermonde 50 B3
Dendre 50 B4
Dendrohóri 79 D3
Denekamp 17 E2
Den Haag 16 B3
Den Helder 16 C1
Denia 45 E1
Denizli 115 F4
Denkendorf 55 F2
Dennington 11 D1
Denny 4 C2
Den Oever 16 C1
Dent de Vaulion 27 D3
De Panne 50 A3
Đeravica 76 C2
Derby 6 C3
Derbyshire 6 C3
Der Chantecoq, L du 20 C4
Đerdap, H.E. 73 F2
Đerdap, Klisura 73 E3
Derekoy 115 E2
Derenburg 52 C1
Derg, L (Clare) 12 C4
Derg, L (Donegal) 12 C2
Der Grabow 49 D1
Dermatás, Akr 83 F1

Dermbach........... 52 B3
Derneburg......... 52 B1
Derravaragh, L ... 13 D3
Derrynasaggart
  Mts........... 14 B4
Derryveagh Mts 12 C1
Deruta........... 63 E1
Dervaig........... 4 B1
Derval........... 23 D4
Dervéni........... 87 D1
Derventa........... 71 E3
Derviziana......... 82 B2
Derwent (Derbys). 6 C3
Derwent (Durham).. 5 E4
Derwent (Yorks) 7 D1
Derwent Water 5 D4
Desborough......... 9 F1
Descartes......... 25 D3
Desenzano......... 60 B1
Desertas......... 42 A3
Desfiladero de
  Despeñaperros ... 44 A1
Desfiladero de la
  Hermida 35 F2
Desfiladero de los
  Beyos......... 35 E2
Desfiladero del
  Teverga......... 35 D2
Desfina........... 83 E4
Desimirovac....... 73 D4
Desio........... 60 A1
Deskáti........... 83 D1
Desna........... 111 F3
Despotikó, N 88 B3
Despotovac....... 73 E3
Despotovo......... 72 B2
Dessau........... 53 D1
Destriana......... 35 D3
Desulo........... 66 B3
Desvres........... 19 E1
Deta........... 114 C1
Đetinja........... 72 C4
Detmold........... 52 A1
Dettelbach......... 55 E1
Dettifoss......... 96 C1
Deurne........... 17 D3
Deutsche
  Alpenstraße....... 55 E4
Deutsche Bucht 47 E2
Deutschkreutz 57 F3
Deutschlandsberg .. 70 B1
Deutsch-Wagram ... 57 F2
Deux-Alpes, les .. 31 D2
Deux-Sèvres....... 24 C3
Deva........... 114 C1
Deve Bair 77 E2
Deventer......... 17 D2
Deveron........... 3 E3
Devetak......... 72 B4
Devil's Bridge..... 8 C1
Devil's Elbow 3 D4
Devizes........... 9 E2
Devnja........... 115 E2
Dewsbury......... 6 C2
Deza........... 36 C4
Diablerets, les ... 27 E3
Diablerets, les Mt.. 27 E3
Diafáni........... 93 D2
Diakófti........... 90 A1
Diakoftó........... 86 C1
Diamante......... 67 E2
Día, N........... 91 E3
Diano Marina 31 F3
Diápora Nissiá ... 87 E1
Diavlos Aloníssou . 84 B2
Diavlos Oreón 83 F3
Diavlos
  Pelagoníssou ... 84 B2
Diavlos Skiáthou .. 84 A2
Diavlos Skopélou .. 84 A2
Diavlos Trikeríou .. 83 F3
Diavlos Zákinthou.. 86 A1
Diavolítsi......... 86 C3
Diavolo, Pso del .. 64 A2
Diavolórema....... 81 E2
Diavlos
Dibbersen......... 48 A3
Dicmo........... 75 D1
Dicomano......... 61 D2
Didima........... 87 E2
Didimo, Óros 87 E2
Didimótiho....... 81 F1
Die........... 30 C2
Dieburg......... 52 A4
Diedorf........... 52 B2

Diego Alvaro 39 E2
Diekirch........... 21 D2
Diemel........... 52 A2
Diemelstadt....... 52 A2
Diepholz......... 17 F2
Dieppe........... 19 E2
Dierdorf......... 51 E4
Dieren........... 17 D3
Diesdorf......... 48 B4
Dießen........... 56 A1
Diest........... 50 C3
Dietenheim....... 55 E3
Dietfurt......... 55 F2
Dietikon......... 27 F2
Dietmannsried ... 55 E4
Dieulefit......... 30 C2
Dieulouard 21 D4
Dieuze........... 21 D4
Diez........... 51 F4
Diezma........... 44 A3
Differdange 21 D3
Digerkampen 100 B3
Digermulen 94 A4
Dignano......... 59 E3
Digne-les-Bains .. 31 D3
Digoin........... 26 B3
Dijle........... 50 C3
Dijon........... 26 C2
Dikanäs......... 97 F3
Díkea........... 81 F1
Díkela........... 81 E2
Diksmuide....... 50 A3
Diktéo Ándro 91 E4
Diktinéon 90 B3
Dikti, Óros 91 E4
Dilessi........... 84 B4
Dilináta......... 82 B4
Dilj........... 71 E2
Dillenburg......... 51 F3
Dillingen (Bayern). 55 E2
Dillingen
  (Saarland) 54 A2
Dilofos........... 81 F1

Dílos........... 88 C2
Dílos, N......... 88 C2
Dimena........... 87 E2
Dímitra........... 83 E1
Dimitrítsi......... 80 B2
Dimitrovgrad (BG) 115 D3
Dimitrovgrad
  (Srbija)......... 77 F1
Dimitsána......... 86 C2
Dinami........... 67 E4
Dinan........... 18 B4
Dinant........... 50 C4
Dinar........... 115 F4
Dinara Mt....... 75 D1
Dinara (Reg)..... 75 D1
Dinard........... 18 B4
Dinbych......... 6 B3
Dinbych-y-pysgod .. 8 B2
Dingelstädt....... 52 B2
Dingle........... 14 A3
Dingle........... 105 D4
Dingle (Reg)..... 14 A3
Dingle B......... 14 A3
Dingli........... 68 B4
Dinglingen 54 C3
Dingolfing......... 56 B2
Dingwall......... 2 C3
Dinjiška......... 70 C4
Dinkelsbühl....... 55 E2
Dinklage......... 17 F2
Dinslaken......... 17 D3
Dío........... 79 F4
Diónissos......... 87 F1
Dióriga Korínthou .. 87 E1
Dipótama......... 80 C1
Diráhio........... 86 C3
Dippoldiswalde ... 53 E2
Dirfís, Óros 84 B3
Dirrachium
Disentis......... 58 A3
Disgrazia, Mte ... 58 B3
Dispílio......... 79 D3
Diss........... 11 D1
Dissen........... 17 F2

Dístomo........... 83 E4
Dístos........... 84 B4
Ditikí Rodópi 80 C1
Dittaino......... 69 D3
Ditzingen......... 55 D2
Divača........... 70 A3
Divaráta......... 82 B4
Divčibare......... 72 C4
Dives........... 18 C3
Dives R......... 18 C3
Divič........... 72 B4
Divjakë......... 76 C4
Divljana......... 77 E1
Divonne......... 27 D3
Divor, Bgem do .. 38 B4
Divor, Rib de .. 38 B4
Divoúnia, Ni 92 C2
Divri........... 83 E3
Divuša........... 71 D3
Djupini......... 96 A3
Djupvik......... 94 C2
Djuräs........... 105 F2
Djursland 108 B2
Dmitrov......... 111 F2
Dnepr........... 111 E3
Dneprodzeržinskoje
  Vodochranilišče .. 113 F2
Dneprovskij
  Liman......... 113 F3
Dnestr........... 112 C3
Dnestrovskij
  Liman......... 113 F4
Dno........... 111 D2
Dobanovci 72 C3
Dobbiaco......... 59 E2
Dobel........... 54 C2
Dobele......... 110 C3
Döbeln......... 53 E2
Doberlug-
  Kirchhain 53 E1
Döbern......... 53 F1
Dobersberg 57 E1
Dobieszczyn 49 E2

Doboj........... 71 F3
Dobošnica......... 71 F3
Dobra (PL)....... 49 F2
Dobra (Srbija)... 73 E3
Dobra R......... 70 C3
Dobra Voda....... 73 D4
Dobra Voda Mt... 77 D3
Dobrašinci....... 77 F3
Dobratsch......... 59 F2
Dobrčane......... 77 D2
Döbriach......... 59 F2
Dobrič........... 115 E2
Dobrica......... 73 D2
Dobričevo......... 73 D2
Dobrinj......... 70 B3
Dobrna......... 70 B1
Dobromani 75 F2
Dobro Polje....... 76 A1
Dobrovnik......... 70 C1
Dobrun......... 72 C4
Dobruš......... 111 E4
Dobruševo......... 77 E4
Dobrzany......... 49 F2
Döbšiná......... 112 B3
Docksta......... 102 A2
Doc Penfro....... 8 B2
Dodekánissa 89 E3
Dodóni........... 82 B1
Doesburg......... 17 D3
Doetinchem 17 D3
Dogliani......... 31 F2
Doïráni......... 79 F2
Doïránis, L....... 79 F2
Doiras, Emb de.. 34 C1
Dojransko Ez 77 F3
Dokanj........... 72 B3
Dokka........... 104 C2
Dokkum......... 47 D3
Dokós, N......... 87 E2

Doksy........... 53 F3
Dolac........... 76 C2
Dol-de-Bretagne .. 18 B4
Dole........... 26 C2
Dôle, la......... 27 D3
Dølemo......... 104 B4
Dolenci......... 77 D4
Dolenja Vas...... 70 B2
Dolenjske Toplice .. 70 B2
Dolga Vas....... 71 D1
Dolhi........... 79 E4
Dolina........... 112 C3
Doljani......... 71 D4
Doljevac......... 77 D1
Dolla........... 12 C4
Döllach......... 59 E2
Dollar........... 5 D2
Dolle........... 48 C3
Dolní Dvořiště .. 57 D2
Dolno Kosovrasti .. 77 D3
Dolo........... 61 D1
Dolomiti......... 59 D3
Dolomiti Bellunesi, Parco
  Naz dello 59 D3
Dolores......... 45 D2
Dolovo......... 73 D2
Dol Poustevna .. 53 F2
Domaševo......... 75 F2
Domažlice......... 56 B1
Dombås......... 100 B3
Dombasle 21 D4
Dombóvár 114 B1
Domburg......... 16 B3
Domène......... 30 C1
Doméniko......... 83 E1
Domèvre-en-
  Haye......... 21 D4
Domfront......... 18 C4
Dömitz......... 48 C3
Domme........... 29 D2

Dommitzsch 53 D2
Domnista......... 83 D3
Domodossola....... 58 A4
Domokós......... 83 E2
Dompaire 27 D1
Dompierre 26 B3
Domrémy 20 C4
Domusnovas 66 B4
Domžale......... 70 B2
Don (England) .. 7 D2
Don (Scotland) .. 3 E4
Donaghadee 13 E2
Doña María Ocaña .. 44 B3
Doña Mencía 43 F2
Doñana,
  Parque Nac de.. 43 D3
Donau........... 56 C2
Donaueschingen .. 54 C4
Donauwörth 55 E2
Donawitz......... 57 E4
Don Benito 39 E4
Doncaster 7 D2
Donegal......... 12 C2
Donegal B....... 12 C2
Donegal (Co) .. 12 C1
Dongen......... 16 C3
Donges......... 23 D4
Donington 7 E3
Donja Bebrina .. 71 F3
Donja Brela 75 E2
Donja Brezna .. 76 B2
Donja Bukovica .. 76 B2
Donja Kamenica .. 72 C3
Donja Šatornja .. 73 D3
Donje Crniljevo .. 72 C3
Donje Dragovlje .. 77 E1
Donje Ljupče 77 D2
Donji Andrijevci .. 71 F3
Donji Barbeš.... 77 E1
Donji Kanzanci .. 75 D1
Donji Lapac 71 D4
Donji Malovan .. 75 E1
Donji Miholjac .. 71 E2

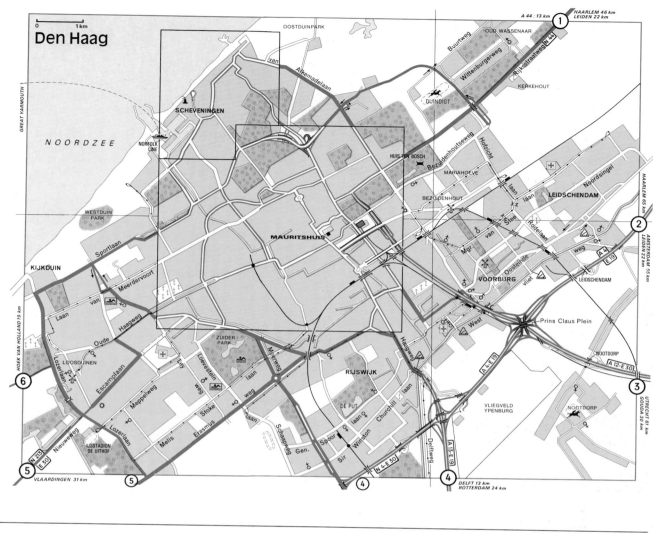

Den Haag

NOORDZEE

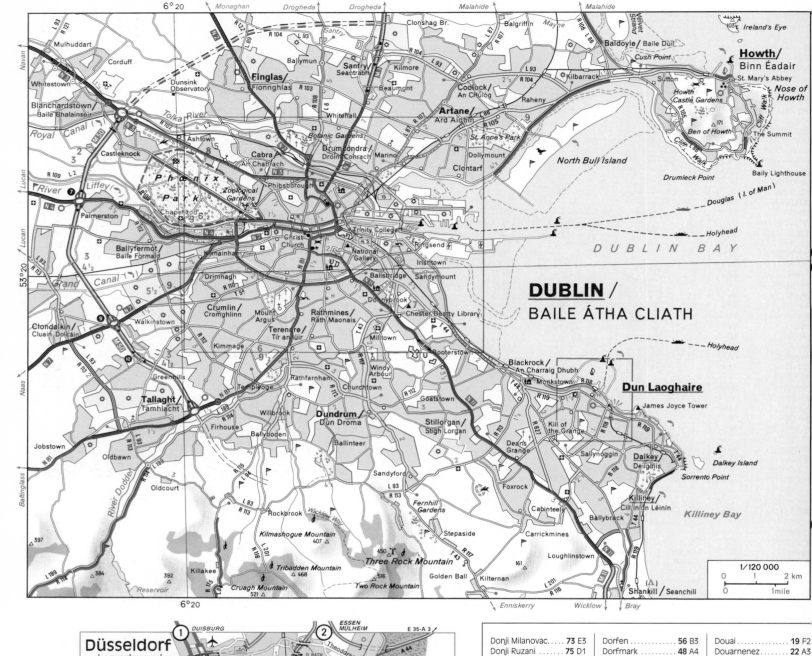

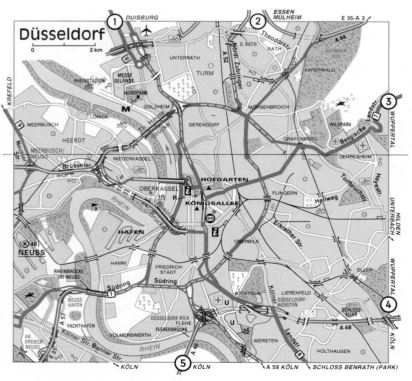

Donji Milanovac..... 73 E3	Dorfen............. 56 B3	Douai............. 19 F2
Donji Ruzani 75 D1	Dorfmark........... 48 A4	Douarnenez........ 22 A3
Donji Seget 75 D2	Dorgali........... 66 C2	Doubs............. 26 C3
Donji Vakuf 71 E4	Dório............. 86 C3	Doubs (Dépt)...... 27 D2
Donji Vijačani 71 E3	Dorkáda........... 80 A2	Doucier........... 27 D3
Donji Zemunik 74 C1	Dorking........... 10 C3	Doudeville........ 19 D2
Donjon, le 26 B3	Dormagen.......... 17 E4	Doué............. 24 C2
Dønna 97 D3	Dormans........... 20 A3	Douglas (I of Man) . 6 A1
Donnemarie-	Dornbirn.......... 58 B2	Douglas (Scotland).. 4 C2
Dontilly 20 A4	Dornburg.......... 52 C3	Doukáto, Akr...... 82 B3
Donnersbachwald .. 57 D4	Dorndorf.......... 52 B3	Doulaincourt...... 20 C4
Dønnes 97 D2	Dornes............ 26 A3	Doulevant-le-
Donon 21 E4	Dornie............ 2 B3	Château 20 C4
Donon, Col du 21 E4	Dornoch........... 3 D3	Doullens.......... 19 F2
Donostia-San	Dornoch Firth...... 3 D3	Doulus Head 14 A4
Sebastián 36 C1	Dornstetten........ 54 C3	Doune............ 4 C2
Donoússa, N 89 D3	Dornum........... 47 E3	Doupov........... 53 E3
Donzenac 29 D2	Dorog............ 112 B4	Dourdan 19 E4
Donzère........... 30 B2	Dorogobuž........ 111 E3	Dourgne.......... 32 A1
Donzy............ 26 A2	Dorohoi........... 113 D3	Douro............ 34 A4
Doorn............ 16 C3	Dorotea........... 101 F1	Douro, R......... 34 A4
Doornik 50 A4	Dörpstedt......... 48 A1	Douvaine......... 27 D3
Dora Baltéa 27 E4	Dorset 9 D3	Douve............ 18 B3
Dora Riparia 31 E1	Dorsten........... 17 E3	Douvres.......... 18 C3
Dorat, le 25 D4	Dortan 27 D3	Dover............ 11 D3
Đorče Petrov...... 77 D3	Dortmund.......... 17 E3	Dover, Str of 11 D3
Dorchester........ 9 D3	Dortmund-Ems-	Dovre............ 100 C3
Dordives 25 F1	Kanal............ 17 E2	Dovrefjell........ 100 C3
Dordogne 29 E1	Dorum............ 47 F3	Dovsk............ 111 E4
Dordogne (Dépt)... 28 C2	Dörzbach......... 55 D1	Down 13 E2
Dordogne R....... 28 B2	Dosbarrios 40 B3	Downham Market .. 10 C1
Dordrecht......... 16 C3	Dos Hermanas 43 D3	Downpatrick 13 E2
Dore 29 F1	Dosse............ 49 D3	Dowra............ 12 C2

Doxarás 83 E2
Doxáto 80 C2
Dozulé 19 D3
Drac 30 C2
Dračevo 77 E3
Drachten 17 D1
Drag 94 A4
Dragalovci 71 E3
Dragaš 77 E3
Drăgăşani 115 D1
Dragaši 76 B1
Draginac 72 C3
Draginje 72 C3
Dragočaj 71 E3
Dragocvet 73 D4
Dragoevo 77 E3
Dragoman 114 C2
Dragonera, I 45 E3
Dragoni 64 B3
Dragør 108 C3
Dragoš 77 E4
Dragotiná 82 A2
Dragović 71 E2
Dragovića Polje . . 76 B2
Dragozetići 70 B3
Dragsfjärd 107 D3
Dragsvik 100 A3
Draguignan 31 D4
Dráma 80 C2
Dráma (Nomos) . . 80 C1
Drammen 104 C3
Drammen selva . . 104 C3
Drangajökull 96 A1
Drangedal 104 C3
Dranske 49 D1
Drápano, Akr 90 C3
Drasenhofen 57 F1
Drau 59 F2
Dráva 71 E2
Dravograd 70 B1
Drawno 49 F2

Drawsko
  Pomorskie . . . 112 A1
Draženov 56 B1
Draževac 72 C3
Drebkau 53 F1
Dreki 96 C2
Drenewydd 9 D1
Drenovac 77 E2
Drenovci 72 B3
Drenovo 77 E3
Drenthe 17 D1
Drépano
  (Makedonía) . . . 79 E3
Drépano
  (Pelopónissos) . . 87 E2
Drépano, Akr
  (Anáfi) 91 E1
Drépano, Akr
  (Makedonía) . . . 80 B4
Dresden 53 E2
Dreux 19 E4
Drežnik-Grad 70 C3
Driebergen 16 C3
Driebes 40 B2
Driméa 83 E3
Drimós 79 F3
Drin 76 C3
Drina 76 A1
Drini i Zi 77 D3
Drinit, Gjiri i 76 B3
Drinjača 72 B4
Drinjača R 72 B4
Drinovci 75 E2
Driopída 88 A2
Driós 88 C3
Drisht 76 C3
Driva 100 B2
Drlače 72 C4
Drnholec 57 F1
Drniš 75 D1
Drnje 71 D1

Drnovo 70 C2
Drøbak 105 D3
Drobeta-Turnu
  Severin 114 C1
Drochtersen 48 A2
Drogheda 13 D3
Drogobyč 112 C3
Droichead Átha . . 13 D3
Droichead Nua . . 13 D4
Droitwich 9 E1
Drokija 113 E3
Dromcolliher 14 B3
Drôme (Dépt) . . . 30 C2
Drôme R 30 C2
Dromore (Down) . . 13 E2
Dromore (Tyrone) . 13 E2
Dronero 31 E2
Dronfield 7 D2
Drongaráti 82 B4
Dronne 28 C1
Dronninglund . . . 108 B2
Dronten 16 C2
Drosendorf Stadt . 57 E1
Drossáto 79 F2
Drosseró 79 E2
Drossiá 84 A4
Drossohóri 83 E4
Drossopigí (Árta) . 82 C2
Drossopigí
  (Ioánina) 78 C4
Drossopigí
  (Makedonía) . . . 79 D3
Drottningholm . . 106 B4
Droué 25 E1
Drulingen 21 E3
Drumkeeran 12 C2
Drummore 4 B4
Drumnadrochit . . . 2 C3
Drumochter,
  Pass of 2 C4
Drumshanbo 12 C2

Drusenheim 21 F4
Druskininkai . . . 110 C4
Druten 16 C3
Drvenik (HR) 75 D2
Drvenik (HR) 75 E2
Dryburgh 5 D3
Drymen 4 C2
Duben 53 E1
Dubesar 113 E3
Dubî 53 E3
Dubica 71 D3
Dublin 13 E4
Dublin (Co) 13 D4
Dubna 111 F2
Dubňany 57 F1
Dubno 113 D2
Dubona 73 D3
Duboštica 71 F4
Dubovac 73 D2
Dubovsko 71 D4
Dubrava (HR) . . . 71 D2
Dubrava (Pelješac) 75 F2
Dubrava Stara . . . 71 D2
Dubrave 71 F3
Dubrave Donje . . 72 B3
Dubravica 73 D3
Dubrovnik 76 A2
Ducey 18 B4
Ducherow 49 E2
Duchkov 53 E3
Duchovščina . . . 111 E3
Duclair 19 D3
Dudelange 21 D3
Duderstadt 52 B2
Dudley 9 E1
Dudweiler 54 B2
Dueñas 35 E4
Duero, R 35 D4
Duesund 104 A1
Dufftown 3 D3
Duga Poljana . . . 76 C1

Duga Resa 70 C3
Dugi Otok 74 C1
Dugi Rat 75 D2
Dugo Selo 70 C2
Duingt 27 D4
Duino 59 F3
Duisburg 17 D3
Dukagjin 76 C3
Dukat 77 E2
Duleek 13 D3
Dulje 77 D2
Dülken 17 D3
Dülmen 17 E3
Dulnain Bridge . . . 3 D4
Dulovo 115 E2
Dumbarton 4 C2
Dumbria 34 A1
Dumfries 4 C3
Dumfries and
  Galloway 4 C3
Dun 20 C3
Dunafőldvár . . . 112 B4
Dunajevcy 113 D3
Dunărea 113 E3
Dunaújváros . . . 112 B4
Dunav 72 B2
Dunav 114 D2
Dunbar 5 E2
Dunblane 4 C2
Duncansby Head . . 3 E2
Dundalk 13 D3
Dundalk B 13 E3
Dun Dealgan . . . 13 D3
Dundee 5 D1
Dundonnell 2 C3
Dundrum B 13 E2
Dunfanaghy 12 C1
Dunfermline 5 D2
Dungannon 13 D2
Dungarvan 14 C4

Dungarvan
  Harbour 14 C4
Dungeness 11 D3
Dungiven 13 D1
Dunglow 12 C1
Dunje 77 E4
Dunkeld 5 D1
Dunkerque 19 F1
Dún Laoghaire . . 13 E4
Dun-le-Palestel . . 25 E4
Dunmanus B . . . 14 A4
Dunmanway 14 B4
Dunmore 12 B3
Dunmore East . . 15 D4
Dunnamanagh . . 13 D1
Dún na nGall . . . 12 C2
Dunnet 3 D2
Dunnet Head . . . 3 D2
Dunoon 4 C2
Duns 5 E2
Dunshaughlin . . . 13 D3
Dunstable 9 F2
Dunster 8 C3
Dun-sur-Auron . . 25 F3
Dunvegan 2 B3
Dunvegan Head . . 2 B3
Duolbbadasgai'sa . 95 E1
Đurakovac 76 C2
Durance 30 C3
Durango 36 B1
Duran, Pso 59 D3
Duras 28 C2
Duratón, R 40 A1
Durban-Corbières . 32 B2
Durbuy 50 C4
Dúrcal 44 A3
Đurđđevac 71 D2
Đurđđevića Tara . 76 B1
Đurđevik 72 B4
Düren 51 D3
Durham 5 E4

Durham (Co) 5 E4
Durlach 54 C2
Durlas 14 C3
Durmanec 70 C2
Durmitor 76 B2
Durness 2 C1
Dürnkrut 57 F2
Dürnstein 57 E2
Durrës 76 C4
Durrësit, Gjiri i . . 76 C4
Durrow 12 C4
Dursey I 14 A4
Dursley 9 D2
Durtal 23 E4
Duruelo de la
  Sierra 36 B3
Dusina 75 F1
Düsseldorf 17 E4
Duved 101 D2
Duvno 75 E1
Duži (BH) 75 F1
Duži (BH) 76 A2
Dverberg 94 A3
Dvor 71 D3
Dyfed 8 C1
Dyje 57 E1
Dyrnes 100 B1
Dyrøya 94 B3
Džami tepe 77 F3
Džaniči 75 F1
Džep 77 E1
Dzermiádo 91 E4
Dzeržinsk 111 D4
Dzierżoniów . . . 112 A2
Dziwnów 49 E1
Džumajlija 77 E3
Dźwirzyno 49 F1

E

Eaglescliffe 5 E4
Eani 79 D4
Earith 10 C1
Earlston 5 D2
Earn 5 D1
Easingwold 7 D1
Easky 12 B2
Eastbourne 10 C3
East Dereham 7 F3
Easter Ross 2 C3
East Grinstead 10 C3
East Kilbride 4 C2
Eastleigh 9 E3
East Linton 5 D2
East Retford 7 D2
East Sussex 10 C3
Eaux-Bonnes 37 D2
Eauze 28 B3
Ebbw Vale 9 D2
Ebeleben 52 C2
Ebeltoft 108 B3
Eben 59 F1
Ebenfurth 57 F3
Ebensee 56 C3
Eberbach 55 D1
Ebermannstadt . . . 52 C4
Ebern 52 C4
Eberndorf 70 B1
Ebersbach 53 F2
Ebersberg 56 B3
Eberstein 70 B1
Eberswalde 49 E3
Ebmath 53 D3
Eboli 64 C4
Ebrach 52 C4
Ebreichsdorf 57 F3
Ebreuil 26 A4
Ebro, Emb del . . . 35 F2
Ebro, R 37 D4
Ebstorf 48 B3
Eccleshall 6 C3
Eceabat 115 E3
Echallens 27 D3
Echarmeaux, les . 26 B4

Echarri-Aranaz 36 C2
Echegárate,
  Pto de 36 B1
Echelles, les 30 C1
Echt 17 D4
Echte 52 B2
Echternach 21 D2
Écija 43 E2
Ečka 72 C2
Eckartsberga 52 C2
Eckernförde 48 A1
Eckerö 106 C3
Ecommoy 23 F4
Ecos 19 E3
Ecouché 18 C4
Ecrins, les 31 D2
Ecrins, Massif des . 31 D2
Ecrins,
  Parc Nat des . . . 31 D2
Ecueillé 25 E3
Ed 105 D4
Eda glasbruk . . . 105 D3
Edam 16 C2
Edane 105 E3
Eday 3 E1
Eddrachillis B 2 C2
Ede 16 C3
Edelény 112 B3
Edelweißspitze . . . 59 E2
Eden 5 D4
Edenderry 13 D4
Edenkoben 54 C2
Eder 52 A3
Eder-Stausee 52 A3
Édessa 79 D3
Edewecht 47 E3
Edgeworthstown . . 12 C3
Edinburgh 5 D2
Edipsós 83 F3
Edirne 115 E3
Edland 104 B3
Edolo 58 C3
Edremit 115 E4
Edsåsdalen 101 D2
Edsbro 106 B3
Edsbyn 101 E4
Edsele 101 F2

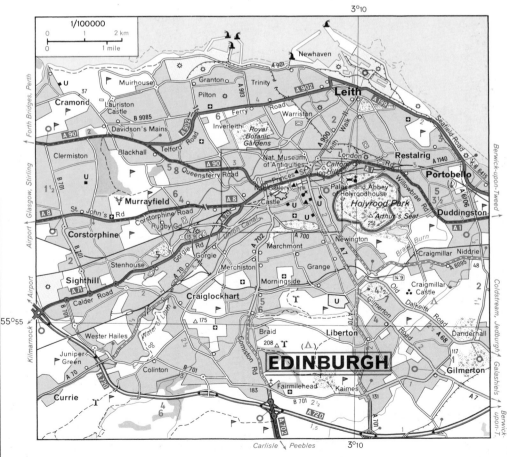

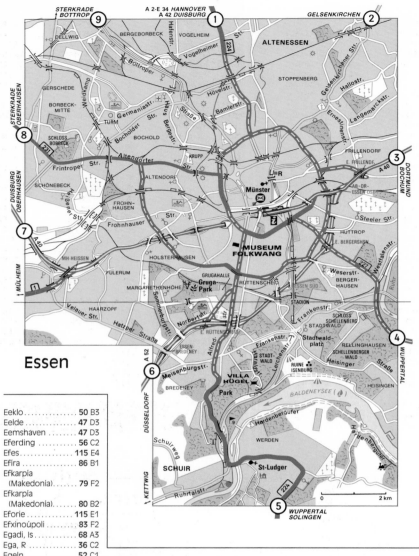

Essen

Eeklo 50 B3
Eelde 47 D3
Eemshaven 47 D3
Eferding 56 C2
Efes 115 E4
Efira 86 B1
Efkarpía
   (Makedonía) 79 F2
Efkarpía
   (Makedonía) 80 B2
Eforie 115 E1
Efxinoúpoli 83 F2
Egádi, Is 68 A3
Ega, R 36 C2
Egeln 52 C1
Egéo Pélagos 84 A1
Eger 112 B3
Egersund 104 A4
Egeskov 108 B4
Egestorf 48 A3
Egg 58 B1
Eggenburg 57 E2
Eggenfelden 56 B2
Eggesin 49 E2
Eggum 94 A3
Eghezée 50 C4
Egiáli 89 D3
Egie 87 D4
Egilsstaðir 96 C2
Égina 87 E2
Égina, N 87 F2
Eginio 79 F3
Égio 83 E4
Égira 87 D1
Egletons 29 E1
Eglinton 13 D1
Egloffstein 55 F1
Egmond aan Zee . . 16 C2
Egósthena 87 E1
Egremont 5 D4
Egtved 108 A3
Egües 36 C2
Eguzon 25 E3
Ehinádes Nissiá . . . 82 C4
Ehingen 55 D3
Ehinos 81 D2
Ehra-Lessien 48 B4
Ehrang-Pfalzel 54 A1
Ehrenberg 52 B3
Ehrenhausen 70 C1
Ehrwald 58 C1
Eibar 36 B1
Eibenstock 53 D3
Eibiswald 70 B1
Eichstätt 55 F2
Eide 100 B2

Eider 48 A2
Eidfjord 104 B2
Eidfjorden 104 B2
Eiði 96 A3
Eidkjosen 94 B2
Eidsborg 104 B3
Eidsbugarden . . . 100 B3
Eidsdal 100 B2
Eidsfjorden 94 A3
Eidsfoss 104 C3
Eidsvåg 100 B2
Eidsvoll 105 D2
Eigg 2 B4
Eigeland 104 A2
Eiken 104 B4
Eikeren 104 C3
Eikesdal 100 B2
Eilean Donan Castle . 2 B3
Eilenburg 53 D2
Eilsleben 52 C1
Einbeck 52 B2
Eindhoven 16 C4
Einsiedeln 58 A2
Eisenach 52 B3
Eisenberg 53 D3
Eisenerz 57 D3
Eisenerzer Alpen . . 57 D4
Eisenhüttenstadt . . 49 F4
Eisenkappel 70 A1
Eisenstadt 57 F3
Eisfeld 52 C3
Eišiškés 110 C4
Eisleben 52 C2
Eisriesenwelt-
   Höhle 59 E1
Eitorf 51 E3
Eivissa 45 D4
Ejea de los
   Caballeros 37 D3
Ejulve 41 E2

Ekára 83 E2
Ekenäs 107 E3
Ekshärad 105 E3
Eksjö 109 D1
Elafohóri 81 E1
Elafoníssi 87 E4
Élafos 82 B2
El Algar 45 D2
El Almendro 42 C2
El Aquián 44 B4
El Arahal 43 E3
El Arenal 45 E3
Elassóna 83 E1
El Atazar, Emb de . 40 B1
Eláti (Makedonía) . 79 E4
Eláti (Thessalía) . . 83 D2
Eláti Mt 82 B3
Elátia 83 F3
Elatohóri 79 E3
Elatoú 83 D4
Elatóvrissi 83 D3
Elba, Isola d' 62 C2
El Barco de Ávila . . 39 E2
Elbasan 76 C4
Elbe 48 B3
Elbe-Lübeck-Kanal . 48 B2
El Berrón 35 D1
Elbe-Seitenkanal . . 48 B4
Elbeuf 19 D3
Elbigenalp 58 C2
Elbingerode 52 C2
Elbląg 110 B4
El Bodón 39 D2
El Bonillo 40 C4
El Bosque 43 E3
El Burgo 43 E3
El Burgo de Osma . 36 A3
El Burgo Ranero . . 35 E3
El Cabaco 39 E2
El Caló 45 D4

El Campo de
   Peñaranda 39 F1
El Carpio 43 F2
El Carpio de Tajo . 39 F3
El Casar de
   Talamanca 40 B2
El Castillo de las
   Guardas 43 D2
El Centenillo 44 A1
El Cerro de
   Andévalo 42 C2
Elche 45 D2
Elche de la Sierra . 44 C1
El Coronil 43 D3
El Cubillo 41 D3
El Cubo de
   Don Sancho 39 D1
El Cubo de Tierra del
   Vino 39 E1
El Cuervo 43 D3
Elda 45 D1
Elde 48 C3
Eldena 48 C3
Elefsína 87 F1
Eleftherés
   (Makedonía) 80 C2
Eleftherés
   (Stereá Eláda) . . . 87 E1
Eleftherés
   (Thessalía) 83 E1
Eléfthero 78 C4
Eleftherohóri 79 D4
Eleftheroúpoli 80 C2
El Ejido 44 B4
Elemir 72 C2
Elena 115 D2
Eleófito 82 C3
Eleohóri 80 C3
Eleohória 80 A3
Eleónas 83 E4
Eleoússa 93 F1

El Escorial 40 A2
El Espinar 40 A2
El Figueró 32 B4
El Formigal 37 D2
Elgå 100 D3
Elgin 3 D3
Elgóibar 36 B1
Elgol 2 B4
El Grado 37 E3
El Grado, Emb de . 37 E3
El Grao 41 E4
El Grau 41 F3
Elhovo 115 E2
El Hoyo de Pinares . 40 A2
Eliá 87 D4
Elie 5 D2
Elikónas, Óros 83 F4
Elimäki 107 F2
Eliniko 86 C2
Elinohóri 81 F1
Elizondo 36 C1
Ełk 110 C4
Ellesmere 6 B3
Ellesmere Port 6 B2
Ellingen 55 E2
Ellon 3 E4
Ellös 108 C1
Ellrich 52 B2
Ellwangen 55 E2
El Madroño 42 C2
El Maestrazgo 41 E2
Elmas 66 B4
El Masnou 32 B4
El Molar 40 B2
El Molinillo 40 A3
El Moral 44 C2
Elmshorn 48 A2
Elne 32 B2
Elnesvågen 100 B2
Elóna 87 D3
Elopía 83 F4
Elorn 22 B2
Élos (Kríti) 90 B3
Élos
   (Pelopónissos) . . 87 D4
Eloúnda 91 E3
Eloyes 27 D1
El Pardo 40 A2
El Paular 40 A1
El Pedernoso 40 B3
El Pedroso 43 D2
El Perelló
   (Catalunya) 41 F2
El Perelló
   (Valencia) 41 E4
Elphin 12 C3
El Picazo 40 C4
El Pinell de Brai . . 41 F1
El Pobo de
   Dueñas 41 D2
El Pont
   d'Armentera 37 F4
El Portal 43 D4
El Port de la Selva . 32 C3
El Port de Llança . . 32 B3
El Prat de
   Llobregat 32 A4
El Puente 36 A1
El Puente del
   Arzobispo 39 F3
El Puerto de
   Sagunto 41 E3
El Puerto de Santa
   María 43 D4
El Real de la Jara . 43 D2
El Real de
   San Vicente 39 F2
El Remolcador,
   Pto 41 E3
El Robledo 39 F4
El Rocío 42 C3
El Romeral 40 B3
El Rompido 42 C3
El Ronquillo 43 D2
El Royo 36 B3
El Rubio 43 E3
Elsa 60 C4
El Saler 41 E4
El Salobral 40 C4
El Saucejo 43 E3
Elsdorf 17 D4
Elserdorf 55 F2
El Serrat 32 A2
Elsfleth 47 F3

Elsterberg 53 D3
Elsterwerda 53 E2
El Tiemblo 40 A2
Eltisley 9 F1
Eltmann 52 C4
El Toboso 40 B3
El Torcal 43 F3
Eltz 51 E4
El Vado, Emb de . . 40 B1
Elvanfoot 4 C3
Elvas 38 C4
Elvekrok 100 B3
El Vellón, Emb de . 40 A2
Elven 22 C4
El Vendrell 37 F4
Elverum 105 D2
El Vicario, Emb de . 40 A4
El Villar de Arnedo . 36 C2
El Viso 43 E1
El Viso del Alcor . . 43 D2
Elx 45 D2
Ely 10 C1
Elygsfors 109 E2
Elzach 54 C3
Elze 52 B1
Emån 109 E2
Embessós 82 C3
Embid 41 D1
Embid de Ariza . . . 36 C4
Émbonas 93 E1
Emboriós (Híos) . . 89 D1
Emboriós (Sími) . . 93 E1
Embrun 31 D2
Emden 47 E3
Emet 115 F4
Emilia-Romagna . . 60 C3
Emlichheim 17 E2
Emmaboda 109 E2
Emmeloord 16 C2
Emmen 17 E1
Emmendingen 54 C3
Emmerich 17 D3
Emocriós 89 E1
Em. Papás 80 B2
Empoli 60 C4
Empúries 32 C3
Ems 17 E1
Emsdetten 17 E2
Ems-Jade-Kanal . . 47 E3
Emskirchen 55 E1
Enafors 101 D2
Enäjärvi 103 E4
Enånger 101 F4
Encamp 32 A2
Encausse 37 E1
Encinas de Abajo . 39 E1
Encinasola 42 C1
Encinedo 34 C3
Endelave 108 B3
Endrinal 39 E2
Enego 59 D3
Enfesta 34 A2
Eng 59 D1
Engadin 58 B3
Engarés 88 C3
Engelberg 27 F3
Engelhartszell 56 C2
Engeløya 97 E1
Engelsdorf 53 D2
Engelskirchen 17 E4
Engen 58 A1
Enger 17 F2
Engerdal 101 D3
Enghien 50 B3
England 9 F1
English Channel . . 10 A4
Engstingen 55 D3
Enguera 41 E4
Enguidanos 41 D3
Enhammarsfjärden
   . . . . 101 F4
Enipéas 83 E2
Enkhuizen 16 C2
Enköping 106 B3
Enna 68 C3
Enneberg 59 D2
Ennell, L 12 C3
Ennepetal 17 E4
Ennezat 26 A4
Ennis 12 B4
Enniscorthy 15 D3
Enniskerry 13 D4
Enniskillen 13 D2
Ennistimon 12 B4

Enns . . . . 57 D
Enns R . . . . 57 D
Eno . . . . 103 F
Enol, L . . . . 35 E
Enonkoski . . . . . . 103 F
Enontekiö . . . . 95 D
Énos, Óros . . . . . . 86 A
Enschede . . . . 17 E
Ensisheim . . . . 27 E
Entlebuch . . . . 27 F
Entraygues-sur-
   Truyère . . . . 29 E
Entredichos . . . . . 40 C
Entre-os-Rios . . . . 34 A
Entrepeñas,
   Emb de . . . . 40 C
Entrevaux . . . . 31 E
Entrèves . . . . 27 E
Entroncamento . . . 38 B
Envalira, Pto de . . 32 A
Envermeu . . . . 19 E
Enviken . . . . 101 E
Enz . . . . 54 C
Enza . . . . 60 B
Enzklösterle . . . . . 54 C
Eochaill . . . . 14 C
Eolie o Lipari, Is . . 69 D
Eo, R . . . . 34 C
Epanomí . . . . 79 F
Epe . . . . 17 D
Epernay . . . . 20 B
Epernon . . . . 19 E
Epidávrou, Kólpos . 87 E
Epidávrou Limirás,
   Kólpos . . . . 87 E
Épila . . . . 36 C
Epinac . . . . 26 B
Epinal . . . . 27 D
Epine, l' . . . . 20 B
Episkopí (Kríti) . . . 90 C
Episkopí (Kríti) . . . 91 E
Episkopí
   (Makedonía) . . . . 79 E
Episkopí
   (Pelopónissos) . . 87 E
Epitálio . . . . 86 B
Eppan . . . . 59 D
Epping . . . . 10 C
Eppingen . . . . 55 D
Epsom . . . . 10 C
Eptahóri . . . . 78 C
Eptálofos . . . . 83 E
Epte . . . . 19 E
Epworth . . . . 7 D
Eraclea . . . . 59 E
Eraclea-Mare . . . . 59 E
Eräjärvi . . . . 103 D
Erásmio, N . . . . . . 81 D
Eratini . . . . 83 E
Eratinó . . . . 80 C
Erátira . . . . 79 D
Erba . . . . 58 B
Erbach . . . . 55 D
Erbalunga . . . . 33 F
Erbendorf . . . . 53 D
Ercina, L de la . . . 35 E
Ercolano . . . . 64 B
Érd . . . . 112 B
Erdek . . . . 115 E
Erdevik . . . . 72 B
Erding . . . . 56 A
Erdre . . . . 23 D
Erdut . . . . 72 B
Eresma, R . . . . 40 A
Eressós . . . . 85 E
Erétria . . . . 84 B
Erezée . . . . 50 C
Erfde . . . . 48 A
Erft . . . . 17 D
Erftstadt . . . . 51 E
Erfurt . . . . 52 C
Erges, R . . . . 39 D
Ergoldsbach . . . . . 56 B
Eriboll, L . . . . 2 C
Erice . . . . 68 A
Ericeira . . . . 38 A
Ericht, L . . . . 2 C
Erikoússa, N . . . . . 78 A
Eriksberg . . . . . . 106 A
Eriksmåle . . . . . . 109 E
Erillas . . . . 43 E
Erimanthos . . . . . . 86 C
Erímanthos, Óros . 86 C
Eripol, Pto del . . . 37 D

Erithrés	87 E1	Escalante	36 A1
Erkelenz	17 D4	Escaldes, les	32 A2
Erkner	49 E4	Escalona	40 A2
Erla	37 D3	Escalonilla	40 A3
Erlangen	55 F1	Escalos de Cima	38 C2
Erlsbach	59 E2	Escandón, Pto de	41 D2
Ermenonville	19 F3	Esca, R	37 D2
Ermidas-Aldeia	42 A1	Escarène, l'	31 E3
Ermióni	87 E2	Escároz	37 D2
Ermoúpoli	88 B2	Escatrón	37 D4
Ermsleben	52 C2	Esch (D)	51 F4
Erndtebrück	17 F4	Esch (L)	21 D2
Erne	13 D3	Eschede	48 B4
Ernée	23 E3	Eschenbach	53 D4
Erne, R	12 C2	Eschershausen	52 B1
Ernstinovo	71 F2	Eschwege	52 B2
Ernstbrunn	57 F2	Eschweiler	51 D3
Erquy	22 C2	Escombreras	45 D3
Errazu	36 C1	Escorihuela	41 E2
Errigal Mt	12 C1	Escudo, Pto del	35 F2
Erris Head	12 A2	Escúllar	44 B3
Erskine Bridge	4 C2	Escurial	39 E4
Erstein	21 E4	Esens	47 E3
Ervenik	75 D1	Esera, R	37 E2
Ervidel	42 B1	Esgueva	35 F4
Ervy	26 B1	Esguevillas de Esgueva	35 F4
Erwitte	17 F3	Esher	9 F2
Erzberg	57 D3	Esino	61 E4
Erzen	76 C4	Esk	5 D3
Erzgebirge	53 E3	Eskifjörður	96 C1
Esbjerg	108 A3	Eskilstuna	106 A4
Esblada	37 F4	Eskisehir	115 F3
Esbo	107 E3		
Escabas, R	40 C2		
Escairón	34 B2		
Escalada	35 F2		

Eskoriatza	36 B1	Essen (Niedersachsen)	17 E2
Esla, R	35 D4	Essen (Nordrhein-Westfalen)	17 E3
Eslarn	56 B1	Essenbach	56 B2
Eslohe	17 F4	Essex	11 D2
Eslöv	109 D3	Essimi	81 E2
Espa	105 D2	Esslingen	55 D2
Espadañedo	34 C3	Essonne	25 F1
Espadán, Sa de	41 E3	Essoyes	26 B1
Espalion	29 E3	Est, Canal de l'	27 D1
Esparreguera	32 A4	Estaca, Pto de la	42 A4
Espedal	100 C3	Estacas de Trueba, Pto de las	35 F2
Espejo	43 F2	Estadilla	37 E3
Espelette	28 A4	Estagel	32 B2
Espelkamp	17 F2	Estaires	19 F1
Espenschied	51 F4	Estarreja	38 B1
Espera	43 D3	Estats, Pic d'	37 F2
Esperó, Pta	45 F2	Estavayer	27 E3
Espichel, C	38 A4	Este	61 D1
Espiel	43 E1	Estella	36 C2
Espigüete	35 E2	Estepa	43 E3
Espinama	35 E2	Estepona	43 E4
Espinho	34 A4	Esteras de Medina	36 B4
Espinilla	35 F2	Esterel	31 E4
Espinosa de Cerrato	35 F4	Esternay	20 A4
Espinosa de los Monteros	36 A1	Esterri d'Àneu	37 F2
Espoo	107 E3	Estissac	26 B1
Esporles	45 E3	Estói	42 B3
Esposende	34 A4	Estoril	38 A4
Espot	37 F2	Estrela, Sa da	38 A3
Espuña, Sa de	44 C2	Estrella	44 A1
Esquedas	37 D3	Estremadura	38 A3
Esquivias	40 A2	Estremoz	38 C4
Essarts, les	24 B3		
Esse	102 C1		

Estret de Collegats	37 F3	Euskirchen	51 E3
Estrées-St-Denis	19 F3	Eußenhausen	52 B3
Esztergom	112 B4	Eutin	48 B2
Etables	22 C2	Evangelismós	83 E1
Etain	20 C3	Evangelistria	83 F4
Etampes	19 F4	Evaux-les-Bains	25 F4
Etaples	19 E1	Évdilos	89 D2
Etel	22 B4	Evendorf	48 B3
Etelhem	109 F4	Evenes	94 B3
Etive, L	4 B1	Evenskjær	94 B3
Etna, M	69 D3	Evergem	50 B3
Etne	104 A3	Everöd	109 D3
Etolía-Akarnanía	82 C3	Evertsberg	101 E4
Etolikó	82 C4	Evesham	9 E1
Etrépagny	19 E3	Evian	27 D3
Etretat	19 D2	Evinohóri	83 D4
Ettelbruck	21 D2	Évinos	83 D3
Etten	16 C3	Evisa	33 F3
Ettenheim	54 C3	Evje	104 B4
Ettington	9 E1	Évlalo	81 D2
Ettlingen	54 C2	Evolène	27 E4
Eugénie-les-Bains	28 B4	Évora	38 B4
Eume, Emb del	34 B1	Évoramonte	38 B4
Eume, R	34 B1	Evran	18 B4
Eupen	51 D4	Evrecy	18 C3
Eura	107 D2	Evreux	19 E3
Eurajoki	107 D2	Evritanía	83 D2
Euratsfeld	57 D3	Evron	23 E3
Eure, R	19 E4	Evropós	79 F2
Eure (Dépt)	19 E3	Évros	81 F2
Eure-et-Loir	25 E1	Évros R	81 F2
Euro Disney	19 F4	Evrostína	87 D1
Europabrücke	59 D2	Evrótas	87 D3
Europoort	16 B3	Evry	19 F4
Euskadi	36 B2		

Évzoni	79 F2
Exaplátanos	79 E2
Éxarhos	83 F4
Excideuil	29 D1
Exe	8 C3
Exeter	8 C3
Exmes	19 D4
Exmoor Nat Pk	8 C3
Exmouth	8 C3
Exohí (Ípiros)	78 C4
Exohí (Makedonía)	79 E3
Exohí (Makedonía)	80 B1
Exómvourgo	88 C2
Exter	17 F2
Extremadura	39 E4
Eydehavn	104 C4
Eye	9 F1
Eyemouth	5 E2
Eye Pen	2 B2
Eygues	30 C2
Eyguières	30 C4
Eygurande	29 E1
Eyjafjörður	96 A1
Eymet	28 C2
Eymoutiers	29 D1
Eyre	28 B3
Eyrieux	30 B2
Eysturoy	96 A3
Eyzies, les	29 D2
Ezcaray	36 B2
Eze	31 E3
Ezine	115 E4

F

Faak	59 F2	Fällfors	98 B4
Fabara	37 E4	Fallingbostel	48 A4
Fåberg	105 D2	Falmouth	8 B4
Fabero	34 C2	Falset	37 F4
Fåborg	108 B4	Falster	108 C4
Fabriano	61 E4	Falterona Mte	61 D3
Fábricas de Riópar	44 C1	Fălticeni	113 D3
Fabro	63 D1	Falun	105 F2
Facinas	43 D4	Falzarego, Pso	59 D3
Facture	28 A2	Fámjin	96 A4
Faenza	61 D3	Fanad Head	13 D1
Færøerne	96 A3	Fanári (Pelopónissos)	87 E2
Faeto	64 B3	Fanári (Pelopónissos)	86 C2
Fafe	34 A4	Fanári (Thessalía)	83 D2
Fágáras	113 D4	Fanári (Thráki)	81 D2
Fágáraşului, M	113 D4	Fanári, Akr	89 D2
Fågelfors	109 E2	Fanefjord	108 C4
Fagernes (Oppland)	104 C2	Fani i Madh	76 C3
Fagernes (Troms)	94 C2	Fani i Vogël	76 C3
Fagersta	105 F3	Fanjeaux	32 A1
Fairford	9 E2	Fannich, L	2 C3
Fair Head	13 E1	Fano	61 E3
Fair I	3 F3	Fanø	108 A3
Fakenham	7 E3	Fanø Bugt	108 A3
Fakovići	72 C4	Fanós	79 F2
Fakse	108 C4	Faouët, le	22 B3
Fakse Ladeplads	108 C4	Faou, le	22 B3
Falaise	18 C4	Farángi Samariás	90 B4
Falakró, Óros	80 C1	Faràngi Víkou	78 C4
Falássarna	90 B3	Fara Novarese	58 A4
Falcade	59 D3	Fårbo	109 E2
Falces	36 C2	Fardes, R	44 A3
Falconara Marittima	61 F3	Fareham	9 E3
Falcone	69 D2	Fårevejle	108 B3
Falcone, C del	66 A1	Färgelanda	105 D4
Falerna	67 E3	Färila	101 F3
Faliráki	93 F1	Farindola	63 F1
Falkefjellet	95 F1	Faringdon	9 E2
Falkenberg (D)	53 E2	Farini d'Olmo	60 B2
Falkenberg (S)	108 C2	Färjestaden	109 E2
Falkensee	49 D4	Farkadóna	83 E1
Falkenstein	53 D3	Farkaždin	72 C2
Falkirk	4 C2	Farlete	37 D3
Falkland	5 D2	Farmakoníssi	89 F2
Falkonéra, N	87 F3	Farnborough	9 F3
Falköping	109 D1	Farnese	63 D2
Fallersleben	48 B4	Farnham	9 F3
		Faro	42 B3
		Fårö	109 F3
		Fårösund	109 F3

Farra d'Alpago	59 E3
Fársala	83 E1
Farsø	108 A2
Farsund	104 A4
Farum	108 C3
Fasano	65 E3
Fašku Vaskojoki	95 E3
Fastov	113 E2
Fátima	38 B3
Fatmomakke	97 E4
Faucille, Col de la	27 D3
Faucogney	27 D1
Faulquemont	21 D3
Fauquembergues	19 E1
Fauske	97 F2
Fauville	19 D3
Fåvang	100 C3
Favara	68 C4
Favareta	41 E4
Faverges	27 D4
Faverney	27 D1
Faversham	11 D3
Favignana, I	68 A3
Fawley	9 E3
Faxaflói	96 A2
Fayence	31 D4
Fayl-Billot	26 C1
Fayón	37 E4
Fay-sur-Lignon	30 B2
Fažana	70 A4
Feale	14 B3
Fécamp	19 D2
Féclaz, la	31 D1
Feda	104 B4
Feggesund	108 A2
Fehmarn	48 B1
Fehmarnbelt	48 B1
Fehmarnsund	48 B1
Fehrbellin	49 D3
Fehring	57 F4
Fejø	108 B4
Feketić	72 B2
Felanitx	45 F3
Felbertauern-tunnel	59 E2
Feld	59 F2
Feldafing	56 A3
Feldbach	57 F4
Feldberg (Baden-Württemberg)	54 C4
Feldberg (Mecklenburg-Vorpommern)	49 D3

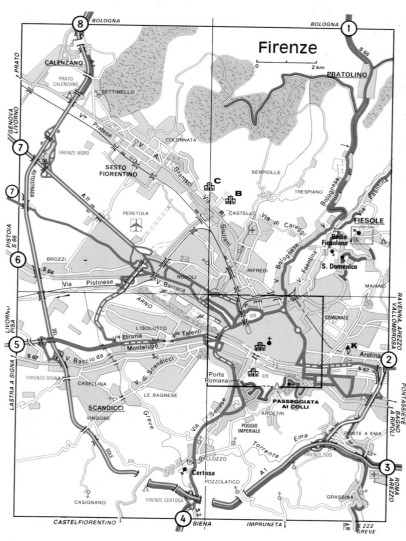

Folkestone Terminal

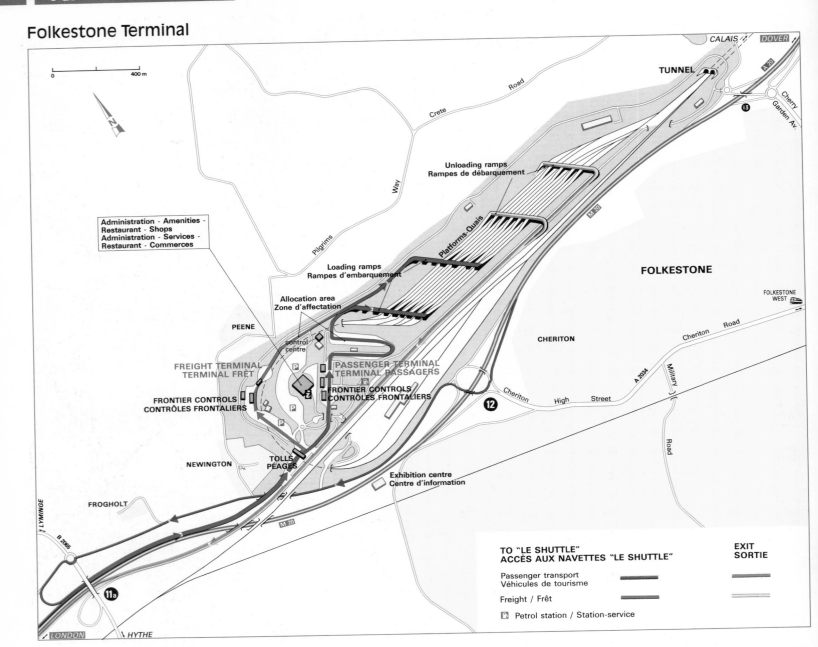

0   400 m

N

Crete   Road

TUNNEL

CALAIS   DOVER

A 20

Cherry Garden Av.

Unloading ramps
Rampes de débarquement

M 20

Pilgrims   Way

Platforms Quais

FOLKESTONE

FOLKESTONE WEST

Administration - Amenities -
Restaurant - Shops
Administration - Services -
Restaurant - Commerces

Loading ramps
Rampes d'embarquement

Allocation area
Zone d'affectation

PEENE

control centre

CHERITON

Cheriton   Road

FREIGHT TERMINAL
TERMINAL FRÊT

PASSENGER TERMINAL
TERMINAL PASSAGERS

FRONTIER CONTROLS
CONTRÔLES FRONTALIERS

FRONTIER CONTROLS
CONTRÔLES FRONTALIERS

A 2034

Military   Road

12

Cheriton   High   Street

NEWINGTON

TOLLS
PÉAGES

Exhibition centre
Centre d'information

FROGHOLT

M 20

11a

LYMINGE

B 2065

TO "LE SHUTTLE"
ACCÈS AUX NAVETTES "LE SHUTTLE"

EXIT
SORTIE

Passenger transport
Véhicules de tourisme

Freight / Frêt

Petrol station / Station-service

LONDON   HYTHE

Feldkirch	58 B2	Ferlach	70 A1
Feldkirchen	59 F2	Ferté-St-Aubin, la	25 E2
Felgueiras	34 A4	Ferté-sous-	
Felixstowe	11 D2	Jouarre, la	20 A3
Fellbach	55 D2	Ferté-Vidame, la	19 D4
Felletin	25 F4	Fertilia	66 A2
Fellingsbro	105 F3	Fervenza, Emb de	34 A1
Felton	5 E3	Festós	91 D4
Feltre	59 D3	Festre, Col du	30 C2
Femer Bælt	108 B4	Festvåg	97 E1
Femundsmarka	101 D3	Fethard	14 C3
Fene	34 B1	Fetlar	3 F1
Fener	59 D3	Fetsund	105 D3
Fenestrelle	31 E1	Feucht	55 F1
Fénétrange	21 E3	Feuchtwangen	55 E2
Feolin Ferry	4 B2	Feunte Dé	35 E2
Fer à Cheval,		Feurs	26 B4
Cirque du	27 E4	Feyzin	30 B1
Feraklós	93 F2	Ffestiniog	6 A3
Ferbane	12 C4	Fflint	6 B2
Ferdinandovac	71 D1	Fiano R.	63 E2
Ferdinandshof	49 E2	Fiastra	61 F4
Fère-		Ficarolo	60 C2
Champenoise	20 B4	Fichtel-gebirge	53 D4
Fère-en-		Fidenza	60 B2
Tardenois	20 A3	Fieberbrunn	59 E1
Fère, la	20 A2	Fier	114 B3
Ferentino	63 F3	Fiera di Primiero	59 D3
Féres	81 F2	Fierzës, Liq i	76 C3
Feria	43 D1	Fiesole	61 D3
Feričanci	71 E2	Fife	5 D2

Ferté-Milon, la	20 A3	Fife Ness	5 D1
Fermanagh	12 C2	Figália	86 C2
Fermo	61 F4	Figeac	29 E2
		Figline Valdarno	61 D4
Fermoselle	34 C4	Figueira da Foz	38 B2
Fermoy	14 C4	Figueira de Castelo	
Fernancaballero	40 A4	Rodrigo	39 D1
Fernán Núñez	43 F2	Figueiró dos	
Ferney-Voltaire	27 D4	Vinhos	38 B2
Fernpaß	58 C1	Figueras	32 B3
Ferrandina	65 D4	Figueres	32 B3
Ferrara	61 D2	Figueruela de	
Ferreira	34 C1	Arriba	34 C3
Ferreira do		Fíhtio	87 D2
Alentejo	42 B1	Filabres, Sa de los	44 B3
Ferreira do Zêzere	38 B3	Filadélfi	80 B3
Ferreiras	42 A3	Filadelfia	67 F3
Ferreras de Abajo	35 D3	Filáki	83 E2
Ferreries	45 F2	Filákio	81 F1
Ferreruela de		Filakopí	88 A4
Huerva	41 D1	Filérimos	93 F1
Ferret, Cap	28 A2	Filey	7 E1
Ferrette	27 E2	Filfola	68 B4
Ferriere	60 B2	Filí	87 F1
Ferrières	25 F1	Filia (Lésvos)	85 F2
Ferrol	34 B1	Fília	
Ferru, M.	66 B3	(Pelopónissos)	86 C1
Ferté-Alais, la	19 F4	Filiátes	82 B1
Ferté-Bernard, la	23 F3	Filiatrá	86 B3
Ferté-Frênel, la	19 D4	Filicudi, I	68 C2
Ferté-Gaucher, la	20 A4	Filiourí	81 E2
Ferté-Macé, la	18 C4		

Filipi	80 C2	Finowfurt	49 E3
Filipiáda	82 C2	Finspång	105 F4
Filipjakov	74 C1	Finsteraarhorn	27 F3
Filipos, Akr.	88 B3	Finsterau	56 C2
Filipstad	105 E3	Finsterwalde	53 E1
Filíra	81 E2	Finström	106 C3
Fillan	100 C1	Fintona	13 D2
Fille-fjell	104 B1	Fintown	12 C1
Filo	83 E2	Fionnphort	4 A1
Filótas	79 D3	Fiorenzuola	
Filottrano	61 F4	d'Arda	60 B2
Finale Emilia	60 C2	Firenze	60 C3
Finale Ligure	31 F3	Firenzuola	61 D3
Fiñana	44 B3	Firminy	30 B1
Finca de la		Firmo	67 E2
Concepción	43 F3	Fischamend Markt.	57 F2
Finchingfield	11 D2	Fischbach	55 F1
Findhorn	3 D2	Fischbeck	48 C4
Finikas	88 B2	Fischen	55 E4
Finikoúndas	86 C4	Fishbourne	9 E3
Finistère	22 B3	Fishguard	8 B1
Finisterre, Emb de	40 A3	Fiskárdo	82 B4
Finja	109 D3	Fiskari	107 E3
Finn	13 D1	Fiskebøl	94 A3
Finneidfjord	97 E3	Fismes	20 A3
Finnentrop	17 F4	Fissíni	85 D1
Finnmark	95 D2	Fisterra	34 A2
Finnmarksvidda	95 D3	Fitero	36 C3
Finnøy	104 A3	Fities	82 C3
Finnsnes	94 B3	Fitjar	104 A2
Finow	49 E3	Fiuggi	63 F3

Fiumicino	63 E3
Fivemiletown	13 D2
Fivizzano	60 B3
Fjällåsen	94 C4
Fjällbacka	105 D4
Fjällnäs	101 D2
Fjärdhundra	106 B3
Fjærland	100 A3
Fjätervålen	101 D3
Fjelie	108 C3
Fjellerup	108 B2
Fjerritslev	108 A2
Fjerze	76 C3
Flå	104 C2
Fladså	108 A3
Fladungen	52 B3
Flaine	27 E4
Flakk	100 C2
Flåm	104 B2
Flamborough Head	7 E1
Flambourári	82 C2
Flámbouro	
(Makedonía)	79 D3
Flámbouro	
(Makedonía)	80 B2
Flamignano	63 F2
Flamouriá	79 D3
Flannan I	2 A2
Flåsjön	101 F1
Flåten	94 C2
Flatey	96 A1

Flatråker 104 A2
Flattnitz 59 F2
Flatval 100 C1
Flèche, la 23 E4
Fleetwood 6 B1
Flekkefjord 104 A4
Flen 106 A4
Flensborg Fjord ... 108 A4
Flensburg 48 A1
Flers 18 C4
Flesberg 104 C3
Flesnes 94 A3
Fleurance 28 C2
Fleurier 27 D3
Fleurus 50 C4
Fleury 19 F4
Fleury-sur-Andelle 19 E3
Fléves, N 87 F2
Flevoland 16 C2
Flexenpaß 58 B2
Flims Waldhaus 58 B2
Flint 6 B2
Flisa 105 D2
Flix 37 E4
Flixecourt 19 F2
Flize 20 C2
Floda 105 D2
Flogny 26 B1
Flöha 53 E3
Flomohóri 87 D4
Flora 77 F3
Florac 29 F3
Flor da Rosa 38 C3
Florennes 50 C4
Florensac 30 A4
Florenville 20 C2
Floreŝty 113 E4
Floriáda 82 C2
Floridia 69 D4
Flórina 79 D2
Flórina (Nomos) 79 D3
Florø 104 A1
Flörsheim-Dalsheim 54 C1
Flötningen 101 D3
Floúda, Akr 92 C1
Floúnda 91 E3
Flüelapass 58 B2
Flüelen 58 A2
Flühli 27 F3
Flumendosa 66 C3
Flumen, R 37 D3
Flumet 27 D4
Fluminimaggiore ... 66 A4
Flums 58 B2
Fluvià, R 32 B3
Foča 76 A1
Foça 115 E4
Foce Verde 63 F3
Fochabers 3 D3
Fockbek 48 A2
Focşani 113 E4
Fódele 91 D3
Foggia 64 C3
Föglö 106 C3
Fohnsdorf 57 D4
Föhr 47 F1
Foiano della Chiana 61 D4
Foinaven 2 C2
Foix 32 A2
Fojnica (BH) 75 F1
Fojnica (BH) 75 F2
Foki 83 E4
Fokstuhø 100 C3
Folda 97 E1
Foldereid 97 D4
Foldfjorden 97 D4
Foleá 80 C2
Folégandros 91 D1
Folégandros, N 91 D1
Følen 104 A3
Folgaria 59 D4
Folgefonna 104 B2
Folgoët, le 22 A2
Folgoso de la Ribera 35 D2
Foligno 63 E1
Folkestad 100 A3
Folkestone 11 D3
Follafoss 101 D1
Folldal 100 C3
Follebu 104 C1

Follina 59 E3
Föllinge 101 E1
Follonica 62 C1
Folmava 56 B1
Folói 86 C2
Fombellida 35 F4
Fond-de-France, le 31 D1
Fondevila 34 B3
Fondi 63 F3
Fondo 59 D3
Fonfría (Aragón) ... 37 D4
Fonfría (Castilla-León) 35 D4
Fongen 101 D2
Fonn 100 A3
Fonni 66 B3
Fonollosa 32 A4
Fonsagrada 34 C2
Fontaine 27 E1
Fontainebleau 19 F4
Fontaine-de-Vaucluse 30 C3
Fontaine-Française 26 C2
Fontaine-Henry 18 C3
Fontaine-le-Dun ... 19 D2
Fontanigorda 60 A3
Fonte Longa 34 B4
Fontenay 26 B2
Fontenay-le-Comte 24 C3
Fontenay-Trésigny 19 F4
Fontevraud-l'Abbaye 25 D2
Fontfroide, Abbaye de 32 B2
Fontgombault 25 D3
Fontibre 35 F2
Fontiveros 39 F1
Fontoy 21 D3
Font-Romeu 32 A2
Fontvieille 30 B4
Fonz 37 E3
Fonzaso 59 D3
Foppolo 58 B3
Forata, Emb de 41 E4
Forbach 21 E3
Forca Canapine 63 F1
Forca Caruso 64 A2
Forca d'Acero 64 A2
Forcall 41 E2
Forcalquier 30 C3
Forcarei 34 A2
Forchheim 55 F1
Forclaz, Col de la ... 27 E4
Forcola di Mte Rest 59 E3
Førde 100 A3
Førdefjorden 104 A1
Förderstedt 52 C1
Fordingbridge 9 E3
Fordongianus 66 B3
Foreland 9 F3
Forenza 64 C3
Foresta di Burgos .. 66 B2
Føresvik 104 A3
Forêt d'Orient, Lac de la 26 B1
Forez, Monts du ... 29 F1
Forfar 5 D1
Forges-les-Eaux ... 19 E3
Forggensee 55 F4
Forio 64 A4
Forlì 61 D3
Forli del Sannio ... 64 A2
Forlimpopoli 61 D3
Formazza 58 A3
Formby 6 B2
Formentera 45 D4
Formentor, C 45 F2
Formerie 19 E3
Formia 64 A3
Formigine 60 C2
Fornaci di Barga ... 60 C3
Fornells 45 F1
Forni Avoltri 59 E2
Forni di Sopra 59 E3
Forno di Zoldo 59 E3
Fornos de Algodres 38 C1
Fornovo di Taro ... 60 B2
Forøy 97 E2

Frankfurt

Forøyar 96 A3
Forres 3 D3
Forsa 101 F3
Forserum 109 D1
Forshaga 105 E3
Forsnes 100 B1
Forssa 107 E2
Forst 53 F1
Fort Augustus 2 C4
Forte dei Marmi ... 60 B3
Forth 55 F1
Forth R. 4 C2
Forth Bridges 5 D2
Forth, Firth of 5 D2
Fort-Mahon 19 E2
Fortore 64 B2
Fortrose 3 D3
Fortuna 45 D2
Fortuneswell 9 D4
Fort William 2 C4
Forvik 97 D3
Fos (Ariège) 37 F2
Fos (Bouches-du-Rhône) 30 C4
Foscagno, Pso di ... 58 C3
Fosnavåg 100 A2
Fossacesia 64 B2
Fossano 31 E2
Fossbakken 94 B3
Fosses 50 C4

Fossli 104 B2
Fossombrone 61 E3
Fotiná 79 E4
Fotolívos 80 B2
Fouesnant 22 B3
Foug 21 D4
Fougères 23 D3
Fougerolles 27 D1
Foula 3 E2
Foulness Pt 11 D2
Fountains Abbey ... 6 C1
Fouras 24 B4
Fourchamboult 26 A2
Fourfourás 91 D4
Foúrka 83 E3
Fourmies 20 B2
Fourná 83 D3
Fournels 29 F2
Fournés 90 B3
Foúrni (Dodekánissa) 89 E2
Fourni (Kríti) 91 E3
Foúrni (Pelopónnissos) 87 E2
Fourniá, Akr 85 E2
Foúrni, N 89 E2
Fours 26 B3
Fousseret, le 37 F1
Foústani 79 E2
Fowey 8 B4
Foxford 12 B2

Foyers 2 C4
Foyle, L 13 D1
Foyle, R 13 D1
Foz 34 C1
Foz do Arelho 38 A3
Foz do Douro 34 A4
Foz Giraldo 38 C2
Frabosa Soprana ... 31 F3
Fraddon 8 B4
Fraga 37 E4
Frailes 44 A3
Fraize 27 E1
Fram 70 C1
Frammersbach 52 B4
Francavilla al Mare .. 64 A1
Francavilla di Sicilia 69 D3
Francavilla Fontana 65 E4
Francavilla in Sinni 65 D4
Francker 16 C1
Francofonte 69 D4
Francolí, R. 37 F4
Francorchamps ... 51 D4
Frangádes 82 C1
Frangísta 83 D3
Frangokástelo 90 C4
Frangy 27 D4

Frankenberg (Hessen) 52 A3
Frankenberg (Sachsen) 53 E3
Frankenburg 56 C3
Frankenmarkt 56 C3
Frankenstein 54 C1
Frankenthal 54 C1
Frankfurt am Main 52 A4
Frankfurt an der Oder 49 F4
Fränk Rezat 55 E2
Fränk Saale 52 B4
Františkovy Lázně ... 53 D4
Franzburg 49 D1
Franz-Josephs-Höhe 59 E2
Frascati 63 E3
Frascineto 67 E2
Frasdorf 56 B3
Fraserburgh 3 E3
Frasno, Pto del 36 C4
Fratel 38 C3
Fratta Polesine 61 D2
Frauenfeld 58 A1
Frauenkirchen 57 F3
Frauenstein 53 E3
Frechen 17 E4
Frechilla 35 E3
Freckenhorst 17 F3

Fredensborg 108 C3
Fredericia 108 B3
Frederikshavn 108 B1
Frederikssund 108 C3
Frederiksværk 108 C3
Fredrika 102 A1
Fredriksberg 105 E3
Fredrikstad 105 D3
Fregenal de la Sierra 42 C1
Fregene 63 E3
Fréhel, Cap 22 C2
Frei 100 B2
Freiberg 53 E3
Freiberger Mulde ... 53 D2
Freiburg (Baden-Württemberg) ... 54 C4
Freiburg (Niedersachsen) 48 A2
Freienhufen 53 E1
Freilassing 56 C3
Freilingen 51 F4
Freising 55 F3
Freistadt 57 D2
Freital 53 E2
Freiwalde 53 E1
Freixedas 38 C1
Freixido 34 C3
Freixo de Espada à Cinta 39 D1
Fréjus 31 D4

Fréjus, Tunnel du... 31 D1
Frenchpark........ 12 C3
Frêne, Col du 31 D1
Freren........... 17 E2
Freshford 12 C4
Freshwater 9 E3
Fresnay-sur-
Sarthe 23 F3
Fresne-St-Mamès . 27 D2
Fresnes-en-
Woëvre 20 C3
Fresno Alhándiga . 39 E1
Fresvikbreen 104 B1
Freudenberg (Baden-
Württemberg) .. 55 D1
Freudenberg (Nord-
rhein-Westfalen) . 17 F4
Freudenstadt 54 C3
Frévent 19 F2
Freyburg 52 C2
Freyenstein 48 C3
Freyung 56 C2
Frí 93 D3
Frias 36 A2
Frías de Albarracín . 41 D2
Fribourg 27 E3
Fridingen 55 D3
Friedberg (A) 57 F3
Friedberg (Bayern) . 55 F3
Friedberg (Hessen) . 52 A4

Friedeburg 47 E3
Friedersdorf 49 E4
Friedland
(Mecklenburg-
Vorpommern) ... 49 D2
Friedland
(Niedersachsen).. 52 B2
Friedrichroda..... 52 B3
Friedrichshafen ... 55 D4
Friedrichskoog ... 47 F2
Friedrichsort 48 A1
Friedrichstadt 47 F1
Friedrichsthal 54 B2
Friesach 57 D4
Friesack 49 D4
Friesland 16 C1
Friesoythe 17 E1
Frigiliana 44 A4
Frihetsli 94 C3
Friis veien 100 C3
Frikes 82 B4
Frilingiánika 90 A1
Frinton-on-Sea ... 11 D2
Friol 34 B2
Fristad 109 D1
Fritsla 108 C1
Fritzlar 52 A3
Friuli-Venezia Giulia . 59 E3
Frizington 5 D4
Frodsham......... 6 B2

Frogner.......... 105 D3
Frohavet......... 100 C1
Frohburg 53 D2
Frohnleiten 57 E4
Froissy 19 F3
Froitzheim 51 D3
Frome 9 D3
Fromentine 24 A3
Frómista 35 F3
Frontenay-Rohan-
Rohan 24 C4
Frontenhausen.... 56 B2
Frontera 42 A4
Frontignan 30 A4
Fronton 29 D3
Frosinone 63 F3
Frosolone 64 B3
Frösön 101 E2
Frosta.......... 100 C1
Frostavallen 109 D3
Frøstrup 108 A2
Frouard 21 D4
Froússa 82 C2
Frövi 105 F3
Frøya 100 B1
Frøyfjorden 100 B1
Frøysjøen 100 A3
Fruges 19 F1
Fruška.......... 72 B2

Frutigen......... 27 E3
Frýdek-Místek.... 112 B3
Ftelia 80 C2
Ftéri (Makedonia)... 79 E4
Ftéri
(Pelopónissos) .. 86 C1
Fthiótida........ 83 E3
Fucecchio 60 C4
Fuencaliente (Castilla-
la-Mancha) 43 F1
Fuencaliente
(Is Canarias) 42 A4
Fuendejalón...... 36 C3
Fuendetodos 37 D4
Fuengirola 43 F4
Fuenlabrada...... 40 A2
Fuenlabrada de
los Montes 39 F4
Fuenmayor 36 B2
Fuensalida 40 A3
Fuensanta de
Martos 43 F2
Fuensanta,
Emb de la.... 44 C1
Fuente-Alamo.... 45 D1
Fuente Alamo.... 45 D2
Fuentecén 35 F4
Fuente de Cantos . 43 D1
Fuente del
Maestre 43 D1

Fuente de Pedro
Naharro 40 B3
Fuente de Piedra.. 43 E3
Fuente el Fresno .. 40 A4
Fuenteguinaldo ... 39 D2
Fuente la Higuera . 45 D1
Fuentelapeña 39 E1
Fuente Obéjuna .. 43 E1
Fuente Palmera .. 43 E2
Fuentepinilla 36 B3
Fuentesauco 39 E1
Fuentes de
Andalucía 43 E2
Fuentes de
Ayódar 41 E3
Fuentes de Ebro .. 37 D4
Fuentes de León .. 43 D1
Fuentes de Nava .. 35 E3
Fuentes de Oñoro . 39 D1
Fuentes de Ropel . 35 D3
Fuentes de
Valdepero.... 35 F3
Fuentidueña 35 F4
Fuentidueña
de Tajo....... 40 B3
Fuerte del Rey ... 44 A2
Fuerteventura ... 42 C4
Fügen.......... 59 D1
Fuglebjerg 108 B4
Fugløysundet ... 94 C2

Fulda............ 52 B3
Fulda R.......... 52 B3
Fulgatore 68 A3
Fulpmes 59 D2
Fulufjället 101 D4
Fumay 20 B2
Fumel 28 C3
Funchal 42 A3
Fundão 38 C2
Funes 59 D2
Fuorn, Pso dal.... 58 C3
Furadouro 38 B1
Furci 64 B2
Furkapass 58 A3
Furnace 4 B2
Furnás 45 D3
Fürstenau 17 E2
Fürstenberg 49 D3
Fürstenfeld 57 F4
Fürstenfeldbruck... 55 F3
Fürstenlager 54 C1
Fürstenwalde ... 49 E4
Fürstenwerder ... 49 E3
Fürstenzell 56 C2
Furtei 66 B3
Fürth 55 E1
Furth 56 B1
Furtwangen 54 C3
Furudal 101 E4

Furuflaten 94 C2
Fuscaldo 67 E2
Fusch 59 E1
Fuschl 56 C3
Fuseta 42 B3
Fushë Arrez 76 C3
Fushë Muhur..... 76 C3
Fusignano 61 D2
Füssen 55 E4
Fustiñana 36 C3
Futa, Pso della... 60 C3
Futog 72 C2
Futrikelv 94 B2
Fuzine 70 B3
Fyn 108 B4
Fyne, L 4 B2
Fynshav 108 B4
Fyresdal 104 B3
Fyresvatn 104 B3
Fyrkat 108 B2

G

Gaaldorf........... 57 D4
Gabarret 28 B3

Gabela 75 F2
Gaberl-Sattel 57 E4
Gabia
la Grande 44 A3
Gabicce Mare 61 E3

Gabriel y Galán,
Emb de 39 E2
Gabrovka......... 70 B2
Gabrovo 115 D2
Gacé 19 D4

Gacilly, la 23 D4
Gacko 76 A2
Gad'ač 113 F1
Gäddede 97 E4
Gadebusch 48 B2

Cádor 44 B3
Gádor, Sa de 44 B3
Gadžin Han 77 E1
Gǎeşti 115 D1
Gaeta 64 A3
Gaeta, Golfo di.... 64 A3
Gagarin 111 F2
Gaggenau 54 C2
Gagnef 105 F2
Gail 59 E2
Gailbergsattel.... 59 E2
Gaildorf 55 D2
Gailey 9 E1
Gaillac......... 29 D3
Gaillimh 12 B3
Gaillon 19 E3
Gainsborough ... 7 D2
Gairloch 2 B3
Gaj 73 D2
Gajdobra 72 B2
Gajsin 113 E3
Gajvoron 113 E3
Gakovo 72 B1
Galan 37 E1
Galanádo 88 C3
Galaniá 90 A2
Galanta 112 A3
Galapagar 40 A2
Galarinós 80 A3
Galaroza 42 C2
Galashiels 5 D2
Galatádes 79 E3
Galatáki........ 84 A3
Galatás
(Argolída) 87 E2
Galatás
(Korinthía) 87 D1
Galáti.......... 113 E4
Galatina 65 F4
Galatiní 79 D3
Galátista 80 A3
Galatone 65 F4
Galaxídi 83 E4
Galdakao 36 B1
Galdhøpiggen ... 100 B3
Galeata 61 D3
Galegos 38 C3
Galende 34 C3
Galera 44 B2
Gagliano del
Capo 65 F4
Galibier, Col du 31 D1
Galicia 34 B2
Galičica 77 D4
Galičnik....... 77 D3
Galikós 79 F3
Galipsós 80 B2
Galisteo 39 D2

Galiz, Pto de 43 D4
Gallarate 60 A1
Gallardon 19 E4
Gallargues 30 B3
Gállego, R 37 D3
Galley Head..... 14 B4
Galliate 60 A1
Gallipoli 65 F4
Gällivare 98 B2
Gallneukirchen .. 57 D2
Gällö 101 E2
Gallo, C. 68 B2
Gallo, R. 41 D2
Galloway Forest
Park........ 4 C3
Gallspach 56 C3
Gallur......... 36 C3
Gälöfjärden 106 B4
Galston 4 C2
Galten 108 B3
Galtür 58 C2
Galty Mts 14 C3
Galveias 38 B3
Gálvez 40 A3
Galway 12 B3
Galway (Co) 12 B3
Galway B 12 B4
Gamaches 19 E2
Gambarie 67 E4
Gaming 57 D3
Gamleby 109 E1
Gammelstaden .. 98 C3
Gammertingen... 55 D3
Gampenjoch 58 C3
Gams 58 B2
Gamvik 95 E1
Gamzigrad 73 E4
Ganacker 56 B2
Gand 50 B3
Gándara 34 B1
Ganderkesee ... 17 F1
Gandesa 41 F1
Gandía....... 41 E4
Gandino 58 B4
Gandria...... 58 A4
Gangáles 91 D4
Ganges 29 F3
Gangi....... 68 C3
Gangkofen ... 56 B2
Gannat 26 A4
Gänserndorf... 57 F2
Gañuelas 45 D2
Gap 31 D2
Garabit, Viaduc de . 29 F2

Gara, L........... 12 C3
Garching 56 B3
Garcia 37 E4
Garcia de Sola,
Emb de 39 F4
Garciaz 39 E3
Gard (Dépt) 30 B2
Gard R. 30 B3
Garda 60 C1
Garda, L di 58 C4
Gardanne 30 C4
Cårdby 109 E2
Garde 109 F4
Garde-Freinet, la . 31 D4
Gardelegen..... 48 C4
Gardermoen 105 D3
Gardiken 97 F3
Gardíki 83 D3
Garding 47 F2
Gardjönäs 97 F3
Gärdnäs 101 E1
Gardone Riviera .. 60 C1
Gardone Val
Trompia 60 B1
Gärdslösa 109 E2
Gardunha, Sa da.. 38 C2
Garður 96 A2
Garešnica 71 D2
Garessio 31 F3
Garforth 7 D2
Gargaliáni 86 B3
Gargano,
Promontorio del.. 64 C2
Garganta 44 B2
Garganta del
Chorro 43 E3
Garganta del
Escalar 37 E2
Garganta la Olla.. 39 E2
Gargantas 40 C2
Gargantas del Sil.. 34 C3
Gargellen 58 B2
Gargilesse 25 E3
Gargnano 58 C4
Gargnäs....... 98 A3
Garigliano 64 A3
Gariglione, Mte .. 67 F3
Garípa 91 E4
Garlasco 60 A2
Garlin....... 28 B4
Carlstorf 48 B3
Garmisch-Parten-
kirchen 55 E4
Carona, R 37 F2
Caronne 28 B2
Carpenberg ... 105 F2
Carphyttan ... 105 F4
Garraf 32 A4

Gent

ZELZATE · TERNEUZEN 39 km · ZELZATE 21 km · ST NIKLAAS 34 km · EVERGEM · OOSTAKKER · WONDELGEM · MARIAKERKE · SINT AMANDSBERG · DESTELBERGEN · GENTBRUGGE · LEDEBERG · HEUSDEN · MELLE · MERELBEKE · ZWIJNAARDE · ZEVERGEM · GONTRODE · O.L.V. VAN LOURDES · Dwight Eisenhowerlaan · Groenstraat · Alfons Braeckmanlaan · BEGIJNHOF · ST-BAAFSKATHEDRAAL · Dendermondsesteenweg · Schelde · Laarnebaan · Brusselsesteenweg · Hundelgemse steenweg · FLANDERS EXPO · Kortrijksesteenweg · Ringvaart · Industrieweg · Scheepen Sifferdok · Grootdok · Voorhaven · Botestr. · Ringvaart · Tramstr. · KNOKKE-HEIST 49 km, EEKLO 20 km · OOSTENDE 66 km, BRUGGE 49 km · DEINZE 17 km · KORTRIJK 45 km · OUDENAARDE 27 km · ANTWERPEN 60 km, ST NIKLAAS 39 km · LAARNE 13 km · AALST 27 km · AALST 33 km, BRUXELLES 55 km · 0 — 2 km

Garrafe de Torio	35	D2
Garray	36	B3
Garrel	17	E1
Garrovillas	39	D3
Garrucha	44	C3
Gars	57	E2
Gartempe	25	E4
Gartow	48	C3
Gartz	49	E3
Garvagh	13	D1
Garvão	42	A2
Garve	2	C3
Garynahine	2	B2
Garz	49	D1
Gaschurn	58	B2
Cassino Torinese	31	E1
Gastoúni	86	B1
Cata (Extremadura)	39	D2
Gata (Valencia)	45	E1
Gata, C de	44	C4
Gata, Sa de	39	D2
Gatčina	111	D1
Gatehouse of Fleet	4	C3
Gateshead	5	E3
Gattinara	31	F1
Gattorna	60	A3
Catwick Airport	10	C3
Caucin	43	E4
Cauja	110	C2
Caula	100	C2
Cauldalen	100	C2
Caulstad	101	D1
Causta	104	C3
Cauting	56	A3
Gavà	32	A4
Gavardo	60	B1
Gavarnie	37	E2
Gavarnie, Cirque de	37	E2
Gavdopoúla, N	90	B4
Gávdos, N	90	C4
Cave d'Oloron	28	A4
Gavi	60	A2
Gavião	38	B3
Gavia, Pso di	58	C3
Cavirate	58	A4
Cävle	106	B2
Gävleborgs Län	101	E3
Cävlebukten	106	B2
Cavoi	66	B2
Gavray	18	B4

Gávrio	88	B1
Gåvsta	106	B3
Gåxsjö	101	E1
Gazzuolo	60	C2
Gdańsk	110	A4
Gdov	111	D1
Gdynia	110	A4
Geaune	28	B4
Gebesee	52	C2
Gebze	115	F3
Gedern	52	A4
Gediz	115	F4
Gediz R	115	E4
Gedser	108	C4
Geel	50	C3
Geertruidenberg	16	C3
Geesthacht	48	B3
Gefell	53	D3
Géfira (Makedonía)	79	F3
Géfira (Pelopónissos)	87	E4
Gefiria	83	E2
Gefrees	53	D4
Gehren	52	C3
Geilenkirchen	17	D4
Geilo	104	C2
Geiranger	100	B3
Geirangerfjorden	100	B3
Geisa	52	B3
Geiselhöring	56	B2
Geisenfeld	55	F2
Geisenhausen	56	B2
Geising	53	E3
Geisingen	54	C4
Geislingen	55	E2
Geismar	52	B2
Geisnes	97	D4
Geithain	53	D2
Gela	68	C4
Gelderland	17	D2
Geldern	17	D3
Geldrop	16	C4
Geleen	17	D4
Gelibolu	115	E3
Gelnhausen	52	A4
Gelsa	37	D4
Gelsdorf	51	E4
Gelsenkirchen	17	E3
Gelting	48	A1
Gembloux	50	C4
Gemeaux	26	C2

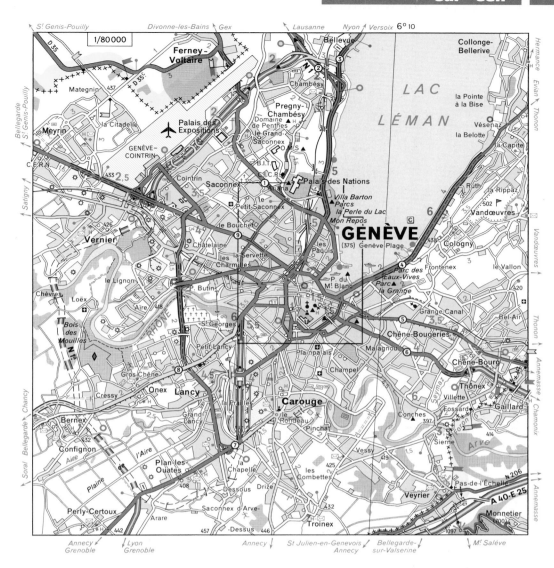

Gémenos	30	C4
Gemert	17	D3
Gemlik	115	F3
Gemona del Friuli	59	F3
Gémozac	28	B1
Gemünd	51	D4
Gemünden (Bayern)	52	B4
Gemünden (Hessen)	52	A3
Gemünden (Rheinland-Pfalz)	54	B1

Genádio	93	E2
Gençay	25	D4
Generalisimo Emb del	41	D3
Generalski Stol	70	C3
General-Toševo	115	E2
Generoso, Mte	58	A4
Genève	27	D4
Genil, R	43	E2
Genisséa	81	D2
Génissiat, Barrage de	27	D4

Genk	50	C3
Genlis	26	C2
Genna Cruxi	66	C3
Gennargentu, Mti del	66	B3
Gennep	17	D3
Gennes	24	C2
Génolhac	29	F3
Genova	60	A3
Genova, Golfo di	60	A4
Genova, Val di	58	C3
Gent	50	B3

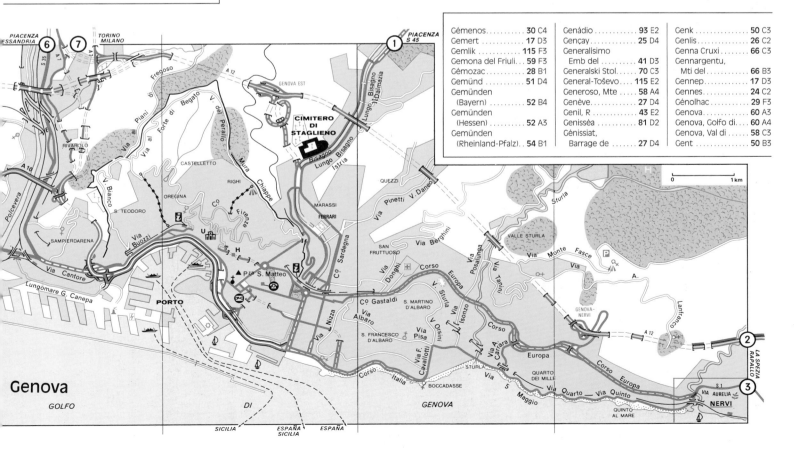

Genova

Genthin 49 D4	Germersheim 54 C2	Ghisonaccia 33 F3	Gillingham (Kent) . . . 11 D2	Gizéla 81 D2	Gleisdorf 57 E4	Gloucestershire 9 D2
Gentioux 29 D1	Gernika-Lumo 36 B1	Ghisoni 33 F3	Gill, L 12 C2	Gizycko 110 B4	Glen Albyn 2 C4	Gložan 72 B2
Genzano di	Gernrode 52 C2	Giali, N. 89 F4	Gilze 16 C3	Gjalicë, M. 77 D3	Glenamoy 12 B2	Głubczyce 112 A2
Lucania 64 C3	Gernsbach 54 C2	Giáltra 83 F3	Gimenells 37 E3	Gjendesheim 100 B3	Glénan, I de 22 B4	Glubokoje 111 D3
Genzano di Roma . . 63 E3	Gernsheim 54 C1	Gianitsá 79 E3	Gimnó 84 B4	Gjermundshavn 104 A2	Glenariff 13 E1	Głuchołazy 112 A2
Georgiani 79 E3	Gerola Alta 58 B3	Gianitsi 84 C4	Gimo 106 B3	Gjesvær 95 D1	Glenarm 13 E1	Gluchov 113 F1
Georgioúpoli 90 C3	Geroliménas 87 D4	Giannádes 82 A1	Gimont 28 C4	Gjirokastër 114 C4	Glenbeigh 14 A4	Glücksburg 48 A1
Georgitsi 87 D3	Gerolstein 51 D4	Giannutri, I di 63 D2	Gingst 49 D1	Gjøra 100 C2	Glen Carron 2 C3	Glückstadt 48 A2
Gera 53 D3	Gerolzhofen 52 B4	Gianoúli 81 F2	Ginosa 65 D4	Gjøv 96 A3	Glen Coe 4 C1	Glumsø 108 C4
Geraardsbergen 50 B3	Gerona 32 B3	Giant's Causeway . . . 13 E1	Ginzling 59 D2	Gjøvik 105 D2	Glencolumbkille . . . 12 C1	Gluščí 72 C3
Gerabronn 55 E2	Geroplátanos 80 B3	Giardini 69 D3	Giogo di Scarperia . . 61 D3	Gjuhezës, Kepi i . . . 114 B4	Glendalough 13 D4	Glyn Ebwy 9 D2
Gerace 67 F4	Gerovo 70 B3	Giáros, N 88 B2	Gioia del Colle 65 E3	Gla 83 F4	Glenelg 2 B4	Gmund (D) 56 A4
Gerakári (Kríti) 90 C4	Gerri de la Sal 37 F3	Giarratana 69 D4	Gioia Tauro 67 E4	Gladbeck 17 E3	Glenfinnan 2 B4	Gmünd (Kärnten) . . . 59 F2
Gerakári	Gerovo 28 C3	Giarre 69 D3	Gióna, Óros 83 E3	Gladenbach 17 F4	Glengarriff 14 A4	Gmünd (Nieder-
(Makedonía) 79 F2	Gers (Dépt) 28 C4	Giat 29 E1	Gioúhtas 91 D4	Gladstad 97 D3	Glenluce 4 C3	österreich) 57 D2
Gerakaroú 80 A3	Gersau 58 A2	Giaveno 31 E1	Gioúra, N. 84 B2	Glafsfjorden 105 E3	Glen More 2 C4	Gmunden 56 C3
Gerakás 87 E4	Gersfeld 52 B4	Giba 66 B4	Giovinazzo 65 D3	Gláma 96 A1	Glen More Forest	Gnarp 101 F3
Gérakas, Akr 84 B2	Gerstetten 55 E2	Gibostad 94 B2	Giovi, Pso dei 60 A3	Glamis 5 D1	Park 3 D4	Gnesta 106 B4
Geráki 87 D3	Gersthofen 55 E3	Gibraleón 42 C2	Girifalco 67 F3	Glamis Castle 5 D1	Glennamaddy 12 C3	Gniezno 112 A1
Gerakiní 80 B4	Gerswalde 49 E3	Gibraltar 43 E4	Giromagny 27 E1	Glamoč 71 E4	Glenrothes 5 D2	Gnjilane 77 D2
Gerakovoúni 83 F3	Gesäuse 57 D3	Gideå 102 A2	Girona 32 B3	Glamorgan 8 C2	Glenties 12 C1	Gnoien 49 D2
Geránia 87 E1	Gescher 17 E3	Gideälven 102 A2	Gironde 28 B1	Glamsbjerg 108 B3	Glifa 83 F3	Gnosjö 109 D2
Gérardmer 27 E1	Geseke 17 F3	Gieboldehausen 52 B2	Gironde (Dépt) 28 B2	Glan 54 B1	Glifáda	Goat Fell 4 B2
Geras 57 E2	Gesualdo 64 B3	Gien 26 A2	Gironella 32 A3	Glandon, Col du . . . 31 D1	(Atikí-Piréas) . . . 87 F1	Goce Delčev 115 D3
Gerbéviller 21 D4	Geta 106 C2	Giengen 55 E2	Girvan 4 C3	Glandorf 17 F2	Glifáda (Fokída) 83 D4	Goch 17 D3
Gerbier de Jonc 30 B2	Getafe 40 A2	Giens 31 D4	Gisburn 6 C2	Glan-	Glikí 82 B2	Godafoss 96 B1
Gerbini 69 D3	Gets, les 27 E4	Gießen 51 F3	Gislaved 109 D2	Münchweiler 54 B1	Glikóvrissi 87 D4	Godalming 9 F3
Gerbstedt 52 C2	Gettorf 48 A1	Giethoorn 17 D2	Gisors 19 E3	Glanshammar 105 F4	Glina 70 C3	Godby 106 C2
Gerena 43 D2	Gevelsberg 17 E4	Gifhorn 48 B4	Gissi 64 B2	Glarus 58 A2	Glittertind 100 B3	Godelheim 52 A2
Gerês 34 B3	Gevgelija 77 F4	Gigha I 4 B2	Gistel 50 A3	Glasgow 4 C2	Gliwice 112 B2	Goderville 19 D3
Gerês, Sa do 34 B3	Gévora, R 38 C4	Giglio, I del 62 C2	Githio 87 D4	Glas Maol 3 D4	Globino 113 F2	Godmanchester 9 F1
Geretsried 56 A3	Gevrey-	Giglio Porto 62 C2	Gittun 98 A2	Glastonbury 9 D3	Globočica 77 D2	Gödöllő 112 B4
Gérgal 44 B3	Chambertin 26 C2	Gignac 30 A4	Giugliano in	Glauchau 53 D3	Gloggnitz 57 E3	Godovič 70 A2
Géfira 87 E4	Gex 27 D3	Gijón 35 D1	Campo 64 B4	Glava 105 D3	Głogów 112 A2	Goduš 72 B3
Geringswalde 53 E2	Geysir 96 B2	Gilching 56 A3	Giuliana 68 B3	Glavatičevo 75 F1	Glomfjord 97 E2	Goeree 16 B3
Gerlitzen 59 F2	Geyve 115 F3	Gilford 13 E2	Giulianova 64 A1	Glavičice 72 B3	Glomma 105 D3	Goes 16 B3
Gerlos 59 D2	Gföhl 57 E2	Giljevo 76 C1	Give 108 A3	Glavnik 77 D1	Glommersträsk 98 B3	Göggingen 55 F3
Gerlospá 59 D1	Ghedi 60 B1	Gilleleje 108 C3	Givors 30 B1	Gledić 73 D4	Gloppet 102 B2	Göhren 49 D1
Gérmas 79 D3	Gheorgheni 113 D4	Gillhov 101 E2	Givry 26 C3	Gledićske pl 73 D4	Glossop 6 C2	Goirle 16 C3
Germering 55 F3	Ghilarza 66 B3	Gillingham (Dorset) . . 9 D3	Givry-en-Argonne . . 20 C3	Gleinalmtunnel 57 E4	Gloucester 9 D2	Góis 38 B2

Goito 60 C1
Gokčanica 73 D4
Gokçe 115 E3
Gol 104 C2
Gola 71 D1
Golada 34 B2
Golaja Pristan' . . . 113 F3
Golczewo 49 F2
Goldbach 52 A4
Goldberg 48 C2
Goldenstedt 17 F1
Golegã 38 B3
Golema reka 77 D3
Golemo Selo 77 E2
Goleniów 49 F2
Goleš 77 E2
Golfe-Juan 31 E4
Golfo Aranci 66 C1
Goli 70 B4
Golija (Crna
  Gora) 76 A2
Golija (Srbija) 76 C1
Goljak 77 D2
Goljaki, M. 70 A2
Goljam Perelik . . . 115 D3
Göllersdorf 57 E2
Golling 59 E1
Golo 33 F3
Golpejas 39 E1
Golspie 3 D3
Golßen 53 E1
Golubac 73 E3
Golubovci 76 B3
Golubovec 70 C2
Golzow 49 D4
Gómara 36 B3
Gomáti 80 B3
Gombrèn 32 A3
Gomecello 39 E1
Gomel' 111 E4
Gomera 42 A4
Gómfi 83 D2
Gommern 52 C1
Goncelin 31 D1
Gondomar (E) 34 A3
Gondomar (P) 34 A4
Gondrecourt 20 C4
Gönen 115 E3
Góni 83 E1
Goniá 90 B3
Goniés 91 D3
Gonnesa 66 B4
Gonnosfanadiga . . . 66 B4
Goole 7 D2
Goor 17 D2
Goppenstein 27 F3
Göppingen 55 D2
Gora 70 C3
Goražde 76 A1
Gördalen 101 D3
Gordes 30 C3
Gorenja Vas 70 A2
Gorey (GB) 18 B3
Gorey (IRL) 15 D3
Gorgona, I di 60 B4
Gorgonzola 60 A1
Gorgopótamos 78 C4
Gorica (BH) 75 E2
Gorica
  (Makedonija) 77 D4
Goričan 71 D1
Gorice 70 B3
Gorinchem 16 C3
Goritsá 87 D3
Gorizia 59 F3
Gorjanci 70 C2
Gorki 111 E3
Gorleston-on-Sea . . 7 F4
Gorlice 112 B3
Görlitz 53 F2
Gorna
  Orjahovica 115 D2
Gornja Dobrinja . . . 72 C4
Gornja Grabovica . . 75 F1
Gornja Kamenica . . 73 F4
Gornja Klina 77 D2
Gornja Ljubovidđa . 72 C4
Gornja Ljuta 75 F1
Gornja Ploča 70 C4
Gornja Radgona . . . 70 C1
Gornja Sabanta . . . 73 D4
Gornja Sanica 71 D4
Gornja Slatina 71 F3
Gornja Toplica 72 C4

Gornja Toponica . . . 73 E4
Gornja Tuzla 72 B3
Gornje Dubočke . . . 76 A2
Gornje Ratkovo . . . 71 E4
Gornje Selo 75 D2
Gornji Grad 70 B2
Gornji Kokoti 76 B3
Gornji Kosinj 70 C4
Gornji Lapac 71 D4
Gornji Lukavac 76 A2
Gornji Milanovac . . 73 D4
Gornji Petrovci 70 C1
Gornji Podgradci . . 71 D3
Gornji Rajič 71 E3
Gornji Stepoš 73 E4
Gornji Vakuf 75 E1
Gornji Zabar 71 F3
Gorno Orizari 77 E3
Goro 61 D2
Gorodišče 113 F2
Gorodn'a 111 E4
Gorodok (RB) 111 D3
Gorodok (UKR) 112 C2
Gorredijk 17 D1
Gorron 23 E3
Gort 12 B4
Gorteen 12 C3
Gortin 13 D2
Górtis 91 D4
Gortmore 12 B3
Gorumna I. 12 B3
Goryn' 113 D2
Góry
  Świętokrzyskie . . 112 B2
Görzke 53 D1
Gorzów
  Wielkopolski 49 F3
Gosaldo 59 D3
Gosau 59 F1
Gosausee 59 F1
Göschenen 58 A3
Gościno 49 F1
Gosforth 5 D4
Goslar 52 B1
Gospič 70 C4
Gospođinci 72 C2
Gosport 9 E3
Gossau 58 B2
Gosselies 50 B4
Gossensass 59 D2
Gostivar 77 D3
Göstling 57 D3
Gostyń 112 A2
Götaälv 108 C1
Göta Kanal 105 E4
Göteborg 108 C1
Göteborgs och
  Bohus Län 108 C1
Götene 105 E4
Gotha 52 C3
Gothem 109 F4
Gotland 109 F4
Gotlands Län 109 F4
Gotska Sandön . . . 106 C4
Göttingen 52 B2
Götzis 58 B2
Gouarec 22 C3
Gouda 16 C3
Gouménissa 79 F2
Goumois 27 E2
Goúra 87 D1
Gourdon 29 D2
Gourin 22 B3
Gournay-en-Bray . . 19 E3
Goúrnes 91 E3
Gourniá 91 E4
Gourock 4 C2
Gouveja 38 C2
Goúves 91 E3
Gouviá 82 A1
Gouzon 25 F4
Goveđari 75 E2
Goverla 113 D3
Gowienica 49 F2
Göynük 115 F3
Gozd 70 A1
Gozo 68 B4
Gozzano 58 A4
Graal-Müritz 48 C1
Graben-Neudorf . . . 54 C2
Grabenstätt 56 B3

Grabovac 75 E2
Grabovci 72 C3
Grabow 48 C3
Gračac 70 C4
Gračanica (BH) 71 F3
Gračanica
  (Crna Gora) 76 B2
Gračanica
  (Kosovo) 77 D2
Gračanica (Srbija) . 72 C4
Graçay 25 E2
Grächen 27 F4
Gradac (Crna Gora) 76 B1
Gradac (HR) 75 E2
Gradac (Srbija) 76 C1
Gradačac 71 F3
Gradara 61 E3
Gradče, Ez 77 F2
Gradec 71 D2
Gradefes 35 E2
Gradeška pl. 77 E3
Gradina 77 F1
Gradisca d'Isonzo . . 59 F3
Gradište (HR) 71 E2
Gradište
  (Makedonija) 77 E2
Grado (E) 35 D1
Grado (I) 59 F4
Gradsko 77 E3
Gradskovo 73 F3
Grafelfing 56 A3
Grafenau 56 C2
Gräfenberg 55 F1
Gräfenhainichen . . . 53 D1
Grafenwöhr 55 F1
Grafing 56 B3
Gragnano 64 B4
Grahovo (BH) 76 A2
Grahovo (SLO) 70 A2
Graiguenamanagh . 15 D3
Grain 11 D2
Grainau 55 F4
Grajewo 110 C4
Gram 108 A3
Gramat 29 D2
Gramatikó 83 E2
Gramatikoú 83 D4
Graměni 80 B2
Graméno 82 B1
Grametten 57 D1
Grammichele 69 D4
Grámos, Óros 78 C3
Grampian 3 E4
Grampian Mts 4 C1
Gramsh 77 D4
Gramzow 49 E3
Gran 105 D2
Granada 44 A3
Granadella 37 E4
Granadilla de
  Abona 42 B4
Granard 12 C3
Gran Canaria 42 B4
Grancey-le-
  Château 26 C2
Grandas 34 C1
Grand Ballon 27 E1
Grand Bois, Col du . 30 B1
Grand-
  Bornand, le 27 D4
Grand-Bourg 25 E4
Grandcamp-Maisy . 18 C3
Grand Canal
  d'Alsace 27 E1
Grand Canyon du
  Verdon 31 D3
Grand-Champ 22 C4
Grand-Colombier . . 27 D4
Grand-Combe, la . . 30 B3
Grand Combin 27 E4
Grand-Couronne . . . 19 D3
Grand-Croix 30 B1
Grande Casse 31 D1
Grande de Europa,
  Punta 43 E4
Grande Dixence,
  Bge de la 27 E4
Grande-Motte, la . . 30 B4
Grande Sassière . . . 31 E1
Grandes Rousses . . 31 D1
Grand-Fougeray . . . 23 D4
Grand-Lemps, le . . . 30 C1
Grand Lieu, L de . . 24 B3
Grand-Lucé, le 23 F4

Grand Morin 20 A4
Grândola 42 A1
Grandpré 20 C3
Grand-Pressigny,
  le 25 D3
Grand Rhône 30 B4
Grandrieu 29 F2
Grand-Serre, le 30 C1
Grands Goulets . . . 30 C2
Grandval, Bge de . . 29 F2
Grandvilliers 19 E3
Grañén 37 D3
Grängärde 105 F3
Grangemouth 5 D2
Grange-Over-
  Sands 6 B1
Grängesberg 105 F3
Grangranges-sur-
  Vologne 27 E1
Granier, Col du 30 C1
Granítis 80 B1
Granítsa 83 D2
Granja (Alentejo) . . 42 C1
Granja (Douro) 34 A4
Granja de
  Torrehermosa . . . 43 E1
Granja, Pto de la . . 43 D1
Gränna 109 D1
Granollers 32 A4
Granón 102 A1
Gran Paradiso 31 E1
Gran San Bernardo,
  Colle del 27 E4
Gran San Bernardo,
  Traforo del 27 E4
Gran Sasso d'Italia . 63 F1
Gransee 49 D3
Gran Tarajal 42 C4
Grantham 7 D3
Grantown-on-Spey . 3 D3
Granville 18 B4
Granvin 104 B2
Grappa, Mte 59 D3
Grasleben 52 C1
Grasmere 5 D4
Grassano 65 D4
Grasse 31 E3
Gråstenn 108 A4
Grästorp 108 C1
Gratangen 94 B3
Gratini 81 E2
Gratkorn 57 E4
Graubünden 58 B2
Graulhet 29 D4
Graus 37 E3
Gravalos 36 C3

Gravdal 97 E1
Grave 17 D3
Grave, la 31 D1
Gravelines 19 F1
Gravellona-Toce . . . 58 A4
Grave, Pointe de . . . 28 A1
Gravesend 11 D2
Graviá 83 E3
Gravina in Puglia . . 65 D3
Gravona 33 F3
Gravoúna 80 C2
Gray 26 C2
Grays Thurrock 10 C2
Grazalema 43 E3
Graz 57 E4
Grazzanise 64 A3
Grdelica 77 E1
Great Blasket I. . . . 14 A3
Great Driffield 7 D1
Great Dunmow 11 D2
Great Grimsby 7 E2
Great Malvern 9 D1
Great Ormes Head . 6 A2
Great Ouse 7 E3
Great Torrington . . . 8 C3
Great Yarmouth . . . 7 F4
Grebbestad 105 D4
Greccio 63 E2
Greding 55 F2
Gredos 39 F2
Gredos, Sa de 39 F2
Greenhead 5 D3
Greenlaw 5 E2
Greenock 4 C2
Greenodd 6 B1
Greggio 31 F1
Gregolímano 83 F3
Greifenburg 59 E2
Greiffenberg 49 E3
Greifswald 49 D1
Greifswalder
  Bodden 49 D1
Grein 57 D2
Greiz 53 D3
Grená 108 B2
Grenade (Haute-
  Garonne) 29 D4
Grenade (Landes) . . 28 B4
Grenchen 27 E2
Grenoble 30 C1
Grense Jakobselv . . 95 F1
Gréoux-les-Bains . . 31 D3
Gressåmoen 101 E1
Gresse 30 C2
Gressoney-la-
  Trinite 27 F4

Gressoney-
  St-Jean 27 F4
Gresten 57 D3
Grésy 31 D1
Greußen 52 C2
Greve 61 D2
Greven 17 E2
Grevená 79 D4
Grevená (Nomos) . . 79 D4
Grevenbroich 17 E3
Grevenbrück 17 F4
Grevenitio 82 C1
Grevesmühlen 48 B2
Greve Strand 108 C3
Greyabbey 13 E2
Greystones 13 E4
Grez-en-Bouère . . . 23 E3
Grezzana 60 C1
Grgur 70 B4
Gria, Akr. 88 B1
Grianan of Aileach . 13 D1
Griebenow 49 D2
Gries 59 D2
Gries im Sellrain . . 58 C2
Grieskirchen 56 C3
Griffen 70 B1
Grignan 30 B2
Grigno 59 D3
Grignols 28 B3
Grimaldi 67 E3
Grimaud 31 D4
Grimma 53 D2
Grimmen 49 D2
Grimone, Col de . . . 30 C2
Grimsbu 100 C3
Grimselpass 27 F3
Grimsey 96 B1
Grimstad 104 B4
Grindaheim 104 C2
Grindavík 96 A3
Grindelwald 27 F3
Grindsted 108 A3
Griñón 40 A2
Grintavec 70 B2
Gripsholm 106 B4
Grisignano 61 D1
Gris Nez, Cap 19 E1
Grisolles 29 D4
Grisslehamn 106 B3
Gríva 79 E2
Grizáno 83 D1
Grk 71 F3
Grljan 73 F3
Grmec 71 D4
Grøa 100 B2
Gröbming 59 F1
Grocka 73 D3

Gröditz 53 E2
Grodno 110 C4
Groenlo 17 D3
Gröer Arber 56 B1
Groitzsch 53 D2
Groix 22 B4
Groix, I de 22 B4
Grömitz 48 B2
Gronau 17 E2
Grönenbach 55 E4
Grong 97 D4
Grönhögen 109 E3
Groningen 47 D3
Groningen (Prov) . . 47 D3
Grönskåra 109 E2
Grønsund 108 C4
Gropello Cairoli . . . 60 A2
Groscavallo 31 E1
Grosio 58 C3
Grosne 26 C3
Gross Beerberg . . . 52 C3
Gross Bösenstein . . 57 D4
Großbreitenbach . . 52 C3
Großburgwedel . . . 48 A4
Großenbrode 48 B1
Großenhain 53 E2
Großenkneten 47 E4
Großenzersdorf . . . 57 F2
Grosse Pierre 27 E1
Grosse Röder 53 E2
Grosser Plöner
  See 48 B2
Grosseto 62 C1
Gross Feldberg 51 F4
Gross-Gerau 54 C1
Groß Gerungs 57 D2
Großglockner 59 E2
Großglockner
  Hochalpenstraße . 59 E2
Großhabersdorf . . . 55 E1
Groß Otscher 57 E3
Großpetersdorf . . . 57 F4
Gross Priel 57 D3
Gross Rachel 56 C2
Großraming 57 D3
Großraschen 53 E1
Groß Reken 17 E3
Großröhrsdorf 53 F2
Groß Rosennock . . . 59 F2
Grossschönau 53 F2
Groß-Schönebeck . 49 E3
Groß Siegharts 57 E2
Gross-Umstadt 55 D1
Großvenediger 59 E2
Großweil 56 A4
Grostenquin 21 D3

Grosuplje 70 B2
Grötlingbo 109 F4
Grøtsundet 94 C2
Grotta di
  Nettuno 66 A2
Grottaglie 65 E4
Grottaminarda 64 B3
Grottammare 61 F4
Grotte di Pertosa . . 64 C4
Grotteria 67 F4
Grouin, Pte du . . 18 B4
Grove 34 A2
Grövelsjön 101 D3
Grovfjord 94 B3
Grubišno Polje 71 D2
Gruda 76 A3
Grude 75 E2
Grudziądz 112 B1
Gruinard B. 2 C3
Gruissan 32 B2
Grums 105 E3
Grünau 56 C3
Grünberg 52 A3
Grünburg 57 D3
Grundarfjörður . . . 96 A2
Grundforsen 101 D4
Grundlsee 56 C3
Grundlsee L 56 C3
Grundsund 108 C1
Grundtjärn 101 F2
Grünstadt 54 C1
Grünwald 56 A3

Grupčin 77 D3
Gruyères 27 E3
Gruža 73 D4
Gruža R 73 D4
Grycksbo 105 F2
Gryfice 49 F2
Gryfino 49 E3
Gryllefjord 94 B2
Grythyttan 105 E3
Grytøya 94 B3
Grza 73 E4
Gschütt, Paß 59 F1
Gstaad 27 E3
Gstadt 56 B3
Guadahortuna 44 A2
Guadaira, R 43 E3
Guadajira, R 39 D4
Guadajoz, R 43 F2
Guadalajara 40 B2
Guadalaviar 41 D2
Guadalaviar, R 41 D2
Guadalcacín,
  Emb de 43 D3
Guadalcanal 43 D1
Guadalén, Emb de . . 44 A1
Guadalén, R 44 B1
Guadalest 45 E1
Guadalete, R 43 D4
Guadalfeo, R 44 A4
Guadalhorce, R 43 E4
Guadalimar, R
  (Andalucía) 43 D3

Guadalimar, R
  (Andalucía) 44 B2
Guadalmellato,
  Emb de 43 F2
Guadalmena,
  Emb de 44 B1
Guadalmena, R 44 B1
Guadalmez, R 43 F1
Guadalope, R 41 E2
Guadalquivir, R . . . 43 D3
Guadal, R 44 B2
Guadalteba-Guadalhorce,
  Emb del 43 E3
Guadalupe 39 E3
Guadalupe, Sa de . . 39 E3
Guadarrama 40 A2
Guadarrama,
  Pto de 40 A2
Guadarrama, R 40 A2
Guadarrama,
  Sa de 40 A1
Guadarranque,
  Emb del 43 E4
Guadasuar 41 E4
Guadazaón, R 40 C3
Guadiamar, R 43 D3
Guadiana Menor,
  R 44 B2
Guadiana, R 39 F4
Guadiaro 43 E4
Guadiaro, R 43 E4
Guadiato, R 43 E2

Guadiela, R 40 C2
Guadix 44 B3
Guajaraz, Emb de . . 40 A3
Gualdo Tadino 61 E4
Guara, Sa de 37 E3
Guarda 38 C1
Guardamar del
  Segura 45 D2
Guardiagrele 64 A2
Guardia
  Sanframondi 64 B3
Guardias Viejas 44 B4
Guardo 35 E2
Guareña 39 D4
Guarrizas, R 44 A1
Guarromán 44 A2
Guastalla 60 C2
Gubbio 61 E4
Guben 53 F1
Guberevac 73 D4
Gubin 53 F1
Guča 73 D4
Guca Gora 71 E4
Gúdar, Sa de 41 E2
Gudavac 71 D3
Gudbrandsdalen . . 100 C3
Guderup 108 A4
Gudhjem 109 D4
Gudingen 109 E1
Gudow 48 B3
Gudvangen 104 B2
Guebwiller 27 E1

Guémené 22 B3
Guémené-Penfao . . 23 D4
Güeñes 36 B1
Guer 23 D3
Guérande 22 C4
Guerche-de-
  Bretagne, la 23 D3
Guerche, la 26 A3
Guéret 25 E4
Guérigny 26 A2
Guerlédan, L de . . 22 C3
Guernsey 18 A3
Guéthary 28 A4
Gueugnon 26 B3
Güglingen 55 D2
Guglionesi 64 B2
Guía 42 B4
Guía de Isora 42 A4
Guidonia 63 E2
Guignes 19 F4
Guijo de Granadilla . 39 D2
Guijuelo 39 E2
Guildford 9 F3
Guillaumes 31 E3
Guillena 43 D2
Guillestre 31 D2
Guillon 26 B2
Guilvinec 22 A3
Güímar 42 B4
Guimarães 34 A4
Guimiliau 22 B2

Guînes 19 E1
Guingamp 22 C2
Guipavas 22 A2
Guisborough 5 F4
Guiscard 19 F3
Guise 20 A2
Guissona 37 F3
Guitiriz 34 B1
Guîtres 28 B2
Gujan-Mestras 28 A2
Gulbene 110 C2
Guldborg Sund . . . 108 C4
Gullesfjorden 94 A3
Gullfoss 96 B2
Gullkrona fjärd . . . 107 D3
Gullspång 105 E4
Gumiel de Hizán . . 36 A3
Gummersbach 17 E4
Gundelfingen 55 E3
Gundelsheim 55 D2
Gunnarn 97 F4
Gunnarsbyn 98 B3
Gunnärsfjärden . . 98 C3
Gunnarskog 105 E3
Gunten 27 F3
Günterode 52 B2
Guntín de Pallares . 34 B2
Günzburg 55 E3
Gunzenhausen 55 E2
Gurk 70 A1
Gurk R. 59 F2

Gurrea de Gállego . . 37 D3
Gusev 110 B4
Gusinje 76 C2
Guspini 66 B3
Güssing 57 F4
Güsten 52 C1
Güstrow 48 C2
Gutcher 3 F1
Gutenstein 57 E3
Gütersloh 17 F3
Gutulia 100 D3
Gützkow 49 D2
Guyhirn 10 C1
Gvardejsk 110 B4
Gvarv 104 C3
Gvozd 76 B2
Gweebarra B. 12 C1
Gwent 9 D2
Gwynedd 6 A3
Gy 27 D2
Gyöngyös 112 B4
Győr 112 A4
Gysinge 106 A3
Gyula 112 C4

H

Haag (A) 57 D3
Haag (D) 56 B3
Haag am Hausruck . 56 C3
Haaksbergen 17 D2
Haamstede 16 B3
Haapajärvi 103 D1
Haapajärvi L 103 D1
Haapakoski 103 E2
Haapamäki (Keski-
  Suomen Lääni) . . 102 C3
Haapamäki
  (Oulun Lääni) . . . 103 D1
Haapavesi 103 D1
Haapsalu 110 B2
Haar 56 A3
Haaren 17 F3
Haarlem 16 B2
Habay 20 C2
Habo 109 D1
Habsheim 27 E1
Hachenburg 51 F3
Hachmühlen 52 A1
Hackås 101 E2
Hadamar 51 F4
Haddington 5 D2
Hadersdorf 57 E2
Haderslev 108 A4
Hadleigh 11 D2
Hadmersleben 52 C1
Hadrian's Wall 5 E3
Hadselfjorden 94 A3
Hadsten 108 B2
Hadsund 108 B2
Hadžići 75 F1
Haganj 71 D2
Hægebostad 104 B4
Hagen
  (Niedersachsen) . . 47 F3
Hagen (Nordrhein-
  Westfalen) 17 E4
Hagenow 48 B3
Hagetmau 28 B4
Hagfors 105 E3
Häggdånger 101 F3
Haggenås 101 E2
Hagondange 21 D3
Hague, Cap de la . . 18 B2
Hahn 47 F3
Hahnbach 55 F1
Haigerloch 55 D3
Hailsham 10 C3
Hailuoto 99 D4

Hainaut 50 B4
Hainburg 57 F2
Hainfeld 57 E3
Hainichen 53 E2
Hajdúböszörmény . 112 C4
Hajdučica 73 D2
Hajdúszoboszló . . 112 C4
Hajla 76 C2
Hajnówka 112 C1
Hakarp 109 D1
Hakkas 98 B2
Häkkilä 103 D2
Halámky 57 D2
Halbe 53 E1
Halberstadt 52 C1
Halden 105 D4
Haldensleben 48 C4
Halesowen 9 E1
Halesworth 11 E1
Halhjem 104 A2
Halifax 6 C2
Halikko 107 E2
Halju 95 D4
Halkeró 80 C2
Hálki
  (Dodekánissa) . . . 93 E1
Halki (Kikládes) . . . 88 C3
Hálki (Thessalía) . . 83 E1
Halkiádes 83 E2
Halkída 84 B4
Halkidikí 80 B3
Hálki, N 93 E1
Halkidóna 79 F3
Halkió 85 F4
Halkío 87 D1
Halkodóni, Óros . . 83 E2
Hallands Län 108 C2
Halle (B) 50 B3
Halle (Nordrhein-
  Westfalen) 17 F3
Halle
  (Sachsen-Anhalt) . . 53 D2
Hällefors 105 E3
Hälleforsnäs 105 F4
Hallein 56 C3
Hällekis 105 E4
Hallenberg 17 F4
Hallencourt 19 E2
Hällesjö 101 F2
Hällevadsholm . . . 105 D4
Halligen 47 F1
Hallingdal 104 C2
Hallingskarvet . . . 104 B2
Hall in Tirol 59 D1

Hällnäs 102 A1
Hallsberg 105 F4
Hallstadt 52 C4
Hallstahammar . . . 105 F3
Hallstatt 59 F1
Hallstavik 106 B3
Halluin 19 F1
Halmstad 108 C2
Hals 108 B2
Halsa 100 B2
Halsafjorden 100 B2
Hälsingtuna 101 F3
Halsskov 108 B3
Halstead 11 D2
Halsteren 16 B3
Haltdålen 101 D2
Haltern 17 E3
Halti-Haldi 94 C3
Halver 17 E4
Ham 19 F2
Hamar 105 D2
Hamarøy 94 A4
Hamburg 48 A3
Hambye 18 B4
Hamdorf 48 A2
Hämeenkyrö 102 C3
Hämeen Lääni 102 C3
Hämeenlinna 107 E2
Hämelerwald 52 B1
Hameln 52 A1
Hamersleben 52 C1
Hamili, N 92 C2
Hamilton 4 C2
Hamina 103 F4
Hamm 17 E3
Hammarland 106 C3
Hammarstrand . . . 101 F2
Hammaslahti 103 F2
Hammel 108 B3
Hammelburg 52 B4
Hammerdal 101 E2
Hammerfest 95 D1
Hammershus 109 D4
Hamneidet 94 C2
Hamningberg 95 F1
Hamoir 50 C4
Hampshire 9 E3
Hamra 101 E3
Hamra (Reg) 101 E3
Hamre 104 B4
Hamzali 77 F3
Hamzići 75 F2
Hanákia 86 B2
Haria 42 C3
Hanau 52 A4
Handrás 91 F4

Hanerau-
  Hademarschen . . . 48 A2
Hangö 107 E3
Hangon
  läntinenselkä . . . 107 D3
Hangö västra
  fjärd 107 D3
Haniá (Haniá) 90 B3
Haniá (Lakonía) . . . 87 B3
Haniá (Nomos) 90 B3
Hánia (Thessalía) . . 83 F2
Hani i Hotit 76 B3
Hanión, Kólpos . . . 90 B3
Haniótis 80 B4
Hankamäki 103 E1
Hankasalmen as. . . 103 D3
Hankasalmi 103 D3
Hanko 107 E3
Hannover 48 A4
Hannut 50 C4
Hanöbukten 109 D3
Han Pijesak 72 B4
Hansnes 94 C2
Han-sur-Lesse 50 C4
Hanstedt 48 A3
Hanstholm 108 A2
Haparanda 98 C3
Harads 98 B3
Harafjärden 96 C3
Haraldshaugen . . . 104 A3
Haranes 97 D4
Haravgi 79 E3
Harburg (Bayern) . . 55 E2
Harburg
  (Hamburg) 48 A3
Hårby 108 B4
Hardangerfjorden . 104 A2
Hardangerjøkulen . 104 B2
Hardangervidda . . . 104 B2
Hardbakke 104 A1
Hardegg 57 E1
Hardegsen 52 B2
Hardelot 19 E1
Hardenberg 17 D2
Harderwijk 16 C2
Hardheim 55 D1
Hardwick Hall 7 D3
Hareid 100 A1
Harelbeke 50 A3
Haren (D) 17 E1
Haren (NL) 47 D3
Harewood 6 C2
Hária 42 C3
Haringvlietdam 16 B3
Haritoméni 80 B2

Härjångsfjällen . . . 101 D2
Harjavalta 107 D2
Harjunpää 107 D1
Hårkan 101 E2
Härkmeri 102 B3
Harlech 6 A3
Harlesiel 47 E3
Harleston 11 D1
Harlingen 16 C1
Harlow 10 C2
Harmånger 101 F3
Harmanli 115 E3
Härnösand 101 F3
Haro 36 B2
Harokopió 86 C4
Haroldswick 3 F1
Harouè 21 D4
Harøyfjorden 100 A2
Harpenden 9 F2
Harplinge 108 C2
Harpstedt 17 F1
Harris 2 A2
Harrislee 47 F1
Harrogate 6 C1
Härryda 108 C1
Harsefeld 48 A3
Harsprånget 98 B2
Harstad 94 B3
Harsvik 96 C3
Hartberg 57 F4
Hårteigen 104 B2
Hartha 53 E2
Hartkjölen 101 E1
Hartland Pt 8 B3
Hartlepool 5 F4
Hartmannsdorf . . . 53 E3
Hartola 103 D3
Harwich 11 D2
Harz 52 B2
Harzgerode 52 C2
Hase 17 E2
Haselünne 17 E2
Haskovo 115 D3
Haslach (A) 56 C2
Haslach (D) 54 C3
Hasle 109 D4
Haslemere 9 F3
Haslev 108 C4
Hasparren 28 A4
Hassela 101 F3
Hasselfelde 52 C2
Hasselt 50 C3
Haßfurt 52 C4
Hássia, Óri 83 D1
Hässleholm 109 D3

Hastière 50 C4
Hastings 11 D3
Hasvik 95 D1
Hatě 57 E1
Hatfield 9 F2
Hațeg 114 C1
Hatfjelldal 97 E3
Hattem 17 D2
Hattfjelldal 97 E3
Hattingen 17 E3
Hattula 107 E2
Hattuvaara
  (Lieksa) 103 F1
Hattuvaara
  (Ilomantsi) 103 F2
Hatvan 112 B4
Hatvik 104 A2
Hatzí 82 C2
Haubourdin 19 F1
Hauge 104 A4
Haugesund 104 A3
Hauho 107 E2
Haukelifjell 104 B2
Haukeligrend 104 B2
Haukipudas 99 D3
Haukivesi 103 E3
Haukivuori 103 E3
Haunstetten 55 F3
Hausach 54 C3
Hausham 56 A4
Hausjärvi 107 E2
Haus 59 F1
Haute-Corse 33 F3
Hautefort 29 D1
Haute-Garonne . . . 29 D4
Haute-Loire 29 F2
Haute-Marne 26 C1
Hautes-Alpes 31 D2
Haute-Saône 27 D1
Haute-Savoie 27 D4
Haute-Vienne
  (Dépt) 29 D1
Hauteville-
  Lompnes 27 D4
Hautmont 20 B2
Haut-Rhin (Dept) . . 27 E1
Havant 9 F3
Hävári 86 B1
Havdalsfjellet 97 E4
Havdáta 82 B4
Havel 49 D4
Havelange 50 C4
Havelberg 48 C3
Haverfordwest 8 B2

Haverhill 11 D1
Haverö 101 E3
Havneby 108 A4
Havøysund 95 D1
Havraň 53 E3
Havre, Le 19 D3
Hawes 6 C1
Hawick 5 D3
Hawkhurst 11 D3
Hayange 21 D3
Haye-du-Puits, la . . 18 B3
Haye-Pesnel, la . . . 18 B4
Hayle 8 A4
Hay-on-Wye 9 D1
Haywards Heath . . . 10 C3
Hazebrouck 19 F1
Headford 12 B3
Heanor 7 D3
Héas 37 E2
Heathfield 10 C3
Heathrow Airport . . . 9 F2
Hebrides, Outer 2 A2
Hebrides,
  Sea of the 2 A3
Heby 106 B3
Hechingen 55 D3
Hecho 37 D2
Hechtel 50 C3
Hecklingen 52 C1
Hedal 104 C2
Heddal 104 C3
Hédé 23 D3
Hede 101 E3
Hedemora 105 F3
Hedenäset 98 C2
Hedensted 108 B3
Hedesundafjärdarna
  . . . . 106 B3
Hedeviken 101 E3
Hedmark 104 C1
Hedon 7 E2
Heemstede 16 C2
Heerde 17 D2
Heerenveen 17 D1
Heerlen 51 D3
Heeze 16 C4
Hegge 104 C1
Hegra 101 D2
Heia 94 C3
Heide 47 F2
Heidelberg 54 C1
Heidenau 53 E2
Heidenheim 55 E2
Heidenreichstein . . 57 D2
Heikkila 99 F2

Heilbronn 55 D2
Heiligenberg 55 D4
Heiligenblut 59 E2
Heiligenhafen 48 B1
Heiligenhafen 17 F3
Heiligenkreuz 57 F4
Heiligenstadt 52 B2
Heilsbronn 55 E1
Heimari 103 E3
Heimdal. 100 C2
Heimertingen 55 E3
Heinävaara 103 F2
Heinävesi. 103 E2
Heinola 107 F1
Heinolan mlk 107 F1
Heinsberg 17 D4
Heist 50 A3
Heist-op-den-
Berg 50 C3
Hejde 109 F4
Hekla 96 B2
Hekuravë, Maj'e . . 76 C2
Helagsfjället. 101 D2
Hélatros, Akr 93 D3
Heldeburg 52 C4
Heldrungen 52 C2
Helechal. 43 E1
Helensburgh 4 C2
Helgåa (N) 101 D1
Helgå (S) 109 D1
Helgasjön 109 D2
Helgoland 47 E2
Hella Is 96 B2
Hella N. 104 B1
Hellemofjorden . . 97 E3
Hellendoorn 17 D2
Hellesylt 100 A3
Hellevoetsluis . . . 16 B3
Hellin 44 C1
Hellvik 104 A4
Helmbrechts 53 D4
Helme 52 C2
Helmond 17 D3
Helmsdale 3 D2
Helmsley 7 D1
Helmstadt 55 D1
Helmstedt. 52 C1
Helpter Berge . . . 49 E2
Helsa 52 B2
Helsingborg. . . . 108 C3
Helsinge 108 C3
Helsingfors. 107 F3
Helsingør 108 C3
Helsinki 107 F3
Helston. 8 B4
Helvetinjärvi . . . 102 C3
Helvick Head. . . . 14 C4
Hemau 55 F2
Hemavan 97 E3
Hemel Hempstead. . 9 F2
Hemer 17 E3
Hemme 100 C2
Hemmoor. 48 A2
Hemnefjorden . . 100 C1
Hemnes 105 D3
Hemnesberget . . 97 E2
Hemsedal 104 C2
Hemsedal V 104 C2
Henares, R 40 B2
Hendaye. 28 A4
Hengelo. 17 D2
Hengersberg . . . 56 B2
Hengstpaß 57 D3
Hénin-Beaumont. . 19 F1
Henley 9 E1
Henley-on-Thames . . 9 F2
Henneberg 52 B3
Hennebont. 22 B3
Hennef 51 E3
Hennigsdorf 49 D4
Henrichemont. . . 25 F2
Henstedt-Ulzburg . 48 A2
Henstridge 9 D3
Hepoköngäs 99 E4
Heppenheim 54 C1
Heraclea 77 D1
Hérault 29 F4
Hérault (Dépt) . . 30 A4
Herbault 25 E2
Herbertingen . . . 55 D3
Herbiers, les 24 B3
Herbignac 22 C4
Herbolzheim 54 C3
Herborn 51 F3

Herbrechtingen 55 E2
Herbstein 52 A3
Herceg Novi 76 A3
Hercegovac 71 D2
Hercegov Goleša . . 76 B1
Hereford 9 D1
Hereford and
Worcester 9 D1
Herencia 40 B4
Herentals. 50 C3
Herford 17 F2
Héricourt 27 E2
Heringsdorf 49 E2
Herisau 58 B2
Hérisson 26 A3
Herk 50 C3
Herleshausen 52 B3
Hermagor 59 F2
Herma Ness 3 F1
Hermannsburg 48 B4
Hermansverk 104 B1
Hermenault, l' 24 C3
Herment 29 E1
Hermeskeil 54 B1
Hermigua 42 A4
Hermsdorf 53 D3
Hernani 36 C1
Hernansancho 39 F1
Herne 17 E3
Herne Bay 11 D3
Herning 108 A3
Heroldsberg 55 F1
Herónia 83 F4
Herøy 100 A3
Herrala 107 F2
Herre 104 C3
Herrenberg 55 D3
Herrenchiemsee . . 56 B3
Herrera
(Andalucía) 43 E3
Herrera (Aragón) . 37 D4
Herrera Mt 37 D4
Herrera de
Alcántara 38 C3
Herrera del Duque . 39 F4
Herrera de
Pisuerga 35 F3
Herrera, Pto de . . 36 B2
Herreruela 39 D3
Herrestad 108 C1
Herrieden 55 E2
Herrljunga 109 D1
Herrnburg 48 B2
Herrnhut 53 F2
Herrsching 56 A3
Herrskog 102 A2
Hersbruck 55 F1
Herselt 50 C3
Hérso 79 F2
Hersónissos
Akrotiri 90 C3
Hersónissos
Methánon . . . 87 E2
Hersónissos
Spinalónga . . 91 E3
Herstal 51 D3
Herten 17 E3
Hertford 9 F2
Hertfordshire . . . 9 F2
Hervás 39 E2
Herzberg
(Brandenburg) . 53 E1
Herzberg
(Niedersachsen) . 52 B2
Herzogenaurach . 55 E1
Herzogenburg . . 57 E2
Herzsprung 49 D3
Hesdin 19 E2
Hesel 47 E3
Hessen 52 A3
Hesseng 95 F2
Hessisch-
Lichtenau 52 B2
Hessisch
Oldendorf 52 A1
Hestfjørdur 96 A4
Hetekylä 99 E3
Hetin 72 C1
Hettange 21 D3
Hettstedt 52 C2
Heubach 55 E2
Heuchin 19 F1

Heukuppe 57 E3
Hevlin 57 F1
Hexham 5 E3
Heyrieux 30 C1
Heysham 6 B1
Hiddensee 49 D1
Hieflau 57 D3
Hiekkasärkät 102 C1
Hierbas 41 E3
Hierro 42 A4
Hiersac 28 C1
Hietaniemi 95 F4
Higham Ferrers . . . 9 F1
Highland 2 C3
High Peak 6 C2
High Willhays 8 C3
High Wycombe . . . 9 F2
Higuera de Arjona . 44 A2
Higuera de la
Serena 43 E1
Higuera de la
Sierra 43 D2
Higuera de Vargas . 42 C4
Higuera la Real . . . 42 C1
Higueruela 41 D4
Hiidenportti 103 E1
Hiiumaa 110 B1
Híjar 37 D4
Hilchenbach 17 F4
Hildburghausen . . 52 C3
Hilden 17 E4
Hilders 52 B3
Hildesheim 52 B1
Hiliomódi 87 E1
Hillegom 16 B2
Hillerød 108 C3
Hillesøy. 94 B2
Hillswick 3 F1
Hiloús, Akr 92 C1
Hilpoltstein 55 F2
Hiltula 103 E3
Hilvarenbeek . . . 16 C4
Hilversum 16 C2
Himanka 102 C1
Hímaros 80 A2
Himmerland . . . 108 B2

Hinckley 9 E1
Hindelang 55 E4
Hindhead 9 F3
Hindsholm 108 B3
Hinnøya 94 A3
Hinodejo 36 B3
Hinojares 44 B2
Hinojosa de Duero . 39 D1
Hinojosa del
Duque 43 E1
Hinterrhein 58 B3
Hintersee (Bayern) . 56 B4
Hintersee (Mecklenburg-
Vorpommern) . . 49 E2
Hinterstoder 57 D3
Hintertux 59 D2
Hinterweidenthal . . 54 B2
Híos 85 F4
Híos, N 85 E4
Hirschau. 55 F1
Hirschberg 53 D3
Hirschegg 58 B3
Hirsingue 27 E2
Hirson 20 B2
Hîrşova 115 E1
Hirtshals 108 B1
Hirvasvaara 99 E2
Hirvensalmi 103 E3
Hirvilahti 103 E3
Hirwaun 8 C2
Hisarja 115 D2
Histria 115 E1
Hitchin 9 F2
Hitra 100 C1
Hitzacker 48 B3
Hjälmaren 105 F4
Hjartdal 104 C3
Hjellestad 104 A2
Hjelmeland . . . 104 A3
Hjelmsøya 95 D1
Hjo 109 D1
Hjørring 108 B1
Hjørundfjorden . 100 A2
Hlebine 71 D1
Hlemoútsi 86 B1
Hlomó, Óros . . . 83 F3

Hluboká 57 D1
Hobro. 108 B2
Höchberg 55 D1
Hochdorf 27 F2
Hochfeiler. 59 D2
Hochfelden 21 E4
Hochgolling 59 F1
Hochgrabe 59 E2
Hochosterwitz . . 70 B1
Hochreichart . . . 57 D4
Hochschober . . . 59 E2
Hochschwab . . . 57 D3
Hochspeyer 54 C1
Höchst 55 D1
Höchstadt 55 E1
Höchstädt 55 E1
Hochtannbergpaß . 58 B2
Hochtor (Osttirol) . 59 E2
Hochtor
(Steiermark) . . . 57 D3
Hockenheim . . . 54 C2
Hoddesdon 9 F2
Hodenhagen . . . 48 A4
Hœdic 22 C4
Hódmezővásárhely 114 B1
Hodnet 6 B3
Hodonín 57 F1
Hodoš 70 C1
Hodovo 75 F2
Hoedekenskerke . 16 B4
Hoek van Holland . 16 B3
Hoemsbu 100 B2
Hof 53 D4
Hofgeismar 52 A2
Hofheim 52 B4
Hofles 97 D4
Höfn 96 C2
Hofolding 56 A3
Hofors 105 F2
Hofsjökull 96 B2
Höganäs 108 C3
Høgebru 100 A3
Höglekardalen . . 101 E2
Högsäter 105 D4
Högsby 109 E2
Høgset. 100 B2

Hohe Acht 51 E4
Hohenau 57 F2
Hohenberg 57 E3
Hohenems 58 B2
Hohengandern 52 B2
Hohenlimburg 17 E4
Hohenlinden 56 B3
Hohenlockstedt . . . 48 A2
Hohenmölsen 53 D2
Hohenpeißenberg . . 56 A4
Hohenseeden 48 C4
Hohenstein 53 D3
Hohentauern 57 D4
Hohenwestedt . . . 48 A2
Hohenzollern 55 D3
Hoher Zinken 56 C3
Hohe Tauern 59 E2
Hohe Tauern,
Nat Pk 59 E2
Höhlakas 93 E2
Hohneck 27 E1
Hohwachter
Bucht. 48 B1
Hohwald, le 21 E4
Hojer. 108 A4
Hokksund 104 C3
Hol. 104 C2
Holbæk 108 C3
Holbeach 7 E3
Holdorf 17 F2
Holíč 57 F1
Höljes 101 D4
Höljäkkä 103 E1
Hollabrunn 57 E2
Høllen 104 B4
Hollenstedt 48 A3
Höllental 57 E3
Holles 97 D4
Hollfeld 52 C4
Hollingsholm . . . 100 B2
Hollola 107 F2
Hollum 16 C1
Hollywood 13 D4
Holm (N) 97 D3
Holm (S) 101 F2
Hólmavík 96 A1

Holmec 70 B1
Holmen 105 D2
Holmestrand 104 C3
Holmfirth 6 C2
Holmön 102 B1
Holmsjön 101 E3
Holmslands Klit. . . 108 A3
Holmsund 102 B1
Holomóndas,
Óros 80 B3
Holstebro 108 A2
Holsted 108 A3
Holsworthy 8 C3
Holt 7 F3
Holwerd. 47 D2
Holy Cross Abbey . 14 C3
Holyhead 6 A2
Holy I (Anglesey) . 6 A2
Holy I
(Northumberland) . 5 E2
Holywell 6 B2
Holywood 13 E2
Holzappel 51 F4
Holzgau 58 C2
Holzkirchen 56 A3
Holzleitner Sattel . 58 C2
Holzminden 52 A2
Homberg
(Hessen) 52 A3
Homberg (Nordrhein-
Westfalen) 17 D3
Homburg 54 B2
Hommelstø 97 D3
Hommelvik 100 C2
Hommersåk. . . . 104 A3
Homoljske
planine 73 E3
Hondarribia
Fuenterrabia. . . 36 C1
Hondón de las
Nieves 45 D2
Hönebach 52 B3
Hønefoss 104 C3
Honfleur 19 D3
Høng 108 B3
Hónikas 87 D2

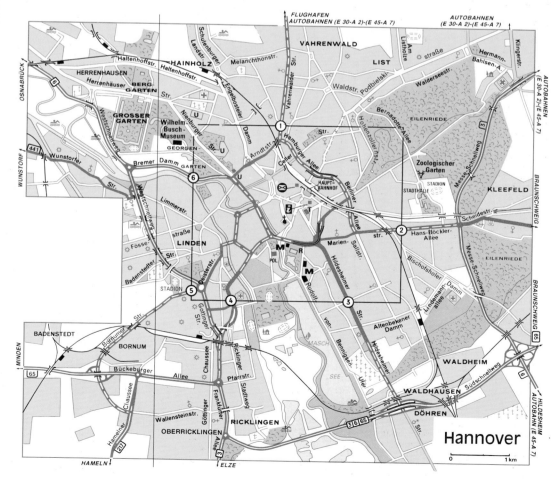

Hannover

0   1 km

Honiton 9 D3
Honkajoki 102 B3
Honningsvåg 95 E1
Honrubia 40 C3
Honrubia de la
 Cuesta 36 A3
Hontalbilla 40 A1
Hontoria del Pinar . 36 A3
Hooge 47 F1
Hoogeveen 17 D2
Hoogezand 47 D3
Hoogstraten 50 C2
Hook Head 15 D4
Höör 109 D3
Hoorn 16 C2
Hopetoun House 5 D2
Hopfgarten 59 D1
Hopperstad 104 B1
Hóra
 (Dodekánissa) 89 E2
Hóra
 (Pelopónissos) . . . 86 C3
Hora Svatého
 Šebestiána 53 E3
Horažd'ovice 56 C1
Horb 54 C3
Hörby 109 D3
Horcajo de los
 Montes 39 F4
Horcajo de
 Santiago 40 B3
Horcajo de
 Trevélez 44 A3
Horcajo-
 Medianero 39 E2
Horche 40 B2
Hordaland 104 B2
Horden 5 E4
Horeftó 83 F2

Horezu 115 D1
Horgen 58 A2
Horgoš 72 C1
Horley 10 C3
Horn (A) 57 E2
Horn (Baden-
 Württemberg) . . . 55 D4
Horn (N) 97 D3
Horn (Nordrhein-
 Westfalen) 52 A2
Hornachos 43 D1
Hornachuelos 43 E2
Hornavan 98 A2
Hornberg 54 C3
Hornbjarg 96 A1
Hornburg 52 B1
Horncastle 7 E3
Horndal 106 A3
Horneburg 48 A3
Hörnefors 102 A2
Hörnerkirchen 48 A2
Hornet 100 C2
Hornindal 100 A3
Hornindalsvatn . . . 100 A3
Hørning 108 B3
Horni Počernice 53 F3
Hornisgrinde 54 C3
Horni Slavkov 53 E4
Hornos 44 B2
Hornoy 19 E2
Hornsea 7 E2
Hörnum 47 F1
Hořovice 53 F4
Horsens 108 B3
Horsham 10 C3
Hørsholm 108 C3
Horšovký Týn 56 B1
Horst 48 B3
Horstmar 17 E2

Hortafjorden 97 D3
Horten 104 C3
Hortezuela 36 B4
Hortiátis 80 A3
Hospental 58 A3
Hospital 14 C3
Hospital de
 Orbigo 35 D3
Hossa 99 F3
Hossegor 28 A4
Hostalric 32 B4
Hotagen 101 E1
Hotagen L. 101 E1
Hotagsfjällen 101 E1
Hoting 101 F1
Hotton 50 C4
Houat 22 C4
Houches, les 27 E4
Houdain 19 F1
Houdan 19 E4
Houeillès 28 B3
Houffalize 51 D4
Houghton-le-
 Spring 5 E4
Houlgate 18 C3
Houmnikó 80 B2
Hoúni 83 D3
Hourtin 28 A2
Houtskår 107 D3
Hov 108 B3
Hovärken 101 D3
Hovden 104 B3
Hove 10 C3
Hovet 104 B2
Hovmantorp 109 E2
Høvringen 100 C3
Howden 7 D2
Howth 13 E4
Höxter 52 A2

Hoy 3 D1
Hoya 17 F1
Høyanger 100 A3
Hoyerswerda 53 F2
Hoylake 6 B2
Høylandet 97 D4
Hoym 52 C1
Hoyos 39 D2
Höytiainen 103 F2
Hoz de Beteta 40 C2
Hozoviótissa 89 D3
Hracholuská přehr
 nádrž 53 E4
Hradec-Králove . . . 112 A2
Hrádek 57 E1
Hrádek nad Nisou . . 53 F2
Hranice
 (Severomoravský) 112 A3
Hranice
 (Západočeský) . . . 53 D4
Hrasnica 75 F1
Hrastnik 70 B2
Hrastovlje 70 A3
Hřensko 53 F2
Hrísey 96 B1
Hríssafa 87 D3
Hrissí, N 91 E4
Hrissó 80 B2
Hrissoskalítissa 90 B3
Hrissoúpoli 80 C2
Hrissovítsi 86 C2
Hristiani, N 91 D1
Hristianó 86 C3
Hristós 89 D2
Hrómio 79 D4
Hrtkovci 72 C3
Hrušovany 57 F1
Hrvace 75 D1
Hrvatska 70 C2

Hückeswagen 17 E4
Hucknall 7 D3
Hucqueliers 19 E1
Huddersfield 6 C2
Hude 47 F3
Huébra, R 39 E1
Huedin 112 C4
Huélago 44 A3
Huélamo 40 C2
Huelgoat 22 B3
Huelma 44 A2
Huelva 42 C2
Huelva, Riv. de 43 D2
Huércal-Overa 44 C3
Huérguina 41 D3
Huerta del Rey 36 A3
Huerta de
 Valdecarábanos . . 40 A3
Huertahernando . . . 40 C2
Huerto 37 E3
Huerva, R 37 D4
Huesa 44 B2
Huesca 37 D3
Huéscar 44 B2
Huesna, Emb de . . . 43 D2
Huete 40 B3
Huétor-Santillán . . . 44 A3
Huétor-Tájar 43 F3
Hüfingen 54 C4
Huisne 23 F3
Huittinen 107 D2
Huizen 16 C2
Hulst 16 B4
Hultsfred 109 E2
Humada 35 F3
Humanes 40 B1
Humber Bridge 7 D2

Humber, R. 7 E2
Humberside 7 D2
Humberside
 (Airport) 7 D2
Humenné 112 C3
Humppila 107 E2
Hundested 108 C3
Hundorp 100 C3
Hunedoara 114 C1
Hünfeld 52 B3
Hungerford 9 E2
Hunnebostrand . . . 105 D4
Húnaflói 96 A1
Hunspach 21 F3
Hunsrück 54 B1
Hunstanton 7 E3
Hunte 17 F1
Huntingdon 9 F1
Huntly 3 E3
Hurdal 105 D2
Huriel 25 F4
Hurones,
 Emb de los 43 D3
Hurskaala 103 E3
Hürth 17 E4
Hurum 104 C1
Hurup 108 A2
Husafell 96 B2
Húsavík Is 96 B1
Husavik N 104 A2
Husbands
 Bosworth 9 F1
Hushinish 2 A2
Huşi 113 E4
Huskvarna 109 D1
Husnes 104 A2
Hustadvika 100 B2
Hustopeče 57 F1
Husum (D) 47 F1

Husum (S) 102 A2
Hutovo 75 F2
Hutovo Blato 75 F2
Hüttenberg 57 D4
Hüttschlag 59 E1
Huttula 103 D3
Huttwil 27 F2
Huy 50 C4
Hvalba 96 A4
Hvalfjörður 96 A1
Hvalpsund 108 A2
Hvalvík 96 A3
Hvar 75 D2
Hvar I. 75 E2
Hvarski kan 75 D2
Hveragerði 96 A1
Hveravellir 96 B2
Hvidbjerg 108 A2
Hvide Sande 108 A3
Hvítá 96 B2
Hvittingfoss 104 C3
Hvitträsk 107 E3
Hvolsvöllur 96 B3
Hwlffordd 8 B2
Hyde 6 C2
Hyen 100 A3
Hyères 31 D4
Hyères, Iles d' 31 D4
Hylsfjorden 104 A3
Hyltebruk 108 C2
Hyrynsalmi 99 E4
Hythe 11 D3
Hyvinkää 107 E2
Hyypiö 99 D2

I

Ía 91 E1
Ialomiţa 115 E1
Iaşi 113 E3
Íasmos 81 D2
Ibañeta, Pto 36 C1
Ibar 73 D4
Ibbenbüren 17 E2
Ibestad 94 B3
Ibi 45 E1
Ibias, R 34 C2
Ibiza 45 D4
Ibiza I 45 D3
Iblei, Mti. 69 D4
Ičn'a 113 F1
Icod de los Vinos . . 42 A4
Idanha a Nova 38 C2
Idar-Oberstein 54 B1
Idéo Ándro 91 D4
Ídi, Óros 91 D4
Idoméni 79 F2
Iddoš 72 C1
Ídra 87 F2
Ídra, N 87 F3
Ídras, Kólpos 87 E2
Idre 101 D3
Idrigill Pt 2 B3
Idrija 70 A2
Idrijca 70 A2
Idro 58 C4
Idstein 51 F4
Ieper 50 A3
Ierápetra 91 E4
Ierissós 80 B3
Ieropigí 78 C3
If, Château d' 30 C4
Ifestía 85 D1
Ifjord 95 E1
Ifjordfjellet 95 E1
Igalo 76 A3
Iga Vas 70 B2
Iggesund 101 F3
Iglesias 66 B4
Igls 59 D2
Igoumenítsa 82 B2
Igrane 75 E2
Igualada 37 F4

Ihtiman 115 D2
Ii 99 D3
Iljarvi 95 E2
Iijoki 99 D3
Iisalmi 103 E1
Iisvesi 103 E2
IJmuiden 16 B2
IJssel 17 D3
IJsselmeer 16 C2
IJsselmuiden 17 D2
IJzendijke 16 B4
IJzer 50 A3
Ikaalinen 102 C3
Ikaría, N 89 D2
Ikast 108 A3
Ilandža 73 D2
Ilanz 58 B3
Ilche 37 E3
Ilchester 9 D3
Ile-Bouchard, l' 25 D3
Ile-Rousse, l' 33 F2
Ilfracombe 8 C3
Ílhavo 38 B1
Ília 83 F3
Ilía 86 B1
Il'ičevsk 113 F4
Ílida 75 F1
Ilijas 71 F4
Ilíki 84 A4
Ilíki, L 84 A4
Iliókastro 87 E2
Ilirska Bistrica 70 B3
Ilkeston 7 D3
Ilkley 6 C2
Illana 40 B2
Illano 34 C1
Illar 44 B3
Ille 23 D3
Ille et Rance,
 Canal d' 23 D3
Ille-et-Vilaine 23 D3
Iller 55 E4
Illertissen 55 E3
Illescas 40 A2
Ille-sur-Têt 32 B2
Illhæusern 27 E1
Illingen 55 D2

Illmitz 57 F3
Illora 44 A3
Illueca 36 C4
Ilm 52 C3
Ilmajoki 102 C2
Ilmenau R 48 B3
Ilmenau 52 C3
Il'men, Ozero 111 D1
Ilminster 9 D3
Ilok 72 B2
Ilomantsi 103 F2
Ilova 71 D2
Ilovik 70 B4
Ilsenburg 52 B1
Ilsfeld 55 D2
Imathía 79 E3
Imatra 103 F4
Ímeros 81 E2
Imitós 87 F1
Immenstaad 55 D4
Immenstadt 55 E4
Immingham 7 E2
Immingham Dock . . . 7 E2
Imola 61 D3
Imotski 75 E1
Imperia 31 F3
Imphy 26 A3
Impruneta 61 D4
Imst 58 C2
Ina 49 F3
Inari 95 E3
Inarijärvi 95 E3
Inarijoki 95 E3
Inca 45 F2
Inchnadamph 2 C2
Inchtree 2 C4
Incisa in
 Val d'Arno 61 D4
Incudine, M 33 F4
Indal 101 F3
Indalsälven 101 E2
Indija 72 C2
Indre 25 D2
Indre (Dépt) 25 E3
Indre-et-Loire 25 D2
Infiesto 35 E1
Ingå 107 E3
Ingelmunster 50 A3
Ingleton 6 C1

Ingolstadt 55 F2
Ingrandes 23 E4
Ingul 113 F3
Ingulec 113 F3
Ingulec R. 113 F3
Ingwiller 21 E3
Iniesta 41 D4
Inió 107 D2
Iniön aukko 107 D2
Inis 12 B4
Inis Córthaidh 15 D3
Inishbofin 12 A3
Inishcrone 12 B2
Inisheer 12 B4
Inishkea 12 A2
Inishmaan 12 B4
Inishmore 12 B4
Inishmurray 12 C2
Inishowen 13 D1
Inishowen Head . . . 13 D1
Inishshark 12 A3
Inishtrahull 13 D1
Inishturk 12 A3
Inkee 99 E3
Inkoo 107 E3
Inn (CH) 58 B3
Inn (D) 56 B3
Innbygda 104 C1
Inndyr 97 E2
Innellan 4 B2
Innerleithen 5 D2
Inner Sd 2 B3
Innfield 13 D3
Innhavet 97 F1
Innichen 59 E2
Inning 56 A3
Innsbruck 59 D2
Innset 94 B3
Innvik 100 A3
Inói (Pelopónissos) . 86 B1
Inói (Stereá Eláda) . 84 A4
Inoússes 85 F4
Inoússes, N 85 F4
Inowrocław 112 A1
Ins 27 E2
Insko 49 F2
Interlaken 27 F3
Întorsura Buzăuli . . 113 D4
Inveraray 4 B1

Inverbervie 3 E4
Invergarry 2 C4
Invergordon 3 D3
Inverkeithing 5 D2
Invermoriston 2 C4
Inverness 2 C3
Inverurie 3 E4
Inzell 56 B3
Ioánina 82 C1
Ioánina (Nomos) . . . 82 B1
Ioanínon, L 82 C1
Iona 4 A1
Ionia 79 F3
Iónia Nissiá 82 A2
Íos 88 C4
Íos, N. 88 C4
Ipáti 83 E3
Ipéria 83 E2
Iphofen 55 E1
Ípiros 82 B2
Ipsili Ráhi 80 C2
Ípsos 82 A1
Ipsoúnda 86 C2
Ipswich 11 D2
Iput' 111 E4
Iráklia (Makedonía) . 80 A2
Iráklia (Stereá
 Eláda) 83 E3
Iráklia, N. 88 C3
Iráklio 91 D3
Iráklio (Nomos) . . . 91 D4
Irati, R 36 C2
Irbes Šaurums . . . 110 B2
Irdning 57 D4
Iregua, R 36 B2
Iréo (Argolída) 87 D2
Iréo (Dodekánissa) . 89 E2
Iréo (Korinthía) . . . 87 E1
Iréo, Akr 87 E1
Íria 87 E2
Irig 72 C2
Irish Sea 13 F3
Iriški venac 72 C2
Irixoa 34 B1
Irnijärvi 99 E3
Iron-Bridge 9 D1
Irschenberg 56 B3
Irsina 65 D4
Irún 36 C1

Irurzun 36 C2
Irvine 4 C2
Irvinestow 12 C2
Irxleben 52 C1
Isaba 37 D2
Isaccea 113 E4
Ísafjarðardjúp 96 A1
Ísafjörður 96 A1
Ísala 115 E3
Isane 100 A3
Isar 56 B2
Isarco 59 D2
Isbister 3 F1
Iscar 35 E4
Ischgl 58 C2
Ischia 64 A4
Ischia, I d' 64 A4
Ise 105 D3
Isefjord 108 C3
Iselle 58 A3
Iselsberg 59 E2
Iseo 60 B1
Iseo, L d' 58 B4
Iseran, Col de l' . . . 31 E1
Isère (Dépt) 30 C1
Isère (R) 30 C1
Iserlohn 17 E3
Isernia 64 A3
Isfjellet 94 C2
Isfjorden 100 B2
Ishavsleden 94 C3
Ishëm 76 C4
Ishëm R 76 C4
Isigny 18 C3
Isili 66 B3
Iskår 115 D2
Is'kuras 95 E2
Isla 3 D4
Isla 36 A1
Isla Cristina 42 C3
Isla Mayor 43 D3
Island Magee 13 E2
Islay 4 A2
Isle 28 C2
Isle-Adam, l' 19 F3
Isle-de-Noé, l' 9 D1
Isle-en-Dodon, l' . . 37 F1
Isle-Jourdain, l'
 (Gers) 28 C4

Isle-Jourdain, l'
 (Vienne) 25 D4
Isle of Man 6 A1
Isle of Portland 9 D4
Isle of Whithorn 4 C4
Isle of Wight 9 E4
Isleornsay 2 B4
Isles of Scilly 8 A4
Isle-sur-la-
 Sorgue,l' 30 C3
Isle-sur-le-
 Doubs, l' 27 D2
Isle-sur-Serein, l' . . 26 B2
Ismaning 55 F3
Isnäs 107 F2
Isny 55 E4
Iso-Evo 107 E2
Isojärvi 103 D3
Isojoki 102 B3
Isokylä 99 E3
Isokyrö 102 B2
Isola 31 E3
Isola del Gran Sasso
 d'Italia 63 F1
Isola della Scala . . . 60 C1
Isola del Liri 64 A3
Isola di Capo
 Rizzuto 67 F3
Isona 37 F3
Isonzo 59 F3
Isorella 60 B1
Iso-Syöte 99 E3
Ispica 69 D4
Issambres, les 31 D4
Issel 17 D3
Issigeac 28 C2
Issoire 29 F1
Issóvla, M. 86 C2
Íssoma 86 C1
Issoudun 25 E3
Is-sur-Tille 26 B2
Issy-l'Evêque 26 B3
Ist 74 B1
Istán 43 E4
İstanbul 115 F3
Istarske Toplice . . . 70 A3
Istérnia 88 B2
Istha 52 A2
Isthmía 87 E1

Istibanja. 77 F2	Ittiri 66 A2	Ixiá 93 F1
Istiéa 83 F3	Itz 52 C4	Ixworth 11 D1
Istindan 94 B3	Itzehoe. 48 A2	Iž 74 C1
Istok 76 C2	Ivaceviči 112 C1	Izeda 34 C4
Istres 30 C4	Ivajlovgrad 115 E3	Izegem 50 A3
Ístrios 93 E2	Ivalo 95 E3	Izernore 26 C4
Isturits et d'Oxocelhaya,	Ivalojoki Ävvil . . . 95 E3	Izlake 70 B2
Grottes d' 28 A4	Ivančice 57 F1	Izmail 113 E4
Itä-Aure 102 C3	Ivančiči 71 F4	Izmir 115 E4
Itaïnen	Ivančna Gorica. . . 70 B2	Izmit 115 F3
Suomenlahti. . . . 107 F2	Ivanec 70 C1	Iznájar 43 F3
Itanós 91 F3	Ivangrad 76 C2	Iznájar, Emb de. . . 43 F3
Itéa (Flórina) 79 D2	Ivanič Grad 71 D3	Iznallos 44 A3
Itéa (Grevená) . . . 79 D4	Ivanjica 73 D4	Iznik 115 F3
Itéa (Stereá Eláda) . . 83 E4	Ivanjska 71 E3	Iznik Gölü 115 F3
Itéa (Thessalía) . . . 83 E2	Ivankovo 71 F2	Izoard, Col d' 31 D2
Itéas, Kólpos 83 E4	Ivano-Frankovsk . . 113 D3	Izola 70 A3
Itháki 82 B4	Ivanščica 70 C2	Iz Veli 74 C1
Itháki, N 82 B4	Ivan Sedlo 75 F1	Izvor (Makedonija) . . 77 D4
Ithómi 86 C3	Ivanska 71 D2	Izvor
Iti 83 E3	Iveland 104 B4	(Makedonija) 77 E1
Ítilo 87 D4	Iveragh 14 A4	Izvor (Srbija) 73 E4
Íti, Óros. 83 E3	Ívira 80 B2	
Iton 19 E3	Ivíron 80 C4	
Itri 64 A3	Ivrea 31 F1	
Itta 52 B3	Ivry-la-Bataille . . . 19 E4	

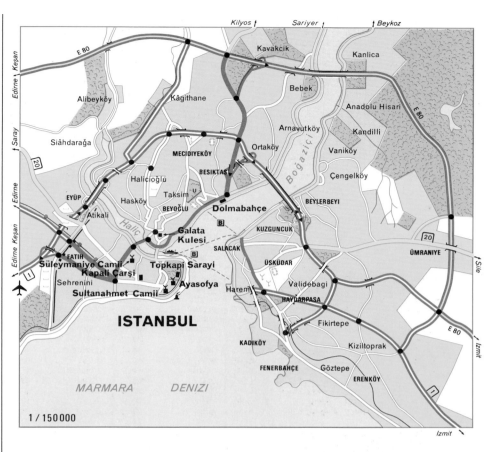

J

	Jäminkipohja. 102 C3	Jasenica (BH) 71 D3
	Jämjö. 109 E3	Jasenica (Srbija) . . . 73 D3
	Jammerbugten . . . 108 A2	Jasenovac 71 D3
Jaala 107 F2	Jamnička Kiselica . . 70 C2	Jasenovo
Jääsjärvi 103 D3	Jämsä. 103 D3	(Crna Gora) 76 B2
Jabalón, R 44 A1	Jämsänkoski 103 D3	Jasenovo (Srbija) . . 76 B1
Jabbeke 50 A3	Jämtlands Län 101 E2	Jasenovo
Jablanac. 70 B4	Janakkala 107 E2	(Vojvodina). 73 D2
Jablan Do 76 A2	Jance 77 D3	Jasień 53 F1
Jablanica 75 F1	Jandía, Pta de 42 C4	Jasika 73 E4
Jablanica (Reg) . . . 77 D4	Jándula, Emb del . . 44 A1	Jasikovo 73 E3
Jablanica R 77 D1	Jandula, R 44 A1	Jaslo 112 C3
Jablaničko jez 75 F1	Jänisselkä 103 F2	Jasmund 49 D1
Jablonec nad	Janja 72 B3	Jastrebarsko 70 C2
Nisou. 112 A2	Janjevo 77 D2	Jastrowie 112 A1
Jablonné v	Janjina 75 E2	Jászberény 112 B4
Podještědí 53 F3	Jankov kamen 76 C1	Jau, Col de 32 B2
Jabugo 42 C2	Jaňona 39 D2	Jaufenpass. 59 D2
Jabuka (BH) 76 A1	Jantra 115 D2	Jaunay-Clan 25 D3
Jabuka (Srbija) . . . 76 B1	Janville 25 E1	Jaunpass 27 E3
Jabuka	Janzé 23 D3	Jausiers 31 D2
(Vojvodina). 73 D2	Japetić 70 C2	Javalambre 41 D3
Jabuka, I 74 C2	Jäppilä 103 E2	Javalambre,
Jabukovac (HR) 71 D3	Jaraba 36 C4	Sa de 41 E3
Jabukovac (Srbija) . . 73 F3	Jarafuel 41 D4	Javalón 41 D2
Jabukovik 77 E1	Jaraicejo 39 E3	Javea 45 E1
Jaca 37 D2	Jaráiz 39 E2	Javenitz 48 C4
Jáchymov 53 E3	Jarak 72 C3	Javie, la 31 D3
Jadar (BH) 72 C4	Jarama, R 40 B2	Javor 76 C1
Jadar (Srbija) 72 B3	Jarandilla de la	Javořice 57 D1
Jäder 106 A3	Vera 39 E2	Javornjača 71 D4
Jaderberg 47 F3	Järbo 106 A2	Javorov 112 C2
Jadovik 76 B1	Jarcevo 111 E3	Jävre 98 B4
Jadovnik 71 D4	Jard 24 B3	Javron 23 E3
Jadranska Lešnica. . 72 B3	Jæren 104 A4	Jedburgh 5 D3
Jadransko More . . . 74 B2	Jaren 105 D2	Jedincy 113 D3
Jadraque 40 B1	Jargeau 25 E1	Jędrzejów 112 B2
Jaén 44 A2	Jarkovac 73 D2	Jeesiö 95 E4
Jagodnjac 71 F2	Jarmen 49 D2	Jeetze 48 B3
Jagotin 113 F2	Jarmenovci 73 D3	Jegun 28 C4
Jagst 55 E2	Jarnac. 28 B1	Jegunovce 77 D3
Jagsthausen 55 D2	Jarnages 25 E4	Jēkabpils 110 C3
Jahorina 76 A1	Järna (Kopparbergs	Jektevik 104 A2
Jahorina (Reg) 76 A1	Län) 105 E2	Jelah 71 E3
Jajce 71 E4	Järna (Stockholms	Jelašca 76 A1
Jäkkvik 97 F2	Län) 106 B4	Jelenia Góra 112 A2
Jakobselv 95 F2	Jarny 21 D3	Jelenje 70 B3
Jakobstad 102 C1	Jarocin 112 A2	Jelgava 110 C3
Jakšić 71 E2	Jaroměřice 57 E1	Ježevica 72 C4
Jakupica 77 E3	Jarosław 112 C2	Jičín. 112 A2
Jalasjärvi 102 C3	Järpen 101 E2	Jiekkevarre 94 C2
Jaligny 26 A3	Jarrow 5 E3	Jelsa (HR) 75 E2
Jalón, R 36 C3	Järvelä 107 F2	Jelsa (N) 104 A3
Jalovik Izvor 73 F4	Järvenpää 107 E2	Jelsi 64 B3
Jambol 115 E2	Järvsö. 101 F3	Jemnice 57 E1
Jamena 72 B3	Jaša Tomić 73 D2	Jena 52 C3
Jämijärvi 102 C3	Jasenak 70 B3	Jenbach 59 D1

Jennersdorf 57 F4	Jimena de la	Jošavka. 71 E3	Jungfrau 27 F3
Jeppo 102 C2	Frontera 43 E4	Josenfjorden. 104 A3	Junik 76 C2
Jerez de la	Jindřichovice 53 D3	Jose Toran, Emb de. 43 E2	Juniville 20 B3
Frontera 43 D3	Jindřichuv Hradec. . 57 D1	Josipdol 70 C3	Junkeren 97 E2
Jerez de	Jirkov 53 E3	Josipovac 71 F2	Junosuando. 95 D4
los Caballeros . . 42 C1	Jiu 115 D2	Josselin 22 C3	Junsele 101 F2
Jérica 41 E3	Jizera 53 F3	Jostedalsbreen . . . 100 A3	Juntusranta 99 F3
Jerichow 49 D4	Joachimsthal 49 E3	Jotunheimen 100 B3	Juojärvi 103 E2
Jerisjärvi 95 D4	Jockfall 98 C2	Jou, Coll de 32 A3	Juoksenki 98 C2
Jerpoint Abbey. . . . 15 D3	Jódar 44 A2	Joué 25 D2	Juorkuna 99 E4
Jersey 18 A3	Jodoigne 50 C3	Jougne 27 D3	Jura 4 B2
Jerte 39 E2	Joensuu 103 F2	Joutjärvi 107 F2	Jura (Canton) 27 E2
Jerte, R. 39 E2	Jõgeva 110 C1	Joutsa 103 D3	Jura (Dépt) 27 D3
Jerxheim 52 B1	Johanngeorgenstadt	Joutseno 103 E4	Jura, Sd of. 4 B2
Jerzu 66 C3	. . . . 53 D3	Joutsijärvi 99 E2	Jurbarkas 110 C3
Jesenice (CS) 53 E4	John o'Groats 3 D2	Joyeuse 30 B2	Jurjevo 70 B4
Jesenice (SLO) 70 A1	Johnstone 4 C2	Juankoski 103 E2	Jürmala 110 C2
Jeseník 112 A2	Johovac 71 F3	Juan-les-Pins 31 E4	Jurmofjärden 107 D3
Jesi 61 F4	Joigny. 26 A1	Júcar, R 41 E4	Jurmu. 99 E3
Jesolo 59 E4	Joinville 20 C4	Jüchen 17 D4	Juromenha 38 C4
Jessen 53 D1	Jokela 107 E2	Juchnov 111 F3	Jurva 102 B2
Jessheim 105 D3	Jokijärvi 99 E3	Judaberg 104 A3	Jussey 27 D1
Jeßnitz 53 D2	Jokikylä 99 E4	Judenau 57 E2	Justel 34 C3
Jetzelsdorf 57 E2	Jokioinen 107 E2	Judenburg 57 D4	Jüterbog 53 E1
Jeumont 20 B1	Jokkmokk 98 B2	Judio 43 F1	Juuka 103 E2
Jevenstedt 48 A2	Jökulsá-á Fjöllum . . 96 C1	Juelsminde 108 B3	Juupajoki 103 D3
Jever 47 E3	Joloskylä 99 D3	Jugenheim 54 C1	Juurusvesi 103 E2
Jevišovice 57 E1	Jølstravatnet 100 A3	Jugon 22 C3	Juva (Mikkelin
Jevnaker 105 D2	Jomala 106 C3	Jugorje. 70 B2	Lääni) 103 E3
Jezerane 70 C3	Jönåker 106 A4	Juillac. 29 D1	Juva (Turun ja Porin
Jezerce 77 D2	Jondal 104 B2	Juist 47 E3	Lääni) 107 D2
Jezercë, M 76 C2	Jongunjärvi 99 E3	Jukkasjärvi. 94 C4	Juvigny-le-Tertre . . . 18 C4
Jezero 71 E4	Joniškis 110 C3	Jülich 17 D4	Juvigny-sous-
Jezero Šćit 75 E1	Jönköping 109 D1	Julierpass 58 B3	Andaine 18 C4
Jezersko 70 B1	Jönköpings Län . . . 109 D2	Jullouville 18 B4	Juvola 103 E3
Ježevica 72 C4	Jonzac. 28 B1	Jumaliskylä 99 F4	Juzennecourt 26 C1
Jičín. 112 A2	Jordbro 106 B4	Jumeaux 29 F1	Južna Morava 73 E4
Jiekkevarre 94 C2	Jordbruksveien . . . 95 D2	Jumièges 19 D3	Južnyj Bug 113 E2
Jihlava 57 E1	Jormlien 97 E4	Jumilhac-	Jyderup 108 B3
Jihlava R. 57 E1	Jörn 98 B4	le-Grand 29 D1	Jylland 108 A3
Jijona 45 E1	Joroinen 103 E3	Jumilla 45 D1	Jyrkkä 103 E1
Jiloca, R 41 D2	Jørpeland 104 A3	Jumilla, Pto de 45 D1	Jyväskylä, R 103 D3
Jilové u Prahy 53 D1	Jørstadmoen 105 D2	Juminen 103 E1	
Jimbolia 114 C1	Jošanica 73 D4	Jumisko 99 E2	
Jimena 44 A2	Jošanička Banja . . . 76 C1	Juneda 37 F4	

K

Kaakamo 99 D3
Kaamanen 95 E3
Kaamaskoki 95 E2
Kaaresuvanto 95 D3
Kaarina 107 D2
Kaatsheuvel 16 C3
Kaavi 103 E2
Kaavinjärvi 103 E2
Kåbdalis 98 B3
Kablart 72 C4
Kač 72 C2
Kačanik 77 D2
Kačarevo 73 D2
Kachul 113 E4
Kačikol 77 D2
Kadaň 53 E3
Kadi Bogaz 73 F4
Kadrifakovo 77 E3
Kafiréas, Akr 84 C4
Kafiréa, Stenó 88 B1
Kåfjord 95 E1
Kåfjorden 94 C2
Kaga 106 A4
Kagarlyk 113 E2
Kahla 52 C3
Kaiáfas 86 B2
Kailbach 55 D1
Kaïmaktsalán 79 E2
Kainasto 102 B3
Kaindorf 57 E4
Kaipola 103 D3
Kairala 95 F4
Kaisergebirge 59 D1
Kaiserslautern 54 B1
Kaisheim 55 E2
Kaitumälven 94 C4
Kaiudđerovo 73 E2
Kajaani 99 E4
Kakan 74 C1
Kakanj 71 F4
Kaki Thálassa 88 A1
Kakí Vigla 87 F1
Kakslauttanen 95 E3
Kalajoki 102 C1
Kalajoki R. 102 C1
Kalak 95 E1
Kalamáki
(Lárissa) 83 F2
Kalamáki
(Magnissía) 84 A2
Kalamáki, Akr 85 D2
Kalamáta 86 C3
Kalambáka 83 D1
Kalambáki 80 C2
Kalámi 89 E1
Kalamiótissa 91 F1
Kalamítsi
(Makedonía) 80 B4
Kalamítsi (Stereá
Eláda) 82 B3
Kálamos, N 82 C3
Kalamotí 85 F4
Kalamotó 80 A3
Kalándra 80 A4
Kalá Nerá 83 F2
Kalá Nissiá 87 E1
Kalanti 107 D2
Kalapódi 83 F3
Kalaraš 113 E3
Kälarne 101 F2
Kalavárda 93 E1
Kalávrita 86 C1
Kal'azin 111 F1
Kalbe 48 C4
Kalce 70 A2
Kaldakvísl 96 B2
Kaléndzi (Ípiros) . . . 82 C2
Kaléndzi
(Pelopónissos) . . . 86 C1
Kalenić 73 D4
Kalérgo 84 C4
Kalesija 72 B3
Kalí 74 C1
Kaliakoúda 83 D3
Kaliáni 87 D1
Kalidromo, Óros . . . 83 E3
Kalifitos 80 C2
Kalí Liménes 91 D4
Kalí Limni 93 D3
Kalimassiá 85 F4
Kalimenci, Ez 77 F2

Kálimnos 89 F3
Kálimnos, N 89 E3
Kaliningrad 110 B4
Kalinkoviči 113 E1
Kalinovik 75 F1
Kalipéfki 79 E4
Kaliráhi 79 D4
Kalithéa
(Dodekánissa) . . . 93 F1
Kalithéa
(Ilía) 86 C2
Kalithéa
(Makedonía) 80 B2
Kalithéa
(Messinía) 86 C3
Kalithéa (Stereá
Eláda) 83 D3
Kalithéa (Thessalía) . . 80 B4
Kalithiés 93 F1
Kalithiro 83 D2
Kalivári 88 B1
Kalíves (Kríti) 90 C3
Kalíves (Thássos) . . . 80 C3
Kalivia
(Ahaía) 86 C1
Kalivia (Atiki-
Piréas) 87 F1
Kalivia (Etolía-
Akarnanía) 82 C3
Kalivia
(Korinthía) 87 D1
Kalivia Varikoú 79 F4
Kalix 98 C3
Kalixälven 98 C2
Kaljord 94 A3
Kalkar 17 D3
Kalkkinen 107 F1
Kall 101 D2
Kallaktjåkkå 94 B4
Kallavesi 103 E2
Källby 102 C1
Källby 105 E4
Kallinge 109 E3
Kallio 102 C3
Kalliojoki 99 F4
Kallislahti 103 E3
Kallmünz 55 F2
Kallsjön 101 D1
Kalmar 109 E2
Kalmar Län 109 E2
Kalmar sund 109 E2
Kalmit 54 C2
Kalna 73 F4
Kalnik 71 D2
Kalnik Mt 71 D2
Kalocsa 112 B4
Kalogerikoú 87 D2
Kalogriá 86 B1
Kalohóri 83 D1
Kaló Horió 91 E4
Kalókastro 80 A2
Kaló Neró 86 C3
Kaloní (Lésvos) 85 F2
Kaloní
(Pelopónissos) . . . 87 E2
Kalonís, Kólpos 85 E2
Kaloskopí 83 E3
Kalotássi, Akr 89 D4
Kalø Vig 108 B3
Kalpáki 78 C4
Kals 59 E2
Kalsdorf 57 E4
Kaltenkirchen 48 A2
Kaltennordheim 52 B3
Kaltern 59 D3
Kaltezés 87 D2
Kaluga 111 F3
Kalundborg 108 B3
Kaluš 112 C3
Kalvåg 104 A1
Kalvehave 108 C4
Kälviä 102 C1
Kalvola 107 E2
Kalvträsk 98 B4
Kamáres (Kríti) 91 D4
Kamarés (Páros) . . . 88 C3
Kamáres
(Pelopónissos) . . . 83 D4
Kamáres (Sifnos) . . . 88 B3
Kamári 91 E1
Kamariótissa 81 E3
Kambanós, Akr 88 B1
Kambiá 85 E4

Kámbos (Kríti) 90 B3
Kámbos
(Pelopónissos) . . . 86 C3
Kámbos (Stereá
Eláda) 83 D4
Kamčija 115 E2
Kamen 17 E3
Kamenari 76 A3
Kaména Voúria 83 F3
Kamenec-
Podol'skij 113 D3
Kamenica 77 F2
Kamenice 57 D1
Kaméni, N 91 E1
Kamenjak, Rt 70 A4
Kamenka 113 F2
Kamensko (HR) 71 E2
Kamensko (HR) 75 E1
Kamenz 53 F2
Kamień Pomorski . . . 49 E2
Kamieński, Zalew . . . 49 E2
Kamilári 91 D4
Kaminia 86 B1
Kámiros 93 E1
Kámiros Kastélo 93 E1
Kamnik 70 B2
Kamp 57 E2
Kamp-Bornhofen . . . 51 E4
Kampen (D) 47 F1
Kampen (NL) 17 D2
Kamp-Lintfort 17 D3
Kanal 70 A2
Kanála 88 A2
Kanal Dunav-Tisa-
Dunav 73 D2
Kanália 55 D4
Kándanos 90 B3
Kánava 88 A4
Kandel 54 C2
Kandel Mt 54 C3
Kandern 54 C4
Kandersteg 27 F3
Kándia 87 E2
Kandila
(Pelopónissos) . . . 87 D2
Kandíla (Stereá
Eláda) 82 C3
Kandili 84 A3
Kandíra 115 F3
Kandrše 70 B2
Kanestraum 100 B2
Kanev 113 F2
Kanfanar 70 A3
Kangádio 86 B1
Kangasala 107 E1
Kangaslampi 103 E2
Kangasniemi 103 D3
Kangosjärvi 95 D4
Kanjiža 72 C1
Kankaanpää 102 C3
Kannonkoski 103 D2
Kannus 102 C1
Kannusjärvi 103 E4
Kanturk 14 B3
Kaona 73 D4
Kaonik (BH) 71 F4
Kaonik (Srbija) 73 E4
Kapandríti 87 F1
Kaparéli 83 F4
Kapariá 88 B2
Kapele, Vrh 70 C3
Kapellskär 106 C3
Kapélo, Akr 90 A2
Kapfenberg 57 E3
Kaplice 57 D2
Kaposvár 114 B1
Kapp 105 D2
Kappel 51 E4
Kappeln 48 A1
Kappelshamnsviken
. . . . 109 F3
Kaprije 74 C1
Kaprun 59 E1
Kapsáli 90 A2
Kapsas 87 D2
Kapsoúri 88 B1
Kapuvár 112 A4
Karabiga 115 E3
Karaburun 115 E4
Karačev 111 F4
Karadeniz Boğazı . . . 115 F3
Karan 72 C4
Karasjåkka 95 E2

Karasjok 95 E2
Karasu 115 F3
Karats 98 A2
Karavás 90 A1
Karavómilos 83 D3
Karavónissia 92 C2
Karavostássis 91 D1
Karcag 112 B4
Kardámena 89 F3
Kardámili 85 E4
Kardamíli 86 C3
Kardeljevo 75 E2
Kärdla 110 B1
Karditsa 55 D4
Karditsa (Nomos) . . . 55 D4
Kårdžali 115 D3
Karerpass 59 D3
Karesuando 95 D3
Karfás 85 F4
Karhukangas 99 D4
Karhula 103 F4
Karhunkierros 99 F2
Karhutunturi 95 F4
Kariá
(Pelopónissos) . . . 87 D2
Kariá (Stereá
Eláda) 83 F3
Kariés
(Makedonía) 80 C4
Kariés
(Pelopónissos) . . . 87 D3
Karigasniemi 95 E2
Karijoki 102 B3
Karinainen 107 D2
Kariótisa 79 E3
Karis 107 E3
Karítena 86 C2
Karjaa 107 E3
Karjalohja 107 E3
Karkaloú 86 C2
Karkinágri 89 D2
Karkku 107 D1
Kärkölä 107 E2
Karleby 102 C1
Karlevi 109 E3
Karlino 49 F1
Karlobag 70 C4
Karlovac 70 C3
Karlovássi 89 E1
Karlovo 115 D2
Karlovy Vary 53 E4
Karlsborg 105 E4
Karlsburg 49 D2
Karlsfeld 55 F3
Karlshamn 109 D3
Karlshuld 55 F2
Karlskoga 105 E4
Karlskrona 109 E3
Karlsøy 94 C2
Karlsruhe 54 C2
Karlstad 105 E3
Karlstadt 52 B4
Karlštejn 53 F4
Karlstift 57 D2
Karmøy 104 A3
Karnezéika 87 E2
Kärnten 59 F2
Karolinerleden 101 E2
Karow 48 C2
Kärpankylä 99 F2
Kárpathos 93 D3
Kárpathos, N 93 D3
Karpeníssi 83 D3
Karperí 80 A2
Karperó 79 D4
Kärsämäki 103 D1
Kårsatjåkka 94 B4
Kärsava 111 D2
Karstädt 48 C3
Karstula 103 D2
Kartal 115 F3
Kartéri (Ípiros) 82 B2
Kartéri
(Pelopónissos) . . . 87 D1
Karterós 91 D3
Kártsino, Akr 84 C3
Karttula 103 E2
Kartuzy 110 A4
Karungi 98 C3
Karunki 98 C3
Karup 108 A2

Karvala 102 C2
Kärväskylä 103 D2
Karvia 102 C3
Karviná 112 B3
Karvoskylä 103 D1
Karvounári 82 B2
Karwendelgebirge . . . 59 D1
Kašalj 76 C1
Kašin 111 F1
Kašina 70 C2
Kaskinen 102 B3
Kasko 102 B3
Káspakas 85 D1
Kašperské Hory 56 C1
Kassándra 80 B4
Kassándras,
Kólpos 80 B4
Kassándria 80 A4
Kassel 52 A2
Kassiópi 82 A1
Kassópi 82 B2
Kássos, N 93 D3
Kastaniá
(Makedonía) 79 E3
Kastaniá
(Pelopónissos) . . . 87 D1
Kastaniá
(Thessalía) 82 C1
Kastaniá
(Thessalía) 83 D2
Kastaniés 81 F1
Kastaniótissa 83 F3
Kastéla 84 B4
Kastelhoms 106 C3
Kastéli (Kríti) 90 B3
Kastéli (Kríti) 91 E4
Kastellaun 51 E4
Kastelórizo 93 F2
Kastélou, Akr 93 D3
Kastelruth 59 D3
Kaštel Stari 75 D1
Kaštel Žegarski 75 D1
Kasterlee 50 C3
Kastl 55 F1
Kastorf 48 B2
Kastóri 87 D3
Kastoriá 79 D3
Kastoriá (Nomos) . . . 78 C3
Kastoriás, L 79 D3
Kastós, N 82 C4
Kastráki (Kikládes) . . 88 C3
Kastráki (Stereá
Eláda) 82 C3
Kastráki (Thessalía) . . 83 D1
Kastrakíou, Teh L . . . 82 C3
Kastri
(Pelopónissos) . . . 87 D2
Kastrí (Stereá
Eláda) 83 E3
Kastrí (Thessalía) . . . 83 F1
Kástro
(Pelopónissos) . . . 86 B1
Kástro (Skiathos) . . . 84 A3
Kástro (Stereá
Eláda) 83 F4
Kastrossikiá 82 B2
Katáfito 80 B1
Katáfourko 82 C3
Katahás 79 F3
Katákolo 86 B2
Katálako 85 D1
Kátano, Akr 88 A3
Katápola 89 D3
Katára 82 C1
Katastári 86 A1
Katavía 93 E2
Katelimátsa 91 F1
Kateliós 86 A1
Kateríni 79 F4
Katerloch 57 E4
Kefalári 87 D2
Kefalás, Akr 80 C3
Katharó 91 E4
Katheni 84 B4
Katići 76 C1
Kätkäsuvanto 95 D3
Katlanovo 77 E3
Katlanovska Banja . . 77 E3
Katlenburg-Duhm . . 52 B2
Káto Ahaía 86 B1
Káto Alissós 86 B1
Káto Asséa 87 D2
Káto Dolianá 87 D2
Káto Figália 86 C2
Káto Gadzéa 83 F2

Katohí 82 C4
Káto Kamíla 80 B2
Káto Klinés 79 D2
Káto Makrinoú 83 D4
Katoméri, Akr 88 C3
Káto
Moussounítsa . . . 83 E3
Káto Nevrokópi 80 B1
Káto Ólimbos 83 E1
Káto Tithoréa 83 E4
Katoúna (Lefkáda) . . 82 B3
Katoúna (Stereá
Eláda) 82 C3
Káto Vassiliki 83 D4
Káto Vérga 86 C3
Káto Vérmio 79 E3
Káto Vlassía 86 C1
Katowice 112 B2
Káto Zahloroú 86 C1
Káto Zákros 91 F4
Katrineholm 106 A4
Katschberg 59 F2
Katschberg-
Tunnel 59 F2
Kattegat 108 C2
Katwijk aan Zee . . . 16 B2
Kaub 51 F4
Kaufbeuren 55 E3
Kauhajärvi 102 C2
Kauhajoki 102 B3
Kauhaneva-
Pohjankangas . . . 102 C3
Kauhava 102 C2
Kaukonen 95 E4
Kaunas 110 C3
Kaupanger 104 B1
Kaušany 113 E4
Kaustinen 102 C2
Kautokeino 95 D3
Kautokeinoelva 95 D3
Kauttua 107 D2
Kavadarci 77 E3
Kavajë 76 C4
Kavála 80 C2
Kavála (Nomos) 80 C2
Kaválas, Kólpos 80 C2
Kavarna 115 E2
Kavili 81 F1
Kavírio-Hlói 81 E4
Kävlinge 108 C3
Kávos 82 A2
Kavoússi 91 F4
Käylä 99 E2
Kaysersberg 27 E1
Kazan 73 D2
Kazáni 73 D2
Kazanlâk 115 D2
Kazárma 86 C3
Kazatin 113 E2
Kazimierz Dolny . . . 112 C2
Kazincbarcika 112 B3
Kdyně 56 B1
Kéa 88 A2
Keadew 12 C2
Keady 13 D2
Keähkkiljohka 95 D3
Keal, L na 4 B1
Kéa Meriá 88 A2
Kéa, N 88 A2
Kéas, Stenó 88 A2
Kebnekaise 94 B4
Kebnekaise Mt 94 B4
Kebock Head 2 B2
Kecskemét 112 B4
Kédainiai 110 C3
Kédros 83 D2
Kędzierzyn-
Koźle 112 B2
Keel 12 A2
Keerbergen 50 C3
Kefalári 87 D2
Kefalás, Akr 80 C3
Kefáli, Akr 90 A2
Kefaloniá, N 82 B4
Kéfalos 89 F4
Kéfalos, Akr 88 A2
Kefalóvrisso
(Ípiros) 78 C4
Kefalóvrisso
(Pelopónissos) . . . 86 C3
Kefalóvrisso (Stereá
Eláda) 82 C4
Kefalóvrisso
(Thessalía) 83 D1

Keflavík 96 A2
Kehl 54 C3
Kehlstein 56 C4
Kehrókambos 80 C2
Kéhros 81 E2
Keighley 6 C2
Keimaneigh,
Pass of 14 B4
Keitele 103 D2
Keitele L. 103 D2
Keith 3 D3
Kéla 79 D2
Kelankylä 99 E3
Kelberg 51 E4
Kelbra 52 C2
Këlcyrë 114 C4
Kelebija 72 B1
Kelefá 87 D4
Kelheim 55 F2
Kellinghusen 48 A2
Kellojärvi 99 F4
Kellokoski 107 E2
Kells 13 D3
Kelso 5 E2
Kelujärvi 95 E4
Kemberg 53 D1
Kembs 27 E1
Kemi 99 D3
Kemihaara 95 F4
Kemijärvi 99 E2
Kemijärvi L. 99 E2
Kemijoki 99 D2
Keminmaa 99 D3
Kemiö 107 D3
Kemnath 53 D4
Kempele 99 D4
Kempen 17 D4
Kempenich 51 E4
Kempten 55 E4
Kendal 6 C1
Kéndras, Akr 88 B3
Kendrikó 79 F2
Kenilworth 9 E1
Kenmare 14 A4
Kenmare River 14 A4
Kennacraig 4 B2
Kenoúrgio 83 D3
Kent 11 D3
Kentallen 4 B1
Kenzingen 54 C3
Keramía 85 E4
Keramídi 83 F2
Keramítsa 82 B1
Kéramos 85 E4
Keramotí 81 D2
Kerassiá (Évia) 84 A3
Kerassiá (Thessalía) . . 83 F2
Kerassiés 79 E3
Kerassohóri 83 D3
Kerassóna 82 C2
Kérata, Akr 83 F3
Keratéa 87 F1
Kerava 107 E2
Kerdília, N. 80 B3
Kérês 72 C1
Kerí 86 A2
Kerimäki 103 F3
Kerken 17 D3
Kerketéas, Óros . . . 89 E1
Kerkétio, Óri. 83 D2
Kerkini, Óros 80 A1
Kerkínis, L 80 A2
Kérkira 82 A1
Kérkira, N 82 A1
Kerkonkoski 103 D2
Kerkrade 51 D3
Kernascléden 22 B3
Kéros, N 88 C3
Kerpen 17 D4
Kerrera 4 B1
Kerry 14 B3
Kerry Head 14 A3
Kerteminde 108 B3
Kértezi 86 C1
Kerzers 27 E2
Kesälahti 103 F3
Keşan 115 E3
Kesch, Piz 58 B3
Kesh 12 C2
Keski-Suomen
Lääni 103 D2
Kessariani 87 F1
Kestilä 99 D4
Keswick 5 D4

Keszthely	112 A4	Keukenhof	16 B2	Key, L	12 C3
Kętrzyn	110 B4	Keurusselkä	103 D3	Keynsham	9 D2
Kettering	9 F1	Keuruu	102 C3	Kežmarok	112 B3
Kettletoft	3 E1	Kevelaer	17 D3	Kianí	81 F1
Kettwig	17 E4	Kevo	95 E2	Kiantajärvi	99 F3
Ketzin	49 D4	Kevo (Nat Pk)	95 E2	Kiáto	87 D1

Kiberg	95 F1	Kiefersfelden	56 B4	Kiental	27 F3
Kičevo	77 D3	Kiekinkoski	99 F4	Kierinki	99 D1
Kidderminster	9 D1	Kiel	48 A1	Kietz	49 F4
Kidlington	9 E2	Kielce	112 B2	Kifissiá	87 F1
Kidsgrove	6 C3	Kielder Reservoir	5 E3	Kifissos	83 F4
Kidwelly	8 C2	Kieler Bucht	48 A1	Kifjord	95 E1

Kihlanki	95 D4
Kihniö	102 C3
Kihti Skiftet	107 D3
Kiihtelysvaara	103 F2
Kiikala	107 E2
Kiikka	107 D2

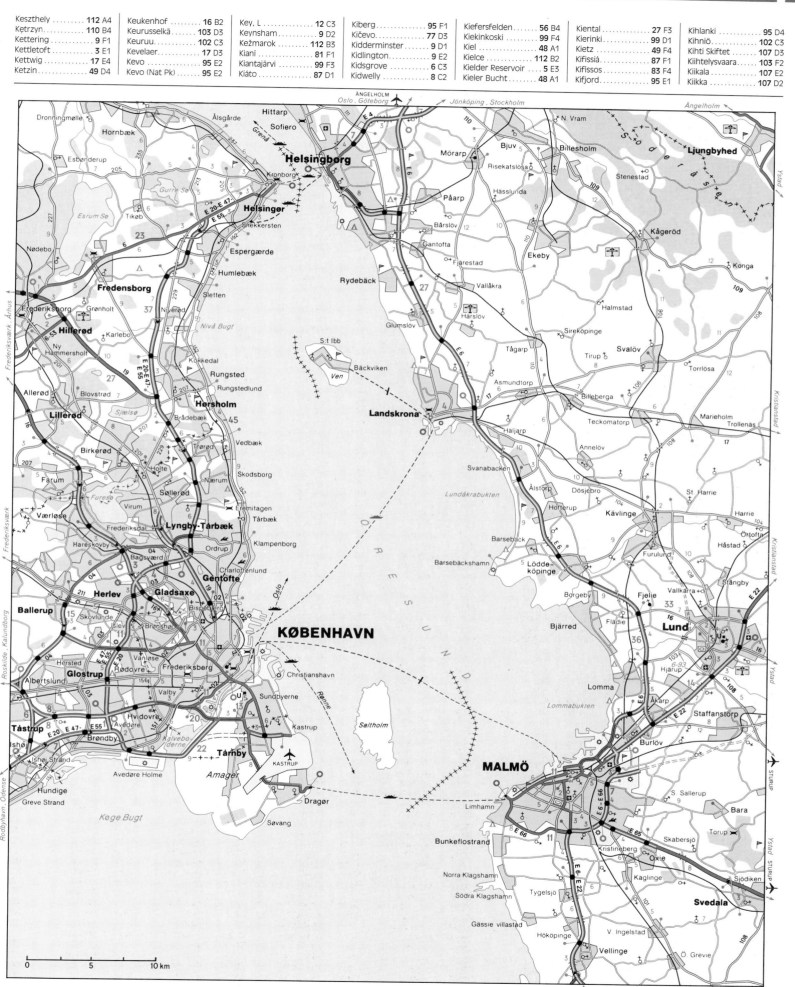

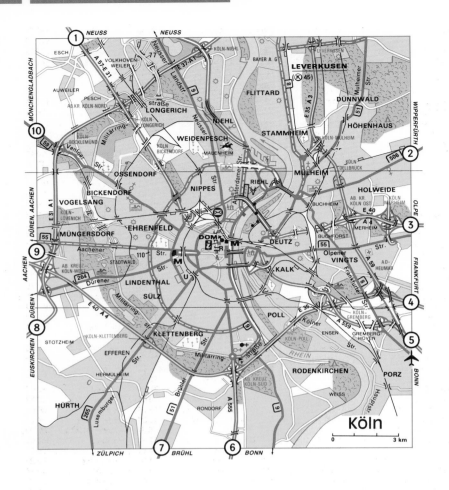

Köln

Kiikoinen 107 D1
Kiimanen 99 E4
Kiiminginjoki 99 D3
Kiiminki 99 D3
Kiiskilä 102 C1
Kiistala 95 E4
Kijev 113 E2
Kijevo (HR) 75 D1
Kijevo (Kosovo) 77 D2
Kijevskoje Vodochranilišče .. 113 E2
Kikinda 72 C1
Kiklades 88 B2
Kil 105 E3
Kila 79 D3
Kiláda (Makedonía) . 79 E3
Kiláda (Pelopónissos) .. 87 E2
Kilafors 101 F4
Kilbaha 12 A4
Kilbeggan 12 C4
Kilbirnie 4 C2
Kilboghamn 97 E2
Kilbotn 94 B3
Kilbrannan Sd. 4 B2
Kilchoan 2 B4
Kilcock 13 D4
Kilcormac 12 C4
Kilcreggan 4 C2
Kilcullen 13 D4
Kildare 13 D4
Kildare (Co) 13 D4
Kildorrery 14 C3
Kilfenora 12 B4
Kilgarvan 14 B4
Kilija 113 E4
Kilingi-Nõmme ... 110 C2
Kilíni 86 B1
Kilíni, Óros 87 D1
Kilkee 12 A4
Kilkeel 13 E3
Kilkenny 15 D3
Kilkenny (Co) 15 D3
Kilkhampton 8 B3

Kilkieran B 12 A3
Kilkís 79 F2
Kilkis (Nomos) 79 F2
Killadysert 12 B4
Killala B 12 B2
Killaloe 12 B4
Killarney 14 B4
Killary Harbour 12 A3
Killashandra 12 C3
Killenaule 14 C3
Killimer 12 B4
Killin 4 C1
Killinkoski 102 C3
Killorglin 14 A3
Killybegs 12 C2
Killyleagh 13 E2
Kilmaine 12 B3
Kilmallock 14 B3
Kilmarnock 4 C2
Kilmartin 4 B2
Kilmore Quay 15 D4
Kilmurry 12 B4
Kilninver 4 B1
Kilnsea 7 E2
Kilpisjärvi 94 C3
Kilpisjärvi *L* 94 C3
Kilrea 13 D1
Kilronan 12 B4
Kilrush 12 B4
Kilsyth 4 C2
Kiltamagh 12 B3
Kiltealy 15 D3
Kilwinning 4 C2
Kılyos 115 F3
Kimássi 84 A3
Kiméria 81 D2
Kími 84 B3
Kímina 79 F3
Kimis, Órmos 84 B4
Kimísseos Theotókou ... 87 D2
Kimito 107 D3
Kimolos 88 B4
Kimolos, N 88 B4

Kimólou Sifnou, Stenó 88 B3
Kimry 111 F2
Kimstad 105 F4
Kínaros, N 89 D3
Kinbrace 3 D2
Kincardine 5 D2
Kindberg 57 E3
Kindelbrück 52 C2
Kinéta 87 E1
Kingisepp 111 D1
Kingissepp 110 B2
Kingsbridge 8 C4
Kingscourt 13 D3
King's Lynn 7 E3
Kingston 9 F2
Kingston-upon-Hull 7 E2
Kingswear 8 C4
Kington 9 D1
Kingussie 3 D4
Kínira 81 D3
Kinlochbervie 2 C2
Kinlochewe 2 C3
Kinloch Rannoch 4 C1
Kinna 108 C1
Kinnairds Head 3 E3
Kinnasniemi 103 F2
Kinnegad 13 D3
Kinnitty 12 C4
Kinnula 103 D2
Kinross 5 D2
Kinsale 14 B4
Kinsarvik 104 B2
Kintaus 103 D3
Kintore 3 E4
Kintyre 4 B2
Kinvarra 12 B4
Kinzig 54 C3
Kióni 82 B4
Kiparíssi 87 E3
Kiparissía 86 C3
Kiparissiakós Kólpos 86 B2

Kiparissías, Óri 86 C3
Kipárissos 83 E2
Kípi (Ípiros) 78 C4
Kípi (Thráki) 81 F2
Kipinä 99 D3
Kípos, Akr 81 E3
Kipourío 79 D4
Kippure 13 D4
Kipséli 83 E2
Kir 76 C3
Kirá Panagiá, N 84 B2
Kirchbach 57 E4
Kirchberg (Niederösterreich) 57 E2
Kirchberg (Rheinland-Pfalz) .. 54 B1
Kirchberg (Sachsen) 53 D3
Kirchberg (Tirol) .. 59 E1
Kirchberg an der Pielach 57 E3
Kirchdorf 57 D3
Kirchenlamitz 53 D4
Kirchenthumbach .. 53 D4
Kirchhain 52 A3
Kirchheim (Baden-Württemberg) ... 55 D2
Kirchheim (Hessen) 52 B3
Kirchheimbolanden . 54 C1
Kirchheim unter Teck 55 D2
Kirchhundem 17 F4
Kirchlengern 17 F2
Kirchmöser 49 D4
Kirchschlag 57 F3
Kiriakí 81 F1
Kiriáki 83 F4
Kiriši 111 E1
Kırkağaç 115 E4
Kirkby Lonsdale 6 B1
Kirkby Stephen 5 E4
Kirkcaldy 5 D2
Kirkcolm 4 B3

Kirkcudbright 4 C3
Kirkenær 105 D2
Kirkenes 95 F2
Kirkeøy 105 D4
Kirkestinden 94 B3
Kirkham 6 B2
Kirki 81 E2
Kirkintilloch 4 C2
Kirkjubøur 96 A4
Kirkkonummi 107 E3
Kirklareli 115 E3
Kirkonmaanselkä .. 103 F4
Kirkwall 3 E1
Kirn 54 B1
Kirov 111 F3
Kirovograd 113 F2
Kirovsk 111 D1
Kirriemuir 5 D1
Kirtorf 52 A3
Kiruna 94 C4
Kisa 109 E1
Kisac 72 C2
Kiseljak (Loznica) .. 72 B3
Kiseljak (Sarajevo) .. 75 F1
Kiseljak (Tuzla) 71 F3
Kišin'ov 113 E3
Kisko 107 E3
Kiskőrös 112 B4
Kiskunfélegyháza . 112 B4
Kiskunhalas 114 B1
Kissámou, Kólpos ... 90 B3
Kißlegg 55 E4
Kissoú Kámbos 90 C4
Kistanje 75 D1
Kisújszállás 112 B4
Kisvárda 112 C3
Kíta 87 D4
Kitee 103 F3
Kithira 90 A2
Kithira, N 90 A2
Kithnos 88 A2
Kithnos, N 88 A2
Kíthnou, Stenó 88 A2
Kitinen 95 E4
Kitka 99 E2
Kitriés, Akr 86 C3
Kittilä 95 E4
Kittsee 57 F2
Kitzbühel 59 E1
Kitzingen 55 E1

Klazienaveen 17 E2
Kleinhaugsdorf 57 E2
Kleinheubach 55 D1
Kleinwalsertal 55 E4
Klekovača 71 D4
Klenike 77 E2
Klenovica 70 B3
Kleppe 104 A3
Kleppestø 104 A2
Kleve 17 D3
Kličevac 73 D2
Klimoviči 111 E4
Klimpfjäll 97 E4
Klin 111 F2
Klina 76 C2
Klinča Selo 70 C2
Klincy 111 E4
Klingenbach 57 F3
Klingenthal 53 D3
Klinovec 53 E3
Klintehamn 109 F4
Klippan 108 C3
Klippen 97 E3
Klippitztörl 57 D4
Klis 75 D1
Klissoúra 79 D3
Klisura (Makedonija) 77 F3
Klisura (Srbija) 77 E1
Klitoría 86 C1
Klitten 53 F2
Klixbüll 47 F1
Kljajićevo 72 B2
Ključ 71 D4
Kłodzko 112 A2
Kløfta 105 D3
Klokkarvik 104 A2
Klokočevac 73 F3
Klos 76 C4
Kloštar 71 D2
Kloštar Ivanić 71 D2
Klösterle 58 B2
Klosterneuburg 57 F2
Klosters 58 B2
Kloten 58 A2
Klötze 48 C4
Klöverträsk 98 B3
Klövsjö 101 E3
Kluczbork 112 A2
Klupe 71 E3
Klütz 48 B2
Knapdale 4 B2
Knappogue Castle .. 12 B4
Knäred 109 D2
Knaresborough 6 C1
Knarvik 104 A2
Kneginec 71 D1
Kneža 115 D2
Knežak 70 B3
Kneževi Vinogradi . 71 F2
Kneževo 71 F2
Knežica 71 D3
Knežina 72 B4
Knić 73 D4
Knidi 79 D4
Knighton 9 D1
Knight's Town 14 A4
Knin 75 D1
Knittelfeld 57 D4
Knivskjellodden ... 95 D1
Knivsta 106 B3
Knjaževac 73 F4
Knockmealdown Mts. 14 C3
Knokke-Heist 50 A3
Knole House 10 C3
Knossós 91 D3
Knutsford 6 C2
Koarvikodds 95 E3
Kobarid 70 A2
Kobbfjorden 95 D1
Kobel'aki 113 F2
København 108 C3
Kobern-Gondorf ... 51 E4
Kobišnica 73 F3
Koblenz 51 E4
Kobrin 112 C1
Koca D 115 F3
Kočani 77 F2
Kočerin 75 E2
Kočevje 70 B2
Kočevski rog 70 B2
Kochel 56 A4

Kocher 55 E2
Kodiksami 107 D2
Kodisjoki 107 D2
Köflach 57 E4
Køge 108 C3
Køge Bugt 108 C3
Kohtla-Järve 110 C1
Koikkala 103 E3
Koirakoski 103 E1
Koitajoki 103 F2
Koitelainen 95 E4
Koitere 103 F2
Koivujärvi 103 D1
Koivusuo 103 F2
Kokála 87 D4
Kokar 106 C3
Kokári 89 E1
Kökarsfjärden 106 C3
Kokemäenjoki 107 D1
Kokemäki 107 D2
Kokin Brod 76 B1
Kókino Neró 83 F1
Kokkola 102 C1
Kokotí 83 F3
Koksijde-Bad 50 A3
Kola 71 E3
Koláka 83 F4
Kolari (SF) 98 C1
Kolari (Srbija) 73 D3
Kolåsen 101 D2
Kolašin 76 B2
Kolbäck 105 F3
Kołbacz 49 F2
Kołbaskowo 49 E2
Kolbermoor 56 B3
Kolby Kås 108 B3
Kolding 108 A3
Kolho 103 D3
Koli 103 F2
Kolima 103 D2
Kolimvári 90 B3
Kolin 112 A3
Kolindrós 79 F3
Kolines 87 D2
Kolka 110 B2
Kolkanlahti 103 D2
Kolkasrags 110 B2
Kölleda 52 C2
Kolmården 106 A4
Köln 17 E4
Koło 112 B1
Kołobrzeg 49 F1
Koločep 75 F2
Kolomyja 113 D3
Koloveč 56 B1
Kolovrat 76 B1
Kolpino 111 D1
Kolsva 105 F3
Kolubara 72 C3
Kolvereid 97 C4
Komagfjord 95 D2
Kómanos 79 D3
Komar 71 E4
Kómara 81 F1
Komarnica 76 B2
Komárno 112 B4
Kombóti 82 C2
Kómeno 82 C3
Kómi (Kikládes) ... 88 B2
Kómi (Híos) 89 D1
Komilío 82 B3
Komin 70 C2
Kómito 88 B1
Komiža 75 D2
Komló 114 B1
Komninádes 78 C3
Komniná (Makedonía) 79 D2
Komniná (Thráki) . 81 D2
Komorane 77 D2
Komotiní 81 E2
Komovi 76 B2
Komrat 113 E4
Komulanköngäs ... 99 E4
Konak 73 D2
Konakovo 111 F2
Končanica 71 D2
Kondiás 85 D1
Kondopoúli 85 D1
Kondós, Akr 88 B3
Kondovázena 86 C1
Kondrić 71 F2
Konečka pl 77 D2
Køng 108 C4

Kiukainen 107 D2
Kiuruvesi 103 D1
Kiutaköngäs 99 E2
Kivalo 99 D3
Kivéri 87 D2
Kivi 88 B2
Kivijärvi 103 D2
Kivijärvi *L* (Keski-Suomen Lääni) 103 D2
Kivijärvi *L* (Kymen-Lääni) ... 103 E4
Kivilahti 103 F2
Kivitaipale 99 E2
Kivotós 79 D4
Kizário 81 E2
Kjellerup 108 A2
Kjerringøy 97 E1
Kjerringvåg 100 C1
Kjerringvik 101 D1
Kjølifjell 101 D2
Kjøllefjord 95 E1
Kjøpsvik 94 B4
Kjustendil 114 C3
Klæbu 100 C2
Kladanj 72 B4
Kladnica 76 C1
Kladnice 75 D1
Kladno 53 F4
Kladovo 73 F2
Klagenfurt 70 A1
Klaipėda 110 B3
Klaksvik 96 A3
Klana 70 B3
Klanac 70 C4
Klanxbüll 47 F1
Klarälven 105 E2
Klašnice 71 E3
Klässbol 105 E3
Klašterec 53 E3
Klasvík 96 A3
Klaukkala 107 E2
Klausen 59 D2
Klausenpass 58 A2

Köngernheim 54 C1
Konginkangas. . . 103 D2
Kongsberg 104 C3
Kongselva 94 A3
Kongsfjord 95 F1
Kongsvinger 105 D3
Kœnigsbourg . . . 27 E1
Königsbrück 53 E2
Königsbrunn 55 F3
Königsee 52 C3
Königsfeld 54 C3
Königslutter 52 B1
Königsschlösser . . 55 F4
Königssee 56 C4
Königssee L 56 C4
Königstein (Hessen). 51 F4
Königstein (Sachsen) . . . 53 F2
Königswiesen . . . 57 D2
Königswinter . . . 51 E3
Königs-Wusterhausen . . . 49 E4
Konin 112 A1
Koniskós 83 D1
Konistres. 84 B4
Kónitsa 78 C4
Konj 75 E1
Konjevrate 75 D1
Konjic 75 F1
Konjsko 76 A2
Konjuh 71 F4
Konkämäälven . . . 94 C3
Könnern 52 C2
Konnevesi 103 D2
Konnevesi L 103 D2
Könönpelto 103 E3
Konopiště 77 E3
Konotop 113 F1
Konsko 77 F4
Konsmo. 104 B4
Konstantinovy Lázně . . . 53 E4
Konstanz. 55 D4
Kontich 50 B3
Kontiolahti 103 F2
Kontiomäki 99 E4
Konttajärvi 98 C2
Konz 54 A1
Kopaída 83 F4
Kopáni 82 C2
Kopanós. 79 E3
Kopaonik 77 D1
Koparnes 100 A2
Kópasker 96 C1
Köpenick 49 E4
Koper 70 A2
Kopervik 104 A3
Köping 105 F3
Köpingsvik 109 E2
Koplik 76 B3
Köpmanholmen . 102 A2
Koporiće 77 D1
Koppang 100 C3
Kopparberg 105 F3
Kopparbergs Län . 105 E2
Kopparleden . . . 101 E2
Kopperby 48 A1
Kopperveien 100 D3
Koprivna 71 F3
Koprivnica (BH) . . 71 D1
Koprivnica (Srbija). 73 F3
Korab 77 D3
Kórakas, Akr 88 C3
Koralpe. 70 B1
Korana 70 C3
Korbach 52 A2
Korbevac 77 E2
Korbovo. 73 F2
Korçë 114 C3
Korčula 75 E2
Korčula I. 75 E2
Korčulanski kan. . . 75 E2
Korensko sedlo . . 70 A1
Kórfos 87 E2
Korgåsen. 95 F2

Korgen 97 E3
Koria 107 F2
Korifássi. 86 C3
Koríkio Ándro . . . 83 E4
Kórimvos. 81 F1
Korini 83 F4
Korinós. 79 F4
Korinthía 87 D1
Korinthiakós Kólpos . . . 87 D1
Kórinthos 87 E1
Korissía 88 A2
Korissós 79 D3
Korita (BH) 76 A2
Korita (Crna Gora) . 76 B2
Korita (Mljet). . . . 75 F2
Korithí. 86 A1
Koritnik 76 C1
Koritnik, M. 77 D3
Korneuburg 57 F2
Kornofoléa 81 F2
Kornwestheim . . . 55 D2
Koromacno 70 B4
Koróni 86 C4
Korónia 83 F4
Korónia, L 80 A3
Koronída 88 C3
Koronissía 82 C3
Kóronos 88 C3
Koronoúda 80 A2
Koropí. 87 F1
Köros. 112 B4
Korosten' 113 E2
Korostyšev 113 E2
Korouoma. 99 E2
Korpilahti 103 D3
Korpilombolo . . . 98 C2
Korpo 107 D3
Korppoo 107 D3
Korsberga 109 E2
Korsfjorden 104 A2
Korsholm 102 B2
Korsnäs 102 B2
Korsør 108 B4
Korsun-Ševčenkovskij . 113 F2
Korsvoll 100 B2
Kortesjärvi 102 C2
Kórthio 88 B2
Kortrijk 50 A3
Kortteenperä . . . 99 D2
Korvala 99 D2
Korvaluoma 102 C3
Korvatunturi 95 F3
Kos 89 F3
Kosančić 77 D1
Kosanica 76 B1
Kościan 112 A2
Kościerzyna 110 A4
Kosel. 77 D4
Koserow. 49 E1
Košice 112 C3
Kosjerić 72 C4
Koška 71 F2
Koskenkorva 102 B2
Koskenpää 103 D3
Koski (Hameen Lääni) . . 107 E2
Koski (Turun ja Porin Lääni). . . 107 D2
Kóskina 84 B4
Koskue 102 C3
Kosmaj 73 D3
Kosmás 87 D3
Kósmio 81 E2
Kos, N 89 F3
Kosovo. 77 D2
Kosovo Polje . . . 77 D2
Kosovska Kamenica. 77 D2

Kössen 59 E1
Kósta 87 E3
Kostajnica 71 D3
Kostanjevac 70 C2
Kostanjevica 70 C2
Kostenec 115 D3
Koster 105 D4
Kostolac. 73 D3
Kostonjärvi 99 E3
Kostopol' 113 D2
Kóstos 88 C3
Kostrzyn 49 F4
Kosturino 77 F3
Kosula. 103 E2
Koszalin 110 A4
Köszeg. 112 A4
Kotala (Keski-Suomen Lääni). . . 102 C3
Kotala (Lapin Lääni) . . . 99 E1
Kótas. 79 D3
Kotel 115 E2
Kóthen. 53 D1
Kotka 103 F4
Kotor 76 B3
Kotoriba 71 D1
Kotorsko 71 F3
Kotor Varoš 71 E4
Kotovsk 113 E3
Kotraža 73 D4
Kótronas 87 D4
Kotroniá 81 F2
Kötschach-Mauthen . . . 59 E2
Köttsjön 101 F2
Kötzting 56 B1
Koufália. 79 F3
Koufoníssi (Kikládes) . . 88 C3
Koufoníssi (Kríti) . 91 F4
Koufós 80 B4
Kouklii. 82 B1
Koukounariés . . . 84 A2
Koúla. 81 D1
Kouméika 89 E2
Koúndouros 88 A2
Kounoupéli 86 B1
Koura 102 C2
Koúrenda 82 B1
Kourkoulí 84 A3
Kournás 90 C3
Kouroúta 86 B2
Koutselió 82 C1
Koutsó 81 D2
Koutsóhero 83 E1
Kouvola 107 F2
Kovačica 72 C2
Kovel' 112 C2
Kovero 103 F2
Kovin. 73 D3
Kozáni 79 D3
Kozáni 79 D3
Kozara 71 D3
Kozarac (BH) 71 D3
Kozarac (HR). . . . 71 F2
Koželʹsk 111 F3
Kozica 75 E2
Kozina 70 A3
Kozjak 77 E4
Kozluk 72 B3
Kožuf 77 F4
Kragenæs 108 B4
Kragerø 104 C4
Kragujevac 73 D4
Krajišnik 73 D2
Krajkovac 77 D1
Krajn 76 C3
Krajnik Dln 49 E3
Krakhella 104 A1
Krakow. 48 C2
Kraków 112 B2

Kralovice. 53 E4
Kralupy 53 F3
Kramfors. 101 F2
Kranenburg 17 D3
Krani 77 E4
Kraniá Elassónas . 79 E4
Kraniá (Makedonía) . . 79 D4
Kraniá (Thessalía) . 82 C1
Kranichfeld 52 C3
Kranídi 87 E2
Kranj 70 A2
Kranjska Gora . . . 70 A1
Krapina 70 C2
Krapinske Toplice . 70 C2
Krašić. 70 C2
Kråslava 111 D3
Kraslice 53 D3
Krasná Lipa 53 F2
Krásnik 112 C2
Krasno Polje 70 C4
Krasnyj Cholm . . 111 F1
Krasnystaw 112 C2
Kráthio. 87 D1
Krmčine 74 C1
Krátigos 85 F3
Kratovo 77 E2
Kratovska-Stena . . 72 C4
Krauchenwies . . . 55 D3
Krautheim 55 D1
Kravarsko 70 C2
Krefeld 17 D4
Kremasti (Pelopónissos) . 87 E3
Kremasti (Ródos) . 93 F1
Kremastón, Teh L . 83 D3
Kremenčug 113 F2
Kremenčugskoje Vodochranilišče . 113 F2
Kremenec 113 D2
Kremidi, Akr 87 E4
Kremmen 49 D3
Kremna 72 C4
Kremnica 112 B3
Krems 57 E2
Kremsmünster . . 57 D3
Krepoljin 73 E3
Kreševo 75 F1
Krestcy 111 E1
Kréstena 86 B2
Kreuth 56 A4
Kreuzbergpass . . 59 E2
Kreuzlingen 58 A1
Kreuztal 17 F4
Kria Vrissi (Évia) . 84 A3
Kría Vríssi (Makedonía) . 79 E3
Krikelo 83 D3
Krikelos 82 C3
Krikelos, Akr 89 F4
Krimml 59 D2
Krimmler Wasserfälle . 59 D2
Krimpen 16 C3
Krinídes 80 C2
Krionéri (Makedonía) . . 80 A2
Krionéri (Pelopónissos) . 86 C3
Krionéri (Pelopónissos) . 87 D1
Kriopigí. 80 B4
Kriós, Akr 90 B4
Kristalopigi 78 C3
Kristdala 109 E2
Kristiansand 104 B4
Kristianstad 109 D3
Kristianstads Län . 109 D3
Kristiansund 100 B2
Kristiinankaupunki . . 102 B3
Kristineberg 98 A4
Kristinehamn. . . . 105 E4

Kristinehov. 109 D3
Kristinestad 102 B3
Krithéa 79 F2
Krithína, Óros. . . 87 E4
Kritikó Pélagos . . 90 B2
Kríti, N. 91 E3
Kritinía 93 E1
Kritsá 91 E4
Kriva Feja 77 E2
Krivaja (BH) 71 F4
Krivaja (Vojvodina) . 72 B1
Kriva Palanka . . . 77 E2
Kriva reka. 77 E2
Krivogaštani 77 E4
Krivoj Rog 113 F3
Krivolak. 77 E3
Križanov. 57 E1
Križevci 71 D2
Krk 70 B3
Krk I. 70 B3
Krka 112 C2
Krka 70 B2
Krka R 75 D1
Krkonoše 112 A2
Krmčine 74 C1
Krn 70 A2
Krnjača 72 C3
Krnjak 70 C3
Krnjeuša 71 D4
Krnjevo 73 D3
Krnov 112 A3
Krnovo 76 B2
Krøderen 104 C2
Krokeés 87 D3
Krokeide 104 A2
Krokek 106 A4
Krokílio 83 D4
Krokom 101 E2
Krókos 79 E4
Kroksjö 98 A4
Krolevec 113 F1
Kröller Müller . . . 17 D3
Kromĕříž 112 A3
Kronach 52 C4
Kronobergs Län . . 109 D2
Kronoby 102 C1
Kronshagen 48 A1
Kronštadt 111 D1
Kröpelin 48 C2
Kropp 48 A1
Kroppenstedt . . . 52 C1
Krosno 112 C3
Krosno Odrzańskie . 53 F1
Krotoszyn 112 A2
Kroussónas 91 D4
Krovili, Pal. 81 E2
Krrabe, M 76 C3
Krško 70 C2
Krstac 76 A2
Krstača 76 C2
Krstinja 70 C3
Kruë i Fushës . . . 76 C3
Kruiningen 16 B4
Krujë 76 C4
Krumbach 55 E3
Krumpendorf . . . 70 A1
Krün. 55 F4
Krupà 53 E4
Krupac (BH) 76 B2
Krupac (Crna Gora) . 76 B2
Krupac (Srbija) . . 77 E1
Krupaja 73 E3
Krupa na Vrbasu . 71 E4
Krupanj 72 C3
Krupište 77 E3
Krupka 53 E3
Kruså 108 A4
Kruščica 71 E4
Kruščica, Jezero . . 70 C4
Kruševac 73 E4
Kruševica 73 D3
Kruševo 77 E4
Krute 76 B3
Kruunupyy. 102 C1

Krvavec 70 B2
Krynica 112 B3
Krzeszyce 49 F4
Kteniás, Óros . . . 87 D2
Ktísmata 82 B1
Kubitzer Bodden . 49 D1
Küblis 58 B2
Kučaj 73 E4
Kučevište 77 D2
Kučevo 73 E3
Kučište 76 C2
Kučina Kosa 71 D4
Kudowa-Zdrój . . 112 A2
Kufstein 59 D1
Kühlungsborn . . . 48 C2
Kuhmalahti 103 D3
Kuhmo 99 F4
Kuhmoinen 103 D3
Kuivajärvi 99 F4
Kuivajoki 99 D3
Kuivalahti 107 D2
Kuivaniemi 99 D3
Kuivasjärvi 102 C3
Kuivi 95 E2
Kuk. 70 C4
Kukavica 77 E1
Kukës 76 C3
Kukkia 107 E1
Kukko 102 C2
Kukujevci 72 B2
Kukulje 71 E3
Kula (BG) 114 C2
Kula (TR) 115 F4
Kula (Vojvodina) . 72 B2
Kuldīga 110 B3
Kulennoinen . . . 103 F3
Kulen Vakuf 71 D4
Kulina 73 E4
Kulju 107 E1
Kulkjica 74 C1
Kullaa 107 D1
Kulm 27 F2
Kulmbach 52 C4
Kuloharju 99 E2
Külsheim 55 D1
Kultakero 99 E1
Kultsjön 97 E4
Kum 70 B2
Kumane 72 C2
Kumanovo 77 E2
Kumla 105 F4
Kumlinge 106 C3
Kummavuopio . . 94 C3
Kummerower See . 49 D2
Kumputunturi . . . 95 E4
Kumrovec 70 C2
Kungälv 108 C1
Kungsbacka 108 C1
Kungshamn 105 D4
Kungsör 105 F3
Kunoy 96 A3
Kunrau 48 B4
Kunszentmárton . 112 B4
Künzelsau 55 D2
Kuolimo 103 E4
Kuolio 99 E3
Kuopio 103 E2
Kuopion Lääni . . 103 E2
Kuorboaivi 95 E2
Kuorevesi 103 D3
Kuortane. 102 C2
Kuortovare 94 C3
Kuortti 103 D3
Kupa 70 B3
Kupa 70 C3
Kupferzell 55 D2
Kupinova Glava . . 73 E3
Kupinovo 72 C3
Kupres 75 E1
Kupreška vrata . . 75 E1
Kurfar. 59 D3
Kurikka 102 B2
Kuřim 57 F1

Kuršėnai 110 C3
Kuršskij Zaliv. . . . 110 B3
Kursu 99 E2
Kuršumlija 77 D1
Kuršumlijska Banja . 77 D1
Kurtakko 95 D4
Kuru 102 C3
Kusadak 73 D3
Kuşadasi 115 E4
Kusel 54 B1
Küsnacht 58 A2
Küssnacht 58 A2
Kustavi 107 D2
Küstenkanal 17 E1
Kütahya 115 F3
Kutina 71 D2
Kutjevo 71 E2
Kutná-Hora 112 A3
Kutno 112 B1
Kuttanen 95 D3
Kuttura 95 E3
Kúty 57 F2
Kuumu 99 F4
Kuusamo 99 E2
Kuusamojärvi. . . 99 F2
Kuusankoski. . . . 107 F2
Kuusjärvi 103 E2
Kuusjoki 107 E2
Kuvšinovo 111 E2
Kuzma 70 C1
Kuzmin. 72 B3
Kvæfjord 94 A3
Kvaløy 94 B2
Kvaløya. 95 D1
Kvalsund 95 D1
Kvalvøg 100 B2
Kvam 100 C3
Kvænangen 94 C2
Kvænangsbotn. . . 95 D2
Kvanndal 104 B2
Kvanne 100 B2
Kværndrup 108 B4
Kvarner 70 B4
Kvarnerič 70 B4
Kvernes 100 B2
Kvevlax 102 B2
Kvikkjokk 98 A2
Kvikne 100 C2
Kvina 104 B4
Kvinesdal 104 B4
Kvinesdal V. 104 B4
Kvisvik 100 B2
Kviteseid 104 B3
Kvitnes 100 B2
Kvitsøy 104 A3
Kwidzyn. 110 B4
Kyjov 57 F1
Kylänpää. 102 B2
Kylänlahti 103 F1
Kyleakin 2 B3
Kyle of Lochalsh . 2 B3
Kyle of Tongue . . 2 C2
Kylerhea 2 B3
Kylestrome 2 C2
Kyll 51 D4
Kyllburg 51 D4
Kylmäkoski 107 E2
Kylmälä 99 D4
Kymen Lääni . . . 103 F4
Kynsivesi 103 D3
Kyritz 49 D3
Kyrksæterøra . . . 100 C2
Kyrkslätt 107 E3
Kyrönjoki 102 C2
Kyrösjärvi 102 C3
Kyselka 53 E3
Kyšice 53 F4
Kyyjärvi 102 C3
Kyyvesi 103 E3

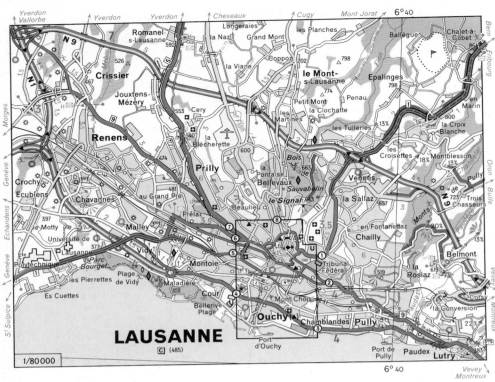

LAUSANNE
1/80 000
C (485)

Landstuhl **54** B2
Landverk **101** D2
Lanersbach **59** D2
Lanesborough **12** C3
Langáda (Híos) **85** F4
Langáda
(Pelopónissos) . . . **87** D4
Langadás **79** F3
Langádas **87** D3
Langa de Duero . . . **36** A3
Langádia **86** C2
Langadíkia **80** A3
Langangen **104** C4
Langeac **29** F2
Langeais **25** D2
Langeland **108** B4
Langelandsbælt . . . **108** B4
Langelmäki **103** D3
Langelmävesi **103** D3
Langelsheim **52** B1
Langenargen **55** D4
Langenau **55** E3
Langenberg **53** D3
Langenbruck **55** F2
Langenburg **55** D2
Langeneß **47** F1
Langenfeld **17** E4
Längenfeld **58** C2
Langenhagen **48** A4
Langenhahn **51** F3
Langen (Hessen) . . **52** A4
Langen
(Niedersachsen) . . **47** F3
Langenlois **57** E2
Langenthal **27** F2
Langenwang **57** E3
Langenzenn **55** E1
Langeoog **47** E3
Långeserud **105** E3
Langeskov **108** B3
Langesund **104** C4
Langevåg **100** A2
Langevåg **104** A3
Långfjället **101** D3
Langfjord **95** D2
Langfjorden **95** E1
Langfjordjøkelen . . **94** C2
Langforden **100** B2
Langhirano **60** B2
Langholm **5** D3
Langjökull **96** B2
Langnau **27** F2
Langogne **29** F2
Langon **28** B2
Langøya **94** A3
Langport **9** D3
Langres **26** C1
Langrune **18** C3
Långsele **101** F2
Långshyttan **105** F2
Långträsk **98** B3
Lanjarón **44** A3
Lanke **49** E3
Länkipohja **103** D3
Lanmeur **22** B2
Lannemezan **37** E1
Lannilis **22** A2
Lannion **22** B2
Lanouaille **29** D1
Lans-en-Vercors . . **30** C1
Lanslebourg **31** E1
Lanta **29** D4
Lantosque **31** E3
La Nuez de Arriba . **35** F3
Lanusei **66** C3
Lanvollon **22** C2
Lanzahita **39** F2
Lanzarote **42** C3
Lanzo Torinese . . . **31** E1
Laois **12** C4
La Oliva
(Is Canarias) **42** C4
La Oliva (Navarra) . **36** C2
Laon **20** A3
La Orotava **42** B4
La Paca **44** C2
Lapalisse **26** B4
La Palma **42** A4
La Palma del
Condado **42** C2
La Panadella **37** F4
Lápas **86** B1
Lapa, Sa da **38** C1
Laperdiguera **37** E3

La Pinilla **36** A4
Lapinjärvi **107** F2
Lapin Lääni **95** E4
Lapinlahti **103** E2
La Platja d'Aro . . . **32** B4
La Plaza **35** D2
Lapleau **29** E1
Laplume **28** C3
La Pobla **41** E4
La Pobla de Lillet . **32** B4
La Pobla de
Massaluca **37** E4
La Pobla de Segur . **37** F3
La Pobla de
Vallbona **41** E3
Lapoutroie **27** E1
Lapovo **73** D3
Lappajärvi **102** C2
Lappajärvi L **102** C2
Lappalaisten-
Kesätuvat **95** D3
Lappea **98** C2
Lappeenranta . . . **103** F4
Lappfjärd **102** B3
Lappfors **102** C2
Lappi **107** D2
Lappoå **102** C2
Lappohja **107** E3
Lappträsk **98** C3
Lappträsk **107** F2
Lappvesi **106** C3
Lapua **102** C2
Lapuanjoki **102** C2
La Puebla de
Almoradiel **40** B3
La Puebla de
Cazalla **43** E3
La Puebla de Híjar . **37** D4
La Puebla de
los Infantes **43** E2
La Puebla del Río . **43** D3
La Puebla de
Montalbán **39** F3
La Puebla de
Valverde **41** E3
La Pueblanueva . . **39** F3
La Puerta de
Segura **44** B1
Lapväärtti **102** B3
L'Aquila **63** F2
La Rábida **42** C3
La Rábita **44** B4
Laracha **34** A1
Laragh **13** D4
Laragne-
Montéglin **30** C3
La Rambla **43** F2
Lärbro **109** F3
Larche (Alpes-de-
Haute-Provence) . **31** E2
Larche (Corrèze) . **29** D2
Larche, Col de . . . **31** E2
Lærdalsøyri **104** B1
Lardarello **60** C4
Lárdos **93** F2
Lárdos, Akr **93** F2
Laredo **36** A1
Laren **16** C2
Largentière **30** B2
Largs **4** C2
Lárimna **84** A4
La Rinconada **43** D2
Larino **64** B2
La Rioja **36** B2
Lárissa **83** E1
Lárissa (Nomos) . . **83** E2
Larmor **22** B4
Larne **13** E2
La Robla **35** D2
La Roca **32** B4
La Roca de la
Sierra **39** D4
Larochette **21** D2
La Roda
(Andalucía) **43** E3
La Roda (Castilla-la-
Mancha) **40** C4
Laroles **44** B3
Laroquebrou **29** E2
Laroque-d'Olmes . **32** A2
Laroque-Timbaut . **28** C3
Larouco **34** B3
Larraga **36** C2
Larrau, Pto de . . . **37** D2

L

Laa an der Thaya . . . **57** F2
La Adrada **39** F2
Laage **48** C2
Laakajärvi **103** E1
La Alberca **39** E2
La Alberca de
Záncara **40** C3
La Alberguería de
Argañán **39** D2
La Albuera **38** C4
La Albufera **41** E4
La Alcarria **40** C2
La Algaba **43** D2
La Almarcha **40** C3
La Almunia de Doña
Godina **36** C4
La Antillas **42** C3
La Azohía **45** D3
Labacolla **34** A2
La Baells, Emb de . . **32** A3
Labajos **40** A1
La Bañeza **35** D3
La Barca de la
Florida **43** D3
Labasheeda **12** B4
Labastida **36** B2
Labastide-
Clairence **28** A4
Labastide-Murat . . . **29** D2
Labastide-
Rouairoux **32** B1
Labe **53** F3
Labin **70** A3
Labinot Fushë **76** C4
La Bisbal de Falset . **37** E4
La Bisbal
d'Empordà **32** B3
Laboe **48** A1
Labouheyre **28** A3
Labouret, Col du . . . **31** D3
La Bóveda de Toro . **35** D4
La Brède **28** B2
Labrit **28** B3
Labruguière **32** B1
Labudnjača **72** B2
Laç **76** C4
La Cabrera **40** B1
Lacalahorra **44** B3
La Campana **43** E2
Lacanau **28** A2
Lacanau-Océan . . . **28** A2

Lacapelle-Marival . . . **29** D2
Laćarak **72** B3
La Carlota **43** E2
La Carolina **44** A1
Lacaune **32** B1
Lacaune, Mts de . . . **32** B1
La Cava **41** F2
La Cazada de
Oropesa **39** E3
Lacedonia **64** C3
Läckö **105** E4
Lac Léman **27** E3
La Codosera **38** C3
Laconi **66** B3
La Coronada **39** E4
La Coruña **34** A1
Lacq **28** B4
La Cumbre **39** E3
La Espina **35** D1
Ladbergen **17** E2
Ládi **81** F1
Ladispoli **63** E2
Ladoeiro **38** C3
Ladožskoje
Ozero **111** D1
Láerma **93** E2
La Felguera **35** D1
Laferté **27** D1
Laffrey **30** C2
Láfka **87** D1
Láfkos **83** F2
Lafnitz **57** F4
La Franca **35** E1
Lafrançaise **29** D3
La Fregeneda **39** D1
La Frontera **40** C2
La Fuente de San
Esteban **39** D2
Lagan **109** D2
Lagan R **109** D2
Laganá, Kólpos **86** A2
Laganás **86** A2
Lagarfljót **96** C2
La Garganta **34** C1
La Garriga **32** B4
Lagartera **39** E3
Lagastrello, Pso di . **60** B3
Lage **17** F3
Lågen
(Buskerud) **104** C3
Lågen
(Oppland) **100** C3
Laggan **2** C4

Laggan, L **2** C4
Laginá
(Makedonía) **79** F3
Laginá (Thráki) . . . **81** F2
La Gineta **40** C4
Lagnieu **26** C4
Lagny **19** F4
Lago **67** E3
Lagoa **42** A2
Lagoaça **34** C4
Lagonegro **65** D4
Lagoníssi **87** F2
Lagos **42** A2
Lágos **81** D2
Lagów **49** F4
La Granjuela **43** E1
Lagrasse **32** B2
Laguardia **36** B2
La Guardia **40** B3
La Guardia de Jaén . **44** A2
Laguarres **37** E3
Laguarta **37** E2
Laguiole **29** E2
Laguna de Duero . . **35** E4
Lahanás **80** A2
La Hermida **35** E2
La Herradura **44** A4
Lahinch **12** B4
Lahn **17** F4
Lahnstein **51** E4
Laholm **108** C2
Laholmsbukten . . . **108** C2
La Horcajada **39** E2
La Horra **35** F4
Lahr **54** C3
Lahti **107** F2
Laichingen **55** D3
Laide **2** B3
La Iglesuela del Cid . **41** E2
Laignes **26** B1
Laigueglia **31** F3
Laihia **102** B2
Laïliás **80** B1
Laimbach **57** D2
Laimoluokta **94** C3
Lainate **60** A1
Lainioälven **95** D4
Lairg **2** C2
Laissac **29** E3
Laïsta **78** C4
Laisvall **97** F3
Laitikkala **107** E2
Laitila **107** D2
La Jana **41** F2

Laggan, L **2** C4
Lajkovac **72** C3
La Jonquera **32** B3
Laká **82** A2
Lakavica **77** E3
Lake District
Nat Pk **5** D4
Laki **89** E3
Láki **90** B3
Lákmos, Óri **82** C1
Lákoma **81** E3
Lákones **82** A1
Lakonía **87** D3
Lakonikós Kólpos . . **87** D4
Lakópetra **86** B1
Laksefjorden **95** E1
Lakselv **95** D2
Laktaši **71** E3
La Laguna **42** B4
La Lantejuela **43** E3
Lálas **86** C2
Lalbenque **29** D3
L'Alcudia **41** E4
L'Aldea **41** F2
Lalín **34** B2
Lalinac **73** F4
Lalinde **28** C2
La Línea de la
Concepción **43** E4
Laliótis **87** D1
Lalm **100** C3
La Losa **44** B2
Lalouvesc **30** B1
Lalueza **37** E3
La Luisiana **43** E2
Lalzit, Gjiri i **76** C4
Lam **56** B1
Lama dei Peligni . . . **64** A2
La Magdalena **35** D2
Lamalou **30** A4
La Manche **10** A4
La Manga del
Mar Menor **45** D2
Lamarche **27** D1
La Marmora, P **66** B3
Lamarque **28** B2
Lamastre **30** B2
Lambach **56** C3
Lamballe **22** C3
Lambesc **30** C4
Lámbia **86** C1
Lambíri **83** D4
Lámbou Míli **85** F2
Lambrecht **54** C2
Lamego **34** B4

La Mesa Roldán **44** C3
Lamía **83** E3
Lamlash **4** B2
Lammermuir Hills . . . **5** D2
Lammhult **109** D2
Lammi **107** E2
La Molina **32** A3
Lamotte-Beuvron . . **25** E2
Lampaul **22** A2
Lampedusa **68** A4
Lampedusa, I di . . . **68** A4
Lampertheim **54** C1
Lampeter **8** C1
L'Ampolla **41** F2
Lamstedt **47** F3
La Mudarra **35** E4
La Muela **36** C4
Lamure **26** B4
Lana **58** C3
Lanaja **37** D3
Lanaken **51** D3
Lanark **4** C2
La Nava de
Ricomalillo **39** F3
La Nava de
Santiago **39** D4
Lancashire **6** B2
Lancaster **6** B1
Lanchester **5** E4
Lanciano **64** A2
Landau (Bayern) . . . **56** B2
Landau (Rheinland-
Pfalz) **54** C2
Landeck **58** C2
Landerneau **22** B2
Landes **28** B3
Landes de
Lanvaux **22** C3
Landete **41** D3
Landévennec **22** A3
Landivisiau **22** B2
Landivy **18** C4
Landmannalaugar . . **96** B2
Landquart **58** B2
Landrecies **20** A2
Landriano **60** A1
Landsberg (Bayern) . **56** A3
Landsberg (Sachsen-
Anhalt) **53** D2
Land's End **8** A4
Landshut **56** B2
Landskapet
Åland **106** C3
Landskrona **108** C3

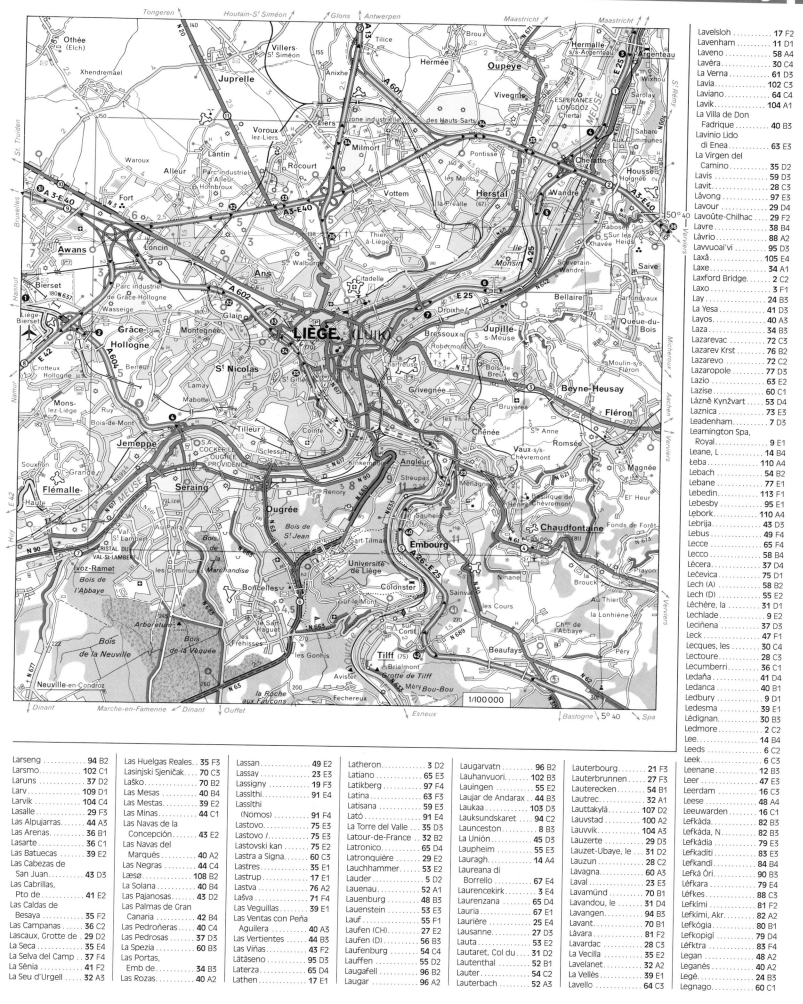

Lavelsloh 17 F2
Lavenham 11 D1
Laveno 58 A4
Lavéra 30 C4
La Verna 61 D3
Lavia 102 C3
Laviano 64 C4
Lavik 104 A1
La Villa de Don
  Fadrique 40 B3
Lavinio Lido
  di Enea 63 E3
La Virgen del
  Camino 35 D2
Lavis 59 D3
Lavit 28 C3
Lavong 97 E3
Lavour 29 D4
Lavoûte-Chilhac 29 F2
Lavre 38 B4
Lávrio 88 A2
Lavvuoai'vi 95 D3
Laxå 105 E4
Laxe 34 A1
Laxford Bridge 2 C2
Laxo 3 F1
Lay 24 B3
La Yesa 41 D3
Layos 40 A3
Laza 34 B3
Lazarevac 72 C3
Lazarev Krst 76 B2
Lazarevo 72 C2
Lazaropole 77 D3
Lazio 63 E2
Lazise 60 C1
Lázně Kynžvart 53 D4
Laznica 73 E3
Leadenham 7 D3
Leamington Spa,
  Royal 9 E1
Leane, L 14 B4
Łeba 110 A4
Lebach 54 B2
Lebane 77 E1
Lebedin 113 F1
Lebesby 95 E1
Łebork 110 A4
Lebrija 43 D3
Lebus 49 F4
Lecce 65 F4
Lecco 58 B4
Lécera 37 D4
Lečevica 75 D1
Lech (A) 58 B2
Lech (D) 55 E2
Léchère, la 31 D1
Lechlade 9 E2
Leciñena 37 D3
Leck 47 F1
Lecques, les 30 C4
Lectoure 28 C3
Lecumberri 36 C1
Ledaña 41 D4
Ledanca 40 B1
Ledbury 9 D1
Ledesma 39 E1
Lédignan 30 B3
Ledmore 2 C2
Lee 14 B4
Leeds 6 C2
Leek 6 C3
Leenane 12 B3
Leer 47 E3
Leerdam 16 C3
Leese 48 A4
Leeuwarden 16 C1
Lefkáda 82 B3
Lefkáda, N. 82 B3
Lefkádia 79 E3
Lefkáditi 83 E3
Lefkandí 84 B4
Lefká Óri 90 B3
Lefkara 79 E4
Léfkes 88 C3
Lefkími 81 F2
Lefkími, Akr. 82 A2
Lefkógia 80 B1
Lefkopigí 79 D4
Léfktra 83 F4
Legan 48 A2
Leganés 40 A2
Legé 24 B3
Legnago 60 C1

Larseng 94 B2
Larsmo 102 C1
Laruns 37 D2
Larv 109 D1
Larvik 104 C4
Lasalle 29 F3
Las Alpujarras 44 A3
Las Arenas 36 B1
Lasarte 36 C1
Las Batuecas 39 E2
Las Cabezas de
  San Juan 43 D3
Las Cabrillas,
  Pto de 41 E2
Las Caldas de
  Besaya 35 F2
Las Campanas 36 C2
Lascaux, Grotte de . 29 D2
La Selva del Camp . 37 F4
La Sénia 41 F2
La Seu d'Urgell ... 32 A3

Las Huelgas Reales .. 35 F3
Lasinjski Sjeničak ... 70 C3
Laško 70 B2
Las Mesas 40 B4
Las Mestas 39 E2
Las Minas 44 C1
Las Navas de la
  Concepción 43 D3
Las Navas del
  Marqués 40 A2
Lastra a Signa 60 C3
Lastres 35 E1
Lastrup 17 E2
Lastva 76 A2
Lašva 71 F4
Las Veguillas 39 E1
Las Ventas con Peña
  Aguilera 40 A3
Las Vertientes ... 44 B3
Las Viñas 43 F2
Lätäseno 95 D3
Laterza 65 D4
Lathen 17 E1

Lassan 49 E2
Lassay 23 E3
Lassigny 19 F3
Lassíthi 91 E4
Lassíthi
  (Nomos) 91 F4
Lastovo 75 E3
Lastovo I 75 E3
Lastovski kan ... 75 E2
Lastva 76 A2
Laterza 65 D4

Latheron 3 D2
Latiano 65 E3
Latikberg 97 F4
Latina 63 F3
Latisana 59 E3
Lató 91 E4
La Torre del Valle .. 35 D3
Latour-de-France .. 32 B2
Latronico 65 D4
Latronquière 29 E2
Lauchhammer 53 E2
Lauchröden 52 B3
Lauder 5 D2
Lauenau 52 A1
Lauenburg 48 B3
Lauenstein 53 E3
Lauf 55 F1
Laufen (CH) ... 27 E2
Laufen (D) 56 B3
Laufenburg ... 54 C4
Lauffen 55 D2
Laugafell ... 96 B2
Laugar 96 A2

Laugarvatn 96 B2
Lauhanvuori 102 B3
Lauingen 55 E2
Laujar de Andarax . 44 B3
Laukaa 103 D3
Lauksundskaret .. 94 C2
Launceston 8 B3
La Unión 45 D3
Laupheim 55 E3
Lauragh 14 A4
Laureana di
  Borrello 67 E4
Laurencekirk 3 E4
Laurenzana 65 D4
Lauria 67 E1
Laurière 25 E4
Lausanne 27 D3
Lauta 53 E2
Lautaret, Col du .. 31 D2
Lautenthal 52 B1
Lauter 54 C2
Lauterbach ... 52 A3

Lauterbourg 21 F3
Lauterbrunnen 27 F3
Lauterecken 54 B1
Lautrec 32 A1
Lauttakylä 107 D2
Lauvstad 100 A2
Lauvvik 104 A3
Lauzerte 29 D3
Lauzet-Ubaye, le .. 31 D2
Lauzun 28 C2
Lavagna 60 A3
Laval 23 E3
Lavamünd 70 B1
Lavandou, le ... 31 D4
Lavangen 94 B3
Lavant 70 B1
Lávara 81 F2
Lavardac ... 28 C3
La Vecilla .. 35 E2
La Vellès .. 39 E1
Lavello ... 64 C3

Legnano 60 A1
Legnica 112 A2
Legrad 71 D1
Legrená 87 F2
Léguevin 29 D4
Legutiano 36 B1
Le Havre 19 D3
Lehená 86 B1
Lehnin 49 D4
Léhovo 79 D3
Lehrberg 55 E1
Lehre 52 B1
Lehrte 52 B1
Lehtimäki 102 C2
Lehtovaara (Lapin
  Lääni) 99 D1
Lehtovaara (Oulun
  Lääni) 103 E1
Leibnitz 70 B1
Leicester 9 F1
Leicestershire 9 E1
Leiden 16 B3
Leie 50 B4
Leighton Buzzard 9 F2
Leikanger 100 A3
Leiknes 97 F1
Leine 48 A4
Leinefelde 52 B2
Leini 31 E1
Leipheim 55 E3
Leipzig 53 D2
Leira (Møre og
  Romsdal) 100 B2
Leira (Oppland) 104 C2
Leirbotn 95 D2
Leiria 38 B2
Leiro 34 B2
Leirpollskogen 95 F1
Leirvåg 104 A1
Leirvik (Færøerne) . . 96 A3
Leirvik
  (Hordaland) 104 A3

Leirvik (Sogn og
  Fjordane) 104 A1
Leisnig 53 E2
Leiston 11 E1
Leitáriegos, Pto de . . 34 C2
Leith 5 D2
Leitha 57 F2
Leitir Ceanainn 12 C1
Leitzkau 52 C1
Leivonmäki 103 D3
Leiza 36 C1
Lek 16 C3
Léka 89 E1
Leka 97 D3
Lekáni 80 C2
Lekeitio 36 B1
Lekenik 71 D2
Leknes (Møre og
  Romsdal) 100 A2
Leknes
  (Nordland) 97 E1
Łeknica 53 F1
Leksand 101 E4
Leksvik 100 C1
Leland 97 D3
Lelång 105 D4
Lelija 76 A1
Lelystad 16 C2
Lelystad-Haven 16 C2
Léman, Lac 27 E3
Le Mans 23 F3
Lembach 21 E3
Lembeye 28 B4
Lemförde 17 F2
Lemgo 17 F2
Lemgow 48 C3
Lemi 103 E4
Lemland 106 C3
Lemmenjoki 95 E3
Lemmenjoki
  (Nat Pk) 95 E3

Lemmenjoki R 95 E3
Lemmer 16 C1
Lemonodássos 87 F2
Lempäälä 107 E1
Lempdes 29 F1
Lemvig 108 A2
Lenart 70 C1
Lencloître 25 D3
Lend 59 E1
Léndas 91 D4
Lendava 71 D1
Lendava R 70 C1
Lendinara 61 D2
Lengefeld 53 E3
Lengenfeld 53 D3
Lengerich 17 E2
Lenggries 56 A4
Lenhovda 109 E2
Lenk 27 E3
Lenne 17 F4
Lennestadt 17 F4
Lens 19 F2
Lensahn 48 B2
Lentföhrden 48 A2
Lenti 114 A1
Lentiira 99 F4
Lenting 55 F2
Lentini 69 D3
Lentua 99 F4
Lenvik 94 B3
Lenzburg 27 F2
Lenzen 48 C3
Lenzerheide
  Valbella 58 B3
Lenzkirch 54 C4
Leoben 57 E4
Leobersdorf 57 F3
Leogang 59 E1
Leominster 9 D1
Léon 28 A3
León 35 D2
León, Mtes de 35 D2

Leonberg 55 D2
Léoncel 30 C2
Leondári
  (Pelopónissos) . . . 86 C2
Leondári
  (Thessalía) 83 E2
Leóndio 87 D2
Leonessa 63 E1
Leonforte 68 C3
Leonídio 87 E3
Leopoldsburg 50 C3
Leopoldsdorf 57 F2
Leopoldsteinersee . . 57 D3
Leovo 113 E4
Lepel' 111 D3
Lepenoú 80 C3
Lepenski vir 73 E3
Lepetane 76 B3
Lepoglava 70 C1
Leposavić 77 D1
Lépoura 84 B4
Leppäjärvi 95 D3
Leppävirta 103 E2
Leptokariá
  (Makedonía) 79 F4
Leptokariá (Thráki) . . 81 E2
Lercara Friddi 68 B3
Léré 26 A2
Lerici 60 B3

Lérida 37 E4
Lerin 36 C2
Lérins 31 E4
Lerma 35 F3
Lermoos 58 C1
Lérni 87 D2
Léros, N 89 E3
Lerum 108 C1
Lerwick 3 F2
Les 37 F2
Lešak 76 C1
Lešani 77 D4
Les Borges
  Blanques 37 F4
L'Escala 32 C3
Lescar 28 B4
Lesce 70 A2
Lešće 70 C3
Lescun 37 D2
Leshnicë 77 D4
Lesima, Mte 60 A2
Lesina 64 C2
Lesina, L di 64 C2
Lesja 100 B3
Lesjöfors 105 E3
Leskovac 77 E1
Les Llosses 32 A3
Lesneven 22 B2
Lešnica 72 B3
Lesparre-Médoc 28 A1

L'Espina 41 F2
L'Espluga de
  Francolí 37 F4
L'Espunyola 32 A3
L'Estartit 32 C3
Lestelle-
  Bétharram 37 E1
Lestijärvi 102 C2
Lestijoki 102 C1
Lestkov 53 E4
Lésvos, N 85 F2
Leszno 112 A2
Letchworth 9 F2
Letenye 114 A1
Letino 64 A3
Letmathe 17 E4
Letterfrack 12 A3
Letterkenny 12 C1
Lettermullan 12 A3
Letur 44 C1
Letuš 70 B1
Letzlingen 48 C4
Leuca 65 F4
Leuchars 5 D1
Leuk 27 F3

Leukerbad 27 E3
Leuna 53 D2
Leutenberg 52 C3
Leutershausen 55 E1
Leutkirch 55 E4
Leutschach 70 B1
Leuven 50 C3
Leuze 50 B4
Levajok 95 E2
Levanger 101 D1
Levanjska Varoš 71 F2
Levant, I du 31 D4
Levanto 60 B3
Levanzo, I di 68 A3
Levásjoki 102 B3
Levene 108 C1
Leven (England) 7 D2
Leven (Scotland) 5 D1
Levens 31 E3
Leverano 65 F4
Leverburgh 2 A3
Leverkusen 17 E4
Levet 25 F3
Levi 95 E3
Levice 112 B3
Levico Terme 59 D3
Levídi 87 D2
Levie 33 F4
Levier 27 D3
Levítha, N 89 E3
Levoča 112 B3
Levroux 25 E3
Lévy, Cap 18 B2
Lewes 10 C3
Lewis 2 B2
Leyburn 6 C1
Leyland 6 B2
Leyre 37 D2
Leysdown-
  on-Sea 11 D3
Leysin 27 E3
Lézardrieux 22 C2
Lézat 37 F1
Lezay 24 C2
Lezhë 76 C3
Lézignan-
  Corbières 32 B2
Ležimir 72 C2
Lezoux 29 F1
Lezuza 40 C4
L'gov 111 F4
L'Hospitalet de
  l'Infant 37 F4
Liabygda 100 B2
Liákoura 83 E3
Lianokládi 83 E3
Liathach 2 C3
Liberec 112 A2
Libochovice 53 F3
Libourne 28 B2
Librazhd 77 D4
Librilla 45 D2
Licata 68 C4
Licciana Nardi 60 B3
Lich 52 A4
Lichfield 9 E1
Lichoslavl' 111 F2
Lichtenberg 53 D3
Lichtenfels 52 C4
Lichtenstein 53 D3
Lichtenvoorde 17 D3
Lička Jesenica 70 C4
Lički Osik 70 C4
Ličko Lešće 70 C4
Lida 110 C4
Liddel Water 5 D3
Liden 101 F2
Lidhult 109 D2
Lidingö 106 B4
Lidköping 105 E4
Lido degli Estensi . . 61 D2
Lido delle Nazioni . . 61 D2
Lido di Camaiore . . . 60 B3
Lido di Classe 61 D3
Lido di Jesolo 59 E4
Lido di Metaponto . . 65 E4
Lido di Ostia 63 E3
Lido di Savio 61 D3
Lido di Spina 61 D2
Lido di Venezia 61 D1
Lidoríki 83 E4
Lido Silvana 65 E4
Lidzbark
  Warmiński 110 B4

Lille

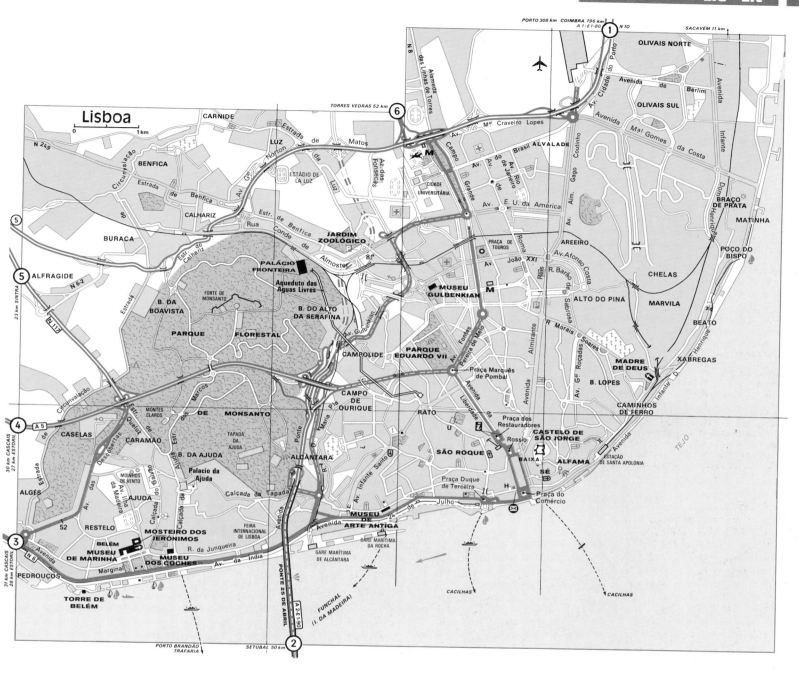

Lisboa

Liebenwalde	49 D3	Lignières	25 F3
Lieberose	53 F1	Ligny-en-Barrois	20 C4
Liège	51 D4	Ligny-le-Châtel	26 B1
Liège (Prov.)	51 D4	Ligourió	87 E2
Lieksa	103 F1	Ligueil	25 D3
Lienz	59 E2	Liguria	60 A3
Liepāja	110 B3	Liháda	83 F3
Lier	50 C3	Liikasenvaara	99 E2
Liérganes	35 F2	Lijeva Rijeka	76 B2
Liernais	26 B2	Lijevi Dubravčak	71 D2
Lieser	59 F2	Lika	70 C4
Liesjärvi	107 E2	Likenäs	105 E2
Liestal	27 E2	Likeo, Óri	86 C2
Lieto	107 D2	Likódimo, Óros	86 C3
Liétor	44 C1	Likófos	81 F2
Lieurey	19 D3	Likoporiá	87 D1
Lievestuore	103 D3	Likórahi	78 C4
Liévin	19 F1	Likóstomo	80 C2
Liezen	57 D3	Likouría	86 C1
Liffey	13 D4	Liland	94 B3
Liffol-le-Grand	20 C4	Lílea	83 E3
Lifford	13 D1	Lilienfeld	57 E3
Liffré	23 D3	Liljendal	107 F2
Lifjell	104 C3	Lilla Edet	108 C1
Ligiá	86 B1	Lillby	102 C2
Lignano		Lille	19 F1
Sabbiadoro	59 F4	Lille Bælt	108 A3
Ligné	23 D4	Lillebonne	19 D3

Lillehammer	105 D2	Liminpuro	99 E4
Lillerød	108 C3	Limljani	76 B3
Lillers	19 F1	Límnes	87 E2
Lillesand	104 B4	Limni	84 A3
Lillestrøm	105 D3	Limniá	80 C2
Lillhärdal	101 E3	Limnítsa	83 D4
Lillo	40 B3	Límnos, N	85 D1
Lillögda	102 A1	Limoges	29 D1
Lillsholmsjön	101 E1	Limogne	29 D3
Lim	76 B1	Limone Piemonte	31 E3
Limáni		Limonest	26 C4
Hersoníssou	91 E3	Limours	19 E4
Limáni Litohórou	79 F4	Limoux	32 B2
Lima, R	34 A3	Lin	77 D4
Limavady	13 D1	Linares	44 A2
Limbach	53 D3	Linares del Arroyo,	
Limbara, M	66 B2	Emb de	36 A3
Limburg (B)	50 C3	Linares de Mora	41 E2
Limburg (D)	51 F4	Linares de Riofrío	39 E2
Limburg (NL)	17 D4	Linariá	84 C3
Limenária	80 C3	Linas, M	66 B4
Limerick	14 B3	Lincoln	7 D3
Limerick (Co)	14 B3	Lincolnshire	7 D3
Limfjorden	108 A2	Lindås	104 A2
Limia, R	34 A3	Lindau	55 D4
Limingen	97 E4	Linden	52 C4
Liminka	99 D4	Lindenberg	55 E4

Lindesberg	105 F3	Lioran, le	29 E2
Lindesnes	104 B4	Lipar	72 B2
Lindhem	106 A4	Lipari	69 D2
Lindö	106 A4	Lipari, I	69 D2
Líndos	93 F2	Lipenská přehr	
Lindoso	34 B3	nádrž	56 C2
Lindow	49 D3	Liperi	103 F2
Lindsdal	109 E2	Lipiany	49 F3
Lingbo	106 A2	Lipica	70 A3
Linge	100 B2	Lipik	71 D2
Lingen	17 E2	Lipkovo	77 E2
Linguaglossa	69 D3	Lipljan	77 D2
Linken	49 E2	Lipno	57 D2
Linköping	106 A4	Lipova	112 C4
Linlithgow	5 D2	Lipovac	72 B3
Linnansaari	103 E3	Lippe	17 E3
Linnhe, L	4 B1	Lippstadt	17 F3
Linosa, I di	68 A4	Lipsí	89 E2
Linsell	101 E3	Lipsí, N	89 E2
Linslade	9 F2	Liptovský Mikuláš	112 B3
Linthal	58 A2	Liqenas	77 D4
Linyola	37 F3	Lírkia	87 D2
Linz (A)	57 D2	Lis	76 C3
Linz (D)	51 E4	Lisac	71 E4
Lion	18 C3	Lisboa	38 A4
Lion-d'Angers, le	23 E4	Lisburn	13 E2
Lioni	64 C4	Liscia	66 B1
Lióprasso	83 D1	Lisdoonvarna	12 B4

Lisieux	19 D3	
Lisina	71 E4	
Liskeard	8 B4	
Lisková	56 B1	
Lisle	29 D3	
Lismore (GB)	4 B1	
Lismore (IRL)	14 C4	
Lisnaskea	13 D2	
Lišnja	71 E3	
Lison, Source du	27 D3	
Lisovići	71 F3	
Lisse	16 C2	
List	47 F1	
Listafjorden	104 A4	
Lištica	75 E2	
Listowel	14 B3	
Lit	101 E2	
Lit-et-Mixe	28 A3	
Lithakiá	86 A2	
Lithári, Akr	84 C3	
Líthines	91 F4	
Líthino, Akr	91 D4	
Lithio	85 E4	
Liti	79 F3	
Litija	70 B2	
Litóhoro	79 F4	
Litoměřice	53 F3	
Litomyšl	112 A3	

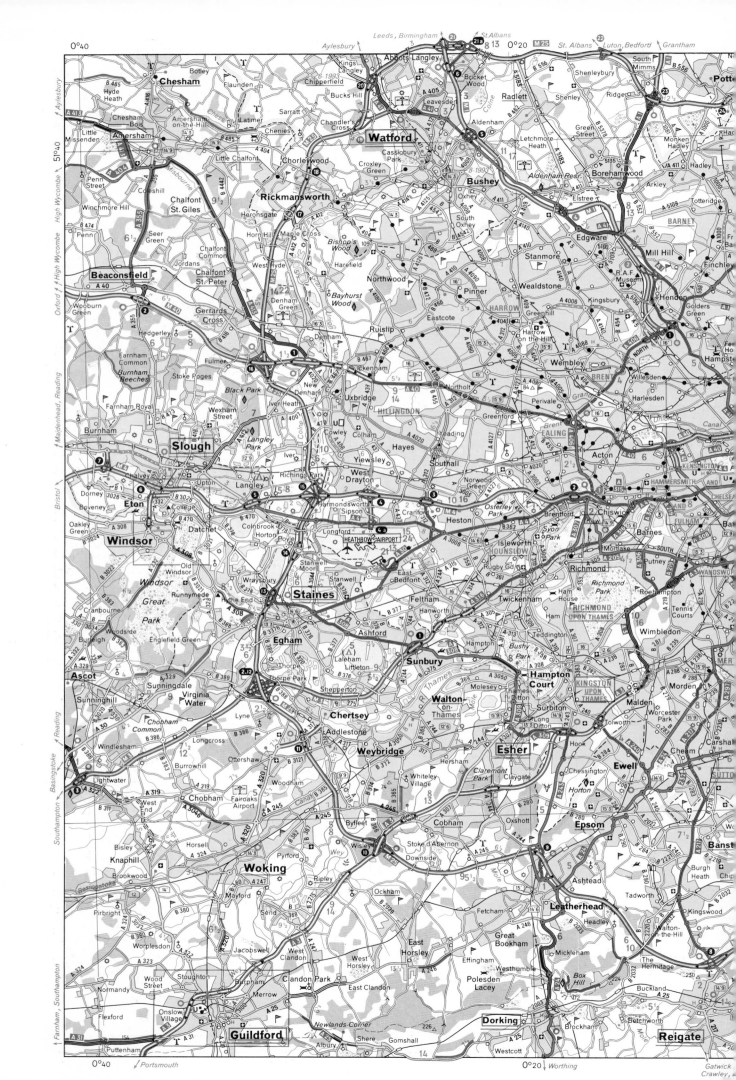

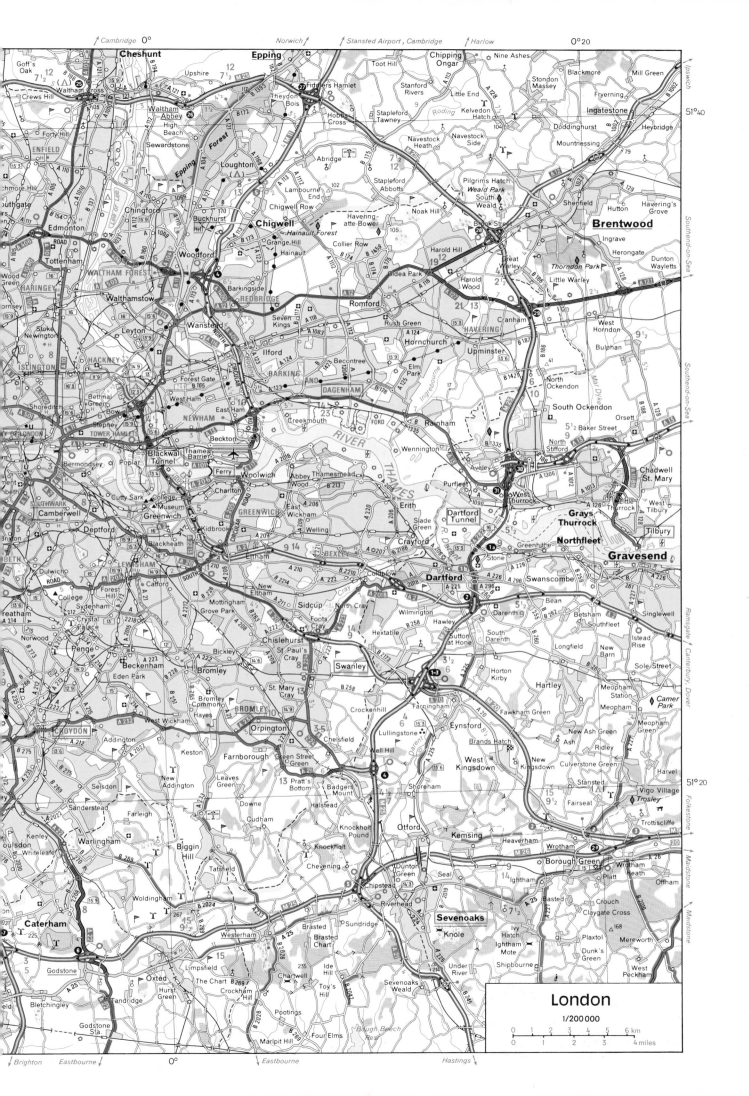

London

1/200 000

0 1 2 3 4 5 6 km

0 1 2 3 4 miles

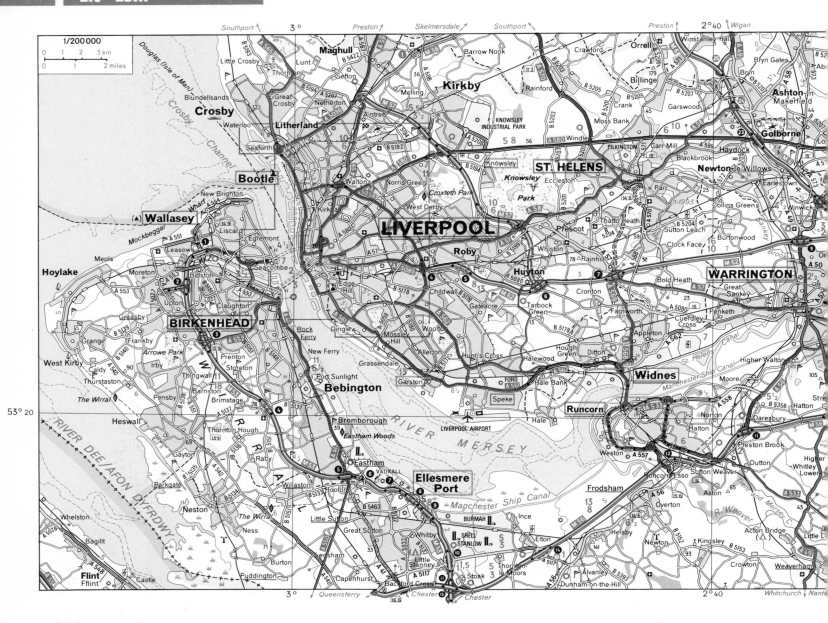

Litschau 57 D1	Livno 75 E1	Ljungby 109 D2	Llanwrtyd-Wells 8 C1	Lochearnhead 4 C1	Løfallstrand 104 A2	Loir 25 E1
Littlehampton 10 C3	Livo 99 E3	Ljungbyhed 109 D3	Llanymyddfri 8 C1	Lochem 17 D2	Lofário 81 E2	Loire 23 E4
Little Minch, The .. 2 A3	Livojärvi 99 E2	Ljungdalen 101 D2	Llarga 41 E4	Loches 25 D3	Lofer 59 E1	Loire (Dépt) 29 F1
Little Moreton Hall .. 6 C3	Livojoki 99 E3	Ljungsbro 105 F4	Llavorsi 37 F2	Loch Garman 15 D3	Löffingen 54 C4	Loire-Atlantique ... 23 E4
Littleport 10 C1	Livold 70 B3	Ljungskile 108 C1	Lleida 37 E4	Lochgelly 5 D2	Lofoten 97 E1	Loir-et-Cher 25 E2
Litvínov 53 E3	Livorno 60 C4	Ljusdal 101 F3	Llera 43 D1	Lochgilphead 4 B2	Lofsdalen 101 D3	Loiret 25 E2
Livaara 99 F3	Livorno Ferraris ... 31 F1	Ljusnan 101 E3	Llerena 43 D1	Lochinver 2 C2	Lofthus 104 B2	Loiri 66 B3
Liváda, Akr 88 C2	Livron 30 B2	Ljusne 101 F4	Lles 32 A3	Lochmaben 5 D3	Loftus 5 F4	Loiron 23 E3
Livade 70 A3	Lixoúri 82 B4	Ljutići 76 B1	Llessui 37 F2	Lochmaddy 2 A3	Log 70 A2	Loitz 49 D2
Livaderó (Dráma) .. 80 C2	Lizard 8 B4	Ljutoglav 77 D2	Lleyn Pen 6 A3	Loch Ness 2 C3	Logarska dolina ... 70 B1	Loja 43 F3
Livaderó (Kozáni) .. 79 E4	Lizard Pt 8 B4	Ljutomer 70 C1	Lliria 41 E3	Lochranza 4 B2	Logatec, D. 70 A2	Lojsta 109 F4
Livádi (Kíthira) 90 A2	Lizy 19 F3	Llagostera 32 B3	Llívia 32 A2	Lochvica 113 F2	Logroño 36 B2	Lokalahti 107 D2
Livádi (Makedonía) .. 80 A3	Lizzano in	Llanberis 6 A3	Llobregat, R 32 A3	Lochy, L 2 C4	Logrosán 39 E3	Lokan Tekojärvi... 95 F3
Livádi (Sérifos) 88 A3	Belvedere 60 C3	Llanca 32 C3	Llodio 36 B1	Löcknitz 49 E2	Løgstør 108 A2	Løken 105 D3
Livádi (Thessalía) ... 79 E4	Ljeskove Vode 71 E3	Llandeilo 8 C2	Lloret de Mar 32 B4	Locle, le 27 E2	Løgten 108 B3	Lokeren 50 B3
Livadiá	Ljig 72 C3	Llandovery 8 C1	Llucmajor 45 F3	Locmariaquer 22 C4	Løgumkloster 108 A4	Loket 53 E4
(Makedonía) 80 A2	Ljubaništa 77 D4	Llandrindod Wells .. 9 D1	Llynclys 6 B3	Locminé 22 C3	Lohals 108 B4	Lokka 95 F4
Livadiá	Ljubata, D. 77 E2	Llandudno 6 A2	Lnáre 56 C1	Locorotondo 65 E3	Lohberg 56 B1	Lokn'a 111 E2
(Stereá Eláda) ... 83 F4	Ljubelj 70 A1	Llandysul 8 C1	Loanhead 5 D2	Locquirec 22 B2	Lohilahti 103 E3	Løkken (N) 100 C2
Livádi (Tílos) 89 F4	Ljubija 71 D3	Llanelli 8 C2	Loano 31 F3	Locri 67 F4	Lohiniva 99 D1	Løkken (S) 108 B1
Livadítis 80 C1	Ljubinje 75 F2	Llanerchymedd 6 A2	Löbau 53 F2	Locronan 22 B3	Lohja 107 E3	Lokrum 76 B2
Livadohóri 85 D1	Ljubiš 72 C4	Llanes 35 E1	Löbejün 53 D2	Loctudy 22 B3	Lohjanjärvi 107 E2	Lokve (HR) 70 B3
Livanátes 83 F3	Ljubišnja 76 B1	Llanfairfechan 6 A2	Lobenstein 52 C3	Lodè 66 C2	Lohne 17 F2	Lokve (SLO) 70 A2
Livari 76 B3	Ljubljana 70 B2	Llanfair-ym-Muallt .. 9 D1	Łobez 49 E2	Lodève 30 A4	Löhne 17 F2	Lokve (Vojvodina) .. 73 D2
Livarot 19 D4	Ljubno 70 B1	Llanfyllin 6 B3	Löbnitz 49 D1	Lodi 60 B1	Lohr 52 B4	Lolland 108 B4
Livenza 59 E4	Ljubojno 77 E4	Llangadog 8 C2	Lobo 36 A4	Lodosa 36 C2	Lohtaja 102 C1	L'Olleria 45 E1
Liverà 79 D3	Ljubostinja 73 D4	Llangefni 6 A2	Lobón 39 D4	Lodòve 30 A4	Loiano	Lom (BG) 115 D2
Liverdun 21 D4	Ljuboten 77 D2	Llangollen 6 B3	Loburg 53 D1	Løding 97 E1	Rioveggio 60 C3	Lom (CS) 53 E4
Livernon 29 D2	Ljubovija 72 C4	Llangurig 8 C1	Locana 31 E1	Lødingen 94 A3	Loibltunnel 70 A1	Lom (N) 100 B3
Liverpool 6 B2	Ljubuša 75 E1	Llanidloes 8 C1	Locarno 58 A3	Loimaa 107 E2	Loimaa 107 E2	Loma Negra 36 C3
Liverpool B 6 B2	Ljubuški 75 E2	Llano, Pto 39 E3	Lochaline 4 B1	Łódź 112 B2	Loimaan kunta ... 107 D2	Lomazzo 60 A1
Livigno 58 C3	Ljugarn 109 F4	Llanrhystud 8 C1	Lochboisdale 2 A3	Loeches 40 B2	Loimijoki 107 D2	Lombarda,
Livingston 5 D2	Ljungan 101 F3	Llanrwst 6 A3	Lochcarron 2 B3	Loen 100 A3	Loing 26 A2	Colle della 31 E3

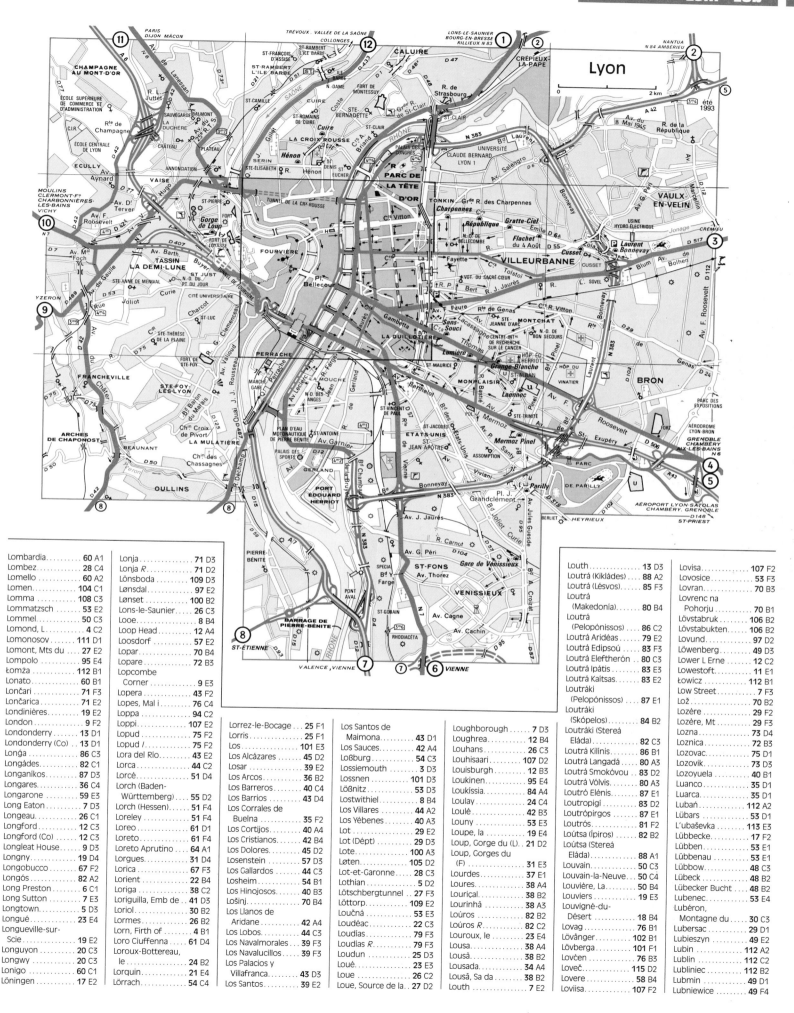

Lyon

Lombardia 60 A1
Lombez 28 C4
Lomello 60 A2
Lomen 104 C1
Lomma 108 C3
Lommatzsch 53 E2
Lommel 50 C3
Lomond, L 4 C2
Lomonosov 111 D1
Lomont, Mts du 27 E2
Lompolo 95 E4
Łomża 112 B1
Lonato 60 B1
Lončari 71 F3
Lončarica 71 E2
Londinières 19 E2
London 9 F2
Londonderry 13 D1
Londonderry (Co) . . 13 D1
Longa 86 C3
Longádes 82 C1
Longaníkos 87 D3
Longares 36 C4
Longarone 59 E3
Long Eaton 7 D3
Longeau 26 C1
Longford 12 C3
Longford (Co) 12 C3
Longleat House 9 D3
Longny 19 D4
Longobucco 67 F2
Longós 82 A2
Long Preston 6 C1
Long Sutton 7 E3
Longtown 5 D3
Longué 23 E4
Longueville-sur-
   Scie 19 E2
Longuyon 20 C3
Longwy 20 C3
Lonigo 60 C1
Löningen 17 E2

Lonja 71 D3
Lonja R. 71 D2
Lönsboda 109 D3
Lønsdal 97 E2
Lønset 100 B2
Lons-le-Saunier 26 C3
Looe 8 B4
Loop Head 12 A4
Loosdorf 57 E2
Lopar 70 B4
Lopare 72 B3
Lopcombe
   Corner 9 E3
Lopera 43 F2
Lopes, Mal i 76 C4
Loppa 94 C2
Loppi 107 E2
Lopud 75 F2
Lopud I 75 F2
Lora del Río 43 E2
Lorca 44 C2
Lorcé 51 D4
Lorch (Baden-
   Württemberg) 55 D2
Lorch (Hessen) 51 F4
Loreley 51 F4
Loreo 61 D1
Loreto 61 F4
Loreto Aprutino 64 A1
Lorgues 31 D4
Lorica 67 F3
Lorient 22 B4
Loriga 38 C2
Loriguilla, Emb de . . 41 D3
Loriol 30 B2
Lormes 26 B2
Lorn, Firth of 4 B1
Loro Ciuffenna 61 D4
Loroux-Botbereau,
   le 24 B2
Lorquin 21 E4
Lörrach 54 C4

Lorrez-le-Bocage . . . 25 F1
Lorris 25 F1
Los 101 E3
Los Alcázares 45 D2
Losar 39 E2
Los Arcos 36 B2
Los Barreros 40 C4
Los Barrios 43 D4
Los Corrales de
   Buelna 35 F2
Los Cortijos 40 A4
Los Cristianos 42 B4
Los Dolores 45 D2
Lote 100 A3
Løten 105 D2
Los Gallardos 44 C3
Losheim 54 B1
Los Hinojosos 40 B3
Lošinj 70 B4
Los Llanos de
   Aridane 42 A4
Los Lobos 44 C3
Los Navalmorales . . 39 F3
Los Navalucillos . . . 39 F3
Loudun 25 D1
Los Palacios y
   Villafranca 43 D3
Los Santos 39 E2

Los Santos de
   Maimona 43 D1
Los Sauces 42 A4
Loßburg 54 C3
Losar 39 E2
Lossiemouth 3 D3
Lossnen 101 D3
Lößnitz 53 D3
Lostwithiel 8 B4
Los Villares 44 A2
Los Yébenes 40 A3
Lot 29 E2
Lot (Dépt) 29 D3
Lot-et-Garonne 28 C3
Lothian 5 D2
Lötschbergtunnel . . . 27 F3
Löttorp 109 E2
Loučná 53 E3
Loudéac 22 C3
Loudias 79 E3
Loudias R. 79 E3
Loudun 25 D1
Loué 23 E3
Loue 26 C2
Loue, Source de la . . 27 D2

Louth 13 D3
Loutrá (Kikládes) . . . 88 A2
Loutrá (Lésvos) 85 F3
Loutrá
   (Makedonía) 80 B4
Loutrá
   (Pelopónissos) . . . 86 C2
Loutrá Aridéas 79 E2
Loutrá Edipsoú 83 F3
Loutrá Eleftherón . . 80 C3
Loutrá Ipátis 83 E3
Loutrá Kaítsas 83 E2
Loutráki
   (Pelopónissos) . . . 87 E1
Loutráki
   (Skópelos) 84 B2
Loutráki (Stereá
   Eláda) 82 C3
Loutrá Killínis 86 B1
Loutrá Langadá 80 A3
Loutrá Smokóvou . . 83 D2
Loutrá Vólvis 80 A3
Loutró Elénis 87 E1
Loutropigi 83 D2
Loutrópirgos 87 E1
Loutrós 81 F2
Loútsa (Ípiros) 82 B2
Loútsa (Stereá
   Eláda) 88 A1
Louvain 50 C3
Louvain-la-Neuve . . 50 C4
Loures 38 A4
Lourical 38 B2
Lourinhã 38 A3
Loúros 82 B2
Loúros R. 82 C2
Lousã 38 B2
Lousada 34 A4
Lousã, Sa da 38 B2
Louth 7 E2

Loughborough 7 D3
Loughrea 12 B4
Louhans 26 C3
Louhisaari 107 D2
Louisburgh 12 B3
Loukinen 95 E4
Loukíssia 84 A4
Loulay 24 C4
Loulé 42 B3
Louny 53 E3
Loupe, la 19 E4
Loup, Gorge du (L.) . 21 D2
Loup, Gorges du
   (F) 31 E3
Lourdes 37 E1
Loures 38 A4
Lourical 38 B2
Lourinhã 38 A3
Loúros 82 B2
Loúros R. 82 C2
Lovag 76 B1
Lövånger 102 B1
Lövberga 101 F1
Lovćen 76 B3
Loveč 115 D2
Lovere 58 B4
Loviisa 107 F2

Lovisa 107 F2
Lovosice 53 F3
Lovran 70 B3
Lovrenc na
   Pohorju 70 B1
Lövstabruk 106 B2
Lövstabukten 106 B2
Lovund 97 D2
Löwenberg 49 D3
Lower L Erne 12 C2
Lowestoft 11 E1
Łowicz 112 B1
Low Street 7 F3
Lož 70 B2
Lozère 29 F2
Lozère, Mt 29 F3
Lozna 73 D4
Loznica 72 B3
Lozovac 75 D1
Lozovik 73 D3
Lozoyuela 40 B1
Luanco 35 D1
Luarca 35 D1
Lubań 112 A2
Lübars 53 D1
L'ubaševka 113 E3
Lübbecke 17 F2
Lübben 53 E1
Lübbenau 53 E1
Lübbow 48 C3
Lübeck 48 B2
Lübecker Bucht 48 B2
Lubenec 53 E4
Lubéron,
   Montagne du 30 C3
Lubersac 29 D1
Lubieszyn 49 E2
Lublin 112 A2
Lublin 112 C2
Lubliniec 112 B2
Lubmin 49 D1
Lubniewice 49 F4

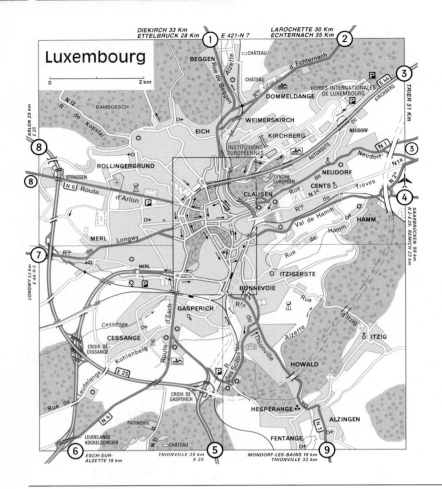

Luxembourg

Ludwigshafen (Rheinland-Pfalz) **54** C1	Lun **70** B4	Lutzelbourg **21** E4
Ludwigslust **48** C3	Luna ....., Emb	Lützen............. **53** D2
Ludwigstadt **52** C3	Barrios de **35** D2	Lutzerath........ **51** E4
Luère, Col de la .. **26** C4	Luna, R. **35** D2	Lutzmannsburg .. **57** F3
Lug **75** E1	Lunas **30** A4	Lützow............ **48** B2
Lug R. **73** D3	Lund **108** C3	Luumäki.......... **103** F4
Luga **111** D1	Lunde (Sogn og	Luupuvesi........ **103** D1
Luga R. **111** D1	Fjordane) **100** A3	Luusua **99** E2
Lugagnano Val	Lunde (Telemark) .. **104** C3	Luvia............. **107** D2
d'Arda **60** B2	Lunden **47** F2	Luxembourg **21** D2
Lugano **58** A4	Lundy **8** B3	Luxembourg (Grand-Duché) **21** D2
Lugau **53** D3	Lune............. **6** B1	
Lügde **52** A1	Lüneburg **48** B3	Luxembourg (Prov.) **20** C2
Lugnano in	Lunel **30** B4	
Teverina **63** E2	Lünen **17** E3	Luxeuil........... **27** D1
Lugnaquillia Mt **13** D4	Lünersee **58** B2	Luynes **25** D2
Lugo (E) **34** B2	Lunéville **21** D4	Lužani............ **71** E3
Lugo (I) **61** D2	Lungern **27** F3	Luzarches **19** F3
Lugoj **114** C1	Lungro **67** E2	Luzech **29** D3
Lugones **35** D1	Luninec **113** D1	Luzern **27** F2
Luhačovice **112** A3	Luodonselkä **99** D4	Lužnica **77** E1
Luhalahti **102** C3	Luogosanto **66** B1	Lužnice **57** D1
Luhanka **103** D3	Luonteri......... **103** E3	Luz-St-Sauveur ... **37** E2
Luhtapohja **103** F2	Luopioinen **107** E1	Luzy............. **26** B3
Luik **51** D4	Luosto **99** D1	Luzzara **60** C2
Luimneach **14** B3	Luoto **102** C1	Luzzi **67** E2
Luiña **35** D1	Lupoglav **71** D2	L'vov............ **112** C2
Luing **4** B1	Luque **43** F2	Lychen **49** D3
Luino **58** A4	Lurbe-St-Christau .. **37** D1	Lyckebyån........ **109** E3
Luiro **95** F4	Lurcy-Lévis **26** A3	Lycksele **98** A4
Luisenburg **53** D4	Lure............. **27** D1	Lydd **11** D3
Luka (BH) **75** F1	Lure, Mgne de.... **30** C3	Lydney **9** D2
Luka (HR) **74** C1	Lurgan **13** E2	Lye.............. **109** F4
Luka (Srbija) **73** E3	Luri **33** F2	Lygna............ **104** B4
Lukavac **71** F3	Lurisia **31** E3	Lyme B **9** D3
Lukavica **71** F3	Lurøy **97** D2	Lyme Regis **9** D3
Lukovica **70** B2	Lury **25** E3	Lymington........ **9** E3
Lukovit.......... **115** D2	Lušci Palanka **71** D4	Łyna **110** B4
Lukovo (Makedonija) **77** D4	Lushnjë **76** C4	Lyndhurst **9** E3
Lukovo (Srbija) **73** E4	Lusi **107** F1	Lyness............ **3** D1
Lukovo (Srbija) **77** D1	Lusignan **24** C3	Lyngdal **104** B4
Lukovo Šugarje ... **70** C4	Lusigny **26** B1	Lyngen **94** C2
Luleå **98** C3	Lusk **13** E3	Lyngseidet **94** C2
Luleälven **98** B3	Luso. **38** B2	Lyngsnes **97** D4
Lüleburgaz **115** E3	Lussac **28** B2	Lynmouth **8** C3
Lumbarda **75** E2	Lussac-les-Châteaux **25** D4	Lynton **8** C3
Lumbier **36** C2		Lyon **26** C4
Lumbrales **31** D1	Lussan **30** B3	Lyons-la-Forêt **19** E3
Lumbres **19** F1	Lussau **53** F3	Lys **19** F1
Lumezzane **60** B1	Lustenau **58** B2	Lysá **53** F3
L'udinovo **111** F3	Luster. **100** B3	Lysefjorden **104** A3
Ludlow **9** D1	Lustrafjorden **100** B3	Lyseheiene **104** B3
Ludvika.......... **105** F3	Lütjenburg **48** B2	Lysekil........... **108** C1
Ludwigsburg **55** D2	Luton **9** F2	Lyss **27** E2
Ludwigsfelde..... **49** D4	Lutterberg **52** A2	Lysvik **105** E3
Ludwigshafen (Baden-Württemberg) **55** D4	Lutterworth........ **9** E1	Lytham St Anne's. . **6** B2
	Lutto **95** F3	

Lubniewsko, Jez **49** F4	Lučani. **73** D4	Lucera............ **64** C3	Ludbreg. **71** D1
Lubny **113** F2	Lúcar **44** B3	Lüchow **48** C3	Lude, le **23** F4
L'uboml' **112** C2	Lucca **60** C3	Luciana **39** F4	Lüdenscheid...... **17** E4
Lubrín **44** C3	Luče **70** B2	Lucito **64** B2	Ludiente **41** E3
Lubsko........... **53** F1	Luce B. **4** B3	Luck **113** D2	Lüdinghausen **17** E3
Lubsza **53** F1	Lucena **43** F3	Lucka **53** D2	Ludlow **9** D1
Lübtheen **48** B3	Lucena del Cid ... **41** E3	Luckau **53** E1	Ludvika. **105** F3
Lübz **48** C3	Lucenay-l'Evêque ... **26** B2	Luckenwalde **53** E1	Ludwigsburg **55** D2
Luc............. **18** C3	Luc-en-Diois **30** C2	Luc, le **31** D4	Ludwigsfelde..... **49** D4
Lucainena de las Torres........ **44** C3	Lučenec. **112** B3	Lucomagno, Pso del ... **58** A3	Ludwigshafen (Baden-Württemberg) **55** D4
Lucan............ **13** D4	Luceni........... **36** C3	Luçon **24** B3	

M

Maakalla.......... **102** C1	Macgillycuddy's Reeks **14** A4	Maddalena La. **66** B1	Maesteg **8** C2	Magoúla........... **86** B2	Mainz **51** F4	Makrihóri (Thessalía) **83** E1
Maalanti........... **102** B2	Machault **20** B3	Maddaloni **64** B3	Mafra **38** A3	Magro, R **41** D4	Maira **31** E2	Makrinítsa **83** F2
Maam Cross **12** B3	Machecoul **24** B3	Madeira, Arquipélago da ... **42** A3	Magacela **39** E4	Magura **77** D2	Mairena del Alcor. . . **43** D2	Makrinóros **82** C3
Maaninka **103** E2	Machero **39** F4	Madeira, I da **42** A3	Magallón **36** C3	Maherádo **86** A1	Maisach **55** F3	Makriráhi **83** E3
Maaninkavaara..... **99** E2	Machichaco, C. ... **36** B1	M'adel' **111** D3	Magaña **36** B3	Mahlu **103** D2	Maison-Neuve..... **26** B1	Makriplágio **80** C2
Maanselkä **103** E1	Machine, la **26** A3	Madeleine, Col de la **31** D1	Magaz. **35** F3	Mahón **45** F2	Maisons-Blanches, les **25** D4	Makrívrahos, Akr. ... **81** E3
Maarestatunturit .. **95** E3	Machrihanish **4** B3	Madero, Pto del .. **36** C3	Magdalena, Pto de la **35** D2	Mahora **41** D4	Maissau **57** E2	Makrohóri **79** E3
Maarianhamina ... **106** C3	Machynlleth **6** A3	Maderuelo **36** A1	Magdeburg **52** C1	Mähring **53** D4	Maiziéres **21** D3	Makroníssi **88** A2
Maarianvaara **103** E2	Mackendorf **52** C1	Madesimo **58** B3	Magenta **60** A1	Maia **34** A4	Maja **70** C3	Maksniemi **99** D3
Maas **16** C3	Mackenrode. **52** B2	Madine, Lac de ... **20** C3	Magerøya **95** E1	Maials **37** E4	Majales, Pto de los . **40** A4	Mala **14** B4
Maaseik **51** D4	Mačkovci **70** C1	Madon **21** D4	Maggía **58** A3	Maîche **27** E2	Majdanpek **73** E3	Malå **98** A4
Maasmechelen ... **51** D3	Macocha **57** F1	Madona **110** C2	Maggiore, L **58** A4	Maida **67** F3	Majevica **72** B3	Mala Bosna **72** B1
Maassluis **16** B3	Macomer **66** B2	Madonie Nebrodi .. **68** C3	Maghera **13** D1	Maidenhead **9** F2	Majšperk **70** C1	Malacky **57** F2
Maastricht **51** D3	Mâcon **26** C4	Madonna di Campiglio. **58** B3	Magherafelt **13** D2	Maidstone **11** D3	Makarska **75** E2	Maladeta **37** E2
Määttälänvaara ... **99** F2	Macotera **39** F1	Madrid. **40** A2	Mágina **44** A2	Maiella, la. **64** A2	Makce **73** E3	Malaga **43** F4
Mablethorpe **7** E2	Macroom **14** B4	Madrid (Prov.) ... **40** A2	Magione. **61** E4	Maienfeld **58** B2	Makedonía **79** F2	Malagón **40** A4
Macael **44** C3	Macugnaga **27** F4	Madridejos **40** B3	Maglaj **71** F3	Maignelay **19** F3	Makedonija **77** E3	Malahide **13** E4
Mação **38** B3	Mačvanska Mitrovica **72** C3	Madrigal de las Altas Torres........ **39** F1	Magliano di Marsi .. **63** F2	Maigue **14** B3	Makedonski Brod.. **77** D3	Malaja Višera **111** E1
Macclesfield **6** C3	Mačvanski Pričinović **72** C3	Madrigal de la Vera . **39** F2	Magliano in Toscana **63** D2	Mailly-le-Camp ... **20** B3	Makó. **114** B1	Malaja Viska **113** F2
Macduff **3** E3	Madara. **115** E2	Madrigalejo **39** E4	Magliano Sabina .. **63** E2	Main **55** D1	Makovo **77** E4	Mala Kapela **70** C3
Maceda **34** B3	Maddalena, Arc della **66** B1	Madrona **40** A1	Maglić **73** D4	Mainar **36** C4	Makrakómi **83** E3	Mala Krsna **73** D3
Macedo de Cavaleiros **34** C4	Maddalena, Colle della......... **31** E2	Madrona, Sa. **44** A1	Maglić Mt **76** A1	Mainburg. **55** F2	Mákri **81** E2	Malalbergo **61** D2
Macelj........... **70** C1	Maddalena, I **66** B1	Madroñera **39** E3	Maglie **65** F4	Maine-et-Loire.... **23** E4	Makríamos **80** C3	Malámata **83** D4
Macerata **61** F4	Maël-Carhaix **22** B3	Magnac-Laval **25** D4	Maintenon **19** E4	Makrígialos **79** F3	Malandríno **83** E4
Macerata Feltria **61** E3	Maella **37** E4	Magnor **105** D3	Mainistir na Búille .. **12** C3	Makrigialós **91** F4	Malangen **94** B2
		Magny-en-Vexin ... **19** E3	Mainland (Orkney) . **3** D1	Makrihóri (Makedonía). ... **80** C2	Mälaren **106** B3
			Mainland (Shetland) . **3** F2		Mala Subotica **71** D1
		Magnissía......... **83** E2			Malaucène **30** C3

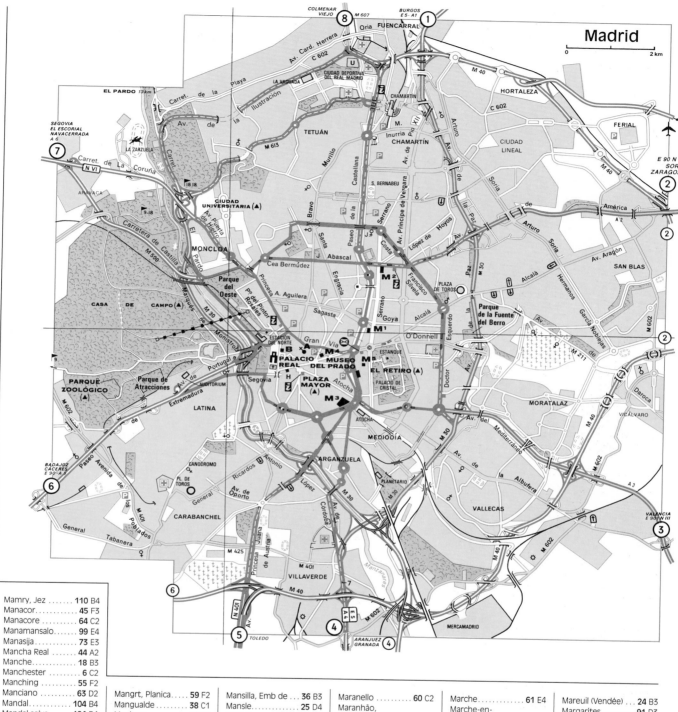

Madrid

Malax 102 B2
Malbork 110 B4
Malbuisson 27 D3
Malcata, Sa de . . . 39 D2
Malcesine 58 C4
Malchin 49 D2
Malchiner See 49 D2
Malchow 49 D2
Maldegem 50 B3
Maldon 11 D2
Malé 58 C3
Maléas, Akr 87 E4
Maleme 90 B3
Malène, la 29 F3
Malente
  Gremsmühlen 48 B2
Male Pijace 72 C1
Máles 91 E4
Malesherbes 25 F1
Malessina 83 F3
Malestroit 22 C3
Malgomaj 97 F4
Malgrat de Mar 32 B4
Mália 91 E3
Malicorne 23 E4
Mali Haian 70 C4
Mali Iđđos 72 B2
Mali kanal 72 B2
Mali Lošinj 70 B4
Malin 113 E2
Malines 50 B3
Malin Head 13 D1
Malinska 70 B3
Mali Poževerac 73 D3
Mališevo 77 D2
Maliskylä 103 D1
Malit, Maj'e 76 C3
Mali Zvornik 72 B4
Maljen 72 C4
Malko Târnovo 115 E2
Mallaig 2 B4
Mållejus 95 D2
Mallén 36 C3
Mallersdorf-
  Pfaffenberg 56 B2
Malles Venosta 58 C2
Mallnitz 59 E2
Mallorca 45 E2
Mallow 14 B4
Mallwyd 6 A3
Malm 101 D1
Malmberget 98 B2
Malmédy 51 D4
Malmesbury 9 D2
Malmköping 106 A1
Malmö 108 C3
Malmöhus Län 109 D3
Malmslätt 106 A4
Malo 59 D4
Maloja 58 B3
Malojaroslavec 111 F3
Malo Konjari 77 E4
Malo-les-Bains 19 F1
Malónas 93 F1
Malori 64 B4
Måløy 100 A3
Malpartida de
  Cáceres 39 D3
Malpartida de
  Plasencia 39 E2
Malpica (E) 34 A1
Malpica (P) 38 C3
Mals 58 C2
Målselv 94 B3
Målselva 94 B3
Målsnes 94 B3
Malsta 101 F3
Malta 59 F2
Malta/ 68 B4
Maltby 7 D2
Maltiotunturi 95 F4
Malton 7 D1
Maluenda 36 C4
Malung 105 E2
Malungsfors 101 D4
Malveira 38 A4
Malvik 100 C2
Malzieu-Ville, le . . . 29 F2
Mamaia 115 E1
Mamarrosa 38 B1
Mamers 23 F3
Mammola 67 F4
Mamonovo 110 B4
Mampodre 35 E2

Mamry, Jez 110 B4
Manacor 45 F3
Manacore 64 C2
Manamansalo 99 E4
Manasija 73 E3
Mancha Real 44 A2
Manche 18 B3
Manchester 6 C2
Manching 55 F2
Manciano 63 D2
Mandal 104 B4
Mandal selva 104 B4
Mandamádos 85 F2
Mandas 66 B3
Mandela 63 F2
Mandelieu 31 E4
Manderscheid 51 E4
Mandinia 87 D2
Mandoúdi 84 A3
Mandráki 89 F4
Mándra (Stereá
  Eláda) 87 F1
Mándra (Thráki) 81 F2
Mandre 70 B4
Mandrikó 93 E1
Mandrioli, Pso dei . . 61 D3
Manduria 65 E4
Måne 104 C3
Manerbio 60 B1
Manětin 53 E4
Manfredonia 64 C2
Manfredonia, G di . . 64 C2
Mangalia 115 E2
Mángana 81 D2
Manganári 88 C4
Manger 104 A2
Mangerton Mt. 14 B4

Mangrt, Planica 59 F2
Mangualde 38 C1
Maniago 59 E3
Manilva 43 E4
Man, I of 6 A1
Máni
  (Pelopónissos) . . 87 D4
Máni (Thráki) 81 F1
Manisa 115 E4
Mánises 41 E4
Manjača 71 E4
Mank 57 E3
Mankarbo 106 B3
Manlleu 32 B3
Mannersdorf 57 F3
Mannheim 54 C1
Mannu 66 B4
Manojlovac slap . . . 75 D1
Manojlovce 77 E1
Manoppello 64 A2
Manorhamilton 12 C2
Manosque 30 C3
Manresa 32 A4
Manschnow 49 F4
Mansfeld 52 C1
Mansfield 7 D3
Mansilla de las
  Mulas 35 E3

Mansilla, Emb de . . 36 B3
Mansle 25 D4
Manteigas 38 C2
Mantes 19 E4
Mantiel 40 C2
Mäntlahti 103 F4
Mantorp 109 E1
Mantova 60 C2
Mäntsälä 107 F2
Mänttä 103 D3
Mäntyharju 103 E3
Mäntyjärvi 99 E2
Mäntyluoto 102 B3
Manzanal, Pto del . . 35 D2
Manzanares 40 B4
Manzanares el
  Real 40 A2
Manzaneda 34 C3
Manzanera 41 E3
Manzat 26 A4
Manziana 63 E2
Maó 45 F2
Maqellarë 77 D3
Maqueda 40 A2
Maramureş 112 C3
Maranchón 40 C1
Maranchón,
  Pto de 40 C1

Maranello 60 C2
Maranhão,
  Bgem do 38 B4
Marano 59 F3
Marano di Napoli . . 64 B4
Marano, L di 59 F4
Marans 24 B4
Marão, Sa do 34 B4
Marássia 81 F1
Maratea 67 E2
Marateca 38 A4
Marathéa 83 D2
Marathiá, Akr 86 A2
Marathiás 83 D4
Marathókambos . . . 89 E1
Marathónas 87 F1
Marathópoli 86 B3
Márathos 83 F2
Marbach 55 D2
Mårbacka 105 E3
Marbella 43 E4
Marburg 17 F4
Marby 101 E2
Marčana 70 A4
March (A) 57 F2
March (GB) 10 C1
Marchamalo 40 B2
Marchaux 27 D2

Marche 61 E4
Marche-en-
  Famenne 50 C4
Marchegg 57 F2
Marchena 43 E3
Marchenoir 25 E1
Marchiennes 20 A1
Marciac 28 C4
Marciana Marina . . 62 C1
Marcianise 64 B3
Marcigny 26 B4
Marcilla 36 C3
Marcillac-Vallon . . . 29 E3
Marcillat-en-
  Combraille 25 F4
Marcilly-le-Hayer . . 20 B4
Marcksolsheim 27 E1
Marco de
  Canaveses 34 A4
Marcoule 30 B3
Mære 101 D1
Maree, L 2 C3
Mare Ligure 60 A4
Marene 31 E2
Marennes 28 A1
Marentes 34 C2
Maréttimo, I- 68 A3
Mareuil (Dordogne) . 28 C1

Mareuil (Vendée) . . 24 B3
Margarites 91 D3
Margaríti 82 B2
Margate 11 D2
Margherita di
  Savoia 65 D3
Marguerittes 30 B3
María 44 C2
María Cristina,
  Emb de 41 E3
Mariannelund 109 E1
Mariánské Lázně . . 53 E4
Maria Saal 70 A1
Maria Taferl 57 E2
Mariazell 57 E3
Maribo 108 B4
Maribor 70 C1
Mariborsko
  Pohorje 70 C1
Marica 115 D3
Mariefred 106 B4
Mariehamn 106 C4
Marienberg 53 E3
Marienborn 52 C1
Marienburg 51 E4
Marienstedt 48 B3
Mariestad 105 E4
Marignane 30 C4

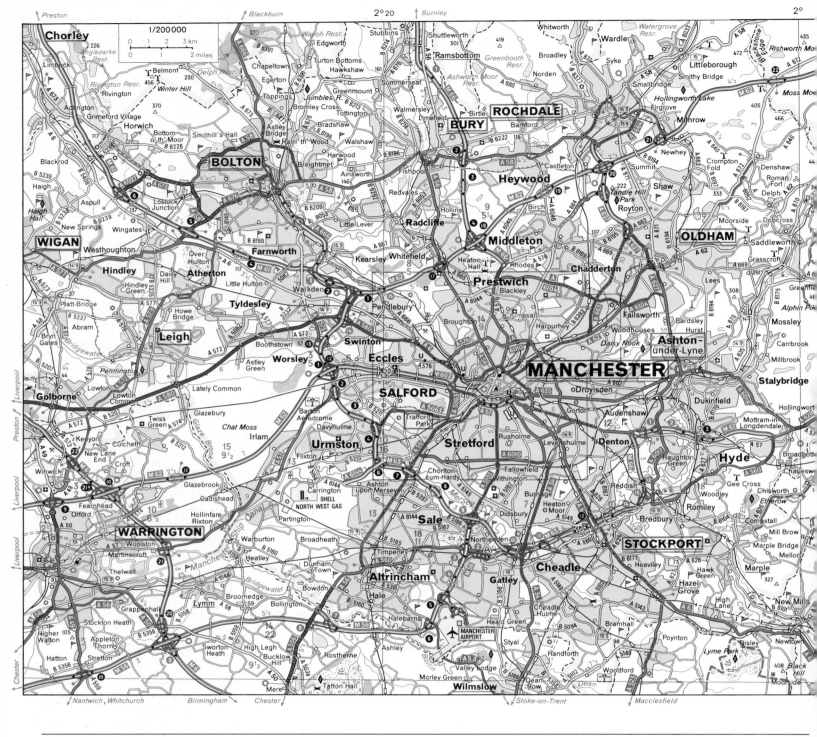

Marigny............ 18 B3	Marineo 68 B3	Markkleeberg 53 D2	Marl............... 17 E3	Maronías, Akr....... 81 E2	Märsta 106 B3	Martinengo 60 B1
Marigny-le-Châtel .. 20 B4	Marines 19 E3	Markneukirchen.... 53 D4	Marlborough 9 E2	Maronne........... 29 E2	Marstal........... 108 B4	Martinet.......... 32 A3
Marija Bistrica 70 C2	Maringues......... 26 A4	Markópoulo (Atiki-	Marle............. 20 B2	Maros 114 B1	Marstrand......... 108 C1	Martingança 38 A2
Marijampolė...... 110 C4	Marinha Grande .. 38 A2	Piréas)........... 84 B4	Marlow (D)........ 48 C2	Marostica 59 D4	Marta 63 D2	Martinniemi 99 D3
Marikirk........... 3 E4	Marinkainen....... 102 C1	Markópoulo (Atikli-	Marlow (GB) 9 F2	Marotta 61 E3	Martano 65 F4	Martíno 83 F4
Marín............ 34 A2	Marino 63 E3	Piréas)........... 87 F1	Marmande 28 C3	Márpissa 88 C3	Martel............ 29 D2	Martín, R 41 E1
Marina 75 D2	Marismas,	Markópoulo	Marmara Denizi ... 115 E3	Marquartstein 56 B3	Martelange........ 21 D2	Martinščica 70 B4
Marina di	Pto de las....... 43 D2	(Kefaloniá) 86 A1	Marmári 88 A1	Marquíon 19 F2	Martelange........ 21 D2	Martis 66 B2
Camerota..... 67 D2	Marjaniemi 99 D4	Markovac (Srbija) ... 73 D3	Mármaro 85 F4	Marquise 19 E1	Martes, Sa de 44 A2	Martjanci 70 C1
Marina di Campo .. 62 C2	Marjina Gorka 111 D4	Markovac	Marmolada, Mte... 59 D3	Marradi 61 D3	Marthon 28 C1	Martofte 108 B3
Marina di Carrara .. 60 B3	Markaryd 109 D3	(Vojvodina)....... 73 D2	Marmolejo 43 F2	Marraskoski 99 D2	Martignacco 59 F3	Martonvaara 103 F2
Marina di Castagneto-	Markdorf 55 D4	Markov manastir ... 77 E3	Marmoutier 21 E4	Marsaglia 60 A2	Martigné-	Martorell 32 A4
Donoratico....... 62 C1	Marken........... 16 C2	Markranstädt...... 53 D2	Marnay........... 27 D2	Marsala 68 A3	Ferchaud 23 D4	Martigny 27 E4	Martos............ 44 A2
Marina di	Markermeer....... 16 C2	Markstein, le 27 E1	Marne............ 47 F2	Marsberg 17 F3	Martigny-les-Bains . 27 D1	Martti 95 F4
Gioiosa Jonica..... 67 F4	Market Drayton 6 C3	Marktbreit......... 55 E1	Marne (Dépt) 20 B4	Marsciano 63 E1	Martigues 30 C4	Marttila 107 E2
Marina di Grosseto . 62 C1	Market Harborough . 9 F1	Markt Erlbach 55 E1	Marne R........... 19 F4	Marseillan 30 A4	Martim Longo 42 B2	Marvão 38 C3
Marina di Massa .. 60 B3	Markethill 13 D2	Marktheidenfeld ... 55 D1	Marne au Rhin, Canal	Marseille 30 C4	Martin 112 B3	Marvejols 29 F2
Marina di	Market Rasen....... 7 D2	Markt Indersdorf ... 55 F3	de la 20 C4	Marseille-en-	Martina 58 C2	Marxwalde 49 E4
Pietrasanta 60 B3	Market Weighton ... 7 D2	Marktl 56 B3	Marnitz........... 48 C3	Beauvaisis........ 19 E3	Martina Franca ... 65 E3	Maryport 5 D1
Marina di Pisa 60 C4	Markgröningen ... 55 D2	Marktoberdorf 55 E4	Marofa 39 D1	Marsico Nuovo ... 64 C4	Martin Brod 71 D4	Mary, Puy 29 E2
Marina di Ragusa .. 69 D4	Markina 36 B1	Marktredwitz 53 D4	Marolles-les-	Marske-by-the-Sea .. 5 F4	Martinci Čepinski .. 71 F2	Marzagran 20 B3
Marina di Ravenna .. 61 D2	Märkisch	Markt St Florian ... 57 D3	Braults.......... 23 F3	Mars-la-Tour...... 21 D3	Martin de la Jara .. 43 E3	Mas-Cabardès 32 B1
Marinella 68 B3	Buchholz 53 E1	Markušica 71 F2	Marónia........... 81 E2	Mars-la-Tour...... 21 D3	Martin de Yeltes .. 39 D1	Mas-d'Agenais, le... 28 C3

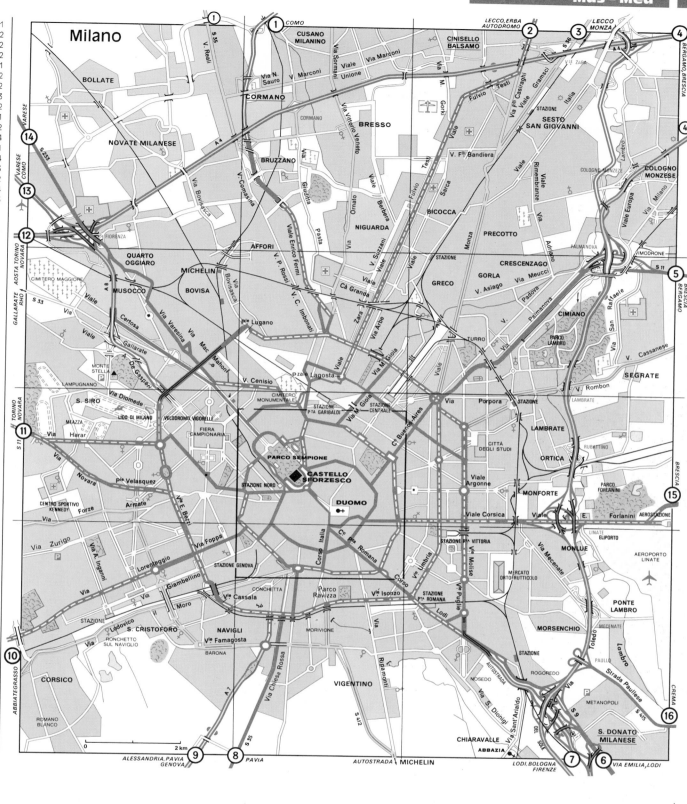

Monaco (map)

Monaco · VENTIMIGLIA MENTON · MENTON A 8 · A 8 · MENTON · COUNTRY CLUB · NICE · G DE CORNICHE · D 53 · D 2564 · N 7 · ST-ROMAN · LA ROUSSA · Guynemer · CORNICHE INFÉRIEURE · N 98 · MONTE-CARLO BEACH · Rte de la Turbie · MONT DES MULES · FAUSSIGNANA · AUREILLA · BEAUSOLEIL · BORDINA · CORNICHE · MONTE-CARLO · Casino · MONTE-CARLO SPORTING-CLUB · PLAGE DU LARVOTTO · HALL DU CENTENAIRE · MOYENNE CORNICHE · LES MONEGUETTI · LES RÉVOIRES · tunnel en construction · PORT · LA CONDAMINE · JARDIN EXOTIQUE · MONACO · PALAIS · MUSÉE OCÉANOGRAPHIQUE · NICE EZE, A 8 · N 7 · LES SALINES · FONTVIEILLE · ST-ANTOINE · STADE LOUIS II · CIRQUE · HELIPORT · PORT DE CAP-D'AIL · PLAGE MARQUET · CAP-D'AIL VILLEFRANCHE-S-MER · N 98 · LA TURBIE · 0 — 300 m

Mer Adriatique 74 B2
Meråker 101 D2
Meran 59 D2
Merano 59 D2
Merate 60 A1
Mercadal 45 F1
Mercante, Pso di ... 67 E4
Mercantour, Parc Nat du 31 E3
Mercatale (Marche) 61 E3
Mercatale (Toscana) 61 D4
Mercatino Conca ... 61 E3
Mercato San Severino 64 B4
Mercato Saraceno .. 61 D3
Mercëz 77 D1
Mercoeur 29 D2
Mer de Crète 90 C2
Merdrignac 22 C3
Mer du Nord 16 A2
Mere 9 D3
Mer Égée 85 D4
Méréville 25 F1
Mergozzo 58 A4
Méribel 31 D1
Mérida 39 D4
Mérignac 28 B2
Mérihas 88 A2
Merijärvi 99 D4
Merikarvia 102 B3
Mering 55 F3
Merkendorf 55 E2
Merklingen 55 D3
Merlerault, le 19 D4
Mer Noir 115 F1
Merošina 77 D1
Merrenkurkku 102 B2
Merrick 4 C3
Mers 19 E2
Mersch 21 D2
Merseburg 53 D2
Merthyr Tydfil 8 C2
Mértola 42 B2
Méru 19 F3
Méry 20 B4
Merville (Calvados) .. 18 C3
Merville (Pas-de-Calais) 19 F1
Merzig 54 A2
Mesagne 65 F3
Mesão Frio 34 B4
Meschede 17 F3
Mescherin 49 E3
Meschers 28 A1
Mešeišta 77 D4
Mesići 76 A1
Mesihovina 75 E1
Meslay 23 E3
Mesocco 58 B3
Mesola 61 D2
Mesón do Vento .. 34 B1
Mesoraca 67 F3
Mespelbrunn 52 A4
Messanagrós 93 E2
Messarás, Órmos .. 91 D4
Messariá 88 B1
Meßdorf 48 C4
Messei 18 C4
Méssi 81 D2
Messíni 86 C3
Messinia 86 C3
Messiniakós Kólpos 86 C4
Messlingen 101 D2
Messohóra 82 C2
Messohóri (Kárpathos) 93 D3
Messohóri (Thessalía) 83 E1
Messolóngi 82 C4
Messongi 82 A2
Messopótamo 82 B2
Messótopos 85 E2
Meßstetten 55 D3
Mestá 85 E4
Mesta 115 D3
Mestanza 44 A1
Mésti 81 E2

Mestlin 48 C2
Mestre 61 D1
Mesvres 26 B3
Metajna 70 C4
Meta, la 64 A2
Metalika 76 B1
Metalikó 79 F2
Metalio 83 E3
Metamórfossi (Halkidikí) 80 B4
Metamórfossi (Kilkís) 79 F2
Metangítsi 80 B4
Metanopoli 60 A1
Metauro 61 E3
Metaxádes 81 F1
Metéora 83 D1
Méthana 87 E2
Methil 5 D2
Methóni (Makedonía) 79 F3
Methóni (Pelopónissos) .. 86 C3
Metković 75 F2
Metlika 70 C2
Metnitz 57 D4
Metóhi (Ahaïa) .. 86 B1
Metóhi (Argolída) 87 E2
Metóhi (Évia) 84 B3
Metóhi (Thessalía) . 83 F2
Metsäkyla 99 E3
Metsäkylä 103 F4
Metsämaa 107 E2
Métsovo 82 C1
Mettingen 17 E2
Mettlach 54 A1
Mettmann 17 E4
Metz 21 D3
Metzervisse 21 D3
Metzingen 55 D3
Meulan 19 E3
Meung 25 E2
Meursault 26 C3
Meurthe-et-Moselle 21 D4
Meuse 20 C3
Meuse (Dépt.) 20 C3
Meuselwitz 53 D2
Mevagissey 8 B4
Meximieux 26 C4
Meyenburg 48 C3
Meymac 29 D1
Meyrand, Col de .. 30 B2
Meyrueis 29 F3
Meyzieu 26 C4
Mezas 39 D2
Mezdra 115 D2
Mèze 30 A4
Mézel 31 D3
Mézenc, Mt. 30 B2
Mezőberény 112 C4
Mézières 25 D4
Mézières-en-Brenne 25 E3
Mézin 28 C3
Mezőkövesd 112 B4
Meztúr 112 B4
Mezzano 59 D3
Mezzolombardo .. 58 C3
Mgarr 68 B4
Miajadas 39 E4
Miastko 110 A4
Michalovce 112 C3
Micheldorf 57 D3
Michelstadt 55 D1
Michendorf 49 D4
Middelburg 16 B3
Middelfart 108 B3
Middelharnis 16 B3
Middelkerke-Bad .. 50 A3
Middlesbrough 5 F4
Middleton-in-Teesdale 5 E4
Middlewich 6 C3
Midhurst 9 F3
Midi, Canal du 32 B1
Midi de Bigorre, Pic du 37 E2

Midi d'Ossau, Pic du 37 D2
Midleton 14 C4
Midouze 28 B3
Midsund 100 B2
Mid Yell 3 F1
Miedes 36 C4
Miedwie, Jez. 49 F3
Międzychód 112 A1
Międzylesie 112 A2
Międzyrzec Podlaski 112 C1
Międzyzdroje 49 E2
Miehikkälä 103 F4
Miekojärvi 98 C2
Miélan 28 C4
Mielec 112 B2
Mielno 49 F1
Mieluskylä 103 D1
Miera, R 35 F2
Miercurea-Ciuc ... 113 D4
Mieres 35 D2
Miesbach 56 B3
Mieszkowice 49 E3
Mietoinen 107 D2
Miettila 103 F3
Migennes 26 A1
Migliarino 61 D2
Miglionico 65 D4
Miguel Esteban .. 40 B3
Miguelturra 40 A4
Mihajlovac (Srbija) .. 73 D3
Mihajlovac (Srbija).. 73 F3
Mihajlovgrad 115 D2
Mihas 86 C1
Mihóï 86 B1
Mijas 43 E4
Mijoux 27 D3
Miki 81 D2
Mikines 87 D2
Mikkeli 103 E3
Mikkelin Lääni 103 E3
Mikkelvik 94 B2
Mikleuš 71 E2
Mikonos 88 C2
Míkonos, N. 88 C2
Mikrí Mandínia 86 C3
Mikrí Préspa, L. 78 C3
Mikró Horió 83 D3
Mikrókambos 79 F2
Mikroklissoúra 80 B1
Mikrolímni 78 C3
Mikromiliá 80 C1
Mikrón Dério 81 F1
Mikron Eleftherohóri 79 E4
Mikrópoli 80 B2
Mikulov 57 F1
Milagro 36 C2
Milano 60 A1
Milano Marittimo 61 E3
Milatos 91 E3
Milazzo 69 D2
Mileševo (Srbija) .. 76 B1
Mileševo (Vojvodina) 72 C1
Milestone 14 C3
Miletići 70 C4
Mileto 67 E3
Miletto, Mte 64 B3
Milevsko 57 D1
Milford (GB) 9 F3
Milford (IRL) 13 D1
Milford Haven 8 B2
Milhão 34 C4
Mílii 87 D2
Miliá (Makedonía)... 79 D4
Miliá (Pelopónissos) .. 87 D2
Miliá (Thráki) 81 F1
Milići 72 B4
Miliés 83 F2
Milín 53 F4
Milína 83 F2
Milis 66 B3
Militello in Val di C. .. 69 D4
Miljevina 76 A1
Millas 32 B2
Millau 29 F3
Millesimo 31 F2
Millom 6 B1

Meerane 53 D3
Meersburg 55 D4
Mées, les 31 D3
Mefjordbotn 94 B2
Mefjordvær 94 B2
Méga Dério 81 F2
Mega Horió (Stereá Eláda) 83 D3
Megalohóri 83 D1
Megalópoli 86 C2
Meganíssi 82 B3
Megaplátanos 83 F3
Mégara 87 E1
Megárhi 83 D1
Méga Spíleo 86 C1
Megève 27 E4
Megaló Horió (Agathoníssi) 89 F2
Megaló Horió (Tílos). 89 F4
Megisti 93 F2
Megísti, N 93 F2
Megístis Lávras 80 C4
Meg. Livádi 88 A3
Meg. Panagía 80 B3
Meg. Vólvi 80 B3
Mehamn 95 E1
Mehedeby 106 B2
Mehov Krš 76 C2
Mehun 25 F2
Meigle 5 D1
Meijel 17 D4
Meije, la 31 D2
Meilen 58 A2
Meillant 25 F3
Meimoa 38 C2
Meina 58 A4
Meinerzhagen 17 E4
Meiningen 52 B3

Meira 34 C1
Meira, Sa de 34 C1
Meiringen 27 F3
Meisenheim 54 B1
Meißen 53 E2
Meitingen 55 E3
Mel 59 E3
Melalahti 99 E4
Mélambes 91 D4
Melaniós 85 E4
Melánthio 78 C3
Melátes 82 C2
Melbeck 48 B3
Melbu 94 A3
Meldal 100 C2
Meldola 61 D3
Meldorf 47 F2
Melegnano 60 A1
Mêle, le 19 D4
Melenci 72 C2
Melendugno 65 F4
Melfi 64 C3
Melfjorden 97 E2
Melgaço 34 B3
Melgar de Abajo .. 35 E3
Melgar de Fernamental 35 F3
Melhus 100 C2
Melía 83 E2
Melide 34 B2
Melides 42 A1
Melidóni 91 D3
Meligalás 86 C3
Melilli 69 D4
Mélisey 27 D1
Mélissa 81 D2
Mélissa, Akr 82 B4

Melissáni 82 B4
Melíssi 87 D1
Melissohóri 84 A4
Melissópetra 78 C4
Melissourgós 80 B3
Meliti 79 D2
Melito di Porto Salvo 67 E4
Melivia (Thessalía) .. 83 F1
Melívia (Thráki) 81 D1
Melk 57 E2
Melksham 9 E2
Mellan Fryken 105 E3
Mellansel 102 A2
Melle (D) 17 F2
Melle (F) 24 C4
Mellerstair 5 D2
Mellerud 105 D4
Mellieha 68 B4
Mellin 48 B4
Mellingen 52 C3
Mellrichstadt 52 B4
Mellum 47 F3
Melnica 73 E3
Melnice 70 B3
Mělník 53 F3
Mělník 53 F4
Melogno, Colle di .. 31 F3
Meløy 97 E2
Meløyfjorden 97 E2
Melpers 52 B3
Melrose 5 D2
Melsungen 52 A3
Meltaus 99 D2
Melton Mowbray ... 7 D3
Meltosjärvi 99 D2

Melun 19 F4
Melvich 3 D2
Melvin, L 12 C2
Membrilla 40 B4
Membrio 38 C3
Memmingen 55 E3
Mena 113 F1
Menaggio 58 B4
Menai Bridge 6 A2
Ménalo, Óros 86 C2
Menasalbas 40 A3
Menat 26 A4
Mencal 44 B3
Mendavia 36 B2
Mende 29 F3
Mendelpass 59 D3
Menden 17 E3
Mendenítsa 83 E3
Menderes, B 115 F4
Mendola, Pso della 59 D3
Mendrisio 58 A4
Menée, Col de 30 C2
Menen 50 A3
Menesjärvi 95 E3
Menetés 93 D3
Ménez-Hom 22 B3
Menfi 68 B3
Mengamuñoz 39 F2
Menga, Pto de .. 39 F2
Mengara 61 E4
Mengen 55 D3
Mengeš 70 B2
Menglbar 44 A2
Menídi 82 C2
Ménigoute 24 C3
Meníkio, Óros 80 B2
Mennetou 25 E2
Menor, Mar 45 D2
Menorca 45 F1
Mens 30 C2
Mentana 63 E2
Menthon 27 D4
Menton 31 E3
Méntrida 40 A2
Menuires, les 31 D1

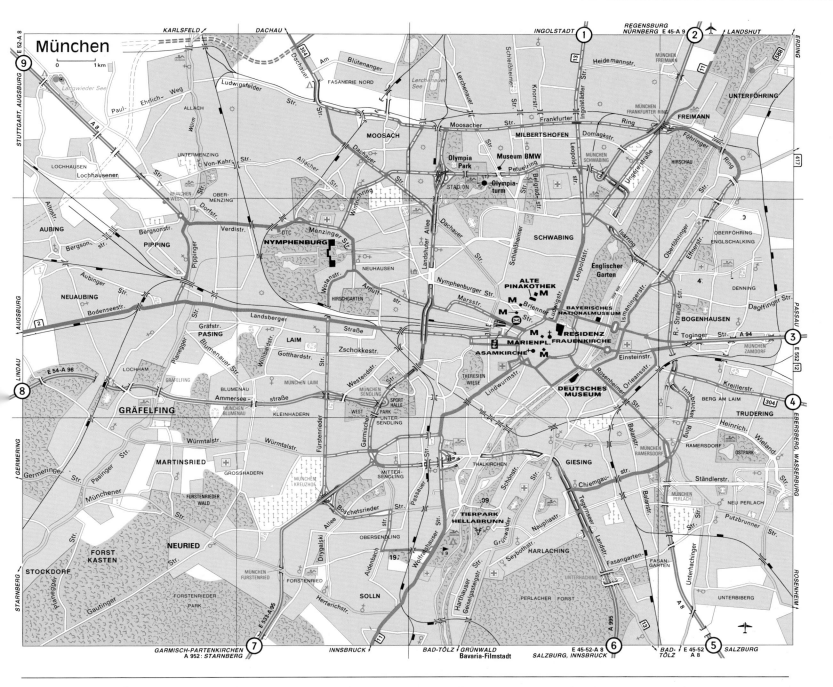

München

Millport	4	C2
Millstatt	59	F2
Millstreet	14	B4
Milltown Malbay	12	B4
Milly	19	F4
Milmarcos	36	C4
Milmersdorf	49	E3
Milna	75	D2
Miločer	76	B3
Milohnič	70	B3
Milopótamos	90	A4
Milos	88	A4
Miloševa Kula	73	E3
Milos, N	88	A4
Miltach	56	B1
Miltenberg	55	D1
Milton Keynes	9	F2
Milutinovac	73	F2
Mimizan	28	A3
Mimizan-Plage	28	A3
Mimoň	53	F3
Mína	87	D4
Mina de São		
Domingos	42	B2
Minas de Riotinto	42	C2
Minaya	40	C4
Minch, The	2	B2
Mincio	60	C1
Mindelheim	55	E3

Minden	17	F2
Mindin	24	A2
Minehead	8	C3
Minerbe	60	C1
Minerbio	61	D2
Minervino Murge	65	D3
Minglanilla	41	D3
Mingorria	39	F1
Mínguez, Pto	41	D2
Mingulay	2	A4
Minho	34	A3
Miničevo	73	F4
Minilla, Emb de la	43	D2
Ministra, Sierra	36	B4
Minkiö	107	E2
Miño, R	34	A2
Minsk	111	D4
Mińsk Mazowiecki	112	B1
Minsterley	9	D1
Minthi, Óros	86	C2
Mintlaw	3	E3
Miokovićevo	71	E2
Mionica	72	C3
Mionnay	26	C4
Mira (E)	41	D3
Mira, R	42	A2
Mira (P)	38	B1
Mirabella		
Imbaccari	68	C4

Mira de Aire	38	B3
Mirador de Coto		
Rondo	34	A2
Mirador del Fito	35	E1
Miraflores	35	F3
Miraflores de la		
Sierra	40	A1
Miramar (F)	31	E4
Miramar (P)	34	A4
Miramare	61	E3
Miramas	30	C4
Mirambeau	28	B1
Mirambélou,		
Kólpos	91	F3
Miramont-de-		
Guyenne	28	C2
Miranda de Ebro	36	B2
Miranda del		
Castañar	39	E2
Miranda do Corvo	38	B2
Miranda do Douro	34	C4
Mirande	28	C4
Mirandela	34	C4
Mirandola	60	C2
Mirano	61	D1
Mirow	49	D3
Mirow	49	D3
Mirsini	87	D4
Mirtiés	89	E3
Mirtóo Pélagos	87	E3
Mirtos	91	E4
Mirtos, Akr	93	E2
Mirtou, Kólpos	82	B4
Mírovice	56	C1
Misi	99	D2
Misilmeri	68	B3

Miravete, Pto de	39	E3
Mirditë	76	C3
Mirebeau		
(Côte-d'Or)	26	C2
Mirebeau (Vienne)	25	D3
Mirecourt	27	D1
Mirepoix	32	A2
Mires	91	D4
Mirgorod	113	F2
Miribel	26	C4
Mirina	85	D1
Mirna	70	B2
Mirna R	70	A3
Miroč	73	E3
Mironovka	113	E2
Miroševce	77	E1
Mirotice	56	C1
Mírovice	56	C1

Miskolc	112	B3
Mislinja	70	B1
Mistelbach	57	F2
Misterbianco	69	D3
Mistrás	87	D3
Mistretta	68	C3
Mistros	84	B4
Misurina	59	E2
Mitchelstown	14	C3
Mittelland-Kanal	17	F2
Mitikas	82	C3
Mitikas Mt	79	E4
Mitilini	85	F2
Mitilinii	89	E1
Mitrašinci	77	E3
Mitrópoli	83	D2
Mitrovica	77	D1
Mitsikéli, Óros	82	B1
Mittelberg (Tirol)	58	C2
Mittelberg		
(Vorarlberg)	58	B2
Mittenwald	55	F4
Mittenwalde	49	E4
Mittersill	59	E1
Mitterteich	53	D4
Mittweida	53	E2
Mizen Head	14	A4
Mjällån	101	F2

Mjällom	102	A2
Mjöbäck	108	C2
Mjölby	109	E1
Mjøndalen	104	C3
Mjøsa	105	D2
Mladá Boleslav	112	A2
Mladá Vožice	57	D1
Mladenovac	73	D3
Mladost, Ez	77	E3
Mlado Nagoričane	77	E2
Mlava	73	E3
Mława	112	B1
Mlini	76	A2
Mlinište	71	D4
Mljet	75	E2
Mljetski Kanal	75	F2
Mnichovo		
Hradiště	53	F3
Moälven	102	A2
Moaña	34	A2
Moate	12	C3
Mocejón	40	A3
Möckern	52	C1
Möckmühl	55	D2
Moclin	44	A3
Modane	31	D1
Modbury	8	C4
Modena	60	C2
Módi	83	E3

Modica	69	D4
Modigliana	61	D3
Mödling	57	F2
Modračko jez	71	F3
Modran	71	E3
Modřany	53	F4
Modrava	56	C1
Modriča	71	F3
Modrište	77	D3
Modugno	65	D3
Moëlan	22	B3
Moelv	105	D2
Moen	94	B3
Moena	59	D3
Moers	17	D3
Moesa	58	B3
Moffat	5	D3
Mogadouro	34	C4
Mogadouro,		
Sa do	34	C4
Mogente	45	D1
Mogila	77	E4
Mogil'ov	111	E4
Mogil'ov-		
Podol'skij	113	E3
Moglia	60	C2
Mogliano Veneto	59	E4
Mogón	44	B2
Mogorrit	41	D2

Moguer 42 C2
Mohács 114 B1
Moher, Cliffs of . . . 12 B4
Mohill 12 C3
Möhkö 103 F2
Móhlos 91 F4
Möhne 17 F3
Moholm 105 E4
Moi 104 A4
Moià 32 A4
Moie 61 E4
Moimenta 34 C3
Moimenta da Beira . 38 C1
Mo i Rana 97 E2
Moirans 30 C1
Moirans-en-
  Montagne 27 D3
Moisdon 23 D4
Moisiovaara 99 F4
Moisling 48 B2
Moissac 29 D3
Moita 38 A4
Mojácar 44 C3
Mojados 35 E4
Mojkovac 76 B2
Mojón Pardo, Pto
  de 36 B3
Mojstrana 70 A1
Mokra Gora 72 C4
Mokra Gora Mts . . . 76 C2
Mokrin 72 C1
Mokronog 70 B2
Mokro Polje 75 D1
Mol (B) 50 C3
Mol (Vojvodina) 72 C1
Mola di Bari 65 E3
Molái 87 D4
Molat 74 B1
Molat I 74 B1
Molatón 41 D4
Mold 6 B3
Moldavija 113 E3
Molde 100 B2
Moldefjorden 100 B2
Moldova Nouã 114 C1
Moldoveanu 113 D4
Møldrup 108 B2
Moledo do
  Minho 34 A3
Molène 22 A2
Molfetta 65 D3
Molières 29 D3
Molina de Aragón . . 40 C2
Molina de Segura . . . 45 D2
Molinella 61 D2
Molinicos 44 C1
Molins de Rei 32 A4
Molise 64 B2
Moliterno 65 D4
Molitg-les-Bains 32 B2
Mólivos, Akr 85 F2
Molkom 105 E3
Möllbrücke 59 F2
Mollerussa 37 F3
Molliens-Vidame . . . 19 E2
Mollina 43 F3
Mölln 48 B2
Mollösund 108 C1
Mölnlycke 108 C1
Molodečno 111 D4
Mologa 111 F1
Mólos 83 E3
Molpe 102 B2
Mols 108 B3
Molsheim 21 E4
Molve 71 D1
Molveno 58 C3
Mombeltrán 39 F2
Mombuey 35 D3
Mommark 108 B4
Momo 60 A1
Møn 108 C4
Monach, Sd of 2 A3
Monadhliath Mts 2 C4
Moná fjärd 102 B2
Monaghan 13 D2
Monaghan (Co) 13 D2
Monasterace
  Marina 67 F4
Monasterboice 13 D3
Monasterevin 13 D4
Monasterio de
  Rodilla 36 A2
Monastier, le 30 B2

Monastir 66 B4
Monastiráki (Stereá
  Eláda) 82 C3
Monastiráki
  (Thráki) 81 F2
Monastíri Doukáto . . 81 E2
Monastiri, N 83 E2
Monbazillac 28 C2
Moncalieri 31 E2
Moncalvo 31 F1
Monção 34 A3
Moncarapacho 42 B3
Moncayo, Sa
  de 36 C3
Mönchdorf 57 D2
Mönchengladbach . 17 D4
Monchique 42 A2
Monchique,
  Sa de 42 A2
Monclar-de-
  Quercy 29 D3
Moncófar 41 E3
Moncontour (Côtes-
  d'Amor) 22 C3
Moncontour
  (Vienne) 24 C3
Moncoutant 24 C3
Monda 43 E4
Mondariz 34 A3
Mondavio 61 E3
Mondego, Cabo 38 A2
Mondego, R 38 B2
Mondéjar 40 B2
Mondello 68 B2
Mondim 34 B4
Mondolfo 61 E3
Mondoñedo 34 C1
Mondorf 21 D3
Mondoubleau 23 F3
Mondoví 31 F2
Mondragon 30 B3
Mondragone 64 A3
Mondsee 56 C3
Moneim 28 B4
Monemvassía 87 E4
Monesi 31 E3
Monesterio 43 D1
Monestier-de-
  Clermont 30 C2
Monestiés 29 E3
Monêtier, le 31 D2
Moneygall 12 C4
Moneymore 13 D2
Monfalcone 59 F3
Monflanquin 28 C2
Monforte 38 C4
Monforte de
  Lemos 34 B2
Mongie, la 37 E2
Mongó 45 E1
Monguelfo 59 D2
Monheim 55 E2
Mönichkirchen 57 F3
Mon-Idée 20 B2
Monifieth 5 D1
Moní, N 87 E2
Monistrol 32 A4
Monistrol-d'Allier . . . 29 F2
Monistrol-sur-
  Loire 30 B1
Mönkebude 49 E2
Monmouth 9 D2
Monnickendam 16 C2
Monodéndri 78 C4
Monódrio 84 B4
Monólithos 93 E2
Monopoli 65 E3
Monor 112 B4
Monóvar 45 D1
Monpazier 28 C2
Monreal 51 E4
Monreal del
  Campo 41 D2
Monreale 68 B3
Monrepós, Pto de . . 37 D2
Monroy 39 D3
Monroyo 41 E2
Mons 50 B4
Monsanto 38 C2
Monsaraz 42 C1
Monschau 51 D4
Monségur 28 C2
Monselice 61 D1
Monserrat 41 E4

Møns Klint 108 C4
Monsols 26 B4
Mönsterås 109 E2
Monsummano
  Terme 60 C3
Montabaur 51 F4
Montagnac 30 A4
Montagnana 61 D1
Montagne Noire 32 B1
Montagnes
  Noires 22 B3
Montagrier 28 C1
Montaigu 24 B3
Montaigu-de-
  Quercy 29 D3
Montaigut 26 A4
Montaione 60 C4
Montalbán 41 E2
Montalbo 40 C3
Montalcino 63 D1
Montalegre 34 B3
Montalieu 26 C4
Montalivet 28 A1
Montalto delle
  Marche 61 F4
Montalto di Castro . 63 D2
Montalto Uffugo . . . 67 E2
Montalvão 38 C3
Montamarta 35 D4
Montana 27 E3
Montaña 37 D3
Montánchez 39 D3
Montanejos 41 E3
Montargil 38 B3
Montargil, Bgem
  de 38 B4
Montargis 25 F1
Montastruc-la-
  Conseillère 29 D4
Montauban (Ille-et-
  Vilaine) 23 D3
Montauban (Tarn-et-
  Garonne) 29 D3
Montbard 26 B2
Montbazens 29 E3
Montbazon 25 D2
Montbéliard 27 E2
Montbenoit 27 D2
Mont Blanc 27 E4
Montblanc 37 F4
Mont Blanc,
  Tunnel du 27 E4
Montbozon 27 D2
Montbrió del
  Camp 37 F4
Montbrison 30 B1
Montbron 28 C1
Montceau-les-
  Mines 26 B3
Montcenis 26 B3
Mont Cenis, Col
  du 31 E1
Montchanin 26 B3
Montcornet 20 B2
Montcuq 29 D3
Mont-de-Marsan . . . 28 B3
Montdidier 19 F3
Mont-Dore, le 29 E1
Monteagudo de las
  Vicarías 36 B4
Montealegre 35 E4
Montealegre del
  Castillo 45 D1
Montebello Ionico . . 67 E4
Montebello
  Vicentino 60 C1
Montebelluna 59 E4
Monte Bianco,
  Traforo di 27 E4
Montebourg 18 B3
Monte-Carlo-
  Monaco 31 E3
Montecarotto 61 E4
Montecatini-
  Terme 60 C3
Montecchio
  Maggiore 60 C1
Montech 29 D3
Montecchio 61 E3
Monte Citerna,
  Pso del 60 C3
Montecorvino
  Rovella 64 B4
Montecristo, I di . . . 62 C2

Monte Croce Carnico,
  Pso di 59 E2
Monte Croce di
  Comelico, Pso . . . 59 E2
Monte da
  Pedra 38 C3
Monte da Rocha,
  Bgem de 42 B2
Montedoro 68 C3
Montefalco 63 E1
Montefalcone di Val
  Fortore 64 B3
Montefalcone nel
  Sannio 64 B2
Montefeltro 61 D3
Montefiascone 63 E2
Montefiore dell'
  Aso 61 F4
Montefiorino 60 C3
Montefrío 43 F3
Montegallo 63 F1
Montegiorgio 61 F4
Monte Giovo, Pso
  di 59 D2
Montegranaro 61 F4
Montegrotto
  Terme 61 D1
Montehermoso 39 D2
Montejicar 44 A2
Montejo de
  Tiermes 36 A4
Montejunto,
  Sa de 38 A3
Monteleone di
  Spoleto 63 E1
Montélimar 30 B2
Montella 64 B4
Montellano 43 D3
Monteluco 63 E1
Montelupo
  Fiorentino 60 C4
Montemaggiore
  Belsito 68 C3
Montemagno 31 F1
Montemayor 43 F2
Montemayor de
  Pililla 35 E4
Montemor-o-Novo . 38 B4
Montemor-o-
  Velho 38 B2
Montemuro,
  Sa do 38 C1
Montendre 28 B1
Montenegro de
  Cameros 36 B3
Montenero di
  Bisaccia 64 B2
Montenero
  Sabino 63 E2
Montepulciano 61 D4
Monte Real 38 B2
Montereale
  (Abruzzo) 63 F1
Montereale
  (Friuli-Venezia) . . 59 E3
Montereau 19 F4
Monte Redondo 38 B2
Monterenzio 61 D3
Monteriggioni 61 D4
Monteroni di
  Lecce 65 F4
Monte Rosa 27 F4
Monterosso al
  Mare 60 B3
Monterotondo 63 E2
Monterotondo
  Marittimo 62 C1
Monterroso 34 B2
Monterrubio de la
  Serena 43 E1
Monterubbiano 61 F4
Montesano sulla
  Marcellana 64 C4
Monte San Savino . . 61 D4
Monte Sant'
  Angelo 64 C2
Montesarchio 64 B3
Montescaglioso 65 D4
Montesilvano
  Marina 64 A1
Montesquieu-
  Volvestre 37 F1
Montesquiou 28 C4
Montet, le 26 A3

Montets, Col des . . . 27 E4
Montevarchi 61 D4
Monteviejo, Pto
  de 35 E2
Montfaucon (Maine-
  et-Loire) 24 B2
Montfaucon-
  d'Argonne 20 C3
Montfaucon-en-
  Velay 30 B1
Montfort 23 D3
Montfort-en-
  Chalosse 28 B4
Montfort-
  l'Amaury 19 E4
Montfort-sur-
  Risle 19 D3
Montgaillard 32 A2
Montgenèvre 31 D2
Montgenèvre, Col
  de 31 D2
Montgiscard 29 D4
Montgomery 9 D1
Montguyon 28 B1
Monthermé 20 C2
Monthey 27 E4
Monthois 20 C3
Monthureux 27 D1
Monti 66 B2
Montichiari 60 B1
Monticiano 61 D4
Montier-en-Der 20 C4
Montignac 29 D2
Montigny-le-Roi 26 C1
Montigny-sur-
  Aube 26 C1
Montijo (E) 39 D4
Montijo (P) 38 A4
Montilla 43 F2
Montioni 62 C1
Montivilliers 19 D3
Montjean 23 E4
Montlhéry 19 F4
Montlieu 28 B1
Montlouis 25 D2
Mont-Louis 32 A3
Montluçon 25 F4
Montluel 26 C4
Montmarault 26 A4
Montmartin 18 B3
Montmédy 20 C3
Montmélian 31 D1
Montmirail
  (Marne) 20 A4
Montmirail
  (Sarthe) 23 F3
Montmirey-le-
  Château 26 C2
Montmoreau 28 C1
Montmorency 19 F4
Montmorillon 25 D4
Montmort 20 B3
Montoggio 60 A3
Montoire 23 F4
Montoito 38 C4
Montone 61 D3
Montorio al
  Vomano 63 F1
Montoro 43 F2
Montòro, Emb de . . 43 F1
Montpellier 30 A4
Montpellier-le-Vieux,
  Chaos de 29 F3
Montpezat-de-
  Quercy 29 D3
Montpezat-sous-
  Bauzon 30 B2
Montpon-
  Ménestérol 28 C2
Montpont 26 C3
Montréal (Aude) . . . 32 A2
Montréal (Gers) 28 C3
Montréal-la-Cluse . . 26 C4
Montredon-
  Labessonnie 32 B1
Montréjeau 37 E1
Montrésor 25 E2
Montresta 66 A2
Montreuil 19 F1
Montreuil-Bellay . . . 24 C2
Montreux 27 E3
Montrevault 24 B2
Montrevel 26 C3

Montrichard 25 E2
Mont-roig del
  Camp 37 F4
Montrond-les-
  Bains 30 B1
Montrose 5 E1
Mont-St-Michel, le . 18 B4
Mont-St-Vincent . . . 26 B3
Montsalvy 29 E2
Montsant, Sa del . . . 37 F4
Montsauche 26 B2
Montsec, Serra de . . 37 F3
Montseny 32 B4
Montseny, Sa de . . . 32 B4
Montserrat 32 A4
Mont-sous-
  Vaudrey 26 C3
Monts-sur-
  Guesnes 25 D3
Montsûrs 23 E3
Montuenga 39 F1
Montuiri 45 F3
Monviso 31 E2
Monza 60 A1
Monzón 37 E3
Monzón de
  Campos 35 F3
Moordorf 47 E3
Moorfoot Hills 5 D2
Moosburg 56 B2
Mór 112 B4
Mora (E) 40 A3
Mora (P) 38 B4
Mora (S) 101 E4
Morača 76 B2
Morača R 76 B2
Morača klisura 76 B2
Móra d'Ebre 37 E4
Mora de Rubielos . . 41 E2
Moraira 45 E1
Moraira, Pta de 45 E1
Morais 34 C4
Moraltika 82 A2
Morakovo, G 76 B2
Móra la Nova 41 F1
Moral de Calatrava . 40 A4
Moraleda de
  Zafayona 44 A3
Moraleja 39 D2
Moraleja de
  Sayago 39 E1
Morales de Rey 35 D3
Morales de Toro . . . 35 E4
Morano Calabro . . . 67 E2
Mora, Pto de la 44 A3
Morar, L 2 B4
Mörarp 108 C3
Morasverdes 39 D2
Morata de Jalón . . . 36 C4
Morata de Tajuña . . 40 B2
Moratalla 44 C2
Morata, Pto de 36 C4
Morava 57 E1
Morava R 112 A3
Moravče 70 B2
Moravci 70 C1
Moravica 73 D4
Moravské
  Budějovice 57 E1
Moravske Toplice . . . 70 C1
Moravský Krumlov . . 57 E1
Moray Firth 3 D3
Morbach 54 B1
Morbegno 58 B3
Morbihan 22 C3
Mörbisch 57 F3
Mörbylånga 109 E3
Morcenx 28 A3
Morciano di
  Romagna 61 E3
Morcone 64 B3
Morcote 58 A4
Morcuera, Pto de
  la 40 A1
Mordelles 23 D3
Morecambe 6 B1
Morecambe Bay 6 B1
Moreda 44 A3
Morée 25 E1
Moreleja del Vino . . 35 D4
Morella 41 E2
Møre og Romsdal . 100 B2
Mores 66 B2
Morestel 30 C1

Moret 19 F4
Moreton 9 E2
Moretonhampstead . . 8 C3
Moreuil 19 F2
Morez 27 D3
Morfasso 60 B2
Mórfio 82 B2
Morgat 22 A3
Morges 27 D3
Morgex 27 E4
Morgins, Pas de . . . 27 E4
Morhange 21 D3
Mori 58 C4
Morina 76 C2
Moritzurg 53 E2
Morjärv 98 C3
Morlaàs 37 E1
Morlaix 22 B2
Mormanno 67 E2
Mormant 19 F4
Mormoiron 30 C3
Mornant 30 B1
Mórnou, Teh L 83 E1
Morón de
  Almazán 36 B4
Morón de la
  Frontera 43 E3
Morosaglia 33 F3
Morović 72 B3
Morpeth 5 E3
Morrón 44 B3
Mörrum 109 D3
Mors 108 A2
Morsbach 17 E4
Mörsil 101 E2
Morsleben 52 C1
Mortagne 28 B1
Mortagne-au-
  Perche 19 D4
Mortagne-sur-
  Sèvre 24 C3
Mortágua 38 B2
Mortain 18 C4
Mortara 60 A2
Morteau 27 D2
Mortrée 19 D4
Morven 3 D2
Moryń 49 E3
Morzine 27 E4
Morzyczyn 49 F2
Mosbach 55 D2
Mosby 104 B4
Mošćenice 70 B3
Mošćenička Draga . . 70 B3
Moschendorf 57 F4
Mosel 51 E4
Moselle (Dépt) 21 D3
Moselle R 27 D4
Moshokariá 83 E1
Moshopótamos 79 E3
Mosjøen 97 E3
Moskenesøya 97 E1
Moskenstraumen . . . 97 E1
Mosko 76 A2
Moskosel 98 B3
Moskva 111 F2
Moskva R 111 F2
Moslavačka gora . . . 71 D2
Mosonmagyaróvár 112 A4
Mosor 75 E2
Mosqueruela 41 E2
Moss 105 D3
Mossala 107 D3
Mossat 3 E4
Mosses, Col des . . . 27 E3
Mössingen 55 D3
Mosta 68 B4
Mostar 75 F2
Mosteiro 34 A2
Mosterhamn 104 A3
Mostiska 112 C2
Móstoles 40 A2
Mostonga 72 B2
Mostrim 12 C3
Mosty 110 C4
Møsvatn 104 B3
Mosvik 101 D1
Mota del Cuervo . . . 40 B3
Mota del Marqués . . 35 E4
Motajica 71 E3
Motala 105 F4
Motala S 106 A4

Mothe-Achard, la ... 24 B3
Motherwell 4 C2
Mothe-St-Héray, la . 24 C4
Motilla del
  Palancar 40 C3
Motovun 70 A3
Motril 44 A4
Motta di Livenza .. 59 E4
Motta S.A. 69 D3
Motta Visconti ... 60 A1
Motte-Chalancon,
  la 30 C2
Motte, la 31 D3
Mottola 65 E4
Mouchard 27 D3
Moudon 27 E3
Moúdros 85 D1
Mougins 31 E4
Mouhijärvi 107 D1
Mouilleron-en-
  Pareds 24 C3
Moulins 26 A3
Moulins-Engilbert . 26 B3
Moulins-la-Marche . 19 D4
Moult 18 C3
Moúnda, Akr 86 A1
Mountain Ash 8 C2
Mount Bellew 12 C3
Mountmellick 13 D4
Mountrath 12 C4
Mount's B 8 A4
Mountsoúna 88 C3
Moura 42 B1
Mourâo 42 C1
Moúrdzeflos, Akr .. 85 D1
Mourenx 28 B4
Mouríki 84 A4
Mourmelon-le-
  Grand......... 20 B3

Mourne........... 13 D2
Mourne Mts 13 E3
Mourniés......... 90 B3
Mourujärvi 99 E2
Mouscron 50 A3
Moustiers-Ste-
  Marie 31 D3
Mouthe........... 27 D3
Mouthier......... 27 D2
Mouthoumet....... 32 B2
Moutier.......... 27 E2
Moûtiers 31 D1
Moutiers-les-
  Mauxfaits 24 B3
Mouy 19 F3
Mouzakéi......... 82 C1
Mouzáki 83 D2
Mouzon 20 C2
Moville.......... 13 D1
Moy 12 B2
Moyenneville 19 E2
Moyeuvre 21 D3
Moyuela 37 D4
Mozajsk 111 F2
Mozirje 70 B1
Mozyr'........... 113 E1
Mrągowo 110 B4
Mrakovica 71 D3
Mramorak 73 D2
Mratinje 76 A1
Mrazovac....... 70 C3
Mrčajevci....... 73 D4
Mrežičko........ 77 E3
Mrkonjić Grad ... 71 E4
Mrkopalj........ 70 B3
Mrzeżyno 49 F1
Mšeno.......... 53 F3
Msta 111 E1
Mstislavl'....... 111 E3

Mú 42 B2
Muć............ 75 D1
Muccia 61 E4
Much........... 17 E4
Much Wenlock.... 9 D1
Mucientes 35 E4
Muck 2 B4
Muckle Roe 3 F1
Muckross House ... 14 B4
Mudanya 115 F3
Mudau 55 D1
Muddus 98 B2
Muel 37 D4
Muelas del Pan ... 35 D4
Muff 13 D1
Muge 38 B3
Mügeln 53 E2
Muggia 59 F4
Mugron 28 B4
Mugueimes 34 B3
Mühlbach 59 E1
Mühlberg 53 E2
Mühldorf....... 56 B3
Mühlen-Eichsen .. 48 B2
Mühlhausen 52 B2
Mühltroff...... 53 D3
Muhniemi 107 F2
Muhos 99 D4
Muhu.......... 110 B2
Muineachán 13 D2
Muine Bheag 15 D3
Muirkirk 4 C3
Muir of Ord..... 2 C3
Mukačevo 112 C3
Mukos 77 E3
Mula 45 D2
Mülacker 54 C2
Mula, R........ 45 D2

Mulargia, L 66 B3
Mulhacén 44 A3
Mülheim 17 E3
Mulhouse 27 E1
Mull 4 B1
Müllheim 54 C4
Mullingar 13 D3
Mull of Galloway .. 4 B4
Mull of Kintyre .. 4 B3
Mull of Oa 4 A2
Müllrose 49 F4
Mull, Sd of 4 B1
Mullsjö 109 D1
Mulrany........ 12 B2
Multia 103 D3
Mumbles, The .. 8 C2
Muñana 39 F2
Münchberg 53 D4
Müncheberg ... 49 E4
München..... 56 A3
Münchhausen ... 17 F4
Münden 52 B2
Mundesley...... 7 F3
Mundford 11 D1
Mundo, R...... 44 C1
Munera 40 C4
Mungia....... 36 B1
Muñico 39 F2
Muniesa....... 37 D4
Munkebo 108 B3
Munkedal 105 D4
Munkfors 105 E3
Münnerstadt ... 52 B4
Muñogalindo ... 39 F2
Munsala 102 B2
Munsfjället 101 E1
Münsingen (CH) . 27 E3
Münsingen (D) .. 55 D3
Munster (F)..... 27 E1

Münster (CH) ... 27 F3
Münster
  (Niedersachsen) .. 48 B3
Münster (Nordrhein-
  Westfalen) 17 E3
Münstertal 54 C4
Münzenberg ... 52 A4
Münzkirchen ... 56 C2
Muodoslompolo .. 95 D4
Muojärvi 99 F2
Muonio 95 D4
Muonioälven ... 95 D4
Muotkatonturit.... 95 E2
Mur 57 E4
Mura 70 C1
Muraglione, Pso
  del.......... 61 D3
Murano 61 D1
Murat 29 E2
Murato 33 F3
Murat-sur-Vèbre . 32 B1
Murau....... 57 D4
Muravera 66 C4
Murça 34 B4
Murchante 36 C3
Murcia 45 D2
Murcia (Reg)... 44 C2
Mur-de-Barrez .. 29 E2
Mur-de-Bretagne . 22 C3
Mureck....... 57 E4
Mure, la 30 C2
Mures....... 112 C4
Muret 29 D4
Murg 54 C2
Murgia....... 36 B1
Muri 27 F2
Murias de Paredes . 35 D2
Murino 76 C2
Muriqan 76 B3

Müritz See........ 49 D3
Murjek........ 98 B2
Murlough Bay ... 13 E1
Murnau 56 A4
Muro 33 F3
Muro de Alcoy ... 45 E1
Murol 29 E1
Murole 102 C3
Muro Lucano ... 64 C4
Muros 34 A2
Mürren 27 F3
Murrhardt..... 55 D2
Murska Sobota .. 70 C1
Mursko Središče... 70 C1
Murten 27 E3
Murter 74 C1
Murter / 74 C1
Murtosa 38 B1
Murtovaara.... 99 F3
Murvica 74 C1
Murviel...... 30 A4
Mürz 57 E3
Mürzsteg..... 57 E3
Mürzzuschlag .. 57 E3
Musala 115 D3
Mussalo 103 F4
Musselburgh ... 5 D2
Musselkanaal ... 17 E1
Mussidan 28 C2
Mussomeli 68 C3
Mussy 26 B1
Mustair...... 58 C1
Mustasaari ... 102 B2
Muste 58 A3
Mustion as ... 107 E3
Mustvee 110 C1
Muta 70 B1
Mutala 102 C3
Mutterstadt ... 54 C1

Mutzschen 53 E2
Muurame 103 D3
Muurasjärvi 103 D1
Muuratjärvi 103 D3
Muurla 107 E2
Muurola....... 99 D2
Muuruvesi 103 E2
Muxía 34 A1
Muy, le 31 D4
Muzillac 22 C4
Muzzana del
  Turgnano ... 59 F3
Mweelrea Mts ... 12 B3
Myckegensjö 101 F2
Mykines....... 96 A3
Myllykoski 107 F2
Myllykylä 102 C3
Myllymäki 102 C2
Mynämäki 107 D2
Mýrdalsjökull ... 96 B3
Myre 94 A3
Myrlandshaugen .. 94 B3
Myrskylä 107 F2
Myrviken 101 E2
Mysen 105 D3
Mysingen 106 B4
Myśla...... 49 F3
Myślibórskie, Jez . 49 F3
Myślibórz.... 49 F3
Mývatn..... 96 B1
Mże 53 E4

N

Naab 55 F1
Naamijoki 98 C2
Naantali 107 D2
Naarajärvi 103 E2
Naarva....... 103 F2
Naas 13 D4
Näätämöjoki ... 95 F2
Nabburg 56 B1
Načeradec 57 D1
Náchod 112 A2
Naddvik 104 B1
Nadela 34 B2
Nădlac 114 C1
Nadur 68 B4
Nadvornaja.... 113 D3
Näfels 58 A2
Nafpaktías, Óri .. 83 D4
Náfpaktos 83 D4
Náfplio 87 D2
Naggen 101 F3
Nagold 54 C3
Nagu 107 D3
Nagyatád 114 A1
Nagykálló 112 C3
Nagykanizsa.. 114 A1
Nagykőrös 112 B4
Nahe 48 A2
Nahe R. 54 B1
Naila 53 D4
Nailloux 32 A1
Nailsworth .. 9 D2
Nairn 3 D3
Najac 29 D3
Nájera 36 B2
Najerilla, R..... 36 B2
Nakkila 107 D1
Nakło 112 A1
Nakovo...... 73 D3
Nakskov...... 108 B4
Näljänkä..... 99 E3
Nalón, R. ... 35 E2
Naltijärvi 95 D3
Namdalseid .. 97 D4

Nämdöfjärden 106 B4
Náměšt 57 E1
Namsen 97 D4
Namsos 97 D4
Namsskogan 97 D4
Namur 50 C4
Namur (Prov).... 50 C4
Nancy 21 D4
Nangis 19 F4
Nannestad 105 D2
Nant 29 F3
Nanterre 19 F4
Nantes 24 B2
Nantes, Canal
  de 22 C3
Nanteuil-le-
  Haudouin 19 F3
Nantiat 25 E4
Nantua 26 C4
Nantwich ... 6 C3
Nao, C de la .. 45 F1
Náoussa (Kikládes).. 88 C3
Náoussa
  (Makedonía).... 79 E3
Napapiiri 99 D2
Napoli...... 64 B4
Napoli, G di 64 A4
Napoule, la ... 31 E4
Narberth 8 B2
Nærbø 104 A4
Narbolia ... 66 B3
Narbonne 32 B1
Narbonne-Plage.. 30 A4
Narcao 66 B4
Narcea, R. 35 D1
Nardó 65 F4
Narew 112 C1
Narila 103 E3
Narkaus 99 D2
Narni 63 E2
Naro 68 C4
Naro-Fominsk.... 111 F2
Nærøy 97 D4
Närpes 102 B3
Närpio 102 B3
Narta 71 D2
Narthiáki 83 E2

Narthiáki, Óros 83 E2
Narva.......... 111 D1
Narvik 94 B3
Nås 105 E2
Näsåker 101 F2
Näsäud 113 D4
Nasbinals 29 F2
Našice 71 E2
Näsijärvi 102 C3
Naso 69 D2
Nassau 51 F4
Nassereith 58 C2
Naßfeld-Paß 59 F2
Nässjö 109 D1
Nastola 107 F2
Næstved 108 C4
Natalinci 73 D3
Nattaset 95 F3
Nattavaara 98 B2
Nättraby 109 E3
Naucelle 29 E3
Nauders 58 C2
Nauen 49 D4
Naul. 13 D3
Naumburg 52 C2
Naunhof 53 D2
Naussac, Bge de... 29 F2
Naustdal 100 A3
Nauvo 107 D3
Nava 35 E1
Nava, Colle di ... 31 F3
Navacelles, Cirque
  de 29 F3
Navacepeda 39 E2
Navacerrada 40 A2
Navacerrada, Pto
  de 40 A1
Navachica 44 A3
Navaconcejo 39 E2
Nava de la
  Asunción 40 A1
Nava del Rey ... 35 E4
Navafria, Pto de .. 40 A1
Navahermosa 39 F3
Navalcán 39 F2
Navalcarnero 40 A2
Navaleno 36 B3

Navalmanzano 40 A1
Navalmoral de la
  Mata 39 E3
Navalperal de
  Pinares 40 A2
Navaluenga 39 F2
Navalvillar de Pela . 39 E4
Navamorcuende.... 39 F2
Navan 13 D3
Navarra 36 C2
Navarredonda de la
  Sierra....... 39 F2
Navarrenx 28 B4
Navarrés 41 E4
Navarrete 36 B2
Navascués 37 D2
Navas del
  Madroño 39 D3
Navas de Oro.... 40 A1
Navas de San Juan . 44 B2
Navasfrías 39 D2
Navatalgordo 39 F2
Nave 60 B1
Navekvarn 106 A4
Navelli 63 F2
Naver, L 2 C2
Naveros 43 D4
Navia 34 C1
Navia de Suarna . 34 C2
Navia, R. 34 C1
Navl'a 111 F4
Náxos 88 C3
Náxos Días 88 C3
Náxos, N 88 C3
Nay. 37 E1
Nazaré 38 A3
Naze, The 11 D2
Nazilli 115 F4
Ndrejaj 76 C2
Ndroq 76 C4
Nea 101 D2
Néa Agathoúpoli .. 79 F3
Néa Alikarnassés.. 91 D3
Néa Anhíalos 83 F2
Néa Artáki.... 84 B4
Néa Éfessos 79 F4
Néa Epidavros 87 E2

Néa Fókeada 80 A4
Neagh, L 13 E2
Néa Hili 81 E2
Néa Iraklítsa 80 C2
Néa Kalikrátia 79 F4
Néa Kariá 81 D2
Néa Karváli 80 C2
Néa Kerassoús 82 C2
Néa Kíos 87 D2
Néa Koróni 86 C3
Néa Mákri 88 A1
Néa Messángala .. 83 F1
Néa Mihanióna .. 79 F3
Néa Moní 85 E4
Néa Moudaniá 80 A4
Néa Péla 79 F3
Néa Péramos (Stereá-
  Eláda) 87 E1
Néa Péramos
  (Makedonía)....... 80 C2
Négrepelisse 29 D3
Neápoli (Kríti) 91 E4
Neápoli
  (Makedonía) 79 D3
Neápoli
  (Pelopónissos) ... 87 E4
Néa Róda 80 B3
Néa Sánda
  (Makedonía).... 79 F2
Néa Sánda (Thráki) . 81 E2
Néa Silata 80 A3
Néa Skióni 80 B4
Néa Stira 84 B4
Néa Triglia 80 A4
Néa Vissa 81 F1
Néa Zoi 79 E2
Néa Zíhni 80 B2
Nebel 47 F1
Nebelhorn 55 E4
Nebljusi 70 C4
Nebra 52 C2
Nechranická přehr
  nádrž.......... 53 E3
Neckar 55 D1
Neckarelz 55 D2
Neckargemünd.... 54 C1
Neckarsteinach.... 54 C1

Neckarsulm 55 D2
Nečujam 75 D2
Neda 34 B1
Nédas 86 C2
Nedelišče 70 C1
Nedervetil 102 C1
Neede 17 D2
Needles, The .. 9 E3
Neermoor 47 E3
Nefyn 6 A3
Negoiu 113 D4
Negorci 77 F3
Negotin 73 F3
Negotino 77 E3
Negra de Urbión, L. 36 B3
Negrar 60 C1
Negratin, Emb del .. 44 B2
Negreira 34 A2
Negru Vodă 115 E2
Neheim-Hüsten .. 17 F3
Neiden 95 F2
Neige, Crêt de la . 27 D3
Neila 36 B3
Neiße.... 53 F1
Nejdek 53 E3
Nekromandío Efiras 82 B2
Neksø 109 D4
Nela, R 36 A1
Nelas 38 C1
Nelidovo 111 E2
Nellim 95 F3
Nelson 6 C2
Neman 110 B3
Neméa 87 D1
Nemirov 113 E3
Nemours 25 F1
Nemunas 110 C3
Nenagh 12 C4
Nene 10 C1
Nénita 85 F4
Nenzing 58 B2
Neohoráki.... 84 A4
Neohóri (Etolia-
  Akarnanía) 82 C4
Neohóri (Évia) 84 B4

Neohóri
  (Fthiótida) 83 E3
Neohóri (Ípiros).... 82 C2
Neohóri (Karditsa) .. 83 D2
Neohóri
  (Magnisía)....... 84 A2
Neohóri
  (Pelopónissos) 86 C2
Neohóri (Thráki) ... 81 F1
Neohóri (Trikala) ... 83 D1
Néo Monastiri 83 E2
Néon Petritsi 80 A2
Néos Marmarás .. 80 B4
Néos Skopós 80 B2
Néouvielle, Pic de . 37 E2
Nephin 12 B2
Nephin Beg Range . 12 B2
Nepomuk 56 C1
Nera 63 E1
Nérac 28 C3
Neráïda
  (Amárandóos) 83 D2
Neráïda (Neohóri) .. 83 D2
Neratovice 53 F3
Nerdvika 100 B1
Neresheim 55 E2
Nereto 63 F1
Neretva 76 A1
Neretva klisura .. 75 F1
Neretvanski kan .. 75 E2
Nerezi 77 D3
Nerezine 70 B4
Nerežišca 75 E2
Neris 110 C3
Néris-les-Bains.. 25 F4
Nerja 44 A4
Néronde 26 B4
Nérondes 26 A3
Nerotriviá 84 A3
Nerpio 44 C2
Nerva 42 C2
Nervesa della
  Battaglia 59 E4
Nervi 60 A3
Nervión, R. 36 B1
Nes (Akershus).... 105 D3
Nes (Buskerud) 104 C2

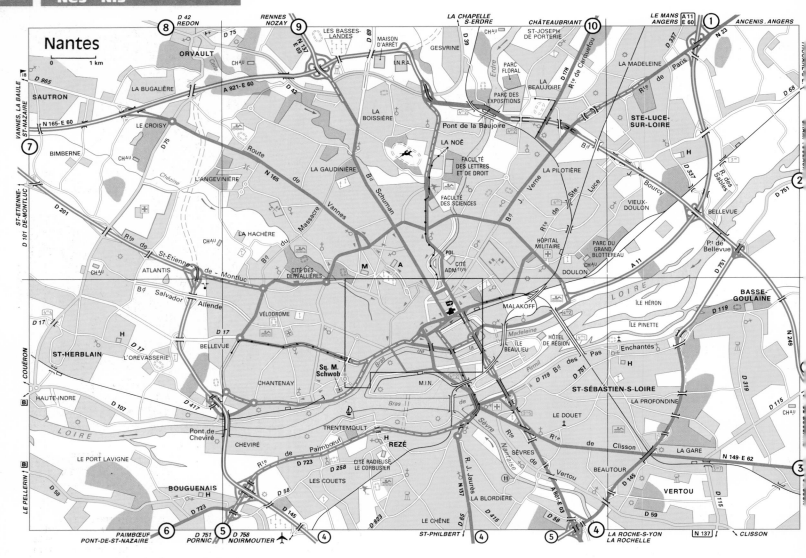

Nantes

Nes (NL)	16	C1
Nesbyen	104	C2
Nesebâr	115	E2
Nesjøen	101	D2
Neskaupstaður	96	C2
Nesle	19	F2
Nesoddtangen	105	D3
Nesseby	95	F1
Nesselwang	55	E4
Ness, L	2	C3
Nestáni	87	D2
Nesterov	112	C2
Nestório	78	C3
Néstos	81	D2
Nesvik	104	A3
Nesviž	111	D4
Neto	67	F3
Netolice	56	C1
Netretić	70	C3
Nettetal	17	D4
Nettuno	63	E3
Neuastenberg	17	F4
Neubeckum	17	F3
Neubourg, le	19	D3
Neubrandenburg	49	D2
Neubukow	48	C2
Neuburg	55	F2
Neuchâtel	27	E2
Neu Darchau	48	B3
Neuenburg	47	E3
Neuenbürg	54	C2
Neuendorf	49	D1
Neuenhaus	17	E2
Neuenkirchen	48	A3
Neuenstadt	55	D2
Neuerburg	54	A1
Neufahrn	56	B2
Neuf-Brisach	27	E1
Neufchâteau (B)	20	C2
Neufchâteau (F)	20	C4
Neufchâtel	20	B3

Neufchâtel-en-Bray	19	E2
Neufelden	56	C2
Neuffen	55	D3
Neugersdorf	53	F2
Neuhaus (Mecklenburg-Vorpommern)	48	B3
Neuhaus (Niedersachsen)	47	F2
Neuhaus (Thüringen)	52	C3
Neuhausen	58	A1
Neuhaus-im-Solling	52	A2
Neuhofen an der Krems	57	D3
Neuillé-Pont-Pierre	25	D2
Neuilly-en-Thelle	19	F3
Neuilly-le-Réal	26	A3
Neuilly-l'Evêque	26	C1
Neuilly-St-Front	20	A3
Neu-Isenburg	52	A4
Neukalen	49	D2
Neukirch	53	F2
Neukirchen (A)	59	D1
Neukirchen (D)	47	F1
Neukloster	48	C2
Neulengbach	57	E2
Neu Lübbenau	53	E1
Neum	75	F2
Neumarkt (D)	55	F1
Neumarkt (Salzburg)	56	C3
Neumarkt (Steiermark)	57	D4
Neumarkt-St Veit	56	B3
Neumünster	48	A2
Neunagelberg	57	D2
Neunburg	56	B1
Neung	25	E2
Neunkirchen (A)	57	F3

Neunkirchen (D)	54	B2
Neuötting	56	B3
Neupölla	57	E2
Neuruppin	49	D3
Neusiedl	57	F3
Neusiedler See	57	F3
Neuss	17	D4
Neustadt (Baden-Württemberg)	54	C4
Neustadt (Brandenburg)	49	D3
Neustadt (Coburg)	52	C4
Neustadt (Hessen)	52	A3
Neustadt (Ingolstadt)	55	F2
Neustadt (Sachsen)	53	F2
Neustadt (Schleswig-Holstein)	48	B2
Neustadt (Thüringen)	53	D3
Neustadt am Rübenberge	48	A4
Neustadt an der Aisch	55	E1
Neustadt an der Waldnaab	53	D4
Neustadt an der Weinstraße	54	C2
Neustadt Glewe	48	C3
Neustift	59	D2
Neustrelitz	49	D3
Neu-Ulm	55	E3
Neuve-Lyre, la	19	D4
Neuves-Maisons	21	D3
Neuvic (Corrèze)	29	E1
Neuvic (Dordogne)	28	C2
Neuville	26	C4
Neuville-aux-Bois	25	E1
Neuville-de-Poitou	25	D3
Neuvy-le-Roi	25	D2

Neuvy-St-Sépulchre	25	E3
Neuvy-sur-Barangeon	25	F2
Neuwied	51	E4
Névache	31	D2
Nevada, Sierra	44	A3
Nevea, Pso di	59	F3
Nevel'	111	D3
Nevers	26	A3
Nevesinje	75	F2
Nevis, L	2	B4
Nevlunghavn	104	C4
New Abbey	4	C3
New Alresford	9	E3
Newark-on-Trent	7	D3
Newbiggin-by-the-Sea	5	E3
Newborough	6	A2
Newbridge	13	D4
Newburgh (Fife)	5	D1
Newburgh (Grampian)	3	E4
Newbury	9	E2
Newcastle	13	E2
Newcastle Emlyn	8	C1
Newcastle-under-Lyme	6	C3
Newcastle-upon-Tyne	5	E3
Newcastle West	14	B3
New Cumnock	4	C3
New Deer	3	E3
New Forest	9	E3
New Galloway	4	C3
Newgrange	13	D3
Newhaven	10	C3
Newmarket (GB)	11	D1
Newmarket (IRL)	14	B3
Newmarket on Fergus	12	B4

Newnham	9	D2
Newport (Dyfed)	8	B1
Newport (Gwent)	9	D2
Newport (I of Wight)	9	E3
Newport (Mayo)	12	B3
Newport (Shropshire)	6	C3
Newport (Tipperary)	12	C4
Newport-on-Tay	5	D1
Newport Pagnell	9	F1
Newquay	8	B4
New Quay	8	C1
New Romney	11	D3
New Ross	15	D3
Newry	13	E2
Newton Abbot	8	C4
Newton-Aycliffe	5	E4
Newton Ferrers	8	C4
Newtonmore	2	C4
Newton Stewart	4	C3
Newtownabbey	13	E2
Newtownards	13	E2
Newtownbutler	13	D2
Newtown (England)	9	D1
Newtown (Wales)	9	D1
Newtownhamilton	13	D2
Newtown St Boswells	5	D3
Newtownstewart	13	D2
Nexon	29	D1
Neyland	8	B2
Nez de Jobourg	18	B2
Nežin	113	F1
Niáta	87	D3
Niaux, Grotte de	32	A2
Nibe	108	D2
Nicastro	67	E3
Nice	31	E4
Nickelsdorf	57	F3
Nicolosi	69	D3

Nicosia	68	C3
Nicotera	67	E4
Nidda	52	A4
Nidderau	52	A4
Nideggen	51	D3
Nidelva	104	B4
Nidri	82	B3
Niebla	42	C2
Niebüll	47	F1
Niechorze	49	F1
Nied	21	D3
Nieddu, M.	66	C2
Niederalteich	56	B2
Niederaula	52	B3
Niederbronn	21	E3
Niederelsungen	52	A2
Niedere Tauern	57	D4
Niederjossa	52	B3
Niederkrüchten	17	D4
Niederösterreich	57	E2
Niedersachsen	48	A4
Niederstetten	55	D1
Niederstotzingen	55	E3
Niederzerf	54	A1
Niefla, Pto de	43	F1
Niegripp	48	C4
Niemegk	53	D1
Niemisel	98	C3
Nienburg (Niedersachsen)	48	A4
Nienburg (Sachsen-Anhalt)	52	C1
Nieras	94	B4
Nierstein	54	C1
Niesky	53	F2
Niesłysz, Jez.	49	F4
Nieuweschans	47	E3
Nieuwpoort	50	A3
Nièvre	26	B2
Niforéka	86	B1
Nigríta	80	B2

Niinivesi	103	D2
Nijar	44	C3
Nijemci	72	B2
Nijkerk	16	C2
Nijmegen	17	D3
Nijverdal	17	D2
Níkea	83	E2
Niki	79	D3
Nikiá	89	F4
Nikifóros	80	C2
Nikíssiani	80	C2
Níkitas	80	B4
Nikkaluokta	94	C4
Nikolajev (L'vov)	112	C3
Nikolajev (Odessa)	113	F3
Nikoléika	86	C1
Nikopol	115	D2
Nikópoli	82	B3
Nikópolis, Órmos	82	B2
Nikšić	76	B2
Nilakka	103	D2
Nilivaara	98	B2
Nilsiä	103	E2
Nîmes	30	B3
Nimféa	81	E2
Nimféo	79	D3
Nímos, N	93	E1
Nin	74	C1
Ninove	50	B3
Niort	24	C4
Nipfjället	101	D3
Nipsa	81	E2
Niš	77	E1
Nisa	38	C3
Nisa, Rib de	38	C3
Nišava	73	E1
Niscemi	68	C4
Niška Banja	77	E1
Nissáki	82	A1
Nissan	109	D2

Nisser . . . 104 B3
Nissilä . . . 103 D1
Nissiros, N . . . 89 F4
Nissum Bredning . 108 A2
Nissum Fjord . . . 108 A2
Nith . . . 4 C3
Niton . . . 9 E4
Nitra . . . 112 B1
Nitry . . . 26 B2
Nittedal . . . 105 D3
Nittenau . . . 56 B1
Nittendorf . . . 55 F2
Nivala . . . 102 C1
Nive . . . 28 A4
Nivelles . . . 50 B4
Nivernais . . . 26 B3
Nivolet, Colle del . . . 31 E1
Niwica . . . 53 F1
Nizke Beskydy . . . 112 C3
Nizza Monferrato . . . 31 F2
Njegoš . . . 76 A2
Njivice . . . 70 B3
Njunis . . . 94 C3
Njupeskär . . . 101 D3
Noailles . . . 19 F3
Noáin . . . 36 C2
Noarvaš . . . 95 D3
Noblejas . . . 40 B3
Nocera . . . 64 B4
Nocera Tirinese . . . 67 E3
Nocera Umbra . . . 61 E4
Noceto . . . 60 B2

Nonancourt . . . 19 E4
Nonant-le-Pin . . . 19 D4
Nonaspe . . . 37 E4
None . . . 31 E2
Nonio . . . 58 A4
Nontron . . . 28 C1
Nónza . . . 33 F2
Noord-Brabant . . . 16 C3
Noord-Holland . . . 16 C2
Noord-Oost-Polder . . . 16 C2
Noordwijk aan Zee . 16 B2
Noordzee . . . 46 B3
Noormarkku . . . 102 B3
Nora . . . 105 F3
Norberg . . . 105 F3
Norcia . . . 63 F1
Nord . . . 20 A1
Nord Beveland . . . 16 B3
Nordborg . . . 108 A4
Nordby (Fanø) . . . 108 A3
Nordby (Samsø) . . . 108 B3
Norddeich . . . 47 E3
Nordeide . . . 100 A3
Norden . . . 47 E3
Nordenau . . . 17 F4
Nordenham . . . 47 E3
Norderney . . . 47 E3
Norderstedt . . . 48 A2
Nordfjord . . . 100 A3
Nordfjordeid . . . 100 A3

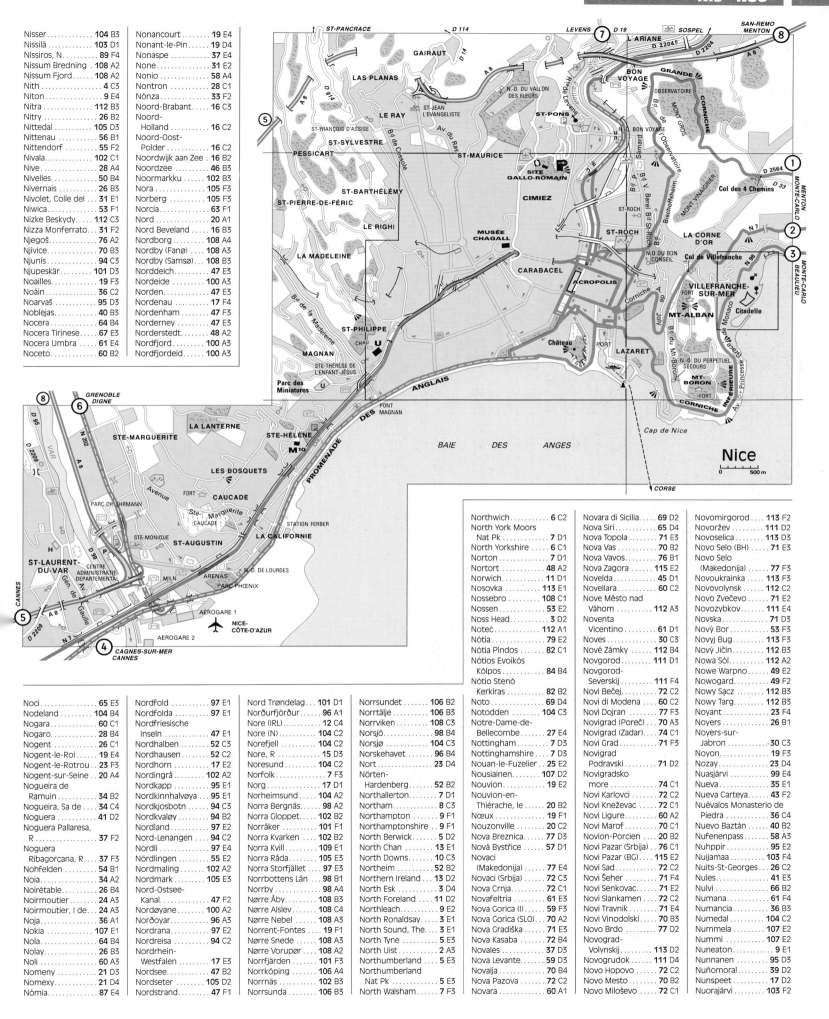

Nice

0   500 m

BAIE DES ANGES

Noci . . . 65 E3
Nodeland . . . 104 B4
Nogara . . . 60 C1
Nogaro . . . 28 B4
Nogent . . . 26 C1
Nogent-le-Roi . . . 19 E4
Nogent-le-Rotrou . . . 23 F3
Nogent-sur-Seine . . . 20 A4
Nogueira de Ramuin . . . 34 B2
Nogueira, Sa de . . . 34 C4
Noguera . . . 41 D2
Noguera Pallaresa, R . . . 37 F2
Noguera Ribagorçana, R . . . 37 F3
Nohfelden . . . 54 B1
Noia . . . 34 A2
Noirétable . . . 26 B4
Noirmoutier . . . 24 A3
Noirmoutier, I de . . . 24 A3
Noja . . . 36 A1
Nokia . . . 107 E1
Nola . . . 64 B4
Nolay . . . 26 B3
Noli . . . 60 A3
Nomeny . . . 21 D3
Nomexy . . . 21 D4
Nómia . . . 87 E4

Nordfold . . . 97 E1
Nordfolda . . . 97 E1
Nordfriesische Inseln . . . 47 E1
Nordhalben . . . 52 C3
Nordhausen . . . 52 C2
Nordhorn . . . 17 E2
Nordingrå . . . 102 A2
Nordkapp . . . 95 E1
Nordkinnhalvøya . . . 95 E1
Nordkjosbotn . . . 94 C3
Nordkvaløy . . . 94 B2
Nordland . . . 97 E2
Nord-Lenangen . . . 94 C2
Nordli . . . 97 E4
Nördlingen . . . 55 E2
Nordmaling . . . 102 A2
Nordmark . . . 105 E3
Nord-Ostsee-Kanal . . . 47 F2
Nordøyane . . . 100 A2
Norðoyar . . . 96 A3
Nordrana . . . 97 E2
Nordreisa . . . 94 C2
Nordrhein-Westfalen . . . 17 E3
Nordsee . . . 47 B2
Nordseter . . . 105 D2
Nordstrand . . . 47 F1

Nord Trøndelag . . . 101 D1
Norðurfjörður . . . 96 A1
Nore (IRL) . . . 12 C4
Nore (N) . . . 104 C2
Norefjell . . . 104 C2
Nore, R . . . 15 D3
Noresund . . . 104 C2
Norfolk . . . 7 F3
Norg . . . 17 D1
Norheimsund . . . 104 A2
Norra Bergnäs . . . 98 B1
Norra Gloppet . . . 102 B2
Norråker . . . 101 F1
Norra Kvarken . . . 102 B2
Norra Kvill . . . 109 E1
Norra Råda . . . 105 E3
Norra Storfjället . . . 97 E3
Norrbottens Län . . 98 B1
Norrby . . . 98 A4
Nørre Åby . . . 108 B3
Nørre Alslev . . . 108 C4
Nørre Nebel . . . 108 A3
Norrent-Fontes . . . 19 F1
Nørre Snede . . . 108 A3
Nørre Vorupør . . . 108 A2
Norrfjärden . . . 101 F3
Norrköping . . . 106 A4
Norrnäs . . . 102 B3
Norrsunda . . . 106 B3

Norrsundet . . . 106 B2
Norrtälje . . . 106 B3
Norrviken . . . 108 C3
Norsjö . . . 98 B4
Norsjø . . . 104 C3
Norskehavet . . . 96 B4
Nort . . . 23 D4
Nörten-Hardenberg . . . 52 B2
Northallerton . . . 7 D1
Northam . . . 8 C3
Northampton . . . 9 F1
Northamptonshire . . 9 F1
North Berwick . . . 5 D2
North Chan . . . 13 E1
North Downs . . . 10 C3
Northeim . . . 52 B2
Northern Ireland . . 13 D2
North Esk . . . 3 D4
North Foreland . . . 11 D2
Northleach . . . 9 E2
North Ronaldsay . . 3 E1
North Sound, The . . 3 E1
North Tyne . . . 5 E3
North Uist . . . 2 A3
Northumberland . . . 5 E3
Northumberland Nat Pk . . . 5 E3
North Walsham . . . 7 F3

Northwich . . . 6 C2
North York Moors Nat Pk . . . 7 D1
North Yorkshire . . . 6 C1
Norton . . . 7 D1
Nortort . . . 48 A2
Norwich . . . 11 D1
Nosovka . . . 113 E1
Nossebro . . . 108 C1
Nossen . . . 53 E2
Noss Head . . . 3 D2
Noteć . . . 112 A1
Nótia . . . 79 E2
Nótia Píndos . . . 82 C1
Nótios Evoikós Kólpos . . . 84 B4
Nótio Stenó Kerkíras . . . 82 B2
Noto . . . 69 D4
Notodden . . . 104 C3
Notre-Dame-de-Bellecombe . . . 27 E4
Nottingham . . . 7 D3
Nottinghamshire . . . 7 D3
Nouan-le-Fuzelier . . 25 E2
Nousiainen . . . 107 D2
Nouvion . . . 19 E2
Nouvion-en-Thiérache, le . . 20 B2
Nœux . . . 19 F1
Nouzonville . . . 20 C1
Nova Breznica . . . 77 D3
Nova Crnja . . . 72 C1
Novafeltria . . . 61 E2
Nova Gorica (I) . . . 59 F3
Nova Gorica (SLO) . . 70 A2
Nova Gradiška . . . 71 E3
Nova Kasaba . . . 72 B4
Nova Levante . . . 59 D3
Novalja . . . 70 B4
Nova Pazova . . . 72 C2
Novara . . . 60 A1

Novara di Sicilia . . . 69 D2
Nova Siri . . . 65 D4
Nova Topola . . . 71 E3
Nova Vas . . . 70 B2
Nova Vavos . . . 76 B1
Nova Zagora . . . 115 E2
Novelda . . . 45 D1
Novellara . . . 60 C2
Nove Město nad Váhom . . . 112 A3
Noventa Vicentino . . . 61 D1
Noves . . . 30 C3
Nové Zámky . . . 112 B4
Novgorod . . . 111 D1
Novgorod-Severskij . . . 111 F4
Novi Bečej . . . 72 C2
Novi di Modena . . . 60 C2
Novi Dojran . . . 77 F3
Novigrad (Poreč) . . . 70 A3
Novigrad (Zadar) . . . 74 C1
Novi Grad . . . 71 F3
Novigrad Podravski . . . 71 D2
Novigradsko more . . . 74 C1
Novi Karlovci . . . 72 C2
Novi Kneževac . . . 72 C1
Novi Ligure . . . 60 A2
Novi Marof . . . 70 C1
Novion-Porcien . . . 20 B2
Novi Pazar (Srbija) . . 76 C2
Novi Pazar (BG) . . . 115 E2
Novi Sad . . . 72 C2
Novi Šeher . . . 71 E4
Novi Senkovac . . . 71 D2
Novi Slankamen . . . 72 C2
Novi Travnik . . . 71 E4
Novi Vinodolski . . . 70 B3
Novo Brdo . . . 77 D2
Novograd-Volynskij . . . 113 D3
Novo Hopovo . . . 72 C2
Novo Mesto . . . 70 B3
Novo Miloševo . . . 72 C1

Novomirgorod . . . 113 F2
Novoržev . . . 111 D2
Novoselica . . . 113 D3
Novo Selo (BH) . . . 71 E3
Novo Selo (Makedonija) . . . 77 F3
Novoukrainka . . . 113 F3
Novovolynsk . . . 112 C2
Novo Zvečevo . . . 71 E2
Novozybkov . . . 111 E4
Novska . . . 71 D3
Nový Bor . . . 53 F3
Novyj Bug . . . 113 F3
Nový Jičín . . . 112 B3
Nowa Sól . . . 112 A2
Nowe Warpno . . . 49 E2
Nowogard . . . 49 F2
Nowy Sącz . . . 112 B3
Nowy Targ . . . 112 B3
Noyant . . . 23 F4
Noyers . . . 26 B1
Noyers-sur-Jabron . . . 30 C3
Noyon . . . 19 F3
Nozay . . . 23 D4
Nuasjärvi . . . 99 E4
Nueva . . . 35 E1
Nueva Carteya . . . 43 F2
Nuévalos Monasterio de Piedra . . . 36 C4
Nuevo Baztán . . . 40 B2
Nufenenpass . . . 58 A3
Nuhppir . . . 95 E2
Nuijamaa . . . 103 F4
Nuits-St-Georges . . . 26 C2
Nules . . . 41 E3
Nulvi . . . 66 B2
Numana . . . 61 F4
Numancia . . . 36 B3
Numedal . . . 104 C2
Nummela . . . 107 E2
Nummi . . . 107 E2
Nuneaton . . . 9 E1
Nunnanen . . . 95 D3
Nuñomoral . . . 39 D2
Nunspeet . . . 17 D2
Nuorajärvi . . . 103 F4

Nuorgam........... 95 E2
Nuoro........... 66 B2
Nurallao........... 66 B3
Nürburg........... 51 E4
Núria........... 32 B3
Nurmes........... 103 E1
Nurmijärvi (Pohjois-
  Karjalan Lääni).... 103 F1

Nurmijärvi (Uudenmaan
  Lääni)........... 107 E2
Nurmo........... 102 C2
Nürnberg........... 55 F1
Nürtingen........... 55 D3
Nus........... 27 E4
Nusse........... 48 B2
Nuštar........... 71 F2

Nuthe........... 49 D4
Nuttlar........... 17 F3
Nuttupera........... 103 D1
Nuutajärvi........... 107 E2
Nuvvos-Ailigas........ 95 E2
Nyåker........... 102 A1
Nybergsund........... 105 E2
Nyborg........... 108 B4

Nybro........... 109 E2
Nyírbátor........... 112 C3
Nyíregyháza........... 112 C3
Nykarleby........... 102 B2
Nykøbing F
  (Storstrøm)........ 108 C4
Nykøbing M
  (Viborg)........ 108 A2

Nykøbing S
  (Vestsjælland).... 108 C3
Nyköping........... 106 B4
Nykvarn........... 106 B4
Nynäshamn........... 106 B4
Nyon........... 27 D3
Nyons........... 30 C3
Nýřany........... 53 E4

Nýrdalur........... 96 B2
Nýrsko........... 56 B1
Nyrud........... 95 F2
Nysa........... 112 A2
Nysa Łużycka........ 53 F1
Nysäter........... 105 E3
Nyseter........... 100 B3
Nysted........... 108 C4

Nyvoll........... 95 D2

O

Oadby........... 9 F1
Oakham........... 9 F1
Oanes........... 104 A3
Óassi........... 87 D1
Oban........... 4 B1
O Barco........... 34 C3
Obbola........... 102 B1
Obdach........... 57 D4
Obdacher Sattel........ 57 D4
Obedska bara........ 72 C3
Obejo........... 43 F2
Oberalppass........... 58 A3
Oberammergau........ 55 F4
Oberau........... 56 A4
Oberaudorf........... 56 B4
Oberdrauburg........ 59 E2
Oberessfeld........... 52 C4
Obergeis........... 52 B3
Obergrafendorf........ 57 E2
Obergrünzburg........ 55 E4
Obergurgl........... 58 C2
Oberhaslach........... 21 E4
Oberhausen........... 17 E3
Oberhof........... 52 C3
Oberjoch-Paß........ 58 C1
Oberkirch........... 54 C3
Oberkirchen........... 17 F4
Oberkochen........... 55 E2
Obermarchtal........ 55 D3
Obernai........... 21 E4
Obernberg........... 56 C3
Obernburg........... 55 D1
Oberndorf (A)........ 56 C3
Oberndorf (D)........ 54 C3
Obernzell........... 56 C2
Oberölsbach........... 55 F1
Oberösterreich........ 56 C2
Oberprechtal........... 54 C3
Oberpullendorf........ 57 F3
Oberseebach........... 21 F3
Obersontheim........ 55 E2
Oberstaufen........... 55 E4
Oberstdorf........... 55 E4
Oberstein........... 54 B1
Obertauern........... 59 F1
Obertraun........... 59 F1
Oberursel........... 51 F4
Obervellach........... 59 E2
Oberviechtach........ 56 B1
Oberwart........... 57 F4
Oberwesel........... 51 E4
Oberwiesenthal........ 53 E3
Oberwölz........... 57 D4
Oberzeiring........... 57 D4
Óbidos........... 38 A3
Obilić........... 77 D2
Obing........... 56 B3
Obiou, l'........... 30 C2
Objat........... 29 D1
Obninsk........... 111 F3
O Bolo........... 34 C3
Obón........... 41 E1
Oborniki........... 112 A1
Obornjača........... 72 C1
Oborovo........... 70 C2
Obrenovac........... 72 C3
Obrež........... 72 C3
Obrov........... 70 A3
Obrovac (Split)........ 75 D1
Obrovac (Zadar)........ 74 C1
Obršani........... 77 E4
Obsteig........... 58 C2
Obudovac........... 71 F3
Obzor........... 115 E2
Obzova........... 70 B3

Očakov........... 113 F3
Oca, Mtes de........ 36 A2
Ocaña........... 40 B3
Oca, R........... 36 A2
Očauš........... 71 E4
Occhiobello........... 61 D2
Occhito, L di........ 64 B3
Očevlje........... 71 F4
Ochagavia........... 37 D2
Ochil Hills........... 5 D1
Ochsenfurt........... 55 E1
Ochsenhausen........ 55 E3
Ochtrup........... 17 E2
Ockelbo........... 106 A2
Öckerö........... 108 C1
Ocreza, R........... 38 C3
Odžaci........... 72 B2
Odžak (BH)........... 71 F3
Odžak (Crna Gora)... 76 B1
Odda........... 104 B2
Odden
  Færgehavn...... 108 B3
Odder........... 108 B3
Oddesund........... 108 A2
Odeceixe........... 42 A2
Odeleite........... 42 B2
Odelzhausen........ 55 F3
Odemira........... 42 A2
Ödemiş........... 115 E4
Odense........... 108 B3
Odenthal........... 17 E4
Oder........... 49 E3

Oderberg........... 49 E3
Oderbruch........... 49 E3
Oderbucht........... 49 E1
Oderhaff........... 49 E2
Oderzo........... 59 E4
Ödeshög........... 109 D1
Odessa........... 113 F4
Odet........... 22 B3
Odiel, R........... 42 C2
Odivelas........... 42 B1
Odivelas, Bgem de.. 42 B1
Odolo........... 60 B1
Odorheiu
  Secuiesc...... 113 D4
Odra........... 112 A2
Oebisfelde........... 48 B4
Oederan........... 53 E3
Oeiras........... 38 A4
Oelde........... 17 F3
Oelsnitz (Plauen)... 53 D3
Oelsnitz (Zwickau).. 53 D3
Oettingen........... 55 E2
Oetz........... 58 C2
Ofanto........... 64 C3
Ofenpass........... 58 C2
Offaly........... 12 C4
Offenbach........... 52 A4

Offenburg........... 54 C3
Offida........... 63 F1
Offranville........... 19 E2
Ofir........... 34 A4
Ofotfjorden........... 94 B3
Oggiono........... 60 A1
Ogliastro Cilento... 67 D1
Oglio........... 58 C4
Ognon........... 27 D2
Ogošte........... 77 E2
Ogražden........... 77 F3
Ogre........... 110 C2
Ogulin........... 70 C3
Ohanes........... 44 B3
Óhi, Óros........... 88 A1
Ohiró........... 80 B1
Ohlstadt........... 56 A4
Ohorn........... 53 F2
Ohrdruf........... 52 C3
Ohre........... 48 B4
Ohře........... 53 E3
Ohrid........... 77 D4
Ohridsko Ez........ 77 D4
Ohringen........... 55 D2
Ohrit, Liq i........... 77 D4
Óhthia........... 82 C3
Ohthoniá........... 84 B4
Oijärvi........... 99 D3
Oijärvi L........... 99 D3
Oikarainen........... 99 D2
Oirschot........... 16 C3
Oise........... 20 B2

Oise (Dépt)........... 19 F3
Oisemont........... 19 E2
Oisterwijk........... 16 C3
Oitti........... 107 E2
Oituz........... 113 D4
Ojakylä........... 99 D4
Öje........... 101 D2
Öjebyn........... 98 B3
Ojén........... 43 E4
Ojos Negros........ 41 D2
Ojuelos Altos........ 43 E1
Öjung........... 101 E2
Okehampton........ 8 C3
Oker........... 48 B4
Oklaj........... 75 D1
Oknö........... 109 E2
Okol........... 76 C2
Oksbøl........... 108 A3
Oksby........... 108 A3
Øksfjord........... 95 D2
Øksfjorden........... 94 A3
Øksfjordjøkelen.... 94 C2
Øksnes........... 94 A3
Okstindan........... 97 E3
Okučani........... 71 E3
Okulovka........... 111 E1
Olafsfjörður........ 96 B1
Olafsvík........... 96 A2
Öland........... 109 E2
Olan, Pic d'........ 31 D2

Olargues........... 32 B1
Olazagutía........... 36 B2
Olbernhau........... 53 E3
Olbia........... 66 B1
Oldcastle........... 13 D3
Oldebroek........... 17 D2
Oldeide........... 100 A3
Olden........... 100 A3
Oldenburg
  (Niedersachsen)... 47 F3
Oldenburg (Schleswig
  Holstein)........ 48 B1
Oldenzaal........... 17 E2
Olderdalen........... 94 C2
Oldervik........... 94 C2
Oldham........... 6 C2
Old Head of
  Kinsale........... 14 B4
Oldmeldrum........ 3 E4
Oldsum........... 47 F1
Oleggio........... 60 A1
Oleiros........... 34 B1
Ølen........... 104 A3
Oléron, Ile d'........ 24 B4
Olesa........... 32 A4
Olešnica........... 112 A3
Oletta........... 33 F2
Olette........... 32 B2
Olevsk........... 113 D2

Ølgod........... 108 A3
Olhão........... 42 B3
Olhava........... 99 D3
Oliana........... 32 A3
Oliana, Emb d'........ 32 A3
Olib........... 70 B4
Olib /........... 70 B4
Oliena........... 66 B2
Oliete........... 37 E4
Olimbía........... 86 C2
Olimbiáda
  (Makedonía)..... 80 B3
Olimbiáda
  (Thessalía)..... 79 E4
Ólimbos........... 93 D2
Ólimbos, Óros
  (Évia)........... 84 B4
Ólimbos, Óros
  (Pieriá)........ 79 E4
Ólinthos........... 80 A4
Olite........... 36 C2
Oliva........... 45 E1
Oliva de la
  Frontera........ 42 C1
Oliva de Mérida... 39 D4
Olivares........... 40 C3
Oliveira de
  Azeméis........ 38 B1
Oliveira de Frades.. 38 B1
Oliveira do Bairro.. 38 B1
Oliveira do Douro.. 34 B4

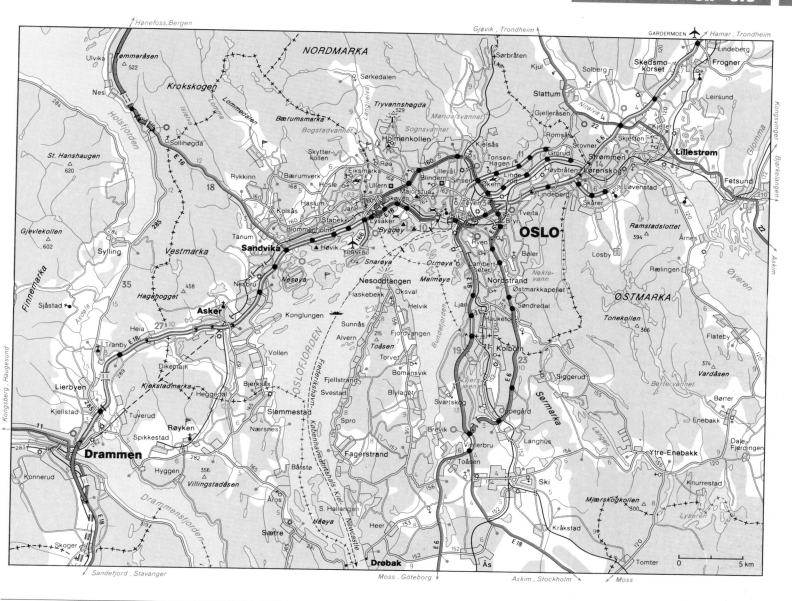

Oliveira do
  Hospital 38 C2
Olivenza 38 C4
Olivenza, R de 38 C4
Olivet 25 E1
Olivone 58 A3
Olleria, Pto de l' . . 41 E4
Ollerton 7 D3
Ollières, les 30 B2
Olliergues 29 F1
Ollioules 31 D4
Ollöla 103 F2
Olmedillo de Roa . . 35 F4
Olmedo (E) 35 E4
Olmedo (I) 66 A2
Olmeto 33 F4
Olocau del Rey . . . 41 E2
Olofström 109 D3
Olombrada 35 F4
Olomouc 112 A3
Olonzac 32 B1
Oloron
  Ste Marie 37 D1
Olost 32 A3
Olot 32 B3
Olovo 71 F4
Olpe 17 F4
Olsberg 17 F3
Olshammar 105 F4
Olst 17 D2
Ølstykke 108 C3
Olsztyn 110 B4
Olszyna 53 F1
Olt 115 D2
Oltedal 104 A3
Olten 27 F2

Oltenia 115 D1
Oltenița 115 E1
Olula del Río 44 C3
Olvega 36 C3
Olvera 43 E3
Omagh 13 D2
Omali 79 D4
Omalós 90 B3
Omarska 71 D3
Ombrone 63 D1
Omegna 58 A4
Omiš 75 E2
Omišalj 70 B3
Omme Å 108 A3
Ommen 17 D2
Omodeo, L 66 B3
Omoljica 73 D3
Omorfohóri 83 E1
Ömossa 102 B3
Oña 36 A2
Oñati 36 B1
Oncala, Pto de . . . 36 B3
Onda 41 E3
Ondara 45 E1
Ondárroa 36 B1
Oneglia 31 F3
Onesse-et-Laharie . 28 A3
Onești 113 D4
Onich 2 C4
Onkamo (Lapin
  Lääni) 99 E2
Onkamo (Pohjois
  Karjalan Lääni) . . 103 F2
Onkivesi 103 E2
Ons, I de 34 A2
Ontaneda 35 F2

Ontiñena 37 E3
Ontinyent 45 E1
Ontojärvi 99 F4
Ontur 45 D1
Onzain 25 E2
Oostburg 16 B4
Oostelijk-Flevoland . 16 C2
Oostende 50 A3
Oosterbeek 17 D3
Oosterend 16 C1
Oosterhout 16 C3
Oostkamp 50 A3
Oostmalle 50 C3
Oost-Vlaanderen . . 50 B3
Oost-Vlieland 16 C1
Ootmarsum 17 E2
Opatija 70 B3
Opatovac 72 B2
Opava 112 A3
Opladen 17 E4
Oplenac 73 D3
Opovo 72 C2
Oppach 53 F2
Oppdal 100 C2
Oppenau 54 C3
Oppenheim 54 C1
Opphaug 100 C1
Oppido Lucano . . . 64 C4
Oppido
  Mamertina 67 E4
Oppland 104 C1
Oputten 16 C2
Opuzen 75 D2
Ora 59 D3

Oradea 112 C4
Oradour-sur-Glane . 25 D4
Oradour-sur-Vayres . 28 C1
Orahova 71 D3
Orahovac 77 D2
Orahovica 71 E2
Oraison 31 D3
Orajärvi 98 C2
Orange 30 B3
Orani 66 B2
Oranienbaum 53 D1
Oranienburg 49 D3
Oranmore 12 B3
Orašac (HR) 75 E2
Orašac (Srbija) . . . 73 D3
Orasi 76 B3
Orašje 71 F3
Orăştie 114 C1
Oravainen 102 B2
Oravais 102 B2
Oravikoski 103 E2
Oraviţa 114 C1
Orb 30 A4
Orba 45 E1
Orbassano 31 E2
Ørbæk 108 B4
Orbe 27 D3
Orbec 19 D3
Orbetello 63 D2
Orbey 27 E1
Orbigo, R 35 D3
Orce 44 B2
Orce, R 44 B2
Orcera 44 B1
Orchej 113 E3
Orchies 20 A1

Orcières 31 D2
Orcival 29 E1
Orco 31 E1
Ordes 34 A1
Ordesa, Parque
  Nac. de 37 E2
Ordino 32 A2
Ordizia 36 C1
Orduña 36 B1
Orduña, Pto de . . . 36 B1
Ore 101 E4
Orea 41 D2
Öreälven 102 A1
Orebić 75 E2
Örebro Län 105 F3
Öregrund 106 B3
Öregrundsgrepen . 106 B2
Orei 83 F3
Orellana de
  la Sierra 39 E4
Orellana, Emb de . . 39 E4
Orellana la Vieja . . 39 E4
Orense 34 B3
Oréo 81 D2
Oreókastro 79 F3
Orestiáda 81 F1
Oresund 108 C3
Orfós, Akr 89 F4
Orgáni 81 E2
Organyà 32 A3
Organyà 37 F3
Orgaz 40 A3
Orgelet 26 C3
Orgères-en-Beauce . 25 E1
Orgon 30 C3
Orgosolo 66 B2

Orhi, Pic d' 37 D1
Orhomenós 83 F4
Oria 44 C3
Oria 65 E4
Oria, R 36 C1
Origny Sainte-
  Benoîte 20 A2
Orihuela 45 D2
Orihuela del
  Tremedal 41 D2
Orimattila 107 F2
Orini 80 B2
Oriolo 65 D4
Oripää 187 D2
Orissaare 110 B2
Oristano 66 B3
Oristano, G di 66 A3
Orivesi 102 C3
Orivesi L 103 F2
Orjahovo 115 D2
Ørjavik 100 B2
Ørje 105 D3
Orjiva 44 A3
Orkanger 100 C1
Örkelljunga 109 D3
Orkla 100 C2
Orkney Is 3 E1
Ørlandet 100 C1
Orlando, C d' 69 D2
Orlane 77 D1
Orlate 77 D2
Orléans 25 E1
Orlická přehr
  nádrž 56 C1
Orlovat 72 C2

Orly 19 F4
Ormério 81 F1
Ormília 80 B4
Órmos 79 F3
Órmos Korthíou . . 88 B1
Órmos Panagías . . 80 B4
Órmos Prínou . . . 80 C3
Ormož 70 C1
Ormsjö 97 F4
Ormsjön 101 F1
Ormskirk 6 B2
Ormtjernkampen . 104 C1
Ornain 20 C4
Ornans 27 D2
Orne (Calvados) . . 18 C4
Orne (Dépt) 20 B3
Orne (Meuse) 21 D3
Ørnes 97 E2
Ornós 88 C2
Örnsköldsvik 102 A2
Or'ol 111 F4
Orolik 72 B2
Oron 72 B1
Oron-la-Ville 27 E3
Oropesa (Castilla la
  Mancha) 39 F3
Oropesa (Valencia) . 41 F3
Orosei 66 C2
Orosei, G di 66 C2
Orosháza 112 B4
Orpierre 30 C3
Orpington 10 C2
Orra 100 C3
Orša 101 E4
Orša 111 E3
Orsajón 101 E4

Orsay 19 F4
Orsières 27 E4
Orsogna 64 A2
Orşova 114 C1
Ørsta 100 A2
Örsundsbro 106 B3
Orta Nova 64 C3
Orta San Giulio 58 A4
Orte 63 E2
Ortegal, C 34 B1
Orth 57 F2
Orthez 28 B4
Ortigueira 34 B1
Ortisei 59 D3
Ortles 58 C3
Ortnevik 104 B1
Orton 5 D4
Ortona 64 A2
Ortrand 53 E2
Örträsk 102 A1
Orubica 71 E3
Orune 66 B2
Orusco 40 B2
Orvalho 38 C2
Orvieto 63 E1
Órvilos, Óros 80 B1
Orvinio 63 F2
Orzinuovi 60 B1
Os 100 D3
Osa de la Vega 40 B3
Osâm 115 D2
Osby 109 D3
Oschatz 53 E2
Oschersleben 52 C1
Oschiri 66 B2
Osečina 72 C3
Oseja de Sajambre . . 35 E2
Osen 96 C4
Osera de Ebro 37 D4
Osijek 71 F2

Osilo 66 B2
Osimo 61 F4
Osinja 71 E3
Osipaonica 73 D3
Osipoviči 111 D4
Osječenica 71 D4
Oskarshamn 109 E2
Oskarström 108 C2
Oslava 57 E1
Oslo 105 D3
Oslo (Fylke) 105 D3
Oslofjorden 104 C3
Ösmo 106 B4
Osnabrück 17 F2
Ośno Lubuskie 49 F4
Osogovija 77 E2
Osogovske
    planine 77 E2
Osoppo 59 E3
Osor 70 B4
Osorno 35 F3
Osøyri 104 A2
Ospedaletti 31 E3
Ospitaletto 60 B1
Oss 16 C3
Óssa 80 A2
Ossa de Montiel . . . 40 B4
Óssa, Óros 83 F1
Ossa, Sa de 38 C4
Ossiach 59 F2
Ossiacher See 59 F2
Óssios Loukás 83 F4
Ossun 37 E1
Ostaškov 111 E2
Østbirk 108 B3
Østby 105 E2
Oste 47 F3
Osted 108 C3
Osterburg 48 C4
Osterburken 55 D1

Österbybruk 106 B3
Østerby Havn 108 B2
Österbymo 109 E1
Österdalälven 101 D3
Østerdalen 100 D3
Österfärnebo 106 A3
Osterfeld 53 D2
Östergötlands Län . 109 E1
Osterhofen 56 B2
Osterholz
    Scharmbeck 47 F3
Osteria del Gatto . . 61 E4
Osterode 52 B2
Osterøya 104 A2
Östersund 101 E2
Östersundom 107 F2
Östervåla 106 B3
Øster Vrå 108 B2
Osterwieck 52 B1
Østfold 105 D3
Ostfriesische
    Inseln 47 D3
Östhammar 106 B3
Ostheim 52 B4
Ostia Antica 63 E3
Ostiglia 60 C2
Östmark 105 E3
Ost'or 113 E1
Ostra 61 E3
Ostrach 55 D4
Östra Gloppet 102 B2
Östra Silen 105 D4
Ostrava 112 B3
Oštrelj 71 D4
Ostritz 53 F2
Ostróda 110 B4
Ostrog 113 D2
Ostrołęka 112 B1
Ostrov (CS) 53 E3
Ostrov (RO) 115 E1

Ostrov (ROS) 111 D2
Ostrowiec
    Świętokrzyski . . . 112 B2
Ostrów
    Mazowiecki 112 B1
Ostrów
    Wielkopolski 112 A2
Ostrožac (BH) 70 C3
Ostrožac (BH) 75 F1
Ostsee 48 C1
Osttirol 59 E2
Ostuni 65 E3
Osuna 43 E3
Oswestry 6 B3
Oświęcim 112 B2
Otanmäki 103 D1
Otava (CS) 56 C1
Otava (SF) 103 E3
Oteren 94 C3
Oteševo 77 D4
Othem 109 F4
Othery 9 D3
Othoní, N 78 A4
Óthris, Óros 83 E3
Otívar 44 A3
Otley 6 C2
Otnes 100 C3
Otočac 70 C4
Otočec 70 B2
Otok 72 B2
Otoka 71 D3
Otra 104 B4
Otranto 65 F4
Otsamo 95 E3
Otta 100 C3
Ottana 66 B2
Ottaviano 64 B4
Ottenschlag 57 E2
Ottensheim 57 D2
Otterburn 5 E3

Otter Ferry 4 B2
Otterlo 17 D3
Otterndorf 47 F2
Otterøy 97 D4
Ottersberg 47 F3
Otterup 108 B3
Ottery St Mary 9 D3
Ottmarsheim 27 E1
Ottnang 56 C3
Ottobeuren 55 E3
Ottobrunn 56 A3
Ottsjö 101 D2
Ottweiler 54 B1
Otwock 112 B1
Otziás 88 A2
Ötztal 58 C2
Ötztaleralpen 58 C2
Ouchy 27 D3
Oucques 25 E1
Oud Beijerland 16 B3
Ouddorp 16 B3
Oude Maas 16 B3
Oudenaarde 50 B3
Oudenbosch 16 C3
Oude-Pekela 47 E3
Ouessant, Ile d' . . . 22 A2
Oughterard 12 B3
Ouistreham 18 C3
Oul 51 D4
Oulainen 99 D4
Oulanka 99 E2
Oulankajoki 99 E2
Oulchy-le-Château . 20 A3
Oulu 99 D3
Oulujärvi 99 E4
Oulujoki 99 D4
Oulun Lääni 99 E4
Oulunsalo 99 D4
Oulx 31 D2
Ounasjoki 99 D2

Oundle 9 F1
Our 54 A1
Ouranópoli 80 B4
Ource 26 C1
Ourcq 20 A3
Ourense 34 B3
Ourique 42 B2
Ourol 34 B1
Ourthe 20 C1
Ourville 19 D2
Ouse, R 7 D2
Oust 37 F2
Outes, Sa de 34 A2
Outokumpu 103 E2
Outomuro 34 B3
Outwell 10 C1
Ouvèze 30 C3
Ouzouer 25 F2
Ouzouer-le-Marché . 25 E1
Ovada 60 A2
Ovanåker 101 F4
Ovar 38 B1
Ovčar Banja 73 D4
Ovedskloster 109 D3
Overath 17 E4
Overbygd 94 C3
Overflakkee 16 B3
Overhalla 97 D4
Överhörnäs 102 A2
Overijse 50 C3
Överkalix 98 C2
Övermark 102 B2
Översjuktan 97 F3
Overtorneå 98 C2
Överum 109 E1
Överuman 97 E3
Oviedo 35 D1
Ovindoli 63 F2

Øvre Årdal 100 B3
Øvre Dividalen 94 C3
Övre Fryken 105 E3
Øvre Pasvik 95 F2
Övre Soppero 95 D4
Ovruč 113 E1
Owel, L 13 D3
Oxelösund 106 B4
Oxford 9 E2
Oxfordshire 9 E2
Oxiá, N 82 C4
Oxiá (Stereá Eláda) . 83 D3
Oxiá (Thessalía) . . . 83 D2
Oxie 108 C3
Oxilithos 84 B4
Ox Mts, The 12 B2
Oyarzun 36 C1
Oybin 53 F2
Øye 104 C1
Øyer 104 C1
Øyeren 105 D3
Oy-Mittelberg 55 E4
Oyntdartfjørður . . . 96 A3
Oyón 36 B2
Oyonnax 27 D4
Øystese 104 B2
Oyten 47 F3
Ozalj 70 C2
Ožbalt 70 B1
Ózd 112 B3
Ozeblin 70 C4
Ozieri 66 B2
Ozren 71 F3
Ozren Devica 73 E4

P

Paakkila 103 E2
Paalasmaa 103 E1
Páamo de Masa,
    Pto de 35 F3
Paar 55 F3
Paasselkä 103 F3
Paavola 99 D4
Pabianice 112 B2
Pacaudière, la 26 B4
Paceco 68 A3
Pachino 69 D4
Packsattel 57 E4
Paço de Sousa 34 A4
Paços de Ferreira . . 34 A3
Pacov 57 D1
Pacy 19 E4
Padasjoki 107 E1
Padej 72 C1
Padđene 75 D1
Paderborn 17 F3
Paderne 42 B2
Padiham 6 C2
Padina 72 C2
Padinska Skela . . . 72 C2
Padirac, Gouffre
    de 29 D2
Padjelanta 97 F1
Padornelo 34 C3
Padova 61 D1
Padrela, Sa da 34 B4
Padrón 34 A2
Padru 66 B2
Padstow 8 B3
Padul 44 A3
Paesana 31 E2
Paestum 64 B4
Pag 70 C4
Pag I 70 B4
Paganico 63 D1
Pagassés, N 83 F2
Pagassitikós
    Kólpos 83 F2
Paglia 63 D1
Pagny 21 D3

Pagóndas (Évia) . . . 84 A3
Pagóndas (Sámos) . 89 E2
Pagoúria 81 D2
Paguera 45 E3
Páhi 87 F1
Pahiá Ámos 91 F4
Pahís, Akr 80 C3
Paide 110 C1
Paignton 8 C4
Päijänne 103 D3
Paimboeuf 23 D4
Paimio 107 D2
Paimpol 22 C2
Painswick 9 E2
Paisley 4 C2
Paistunturit 95 E2
Paittasjärvi 94 C4
Paiva, R 38 B1
Pajala 98 C1
Pájara 42 C4
Pajares, Pto de . . . 35 D2
Paklenica Nac
    Park 70 C4
Pakoštane 74 C1
Pakrac 71 E2
Pakračka Poljana . . 71 D2
Paks 112 B4
Palacios de la
    Sierra 36 A3
Palacios del Sil . . . 34 C2
Palacios de
    Sanabria 34 C3
Palade, Pso del . . . 58 C3
Paládio 81 D2
Paladru 30 C1
Palafrugell 32 C3
Palagía 81 E2
Palagiano 65 E4
Palagonia 69 D3
Palagruža 75 D3
Palaia 60 C4
Palaiseau 19 F4
Palais, le 22 C4
Palamás 83 E2
Palamós 32 C3

Palancia, R 41 E3
Palanga 110 B3
Pala, Pto del 34 C1
Palas de Rei 34 B2
Palata 64 B2
Palatitsía 79 E3
Palatna 77 D1
Palau 66 B1
Palavas 30 B4
Palazzo del Pero . . 61 D4
Palazzolo Acreide . 69 D4
Palazzolo sull'
    Oglio 60 B1
Palazzo San
    Gervasio 64 C3
Palazzuolo sul
    Senio 61 D3
Paldiski 110 C1
Pale 76 A1
Paléa Epídavros . . . 87 E2
Palékastro 91 F4
Palena 64 A2
Palencia 35 E3
Paleohóra (Égina) . . 87 F2
Paleohóra (Kríti) . . 90 B4
Paleohóri (Árta) . . . 82 C2
Paleohóri
    (Grevená) 79 D4
Paleohóri
    (Halkidikí) 80 B3
Paleohóri (Ioánina) . 82 B2
Paleohóri (Lésvos) . 85 F3
Paleohóri
    (Pelopónnissos) . . 87 D3
Paleohóri
    (Thessalía) 83 D1
Paleokastrítsa 82 A1
Paleókastro
    (Halkidikí) 80 A3
Paleókastro
    (Kozáni) 79 D4
Paleókastro
    (Sámos) 89 F2
Paleókastro
    (Séres) 80 B2
Paleókastro (Stereá
    Eláda) 83 D3

Paleokómi 80 B2
Paleópirgos (Stereá
    Eláda) 83 D4
Paleópirgos
    (Thessalía) 83 F1
Paleópoli
    (Ándros) 88 B1
Paleópoli
    (Samothráki) 81 E3
Paleós Kavála 80 C2
Paleós Xánthis 81 D2
Palermo 68 B3
Páleros 82 B3
Palérou, Órm 82 B3
Palestrina 63 F2
Palež 72 B2
Páli 89 F4
Paliano 63 F3
Palić 72 B1
Palidoro 63 E2
Palinges 26 B3
Palinuro 67 D2
Palioúri 80 B4
Paliouriá 79 D4
Paliseul 20 C2
Pälkäne 107 E1
Pålkem 98 B2
Pallas
    Ounastunturi 95 D3
Pallastunturi 95 D4
Pallice, la 24 B4
Palluau 24 B3
Palma 45 E3
Palmaces,
    Emb de 36 B4
Palma del Río 43 E2
Palma di
    Montechiaro 68 C4
Palmadula 66 A2
Palmanova 59 F3
Palmela 38 A4
Palmi 67 E4
Palo del Colle 65 D3
Palojoensuu 95 D3
Palojoki 95 D3
Palokki 103 E2
Palomäki 103 E1

Palomares del
    Campo 40 C3
Palomas 39 D4
Palomas, Pto de
    las 44 B2
Palombara Sabina . 63 E2
Palombera, Pto de . 35 F2
Palomera 41 D2
Pálos, Akr 88 B2
Palos, C de 45 D3
Palos de la
    Frontera 42 C3
Pals 32 C3
Pålsboda 105 F4
Paltamo 99 E4
Paltaselkä 99 E4
Paluzza 59 E2
Pámfila 85 F2
Pamhagen 57 F3
Pamiers 32 A2
Pampilhosa 38 B2
Pampilhosa da
    Serra 38 C2
Pampliega 35 F3
Pamplona 36 C2
Pamporovo 115 D3
Pamukkale 115 F4
Panagía (Ípiros) . . . 82 C2
Panagía (Límnos) . . 85 D1
Panagía
    (Makedonía) 79 D4
Panagía (Thássos) . 81 D3
Panagía (Thessalía) . 82 C1
Panagjurište 115 D2
Panahaïkó, Óros . . . 83 D3
Panarea, I 69 D2
Panaro 60 C2
Pancalieri 31 E2
Pančevo 73 D2
Pančićev vrh 77 D1
Pancorbo 36 A2
Pandánassa 87 E4
Pandeleimónas . . . 79 F4
Pandino 60 B1
Pandokrátor 82 A1
Panes 35 E2

Panetolikó, Óros . . 83 D3
Panetólio 82 C4
Panevėžys 110 C3
Pangbourne 9 E2
Pangéo, Óros 80 B2
Paniza, Pto de 36 C4
Pankajärvi 103 F1
Pankakoski 103 F1
Pankow 49 E4
Panórama
    (Dráma) 80 B2
Panórama
    (Thessaloníki) . . . 80 A3
Panormítis 93 E1
Pánormos
    (Kikládes) 88 B2
Pánormos (Kríti) . . 91 D3
Pántäne 102 B3
Pantelleria 68 A4
Pantelleria, I di . . . 68 A4
Paola 67 E2
Pápa 112 A4
Papádes 84 A3
Papádos 85 F3
Páparis 86 C2
Pápas, Akr 89 D2
Papasídero 67 E2
Papa Stour 3 F1
Papenburg 47 E3
Papíkio 81 D2
Páping 78 C4
Pappenheim 55 F2
Papuk Mt. 71 E2
Papuk (Reg) 71 E2
Parabita 65 F4
Paracin 73 E4
Paracuellos de
    Jiloca 36 C4
Parada de Cunhos . 34 B4
Paradas 43 E3
Paradela 34 B3
Paradíssia 86 C2
Parádissos 81 D2
Parainen 107 D2
Parajes 34 C1
Parakálamos 78 C4
Parákila 85 F2

Paralía (Aháïa) . . . 86 C1
Paralía (Lakonía) . . 87 E3
Paralía
    (Makedonía) 79 F4
Paralía (Stereá
    Eláda) 83 F4
Paralía Akrátas . . . 87 D1
Parália Ástros 87 D2
Paralía Kímis 84 B3
Paralía Kotsikiás . . 84 A3
Paralía Skotínas . . 79 F4
Paralía Tiroú 87 E3
Paralímni 84 A4
Paralovo 77 D2
Paramé 18 B4
Paramera, Pto de . . 39 F2
Paramithía 82 B2
Páramo del Sil 34 C2
Paranésti 80 C2
Parapanda 43 F3
Parapótamos 82 B1
Paraspóri, Akr 93 D2
Paray-le-Monial . . . 26 B3
Parchim 48 C3
Pardubice 112 A3
Paredes 34 A4
Paredes de Coura . 34 A3
Paredes de Nava . . 35 E3
Pareja 40 C2
Pareloup, Lac de . . 29 E3
Parentis-en-Born . . 28 A3
Párga 82 B2
Pargas 107 D2
Parikkala 103 F3
Parîngului, M 114 C1
Paris 19 F4
Parkalompolo 95 D4
Parkano 102 C3
Parla 40 A2
Parlavà 32 B3
Parma 60 B2
Parnassós, Óros . . 83 E4
Parndorf 57 F2
Párnitha, Óros 87 F1
Párnonas, Óros . . . 87 D3
Pärnu 110 C2
Parola 107 E2

Páros 88 C3
Páros, N. 88 B3
Parrett 9 D3
Parsberg 55 F2
Parsdorf 56 A3
Parseierspitze 58 C2
Parşeta 49 F1
Parsteiner See 49 E3
Partakko 95 F2
Partanna 68 B3
Partenen 58 B2
Partenkirchen 55 F4
Partenstein 55 F4
Parthenay 24 C3
Parthéni 89 E3
Partille 108 C1
Partinico 68 B3
Partizani 73 D3
Partizanske Vode . . 72 C4
Partney 7 E3
Partry Mountains . . 12 B3
Pasaia-Pasajes 36 C1
Pas de Calais 11 E3
Pas-de-Calais
   (Dépt) 19 E1
Pas de la Case 32 A2
Pas-en-Artois 19 F2
Pasewalk 49 E2
Pashalítsa 83 E2
Pasikovci 71 E2
Pašman 74 C1
Pašman I 74 C1
Passais 18 C4
Passá-Limáni 85 E4
Passás, N 85 F4
Passau 56 C2
Passavás 87 D4
Passero, C. 69 D4
Passignano sul
   Trasimeno 61 D4
Passwang 27 E2
Pastrana 40 B2
Paštrik 76 C3
Pásztó 112 B4
Patay 25 E1
Pateley Bridge 6 C1
Patéras, Óros 87 E1
Paterna del
   Campo 43 D2
Paterna de Rivera . . 43 D4
Paternion 59 F2
Paterno 69 D3
Paternopoli 64 B3
Patersdorf 56 B2
P'atichatki 113 F2
Patiópoulo 82 C2
Patitíri 84 B2
Pátmos 89 E2
Pátmos, N. 89 E2
Pátra 83 D4
Patraïkós Kólpos . . . 82 C4
Patreksfjörður 96 A1
Patrington 7 E2
Pattada 66 B2
Patterdale 5 D4
Patti 69 D2
Pattijoki 99 D4
Patvinsuo 103 F2
Pau 37 D1
Pauillac 28 B2
Paúl 38 C2
Paularo 59 F2
Paulhaguet 29 F2
Paullo 60 A1
Pavia (I) 60 A2
Pavia (P) 38 B4
Pavilly 19 D3
Pavino Polje 76 B1
Pávliani 83 E3
Pávlos 83 F4
Pavullo nel
   Frignano 60 C3
Paxí 82 A2
Paxí, N 82 A2
Payerne 27 E3
Paymogo 42 C2
Payrac 29 D2
Pazardžik 115 D3
Pazin 70 A3
Pčinja 77 E2
Péage-de-
   Roussillon, le 30 B1
Peak District Nat Pk . 6 C2
Peal de Becerro 44 B2
Peanía 87 F1

Peares, Emb de
   los 34 B2
Peč 76 C2
Peča 70 B1
Peccioli 60 C4
Pečenjevce 77 E1
Pech-Merle,
   Grotte du 29 D3
Pećigrad 70 C3
Pečinci 72 C3
Pecka 72 C4
Peckelsheim 52 A2
Pécs 114 B1
Pécsa Banja 76 C2
Pečúrice 76 B3
Pedaso 61 F4
Pedersker 109 D4
Pedersöre 102 C2
Pédi 93 E1
Pedrafita do
   Cebreiro 34 C2
Pedrafita do Cebreiro,
   Pto de 34 C2
Pedrajas de San
   Esteban 35 E4
Pedralba
   (Castilla-León) . . . 34 C3
Pedralba
   (Valencia) 41 E3
Pedras Salgadas . . . 34 B4
Pedraza de la
   Sierra 40 A1
Pedrera 43 E3
Pedrizas, Pto de
   las 43 F3
Pedro Abad 43 F2
Pedro Bernardo . . . 39 F2
Pedrógão
   (Alentejo) 42 B1
Pedrógão
   (Estremadura) . . . 38 A2
Pedrógão Grande . . 38 B2
Pedrola 36 C3
Pedro Muñoz 40 B2
Peebles 5 D2
Peel 6 A1
Peene 49 D2
Peenemünde 49 E1
Peer Gynt veien . . . 100 C3
Pefkári 80 C3
Pefki 83 F3
Péfkos 78 C3
Pega 38 C2
Pegalajar 44 A2
Pegau 53 D2
Pegli 60 A3
Pegnitz 55 F1
Pego 45 E1
Pego do Altar,
   Bgem de 38 B4
Pegognaga 60 C2
Pegolotte 61 D1
Pehčevo 77 F3
Peine 52 B1
Peio Terme 58 C3
Peíra-Cava 31 E3
Peißenberg 56 A4
Peiting 56 A4
Peitz 53 F1
Pek 73 D3
Péla 79 E2
Péla (Nomos) 79 F3
Pelado 41 D3
Pelagie, Is 68 A4
Pelasgía 83 F3
Pelat, Mt 31 D3
Pełczyce 49 F3
Pelekános 79 D3
Pélekas 82 A1
Peletá 87 E3
Pelhřimov 57 D1
Pélister 77 E4
Pelješac 75 E2
Pelkosenniemi 99 E1
Pellegrino
   Parmense 60 B2
Pellegrue 28 C2
Pellerin, le 24 B2
Pellesmäki 103 E2
Pello 98 C2
Pellworm 47 F1
Pelopónnisos 86 C2

Peloritani, M 69 D2
Peltosalmi 103 E1
Peltovuoma 95 D3
Pélussin 30 B1
Pelvoux, Mt 31 D2
Pembroke 8 B2
Pembroke Dock 8 B2
Pembrokeshire Coast
   Nat Pk 8 B1
Penacova 38 B2
Peña de Francia . . . 39 D2
Peña de Francia,
   Sa de 39 D2
Peña de Oroel 37 D2
Penafiel 34 A4
Peñafiel 35 F4
Peñaflor 43 E2
Peñagolosa 41 E3
Peña Gorbea 36 B1
Peñalara 40 A1
Penalva do
   Castelo 38 C1
Penamacor 38 C2
Peña Mira 34 C3
Peña Nofre 34 B3
Peña Prieta 35 E2
Peñaranda de
   Bracamonte 39 F1
Peñaranda de
   Duero 36 A3
Peñarroya 41 E2
Peñarroya, Emb de . 40 B4
Peñarroya-
   Pueblonuevo 43 E1
Penarth 9 D2
Peña, Sa de la 37 D2
Peña Sagra 35 F2
Peñas, C de 35 D1
Peñascosa 44 C1
Peñas de Cervera . . 36 A3
Peñas de San
   Pedro 44 C1
Peña Trevinca 34 C3
Peña Ubiña 35 D2
Peñausende 35 D4
Pendagií 83 D4
Pendálofo 82 C4
Pendálofos 78 C4
Pendéli 87 F1
Pendéli Mt. 87 F1
Pendeória 83 E4
Pénde Vrísses 80 A2
Pendine 8 B2
Peneda-Gerês,
   Pque Nac da 34 A3
Peneda, Sa da 34 A3
Penedono 38 C1
Penela 38 B2
Pénestin 22 C4
Penha 34 A4
Penhas da Saúde . . 38 C2
Penhas Juntas 34 C4
Penhir, Pte de 22 A3
Penice, Pso del 60 A2
Peniche 38 A3
Penicuik 5 D2
Penig 53 D3
Penkun 49 E3
Penmaenmawr 6 A2
Penmarch, Pte de . . 22 A3
Pennabilli 61 E3
Penne 63 F1
Penne-d'Agenais . . 28 C3
Pennes, Pso di 59 D2
Pennines, The 6 C1
Peñón de Ifach 45 E1
Penrhyndeudraeth . 6 A3
Penrith 5 D4
Penryn 8 B4
Penserjoch 59 D2
Pentland Firth 3 D2
Pentland Hills 5 D2
Pentrefoelas 6 B3
Pen-y-bont 8 C2
Penzance 8 A4
Penzberg 56 A4
Penzlin 49 D2
Peqin 76 C4
Perahóra 87 E1
Peraleda de
   Zaucejo 43 E1
Peralejos de
   las Truchas 40 C2

Perales del
   Alfambra 41 D2
Perales del Puerto . 39 D2
Perales de Tajuña . . 40 B2
Perales, Pto de 39 D2
Peralta 36 C2
Peralta de Alcofea . 37 E3
Peralva 42 B2
Pérama (Ípiros) 82 C1
Pérama (Kérkira) . . 82 A1
Pérama (Kríti) 91 D3
Pérama (Lésvos) . . . 85 F3
Pérama (Stereá
   Eláda) 87 F1
Peraméri 98 C3
Perä-Posio 99 E2
Peräseinäjoki 102 C2
Perast 76 B3
Peratáta 86 A1
Percy 18 B4
Perdido, Mt 37 E2
Pérdika (Égina) 87 F2
Pérdika
   (Ioánina) 82 C2
Pérdika
   (Thesprotía) 82 B2
Perdikáki 82 C3
Perdikas 79 D3
Peréa (Péla) 79 E3
Peréa
   (Thessaloníki) . . . 79 F3
Perejaslav-
   Chmel'nickij 113 F2
Pereruela 35 D4
Pereval
   Jablonickij 113 D3
Pereval
   Srednij Vereckij . . 112 C3
Pereval Užokskij . . . 112 C3
Perg 57 D2
Pergine
   Valsugana 59 D3
Pergola 61 E4
Perho 102 C2
Perhonjoki 102 C2
Periana 43 F3
Périers 18 B3
Périgueux 28 C2
Periklía 79 E2
Perino 60 B2
Períssa 91 E1
Perísta 83 D3
Peristerá 80 A3
Peristéra, N 84 B2
Perithório 80 B1
Perívlepto 83 F2
Perivóli 78 C4
Perivóli, N 83 E2
Perivólio 83 D3
Perjasica 70 C3
Perković 75 D1
Perleberg 48 C3
Perlez 72 C2
Përmet 114 C4
Pernã 107 F2
Pernaja 107 F2
Pernarec 53 E4
Pernes 30 C3
Pernik 114 C2
Perniö 107 E3
Pernitz 57 E3
Pernštejn 57 E1
Péronne 19 F2
Perosa Argentina . . 31 E2
Pérouges 26 C4
Perpignan 32 B2
Perrero 31 E2
Perreux 26 B4
Perros-Guirec 22 B2
Persenbeug 57 D2
Pershore 9 E1
Perstorp 109 D3
Perth 5 D1
Perthus, le 32 B3
Pertisau 59 D1
Pertoča 70 C1
Pertoúli 83 D1
Perttéli 107 E2
Pertunmaa 103 D3
Pertusa 37 E3
Perucác Vrelo 72 C4
Peručko jez 75 D1
Perugia 61 E4

Perušić 70 C4
Péruwelz 50 B4
Pervenchères 23 F3
Pervomajsk 113 F3
Pesaro 61 E3
Pescara 64 A1
Pescasseroli 64 A2
Peschici 64 C2
Peschiera del
   Garda 60 C1
Pescia 60 C3
Pescina 63 F2
Pescocostanzo 64 A2
Pescolanciano 64 A2
Pescopagano 64 C4
Pescorocchiano . . . 63 F2
Peshkopi 77 D3
Pesiökylä 99 E3
Pesmes 26 C2
Pesočani 77 D4
Pêso da Régua 34 B4
Pesoz 34 C1
Pessáni 81 F2
Pessáno 112 A3
Peštani 77 D4
Pešter 76 C2
Pestovo 111 F1
Pešurići 72 B4
Petačinci 77 E1
Petäjäskoski 99 D2
Petäjäves 103 D3
Petalax 102 B2
Petalída, Akr 88 B3
Petalídi 86 C3
Petalií, Nissí 88 A1
Petalión, Kólpos . . . 88 A1
Petaloúdes 93 F1
Pétange 21 D3
Pétas 82 C2
Petehovac 70 B3
Peterborough 9 F1
Peterhead 3 E3
Peterlee 5 E4
Petersfield 9 F3
Petershagen 17 F2
Pethelinós 80 B2
Petilia Policastro . . 67 F3
Petina 64 C4
Petite-Pierre, la . . . 21 E3
Petit Morin 20 A4
Petit St-Bernard,
   Col du 27 E4
Petkula 95 E4
Petlovača 72 C3
Petoússio 82 B2
Petra (E) 45 F3
Pétra (Lésvos) 85 F2
Pétra (Makedonía) . 79 E4
Petralia 68 C3
Petrálona 80 A3
Petraná 79 E4
Petrčane 74 C1
Petrel 45 D1
Petrella, Mte 64 A3
Pétres 79 D3
Petreto-
   Bicchisano 33 F4
Petrič 115 D3
Petrijevki 71 F2
Petrina 86 C3
Petrinja 71 D3
Petrodvorec 111 D1
Petrohóri 83 D4
Petróla 45 D1
Petróna 82 C3
Petroşani 114 C1
Petrotá 81 F1
Petrothálassa 87 E2
Petrotó 83 D2
Petroússa 80 B2
Petrovac (BH) 70 C3
Petrovac (Crna
   Gora) 76 B3
Petrovac (Srbija) . . 73 E3
Petrovaradin 72 C2
Petrovčić 72 C3
Petrovec 77 E3
Petrovice 53 F4
Petrovići 72 B4
Pettenbach 56 C3
Pettigoe 12 C2
Petworth 9 F3
Peuerbach 56 C2
Peura 99 D2
Pewsey 9 E2

Peyrat-le-
   Château 29 D1
Peyrehorade 28 A4
Peyresourde, C de . . 37 E2
Peyriac-Minervois . 32 B1
Peyrolles 30 C4
Peyrol, Pas de 29 E2
Peyruis 31 D3
Pézenas 30 A4
Pezinok 112 A3
Pezoúla 81 D2
Pfaffenhofen 55 F2
Pfäffikon 58 A2
Pfalzgrafenweiler . . 54 C3
Pfarrkirchen 56 B2
Pfeffenhausen 56 B2
Pforzheim 54 C2
Pfreimd 56 B1
Pfronten 55 E4
Pfullendorf 55 D4
Pfullingen 55 D3
Pfunds 58 C2
Pfungstadt 54 C1
Phalsbourg 21 E4
Philippeville 50 C4
Philippsreut 56 C2
Piacenza 60 B2
Piadena 60 B2
Piana 33 E3
Piana d. Albanesi . . 68 B3
Piancastagnaio . . . 63 D1
Piancavallo 59 E3
Piandelagotti 60 C3
Pian delle
   Fugazze, Pso 59 D4
Pian del Voglio 60 C3
Pianella 64 A1
Pianello 61 E4
Pianoro 61 D3
Pianosa, I (Mare
   Adriatico) 64 C1
Pianosa, I (Mare
   Tirreno) 62 B2
Piansano 63 D2
Piapaxaro, P. 34 C2
Pias 42 B1
Piatra-Neamţ 113 D4
Piave 59 E4
Piazza al Serchio . . 60 B3
Piazza Armerina . . . 68 C3
Piazza Brembana . . 58 B4
Piazzola sul
   Brenta 59 D4
Piber 57 E4
Pibeste, P de 37 E1
Pićan 70 A3
Picassent 41 E4
Piccolo San Bernardo,
   Colle del 27 E4
Picerno 64 C4
Pickering 7 D1
Pico 64 A3
Pico, Pto del 39 F2
Pico Ruivo 42 A3
Picos de Europa . . . 35 E2
Picote, Bgem de . . . 34 C4
Picquigny 19 E2
Pídna 79 F3
Piedicavallo 27 F4
Piediluco 63 E2
Piedimonte Matese . 64 B3
Piedrabuena 40 A4
Piedrafita 35 D2
Piedrahíta 39 E2
Piedralaves 39 F2
Piedra, R 36 C4
Piedras Albas 39 D3
Piedra San Martín,
   Collado de la 37 D2
Piedras, Emb de . . . 42 C2
Piedrasluengas,
   Pto de 35 F2
Piedratajada 37 D3
Pieksämäki 103 E3
Pielavesi 103 D2
Pielavesi L 103 F3
Pielinen 103 F1
Pieljekaise 97 F2
Piemonte 31 E2
Piennes 20 C3
Pienza 61 D4
Pieria 79 E4
Piéria, Óri 79 E3

Pierowall 3 E1
Pierre-Buffière 29 D1
Pierre-de-Bresse . . 26 C3
Pierrefitte 20 C3
Pierrefitte-
   Nestaïas 37 E2
Pierrefonds 19 F3
Pierrefontaine-les-
   Varans 27 D2
Pierrefort 29 E2
Pierrelatte 30 B3
Pieskehaure 97 F2
Piešťany 112 A3
Pietersaaren mlk . . . 102 C2
Pietersaari 102 C1
Pietra Ligure 31 F3
Pietralunga 61 E4
Pietraperzia 68 C3
Pietrasanta 60 B3
Pietra Spada, Pso
   di 67 F4
Pietrosu 113 D3
Pieux, les 18 B3
Pieve de' Burgondi
   del Cairo 60 A2
Pieve di Bono 58 C4
Pieve di Cadore . . . 59 E3
Pieve di Soligo 59 E3
Pieve di Teco 31 F3
Pievepelago 60 C3
Pieve Santo
   Stefano 61 D4
Pigádi 83 F3
Pigés 82 C2
Pigí 83 D4
Pigna 31 E3
Pigón, L 82 C1
Pihlajaveden as . . . 102 C2
Pihlajavesi 102 C2
Pihlajavesi L 103 F3
Pihlava 102 B3
Pihtipudas 103 D2
Piikkiö 107 D2
Piippola 103 D1
Piispajärvi 99 F3
Pikal'ovo 111 E1
Pikérmi 87 F1
Piła 112 A1
Pilat-Plage 28 A2
Pilas 43 D3
Pila, Sa de la 45 D2
Pilat, Mt 30 B1
Pilatus 27 F2
Piléa 81 F2
Piles 41 E4
Pilés 93 D3
Píli (Makedonía) . . . 78 C2
Píli (Stereá Eláda) . . 87 F1
Píli (Thessalía) 83 D2
Pilica 112 B2
Pílio 84 A3
Pílio 89 F3
Pílio, Óros 83 F2
Pillon, Col du 27 E3
Pilorí 79 D4
Pílos 86 C3
Pilštanj 70 C2
Pina 37 D4
Piña de Campos . . . 35 E3
Pinar 43 E3
Pineda de la Sierra . 36 A2
Pineda de Mar 32 B4
Pinerolo 31 E2
Pineto 64 A1
Piney 20 B4
Pinhal de Leiria . . . 38 A2
Pinhal Novo 38 A4
Pinhão 34 B4
Pinheiro 34 A4
Pinhel 39 D1
Piniós
   (Pelopónnisos) . . 86 C1
Piniós (Thessalía) . . 83 E1
Pinkafeld 57 F3
Pinneberg 48 A3
Pino 33 F2
Pinofranqueado . . . 39 D2
Pinols 29 F2
Pinoso 45 D1
Pinos Puente 44 A3
Pinsk 113 D1
Pintado, Emb de . . 43 D2
Pintamo 99 E3
Pinto 40 A2

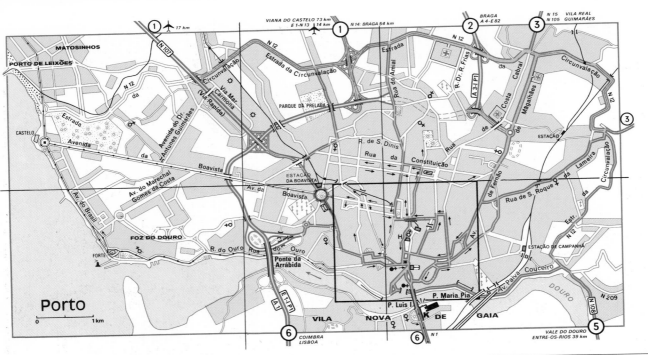

Porto

0 — 1 km

Politiká	84	A4
Poljana (SLO)	70	B1
Poljana (Srbija)	73	D3
Poljčane	70	C1
Polje	71	E3
Poljica	75	E2
Poljice	71	F4
Polla	64	C4
Pölläkkä	103	E2
Pöllau	57	E2
Polle	52	A1
Pollença	45	F2
Pollfoss	100	B3
Pollino, Mte	67	E2
Pollos	35	E4
Polmak	95	E2
Polock	111	D3
Polonnoje	113	D2
Polperro	8	B4
Poltava	113	F2
Polvijärvi	103	F2
Polzela	70	B2
Pomar	37	E3
Pomarance	60	C4
Pomarkku	102	B3
Pombal	38	B2
Pómbia	91	D4
Pomellen	49	E2
Pomezi	53	D4
Pomezia	63	E3
Pomigliano d'Arco	64	B4
Pommersfelden	55	E1
Pomokaira	95	E4
Pomorie	115	E2
Pomorze	110	A4
Pomovaara	95	E4
Pompei	64	B4
Pomposa	61	D2
Poncin	26	C4
Pondoiráklia	79	F2
Pondokómi	79	D3
Ponferrada	34	C1
Ponikovica	72	C4
Pons	28	B1
Ponsacco	60	C4
Pontacq	37	E1
Pontailler	26	C2
Pont-à-Marcq	20	A1
Pont-à-Mousson	21	D3
Pontão	38	B2
Pontardawe	8	C2
Pontardulais	8	C2
Pontarion	25	E4
Pontarlier	27	D3
Pontassieve	61	D3
Pontaubault	18	B4
Pont-Audemer	19	D3
Pontaumur	26	A4
Pont-Aven	22	B3
Pont Canavese	31	E1
Pontcharra	31	D1
Pontchartrain	19	E4
Pontchâteau	23	D4
Pont-Croix	22	A3
Pont-d'Ain	26	C4
Pont-de-Beauvoisin, le	30	C1
Pont-de-Chéruy	26	C4
Pont-de-Claix, le	30	C2
Pont-de-Dore	26	A4
Pont-de-l'Arche	19	E3
Pont-de-Montvert, le	29	F3
Pont-de-Roide	27	E2
Pont-de-Salars	29	E3
Pont-d'Espagne	37	E2
Pont de Suert	37	F2
Pont-de-Vaux	26	C3
Pont-de-Veyle	26	C4
Pont-d'Oléron	28	A1
Pont-d'Ouilly	18	C4
Pont-du-Château	26	A4
Pont-du-Gard	30	B3
Ponte Arche	58	C3
Ponteareas	34	A3
Pontebba	59	F2
Pontecagnano	64	B4
Ponte Caldelas	34	A2
Ponteceno	60	B2
Ponte Ceso	34	A1
Pontecorvo	64	A3
Ponte da Barca	34	A3

Pinzano al Tagliamento	59	E3
Pinzolo	58	C3
Piobbico	61	E4
Piombino	62	C1
Pione	60	B2
Pionsat	26	A4
Piotrków Trybunalski	112	B2
Piove di Sacco	61	D1
Piovene Rocchette	59	D4
Pipéri, N	84	C2
Pipriac	23	D3
Piqueras, Pto de	36	B3
Piran	70	A3
Pir'atin	113	F2
Pireás	87	F1
Pirgadíkia	80	B3
Pirgetós	83	E1
Pirgi (Dráma)	80	B2
Pirgí (Hios)	85	E4
Pirgi (Kérkira)	82	A1
Pírgi (Kozáni)	79	E3
Pírgos (Ílos)	88	C4
Pírgos (Kríti)	91	D4
Pírgos (Makedonía)	79	F3
Pírgos (Pelopónissos)	86	B2
Pírgos (Sámos)	89	E2
Pírgos (Stereá Eláda)	83	F4
Pírgos Diroú	87	D4
Piriac	22	C4
Pirin	115	D3
Pirkkala	107	E1
Pirmasens	54	B2
Pirna	53	F2
Pirok	77	D3
Pirot	77	E1
Pirovac	74	C1
Pirsógiani	78	C4
Pirttikoski	99	E2
Pisa	60	C4
Pisciotta	67	D1
Pisek	56	C1
Piškorevci	71	F2
Pisogne	58	C4
Pisses	88	A2
Pissodéri	79	D3
Pissónas	84	B4
Pissos	28	B3
Pisticci	65	D4
Pistoia	60	C4
Pisuerga, R	35	E4
Piteå	98	B3
Piteälven	98	B3
Pitești	115	D1
Pithagório	89	E2

Pithio (Thessalía)	79	E4
Pithio (Thráki)	81	F1
Pithiviers	25	F1
Pitigliano	63	D2
Pitlochry	3	D4
Pitomača	71	E2
Pittenweem	5	D2
Pivka	70	A3
Pivnica	71	E2
Pivnice	72	B2
Pivsko jezero	76	A2
Pizarra	43	F3
Piz Buin	58	B2
Pizzighettone	60	B2
Pizzo	67	E3
Pizzoli	63	F2
Pjórsá	96	B2
Plabennec	22	A2
Plačenska pl	77	D4
Plačkovica	77	F3
Plagiá (Makedonía)	79	F2
Plagiá (Thráki)	81	E2
Plagne, la	31	D1
Plaisance	28	B4
Pláka (Límnos)	85	D1
Pláka (Pelopónissos)	87	E3
Pláka (Thráki)	81	E2
Pláka, Akr	85	D1
Pláka Litohórou	79	F4
Plakiás	90	C4
Planá	53	E4
Plana	76	A2
Planches-en-Montagne, les	27	D3
Plancoët	22	C3
Plandište	73	D2
Planica Mangrt	70	A1
Plánice	56	C1
Planina (Celje)	70	C2
Planina (Jesenice)	70	A1
Planina (Postojna)	70	A2
Planinica	73	E4
Planitz	53	D3
Plános	86	A1
Plansee	58	C1
Plasencia	39	D2
Plaški	70	C3
Plasy	53	E4
Platamona Lido	66	A2
Platamónas (Kavalá)	80	C2
Platamónas (Piería)	79	F4
Platanákia	79	F2
Platanés	90	C3
Platani	68	B3

Plataniá (Makedonía)	80	C2
Platánia (Pelopónissos)	86	C2
Plataniá (Thessalía)	84	A2
Platanistós	88	A1
Platanítis	83	D4
Plátanos (Kríti)	90	B3
Plátanos (Pelopónissos)	87	D3
Plátanos (Thessalía)	83	F2
Platariá	82	B2
Plateau-d'Assy	27	E4
Plateés	87	E1
Pláti	81	F1
Platiána	86	C2
Platičevo	72	C3
Platikambos	83	E1
Platís Gialós (Kefaloniá)	86	A1
Platís Gialós (Mikonos)	88	C2
Platís Gialós (Sífnos)	88	B3
Platístomo	83	E3
Plattling	56	B2
Plau	48	C3
Plaue	49	D4
Plauen	53	D3
Plauer See (Brandenburg)	49	D4
Plauer See (Mecklenburg-Vorpommern)	48	C3
Plav	76	C2
Plavča	70	C3
Plavna	73	E3
Plavnica	76	B3
Plavnik I	70	B4
Plavnik Mt	70	B4
Playa Blanca	42	C4
Playa de Gandía	41	E4
Playa de San Juan	45	E1
Pleaux	29	E2
Pleine-Fougères	18	B4
Pleinfeld	55	E2
Pleiße	53	D2
Plélan-le-Grand	23	D3
Plélan-le-Petit	22	C3
Pléneuf	22	C2
Plentzia	36	B1
Plépi	87	E2
Plešin	76	C1
Plestin	22	B2
Pleternica	71	E2
Plettenberg	17	F4
Pletvar	77	E3
Pleumartin	25	D3

Pleumeur-Bodou	22	B2
Pleven	115	D2
Pleyben	22	B3
Pliego	44	C2
Plítra	87	D4
Plitvice	70	C3
Plitvička jezera	70	C3
Plitvički Ljeskovac	70	C4
Plješevica	70	C4
Pljevlja	76	B1
Ploaghe	66	B2
Ploče	75	E2
Plochingen	55	D2
Płock	112	B1
Plöckenpaß	59	E2
Plöckenstein	56	C2
Pločno	75	E1
Ploёrmel	22	C3
Ploiești	115	D1
Plomári	85	F3
Plomb du Cantal	29	E2
Plombières	27	D1
Plomin	70	B3
Plön	48	B2
Plonéour-Lanvern	22	A3
Płoń, Jez	49	E2
Płońsk	112	B1
Płoty	49	F2
Plouagat	22	C2
Plouaret	22	B2
Plouay	22	B3
Ploubalay	18	A4
Plœuc	22	C3
Ploudalmézeau	22	A2
Plouescat	22	A2
Plougasnou	22	B2
Plougastel-Daoulas	22	A3
Plougonven	22	B2
Plouguenast	22	C3
Plouha	22	C2
Plouigneau	22	B2
Ploumanach	22	B2
Plouzévédé	22	B2
Plovdiv	115	D3
Plumbridge	13	D2
Plunge	110	B3
Pl'ussa	111	D1
Pluvigner	22	C3
Plužine	76	A1
Plympton	8	C4
Plymstock	8	C4
Plzeň	53	E4
Po	60	C4
Poarta de Fier	114	C1
Pobierowo	49	F1
Poblet	37	F4
Pobrđde	76	C1

Počep	111	F4
Počinok	111	E3
Počitelj	75	F2
Pocking	56	C2
Poćuta	72	C4
Pódareš	77	F3
Podbořany	53	E3
Podčetrtek	70	C2
Podensac	28	B2
Podersdorf	57	F3
Podgajci Posavski	72	B3
Podgarič	71	D2
Podgora	75	E2
Podgorac (HR)	71	F2
Podgorac (Srbija)	73	D3
Podgorica	76	B3
Podgrad	70	A3
Podhum	75	D1
Podjuchy	49	E2
Podkoren	70	A1
Podlugovi	71	F4
Podnovlje	71	F3
Podogorá	82	C3
Podohóri	80	B2
Podol'sk	111	F2
Podol'skaja Vozvyšennost'	113	D3
Podpec	70	B2
Podrašnica	71	E4
Podravska Slatina	71	E2
Podromanija	72	B4
Podsreda	70	C2
Podsused	70	C2
Podturen	71	D1
Podujevo	77	D1
Podunavci	73	D4
Poel	48	C2
Poganovo	77	E1
Poggibonsi	60	C4
Poggio Imperiale	64	C2
Poggio Mirteto	63	E2
Poggio Renatico	61	D2
Poggio Rusco	60	C2
Pöggstall	57	E2
Pogoniani	78	B4
Pogradec	77	D4
Pohja	107	E3
Pohja-Lankila	103	E3
Pohjaslahti (Keski-Suomen Lääni)	102	C2
Pohjaslahti (Lapin Lääni)	99	D2
Pohjois-Karjalan Lääni	103	F2
Pohořelice	57	F1
Pohorje	70	B1
Poiana Brașov	113	D4
Poio	34	A2

Poiré, le	24	B3
Poirino	31	F2
Poissons	20	C4
Poitiers	25	D3
Pöitsamaa	110	C2
Poix	19	E2
Poix-Terron	20	B2
Pojate	73	E4
Pojo	107	E3
Pokka	95	E3
Poklečani	75	E1
Pokljuka	70	A2
Pokupsko	70	C3
Polače	75	E2
Polacra, Pta de la	44	C4
Pola de Allande	34	C1
Pola de Gordón, la	35	D2
Pola de Laviana	35	D2
Pola de Lena	35	D2
Pola de Siero	35	D1
Polán	40	A3
Polcenigo	59	E3
Połczyn-Zdrój	110	A4
Polegate	10	C3
Poles	113	D1
Polesella	61	D2
Polessk	110	B4
Polhov Gradec	70	A2
Policastro	67	D1
Policastro, Golfo di	67	D2
Police	49	E2
Poličnik	74	C1
Policoro	65	D4
Polidéndri	84	B4
Polidrossos	83	E3
Políegos, N	88	B4
Poliégou Folegándrou, Stenó	88	B4
Polígiros	80	A3
Polignano a Mare	65	E3
Poligny	27	D3
Polihnítos	85	F3
Polikárpi	79	E2
Polikástano	78	C3
Polikastro	79	F2
Polimílos	79	E3
Polinéri (Makedonía)	79	D4
Polinéri (Thessalía)	82	C2
Polióhni	85	D1
Polipótamo	79	D3
Polipótamos	84	C4
Poliraho	79	E4
Polirinía	90	B3
Polis, M	77	D4
Políssito	81	D2
Polistena	67	E4
Polithéa	82	C1

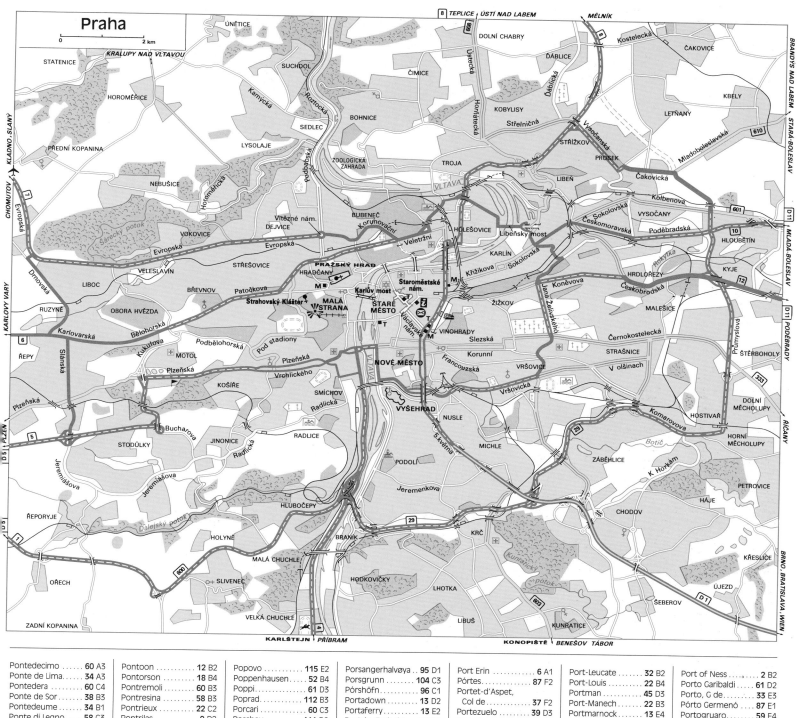

Praha

0   1   2 km

Pontedecimo **60** A3	Pontoon **12** B2	Popovo **115** E2	Porsangerhalvøya .. **95** D1
Ponte de Lima..... **34** A3	Pontorson **18** B4	Poppenhausen .. **52** B4	Porsgrunn **104** C3
Pontedera **60** C4	Pontremoli **60** B3	Poppi............. **61** D3	Pórshöfn.......... **96** C1
Ponte de Sor **38** B3	Pontresina **58** B3	Poprad **112** B3	Portadown **13** D2
Pontedeume **34** B1	Pontrieux **22** C2	Porcari **60** C3	Portaferry **13** E2
Ponte di Legno ... **58** C3	Pontrilas **9** D2	Porchov **111** D2	Portaje, Emb de .. **39** D3
Ponte di Piave ... **59** E4	Ponts **37** F3	Porcuna **43** F2	Porta, la **33** F3
Pontefract **7** D2	Pont-Ste-	Pordenone **59** E3	Portalegre **38** C3
Pontelandolfo **64** B3	Maxence **19** F3	Poreč **70** A3	Portalé, Pto del .. **37** D2
Ponte-Leccia **33** F3	Pont-St-Esprit ... **30** B3	Pori **107** D1	Portalrubio **41** D2
Pontenelle Alpi ... **59** E3	Pont St-Martin ... **31** E1	Porjus **98** B2	Portariá **83** F2
Pont-en-Royans .. **30** C1	Pont-St-Vincent .. **21** D4	Porkkalanselkä ... **107** E3	Portarlington...... **13** D4
Ponte San Pietro .. **60** B1	Pont-Scorff **22** B3	Porma, Emb del .. **35** E2	Port Askaig **4** B2
Pontet, le **30** C3	Ponts-de-Cé, les .. **23** E4	Porma, R **35** E2	Portavogie **13** E2
Ponte Tresa **58** A4	Pontsenni **8** C1	Pornainen **107** F2	Porta-Westfalica .. **51** F1
Pontevico **60** B1	Pont-sur-Yonne .. **26** A1	Pörnbach **55** F2	Port-Bacarès **32** B2
Pontfaverger-	Pontvallain **23** F4	Pornic............ **24** A2	Portbail **18** B3
Moronvilliers .. **20** B3	Pontypool......... **9** D2	Pornichet **24** A2	Portbou **32** C3
Pontgibaud **29** E1	Pontypridd **8** C2	Póros (Kefaloniá) .. **86** A1	Port Charlotte **4** A2
Pontigny **26** B1	Ponza, I **63** D4	Póros (Lefkáda) .. **82** B3	Port, Col de **37** F2
Pontinia.......... **63** F3	Ponziane, I **63** F4	Póros (Póros)..... **87** F2	Port-Cros **31** D4
Pontinvrea **31** F2	Poole **9** E3	Póros, N **87** F2	Port-de-Bouc **30** C4
Pontivy **22** C3	Poperinge **50** A3	Porozina **70** B3	Porte, Col de **30** C1
Pont-l'Abbé **22** A3	Popinci **72** C3	Pórpi **81** D2	Port-Einon **8** C2
Pont-l'Evêque **19** D3	Popoli **64** A2	Porquerolles **31** D4	Portella
Pontlevoy **25** E2	Popovac.......... **73** E4	Porrentruy **27** E2	Femmina Morta **69** D3
Pontoise **19** E3	Popovača **71** D2	Porretta Terme ... **60** C3	Port Ellen **4** A2
Pontones **44** B2	Popova Šapka **77** D3	Porriño **34** A3	Portelo **34** C3
Pontón, Pto del ... **35** E2	Popov Most **76** A1	Porsangen **95** E1	Port-en-Bessin ... **18** C3

Port Erin **6** A1	Port-Leucate **32** B2	Port of Ness **2** B2
Pórtes **87** F2	Port-Louis **22** B4	Porto Garibaldi ... **61** D2
Portet-d'Aspet,	Portman **45** D3	Porto, G de....... **33** E3
Col de **37** F2	Port-Manech **22** B3	Pórto Germenó ... **87** E1
Portadown **13** D2	Portmarnock **13** E4	Portogruaro....... **59** E4
Portaferry **13** E2	Portnacroish **4** B1	Portohéli **87** E2
Portezuelo **39** D3	Portnaguran **2** B2	Pórto Kágio **87** D4
Port Glasgow **4** C2	Portnahaven **4** A2	Pörtom **102** B2
Portglenone **13** E1	Port-Navalo **22** C4	Portomaggiore **61** D2
Porthcawl **8** C2	Porto (F) **33** E3	Portomarín........ **34** B2
Porthmadog **6** A3	Porto (P) **34** A4	Porto-Maurizio **31** F3
Porthmós	Porto Azzurro **62** C1	Porto Moniz....... **42** A3
Elafoníssou **90** A1	Pórto Carrás **80** B4	Portomouro **34** A2
Portící **64** B4	Porto Ceresio **58** A4	Portonovo **34** A2
Portíle de Fier ... **114** C1	Porto Cervo **66** B1	Porto Petro **45** F3
Portilla de la Reina .. **35** E2	Porto Cesareo **65** F4	Porto Pino........ **66** B4
Portillo **35** E4	Porto Cristo **45** F3	Pórto Ráfti **88** A1
Portillo de la	Porto de Envalira .. **32** A2	Porto Recanati ... **61** F4
Canda **34** C3	Porto de Lagos ... **42** A2	Porto Rotondo **66** C1
Portillo de	Porto de Mós..... **38** A3	Portorož **70** A3
Padornelo **34** C3	Porto do	Porto San Giorgio .. **61** F4
Portillo, Pto del... **39** E2	Barqueiro **34** B1	Porto Sant' Elpidio .. **61** F4
Portimão **42** A2	Porto do Son..... **34** A2	Porto Santo **42** A3
Portimo........... **99** D2	Porto Empedocle .. **68** B4	Porto Santo, I de .. **42** A3
Portinatx, Cala de .. **45** D3	Porto Ercole **63** D2	Porto Santo
Portishead **9** D2	Portoferraio **62** C1	Stefano **63** D2
Port-Joinville **24** A3	Portofino **60** A3	Portoscuso **66** A4
Port Láirge **15** D4	Porto Empedocle .. **68** B4	Porto Tolle **61** D2
Portland, Bill of ... **9** D4		Porto Torres...... **66** A2
Port-la-Nouvelle .. **32** B2		
Portlaoise **13** D4		

Porto-Vecchio 33 F4
Portovenere 60 B3
Portpatrick 4 B3
Portree 2 B3
Portrush 13 D1
Port-Ste-Marie 28 C3
Port-St-Louis 30 B4
Port St Mary 6 A1
Portsalon 13 D1
Pörtschach 70 A1
Portsmouth 9 F3
Portstewart 13 D1
Port-sur-Saône 27 D1
Port Talbot 8 C2
Porttipahdan
   tekojärvi 95 E4
Portugalete 36 B1
Portumna 12 C4
Port-Vendres 32 B2
Port William 4 C4
Porvoo 107 F2
Porvoonjoki 107 F2
Porzuna 40 A4
Posada 66 C2
Posadas 43 E2
Pöschenhöhe 56 C3
Pošechonje-
   Volodarsk 111 F1
Posedarje 74 C1
Posets, Pico 37 E2
Posio 99 E3
Positano 64 B4
Poßneck 52 C3
Possidi 80 A4
Possidonía 88 B2
Posta 63 F1
Postavy 111 D3
Postira 75 D2
Postojna 70 B2
Postojnska jama . . . 70 A2
Poštorná 57 F1
Posušje 75 E1
Potamí 80 C1
Potamiá 87 D3
Potamiés 91 E4
Potamós
   (Andikíthira) 90 A2
Potamós (Kíthira) . . . 90 A1
Potamoúla 82 C3
Potenza 64 C4
Potenza R. 61 E4
Potenza Picenza . . . 61 F4
Potes 35 E2
Potídea, N. 80 A4
Potigny 18 C3
Potoci 75 F1
Potok 71 D2
Potós 80 C3
Potpećko jez 76 B1
Potsdam 49 D4
Pottenstein 57 E3
Potters Bar 9 F2
Pöttmes 55 F2
Potton 9 F1
Pouancé 23 D4
Pougues-les-
   Eaux 26 A2
Pouilly (Nièvre) 26 A2
Pouilly (Rhône) 26 B4
Pouilly-en-Auxois . . . 26 C2
Poulaphouca
   Reservoir 13 D4
Poúlari, Akr. 92 C1
Pouldu, le 22 B3
Pouliguen, le 24 A2
Poúlithra 87 E3
Poúnda 88 C3

Poúnda, Akr. 84 B4
Pournári 83 E2
Pournári, Teh L 82 C2
Pourniás, Kólpos . . . 85 D1
Pourri, Mt 31 D1
Poussu 99 F3
Pouyastruc 37 E1
Pouzauges 24 C3
Pouzin, le 30 B2
Považská
   Bystrica 112 B3
Poveda 40 C2
Povlja 75 E2
Povljana 70 C4
Povljen 72 C4
Póvoa de Lanhoso . . 34 A4
Póvoa de Varzim . . . 34 A4
Powerscourt 13 D4
Powys 9 D1
Poysdorf 57 F2
Pöytyä 107 D2
Poza de la Sal 36 A2
Požarevac 73 D3
Požega 72 C4
Požeranje 77 D2
Poznań 112 A1
Pozo Alcón 44 B2
Pozoblanco 43 F1
Pozo Cañada 44 C1
Pozo de
   Guadalajara 40 B2
Pozo Higuera 44 C3
Pozohondo 44 C1
Pozondón 41 D2
Pozozal, Pto. 35 F2
Pozuelo (Castilla-la-
   Mancha) 44 C1
Pozuelo
   (Extremadura) 39 D2
Pozuelo de
   Calatrava 40 A4
Pozzallo 69 D4
Pozzomaggiore 66 B2
Pozzuoli 64 A4
Pozzuolo 59 F3
Präbichl 57 D3
Prača 76 A1
Prachatice 56 C1
Prada, Emb de 34 C3
Pradairo 34 C2
Pradarena, Pso di . . 60 B3
Pradelles 29 F2
Prádena 36 A4
Prades (E) 37 F4
Prades (F) 32 B2
Prado del Rey 43 D3
Pradoluengo 36 A2
Prägraten 59 E2
Praha 53 F4
Prahecq 24 C4
Prahova 115 D1
Prahovo 73 F3
Praia a Mare 67 E2
Praia da Barra 38 B1
Praia da Rocha 42 A2
Praia da Vieira 38 A2
Praia de Mira 38 B1
Praia de Santa
   Cruz 38 A3
Praia de Tocha 38 B2
Prali 31 E2
Pralognan 31 D1
Pra-Loup 31 D2
Prámanda 82 C2
Pramollo, Pso di . . . 59 F2
Prangio 81 F1
Pranjani 72 C4

Prapatnica 75 D1
Prassiá 83 D2
Prassiés 90 C3
Præstø 108 C4
Prat de Compte 41 F1
Pratella 64 A3
Prati di Tivo 63 F1
Prato (Toscana) 60 C3
Prato (Umbria) 63 E1
Pratola Peligna 64 A2
Pratomagno 61 D4
Prato-Sornico 58 A3
Prats-de-Mollo 32 B3
Pravdinsk 110 B4
Pravia 35 D1
Praz 27 E4
Prebold 70 B2
Précy-sous-Thil 26 B2
Predappio 61 D3
Predazzo 59 D3
Preddvor 70 B2
Predeal 113 D4
Predejane 77 E1
Predel 70 A2
Predela 115 D3
Predil, Pso di 59 F2
Predjama 70 A2
Predoi 59 D2
Predošćica 70 B3
Pré-en-Pail 23 E3
Preetz 48 B2
Pregarten 57 D2
Preiner Gscheid 57 E3
Prekaja 71 D4
Preko 74 C1
Preljina 73 D4
Prelog 71 D1
Preločšica 71 D2
Premantura 70 A4
Prémery 26 A2
Premià de Mar 32 B4
Premilcuore 61 D3
Premnitz 49 D4
Premuda 74 B1
Premuda I. 74 B1
Prenj 75 F1
Prenjas 77 D4
Prenzlau 49 E3
Prepolac 77 D1
Přerov 112 A3
Prerow 48 C1
Pré-St-Didier 27 E4
Preševo 77 E2
Presjeka 76 B2
Preslav 115 E2
Presolana, Pso
   della 58 B4
Prešov 112 B3
Prespansko Ez 77 D4
Pressath 53 D4
Pressbaum 57 E2
Prestatyn 6 B2
Presteigne 9 D1
Preste, la 32 B3
Prestfoss 104 C3
Přeštice 56 C1
Preston 6 B2
Prestonpans 5 D2
Prestwick 4 C1
Pretoro 64 A2
Prettau 59 D2
Prettin 53 D1
Pretzsch 53 D1
Preuilly 25 D3
Préveli 90 C4
Préveza 82 B3

Préveza (Nomos) . . . 82 B2
Prevršac 71 D3
Prezid 70 B3
Pribini 71 E4
Priboj (BH) 72 B3
Priboj (Srbija) 76 B1
Příbram 53 F4
Priego 40 C2
Priego de
   Córdoba 43 F3
Prien 56 B3
Prienai 110 C4
Prievidza 112 B3
Prigradica 75 E2
Prijeboj 70 C3
Prijedor 71 D3
Prijepolje 76 B1
Prilep 77 E3
Prilike 73 D4
Priluka 75 E1
Priluki 113 F1
Primaube, la 29 E3
Primel-Trégastel . . . 22 B2
Primišlje 70 C3
Primolano 59 D3
Primorsk 111 D1
Primošten 75 D2
Primstal 54 B1
Princetown 8 C3
Prinés 90 C3
Prínos 80 C3
Prior, C 34 B1
Prip' at' 112 C1
Prisad 77 E3
Prislop 113 D3
Prisoje 75 E1
Priština 77 D2
Pritzerbe 49 D4
Pritzier 48 B3
Pritzwalk 48 C3
Privas 30 B2
Priverno 63 F3
Privlaka (Vincovci) . . 71 F2
Privlaka (Zadar) 70 C4
Prizren 77 D2
Prizzi 68 B3
Prnjavor (BH) 71 E3
Prnjavor (Srbija) . . . 72 B3
Proaza 35 D1
Probištip 77 E2
Probstzella 52 C3
Procida 64 A4
Pródromos 83 F4
Proenca-a-Nova 38 B3
Proevska Banja 77 E2
Profitis Ilias 93 E1
Profondeville 50 C4
Próhoma 79 F3
Prokletije 76 C2
Prokópi 84 A3
Prokuplje 77 D1
Prolom 77 D1
Prómahi 79 E2
Promahónas 80 A1
Promina, V. 75 D2
Promíri 84 A2
Pronsfeld 51 D4
Propriano 33 F4
Proskinás 83 F4
Prosna 112 A2
Prossedi 63 F3
Prossílio 81 D2
Prossotsáni 80 B2
Prostějov 112 A3
Próti 80 B2
Próti, N 86 B3
Protoklissio 81 F1

Prötzel 49 E4
Proussós 83 D3
Provatónas 81 F2
Provence, Canal de . 30 C4
Provenchères 21 E4
Provins 20 A4
Prozor 75 E1
Prudhoe 5 E3
Prukljansko jezero . . 75 D1
Prüm 51 D4
Pruna 43 E3
Prunetta 60 C3
Prut 113 D3
Prut 113 E4
Pružany 112 C1
Prvič 70 B4
Przasnysz 112 B1
Przełęcz Dukielska . 112 C3
Przemyśl 112 C2
Przybiernów 49 F2
Psača 77 E2
Psahná 84 B4
Psáka 82 B2
Psális, Akr. 88 A4
Psará 85 E4
Psarádes 78 C2
Psará, N 85 E4
Psári (Arkadía) 86 C2
Psári (Korinthía) . . . 87 D1
Psári (Mt) 80 C3
Psáthi 88 B4
Psathópirgos 83 D4
Psathotópi 82 C2
Psérimos, N 89 F3
Psihikó 83 E2
Psihró 91 E4
Psínthos 93 F1
Pskov 111 D2
Pskovskoje
   Ozero 111 D2
Ps'ol 113 F2
Pšov 53 E3
Psunj 71 E2
Pteléa 80 C2
Ptéri 83 D3
Ptolemaïda 79 D3
Ptóo 84 A4
Ptuj 70 C1
Puchberg 57 E3
Pučišća 75 E2
Puckeridge 9 F2
Puçol 41 E3
Pudasjärvi 99 E3
Puebla de
   Almenara 40 B3
Puebla de Beleña . . 40 B1
Puebla de
   Benifasar 41 F2
Puebla de Don
   Fadrique 44 B2
Puebla de D.
   Rodrigo 39 F3
Puebla de
   Guzmán 42 C2
Puebla de la
   Calzada 39 D4
Puebla de la Reina . . 39 D4
Puebla de la
   Caramiñal 34 A2
Puebla de Lillo 35 E2
Puebla de Obando . . 39 D3
Puebla de
   Sanabria 34 C3
Puebla de Trives . . . 34 C3
Puebla Tornesa 41 F3
Pueblica de V. 35 D3

Puente de Domingo
   Flórez 34 C3
Puente de Génave . . 44 B1
Puente de los
   Fierros 35 D2
Puente Genil 43 F3
Puente la Reina 36 C2
Puente la Reina
   de Jaca 37 D2
Puentenansa 35 F2
Puente Nuevo,
   Emb de 43 E1
Puentes, Emb de . . . 44 C2
Puentes Viejas,
   Emb de 40 B1
Puente Viesgo 35 F2
Puerto Castilla 39 E2
Puerto de Alcudia . . 45 F2
Puerto de Andratx . . 45 E3
Puerto de la Cruz . . . 42 B4
Puerto de la
   Encina 43 E3
Puerto del Rosario . . 42 C4
Puerto de
   Mazarrón 45 D3
Puerto de
   Pollença 45 F2
Puerto de
   San Vicente 39 F3
Puerto de Sóller . . . 45 E2
Puerto Lápice 40 B4
Puertollano 44 A1
Puerto Lumbreras . . 44 C3
Puerto Real 43 D4
Puerto Serrano 43 E3
Pugets-Théniers . . . 31 E3
Puglia 65 D3
Puhos (Oulun
   Lääni) 99 E3
Puhos (Pohjois-
   Karjalan Lääni) . . . 103 F3
Puhosjärvi 99 E3
Puhovac 71 F4
Puigcerda 32 A3
Puignal 32 A2
Puig-reig 32 A3
Puigsacalm 32 B3
Puiseaux 25 F1
Puisserguier 30 A4
Pujols 28 B2
Pukë 76 C3
Pukiš 72 B3
Pukkila 107 F2
Pula (HR) 70 A4
Pula (I) 66 B4
Pulaj 76 B3
Puławy 112 C2
Pulborough 10 C3
Pulkau 57 E2
Pulkkila 99 D4
Pulpi 44 C3
Pulsnitz 53 E2
Pułtusk 112 B1
Punat 70 B3
Punkaharju 103 F3
Punkalaidun 107 E2
Punta Ala 62 C1
Punta di Penna 64 B2
Puntagorda 42 A4
Punta Križa 70 B4
Punta Raisi 68 B2
Punta Umbría 42 C3
Puokio 99 E4
Puolanka 99 E4
Purbach 57 F3
Purchena 44 B3

Purgstall 57 E3
Purkersdorf 57 E2
Purmerend 16 C2
Purnu 103 D3
Purullena 44 B3
Puruvesi 103 F3
Puškin 111 D1
Püspökladány 112 C4
Pustoška 111 D2
Pusula 107 E2
Puszcza 112 C1
Putanges 18 C4
Putbus 49 D1
Putgarten 49 D1
Putignano 65 E3
Putinci 72 C2
Putivl' 113 F1
Putlitz 48 C3
Puttelange 21 E3
Puttgarden 48 B1
Puula 103 D3
Puumala 103 E3
Puy de Dôme 29 E1
Puy-de-Dôme
   (Dépt) 29 E1
Puy de Sancy 29 E1
Puy-en-Velay, le . . . 30 A2
Puy-Guillaume 26 A4
Puylaurens 29 D4
Puy-l'Evêque 29 D3
Puymirol 28 C3
Puymorens, Col de . 32 A2
Pwllheli 6 A3
Pyhä-Häkki 103 D2
Pyhäjärvi
   (Hameen Lääni) . . 107 E1
Pyäjärvi (Oulun
   Lääni) 103 D1
Pyhäjärvi (Pohjois-
   Karjalan Lääni) . . . 103 F3
Pyhäjärvi (Turun ja
   Porin Lääni) 107 D2
Pyhäjärvi L 103 D1
Pyhäjoki (Oulun
   Lääni) 99 D4
Pyhäjoki (Turun ja
   Porin Lääni) 107 D2
Pyhäjoki R. 99 D4
Pyhälto 103 F4
Pyhäntä
   (Piipola) 103 D1
Pyhäntä (Ristijärvi) . . 99 E3
Pyhäranta 107 D2
Pyhäsalmi 103 D1
Pyhäselkä 103 F2
Pyhäselkä L. 103 F2
Pyhätunturi 99 D2
Pyhatunturi 99 E2
Pyhävuori 102 C2
Pyhitysvaara 99 E3
Pyhrnpaß 57 D3
Pyhtää 107 F2
Pyla 28 A2
Pylkönmäki 103 D2
Pyrénées-
   Atlantiques 28 A4
Pyrénées-
   Orientales 32 B2
Pyrénées, Parc
   Nat des 37 E2
Pyrzyce 49 F3
Pyttis 107 F2

Q

Qaf'e Shllahut 76 C3
Qaf'e Shtamës 76 C4
Quakenbrück 17 E2
Quarré-les-
   Tombes 26 B2
Quarteira 42 B3
Quarto d'Altino 61 D1

Quartu San Elena . . 66 B4
Quatre Chemins . . . 24 B3
Quatretonda 41 E4
Quedlinburg 52 C2
Queenborough 11 D2
Queen Elizabeth
   Forest Park 4 C2
Queensferry 6 B2
Quejigares, Pto de . . 40 A4
Queluz 38 A4

Queralbs 32 B3
Querfurt 52 C2
Quérigut 32 A2
Quero 40 B3
Quesada 44 B2
Quesnoy, le 20 A2
Questembert 22 C4
Quettehou 18 B3
Quiberon 22 C4
Quickborn 48 A2

Quiévrain 50 B4
Quigley's Point 13 D1
Quillan 32 B2
Quillane, Col de la . . 32 A2
Quillebeuf 19 D3
Quimper 22 B3
Quimperlé 22 B3
Quincinetto 31 E1
Quincoces de Yuso . 36 A1
Quingey 27 D2

Quintana
   (Andalucia) 43 E2
Quintana
   (Extremadura) . . . 39 E4
Quintana del
   Puente 35 F3
Quintana Martín
   Galíndez 36 A2
Quintanar de la
   Orden 40 B3

Quintanar de la
   Sierra 36 B3
Quintanar del Rey . . 40 C4
Quintana
   Redonda 36 B3
Quintanilha 34 C4
Quintanilla de
   Onésimo 35 F4
Quintin 22 C3
Quinto 37 D4

Quinzano d'Oglio . . 60 B1
Quipar, R 44 C2
Quiroga 34 C2
Quissac 30 B3
Qukës 77 D4
Quoich, L 2 C4

R

Raab **56** C2
Raab *R* **57** E4
Raabs **57** E1
Raahe **99** D4
Raajärvi **99** D2
Rääkkylä **103** F2
Raalte **17** D2
Raanujärvi **99** D2
Raasay **2** B3
Raasay, Sd of **2** B3
Raattama **95** D4
Rab **70** B4
Rab *I* **70** B4
Rába **112** A4
Rabac **70** B3
Rábade **34** B1
Rabastens **29** D4
Rabastens-de-Bigorre **37** E1
Rabat **68** B4
Rabe **72** C1
Rabka **112** B3
Rabrovo (Makedonija) **77** F3
Rabrovo (Srbija) **73** E3
Rača (Kragujevac) **73** D3
Rača (Radan) **77** D1
Racconigi **31** E2
Rače **70** C1
Rachov **112** C3
Racibórz **112** A2
Račinovci **72** B3
Račišće **75** E2
Radalj **72** B3
Radan **77** D1
Rădăuți **113** D3
Radbuza **56** B1
Rade **48** A3
Råde **105** D3
Radeberg **53** E2
Radebeul **53** E2
Radeburg **53** E2
Radeče **70** B2
Radechov **112** C2
Radenci **70** C1
Radenthein **59** F2
Radevowald **17** E4
Radici, Pso delle **60** C3
Radicondoli **60** C4
Radika **77** D3
Radimlje **75** F2
Radiovce **77** D3
Radlje **70** B1
Radljevo **72** C3
Radnice **53** E4
Radohinës, Maj'e **76** C2
Radojevo **73** D1
Radom **112** B2
Radomsko **112** B2
Radomyšl' **113** E2
Radotin **53** F4
Radovče **76** B2
Radoviči **76** B3
Radoviš **77** F3
Radovljica **70** A2
Radovnica **77** E2
Radøy **104** A2
Radstadt **59** F1
Radstädter Tauernpaß **59** F1
Radstock **9** D2
Raduša **75** E1
Radusa **77** D3
Radviliškis **110** C3
Radzyń Podlaski **112** C2
Raesfeld **17** E3
Raffadali **68** B4
Rafina **88** A1
Ragama **39** F1
Raglan **9** D2
Rago **97** F1
Ragua, Pto de la **44** B3
Raguhn **53** D1
Ragunda **101** F2
Ragusa **69** D4
Rahden **17** F2
Rahes **83** F3
Rahlstedt **48** B3
Raia, Rib de **38** B4
Rain **55** F2
Räisälä **99** E2
Raisduoddarhal'di **94** C2
Raisio **107** D2
Raittijärvi **94** C3
Rajac **73** F3
Raja-Jooseppi **95** F3
Rajamäki **107** E2
Rajince **77** E2
Raka **70** C2
Rakalj **70** A4
Rakitna **70** B2
Rakitnica **71** D2
Rakkestad **105** D3
Rakova Bara **73** E3
Rakovac **71** E3
Rakovica **70** C3
Rakovník **53** E4
Rakvere **110** C1
Ralja **73** D3
Ram **73** D2
Ramacca **69** D3
Ramales de la Victoria **36** A1
Ramallosa **34** A2
Ramberg **97** E1
Rambervillers **21** D4
Rambouillet **19** E4
Rambucourt **20** C4
Ramno **77** D2
Ramnoús **84** B4
Ramor, L **13** D3
Ramsau **56** B4
Ramsau **59** F1
Ramsele **101** F2
Ramsey (Cambridge) **9** F1
Ramsey (I of Man) **6** A1
Ramsgate **11** D3
Ramsjö **101** E3
Ramstein **54** B1
Ramsund **94** B3
Ramundberget **101** D2
Ramvik **101** F2
Rana **97** D3
Ranalt **59** D2
Rance **22** C3
Randaberg **104** A3
Randak **104** B3
Randalstown **13** E2
Randan **26** A4
Randanne **29** E1
Randazzo **69** D3
Randers **108** B2
Randijaure **98** A2
Randow **49** E2
Randsfjorden **105** D2
Råneå **98** C3
Råneälven **98** B2
Rangsdorf **49** E4
Rankweil **58** B2
Rannoch, L **4** C1
Ranovac **73** E3
Rantasalmi **103** E3
Rantsila **99** D4
Ranua **99** D3
Raon-l'Etape **21** E4
Rapallo **60** A3
Rapolano Terme **61** D4
Rapolla **64** C3
Rapperswil **58** A2
Rapsáni **83** E1
Raptópoulo **86** C3
Raša **70** A3
Räsälä **103** E2
Raša *R* **70** A3
Rasbo **106** B3
Rascafría **40** A1
Rasdorf **52** B3
Raseiniai **110** C3
Rasimbegov Most **77** E4
Rasina **73** E4
Raška **76** C1
Rasno **75** E2
Raso, C **38** A4
Rasquera **41** F1
Rastatt **54** C2
Rastede **47** F3
Rastegai'sa **95** E2
Rastenberg **52** C2
Rastenfeld **57** E2
Rasueros **39** F1
Rätan **101** E3
Rateče **70** A1
Ratekau **48** B2
Rates **34** A4
Rathdowney **12** C4
Rathdrum **13** D4
Rathenow **49** D4
Rathfriland **13** E2
Rathkeale **14** B3
Rathlin I **13** E1
Rath Luirc **14** B3
Rathmelton **13** D1
Rathmore **14** B4
Rathmullan **13** D1
Raticosa, Pso della **61** D3
Ratingen **17** E4
Ratkovac **76** C2
Ratkovo **72** B2
Ratten **57** E3
Rattenberg **59** D1
Rattersdorf **57** F3
Rattray **5** D1
Rattray Head **3** E3
Rättvik **101** E4
Ratzeburg **48** B2
Raubling **56** B3
Raucourt-et-Flaba **20** C2
Raudanjoki **99** D2
Raudaskylä **102** C1
Raufarhöfn **96** C1
Raufoss **105** D2
Rauha **103** E4
Rauhamäki **103** D3
Rauland **104** B3
Rauma (N) **100** B3
Rauma (SF) **107** D2
Rauris **59** E1
Rautalampi **103** D2
Rautas **94** C4
Rautavaara **103** E1
Rautio **102** C1
Rautjärvi **103** F3
Ravan **71** F4
Ravanica **73** E4
Ravanjska **70** C4
Ravanusa **68** C4
Ravello **64** B4
Raven **71** D2
Ravenna **61** D2
Ravensbrück **49** D3
Ravensburg **55** D4
Ravna Dubrava **77** E1
Ravna Gora **70** B3
Ravna Reka **73** E3
Ravne na Koroškem **70** B1
Ravnište **77** D1
Ravnje **72** B3
Ravno **75** F2
Ravno Bučje **73** F4
Ravno, G **75** E1
Rawicz **112** A2
Rawtenstall **6** C2
Rayleigh **11** D2
Rayol **31** D4
Räyrinki **102** C2
Ražana **72** C4
Ražanac **70** C4
Razboj **71** E3
Razbojna **77** D1
Raždaginja **76** C1
Razelm **113** E4
Razgrad **115** E2
Razlog **115** D3
Razlovci **77** F2
Raz, Pte du **22** A3
Reading **9** F2
Reales **43** E4
Réalmont **32** B1
Rebais **20** A4
Rebbenesøy **94** B2
Rebordelo **34** C4
Reç **76** C3
Recanati **61** F4
Recco **60** A3
Recey **26** C1
Rechnitz **57** F4
Rečica (HR) **70** C3
Rečica (RB) **111** E4
Recke **17** E2
Recklinghausen **17** E3
Recknitz **48** C2
Recoaro Terme **59** D4
Recuerda **36** A4
Recz **49** F2
Redange **21** D2
Red B **13** E1
Redcar **5** F4
Redditch **9** E1
Redhill **10** C3
Redon **23** D4
Redondela **34** A3
Redondo **38** C4
Redruth **8** B4
Ree, L **12** C3
Rees **17** D3
Reeth **6** C1
Refsnes **94** A3
Reftele **109** D2
Rega **49** F2
Regalbuto **69** D3
Regen **56** B2
Regensburg **56** B2
Regenstauf **56** B2
Reggello **61** D4
Reggio di Calabria **67** E4
Reggiolo **60** C2
Reggio nell' Emilia **60** C2
Reghin **113** D4
Regnitz **55** E1
Reguengos de Monsaraz **42** B1
Rehau **53** D4
Rehburg-Loccum **48** A4
Rehden **17** F2
Rehna **48** B2
Reichenau (A) **57** E3
Reichenau (CH) **58** B2
Reichenbach (Dresden) **53** F2
Reichenbach (Chemnitz) **53** D3
Reichertshofen **55** F2
Reichshoffen **21** E3
Reigate **10** C3
Reignier **27** D4
Ré, Ile de **24** B4
Reillanne **30** C3
Reims **20** B3
Reinach **27** F2
Reinbek **48** B3
Reinberg **49** D1
Reine **97** E1
Reinfeld **48** B2
Reinheim **54** C1
Reinli **104** C2
Reinosa **35** F2
Reinøy **94** C2
Reisaelva **94** C2
Reischenhart **56** B3
Reisjärvi **103** D1
Reiss **3** D2
Reit im Winkl **56** B4
Reitzenhain **53** E3
Reka **70** A3
Rekovac **73** E4
Remagen **51** E4
Rémalard **23** F3
Remeskylä **103** D1
Remich **21** D2
Remiremont **27** D1
Remolinos **36** C3
Remouchamps **51** D4
Remoulins **30** B3
Rempstone **7** D3
Remscheid **17** E4
Rémuzat **30** C2
Rena **105** D2
Renaix **50** B3
Renazé **23** E4
Renchen **54** C3
Rende **67** E2
Rendina (Makedonia) **80** B3
Rendína (Thessalía) **83** D3
Rendsburg **48** A2
Renginio **83** F3
Rengsdorf **51** E4
Reni **113** E4
Renish Pt **2** A3
Renko **107** E2
Renkum **17** D3
Rennebu **100** C2
Rennerod **51** F3
Rennes **23** D3
Rennes-les-Bains **32** B2
Rennesøy **104** A3
Rennweg **59** F2
Reno **61** D2
Rensjön **94** C4
Renwez **20** B2
Réole, la **28** B2
Replot **102** B2
Replotfjärden **102** B2
Repojoki **95** E3
Reposaari **102** B3
République, Col de la **30** B1
Repvag **95** E1
Requena **41** D4
Réquista **29** E3
Rerik **48** C2
Resanovci **71** D4
Resavica **73** E3
Reschenpaß **58** C2
Resen (Makedonija) **77** D4
Resen (Srbija) **77** E2
Resende **34** B4
Resia, Pso di **58** C2
Reșița **114** C1
Resko **49** F2
Resmo **109** E3
Resna **76** B3
Resnik **73** D3
Ressons **19** F3
Restafjorden **94** C2
Restelica **77** D3
Resuttano **68** C3
Retezatului, M **114** C1
Rethel **20** B3
Rethem **48** A4
Rethen **52** B1
Réthimno **90** C3
Réthimno (Nomos) **90** C3
Retiers **23** D3
Retortillo, Emb de **43** E2
Retuerta **41** D1
Retuerta del Bullaque **39** F3
Retuerta, Emb de **36** A3
Retz **57** E2
Reuilly **25** E3
Reus **37** F4
Reusel **16** C4
Reuss **27** F2
Reuterstadt-Stavenhagen **49** D2
Reutlingen **55** D3
Reutte **58** C1
Revard, Mt **27** D4
Revel **29** D4
Revesbotn **95** D1
Revigny **20** C4
Revin **20** B2
Řevnikov **53** F3
Revolcadores **44** C2
Revonlahti **99** D4
Revsnes **104** B1
Rewal **49** F1
Reyðarfjörður **96** C2
Reykholt **96** A2
Reykjavik **96** A2
Rēzekne **111** D2
Rezzato **60** B1
Rezzoaglio **60** A3
Rgotina **73** F3
Rhaeadr **8** C1
Rhayader **8** C1
Rheda-Wiedenbrück **17** F3
Rhede **17** D3
Rhein **17** D3
Rheinbach **51** E4
Rheinberg **17** D3
Rheinböllen **54** B1
Rheine **17** E2
Rheinfelden (CH) **27** F2
Rheinfelden (D) **54** C4
Rheinhausen **17** D3
Rheinland-Pfalz **51** E4
Rheinsberg **49** D3
Rheinwaldhorn **58** B3
Rhêmes N.D. **31** E1
Rhenen **16** C3
Rheydt **17** D4
Rhinau **21** E4
Rhinow **49** D4
Rho **60** A1
Rhondda **8** C2
Rhône **26** C4
Rhône (Dépt) **26** B4
Rhône à Sète, Canal du **30** B3
Rhosneigr **6** A2
Rhossili **8** C2
Rhüden **52** B1
Rhum **2** B4
Rhum, Sd of **2** B4
Rhune, la **28** A4
Rhuthun **6** B3
Rhyl **6** B2
Rhynern **17** E3
Rhynie **3** E4
Riaillé **23** D4
Riákia **79** E3
Rial **34** A2
Riaño **35** E2
Riaño, Emb de **35** E2
Rians **30** C4
Riansares R **40** B3
Rianxo **34** A2
Riaza **36** A4
Ribadavia **34** B3
Ribadelago **34** C3
Ribadeo **34** C1
Riba de Saelices **40** C1
Riba de Santiuste **36** B4
Ribadesella **35** E1
Ribarci **77** E2
Ribariće **76** C1
Riba-roja, Emb de **37** E4
Ribarska Banja **73** E4
Ribas de Campos **35** E3
Ribas de Sil **34** B2
Ribatejo **38** B3
Ribble **6** C2
Ribe **108** A3
Ribeauvillé **27** E1
Ribécourt **19** F3
Ribeira de Pena **34** B4
Ribeira, Emb de la **34** B1
Ribemont **20** A2
Ribera **68** B3
Ribérac **28** C1
Ribera de Cardós **32** A2
Ribera del Fresno **43** D1
Ribes de Freser **32** B3
Ribiers **30** C3
Ribnica (BH) **71** F4
Ribnica (Kočevje) **70** B2
Ribnica (Postojna) **70** A3
Ribnica na Pohorju **70** B1
Ribnik **70** C2
Ribnitz-Damgarten **48** C1
Ribolla **62** C1
Říčany **53** F4
Riccia **64** B3
Riccione **61** E3
Riceys, les **26** B1
Richelieu **25** D3
Richmond (London) **9** F2
Richmond (Yorks) **6** C1
Richtenberg **49** D1
Rickling **48** A2
Ricla **36** C4
Ricobayo, Emb de **35** D4
Riđica **72** B1
Riec **22** B3
Ried (Oberösterreich) **56** C3
Ried (Tirol) **58** C2
Riedenburg **55** F2
Riedlingen **55** D3
Riegel **54** C3
Riegersburg **57** F4
Riego de la Vega **35** D3
Riesa **53** E2
Riesi **68** C4
Riestedt **52** C2
Rietberg **17** F3
Rieti **63** E2
Rieumes **29** D4
Rieupeyroux **29** E3
Rieux **37** F1
Riez **31** D3
Riezlern **58** B2
Rīga **110** C2
Rigáni **83** D4
Rīgas Jūras Līcis **110** B2
Rigeo **83** E2
Rigi **58** A2
Rignac **29** E3
Rignano Flaminio **63** E2
Rihéa **87** E3
Riihimäki **107** E2
Riisitunturi **99** E2
Riistavesi **103** E2
Riječa **72** B4
Rijeka **70** B3
Rijeka Crnojevića **76** B3
Rijssen **17** D2
Riksgränsen **94** B3
Rila **115** D3
Rila *Mts* **115** D3
Rillo **41** D2
Rillo de Gallo **40** C1
Rimavská-Sobota **112** B3
Rimbo **106** B3
Rimini **61** E3
Rîmnicu Sărat **113** E4
Rîmnicu Vîlcea **115** D1
Rímnio **79** E4
Rimske Toplice **70** B2
Rincón de la Victoria **43** F4
Rincón de Soto **36** C2
Rindal **100** C2
Ringaskiddy **14** C4
Ringe **108** B4
Ringebu **100** C3
Ringford **4** C3
Ringkøbing **108** A3
Ringkøbing Fjord **108** A3
Ring of Kerry **14** A4
Ringsaker **105** D2
Ringstad **104** A1
Ringsted **108** C3
Ringvassøy **94** B2
Ringwood **9** E3
Rinia, N **88** C2
Rinkaby **109** D3
Rinns Pt **4** A2
Rinteln **52** A1
Rinvyle Pt **12** A3
Rio **83** D4
Riocavado de la Sierra **36** A3
Riogordo **43** F3
Riola Sardo **66** A3
Riolo Terme **61** D3
Riom **26** A4
Riomaggiore **60** B3
Rio Maior **38** A3
Rio Marina **62** C1
Riom-ès-Montagnes **29** E1
Rionero in Vulture **64** C3
Rio, Punta del **44** B4
Rioseco de Tapia **35** D2
Rioz **27** D2
Ripač **70** C4
Ripanj **73** D3
Riparbella **60** C4
Ripatransone **61** F4
Ripley **7** D3
Ripoli **32** A3
Ripollet **32** A4
Ripon **6** C1
Riquewihr **27** E1
Risan **76** B2
Risbäck **97** E4
Risca **9** D2
Riscle **28** B4
Risle **19** D4
Risnes **104** B4
Risnjak **70** B3
Risør **104** C4
Risøyhamn **94** A3
Risøysundet **94** A3
Rissa **100** C1
Ristiina **103** E3
Ristijärvi **99** E4
Ristilampi **99** D2
Ristovac **77** E2
Risum-Lindholm **47** F1
Ritini **79** E4
Ritoniemi **103** E2
Ritsóna **84** A4
Rittmannshausen **52** B3
Riudoms **37** F4
Riva **58** C4
Rivarolo Canavese **31** E1
Rive-de-Gier **30** B1
Rives **30** C1
Rivesaltes **32** B2
Rivière-Thibouville, la **19** D3

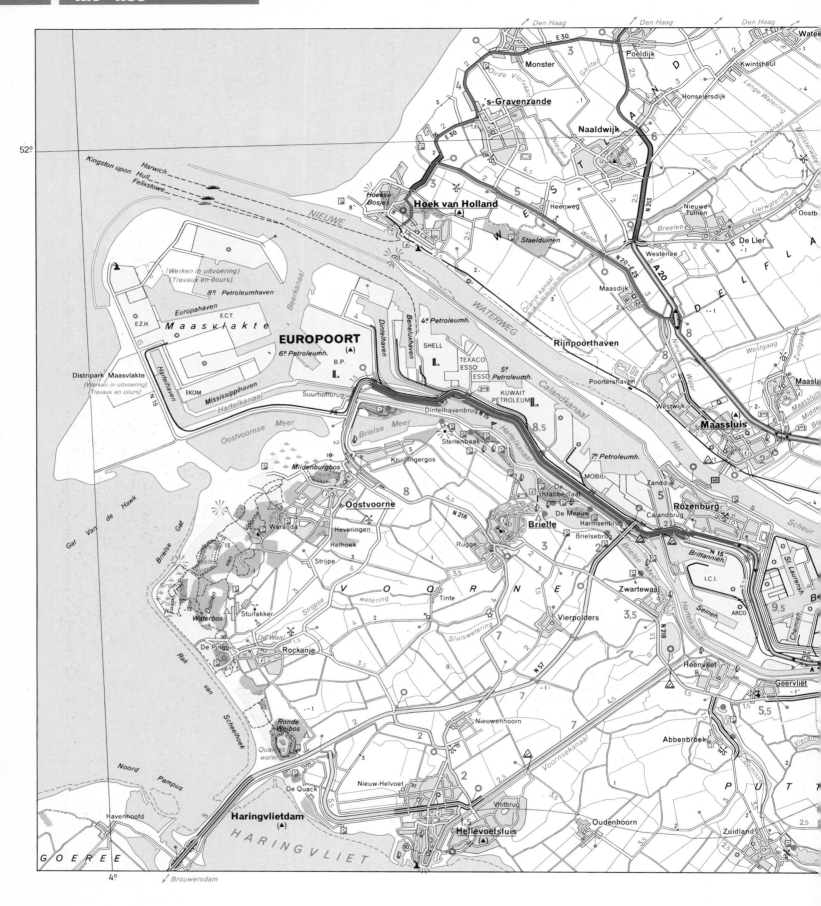

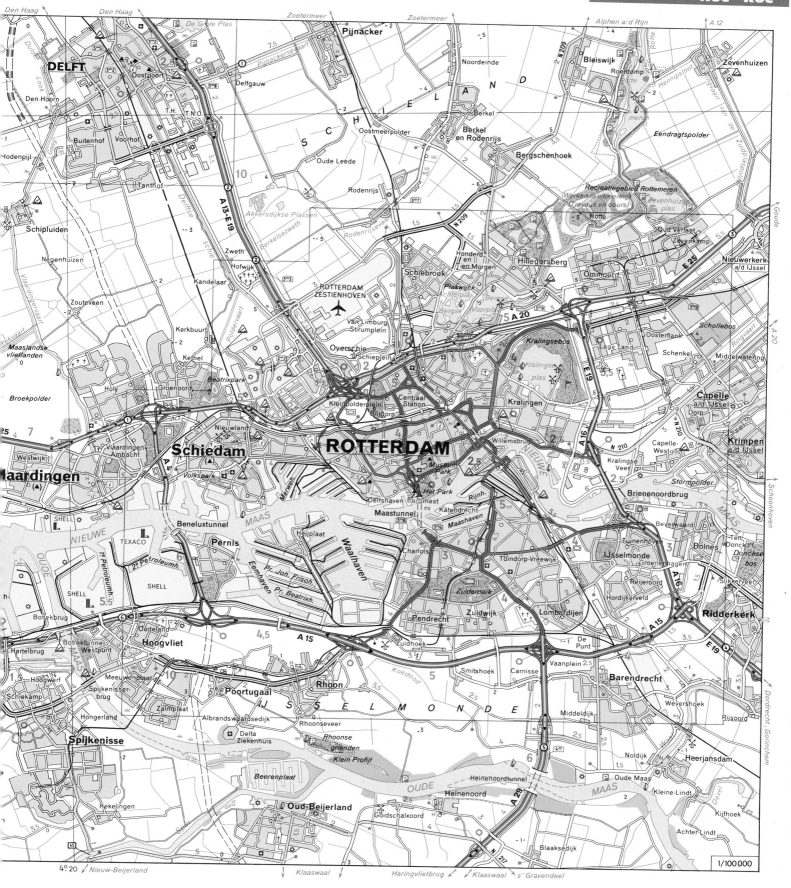

Roccella
  Jonica **67** F4
Rocchetta Sant'
  Antonio **64** C3
Roc de Fraussa **32** B3
Rochdale **6** C2

Roche-Bernard, la .. **22** C4
Rochebonne **30** B2
Roche-Canillac,
  la **29** D2
Roche-Chalais,
  la **28** B2

Rochechouart **28** C1
Roche-Derrien, la .. **22** C2
Roche-en-
  Ardenne, la **51** D4
Rochefort (B). **50** C4
Rochefort (F). **24** B4

Rochefort-en-
  Terre **22** C4
Rochefort-
  Montagne **29** E1
Rochefort-sur-
  Nenon **26** C2

Rochefoucauld, la .. **28** C1
Roche-Guyon, la **19** E3
Rochehaut **20** C2
Rochelle, La **24** B4
Rochemaure **30** B2
Roche-Posay, la ... **25** D3

Rochepot, le **26** C3
Roches, Col des **27** E2
Rocheservière **24** B3
Rochester **11** D2
Roche-sur-Foron,
  la **27** D4

Roche-sur-Yon, la .. **24** B3
Rochette, la **31** D1
Rochlitz **53** D2
Rociana del
  Condado **42** C3
Rockenhausen **54** B1

Rock of Cashel 14 C3
Rocroi. 20 B2
Róda 82 A1
Rodach. 52 C4
Rodacherbrunn 52 C3
Roda de Isábena . . . 37 E3
Rodavgi. 82 C2
Rødberg 104 C2
Rødby 108 B4
Rødbyhavn 108 B4
Rødding (Ribe) 108 A3
Rødding (Viborg) . . 108 A2
Rödeby 109 E3
Rodeiro 34 B2
Rødekro 108 A4
Rodel 2 A3
Rodellar 37 E3
Roden 47 D3
Rödenas 41 D2
Rödermark 52 A4
Rodewisch 53 D3
Rodez 29 E3
Rodiezmo 35 D2
Rodi Garganico 64 C2
Roding 56 B1
Roditis 81 E2
Rodnei, M. 113 D3
Rododáfni 83 D4
Rodohóri 79 E3
Rodolivos 80 B2
Rodön 101 E2
Rodonit, Gjiri i 76 C4
Rodópi
  (Nomos) 81 E2
Rodopi *Mts* 115 D3
Rodopós 79 F2
Rodopós 90 B3
Ródos 93 F1
Ródos, N 93 F2
Rodováni 90 B3
Rodvattnet 102 A1
Rødven 100 B2
Rødvig 108 C4
Roermond 17 D4
Roeselare 50 A3
Rogač 75 D2
Rogača 73 D3
Rogačica (Kosovo) . . 77 E2
Rogačica (Srbija) . . . 72 C4
Rogačov 111 E4
Rogaland 104 A3
Rogaška Slatina 70 C1
Rogatec 70 C2
Rogatica 76 A1
Rogatin 113 D3
Rogätz 48 C4
Rogen 101 D3
Rogen *L.* 101 D3
Roggendorf 48 B2
Roggiano Gravina . . 67 E2
Roggosen 53 F1
Rogliano (F) 33 F2
Rogliano (I) 67 E3
Rognan 97 E2
Rogozna 76 C1
Rogoznica 75 D2
Rohan 22 C3

Rohr 52 B3
Rohrbach (A) 56 C2
Rohrbach (F) 21 E3
Rohrbrunn 52 A4
Rohrer Sattel 57 E3
Roignais 27 E4
Roine Mallasvesi . . 107 E1
Roisel 19 F2
Roissy 19 F4
Rojales 45 D2
Rök 109 D1
Rokiškis 110 C3
Røkland 97 F2
Rokovci 71 F2
Rokua 99 E4
Rokycany 53 E4
Røldal 104 B3
Rolfstorp 108 C2
Rolla 94 B3
Rollag 104 C3
Rolle 27 D3
Rolle, Pso di 59 D3
Rolvsøya 95 D1
Roma 63 E2
Romagnano Sesia . . 31 F1
Roman 113 D4
Romana 66 B2
Romanche 31 D1
Romangordo 39 E3
România 73 D1
Romans 30 C2
Romanshorn 58 B1
Romantische
  straße. 55 E3
Rombas 21 D3
Rombo, Pso del 58 C2
Römhild 52 B4
Romilly 20 B4
Romny 113 F1
Rømø 108 A3
Romont 27 E3
Romorantin 25 E2
Romsdalen. 100 B2
Romsdalsfjorden . . 100 B2
Romsey 9 E3
Rona 2 B3
Ronaldsway 6 A1
Roncade 59 E4
Roncal 37 D2
Ronce 28 A1
Roncegno 59 D3
Roncesvalles 36 C1
Ronchamp 27 D1
Ronchi 59 F3
Ronciglione 63 E2
Roncobilaccio 60 C3
Ronda 43 E3
Rondane 100 C3
Ronda, Serr de 43 E4
Rønde 108 B3
Rondeslottet. 100 C3
Rondissone 31 F1
Rondvassbu. 100 C3
Rönnäng 108 C1
Rønne 109 D4
Ronneburg 53 D3

Ronneby 109 E3
Ronnebyån 109 E3
Rønnede 108 C4
Rönnöfors 101 E1
Ronse 50 B3
Roosendaal. 16 B3
Roperuelos
  del Páramo 35 D3
Ropi 94 C3
Ropinsalmi 94 C3
Ropotovo 77 E3
Roquebillière 31 E3
Roquebrun. 30 A4
Roquebrune-Cap-
  Martin 31 E3
Roquebrussanne,
  la 31 D4
Roquecourbe 32 B1
Roquefort. 28 B3
Roquefort-sur-
  Soulzon 29 F3
Roque-Gageac, la . . 29 D2
Roquemaure 30 B3
Roquesteron 31 E3
Roquetas de Mar . . 44 B4
Roquevaire 30 C4
Rora Head 3 D1
Rore 71 D4
Røros 101 D2
Rørøy 97 D3
Rorschach 58 B1
Rørvig 108 C3
Rørvik (Nord
  Trøndelag) 97 D4
Rørvik (Sør
  Trøndelag) 100 C1
Ros' 113 E2
Rosà 59 D4
Rosal de la Frontera 42 C1
Rosans 30 C2
Rosarito, Emb de . . . 39 E2
Rosarno 67 E4
Roscoff 22 B2
Ros Comáin 12 C3
Roscommon 12 C3
Roscommon (Co) . . . 12 C3
Roscrea 12 C4
Rose (Crna Gora) . . 76 A3
Rose (I) 67 E2
Rosegg 70 A1
Roselend, Cormet
  de 27 E4
Rosell 41 F2
Rosendal 104 A2
Rosenheim 56 B3
Rosenhof 56 B2
Rosenthal 53 F3
Roses 32 C3
Roses, Golfo de 32 C3
Roseto degli
  Abruzzi 64 A1
Rosheim 21 E4
Rosice 57 F1
Rosières 19 F2
Rosiers, les 24 C2
Rosignano
  Marittimo 60 C4

Roșiori de Vede . . . 115 D2
Roskilde. 108 C3
Roški slap 75 D1
Roslavl'. 111 E3
Rosmaninhal 38 C3
Røsnæs 108 B3
Rosolina Mare 61 D1
Rosolini 69 D4
Rosoman 77 E3
Rosova dolina 115 D2
Rosporden 22 B3
Rossano 67 F2
Rossan Pt. 12 C1
Rosscarbery 14 B4
Roßdorf 54 C1
Rosses Point 12 C2
Roßhaupten 55 E4
Rossija 111 E2
Rossio. 38 B3
Rosskreppfjorden . 104 B3
Rosslare 15 D4
Rosslare Harbour . . 15 D4
Roßlau 53 D1
Rosslea 13 D2
Rossön 101 F1
Ross-on-Wye 9 D2
Røssvatnet 97 E3
Roßwein 53 E2
Rosthwaite 5 D4
Røstlandet 97 D1
Roștock 48 C2
Rostrenen 22 B3
Rostrevor 13 E3
Rostujávri 94 C3
Røsvik 94 A4
Rosvik 98 C3
Rota 43 D3
Rotenburg
  (Hessen) 52 B3
Rotenburg
  (Niedersachsen) . . 48 A3
Roth 55 F1
Rötha 53 D2
Rothbury 5 E3
Röthenbach 55 F1
Rothenburg 53 F2
Rothenburg ob der
  Tauber 55 E1
Rothéneuf 18 B4
Rotherham 7 D2
Rothes 3 D3
Rothesay 4 B2
Rothwell. 9 F1
Rotja, Pta 45 D4
Rotonda 67 E2
Rotondella 65 D4
Rotondo, M. 33 F3
Rott (Bayern) 56 A3
Rott (Bayern) 56 B3
Rott *R* 56 B2
Rottach-Egern 56 A4
Rotten 27 E3
Rottenbach 52 C4
Rottenburg (Baden-
  Württemberg) . . . 55 D3
Rottenburg
  (Bayern) 56 B2

Rottenmann 57 D4
Rottenmanner
  Tauern 57 D4
Rotterdam 16 B3
Rottne 109 D2
Rottneros 105 E3
Rottweil 54 C3
Rötz 56 B1
Roubaix. 20 A1
Roudnice. 53 F3
Rouen 19 E3
Rouffach 27 E1
Rougé 23 D4
Rougemont. 27 D2
Rougemont-le-
  Château 27 E1
Rouillac 28 B1
Roujan 30 A4
Roulans 27 D2
Roulers. 50 A3
Roundstone 12 A3
Rousay 3 E1
Roússa 81 E1
Rousses, les 27 D3
Rousset, Col de 30 C2
Rovaniemi 99 D2
Rovato 60 B1
Rovereto 59 D4
Roverud 105 D3
Roviés 83 F3
Rovigo 61 D2
Rovinj 70 A3
Rovišće 71 D2
Rovno 113 D2
Roxen 106 A4
Roxo, Bgem do 42 B1
Royal Canal 12 C3
Royal Leamington
  Spa 9 E1
Royal Tunbridge
  Wells 10 C3
Royan 28 A1
Royat 29 E1
Roybon 30 C1
Roye 19 F3
Royère-de-
  Vassivière 25 E4
Røyrvik 97 E4
Royston 9 F2
Röyttä 98 C3
Rozay-en-Brie 19 F4
Rozier, le 29 F3
Rožmberk 57 D1
Rožmitál 53 F4
Rožňava 112 B3
Rozoy 20 B2
Roztocze 112 C2
Roztoky 53 F3
Rozvadov 56 B1
Rrasë 76 C3
Rrëshen 76 C3
Rrogozhinë 76 C4
Rtanj 73 E4
Rtanj (Reg) 73 E4
Ruabon. 6 B3

Rubbestadneset . . . 104 A2
Rubena. 35 F3
Rubeži. 76 B2
Rubha a'Mhail 4 B2
Rubha Còigeach 2 C2
Rubha Réidh 2 B3
Rubí 32 A4
Rubiães 34 A3
Rubi de
  Bracamonte 39 F1
Rubielos de Mora . . 41 E3
Rubiera 60 C2
Rubio 35 F4
Rudare 77 D1
Rüdersdorf 49 E4
Rüdesheim 51 F4
Rudkøbing 108 B4
Rudn'a 111 E3
Rudna Glava 73 E3
Rudnica (Crna
  Gora) 76 B1
Rudnica (Srbija) . . . 76 C1
Rudnik (Kosovo) . . . 76 C2
Rudnik (Reg) 73 D4
Rudnik (Srbija) 73 D4
Rudo 76 B1
Rudolstadt 52 C3
Rue 19 E2
Ruecas, R 39 E4
Rueda 35 E4
Rueda de Jalón. . . . 36 C3
Ruelle 28 C1
Ruffec 25 D4
Ruffieux 27 D4
Rugby 9 E1
Rugeley 6 C3
Rügen 49 D1
Rugles 19 D4
Rugovska klisura. . . 76 C2
Ruhla. 52 B3
Ruhland 53 E2
Ruhner Berge 48 C3
Ruhpolding 56 B3
Ruhr 17 E3
Ruidera 40 B4
Rūjiena. 110 C2
Ruka 99 E2
Rukatunturi 99 E2
Ruma 72 C2
Rumblar, Emb del . . 44 A2
Rumboci 75 E1
Rumburk 53 F2
Rumengol. 22 B3
Rumenka 72 C2
Rumigny 20 B2
Rumija 76 B3
Rumilly 27 D4
Runcorn 6 B2
Runde 100 A2
Rundvik 102 A2
Runn 105 F2
Runni 103 D1
Runtuna 106 B4
Ruohtir. 95 E2
Ruokojärvi 103 F3
Ruokolahti 103 F3
Ruokovesi 103 E3

Ruokto. 98 B1
Ruoms. 30 B2
Ruotsinpyhtää 107 F2
Ruovesi 102 C3
Rupa 70 B3
Rupea 113 D4
Ruppiner See 49 D3
Rupt 27 D1
Rur 17 D4
Ruše 70 C1
Ruse 115 D2
Ruševo 71 E2
Rush 13 E3
Rushden. 9 F1
Ruski Krstur 72 B2
Rusko. 107 D2
Rusko Selo 72 C1
Rusksele 98 A4
Russborough 13 D4
Rüsselsheim 51 F4
Russenes 95 D1
Russey, le 27 E2
Russi 61 D3
Rust. 57 F3
Rustefjelbma 95 E1
Ruswil 27 F2
Rute. 43 F3
Rüthen 17 F3
Ruthin 6 B3
Rüti 58 A2
Rutigliano 65 E3
Rutledal 104 A1
Ruuhitunturi 99 E2
Ruukki 99 D4
Ruuponsaari 103 D2
Ruurlo 17 D3
Ruvo di Puglia 65 D3
Ruwer 54 A1
Ruynes-en-
  Margeride 29 F2
Ružomberok 112 B3
Ry 108 B3
Rybinsk 111 F1
Rybinskoje
  Vodochranilišče. . 111 F1
Rybnica 113 E3
Rybnik 112 B3
Rychnov
  nad Kněžnou 112 A3
Ryd 109 D3
Ryde. 9 E3
Rye 11 D3
Ryfylke 104 A3
Rygge 105 D3
Rykene 104 B4
Ryl'sk 113 F1
Rymań 49 F1
Rymättylä 107 D2
Rypefjord 95 D1
Rysjedalsvika 104 A1
Ryttylä 107 E2
Rzepin 49 F4
Rzeszów 112 C2
Ržev 111 F2

S

Sääksjärvi 102 C2
Saal. 55 F2
Saalach 59 E1
Saalbach. 59 E1
Saale 52 C1
Saaler Bodden 48 C1
Saales 21 E4
Saalfeld 52 C3
Saalfelden 59 E1
Saane 27 E3
Saanen 27 E3
Saar 54 A1
Saarbrücken 54 B2
Saarburg 54 A1
Saaremaa 110 B2
Saarenkylä 99 D2
Saari 103 F3

Saariharju 99 E3
Saarijärvi 103 D2
Saarikoski 94 C3
Saariselkä 95 F3
Saariselkä (Reg) . . . 95 F3
Saaristomeri 107 D3
Saarland 54 A2
Saarlouis 54 B2
Saas- Fee 27 F4
Šabac 72 C3
Sabadell 32 A4
Sabaudia 63 F3
Sabbioneta 60 C2
Sabero 35 E2
Sabini, Mti 63 E2
Sabiote 44 B2
Sablé 23 E4
Sables-d'Olonne,
  les 24 B3

Sables-d'Or 22 C2
Sæbø 100 A2
Sabóia 42 A2
Sabôr, R. 34 C4
Sabres 28 B3
Sabrosa 34 B4
Sabugal 39 D2
Sæby 108 B2
Sa Calobra 45 E2
Sacavém 38 A4
Sacedon 40 C2
Saceruela 39 F4
Sachsen 53 F2
Sachsen-Anhalt. . . . 48 C4
Sacile 59 E3
Sacra di San
  Michele 31 E1
Sacramenia 35 F4
Sacratif, C 44 A4
Sada 34 B1

Sádaba 36 C2
Sado, R 38 A4
Sadurniño 34 B1
Saelices 40 B3
Safara 42 C1
Säffle 105 E4
Saffron Walden 10 C2
Safonovo 111 E3
Sagard 49 D1
S'Agaró 32 B4
Sagéika 86 B3
Sagfjorden 94 A4
Sagiáda. 82 B1
Sagra, Sa de la 44 B2
Sagres 42 A3
Sagres, Pta de 42 A3
Sagunto 41 E3
Sagvåg 104 A3
Sahagún 35 E3
Sahalahti 107 E1

Šahinoviči 71 E3
Sahl. 108 A2
Sahloinen 103 D3
Saignelégier 27 E2
Saija 95 F4
Saillagouse 32 A3
Saillans 30 C2
Saimaa 103 E3
Saimaanranta 103 E4
Sains-du-Nord. 20 B2
Sains-
  Richaumont 20 B2
St Abb's Head 5 E2
St Aegyd 57 E3
St-Affrique 29 F3
St-Agnant 24 B4
St-Agrève 30 B2
St-Aignan 25 E2
St-Aignan-sur-
  Roë 23 D3

St Alban 29 F2
St Albans 9 F2
St Alban's Head 9 E4
St-Amand-en-
  Puisaye 26 A2
St-Amand-les-
  Eaux 20 A1
St-Amand-
  Longpré 25 D2
St-Amand-
  Montrond 25 F3
St-Amans-des-
  Cots 29 F2
St-Amans. 29 F2
St-Amans-
  Soult. 32 B1
St-Amant 29 F1
St-Amant-Roche-
  Savine 29 F1
St-Amarin 27 E1

St-Ambroix 30 B3
St-Amé. 27 D1
St-Amour 26 C3
St Andrä 70 B1
St Andreasberg 52 B2
St-André-de-
  Cubzac 28 B2
St-André-de-
  l'Eure 19 E4
St-André-de-
  Vézines 29 F3
St-André-les-
  Alpes 31 D3
St Andrews 5 D1
St-Anthème 30 B1
St-Antonin-Noble-
  Val. 29 D3
St Anton 58 C2
St-Arnoult 19 E4
St Asaph 6 B2

St-Astier 28 C2
St-Auban 31 D3
St-Aubin-
d'Aubigné 23 D3
St-Aubin-du-
Cormier 23 D3
St-Aubin 18 C3
St-Aulaye 28 C2
St Austell 8 B4
St-Avold 21 D3
St-Aygulf 31 D4
St-Beauzély 29 E3
St Bees Head 4 C4
St-Benoît-du-
Sault 25 E3
St-Benoît 25 F2
St-Bertrand-de-
Comminges 37 E1
St-Béat 37 F2
St-Bénin-d'Azy 26 A3
St Blasien 54 C4
St-Blin 26 C1
St-Bonnet 31 D2
St-Bonnet-de-
Joux 26 B3
St-Bonnet-le-
Château 30 B1
St-Brévin 24 A2
St-Briac 18 A4
St-Brice-en-Coglès . 18 B4
St Brides B. 8 B2
St-Brieuc 22 C2
St-Calais 23 F3
St-Cast 18 A4
St Catherine's Pt . . . 9 E4
St-Cergue 27 D3
St-Cernin 29 E2
St-Céré 29 D2
St-Chamas 30 C4
St-Chamond 30 B1
St-Chély-d'Apcher . 29 F2
St-Chély-d'Aubrac . 29 E2
St-Chinian 32 B1
St Christophen 57 E2
St-Ciers 28 B1
St-Cirq-Lapopie . . . 29 D3
St-Clair-sur-l'Elle . . 18 C3
St-Clar 28 C3
St-Claud 25 D4
St-Claude 27 D3
St Clears 8 C2
St-Cyprien 29 D2
St-Cyprien-Plage . . 32 B2
St David's 8 B1
St David's Head 8 B1
St-Denis (Charente-
Maritime) 24 B4
St-Denis-d'Orques . 23 E3
St-Denis (Seine-
St-Denis) 19 F4
St-Didier-en-
Velay 30 B1
St-Dié 21 E4
St-Dier-
d'Auvergne 29 F1
St-Dizier 20 C4
St-Donat-sur-
l'Herbasse 30 C1
St-Eloy-les-Mines . . 26 A4
St-Emilion 28 B2
St-Etienne (Alpes-de-
Haute-Provence) . 30 C1
St-Etienne-
Cantalès, Bge de . 29 E2
St-Etienne-de-
Baïgorry 28 A4
St-Etienne-de-
Lugdarès 29 F2
St-Etienne-de-
Montluc 24 B2
St-Etienne-de-
St-Geoirs 30 C1
St-Etienne-de-
Tinée 31 E3
St-Etienne-en-
Dévoluy 31 D2
St-Etienne (Loire) . . 30 B1
St-Fargeau 26 A2
St-Félicien 30 B2
St Finan's B 14 A4
St-Firmin 31 D2
St-Florent (Cher) . . 25 F3
St-Florent (Corse) . 33 F2
St-Florentin 26 B1

St-Flour 29 F2
St-François-
Longchamp 31 D1
St-Fulgent 24 B3
St Gallen (A) 57 D3
St Gallen (CH) 58 B2
St Gallenkirch 58 B2
St-Galmier 30 B1
St-Gaudens 37 F1
St-Gaultier 25 E3
St-Genest-
Malifaux 30 B1
St-Geniez-d'Olt . . . 29 E3
St-Genis-de-
Stonge 28 B1
St-Gengoux-le-
National 26 C3
St-Genis-Laval 30 B1
St-Genix 30 C1
St-Geoire 30 C1
St Georgen (A) 56 C3
St Georgen
am Langsee 70 B1
St Georgen (D) 54 C3
St-Georges 23 E4
St Georges Channel . 8 A1
St-Georges-de-
Didonne 28 A1
St-Georges-en-
Couzan 29 F1
St-Germain-de-
Calberte 29 F3
St-Germain-des-
Fossés 26 A4
St-Germain-du-
Bois 26 C3
St-Germain-du-
Plain 26 C3
St-Germain-du-
Teil 29 F3
St-Germain 19 F4
St-Germain-Laval . . 26 B4
St-Germain-
Lembron 29 F1
St-Germain-les-
Belles 29 D1
St-Germain-
l'Herm 29 F1
St-Gertraud 58 C3
St-Gervais-
d'Auvergne 26 A4
St-Gervais 27 E4
St-Gervais-sur-
Mare 30 A4
St-Géry 29 D3
St-Gildas-de-
Rhuys 22 C4
St-Gildas-des-Bois . 23 D4
St-Gildas, Pte de . . . 24 A2
St Gilgen 56 C3
St-Gilles-Croix-de-
Vie 24 A3
St-Gilles 30 B4
St-Gingolph 27 E3
St-Girons 37 F2
St-Girons-Plage . . . 28 A3
St Goar 51 E4
St Goarshausen 51 E4
St-Gobain 20 A3
St Govan's Head 8 B2
St-Guénolé 22 A3
St-Guilhem-le-
Désert 29 F4
St-Haon-le-Châtel . 26 B4
St Helens 6 B2
St-Hélier 18 B3
St-Hilaire-des-
Loges 24 C3
St-Hilaire-de-
Villefranche 28 B1
St-Hilaire-du-
Harcouet 18 B4
St-Hilaire 32 B1
St-Hippolyte-du-
Fort 29 F3
St-Hippolyte 27 E2
St-Honoré 26 B3
St-Hubert 20 C2
St-Imier 27 E2
St Ingbert 54 B2
St Ives (Cambs) 9 F1
St Ives (Cornwall) . . 8 A4
St-Jacques 23 D3
St-Jacut 18 A4

St Jakob 59 D2
St Jakob im
Rosental 70 A1
St James 18 B4
St-Jean-Brévelay . . 22 C3
St-Jean-Cap-
Ferrat 31 E3
St-Jean-d'Angély . . . 24 C4
St-Jean-de-
Bournay 30 C1
St-Jean-de-Daye . . 18 B3
St-Jean-de-Losne . . 26 C2
St-Jean-de-Luz 28 A4
St-Jean-de-
Maurienne 31 D1
St-Jean-de-Monts . 24 A3
St-Jean-du-Bruel . . 29 F3
St-Jean-du-Gard . . 30 A3
St-Jean-en-
Royans 30 C2
St-Jean-Pied-de-
Port 28 A4
St-Jeoire 27 D4
St Johann im
Pongau 59 E1
St Johann in Tirol . . 59 E1
St John's Pt 13 E2
St-Jouin-de-
Marnes 24 C3
St-Juéry 29 E3
St-Julien-Chapteuil . 30 B2
St-Julien-de-
Vouvantes 23 D4
St-Julien-du-Sault . 26 A1
St-Julien-en-
Genevois 27 D4
St-Julien 26 C3
St-Julien-l'Ars 25 D3
St-Junien 25 D4
St Just 8 A4
St-Just-en-
Chaussée 19 F3
St-Just-en-
Chevalet 26 B4
St-Justin 28 B3
St Keverne 8 B4
St Lambrecht 57 D4
St-Lary-Soulan 37 E2
St-Laurent
(Calvados) 18 C3
St-Laurent-de-la-
Salanque 32 B2
St-Laurent-du-
Pont 30 C1
St-Laurent-en-
Grandvaux 27 D3
St-Laurent-les-
Bains 29 F2
St-Laurent-Médoc . 28 B2
St-Laurent
(Vendée) 24 C3
St-Laurent
(Vienne) 28 C1
St-Léger 26 B3
St Leonhard (I) 59 D2
St Leonhard (Nieder-
österreich) 57 E3
St Leonhard (Tirol) . 58 C2
St-Léonard-de-
Noblat 25 E4
St Lorenzen 59 E2
St-Lô 18 C3
St-Louis 27 E2
St-Loup-Lamairé . . 24 C3
St-Loup-sur-
Semouse 27 D1
St-Luc 27 F3
St-Lunaire 18 B4
St-Lys 29 D4
St-Macaire 28 B2
St Magnus B 3 F1
St-Maixent-l'Ecole . 24 C3
St-Malo-de-la-
Lande 18 B3
St-Malo 18 A4
St-Mamet-la-
Salvetat 29 E2
St-Mandrier 31 D4
St-Marcellin 30 C1
St-Margarethen . . . 48 A2
St Margaret's Hope . 3 E1
St-Mars-la-Jaille . . 23 D4
St-Martin (Charente-
Maritime) 24 B4

St-Martin-
d'Auxigny 25 F2
St-Martin-de-
Belleville 31 D1
St-Martin-de-Crau . 30 B4
St-Martin-de-
Londres 29 F4
St-Martin-de-
Seignan 28 A4
St-Martin-de-
Valamas 30 B2
St-Martin-en-
Bresse 26 C3
St-Martin (Pyrénées-
Orientales) 32 B2
St Martin's 8 A4
St-Martin-Vésubie . 31 E3
St-Martory 37 F1
St Mary's 8 A4
St Märgen 54 C4
St-Mathieu 28 C1
St-Mathieu, Pte
de 22 A3
St-Maurice 27 E4
St Mawes 8 B4
St-Maximin-la-Ste
Baume 31 D4
St-Médard-en-
Jalles 28 B2
St-Méen 22 C3
St Michaelisdonn . . 48 A2
St Michael
(Salzburg) 59 F2
St Michael's Mount . 8 A4
St Michael
(Steiermark) 57 E4
St-Michel-de-
Maurienne 31 D1
St-Michel-en-
Grève 22 B2
St-Michel-en-
l'Herm 24 B4
St-Michel 20 B2
St-Michel-Mont-
Mercure 24 C3
St-Mihiel 20 C3
St Monance 5 D2
St-Moritz 58 B3
St-Nazaire 24 A2
St-Nectaire 29 E1
St Neots 9 F1
St-Nicolas-
d'Aliermont 19 E2
St-Nicolas-de-la-
Grave 28 C3
St-Nicolas-de-
Port 21 D4
St-Nicolas-du-
Pélem 22 C3
St-Niklaas 50 B3
St Niklaus 27 F4
St-Oedenrode 16 C3
St-Omer 19 F1
St Oswald 59 F2
St-Pair 18 B4
St-Palais (Charente-
Maritime) 28 A1
St-Palais (Pyrénées-
Atlantiques) 28 A4
St-Pardoux-la-
Rivière 28 C1
St Paul (A) 70 B1
St-Paul (Alpes-de-
Haute-Provence) . 31 D2
St-Paul (Alpes-
Maritimes) 31 E3
St-Paul-Cap-de-
Joux 29 D4
St-Paul-de-
Fenouillet 32 B2
St-Paulien 29 F2
St-Paul-Trois-
Châteaux 30 B3
St-Père-en-Retz . . . 24 A2
St-Pé-de-Bigorre . . 37 E1
St-Pée 28 A4
St-Péray 30 B2
St Peter in der Au . . 57 D3
St Peter-Ording . . . 47 F2
St Peter Port 18 A3
St-Petersburg 111 D1
St-Philbert 24 B3
St-Pierre (Charente-
Maritime) 24 B4

St-Pierre-
d'Albigny 31 D1
St-Pierre-de-
Chartreuse 30 C1
St-Pierre-de-
Chignac 28 C2
St-Pierre-Eglise . . . 18 B2
St-Pierre-le-
Moûtier 26 A3
St-Pierre
(Morbihan) 22 C4
St-Pierre-sur-
Dives 18 C3
St-Pois 18 C4
St-Pol-de-Léon 22 B2
St-Pol-sur-
Ternoise 19 F2
Ste-Pons-de-
Thomières 32 B1
St-Porchaire 28 B1
St Pölten 57 E2
St-Pourçain 26 A4
St-Privat 29 E2
St-Quay-Portrieux . 22 C2
St-Quentin 20 A2
St-Rambert 30 B1
St-Rambert-
d'Albon 30 B1
St-Rambert-en-
Bugey 26 C4
St-Raphaël 31 E4
St-Renan 22 A2
St-Rémy-de-
Provence 30 B3
St-Rémy-sur-
Durolle 26 B4
St-Riquier 19 E2
St-Romain-de-
Colbosc 19 D3
St-Rome-de-Tarn . . 29 E3
St-Saëns 19 E3
St-Satur 26 A2
St-Saulge 26 A2
St-Sauveur-en-
Puisaye 26 A2
St-Sauveur-
Lendelin 18 B3
St-Sauveur-le-
Vicomte 18 B3
St-Sauveur-sur-
Tinée 31 E3
St-Savin (Gironde) . 28 B2
St-Savinien 24 C4
St-Savin (Vienne) . . 25 D3
St-Seine-l'Abbaye . 26 C2
St-Sernin-sur-
Rance 29 E3
St-Sever
(Calvados) 18 C4
St-Sever (Landes) . . 28 B4
St-Sulpice-les-
Feuilles 25 E4
St-Symphorien-de-
Lay 26 B4
St-Symphorien-
d'Ozon 30 B1
St-Symphorien 28 B3
St-Symphorien-sur-
Coise 30 B1
St-Trivier-de-
Courtes 26 C3
St-Trivier-sur-
Moignans 26 C4
St-Trojan 28 A1
St-Tropez 31 D4
St-Truiden 50 C3
St Ulrich 59 D3
St-Vaast-la-
Hougue 18 B3
St Valentin an der
Haide 58 C2
St Valentin 57 D3
St-Valery 19 E2
St-Valery-en-Caux . 19 D2
St-Vallier 30 B1
St-Vallier-de-
Thiey 31 D3
St-Varent 24 C3
St-Vaury 25 E4
St Veit 70 A1
St-Véran 31 E2
St-Vincent 27 F4
St-Vincent-de-
Tyrosse 28 A4

St Vith 51 D4
St-Vivien-de-
Médoc 28 A1
St-Wandrille 19 D3
St Wendel 54 B1
St Wolfgang 56 C3
St-Yorre 26 A4
St-Yrieix-la-
Perche 29 D1
Ste-Adresse 19 D3
Ste-Anne-d'Auray . . 22 C4
Ste-Baume, la 31 D4
Ste-Croix-du-
Mont 28 B2
Ste-Croix 27 D3
Ste-Croix, Lac de . . 31 D3
Ste-Croix-
Volvestre 37 F1
Ste-Enimie 29 F3
Ste-Foy-la-Grande . 28 C2
Ste-Foy-
l'Argentière 30 B1
Ste-Geneviève-sur-
Argence 29 E2
Ste-Hélène 28 B2
Ste-Hermine 24 B3
Ste-Livrade 28 C3
Ste-Lucie-de-
Tallano 33 F4
Ste-Marie-aux-
Mines 21 E4
Ste-Maure-de-
Touraine 25 D2
Ste-Maxime 31 D4
Ste-Menehould 20 C3
Ste-Mère-Eglise . . . 18 B3
Ste-Odile, Mt 21 E4
Ste-Sévère 25 F3
Ste-Suzanne 23 E3
Ste-Tulle 30 C3
Saintes 28 B1
Stes-Maries-de-la-
Mer 30 B4
Saison R. 37 F1
Saissac 32 B1
Šajkaš 72 C2
Sakarya 115 F3
Sakskøbing 108 B4
Sakule 72 C2
Säkylä 107 D2
Sala 106 A3
Salacgrîva 110 C2
Sala Consilina 64 C4
Salada 41 E3
Salakovac 73 D3
Salamajärvi 102 C2
Salamajärvi L 103 D2
Salamanca 39 E1
Salamína 87 F1
Salamína, N. 87 E1
Salándi 87 E2
Salangen 94 B3
Salar 43 F3
Salardú 37 F2
Salas 35 D1
Salaš 73 E2
Salas de los
Infantes 36 A3
Salazar, R. 37 D2
Salbohed 105 F3
Salbris 25 E2
Salcombe 8 C4
Saldaña 35 E3
Saldus 110 B3
Sale 60 A2
Sålekinna 100 D3
Salem 55 D4
Salemi 68 A3
Sälen 101 D3
Salen (Highland) . . . 2 B4
Salen (Mull) 4 B1
Salernes 31 D4
Salerno 64 B4
Salerno, Golfo di . . 64 B4
Salers 29 E2
Salève, Mt 27 D4
Salgótarján 112 B3
Salgueiro do
Campo 38 C2
Sali 74 C1
Salice Terme 60 A2
Salies-de-Béarn . . . 28 A4
Salies-du-Salat . . . 37 F1
Salignac-Eyvigues . 29 D2

Salihli 115 F4
Salime, Emb de . . . 34 C1
Salina, I. 69 D2
Salinas (Andalucía) . 43 F3
Salinas (Asturias) . . 35 D1
Salinas, C 45 F3
Salindres 30 B3
Sälinkää 107 F2
Salins 27 D3
Salisbury 9 E3
Salla 99 E2
Sallanches 27 E4
Sallent 32 A4
Sallent-de-Gállego . 37 D2
Salles 32 A1
Salles-Curan 29 E3
Salling 108 A2
Salling Sund 108 A2
Salmerón 40 C2
Salmoral 39 F1
Salò 60 B1
Salo 107 E2
Salobreña 44 A4
Salona 75 D1
Salon-de-
Provence 30 C4
Salonta 112 C4
Salorino 38 C3
Salor, R 39 D3
Salou 37 F4
Salou, C de 37 F4
Salpausselkä 107 F2
Salsbruket 97 D4
Salses-le-Château . 32 B2
Salso 68 C3
Salsomaggiore
Terme 60 B2
Salsta 106 B3
Saltash 8 C4
Saltburn-by-the-
Sea 5 F4
Saltcoats 4 C2
Saltee Is 15 D4
Saltfjellet 97 E2
Saltfjorden 97 E2
Salto 34 B2
Saltoluokta 94 B4
Saltvik 106 C3
Saluggia 31 F1
Saluzzo 31 E2
Salvacañete 41 D3
Salvagnac 29 D3
Salvan 27 E4
Salvaterra de
Magos 38 A3
Salvatierra-
Agurain 36 B2
Salvatierra de los
Barros 42 C1
Salvatera de Miño . 34 A3
Salvetat-Peyralès,
la 29 E3
Salvetat-sur-Agout,
la 32 B1
Salviac 29 D2
Sælvig 108 B3
Sálvora, I de 34 A2
Salza 57 E3
Salzach 56 B3
Salzburg 56 C3
Salzburg (Prov) . . . 59 E1
Salzgitter-Bad 52 B1
Salzgitter-
Lebenstedt 52 B1
Salzhausen 48 B3
Salzkammergut . . . 56 C3
Salzkotten 17 F3
Salzwedel 48 C4
Šamac Slavonski . . 71 F3
Sama de Langreo . . 35 D1
Samarína 78 C4
Samatan 28 C4
Sambatiki 87 E3
Sambiase 67 E3
Samboal 40 A1
Sambor 112 C3
Sambre 50 B4
Sambuca di Sicilia . 68 B3
Samedan 58 B3
Sameiro, Mte 34 A4
Samer 19 E1
Sámi 82 B4
Samikó 86 B2
Sammatti 107 E2

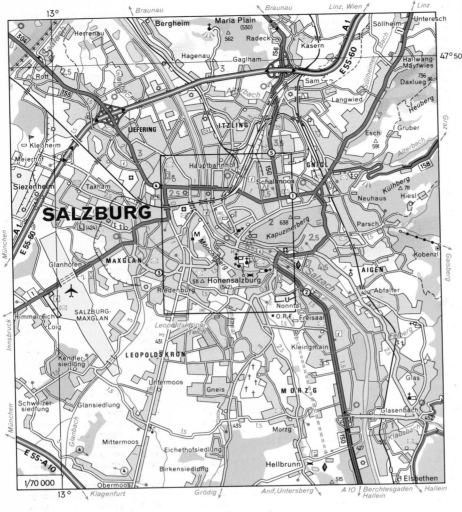

SALZBURG — 1/70 000

Sammichele 65 E3
Samnanger 104 A2
Samobor 70 C2
Samodreža 77 D2
Samoëns 27 E4
Samokov (BG) 115 D3
Samokov (Makedonija) ... 77 D3
Samora Correia ... 38 A4
Samos 34 C2
Samoš 73 D2
Sámos 89 F1
Sámos, N. 89 E1
Samothráki 81 E3
Samothráki, N 81 E3
Samper de Calanda 37 D4
Sampeyre 31 E2
Samsø 108 B3
Samsø Bælt 108 B3
Samtens 49 D1
Samugheo 66 B3
San 112 C2
San Adrián 36 C2
San Adrián, C de ... 34 A1
San Agata de Goti . 64 B3
San Agata di Militello 69 D2
San Agustín 40 B2
San Amaro 34 B2
San Andrea Frius .. 66 B3
San Andrés del Rabanedo 35 D2
San Antioco, I di .. 66 A4
San Antioco 66 B4
San Antonio Abad .. 45 D3
San Antonio 66 B1
San Antonio, C de .. 45 F1
San Bartolomé de las Abiertas 39 F3
San Bartolomé de la Torre 42 C2

San Bartolomeo in Galdo 64 B3
San Benedetto del Tronto 61 F4
San Benedetto in Alpe 61 D3
San Benedetto Po .. 60 C2
San Bernardino ... 58 B3
San Bernardino, Pso del 58 B3
San Biagio Platani 68 B3
San Bonifacio 60 C1
San Candido 59 E2
San Carlos de la Ràpita 41 F2
San Carlos del Valle 40 B4
San Casciano in Val di Pesa 60 C4
San Cataldo (Puglia) 65 F4
San Cataldo (Sicilia) 68 C3
San Cipirello 68 B3
San Clemente, Emb de 44 B2
San Clemente 40 C4
San Colombano al Lambro 60 B2
San Cosme 34 C1
San Cristóbal 42 C1
San Cristóbal de Entreviñas 35 D3
San Cristóbal de la Polantera 35 D3
San Cristóbal de la Vega 39 F1
San Damiano d'Asti 31 F2
San Daniele del Friuli 59 E3

San Daniele Po 60 B2
San Demetrio Corone 67 E2
San Donaci 65 F4
San Donà di Piave . 59 E4
San Emiliano 35 D2
San Esteban de Gormaz 36 A3
San Esteban del Molar 35 D3
San Esteban del Valle 39 F2
San Esteban de Pravia 35 D1
San Fele 64 C4
San Felice a Cancello 64 B3
San Felice Circeo .. 63 F3
San Felices de Los Gallegos 39 D1
San Felice sul Panaro 60 C2
San Felipe 40 C2
San Feliu de Guíxols 32 B4
San Ferdinando di Puglia 64 C3
San Fernando ... 43 D4
San Francisco Javier 45 D4
San Fratello 69 D2
San Gavino Monreale 66 B3
San Gemini 63 E1
San Giacomo 59 D2
San Gimignano ... 60 C4
San Ginesio 61 F4
San Giorgio del Sannio 64 B3
San Giorgio di Nogaro 59 F3
San Giorgio Ionico . 65 E4

San Giorgio 31 E1
San Giorgio Piacentino 60 B2
San Giovanni a Piro 67 D2
San Giovanni di Sinis 66 A3
San Giovanni in Fiore 67 F2
San Giovanni in Persiceto 60 C2
San Giovanni Lupatoto 60 C1
San Giovanni Rotondo 64 C2
San Giovanni Suergiu 66 B4
San Giovanni Valdarno 61 D4
San Giuliano Terme 60 C4
San Giustino 61 D4
San Glorio, Pto de . 35 E2
San Gottardo, Pso del 58 A3
San Ildefonso o la Granja 40 A1
San Isidro 44 C3
San Isidro, Pto de .. 35 E2
San Javier 45 D2
San José (Andalucía) 44 C4
San José (Ibiza) ... 45 D4
San Juan Bautista . 45 D3
San Juan de Alicante 45 E1
San Juan de Aznalfarache .. 43 D2
San Juan de la Peña 37 D2
San Juan del Olmo 39 F2

San Juan de los Terreros 44 C3
San Juan del Puerto 42 C2
San Juan, Emb de . 40 A2
San Just Desvern .. 32 A4
San Just, Sa de 41 E2
San Lazzaro di Savena 61 D2
San Leo 61 E3
San Leonardo de Yagüe 36 A3
San Leonardo 59 D2
San Leonardo, Pso . 64 A2
San Lorenzo (E) ... 36 B2
San Lorenzo (I) ... 63 D1
San Lorenzo de Calatrava 44 A1
San Lorenzo de la Parrilla 40 C3
San Lucido 67 E3
San Luis de Sabanillas 43 E4
San Luis 45 F2
San Marcello 61 F4
San Marcello Pistoiese 60 C3
San Marco Argentano 67 E2
San Marco dei Cavoti 64 B3
San Marco in Lamis 64 C2
San Marino 61 E3
San Martino di Castrozza 59 D3
San Martín de Castañeda 34 C3
San Martín de la Vega 40 B2
San Martín de Mondoñedo 34 C1
San Martín de Montalbán 39 F3
San Martín de Valdeiglesias ... 40 A2
San Mateo 41 F2
San Mateo de Gállego 37 D3
San Mauro Forte .. 65 D4
San Michele all' Adige 59 D3
San Miguel 45 D3
San Miguel de Escalada 35 E3
San Miguel del Arroyo 35 E4
San Miguel de Salinas 45 D2
San Millán 36 A2
San Millán de la Cogolla 36 B2
San Millán de Lara . 36 A3
San Miniato 60 C4
San Nicolás del Puerto 43 E2
San Nicolás de Tolentino 42 B4
San Nicolò Ferrarese 61 D2
San Nicolò Gerrei .. 66 B3
San Ninfa 68 B3
San Pancrazio Salentino 65 F4
San Pedro 44 C3
San Pedro de Alcántara 43 E4
San Pedro del Arroyo 39 F1
San Pedro de Latarce 35 E4
San Pedro del Pinatar 45 D2
San Pedro de Mérida 39 D4
San Pedro Manrique 36 B3
San Pedro, Sa de .. 39 D3
San Pellegrino, Pso 59 D3
San Pellegrino Terme 58 B4
San Piero a Sieve . 61 D3
San Pietro, I di 66 A4

San Pietro in Casale 60 C2
San Pietro Vernotico 65 F4
San Polo d'Enza .. 60 C2
San Quirico d'Orcia 63 D1
San Rafael de Navallana, Emb de 43 F2
San Rafael 40 A2
San Remo 31 F3
San Roque (Andalucía) 43 E4
San Roque (Galicia) 34 A1
San Rufo 64 C4
San Salvador de Cantamuda 35 F2
San Salvador 45 F3
San Salvo 64 B2
San Sebastiano Curone 60 A2
San Sebastián, Emb de 34 C3
San Sebastián ... 42 A4
San Severino Marche 61 F4
San Severo 64 C2
San Silvestre de Guzmán 42 C2
San Sperate 66 B4
San Stefano di Camastra 68 C3
San Stefano Quisquina 68 B3
San Telmo 42 C2
San Valentino alla Muta 58 C2
San Vicente de Alcántara 38 C3
San Vicente de la Barquera 35 F1
San Vicente de la Cabeza 35 D4
San Vicente del Raspeig 45 E1
San Vicenzo 62 C1
San Vigilio di Marebbe 59 D2
San Vigilio, Pso di . 60 C1
San Vitero 34 C4
San Vito al Tagliamento 59 E3
San Vito Chietino .. 64 A2
San Vito dei Normanni 65 E3
San Vito di C. 59 E3
San Vito 66 C4
San Vito lo Capo ... 68 A3
San Vito sullo Ionio 67 F3
San Vittore del Lazio 64 A3
Sana 71 D4
Saná 80 A3
Sanabria, L de ... 34 C3
Sanary 30 C4
Sancergues 26 A2
Sancerre 26 A2
Sanchidrián 39 F1
Sancho, Emb de .. 42 C2
Sanclêr 8 C2
Sancoins 26 A3
Sancti Petri 43 D4
Sancti Spíritus ... 39 D1
Sand (Hedmark) .. 105 D2
Sand (Rogaland) .. 104 A3
Sandane 100 A3
Sandanski 115 D3
Sandarne 101 F4
Sandau 48 C4
Sanday 3 E1
Sandbach 6 C3
Sanddøla 97 D4
Sande (D) 47 E3
Sande (Møre og Romsdal) 100 A2
Sande (P) 34 A4
Sande (Vestfold) .. 104 C3
Sandefjord 104 C3
Sandeid 104 A3
Sandfjellet 95 E1
Sandgerði 96 A2
Sand in Taufers .. 59 D2

Sandnes 104 A3
Sandness 3 F1
Sandnessjøen ... 97 D3
Sando 39 E1
Sandoméri 86 B1
Sandomierz 112 C2
Sandown 9 E3
Sandoy 96 A4
Sandøy 100 A2
Sandrigo 59 D4
Sandringham House 7 E3
Sandstad 100 C1
Sandur 96 A4
Sandviken 106 B2
Sandvikvåg 104 A2
Sandwich 11 D3
Sandy 9 F1
Sânfjället 101 E3
Sangarcia 40 A1
Sangerhausen ... 52 C2
Sangis 98 C3
Sangonera, R. ... 45 D2
Sangro 64 A2
Sangüesa 36 C2
Sanguinaires, Iles .. 33 E4
Sanguinet 28 A3
Sani 80 A4
Sanitz 48 C2
Sankt Olof 109 D3
Sanlúcar de Barrameda 43 D3
Sanlúcar de Guadiana 42 B2
Sanlúcar la Mayor 43 D2
Sanluri 66 B3
Sannainen 107 F2
Sannazzaro 60 A2
Sannicandro di Bari 65 D3
Sannicandro Garganico 64 C2
Sanok 112 C3
Sanquhar 4 C3
Sansepolcro 61 D4
Sanski Most 71 D3
Sant' Agata di Puglia 64 C3
Sant Agustí de Lluçanès 32 A3
Sant Andreu de Llavaneres 32 B4
Sant' Angelo de' Lombardi 64 C3
Sant' Angelo in Vado 61 E4
Sant' Angelo Lodigiano 60 A2
Sant Antoni de C. .. 32 B3
Sant' Antoni, Emb de 37 F3
Sant' Apollinare in Classe 61 D3
Sant' Arcangelo di Romagna 61 E3
Sant Boi de Lluçanès 32 A3
Sant Celoni 32 B4
Sant Cugat 32 A4
Sant' Elia a Pianisi.. 64 B2
Sant' Elpidio a Mare 61 F4
Sant Esteve d'en Bas 32 B3
Sant'Eufemia, Golfodi....... 67 E3
Sant'Eufemia Lamezia 67 E3
Sant Gervàs 37 F3
Sant Hilari Sacalm.. 32 B3
Sant Hipólit de Voltregà 32 A3
Sant Joan de les Abadesses 32 B3
Sant Julià de Lòria . 32 A3
Sant Llorenc de Morunys 32 A3
Sant'Onofrio 67 E3
Sant Pau de Seguries 32 B3
Sant Pere de Roda . 32 C3
Sant Pol de Mar .. 32 B4
Sant Ponç, Emb de. 32 A3

Sant Quirze de Besora 32 B3
Sant Quirze Safaja .. 32 A4
Sant Ramon 37 F3
Sant Sadurní d'Anoia 32 A4
Santa Amalia 39 D4
Santa Ana 40 C4
Santa Anna, Emb de 37 E3
Santa Bàrbara (Catalunya) 41 F2
Santa Bárbara (Andalucía)....... 42 C2
Santa Bárbara Mt.. 44 B3
Santa Catarina 42 B3
Santa Caterina Pittinuri 66 A3
Santa Caterina Valfurva........ 58 C3
Santa Caterina Villarmosa 68 C3
Santa Cesarea Terme........... 65 F4
Santa Clara-a-Velha 42 A2
Santa Clara, Bgem de 42 A2
Santa Coloma de Farners 32 B3
Santa Coloma de Queralt 37 F4
Santa Colombo de Somoza 35 D3
Santa Comba Dão . 38 B2
Santa Comba de Rossas........... 34 C4
Santa Comba 34 A1
Santa Cristina de Lena............ 35 D2
Santa Croce di Magliano........ 64 B2
Santa Cruz de Campezo 36 B2
Santa Cruz de la Palma........... 42 A4
Santa Cruz de la Sierra........... 39 E3
Santa Cruz de la Zarza 40 B3
Santa Cruz del Retamar 40 A2
Santa Cruz de Moya 41 D3
Santa Cruz de Mudela 44 A1
Santa Cruz de Tenerife......... 42 B4
Santa Cruz........ 36 C4
Santa Elena........ 44 A1
Santa Eufemia 43 E1
Santa Eugenia 34 A2
Santa Eulalia del Río 45 D3
Santa Eulalia de Oscos 34 C1
Santa Eulalia...... 41 D2
Santa Eulalia 38 C4
Santa Fe (Andalucía) 44 A3
Santa Fé (Catalunya) 32 B4
Santa Fiora 63 D1
Santa Galdana, Cala 45 F2
Santa Gertrude ... 58 C3
Santa Giusta 66 B3
Santa Inés, Pto de 36 B3
Santa Liestra y San Quílez 37 E3
Santa Lucia d. Mela 69 D2
Santa Luz........ 34 C4
Santa Luzia 42 A2
Santa Magdalena de Pulpis 41 F2
Santa Margarida do Sádão 42 B1
Santa Margarita ... 45 F2
Santa Margherita .. 66 B4
Santa Margherita di Belice 68 B3

Santa Margherita Ligure 60 A3
Santa Maria Capua Vetere 64 B3
Santa Maria, C de .. 42 B3
Santa Maria da Feira 38 B1
Santa Maria d'Angeli 63 E1
Santa Maria del Campo Rus 40 C3
Santa Maria della Versa 60 A2
Santa Maria di Leuca,C 65 F4
Santa Maria la Real de Nieva 40 A1
Santa Maria la Real de Oseira 34 B2
Santa Maria Maggiore 58 A3
Santa Marina 35 E2
Santa Marina del Rey 35 D3
Santa Marinella ... 63 D2
Santa María de Huerta 36 B4
Santa María del Campo 35 F3
Santa María del Páramo 35 D3
Santa Maria de Nieva 44 C3
Santa Maria de Valverde 35 D3
Santa-Maria-Siché . 33 F2
Santa Marta 39 D4
Santa Marta de Penaguião 34 B4
Santa Marta de Tormes 39 E1
Santa Olalla del Cala 43 D2
Santa Olalla 39 F3
Santa Pau 32 B3
Santa Pola 45 E2
Santa Ponsa 45 E3
Santa Sofia 61 D3
Santa Sofia d'Epiro 67 E2
Santa Susanna..... 32 B4
Santa Tecla 34 A3
Santa Teresa di Riva 69 D2
Santa Teresa, Emb de 39 E2
Santa Teresa Gallura 66 B1
Santaella 43 E2
Santana (Estremadura) 38 A4
Santana (Madeira) . 42 A3
Santana de Serra . 42 A2
Santander 35 F1
Santanyí 45 F3
Santarém 38 B3
Santas Martas 35 E3
Santeramo in Colle............ 65 D3
Santes Creus 37 F4
Santesteban...... 36 C1
Santhià 31 F1
Santiago de Alcántara 38 C3
Santiago de Compostela..... 34 A2
Santiago de la Espada 44 B2
Santiago de la Ribera 45 D2
Santiago do Cacém 42 A1
Santiago do Escoural 38 B4
Santibáñez de Béjar 39 E2
Santibáñez de la Peña 35 E2
Santibáñez de la Sierra.......... 39 E2
Santibáñez de Vidriales........ 35 D3
Santillana del Mar... 35 F1
Santiponce 43 D2

Säntis........... 58 B2
Santisteban del Puerto........... 44 B1
Santo Domingo de la Calzada 36 B2
Santo Domingo de Silos 36 A3
Santo Domingo, Ptode 43 D1
Santo Estêvão (Beira Baixa) 38 C2
Santo Estêvão (Estremadura) 38 A4
Santo Estêvão, Rib de 38 A4
Santo Pedro da Torre............ 34 A3
Santo Severa 63 D2
Santo Stefano di Cadore........... 59 E2
Santo Stefano d'Aveto.. 60 B2
Santo Stino di Livenza 59 E4
Santo Tirso 34 A4
Santo Tomé 44 B2
Santok 49 F3
Santolea, Emb de .. 41 E2
Santomera, Emb de 45 D2
Santoña 36 A1
Santo-Pietro-di-Tenda........... 33 F2
Santoríni, N 91 E1
Santuario de San Ignacio de Loyola . 36 C1
Santuario d'Oropa .. 27 F4
Santu Lussurgiu .. 66 B3
Santurtzi 36 B1
Sanxenxo 34 A2
Sanza 67 D1
São Bartolomeu de Messines......... 42 A2
São Brás de Alportel 42 B3
São Cristóvão..... 38 B4
São Domingos..... 42 A1
São Gregório 34 B3
São Jacinto 38 B1
São João da Pesqueira...... 34 B4
São João de Madeira 38 B1
São João de Tarouca 38 C1
São João dos Caldeireiros....... 42 B2
São José da Lamarosa 38 B3
São Leonardo...... 42 C1
São Mamede, Sa de 38 C3
São Manços 42 B1
São Marcos da Serra............ 42 A2
São Marcos do Campo 42 B1
São Martinho das Amoreiras....... 42 A2
São Martinho do Porto............ 38 A3
São Matias 42 B1
São Miguel de Machede 38 B4
São Pedro de Açor 38 C2
São Pedro de Moel............ 38 A2
São Pedro do Sul ... 38 C1
São Romão 38 C2
São Teotónio 42 A2
São Vicente, C de . 42 A2
São Vicente da Beira............ 38 C2
Saône 26 C3
Saône-et-Loire 26 B3
Saorge 31 E3
Sapanca 115 F3
Sapataria 38 A3
Sápes 81 E2
Sapiéndza, N 86 C4
Sa Pobla 45 F2
Sappada 59 E2
Sappee 107 E2

Sapri 67 D1
Säräisniemi 99 E4
Sarajärvi 99 E3
Sarajevo 76 A1
Sarakíni........ 79 E2
Sarakíniko 84 B3
Saramon 28 C4
Sarandáporo 79 E4
Sarandáporos 78 C4
Sarandë 114 C4
Saraváli 86 C1
Saray 115 E3
Sarayköy 115 F4
Šarbanovac 73 E3
Sarbinowo (Gorzów Wlkp) 49 F3
Sarbinowo (Koszalin) 49 F1
Sárbogárd 112 B4
Sarca 58 C3
Sardara 66 B3
Sardegna........ 66 A2
Sardínia 82 C3
Sardoal 38 B3
Sardona, Piz...... 58 B2
Sarek 98 A1
Šarengrad 72 B2
Sarentino 59 D2
Särfjället 101 D2
Sargans 58 B2
Sariá, N 93 D2
Sariñena 37 E3
Sark 18 A3
Särkisalmi 103 F3
Särkisalo 107 D3
Santoríni, N 91 E1
Sari-d'Orcino 33 F3
Sarine 27 E3
Sariñena 37 E3
Sark 18 A3
Santoríni, N 91 E1
Sarlat-la-Canéda .. 29 D2
Sarmitunturi 95 F3
Särna 101 D2
Sarnano 61 F4
Sarnen 27 F2
Sarnico 60 B1
Sarno 64 B4
Sarnthein 59 D2
Sarny 113 D2
Sarö........... 108 C1
Sarón 35 F2
Sarone 59 E3
Saronída........ 87 F2
Saronikós Kólpos ... 87 F1
Saronno 60 A1
Sárospatak 112 C3
Sar Planina 77 D3
Sarpsborg 105 D3
Sarracín 35 F3
Sarral 37 F4
Sarralbe 21 E3
Sarrans, Bge de .. 29 E2
Sarre 21 E3
Sarrebourg 21 E4
Sarreguemines 21 E3
Sarre-Union 21 E3
Sarriá 34 B2
Sarrión 41 E3
Sarroch 66 B4
Sarsina 61 D3
Sars-Poteries 20 B2
Sarstedt 52 B1
Sarteano 63 D1
Sartène 33 F4
Sarthe 23 E4
Sarthe (Dépt) 23 F3
Sárti 80 B4
Sartilly 18 B4
Sarule 66 B2
Sárvár 112 A4
Sarvsjö 101 D2
Sarzana 60 B3
Sarzeau 22 C4
Sarzedas 38 C2
Sasa 77 F2
Sassari 66 A2
Sassello 60 A3
Sassenage 30 C1
Sassenberg 17 F3
Sassenheim 16 B2
Sassetta 62 C1
Saßnitz 49 D1
Sasso 63 E2
Sassoferrato 61 E4
Sassoleone 61 D3
Sasso Marconi 60 C3
Sassuolo 60 C2

Sástago 37 D4
Sasyk, Ozero 113 E4
Sátão 38 C1
Säter 105 F3
Satillieu 30 B1
Satolas 30 C1
Satov 57 E1
Satow 48 C2
Sátres 81 D2
Satrup 48 A1
Sattel 58 A2
Sattledt 57 D3
Satu Mare 112 C3
Saualpe 70 B1
Sauca 36 B4
Saucelle, Emb de .. 39 D1
Sauda 104 A3
Sauðárkrókur 96 B1
Sauerlach 56 A3
Sauerland 17 F4
Saugues 29 F2
Saujon 28 B1
Saukkovaara 99 E4
Sauland 104 C3
Sauldre 26 A2
Saulgau 55 D3
Saulieu 26 B2
Sault 30 C3
Saulx 27 D1
Saulxures 27 E1
Saumur 24 C2
Saundersfoot 8 B2
Sauris 59 E3
Saut du Doubs.... 27 E3
Sautet, Bge du ... 30 C2
Sautusjärvi 94 C4
Sauve 30 B3
Sauveterre-de-Béarn 28 A4
Sauveterre-de-Guyenne 28 B2
Sauveterre-de-Rouergue 29 E3
Sauvo 107 D2
Sauxillanges 29 F1
Sauze d'Oulx 31 E2
Sauze, le 31 D2
Sauze-Vaussais ... 24 C4
Sauzon 22 B4
Sava 65 E4
Sava R 71 E3
Savália 86 B1
Sävar 102 B1
Savelli 67 F2
Savenay 23 D4
Saverdun 32 A1
Saverne 21 E4
Savigliano 31 E2
Savignac-les-Eglises 28 C1
Savignano Irpino .. 64 C3
Savignano sul Rubicone 61 E3
Savigny-sur-Braye .. 23 F4
Saviñán........ 36 C4
Savine, Col de la .. 27 D3
Savines-le-Lac 31 D2
Savinja 70 B1
Savino Selo 72 B2
Savitaipale 103 E4
Sävja 106 B3
Šavnik 76 B2
Savognin 58 B3
Savona 60 A3
Savonlinna 103 E3
Savonranta 103 F3
Sævråsvåg 104 A2
Sävsjö 109 D2
Savudrija 70 A3
Savukoski 95 F4
Sawbridgeworth ... 10 C2
Sawel Mt 13 D1
Sax 45 D1
Saxmundham 11 E1
Saxnäs 97 E4
Sayatón 40 B2
Säynätsalo 103 D3
Säyneinen 103 E2
Sazadón, Pto de 35 D3
Sázava 112 A3

Scaër........... 22 B3
Scafa 64 A2
Scafati 64 B4
Scafell Pikes 5 D4
Scala di Santa Regina 33 F3
Scalasaig........ 4 B2
Scalby 7 D1
Scalea 67 E2
Scalloway 3 F2
Scalpay 2 B3
Scandiano 60 C2
Scanno 64 A2
Scansano 63 D1
Scanzano 65 D4
Scapa Flow 3 D1
Scarba 4 B1
Scarborough 7 D1
Scardovari 61 E2
Scarinish 2 A4
Scarpe 20 A1
Scarriff 12 B4
Ščedro 75 E2
Scey-sur-Saône ... 27 D2
Schaalsee 48 B2
Schachendorf 57 E4
Schafberg 56 C3
Schaffhausen 58 A1
Schafstädt 52 C2
Schagen........ 16 C2
Schaprode 49 D1
Scharbeutz 48 B2
Schärding 56 C2
Scharhörn 47 F2
Scharmützelsee ... 49 E4
Scharnitz 59 D1
Schauinsland Feldberg 54 C4
Scheeßel 48 A3
Scheggia 61 E4
Scheibbs 57 E3
Scheifling 57 D4
Scheinfeld 55 E1
Schelde 50 B3
Schenefeld (Hamburg) 48 A3
Schenefeld (Itzehoe) 48 A2
Scherfede 52 A2
Schermbeck 17 E3
Scheßlitz 52 C4
Scheveningen 16 B3
Schia 60 B3
Schiedam 16 B3
Schieder-Schwalenberg .. 52 A1
Schiehallion 4 C1
Schierling 56 B2
Schiermonnikoog . 47 D3
Schiermonnikoog/. 47 D3
Schiers 58 B2
Schifferstadt 54 C2
Schildau 53 D2
Schilpario 58 C4
Schiltach 54 C3
Schio 59 D4
Schirmeck 21 E4
Schirnding 53 D4
Schkeuditz 53 D2
Schkölen 53 D3
Schladming 59 F1
Schlagsdorf 48 B2
Schlanders 58 C3
Schlangenbad 51 F4
Schleching 56 B3
Schlei 48 A1
Schleiden 51 D4
Schleiz 53 D3
Schleswig 48 A1
Schleswig-Holstein . 48 A1
Schleusingen 52 C3
Schlieben 53 E1
Schliersee 56 B4
Schlitz 52 B3
Schlotheim 52 B2
Schluchsee 54 C4
Schlucht, Col de la .. 27 E1
Schlüchtern 52 B4
Schluderbach 59 E2
Schluderns 58 C3
Schlüsselfeld 55 E1
Schlutup 48 B2

Schmalkalden 52 B3
Schmallenberg ... 17 F4
Schmidmühlen ... 55 F1
Schmilka 53 F2
Schmölln (Mecklenburg-Vorpommern) 49 E3
Schmölln (Thüringen) 53 D3
Schnackenburg ... 48 C3
Schnaittenbach ... 55 F1
Schneeberg (A) ... 57 E3
Schneeberg (Bayern) 53 D4
Schneeberg (Sachsen) 53 D3
Schneverdingen ... 48 A3
Schoberpaß 57 D4
Schöckl......... 57 E4
Schönau 54 C4
Schönberg (A) 59 D2
Schönberg (Bayern). 56 C2
Schönberg (Mecklenburg-Vorpommern) 48 B2
Schönberg (Sachsen) 53 D4
Schönberg (Schleswig-Holstein) 48 B1
Schönbrunn 57 F2
Schönebeck 52 C1
Schöneck 53 D3
Schönecken 51 D4
Schönefeld 49 E4
Schönewalde 53 E1
Schongau 55 F4
Schöningen 52 C1
Schönmünzach ... 54 C3
Schönsee 56 B1
Schönthal 56 B1
Schönwald 54 C3
Schönwalde 48 B2
Schoonhoven 16 C3
Schopfheim 54 C4
Schöppenstedt 52 B1
Schoppernau 58 B2
Schotten 52 A4
Schouwen Duiveland....... 16 B3
Schramberg 54 C3
Schrems 57 D2
Schrobenhausen ... 55 F2
Schröcken 58 B2
Schrozberg 55 E1
Schruns 58 B2
Schuls 58 C2
Schüttorf 17 E2
Schwaan 48 C2
Schwabach 55 E1
Schwäbisch Gmünd 55 D2
Schwäbisch Hall .. 55 D2
Schwabmünchen ... 55 E3
Schwaigern 55 D2
Schwalmstadt-Treysa 52 A3
Schwalmstadt-Ziegenhain 52 A3
Schwandorf 56 B1
Schwanebeck 52 C1
Schwanenstadt... 56 C3
Schwanewede 47 F3
Schwarmstedt ... 48 A4
Schwarza (A)...... 57 E3
Schwarza (D)..... 52 C3
Schwarzach 59 E1
Schwarze Elster ... 53 E1
Schwarzenbach ... 53 D4
Schwarzenbek... 48 B3
Schwarzenberg ... 53 D3
Schwarzenburg ... 27 E3
Schwarzenfeld ... 56 B1
Schwarzheide 53 E2
Schwarzsee 27 E3
Schwarzwald 54 C3
Schwaz......... 59 D1
Schwechat 57 F2
Schwedt........ 49 E3
Schweich 54 A1
Schweinfurt 52 B4
Schweinitz 53 E1
Schwelm........ 17 E4

Schwendi 55 E3
Schwenningen 54 C3
Schwerin 48 C2
Schweriner See 48 C2
Schwerte 17 E3
Schwetzingen 54 C1
Schwielochsee 53 F1
Schwyz 58 A2
Sciacca 68 B3
Scicli 69 D4
Scilla 67 E4
Scilly, Is of 8 A4
Scole 11 D1
Sconser 2 B3
Scopello 58 A4
Scordia 69 D3
Scorff 22 B3
Sčors 113 E1
Scorzè 59 E4
Scotch Corner . . 6 C1
Scotland 2 C4
Scourie 2 C2
Scrabster 3 D2
Scridain, L 4 B1
Scrivia 60 A2
Ščučin 110 C4
Scunthorpe 7 D2
Scuol 58 C2
Seaford 10 C3
Seaham 5 E4
Seaton 9 D3
Seaton Delaval 5 E3
Sebečevo 76 C1
Sebeş 114 C1
Sebež 111 D3
Sebnitz 53 F2
Sečanj 73 D2
Secchia 60 C2
Seckau 57 D4
Seclin 19 F1
Secondigny 24 C3
Sedan 20 C2
Sedano 35 F2
Seda, Rib de 38 C3
Sedbergh 6 C1
Séderon 30 C3
Sedgefield 5 E4
Sedičany 53 F4
Sedico 59 E3
Sedilo 66 B2
Sedini 66 B2
Sedlare 77 D2
Sedlec-Prčice 53 F4
Sée 18 C4
Seebenau 48 B4
Seebergsattel 70 B1
Seeboden 59 F2
Seebruck 56 B3
Seefeld 58 C1
Seehaus 56 C3
Seehausen
   (Magdeburg) 52 C1
Seehausen
   (Stendal) 48 C3
Seeheim 54 C1
Seelisberg 58 A2
Seelow 49 E4
Sées 19 D4
Seesen 52 B1
Seevetal 48 A3
Seewalchen 56 C3
Seewiesen 57 E3
Sefkerin 72 C2
Segesta 68 A3
Segl 58 B3
Segni 63 F3
Segonzac 28 B1
Segorbe 41 E3
Segovia 40 A1
Segrè 23 E4
Segre 37 E3
Segre, R 32 A3
Segura 38 C3
Segura de la
   Sierra 44 B1
Segura de León . . 43 D1
Segura de los
   Baños 41 D1
Segura, R 45 D2
Segura, Sa de . . 44 B2
Sehnde 52 B1
Seia 38 C2
Seiches 23 E4
Seifhennersdorf 53 F2

Seignelay 26 B1
Seil 4 B1
Seiland 95 D1
Seilandsjøkelen 95 D1
Seilhac 29 D1
Seille (Meurthe-et-
   Moselle) 21 D4
Seille (Saône-et-
   Loire) 26 C3
Seinäjoki 102 C2
Seine 19 E3
Seine-et-Marne 19 F4
Seine-Maritime 19 D3
Sein, I de 22 A3
Seitenstetten 57 D3
Seitsemisen 102 C3
Seixal 38 A4
Seixo 34 B3
Sejerø 108 B3
Sejerø Bugt 108 B3
Sejm 113 F1
Sékoulas 86 C2
Šekovići 72 B4
Selargius 66 B4
Selassia 87 D3
Selb 53 D4
Selbekken 100 C1
Selbu 101 D2
Selbusjøen 100 C2
Selby 7 D2
Selce 70 B3
Selçuk 115 E4
Sele 64 C4
Selečka pl 77 E4
Selenter See 48 B1
Sélero 81 D2
Sélestat 21 E4
Selevac 73 D3
Selfoss 96 A2
Séli 79 E3
Selia 90 C4
Selianitika 83 D4
Seligenstadt 52 A4
Selínia 87 F1
Selishtë 76 C3
Selište 73 E3
Selje 100 A3
Seljord 104 C3
Selkämeri 102 B3
Selkirk 5 D3
Sellajoch 59 D3
Sella Nevea 59 F3
Sella, Pso di 59 D3
Selles 25 E2
Sellières 26 C3
Sellin 49 D1
Selm 17 E3
Selmsdorf 48 B2
Selna 71 F3
Selommes 25 E2
Selongey 26 C2
Seløy 97 D3
Selsey 9 F3
Selsey Bill 9 F3
Selters 52 A4
Seltz 21 E4
Sélune 18 C4
Selva 59 D3
Selvino 58 B4
Seman 114 B3
Semeljci 71 F2
Semič 70 B2
Seminara 67 E4
Semizovac 71 F4
Semmering 57 E3
Semmering-Paß 57 E3
Semois 20 C2
Semproniano 63 D1
Semur-en-Auxois . . 26 B2
Semur-en-
   Brionnais 26 B4
Sena 37 E3
Sénas 30 C3
Sendim 34 C4
Senez 31 D3
Senftenberg 53 E2
Sengsengeb 57 D3
Senigallia 61 F3
Senise 65 D4
Senj 70 B3
Senja Ånderdalen . . . 94 B3
Senje 73 E4
Senlis 19 F3

Sennecey-le-Grand . 26 C3
Sennen 8 A4
Sennestadt 17 F3
Sennori 66 A2
Senonches 19 E4
Senones 21 E4
Senorbì 66 B3
Senožeče 70 A2
Sens 26 A1
Senta 72 C1
Šentilj 70 C1
Šentjernej 70 C2
Šentjur 70 C2
Šentvid na
   Šlemenu 70 B1
Sépeaux 26 A1
Šepetovka 113 D2
Sepino 64 B3
Sepúlveda 36 A4
Sequeros 39 E2
Sequillo, R 35 E4
Seraing 50 C4
Seravezza 60 B3
Seregno 60 A1
Serein 26 B2
Serena, Emb de la . . 39 E4
Séres 80 B2
Séres (Nomos) 80 A2
Serfaus 58 C2
Serfopoúla, N 88 B3
Seriate 60 B1
Sérifos 88 A3
Sérifos, N 88 A3
Serifou, Stenó 88 A3
Sermaize-les-
   Bains 20 C4
Sermide 60 C2
Sermoneta 63 F3
Sernancelhe 38 C1
Serón 44 B3
Serón de
   Nágima 36 B4
Seròs 37 E4
Serpa 42 B1
Serpeddì, P 66 B4
Serpis, R 45 E1
Serra 41 E3
Serracapriola 64 B2
Serrada 35 E4
Serradifalco 68 C3
Serradilla 39 D3
Serramanna 66 B4
Serrana, Pto de la . . 39 E3
Serra San Bruno 67 F3
Serravalle Scrivia . . . 60 A2
Serre Chevalier 31 D2
Serre-Ponçon, Bge
   de 31 D2
Serres 30 C2
Serrières 30 B1
Serrota 39 F2
Sersale 67 F3
Sertã 38 B2
Servan 18 B4
Sérvia 79 E4
Servian 30 A4
Servigliano 61 F4
Servol, R 41 F2
Sesa 37 D3
Sesena 40 A2
Sesia 27 F4
Sesimbra 38 A4
Sesklio, N 93 E1
Sesma 36 C2
Sessa Aurunca 64 A3
Sesta Godano 60 B3
Šestanovac 75 E2
Sestino 61 E3
Sesto 59 E2
Sesto Calende 60 A1
Sesto Fiorentino 60 C3
Sesto San
   Giovanni 60 A1
Sestola 60 C3
Sestriere 31 E2
Sestri Levante 60 B3
Sestrunj 74 C1
Sestrunj I 74 C1
Sestu 66 B4
Sesvete 70 C2
Séta 84 B4
Setcases 32 B3
Sète 30 A4
Setenil 43 E3

Setermoen 94 B3
Setesdalen 104 B3
Setesdalsheiene . . . 104 B3
Settebagni 63 E2
Settimo Torinese 31 E1
Settle 6 C1
Settons, les 26 B2
Setúbal 38 A4
Seudre 28 B1
Seui 66 B3
Seulo 66 B3
Seurre 26 C2
Sevastianá 79 E3
Sevenoaks 10 C3
Sévérac-le-
   Château 29 F3
Sever do Vouga . . 38 B1
Severn Bridge 9 D2
Severn, Mouth of
   the 9 D2
Severn,R 9 D2
Sever, R 38 C3
Seveso 60 A1
Sevettijärvi 95 F2
Sevilla 43 D2
Sevilleja de la Jara . . 39 F3
Sevlievo 115 D2
Sevnica 70 C2
Sevojno 72 C4
Sèvre Nantaise 24 C3
Sèvre Niortaise 24 C4
Sévrier 27 D4
Sevsk 111 F4
Sexten 59 E2
Seyches 28 C2
Seyda 53 D1
Seyðisfjörður 96 C2
Seyne 31 D3
Seyne, la 31 D4
Seyssel 27 D4
Sežana 70 A2
Sézanne 20 B4
Sezimovo-Ústí 57 D1
Sezze 63 F3
Sfáka 91 F4
Sfakiá 90 C4
Sfaktiría, N 86 C3
Sferracavallo 68 B2
Sfikiá, L 79 E3
Sfîntu Gheorghe . . 113 D4
Sforzacosta 61 F4
's Gravendeel 16 C3
's Gravenhage 16 B3
Sgùrr Mór 2 C3
Sgùrr na Ciche 2 B4
Shaftesbury 9 D3
Shanklin 9 E4
Shannon 12 B4
Shannon, Mouth
   ofthe 12 A4
Shannon, R 12 B4
Shap 5 D4
Shapinsay 3 E1
Shebenik, Mal i . . 77 D4
Sheelin, L 13 D3
Sheep Haven 12 C1
Sheep's Head 14 A4
's Heerenberg 17 D3
Sheerness 11 D2
Sheffield 6 C2
Shefford 9 F2
Shëmri (Shkodër) . . 76 C3
Shëmri (Tiranë) 76 C4
Shëngjin 76 C3
Sheppey, I of 11 D2
Shepshed 7 D3
Shepton Mallet 9 D3
Sherborne 9 D3
Shercock 13 D3
Sheringham 7 F3
's Hertogenbosch . . . 16 C3
Shetland Is 3 E2
Shiel Bridge 2 C4
Shieldaig 2 B3
Shiel, L 2 B4
Shijak 76 C4
Shinás 79 E3
Shiniás 88 A1
Shin; L 2 C2
Shinos 83 D3
Shinoússa, N 88 C3
Shipston-on-Stour . . . 9 E1
Shíza, N 86 C4
Shkodër 76 B3

Shkodrës, Liq i 76 B3
Shkumbin 76 C4
Sholári 80 A3
Shoreham 10 C3
Shpat, Mal i 77 D4
Shrewsbury 6 B3
Shrewton 9 E3
Shropshire 9 D1
Shupenzë 77 D4
Sía, Pto de la 36 A1
Siátista 79 D4
Sibari 67 E2
Sibbhult 109 D3
Sibbo 107 F2
Sibbofjärden 107 F2
Šibenik 75 D1
Šibenik Mt 75 E2
Sibinj 71 E3
Sibiu 113 D4
Severn,R 9 D2
Sichar, Emb de . . 41 E3
Sicié, Cap 31 D4
Sicignano degli
   Alburni 64 C4
Sicilia 68 B2
Sicó 38 B2
Šid 72 B2
Sidári 82 A1
Sideby 102 B3
Sidensjö 102 A2
Siderno 67 F4
Sideros, Akr 91 F3
Sidiró 81 F2
Sidirókastro 80 A2
Sidirónero 80 C1
Sidlaw Hills 5 D1
Sidmouth 9 D3
Siebenlehn 53 E2
Siedlce 112 C1
Sieg 51 E3
Siegburg 51 E3
Siegen 17 F4
Siegsdorf 56 B3
Siekierki 49 E3
Siena 61 D4
Sieppijärvi 98 C1
Sieradz 112 B2
Sierck 21 D3
Sierentz 27 E1
Sierninghofen 57 D3
Sierpc 112 B1
Sierra Boyera, Emb
   de 43 D4
Sierra de Fuentes . . 39 D3
Sierra de Yeguas . . . 43 E3
Sierre 27 E3
Sievi 102 C1
Sievin as 102 C1
Sifnos, N 88 B3
Sifnou, Stenó 88 B3
Sigean 32 B2
Sigerfjord 94 A3
Siggjarvåg 104 A3
Sighetu
   Marmaţiei 112 C3
Sighişoara 113 D4
Siglufjörður 96 B1
Sigmaringen 55 D3
Signy-l'Abbaye 20 B2
Sigri 85 E2
Sigtuna 106 B3
Sigüenza 36 B4
Sigulda 110 C3
Siiddasjávri 94 B4
Siikainen 102 B3
Siikajoki 99 D4
Siikajoki R 99 D4
Siilinjärvi 103 E2
Sijarinska Banja 77 D1
Sikaminiá 85 F2
Sikås 101 E1
Siki 84 A2
Sikiá (Makedonia) . . 80 B4
Sikiá
   (Pelopónissos) . . . 87 E4
Síkinos 88 C4
Síkinos, N 88 C4
Sikióna 87 D1
Sikoráhi 81 E2
Sikoúrio 83 E1
Sikovuono 95 E3
Síla, La 67 F3
Silandro 58 C3

Silba 70 B4
Silba I 70 B4
Silbaš 72 B2
Sildegapet 100 A2
Şile 115 F3
Siles 44 B1
Siliqua 66 B4
Silistra 115 E1
Silivri 115 E3
Šilo 70 B3
Silo 81 E2
Sil, R 34 C2
Sils 32 B4
Sils im Engadin 58 B3
Siltakylä 107 F2
Šilutè 110 B3
Silvalen 97 D3
Silvaplana 58 B3
Silvares 38 C2
Silves 42 A2
Silvi Marina 64 A1
Silvrettagruppe 58 B2
Silz 58 C2
Simancas 35 E4
Šimandra 80 A3
Šimanovci 72 C3
Simav 115 F4
Simaxis 66 B3
Simbach (Inn) 56 B3
Simbach (Isar) 56 B2
Simbruini, Mti 63 F2
Simeto 69 D3
Sími 93 E1
Šimiči 71 E3
Sími, N 93 E1
Simlångsdalen 108 C2
Simmerath 51 D4
Simmern 54 B1
Simo 99 D3
Simojärvi 99 E2
Simojoki 99 D3
Simola 103 F4
Símonos Pétras 80 C4
Simonsbath 8 C3
Simonswald 54 C3
Simópoulo 86 B1
Simplonpass 27 F3
Simrishamn 109 D3
Sinaia 113 D4
Sinalunga 61 D4
Sinarádes 82 A1
Sinarcas 41 D3
Sindelfingen 55 D2
Sındırgı 115 F4
Sindos 79 F3
Sines 42 A1
Sines, C de 42 A1
Sinettä 99 D2
Sineu 45 F3
Singen 55 D4
Singöfjärden 106 B3
Singra, Pto de 41 D2
Siniscola 66 C2
Sinj 75 D1
Sinjajevina 76 B2
Sinni 65 D4
Sinnicolau Mare . . . 114 C1
Sinopoli 67 E4
Sinsheim 55 D2
Sintra 38 A4
Sinzig 51 E4
Sion 27 E3
Sioule 26 A4
Šipan 75 F2
Šipanska Luka 75 F2
Šipka 115 D2
Sipoo 107 F2
Sipoonselkä 107 F2
Šipovo 71 E4
Sippola 107 F2
Šiprage 71 E4
Sira 104 A4
Sira R 104 B4

Siracusa 69 D4
Sirdalen 104 B4
Sirdalvatn 104 A4
Siret 113 D3
Siret R 113 E4
Sirevåg 104 A4
Sirig 72 C2
Sirino, Mte 65 D4
Sirig 72 C2
Širitovci 75 D1
Sirkka 95 D1
Sirma 95 E2
Sirmione 60 C1
Sirna, N 92 C1
Široko Polje 71 F2
Sirolo 61 F4
Siros, N 88 B2
Siruela 39 F4
Sisak 71 D2
Šišan 70 A4
Sisante 40 C4
Šišljavić 70 C3
Sissa 60 B2
Sissach 27 F2
Sissonne 20 B3
Sisteron 31 D3
Sistiana 59 F3
Sistranda 100 C1
Sitges 32 A4
Sithonia 80 B4
Sitia 91 F4
Sitnica 77 D2
Sittard 17 D4
Sittensen 48 A3
Sittingbourne 11 D3
Siuntio 107 E3
Siuro 107 E1
Siurua 99 D3
Siuruanjoki 99 D3
Siusi 59 D3
Sivac 72 B2
Sivaslı 115 F4
Siviri 80 A4
Sivota 82 B2
Sivros 82 B3
Siziano 60 A1
Sizun 22 B3
Sjælland 108 C3
Sjællands Odde . . . 108 B3
Sjenica 76 C1
Sjeništa 76 A1
Sjøåsen 97 D4
Sjöbo 109 D3
Sjøholt 100 B2
Sjona 97 E2
Sjøtorp 105 E4
Sjoutnäset 97 E4
Sjøvegan 94 B3
Sjulsmark 102 B1
Sjundea 107 E3
Sjusjøen 104 D2
Skåbu 100 C3
Skäckerfjällen 101 D1
Skadarsko jez 76 B3
Skadovsk 113 F4
Skafidiá 86 B2
Skaftá 96 B2
Skaftafell 96 C2
Skagafjörður 96 B1
Skage 97 D4
Skagen 108 B1
Skagern 105 E4
Skagerrak 108 A1
Skaill 3 E1
Skjálfandi 96 B1
Skála (Kefaloniá) . . . 86 A1
Skála (Lésvos) 85 F2
Skála (Pátmos) 89 E4
Skála
   (Pelopónissos) . . . 87 B3
Skála (Stereá
   Eláda) 83 F3
Skála Eressoú 85 E2
Skála Kaliráhis 80 C3
Skaland 94 B2
Skála Oropoú 84 B4
Skála Potamiás 81 D3
Skála Rahoníou 80 C3
Skalavík 96 A4
Skála Volissoú 85 E4
Skälderviken 108 C3
Skálevik 104 B4
Skálfandafljót 96 B2
Skalka 98 A2
Skalohóri (Lésvos) . . 85 E2

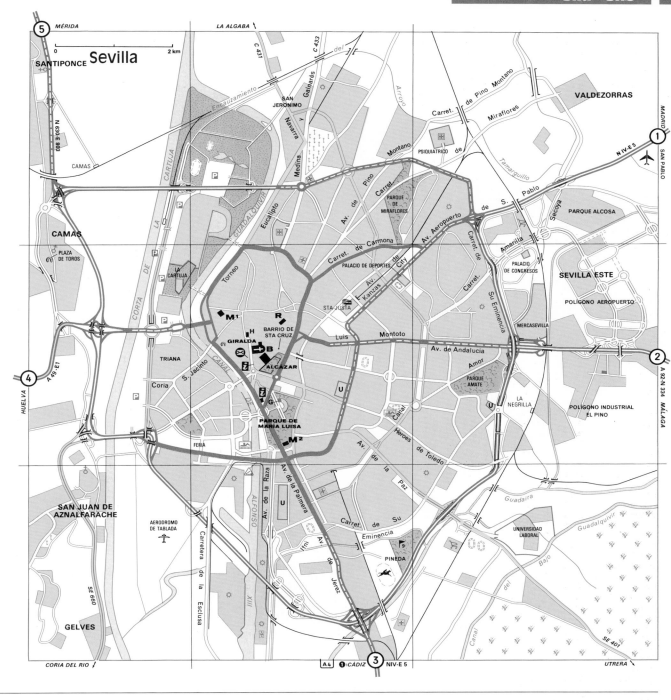

Sevilla

Skalohóri
(Makedonía) ... 79 D3
Skaloti ... 80 C1
Skælskør ... 108 B4
Skamnéli ... 78 C4
Skandáli ... 85 D1
Skandári, Akr ... 89 F3
Skanderborg ... 108 B3
Skandzoúra, N. ... 84 B3
Skåne ... 109 D3
Skånevik ... 104 A3
Skåningsbukt. ... 94 C2
Skånland ... 94 B3
Skänninge ... 106 A4
Skanör
Falsterbo ... 108 C4
Skara ... 109 D1
Skaraborgs Län ... 109 D1
Skaramangás ... 87 F1
Skærbæk ... 108 A4
Skarberget ... 94 B4
Škarda ... 74 B1
Skåre ... 105 E3
Skárfia ... 83 F3
Skärgårdshavet ... 107 D3
Skärhamn ... 108 C1
Skarnes ... 105 D3
Skarplinge ... 106 B2
Skarsvåg ... 95 E1
Skärvången ... 101 E1
Skarżysko-
Kamienna ... 112 B2
Skattungbyn ... 101 E4
Skatval ... 100 C2
Skaulo ... 94 C4
Skaun ... 100 C2
Skee ... 105 D4
Skegness ... 7 E3
Skei (Møre og
Romsdal) ... 100 B2
Skei (Sogn og
Fjordane) ... 100 A3
Skeiðarársandur ... 96 B2
Skela ... 72 C3
Skellefteå ... 98 B4
Skellefteälven ... 98 B4
Skelleftehamn ... 98 B4
Skellig ... 14 A4
Skelmersdale ... 6 B2
Skenderbeut, M i ... 76 C4
Skender Vakuf ... 71 E4
Skepastó ... 80 B2
Skerries ... 13 E3
Ski ... 105 D3
Skiathos ... 84 A2
Skiáthos, N ... 84 A2
Skibbereen ... 14 B4
Skibby ... 108 C3
Skibotn ... 94 C2
Skiddaw ... 5 D4
Skidra ... 79 E3
Skien ... 104 C3
Skierniewice ... 112 B2
Skillingaryd ... 109 D2
Skiloundía ... 86 C2
Skinári, Akr ... 86 A1
Skiniás ... 91 E4
Skinnarbu ... 104 B3
Skinnskatteberg ... 105 F3
Skipagurra ... 95 F1
Skipton ... 6 C2
Skíros ... 84 C3
Skíros, N ... 84 C3
Skíti ... 83 F1
Skive ... 108 A2
Skivjane ... 76 C2
Skjeberg ... 105 D3
Skjelvik ... 97 E2
Skjern ... 108 A3
Skjersholmane ... 104 A3
Skjerstad ... 97 E2
Skjerstadfjorden ... 97 E2
Skjervøy ... 94 C2
Skjønhaug ... 105 D3
Sklavopoúla ... 90 B3
Sklithro ... 83 F1
Šklov ... 111 E3
Skočivir ... 77 E4
Škocjanske jame ... 70 A3
Skodje ... 100 B2
Škofja Loka ... 70 A2
Skofljica ... 70 B2
Skog (Gävleborgs
Län) ... 101 F4

Skog (Västernorrlands
Län) ... 102 A2
Skövde ... 109 D1
Skógafoss ... 96 B3
Skogerøya ... 95 F2
Skoghall ... 105 E3
Skogstorp ... 105 F4
Skokloster ... 106 B3
Skólis ... 86 B1
Skópelos (Lésvos) ... 85 F3
Skópelos (Skópelos) ... 84 B2
Skópelos, N ... 84 B3
Skopí ... 91 F4
Skopiá ... 83 E2
Skopje ... 77 E3
Skopós ... 79 D2
Skopun ... 96 A4
Skorenovac ... 73 D3
Skorovatn ... 97 E4
Skorped ... 101 F2
Skotterud ... 105 D3
Skoulikariá ... 82 C2
Skoúra ... 87 D3
Skoútari
(Makedonía) ... 80 B2
Skoútari
(Pelopónissos) ... 87 D4
Skoutáros ... 85 E2
Skövde ... 109 D1
Skrå ... 79 E2
Skradin ... 75 D1
Skradinski buk ... 75 D1
Skreia ... 105 D2
Skrim ... 104 C3
Skrolsvik ... 94 B3
Skrydstrup ... 108 A4
Skudeneshavn ... 104 A3
Skuleskogen ... 102 A2
Skull ... 14 A4
Skultuna ... 106 A3
Skuodas ... 110 B3
Skuov'gilraš'ša ... 95 D2
Skurup ... 109 D3
Skutskär ... 106 B2
Skutvik ... 94 A4
Skvira ... 113 E2
Skye ... 2 B3
Slagelse ... 108 B3
Slagnäs ... 98 A3
Slânčev Brjag ... 115 E2
Slancy ... 111 D1
Slane ... 13 D3
Slaney ... 15 D3
Slangerup ... 108 C3

Slano ... 75 F2
Slany ... 53 F3
Šlapanice ... 57 F1
Slapská přehr
nádrž ... 53 F4
Slapy ... 53 F4
Šlask ... 112 A2
Slatina (Bor) ... 73 E3
Slatina (BH) ... 71 E3
Slatina (Kraljevo) ... 73 D4
Slatina
(Makedonija) ... 77 D3
Slatina (RO) ... 115 D1
Slatine ... 75 D2
Slatinski Drenovac ... 71 E2
Slavgorod ... 111 E4
Slavinja ... 77 F1
Slavkovica ... 72 C4
Slavkov u Brna ... 57 F1
Slavnik ... 70 A3
Slavonice ... 57 E1
Slavonska Požega ... 71 E2
Slavonski Brod ... 71 E3
Slavonski Kobaš ... 71 E3
Slavuta ... 113 D2
Sławno ... 110 A4
Sławoborze ... 49 F2
Sleaford ... 7 D3

Slea Head ... 14 A3
Sleat, Sd of ... 2 B4
Slettfjellet ... 94 C2
Sliedrecht ... 16 C3
Sliema ... 68 B4
Slieve Bloom Mts ... 12 C4
Slieve Donard ... 13 E3
Slieve Mish Mts ... 14 A3
Slievenamon ... 14 C3
Slieve Snaght ... 13 D1
Sligachan ... 2 B3
Sligeach ... 12 C2
Sligo ... 12 C2
Sligo (Co) ... 12 B3
Sligo B ... 12 C2
Slišane ... 77 D1
Slite ... 109 F4
Sliven ... 115 E2
Sljeme ... 70 C2
Sljivovica ... 72 C4
Slobozia ... 115 E1
Slonim ... 112 C1
Sloten ... 16 C1
Slough ... 9 F2
Slovac ... 72 C3
Slovenska Bistrica ... 70 C1
Slovenija ... 70 A2
Slovenj Gradec ... 70 B1

Slovenske Konjice ... 70 C1
Slovenské
Rudohorie ... 112 B3
Slovinci ... 71 D3
Sluck ... 111 D4
Sluderno ... 58 C3
Sluis ... 16 A4
Sluknov ... 53 F2
Slunj ... 70 C3
Słupsk ... 110 A4
Slyne Head ... 12 A3
Småland ... 109 D2
Smålandsfarvandet 108 B4
Smålands-stenar ... 109 D2
Šmarje ... 70 C2
Šmarješke Toplice ... 70 B2
Šmartin ... 70 B2
Smedby ... 109 E2
Smědeč ... 56 C2
Smederevo ... 73 D3
Smederevska
Palanka ... 73 D3
Smedjebacken ... 105 F3
Smela ... 113 F2
Smigáda ... 81 E2
Smilčić ... 74 C1
Smilde ... 17 D1

Smiltene ... 110 C2
Smojmirovo ... 77 F3
Smokovec ... 70 B3
Smokovljan ... 75 F2
Smøla ... 100 B1
Smolensk ... 111 E3
Smoleviči ... 111 D4
Smólikas, Óros ... 78 C4
Smoljan ... 115 D3
Smorgon ... 111 D4
Smørhamn ... 104 A1
Smygehamn ... 109 D4
Snaefell ... 6 A1
Snæfellsnes ... 96 A2
Snaith ... 7 D2
Snåsa ... 101 D1
Snasahögarna ... 101 D1
Snåsavatnet ... 101 D1
Sneek ... 16 C1
Sneem ... 14 A4
Snežnik ... 70 B3
Śniardwy, Jez ... 110 B4
Snigir'ovka ... 113 F3
Snillfjord ... 100 C2
Snizort, L ... 2 B3
Snøfjord ... 95 D1
Snøhefta ... 100 C3

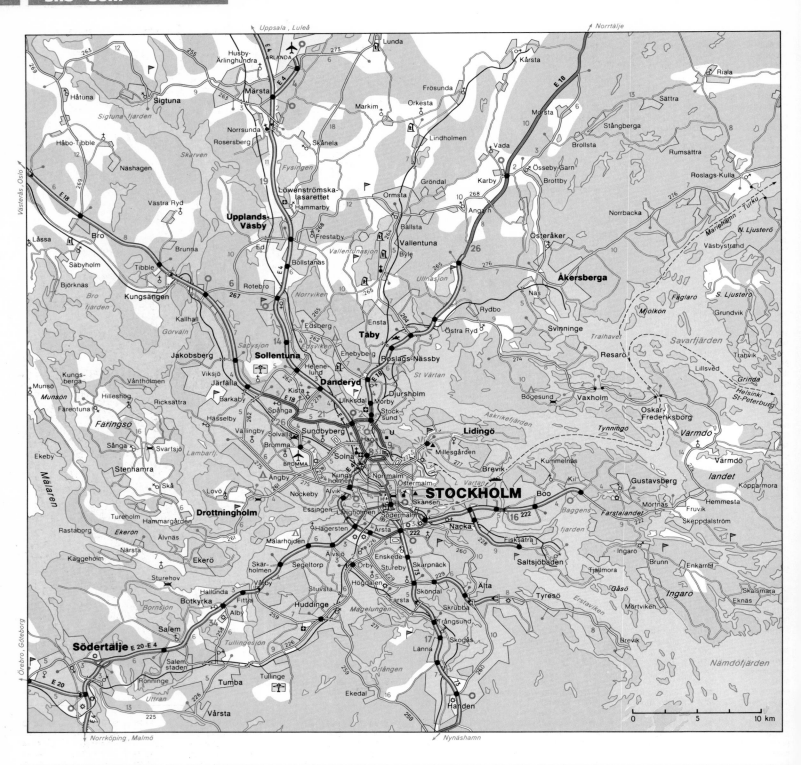

Snøtinden 97 E2	Socol 73 D2	Sofikó 87 E1	Soko Banja 73 E4	Solesmes (Nord) 20 A2	Sóller 45 E2	Sombernon 26 C2
Snowdon 6 A3	Socovos 44 C1	Sofó 83 E2	Sokolac 72 B4	Solesmes (Sarthe) .. 23 E3	Sollerön 101 E4	Sombor............ 72 B2
Snowdonia Forest	Socuéllamos 40 B4	Sögel 17 E1	Sokolov 53 D4	Solevåg 100 A2	Søllested 108 B4	Someren 17 D4
and Nat Pk 6 A3	Sodankylä 95 E4	Sogliano al	Sokołów Podlaski .. 112 C1	Solf 102 B2	Solliès-Pont 31 D4	Somero 107 E2
Soave 60 C1	Söderåkra 109 E3	Rubicone 61 E3	Sokosti 95 F3	Solferino 60 C1	Solnečnogorsk 111 F2	Somerset.......... 9 D3
Sobešlav 57 D1	Söderbärke 105 F3	Soglio 58 B3	Sola (Rogaland) 104 A3	Solholmen 100 B2	Solofra 64 B4	Someş 112 C4
Sobra 75 F2	Söderfors 106 B3	Sogndal 100 B3	Sola (Sogn og	Solignac (Haute-	Solosancho 39 F2	Somiedo, Pto de ... 35 D2
Sobrado de los	Söderhamn 101 F4	Søgne............. 104 B4	Fjordane) 104 A1	Loire) 29 F2	Solothurn 27 E2	Sommarøy 94 B2
Monjes 34 B2	Söderköping 106 A4	Sognefjell 100 B3	Solana de los	Solignac (Haute-	Solsona 32 A3	Sommatino 68 C4
Sobral da Adiça ... 42 C1	Södermanlands	Sognefjorden 104 A1	Barros 39 D4	Vienne) 29 D1	Solrød 108 C3	Somme 19 E2
Sobral de Monte	Län 106 A4	Sognesjøen 104 A1	Solana del Pino ... 43 F1	Soligorsk 111 D4	Solsona 32 A3	Somme (Dépt) 19 F2
Agraço........... 38 A3	Söderskog 109 D3	Sogn og	Solares 35 F2	Solihull 9 E1	Šolta 75 D2	Sommen 109 E1
Sobreira Formosa .. 38 C2	Södertälje 106 B4	Fjordane 100 A3	Solberg 101 F1	Solin 75 D1	Soltau 48 A3	Sömmerda 52 C2
Sobrón, Emb de. .. 36 B2	Sodražica 70 B2	Soham 11 D1	Solbergfjorden 94 B3	Soline 74 B1	Solunska Glava 77 E3	Sommesous 20 B4
Søby 108 B4	Sodupe 36 B1	Sohós 80 A2	Solčava 70 B1	Solingen. 17 E4	Solunto 68 B3	Sommières 30 B3
Soča R........... 70 A2	Soest (D) 17 F3	Soignies 50 B4	Sol'cy 111 D2	Sölkerpaß 57 D4	Solvay 60 C4	Sømna............ 97 D3
Soča R. 70 A2	Soest (NL) 16 C2	Soini 102 C2	Solda 58 C3	Söll 59 D1	Sölvesborg 109 D3	Somolinos 36 A4
Sočanica 77 D1	Soestdijk 16 C2	Soinlahti 103 D1	Sölden 58 C2	Sollana 41 E4	Solvorn 100 B3	Somosierra, Pto
Soccia 33 F3	Sofádes 83 E2	Soissons 20 A3	Soldeu 32 A2	Sollefteå 101 F2	Solway Firth 4 C4	de 36 A4
Sochaczew 112 B1	Sofia 115 D2	Söke 115 E4	Solent, The 9 E3	Sollenau 57 F3	Solynieve 44 A3	Sompio............ 95 F3
Sochaux 27 E2	Sofiero 108 C3	Sokna 104 C2	Solenzara. 33 F4	Sollentuna 106 B3	Soma 115 E4	Somport, Pto de .. 37 D2

Šomrda 73 E3
Soncillo 35 F2
Soncino 60 B1
Søndeled 104 C4
Sønderborg 108 B4
Sønderby 108 B4
Sønder Felding.... 108 A3
Sondershausen.... 52 C2
Søndersø 108 B3
Sondrio 58 B3
Songeons 19 E3
Sonkajärvi 103 E1
Sonnblick 59 E2
Sonneberg 52 C4
Sonnewalde 53 E1
Sonogno 58 A3
Sonsbeck 17 D3
Sonseca 40 A3
Son Servera 45 F3
Sonta 72 B2
Sonthofen 55 E4
Sontra 52 B3
Soome Laht 110 C1
Sopeira 37 F3
Sopilja 76 A1
Sopište 77 D3
Sopoćani 76 C1
Sopot (PL) 110 A4
Sopot (Srbija).... 73 D3
Sopotnica 77 D4
Sopron 112 A4
Sora 64 A3
Soragna 60 B2
Söråker 101 F3
Sørarnøy 97 E2
Sorbas 44 C3
Sorbe, R 40 B1
Sore 28 B3
Soresina 60 B1
Sørfjorden 104 B2
Sør-Flatanger 96 C4
Sørfolda 94 A4
Sörfors 102 A1
Sorga 52 B3
Sorgono 66 B3
Sorgues 30 B3
Sørgutvik 97 D4
Soria 36 B3
Soriano nel
 Cimino 63 E2
Sørkjosen 94 C2
Sørø 108 B3
Soroka 113 E3
Soro, M 69 D3
Soroní 93 E1
Sørøya 95 D1
Sørøysundet 95 D1
Sorraia, R 38 A4
Sørreisa 94 B3
Sorrento 64 A3
Sor, Rib de 38 B3
Sørrollnes 94 B3
Sorsakoski 103 E2
Sorsele 98 A3
Sorso 66 A2
Sort 37 F2
Sortino 69 D4
Sortland 94 A3
Sortlandsundet.... 94 A3
Sør Trøndelag 100 C2
Sorunda 106 B4
Sørvågen 97 E1
Sørvågur 96 A4
Sørvær 94 C1
Sørværøy 97 E1
Sörvattnet 101 D3
Sos del Rey
 Católico 37 D2
Soses 37 E4
Sosnovyj Bor 111 D1
Sosnowiec 112 B2
Sospel 31 E3
Šoštanj 70 B1
Sóstis 81 D2
Šostka 111 F4
Sotaseter 100 B3
Sotillo de la Adrada 39 F2
Sotin 72 B2
Sotíra 79 E2
Sotkamo 99 E4
Soto del Barco ... 35 D1
Soto de los
 Infantes 35 D1
Soto de Luiña 35 D1

Soto de Sajambre .. 35 E2
Sotogrande 43 E4
Sotopalacios 35 F3
Sottomarina 61 D1
Sottunga 106 C3
Sotuélamos 40 C4
Soúda 90 C3
Souesmes 25 F2
Soufflenheim 21 F3
Soufli 81 F2
Soúgia 90 B4
Souillac 29 D2
Souilly 20 C3
Soulac 28 A1
Soulaines-Dhuys.. 20 C4
Soulinári 86 C3
Souliou, Óri 82 B2
Soulópoulo 82 B1
Soultz (Bas-Rhin) . 21 E3
Soultz (Haut-Rhin) . 27 E1
Soúnio 88 A2
Soúnio, Akr 88 A2
Souppes 25 F1
Sourdeval 18 C4
Soure 38 B2
Sournia 32 B2
Souroti 80 A3
Soúrpi 83 F2
Sousceyrac 29 D2
Sousel 38 C4
Soustons 28 A4
Soutelo 34 B2
Souterraine, la .. 25 E4
Southam 9 E1
Southampton 9 E3
Southborough 10 C3
South Downs 9 F3
Southend 4 B3
Southend-on-Sea . 11 D2
Southern Uplands . 4 C3
South Esk 3 D4
South Foreland .. 11 D3
South Molten 8 C3
Southport 6 B2
South
 Queensferry 5 D2
South Ronaldsay.. 3 E1
Southsea 9 F3
South Shields ... 5 E3
South Tyne 5 D3
South Uist 2 A3
Southwell 7 D3
Southwold 11 E1
Souvála 87 F2
Souvigny 26 A3
Sovata 113 D4
Sövdeborg 109 D3
Soverato 67 F3
Soveria Mannelli .. 67 F3
Sovetsk 110 B3
Søvik 100 A2
Sož 111 E4
Sozopol 115 E2
Spa 51 D4
Spaichingen 55 D3
Spakenburg 16 C2
Spalding 7 E3
Spánda, Akr..... 90 B3
Spandau 49 D4
Spangenberg 52 B3
Spanish Pt...... 12 B4
Sparlösa 108 C1
Spárta 87 E1
Spárti 87 D3
Spartivento, C
 (Calabria) 67 E4
Spartivento, C
 (Sardegna) 66 B4
Spárto 82 C3
Spas-Demensk ... 111 F3
Spáta 87 F1
Spatharéi 89 E2
Spathí, Akr (Kíthira) . 90 A1
Spathí, Akr
 (Pelopónissos) .. 87 F2
Spodniji Brnik ... 70 B2
Spean Bridge 2 C4
Speikkogel 57 E4
Spello 63 E1
Spennymoor 5 E4
Sperhiáda 83 E3
Sperhiós 83 E3
Sperillen 104 C2
Sperlonga 63 F3

Sperrin Mts 13 D1
Spétses 87 E3
Spétses, N....... 87 E3
Spetsopoúla, N ... 87 E3
Speyer 54 C2
Spey, R 3 D3
Spezzano
 Albanese 67 E2
Spezzano della Sila . 67 E2
Spiddal 12 B3
Spiekeroog 47 E2
Spielfeld 70 C1
Spiez 27 F3
Spijkenisse 16 B3
Spílea Diroú 87 D4
Spíli 90 C4
Spiliá 83 E1
Spilimbergo 59 E3
Spilsby 7 E3
Spinalónga 91 E3
Spinazzola 65 D3
Spincourt 20 C3
Špionica Donja ... 71 F3
Špišič Bukovica .. 71 E2
Spišská-Nová Ves.. 112 B3
Spital 57 D3
Spittal 59 F2
Spitz 57 E2
Spjelkavik 100 A2
Split 75 D2
Spluga, Pso dello . 58 B3
Splügen 58 B3
Splügenpass 58 B3
Spodsbjerg 108 B4
Špola 113 F2
Spoleto 63 E1
Spornitz 48 C3
Spotorno 60 A3
Spreča 71 F3
Spree 49 E4
Spreewald 53 E1
Spremberg 53 F1
Spresiano 59 E4
Springe 52 A1
Sprogø 108 B4
Spurn Head 7 E2
Spuž 76 B2
Squillace, Golfo di . 67 F3
Squinzano 65 F4
Srb 71 D4
Srbac 71 E3
Srbica 77 D2
Srbija 73 D4
Srbobran 72 C2
Srddevići 75 E1
Srebrenica 72 C4
Središče 70 C1
Sredna Gora 115 D2
Srednje 71 F4
Srednji kanal ... 74 C1
Srednogorie 115 D2
Sredska 77 D3
Sremska
 Kamenica 72 C2
Sremska Mitrovica . 72 C3
Sremska Rača ... 72 B3
Sremski Karlovci . 72 C2
Srnetica 71 D4
Srnice Donje 71 F3
Šroda
 Wielkopolska ... 112 A1
Srpska Crnja 72 C1
Srpske Moravice . 70 B3
Srpski Itebej 73 D1
Srpski Miletić ... 72 B2
Stabbursdalen.... 95 D2
Stade 48 A3
Stádio 87 D2
Stadskanaal..... 17 E1
Stadthagen 52 A1
Stadtilm 52 C3
Stadtkyll 51 D4
Stadtlohn 17 E3
Stadtoldendorf... 52 A2
Stadtroda 52 C3
Stadtsteinach ... 52 C4
Stadt Wehlen ... 53 F2
Staffa 4 A1
Staffanstorp ... 108 C3
Staffelsee 56 A4
Staffelstein 52 C4
Staffin 2 B3
Stafford 6 C3
Staffordshire ... 6 C3

Stágira 80 B3
Stahle 52 A2
Stahovica 70 B2
Staines 9 F2
Stainz 57 E4
Stajovce 77 E2
Stalać 73 E4
Stalida 91 E3
Stall 59 E2
Stallersattel 59 E2
Stalowa Wola 112 C2
Stamford 9 F1
Stamnes 104 A2
Stams 58 C2
Stamsund 94 A4
Stange 105 D2
Stanišić 72 B1
Stanišinci 73 D4
Štanjel 70 A2
Stanke Dimitrov.. 115 D3
Staňkov 56 B1
Stankovci 74 C1
Stanley 5 E4
Stanós 80 B3
Stános 82 C3

Stans 27 F2
Stansstad 27 F2
Stansted 10 C2
Stapar 72 B2
Stara Gradina ... 71 E2
Staraja Russa ... 111 E2
Stara Moravica .. 72 B1
Stara Novalja ... 70 B4
Stara Pazova ... 72 C2
Stara Pl (BG) ... 115 D2
Stara Pl (Srbija).. 73 F4
Stará Role 53 E4
Staravina 77 E4
Stara Vrata 70 C4
Stara Zagora ... 115 D2
Staretina 75 D1
Stargard
 Szczeciński..... 49 F2
Stårheim 100 A3
Stari 77 F3
Stari Bar 76 B3
Stari Begej 72 C2
Starica 111 F2
Starigrad (Hvar) . 75 D2
Starigrad
 (Velebit) 70 B4

Stari Gradac 71 E2
Starigrad
 Paklenica 70 C4
Stari Jankovci ... 72 B2
Stari Log 70 B2
Stari Majdan ... 71 D3
Stari Mikanovci . 71 F2
Starnberg 56 A3
Starnberger See.. 56 A3
Starodub 111 F4
Starogard
 Gdański 110 A4
Starokonstantinov 113 D2
Staro Nagoričane . 77 E2
Staro Petrovo Selo . 71 E3
Staro Slano 76 A2
Starý Smokovec... 112 B3
Staßfurt 52 C1
Statland 97 D4
Staußfurt 52 C2
Stavanger 104 A3
Staveley 7 D3
Stavelot 51 D4
Stavenisse 16 B3
Staveren 16 C1
Stavern 104 C4

Stavrí, Akr 88 C3
Stavrodrómi 86 C1
Stavrohóri 91 F4
Stavrós (Évia) ... 84 B3
Stavrós (Imathía) . 79 E3
Stavrós (Itháki).... 82 B4
Stavrós (Kríti) ... 90 C3
Stavrós (Thessalía) . 83 E2
Stavrós
 (Thessaloníki) ... 80 B3
Stavrós, Akr (Kríti) . 91 D3
Stavrós, Akr
 (Thássos) 81 D3
Stavroúpoli 80 C2
Steblevë 77 D4
Štěchovice 53 F4
Steckborn 58 A1
Steeg 58 C2
Steenbergen 16 B3
Steenvoorde 19 F1
Steenwijk 17 D2
Stefáni (Ípiros) .. 82 B2
Stefáni (Stereá
 Eláda) 87 F1
Šťefaniná 80 B3
Stefanovíkio 83 F2
Stege 108 C4

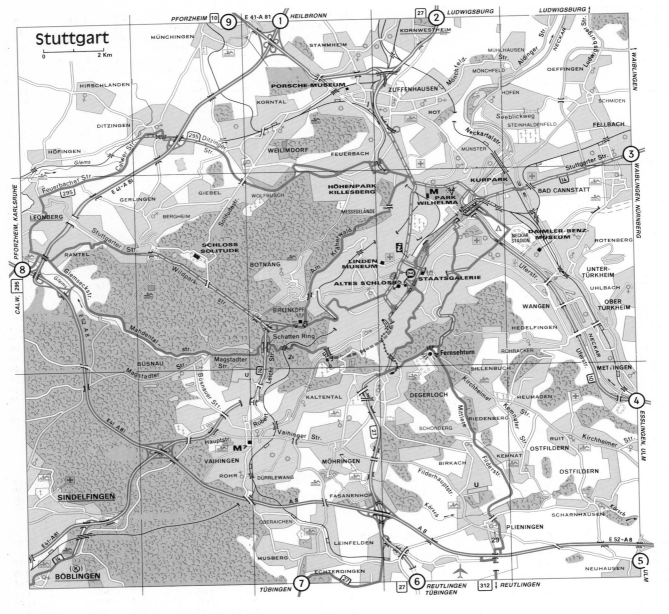

Stuttgart
0   2 Km

Straelen 17 D3
Stragari 73 D4
Strakonice 56 C1
Stralsund 49 D1
Stranda 100 B2
Strandebarm 104 A2
Strandhill 12 C2
Strangford 13 E2
Strangford L. 13 E2
Strängnäs 106 B3
Stranice 70 B1
Stranorlar 12 C1
Stranraer 4 B3
Strasbourg 21 E4
Strasburg 49 E2
Straßburg 70 A1
Straßwalchen 56 C3
Stratford-upon-
  Avon 9 E1
Strathaven 4 C2
Strathclyde 4 C2
Strathy Pt 3 D2
Stratóni 80 B3
Stratoniki 80 B3
Strátos 82 C3
Stratton 8 B3
Straubing 56 B2
Straumen (Bodø) . . . 97 E2
Straumen
  (Fauske) 97 F1
Straumen (Nord
  Trøndelag) 101 D1
Straumsjøen 94 A3
Straumsnes
  (Nordland) 97 E1
Straumsnes
  (Troms) 94 B2
Straupitz 53 E1
Strausberg 49 E4
Straža (Srbija) 73 E4
Straža (Vojvodina) . . 73 D2
Straža 70 B2
Stražbenica 76 B3
Strážný 56 C2
Streatley 9 E2
Street 9 D3
Strehaia 114 C1
Strehla 53 E2
Streitberg 52 C4
Strengberg 57 D3
Stresa 58 A4
Streymoy 96 A3
Strezimirovci 77 E1
Strezovce 77 D2
Stříbro 53 E4
Strimónas 80 B2
Strimonikó 80 A2
Strimonikós
  Kólpos 80 B3
Strmac 71 E2
Strmica 75 D1
Strobl 56 C3
Strofádes, N. 86 A3
Strofiliá 84 A3
Strojkovce 77 E1
Strokestown 12 C3
Stromberg 54 B1
Stromboli, I 69 D2
Stromeferry 2 B3
Strömfors 107 F2
Stromness 3 D1
Strömsbruk 101 F3
Strömsnäsbruk . . . 109 D4
Strömstad 105 D4
Strömsund 101 F1
Ströms vattudal . . . 101 F1
Strongoli 67 F2
Stronsay 3 E1
Stronsay Firth 3 E1
Strontian 2 B4
Stroud 9 D2
Strovlés 90 B3
Strub, Paß 59 E1
Struer 108 A2
Struga 77 D4
Struge 70 B2
Struma 115 D3
Strumble Head 8 B1
Strumica 77 F3
Strumica R. 77 F3
Stryj 112 C3
Stryn 100 A3
Strzelce
  Krajeńskie 49 F3

Stegersbach 57 F4
Steibis 55 E4
Steiermark 57 D4
Steigen 97 E1
Stein (A) 57 E2
Stein (N) 105 D2
Steinach (A) 59 D2
Steinach (D) 52 C3
Steinau 52 A4
Steinbach-
  Hallenberg 52 B3
Stein (Baden-
  Württemberg) 55 D4
Stein (Bayern) 55 E1
Steine 104 A1
Steinestø 104 A2
Steinfeld (A) 59 F2
Steinfeld (D) 17 F2
Steinfurt 17 E2
Steingaden 55 F4
Steinhaus 59 D2
Steinhausen 55 D3
Steinheim (Baden-
  Württemberg) 55 E2
Steinheim (Bayern) . . 55 E3
Steinheim (Nordrhein-
  Westfalen) 52 A2
Steinkjer 101 D1
Steinnuder Meer 48 A4
Steinpaß 59 E1
Steinshamn 100 A2
Steinsland 104 A2
Stekene 50 B3

Stelvio, Parco Naz
  della 58 C3
Stelvio, Pso dello . . . 58 C3
Stená Klissoúras . . . 79 D3
Stenay 20 C3
Stendal 48 C4
Steni 84 B4
Stenlille 108 B3
Stenløse 108 C3
Stenness 3 D1
Stenó 87 D2
Stenó, Akr 88 B2
Stenó Ithákis 82 B4
Sténoma 83 D3
Stenudden 98 A2
Stenungsund 108 C1
Stepanci 77 E3
Stepnica 49 E2
Stepojevac 72 C3
Stereá Eláda 83 D3
Stérna (Makedonía) . 80 C2
Stérna
  (Pelopónissos) . . . 87 D2
Stérna (Thráki) 81 F1
Sternberg 48 C2
Stérnes 90 C3
Sterup 48 A1
Sterza, la 60 C4
Sterzing 59 D2
Stevenage 9 F2
Stevns 108 C4
Stevns Klint 108 C4

Stewarton 4 C2
Steyr 57 D3
Steyrermühl 56 C3
Stia 61 D3
Stigliano 65 D4
Stigtomta 106 A4
Stilfserjoch 58 C3
Stilída 83 E3
Stilo 67 F4
Stimánga 87 D1
Stimfalía, L 87 D1
Štimlje 77 D2
Stintino 66 A1
Štip 77 E3
Stípsi 85 F2
Stíra 84 C4
Stirling 4 C2
Štirovača 70 C4
Štitar 72 C3
Štivan 70 B4
Stjärnhov 106 B4
Stjärnsund 105 F4
Stjernøya 95 D2
Stjernsund 95 D2
Stjørdal 100 C2
Stjørdalselva 101 D2
Stjørnfjorden 100 C1

Stockholms Län . . . 106 B3
Stockport 6 C2
Stocksbridge 6 C2
Stockton-on-Tees . . . 5 E4
Stod 53 E4
Stöde 101 F3
Stogovo 77 D4
Stoke-on-Trent 6 C3
Stokke 104 C3
Stokmarknes 94 A3
Stol 73 E3
Stolac 75 F2
Stolac Mt. 72 C4
Stolbcy 111 D4
Stolberg (Nordrhein-
  Westfalen) 51 D3
Stolberg (Sachsen-
  Anhalt) 52 C2
Stolice 72 B3
Stolice Mt 73 E4
Stolin 113 D1
Stollberg 53 E3
Stöllet 105 E3
Stolpen 53 F2
Stølsheimen 104 B2
Stolzenau 48 A4
Stómio 83 F1
Ston 75 F2
Stone 6 C3
Stonehaven 3 E4
Stonehenge 9 E3
Stonglandet 94 B3
Stopanja 73 E4

Stör 48 A2
Storå 105 F3
Stora Alvaret 109 E3
Stora Blåsjön 97 E4
Stora Lulevatten 98 A2
Stora Sjöfallet 94 B4
Stora Sjöfallet
  (National park) 94 B4
Stora Skedvi 105 F2
Stora Sundby 105 F4
Storavan 98 A3
Storby 106 C3
Stord 104 A2
Stordal 100 B2
Store Bælt 108 B3
Storebø 104 A2
Storebro 109 E2
Store Heddinge . . . 108 C4
Store Molvik 95 F1
Store Mosse 109 D2
Støren 100 C2
Storfjellet 97 F2
Storfjorden 100 B2
Storfors 105 E3
Storforsen 98 B3
Storforshei 97 E2
Storglomvatnet 97 E2
Storkow 49 E4
Storlien 101 D2
Stormi 107 D2
Stornoway 2 B2
Storo 58 C4
Storožinec 113 D3

Storr, The 2 B3
Storsjö 101 D2
Storsjøen 105 D1
Storsjön (Gävleborgs
  Län) 106 B2
Storsjön
  (Ljungdalen) 101 D2
Storsjön
  (Östersund) 101 E2
Storsjouten 97 E4
Storskarven 101 D2
Storslett 94 C2
Storsteinnes 94 C3
Storstrømmen 108 C4
Storuman 97 F4
Storuman L. 97 F3
Storvik (N) 95 D2
Storvik (S) 106 A2
Storvindeln 97 F3
Stotel 47 F3
Stoúpa 86 C3
Stour 11 D2
Stourbridge 9 E1
Stournaréika 83 D2
Stourport 9 D1
Støvring 108 B2
Stowmarket 11 D1
Stow-on-the-Wold . . 9 E2
Strå 61 D1
Strabane 13 D1
Stracin 77 E2
Stradella 60 A2
Stradsett 11 D1

Stubalpe ... 57 D4
Stubbekøbing ... 108 C4
Stubbenkammer ... 49 D1
Štubej ... 73 E3
Štubik ... 73 F3
Stublička Toplice ... 70 C2
Stubline ... 72 C3
Stuckenborstel ... 48 A3
Studena ... 77 E1
Studenci ... 75 E1
Studenica ... 76 C1
Stugun ... 101 F2
Stühlingen ... 54 C4
Stuhr-Brinkum ... 17 F1
Stupnik ... 70 C2
Stura di Demonte ... 31 E3
Sturehov ... 106 B4
Sturminster Newton ... 9 D3
Sturup ... 108 C3
Stuttgart ... 55 D2
Stykkishólmur ... 96 A2
Styr' ... 113 F2
Suances ... 35 F1
Subbiano ... 61 D4
Subiaco ... 63 F2
Subijana ... 36 B2
Subotica ... 72 B1
Subotište ... 72 C3
Suc-au-May ... 29 D1
Suceava ... 113 F3
Sučevici ... 71 D4
Suceviţa ... 113 D3
Suchań ... 49 F2
Suchinići ... 111 F3
Süchteln ... 17 D4
Sucina ... 45 D2
Suck ... 12 C3
Sućuraj ... 75 E2
Sudbury (Derbys) ... 6 C3
Sudbury (Suffolk) ... 11 D2
Suddesjaur ... 98 A3
Sude ... 48 B3

Süderbrarup ... 48 A1
Suðuroy ... 96 A4
Suðuroyarfjørður ... 96 A4
Sueca ... 41 E4
Sueros ... 35 D2
Suffolk ... 11 D1
Suhl ... 52 C3
Suhopolje ... 71 E2
Suho Polje ... 72 B3
Šuica ... 75 E1
Suinula ... 102 C3
Suippes ... 20 B3
Suir, R ... 14 C3
Sukeva ... 103 E1
Sukobin ... 76 B3
Sukošan ... 74 C1
Sukovo ... 77 E1
Sukth ... 76 C4
Sula ... 113 F2
Suldal ... 104 B3
Suldalsvatn ... 104 B3
Sulden ... 58 C3
Sulęcin ... 49 F4
Sulina ... 113 F4
Sulingen ... 17 F2
Sulitjelma ... 97 F2
Sulitjelma Mt ... 97 F2
Sulkava ... 103 E3
Sully ... 25 F2
Sulmona ... 64 A2
Sultanhisar ... 115 F4
Sulz ... 54 C3
Sulzbach (Baden-Württemberg) ... 55 D2
Sulzbach (Saarland) ... 54 B2
Sulzbach-Rosenberg ... 55 F1
Sulzemoos ... 55 F3
Sumartin ... 75 E2
Sumba ... 96 A4
Sumburgh ... 3 F2
Sumburgh Head ... 3 F2

Sümeg ... 112 A4
Šumen ... 115 E2
Sumiainen ... 103 D2
Sumiswald ... 27 F2
Šumperk ... 112 A3
Sumy ... 113 F1
Sunart, L ... 2 B4
Sund ... 106 C3
Sunde (Hordaland) ... 104 A2
Sunde (Sør Trøndelag) ... 100 C1
Sunderland ... 5 E4
Sundern ... 17 F4
Sundini ... 96 A3
Sundom ... 102 B2
Sundsvall ... 101 F3
Sundsvallsbukten ... 101 F3
Suni ... 66 B2
Sunja ... 71 D3
Sunnansjö ... 105 F3
Sunndalen ... 100 C2
Sunndalsøra ... 100 B2
Sunne (Jämtlands Län) ... 101 E2
Sunne (Värmlands Län) ... 105 E3
Sunnemo ... 105 E3
Sunnylvsfjorden ... 100 B3
Suodenniemi ... 107 D1
Suolahti ... 103 D2
Suolijärvet ... 99 E2
Suolijoki ... 99 D2
Suomenlinna ... 107 E3
Suomenniemi ... 103 E3
Suomusjärvi ... 107 E2
Suomussalmi ... 99 F3
Suomutunturi ... 99 E2
Suonenjoki ... 103 E2
Suontee ... 103 D3
Suopelto (Kuopion Lääni) ... 103 D2
Suopelto (Mikkelin Lääni) ... 103 D3

Super-Besse ... 29 E1
Super-Molina ... 32 A3
Supetar ... 75 D2
Supetarska Draga ... 70 B4
Supino ... 63 F3
Šuplja-Stijena ... 76 B1
Surahammar ... 105 F3
Suraž ... 111 E4
Surbo ... 65 F4
Surčin ... 72 C3
Surduc ... 114 C1
Surdulica ... 77 E1
Surdup ... 76 B2
Šûre ... 21 D2
Surgères ... 24 C4
Súria ... 32 A3
Surnadalsøra ... 100 C2
Surrey ... 10 C3
Sursee ... 27 F2
Susa ... 31 E1
Suså ... 108 C4
Sušac ... 75 E3
Susak ... 70 B4
Susak / ... 70 B4
Susch ... 58 B2
Susek ... 72 B2
Sušice ... 56 C1
Suspiro del Moro, Pto del ... 44 A3
Susqueda, Emb de ... 32 B3
Süßen ... 55 D2
Sustenpass ... 58 A3
Susurluk ... 115 F3
Sutinjske Toplice ... 70 C2
Sutivan ... 75 D2
Sutjeska ... 73 D2
Sutjeska nac park ... 76 A1
Sutomore ... 76 B3
Sutri ... 63 E2
Sutterton ... 7 E3
Sutton ... 9 F2

Sutton Coldfield ... 9 E1
Sutton-in-Ashfield ... 7 D3
Sutton-on-Sea ... 7 E3
Suva gora ... 77 D3
Suva pl ... 77 E1
Suva Reka ... 77 D2
Suvasvesi ... 103 E2
Suvereto ... 62 C1
Suvobor ... 72 C4
Suvodol ... 77 E3
Suwałki ... 110 C4
Suze, la ... 23 F4
Suzzara ... 60 C2
Sval'ava ... 112 C3
Svalöv ... 108 C3
Svaneke ... 109 D4
Svanstein ... 98 C2
Svanvik ... 95 F2
Svappavaara ... 94 C4
Svärdsjö ... 105 F2
Svarstad ... 104 C3
Svarta ... 105 E4
Svartevatn ... 104 B3
Svartevatn L. ... 104 B3
Svartisen ... 97 E2
Svaervolthalvøya ... 95 E1
Svattälven ... 105 F3
Svedala ... 108 C3
Sveg ... 101 E3
Svelgen ... 100 A3
Svelvik ... 104 C3
Svendborg ... 108 B4
Svenljunga ... 108 C2
Svensby ... 94 C2
Svenstavik ... 101 E2
Švermov ... 53 F3
Svetac ... 75 D2
Sveti Andrija ... 77 D3
Sveti Ilija ... 75 D1
Sveti Janez ... 70 A2
Sveti Jovan Bigorski ... 77 D3
Sveti Naum ... 77 D4

Sveti Nikita ... 77 D2
Sveti Nikola ... 76 B3
Sveti Nikole ... 77 E3
Sveti Pantelejmon ... 77 D3
Sveti Rok ... 70 C4
Sveti Stefan ... 76 B3
Svetlogorsk (RB) ... 111 E4
Svetlogorsk (ROS) ... 110 B4
Svetlovodsk ... 113 F2
Svetozarevo ... 73 D4
Svetozar Miletić ... 72 B1
Svidník ... 112 C3
Švihov ... 56 B1
Svilaja ... 75 D1
Svilajnac ... 73 E3
Svilengrad ... 115 E3
Svingvoll ... 104 C1
Svinjar ... 71 E3
Svinoy ... 96 A3
Svištov ... 115 D2
Svitavy ... 112 A3
Svodde ... 77 E1
Svolvær ... 94 A4
Svor ... 53 F3
Svorkmo ... 100 C2
Svoronáta ... 86 A1
Svorónos ... 79 F4
Svrljig ... 73 F4
Swadlincote ... 6 C3
Swaffham ... 11 D1
Swale ... 6 C1
Swalmen ... 17 D4
Swanage ... 9 E4
Swanley ... 10 C2
Swanlinbar ... 12 C2
Swansea ... 8 C2
Świdnica ... 112 A3
Świdwin ... 49 F2
Świebodzin ... 112 A2
Świecie ... 112 A1
Świecko ... 49 F4

Świerzno ... 49 F1
Swilly, L ... 13 D1
Swindon ... 9 E2
Swinford ... 12 B3
Świnoujście ... 49 E2
Swords ... 13 D3
Sybil Head ... 14 A3
Syčovka ... 111 F2
Sykäräinen ... 102 C1
Syke ... 17 F1
Sykkylven ... 100 A2
Sylene ... 101 D2
Sylling ... 104 C3
Sylt ... 47 F1
Sylt Ost ... 47 F1
Sylvenstein-Stausee ... 56 A4
Synod Inn ... 8 C1
Syötekylä ... 99 E3
Syre ... 3 D2
Sysmä ... 103 D3
Sysslebäck ... 101 D4
Syväjärvi ... 99 D1
Syväri ... 103 E2
Syvde ... 100 A3
Syvdsnes ... 100 A2
Syyspohja ... 103 E3
Szarvas ... 112 B4
Szczecin ... 49 E2
Szczecinek ... 110 A4
Szczeciński, Zalew ... 49 E2
Szczytno ... 110 B4
Szécsény ... 112 B3
Szeged ... 112 B4
Székesfehérvár ... 112 B4
Szekszárd ... 114 B1
Szentendre ... 112 B4
Szentes ... 112 B4
Szigetvár ... 114 B1
Szolnok ... 112 B4
Szombathely ... 112 A4

T

Tabanovce ... 77 E2
Tábara ... 35 D4
Tabarca, I de ... 45 E2
Taberg ... 109 D1
Tabernas ... 44 B3
Tabernes de Valldigna ... 41 E4
Taboada ... 34 B2
Tábor ... 57 D1
Tábua ... 38 B2
Tabuaço ... 34 B4
Tabuenca ... 36 C3
Täby ... 106 B3
Tachov ... 53 E4
Tadcaster ... 7 D2
Tafalla ... 36 C2
Tafjord ... 100 B3
Taganheira ... 42 A1
Taggia ... 31 F3
Tagliacozzo ... 63 F2
Tagliamento ... 59 E3
Taglio di Po ... 61 D2
Tahal ... 44 C3
Tahkvuori ... 103 E2
Taibilla, Sa de ... 44 C2
Taïgetos, Óros ... 87 D3
Tain ... 3 D3
Tain-l'Hermitage ... 30 B2
Taipadas ... 38 A4
Taipalsaari ... 103 E4
Taivalkoski ... 99 E3
Taivassalo ... 107 D2
Tajera, Emb de la ... 40 C1
Tajo, R ... 40 B2
Tajuña, R ... 40 B2
Takovo ... 73 D4
Taktikoúpoli ... 87 E2
Tálanda ... 87 E4
Talarrubias ... 39 E4
Talaván ... 39 D3

Talave, Emb de ... 44 C1
Talavera de la Reina ... 39 F3
Talavera la Real ... 39 D4
Talayuela ... 39 E2
Talayuelas ... 41 D3
Taldom ... 111 F2
Talgarth ... 9 D1
Talkkunapää ... 95 F3
Talla ... 61 D4
Tallante ... 45 D3
Tallard ... 31 D2
Tällberg ... 101 E4
Tallinn ... 110 C1
Talloires ... 27 D4
Tallow ... 14 C4
Talluskylä ... 103 D2
Talmont ... 24 B3
Tal'noje ... 113 E2
Talsi ... 110 B2
Talvik ... 95 D2
Tamames ... 39 E1
Tamar ... 8 B3
Támara ... 35 F3
Tamarite de Litera ... 37 E3
Tamási ... 112 B4
Tambre, R ... 34 A2
Tâmega, R ... 34 A4
Tamélos, Akr ... 88 A2
Tamiš ... 72 C2
Tammela ... 107 E2
Tammisaari ... 107 E3
Tamnava ... 72 C3
Tampere ... 107 E1
Tamsweg ... 56 C4
Tamworth ... 9 E1
Tana, R ... 40 B2
Tana ... 95 E1
Tana R. ... 95 E1
Tanafjorden ... 95 E1
Tanágra ... 84 A4
Tanagro ... 64 C4
Tanamea, Pso di ... 59 F3
Tanaro ... 31 F2

Tancarville, Pont de ... 19 D3
Tandådalen ... 101 D4
Tandragee ... 13 D2
Tandsbyn ... 101 E2
Tandsjöborg ... 101 E3
Tangerhütte ... 48 C4
Tangermünde ... 48 C4
Tanhua ... 95 F4
Taninges ... 27 E4
Tanlay ... 26 B1
Tann ... 52 B3
Tännäs ... 101 D3
Tanndalen ... 101 D3
Tannheim ... 58 C1
Tannila ... 99 D3
Tanumshede ... 105 D4
Taormina ... 69 D3
Tapa ... 110 C1
Tapia de Casariego ... 34 C1
Tar ... 70 A3
Tara ... 72 C4
Tara R ... 76 B1
Taracena ... 40 B2
Tara klisura ... 76 B2
Tarancón ... 40 B3
Taranto ... 65 E4
Taranto, Golfo di ... 65 E4
Tarare ... 26 B4
Taraš ... 72 C2
Tarašča ... 113 E2
Tarazona ... 36 C3
Tarazona de la Mancha ... 40 C4
Taravo ... 33 F3
Tarayuela ... 41 E2

Tarbert (Western Is) ... 2 B2
Tarbes ... 37 E1
Tarbet ... 4 C1
Tarcento ... 59 F3
Tarčin ... 75 F1
Tardets-Sorholus ... 37 D1
Tardienta ... 37 D3
Targon ... 28 B2
Târgovište ... 115 E2
Tarifa ... 43 D4
Tarm ... 108 A3
Tarmstedt ... 47 F3
Tarn ... 29 D3
Tarn (Dépt) ... 29 E3
Tärnaby ... 97 E3
Tarna, Pto de ... 35 E2
Tärnäsjön ... 97 E3
Tarn-et-Garonne ... 29 D3
Tarn, Gges du ... 29 F3
Tarnobrzeg ... 112 C2
Tarnos ... 28 A4
Tarnów ... 112 B2
Taro ... 60 B2
Tarouca ... 38 C1
Tarp ... 48 A1
Tarporley ... 6 B3
Tarquinia ... 63 D2
Tarragona ... 37 F4
Tarrasa ... 32 A4
Tàrrega ... 37 F4
Tarrekaise ... 98 A2
Tårs ... 108 B4
Tarsia ... 67 E2
Tartas ... 28 B3
Tartu ... 110 C2
Tarvasjoki ... 107 D2
Tarvisio ... 59 F2
Täsch ... 27 F4
Tåsinge ... 108 B4
Tåsjo ... 101 F1
Tåsjön ... 101 F1

Tassin ... 26 C4
Tåstrup ... 108 C3
Tata ... 112 B4
Tatabánya ... 112 B4
Tatarbunary ... 113 E4
Tatry ... 112 B3
Tau ... 104 A3
Tauber ... 55 D1
Tauberbischofsheim ... 55 D1
Taucha ... 53 D2
Tauerntal ... 59 E2
Tauerntunnel ... 59 E2
Taufers i. M. ... 58 C3
Taufkirchen ... 56 B3
Taulé ... 22 B2
Taunton ... 9 D3
Taunus ... 51 F4
Taunussteín ... 51 F4
Tauplitz ... 57 D4
Tauragė ... 110 B3
Taurianova ... 67 E4
Taurion ... 25 E4
Tauste ... 36 C3
Tauves ... 29 E1
Tavankut ... 72 B1
Tavannes ... 27 E2
Tavarnelle Val di Pesa ... 60 C4
Tavastila ... 103 F4
Tavaux ... 26 C2
Taverna ... 67 F3
Tavernelle ... 63 E1
Tavernes ... 31 D4
Tavignano ... 33 F3
Tavira ... 42 B3
Tavistock ... 8 C3
Tavolara, I ... 66 C1
Tavropós ... 83 D2
Tavropoú, Teh L ... 83 D2
Tavşanli ... 115 F3
Taw ... 8 C3
Taxenbach ... 59 E1

Taxiárhis ... 80 B3
Tay ... 5 D1
Tayinloan ... 4 B2
Tay, L ... 4 C1
Taynuilt ... 4 B1
Tayport ... 5 D1
Tayside ... 3 D4
Tazones ... 35 E1
Tczew ... 110 A4
Teano ... 64 A3
Teba ... 43 E3
Tebay ... 5 D4
Tech ... 32 B3
Techendorf ... 59 F2
Tecklenburg ... 17 E2
Tecuci ... 113 E4
Tees ... 5 E4
Teesside ... 5 E4
Teféli ... 91 D4
Tegéa ... 87 D2
Tegel ... 49 E4
Tegelen ... 17 D4
Tegernsee ... 56 A4
Teggiano ... 64 C4
Teguise ... 42 C3
Teide ... 42 B4
Teide Mt. ... 42 A4
Teide, Pque Nac del ... 42 B4
Teignmouth ... 8 C4
Teijo ... 107 D3
Teil, le ... 30 B2
Teilleul, le ... 18 C4
Teisendorf ... 56 B3
Teisko ... 102 C3
Teixeiro ... 34 B1
Teixoso ... 38 C2
Tejeda, Sa de ... 43 F3
Tejo, R ... 38 A3
Tekeriš ... 72 C3
Tekija ... 73 E2
Tekirdağ ... 115 E3
Telč ... 57 E1

Telde ... 42 B4
Telemark ... 104 C3
Télendos, N ... 89 E3
Teleno ... 34 C3
Telese ... 64 B3
Telford ... 6 C3
Telfs ... 58 C2
Telgte ... 17 E3
Tellingstedt ... 48 A2
Telti ... 66 B1
Teltow ... 49 D4
Têmbi ... 83 E1
Tembleque ... 40 B3
Temerin ... 72 C2
Temmes ... 99 D4
Tempelhof ... 49 E4
Tempio Pausania ... 66 B1
Templemore ... 12 C4
Templin ... 49 D3
Temse ... 50 B3
Temska ... 73 F4
Tenala ... 107 E3
Ténaro, Akr ... 87 D4
Tenbury Wells ... 9 D1
Tenby ... 8 B2
Tence ... 30 B2
Tende ... 31 E3
Tende, Col de ... 31 E3
Tende, Colle di ... 31 E3
Tendilla ... 40 B2
Tenerife ... 42 A4
Tenhola ... 107 E3
Tenja ... 71 F2
Tennes ... 94 B3
Tenniöjoki ... 95 F4
Teno ... 95 E2
Tensta ... 106 B3
Tenterden ... 11 D3
Tentudia ... 43 D1
Teolo ... 61 D1
Teovo ... 77 E3
Tepelenë ... 114 C4

Torino

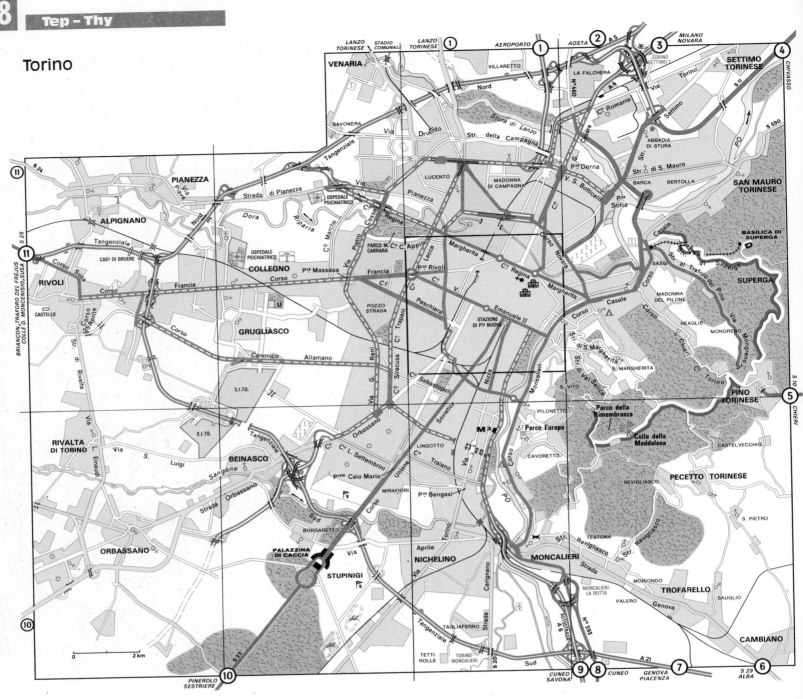

Teplá 53 E4	Terpsithéa 83 D4	Tessy 18 C3	Thanes, K e 76 C4	Thérma Lefkádas . . . 89 D2	Thiessow 49 D1	Thornhill 4 C3
Teplice 53 E3	Ter, R 32 B3	Teste, la 28 A2	Thann 27 E1	Thérmi 79 F3	Thillot, le 27 E1	Thouarcé 24 C2
Tepsa 95 E4	Terracina 63 F3	Tetbury 9 E2	Thannhausen 55 E3	Thérmi 85 F2	Thimariá 81 F2	Thouars 24 C2
Teramo 63 F1	Terra de Basto : 34 B4	Teterev 113 E2	Thaon 27 D1	Thermissia 87 E2	Thímena 89 E2	Thouet 24 C2
Ter Apel 17 E1	Terradets, Emb	Teterow 49 D2	Tharandt 53 E2	Thérmo 83 D4	Thímena, N 89 E2	Thouría 86 C3
Tera, R 35 D3	dels 37 F3	Tetica 44 B3	Tharsis 42 C2	Thermopíles 83 E3	Thiní, Akr 87 E2	Thoúrio 81 F1
Terebovl'a 113 D3	Terråk 97 D4	Tetijev 113 E2	Thássos 80 C3	Thérouanne 19 F1	Thionville 21 D3	Thráki 81 E1
Terena 38 C4	Terralba 66 B3	Tetovo 77 D3	Thássos, N 81 D3	Thespiés 83 F4	Thíra 91 E1	Thrakikó
Terespol 112 C1	Terranova di	Tetrákomo 82 C2	Thatë, Mal i 77 D4	Thesprotía 82 B2	Thíra, N 91 E1	Pélagos 81 D3
Terezino Polje 71 E2	Pollino 67 E2	Tettnang 55 D4	Thau, Bessin de . . . 30 A4	Thesprotikó 82 B2	Thirassía, N 91 E1	Threshfield 9 F1
Terges, Rib de 42 B2	Terrasson-la-	Teuchern 53 D2	Thaya 57 F1	Thessalía 83 E2	Thirsk 7 D1	Threshfield 6 C1
Tergnier 20 A2	Villedieu 29 D2	Teufen 58 B2	Thégonnec 22 B2	Thessaloníki 79 F3	Thisted 108 A2	Thueyts 30 B2
Terjärv 102 C2	Terrenoire 30 B1	Teulada 66 B4	Theil, le 23 F3	Thessaloníki	Thíva 84 A4	Thuile, la 27 E4
Terlizzi 65 D3	Terrassa 32 A4	Teupitz 53 E1	Themar 52 C2	(Nomos) 80 A3	Thiviers 28 C1	Thuin 50 B4
Termas de	Terras de Bouro . . . 34 A3	Teuva 102 B3	Thenon 29 D2	Thetford 11 D1	Thizy 26 B4	Thuir 32 B2
Monfortinho 39 D2	Terriente 41 D2	Tevere 63 E2	Theologós (Stereá	Theux 51 D4	Thoissey 26 C4	Thum 53 E3
Terme Luigiane 67 E2	Terschelling 16 C1	Tewkesbury 9 E2	Eláda) 83 F3	The Wash 7 E3	Tholen 16 B3	Thun 27 E3
Termini Imerese . . . 68 B3	Teruel 41 D2	Texel 16 C1	Theológos	Tholey 54 B1	Thur 58 A1
Terminillo 63 F2	Tervakoski 107 E2	Thabor, Mt 31 D1	(Thássos) 80 C3	Thollon 27 E3	Thüringen 58 B2
Terminillo, Mte 63 F2	Tervo 103 D2	Thale 52 C2	Théoule 31 E4	Thiamis 82 B1	Tholó 86 C3	Thüringen (Land) . . . 52 C3
Termoli 64 B2	Tervola 99 D2	Thalfang 54 B1	Thérain 19 F3	Thiaucourt 21 D3	Tholopotámi 85 E4	Thüringer Wald 52 B3
Terneuzen 16 B4	Tervuren 50 C3	Thalgau 56 C3	Thérma (Ikaría) 89 D2	Thiberville 19 D3	Tholós 80 B2	Thurles 14 C3
Terni 63 E2	Terzaga 40 C2	Thalheim 53 E3	Thermá	Thiéblemont-	Thomastown 15 D3	Thurn, Paß 59 E1
Ternitz 57 E3	Tešanj 71 F3	Thalmässing 55 F2	(Makedonía) 80 B2	Farémont 20 C4	Thônes 27 D4	Thursby 5 D4
Ternopol' 113 D2	Teslić 71 E3	Thalwil 58 A2	Thérma	Thiendorf 53 E2	Thonon 27 D3	Thurso 3 D2
Térovo 82 C2	Tessin 48 C2	Thame 9 F2	(Samothráki) 81 E3	Thiene 59 D4	Thorens-Glières . . . 27 D4	Thury-Harcourt 18 C3
Térpilos 80 A2		Thalgau 56 C3	Thermaïkós	Thiers 26 B4	Thorikó 88 A2	Thusis 58 B3
Terpní 80 B2		Thames, R 11 D2	Kólpos 80 A4	Thiesi 66 B2	Thorne 7 D2	Thy 108 A2

Thyborøn 108 A2
Tibro 109 D1
Tichvin 111 E1
Ticino 60 A1
Ticino R 58 A3
Tidaholm 109 D1
Tidö 106 A3
Tiefenbronn 54 C2
Tiefencastel 58 B3
Tiefensee 49 E4
Tiel 16 C3
Tielt 50 A3
Tienen 50 C3
Tiengen 54 C4
Tierbmesvarri ... 94 C3
Tiercé 23 E4
Tierga 36 C3
Tierp 106 B3
Tiétar, R 39 E2
Tigharry 2 A3
Tighnabruaich ... 4 B2
Tignes 31 D1
Tignes, Bge de ... 31 E1
Tiheró 81 F2
Tihío 79 D3
Tihuţa 113 D4
Tiilikkajärvi 103 E1
Tiistenjoki 102 C2
Tijesno 74 C1
Tijola 44 B3
Tikkakoski 103 D3
Tikkala 103 F2
Tikveš, Ez 77 E3
Tilburg 16 C3
Tilbury 10 C2
Tilissos 91 D3
Tillberga 106 A3
Tillières 19 E4
Tilly-sur-Seulles . 18 C3
Tilos, N 89 F4
Timanfaya, Parque
  Nac. de 42 A4
Timbáki 91 D4
Timbano 81 D2
Timfi, Óros 78 C4
Timfristós 83 D3
Timfristós Mt 83 D3
Timiş 114 C1
Timişoara 114 C1
Timmelsjoch 58 C2
Timmendorfer
  Strand 48 B2
Timok 73 F3
Timoleague 14 B4
Timrå 101 F3
Tímv. Peristéria .. 86 C3
Tinahely 13 D4
Tinchebray 18 C4
Tindari 69 D2
Tinée 31 E3
Tineo 35 D1
Tingáki 89 F3
Tinglev 108 A4
Tingsryd 109 E2
Tingvoll 100 B2
Tingvollfjorden ... 100 B2
Tinja 71 F3
Tinn 104 C3
Tinnsj 104 C3
Tinos 88 C2
Tiñosillos 39 F1
Tinos, N 88 C2
Tiñoso, C 45 D3
Tintagel 8 B3
Tinténiac 23 D3
Tinto, R 42 C2
Tiobraid Árann ... 14 C3
Tione di Trento ... 58 C3
Tipasoja 103 E1
Tipperary 14 C3
Tipperary (Co) ... 12 C4
Tiranë 76 C4
Tirano 58 C3
Tiraspol' 113 E3
Tire 115 F4
Tiree 2 A4
Tirgo-Neamt 113 D4
Tîrgovişte 115 D1
Tîrgu Frumos 113 E3
Tîrgu Jiu 114 C1
Tîrgu Mures 113 D4
Tîrgu Secuiesc ... 113 D4
Tirig 41 F2
Tirintha 87 D2

Tiriolo 67 F3
Tírnavos 83 E1
Tirol 58 C2
Tirós 87 D3
Tirrenia 60 C4
Tirreno, Mare 68 B2
Tirschenreuth 53 D4
Tirso 66 B2
Tirstrup 108 B3
Tirteafuera, R 39 F4
Tisa 72 C2
Tiscar, Pto de 44 B2
Tisnaren 105 F4
Tišnov 57 E1
Tisvildeleje 108 C3
Tisza 112 B4
Tiszafüred 112 B4
Tiszavasvári 112 C3
Titaguas 41 D3
Titaríssios 83 E1
Titel 72 C2
Titisee 54 C4
Titlis 58 A3
Tito 64 C4
Titova Korenica .. 70 C4
Titov Drvar 71 D4
Titov Veles 77 E3
Titov vrh 77 D3
Titran 100 B1
Tittmoning 56 B3
Tiumpan Head ... 2 B2
Tivat 76 B3
Tiveden 105 E4
Tivenys 41 F2
Tiverton 8 C3
Tivissa 41 F1
Tivoli 63 E2
Tjaktjajaure 98 A2
Tjällmo 105 F4
Tjeggelvas 98 A2
Tjeldøya 94 B3
Tjeldstø 104 A2
Tjentište 76 A1
Tjøme 104 C4
Tjong 97 E2
Tjørnuvik 96 A3
Tjøtta 97 D3
Tkon 74 C1
Tobarra 44 C1
Tobercurry 12 B2
Tobermore 13 D2
Tobermory 2 B4
Toberonochy 4 B1
Toblach 59 E2
Toce 58 A3
Tocha 38 B2
Tocina 43 D2
Todi 63 E1
Todmorden 6 C2
Todorići 71 E4
Todtmoos 54 C4
Todtnau 54 C4
Toe Head (GB) ... 2 A2
Toe Head (IRL) ... 14 B4
Töfsingdalen 101 D3
Toft 3 F1
Tofte 104 C3
Toftir 96 A4
Toftlund 108 A4
Tohmajärvi 103 F2
Toholampi 102 C1
Toijala 107 E2
Toivakka 103 D3
Toivala 103 E2
Tojšici 72 B3
Tok 53 F4
Tokaj 112 C3
Toledo 40 A3
Toledo, Mts de ... 40 A3
Tolentino 61 F4
Tolfa 63 D2
Tolga 100 C3
Tollarp 109 D3
Tollense 49 D2
Tølløse 108 C3
Tolmezzo 59 E3
Tolmin 70 A2
Toló 87 D2
Tolox 43 E4
Tolva 99 E2
Tolve 65 D4
Tomar 38 B3

Tomašević 73 D2
Tomaševo 76 B2
Tomašica 71 D3
Tomaszów
  Lubelski 112 C2
Tomaszów
  Mazowiecki ... 112 B2
Tombebœuf 28 C3
Tomelilla 109 D3
Tomelloso 40 B4
Tomiño 34 A3

Tomintoul 3 D4
Tomma 97 D2
Tømmervåg 100 B2
Tomra 100 B2
Tomtabacken 109 D2
Tona 32 B3
Tonale, Pso del ... 58 C3
Tonara 66 B3
Tonbridge 10 C3
Tondela 38 B1
Tønder 108 A4
Tongeren 50 C3
Tongue 2 C2
Tonnay-
  Boutonne 24 C4
Tonnay-Charente . 24 C4
Tonneins 28 C3
Tonnerre 26 B1
Tönning 47 F2
Tønsberg 104 C3
Tonstad 104 B4
Töpen 53 D3
Topeno 107 E2
Topla 70 B1
Toplica 77 D1
Topli Do 73 F4
Topliţa 113 D4
Toploú 91 F4
Topola 73 D3
Topolčani 77 E4
Topol'čany 112 B3
Topólia 90 B3
Topolovnik 73 E3
Topusko 70 C3
Torà bi
  Riubregòs 32 A3
Torano Castello .. 67 E2
Torbay 8 C4
Torble 58 C4
Torcello 61 D1
Torchiarolo 65 F3
Toreno 34 C2
Torgau 53 E2
Torgelow 49 E2
Torhout 50 A3

Torigni 18 C3
Torija 40 B2
Torino 31 E1
Torio, R 35 D2
Torla 37 E2
Törmänen 95 F3
Törmänmäki 99 E4
Tormes, R 39 E1
Tormos 37 D3
Tornavacas 39 E2
Tornavacas, Pto de 39 E2
Torneälven 94 C4
Torneträsk 94 C4
Tornik 76 B1
Tornio 98 C3
Tornionjoki 98 C2
Tornjoš 72 C1
Toro 35 D4
Törökszentmiklós . 112 B4
Toro, Monte 45 F1
Toróni 80 B4
Toropec 111 E2
Torpo 104 C2
Torpoint 8 C4
Torpshammar ... 101 F3
Torquay 8 C4
Torquemada 35 F3
Torralba de
  Calatrava 40 A4

Torrão 42 B1
Torre 38 C2
Torre Annunziata . 64 B4
Torre Baja 41 D3
Torre Beretti 60 A2
Torreblanca 41 F3
Torrecaballeros .. 40 A1
Torrecampo 43 F1
Torre Canne 65 E3
Torrecilla 43 E4
Torrecilla en
  Cameros 36 B2
Torrecillas de la
  Tiesa 39 E3
Torre de Abraham,
  Emb de 40 A3
Torre de D. Chama 34 C4
Torre de
  Embesora 41 E2
Torre de Juan
  Abad 44 B1
Torre del Aguila,
  Emb de 43 D3
Torre de la
  Higuera 42 C3
Torre del Bierzo .. 35 D2
Torre del Campo . 44 A2
Torre del Greco .. 64 B4
Torre del Mar ... 43 F4

Torredembarra ... 37 F4
Torre de
  Moncorvo 34 C4
Torre de Passeri .. 64 A2
Torre d. Impiso .. 68 A3
Torredonjimeno .. 43 F2
Torre Faro 69 E2
Torre Grande 66 A3
Torregrossa 37 F4
Torreira 38 B1
Torrejoncillo 39 D2
Torrejoncillo del
  Rey 40 C3
Torrejón de Ardoz 40 B2
Torrejón de la
  Calzada 40 A2
Torrejón el Rubio . 39 E3
Torrejón-Tajo, Emb
  de 39 E3
Torre la Carcel ... 41 D2
Torrelaguna 40 B1
Torrelapaja 36 C3
Torrelavega 35 F2
Torrellano 45 E2
Torrelobatón 35 E4
Torrelodones 40 A2
Torremaggiore ... 64 B2
Torremegía 39 D4
Torre Mileto 64 C2

Torre Miró, Pto de . 41 E2
Torremocha 39 D3
Torremolinos 43 F4
Torrent 41 E4
Torrente de
  Cinca 37 E4
Torrenueva 44 B1
Torre Orsáia 67 D1
Torre-Pacheco ... 45 D2
Torre Pellice 31 E2
Torreperogil 44 B2
Torres del Río ... 36 B2
Torres Novas 38 B3
Torres Vedras ... 38 A3
Torrevieja 45 D2
Torrico de San
  Pedro 38 C3
Torri del Benaco . 60 C1
Torridon 2 B3
Torridon, L 2 B3
Torriglia 60 A3
Torrijas 41 D3
Torrijo 36 C4
Torrijos 40 A3
Tørring 108 A3
Torrita di Siena .. 61 D1
Torroella de
  Montgrí 32 C3
Torröjen 101 D1

Toulouse

0   1 km

(City map of Toulouse showing districts and surrounding communes including: Montauban-Agen, Villemur-s-Tarn, Fronton, Cornaudric, L'Union, Albi/Gaillac, Lavaur, Gramont, Croix-Daurade, Blagnac, Lalande, Ginestous, Les Cocus, La Salade, Bonnefoy, La Roseraie, Balma, Toulouse Blagnac, Aérospatiale, Les Minimes, Les Sept Deniers, St-Jean-Baptiste, Negreneys, Immaculée Conception, Jolimont, Observatoire, Soupetard, Moscou, St-Martin du Touch, St-Sernin, Capitole, Guilhemery, Côte Pavée, Casselardit, Purpan, Maubec, École Vétérinaire, Les Cappelles, Lardenne, Lestang, Mermoz, Le Busca, Pont des Demoiselles, La Grande Prairie, Le Mirail, La Cx de Pierre, Bagatelle, Cité Universitaire, Université, Basso-Cambo, Reyneire, La Trinité, Bellefontaine, La Fourguette, Rangueil, Montaudran, Pouvourville, La Bourdette, Ramonville-St-Agne, St-Gaudens/Tarbes, Foix, Vieille-Toulouse, Garonne, Castres, Mazamet, Montpellier/Carcassonne, Revel.)

échangeur fin 1993

7-1993

Torrox 43 F4
Torsås 109 E3
Torsby 105 E3
Torshälla 106 A3
Tórshavn 96 A4
Torsken 94 B2
Torsminde 108 A2
Törtoles de
Esgueva 35 F4
Tortoli 66 C3
Tortona 60 A2
Tortorici 69 D2
Tortosa 41 F2
Tortosendo 38 C2
Toruń 112 B1
Torup 108 C2
Tørvikbygd 104 B2
Tory I 12 C1
Toržok 111 F2
Torzym 49 F4
Toscana 60 C4
Toscolano
Maderno 60 C1
Tosenfjorden 97 D3
Toses, Collada de . . 32 A3
Tosno 111 D1
Tossa del Mar 32 B4
Tostedt 48 A3
Totak 104 B3
Totana 44 C2
Tôtes 19 E3
Totes Gebirge 56 C3
Tøtlandsvik 104 A3
Totnes 8 C4
Toucy 26 A1
Toul 21 D4
Toulon (Saône-et-
Loire) 26 B3
Toulon (Var) 31 D4
Toulouse 29 D4
Toumbítsi 86 C2
Touques 19 D3
Touquet-Paris-Plage,
le 19 E1
Tourcoing 19 F1
Tour-
d'Auvergne,la . . 29 E1
Tour-du-Pin, la 30 C1
Tour-Fondue, la . . . 31 D4
Touriñan, C 34 A1
Tourlída 82 C4
Tourmalet, Col du . . 37 E2
Tournai 50 A4
Tournan 19 F4
Tournay 37 E1
Tournoël 26 A4
Tournon-
d'Agenais 28 C3
Tournon-St-
Martin 25 D3
Tournon-sur-
Rhône 30 B2
Tournus 26 C3
Tourouvre 19 D4
Tours 25 D2
Toury 25 E1
Toussuire, la 31 D1
Toutes Aures, Col
de 31 D3
Touvet, le 30 C1
Toužim 53 E4
Tovariševo 72 B2

Tovarnik 72 B2
Tovdal selva 104 B4
Tovel, L di 58 C3
Tøvik 100 B3
Towcester 9 F1
Trabanca 34 C4
Trabancos, R 39 F1
Trabazos 34 C4
Traben-Trarbach . . . 54 B1
Trabla 68 B3
Trabotivište 77 F2
Tracino 68 A4
Trafalgar, C de 43 D4
Trafoi 58 C3
Tragacete 41 D2
Trahiá 87 E2
Trahili 84 B4
Tráhilos, Akr 83 F4
Tráhilos, Akr
(Dodekánissa) . . . 89 F4
Tráhilos, Akr (Stereá
Eláda) 83 E4
Traiguera 41 F2
Traisen 57 E3
Traisen R 57 E3
Traiskirchen 57 E3
Traismauer 57 E2
Trajanova Tabla . . . 73 E2
Trakai 110 C4
Trakošćan 70 C1
Traļee 14 A3
Tralee B 14 A3
Trá Lí 14 A3
Tramagal 38 B3
Tramariglio 66 A2
Tramatza 66 B3
Tramore 15 D4
Tranås 109 D1
Tranche, la 24 B4
Tranco, Emb del . . . 44 B2
Trancoso 38 C1
Trandrandsfjällen . . 101 D4
Tranebjerg 108 B3
Tranemo 109 D2
Tranent 5 D2
Trænfjorden 97 D2
Trani 65 D3
Tranóvalto 79 E4
Tranøy 94 B3
Tranquera, Emb de
la 36 C4
Transilvania 113 D4
Transtrand 101 D4
Trapani 68 A3
Trápeza 86 C1
Trappstadt 52 C4
Trasacco 63 F2
Trasimeno, L 61 D4
Trás os Montes 34 B4
Trassem 54 A1
Trasvase Tajo Segura,
Canal de 40 C4
Traun 57 D3
Traun R 56 C3
Traunkirchen 56 C3
Traunreut 56 B3
Traunsee 56 C3
Traunstein 56 B3
Travemünde 48 B2

Travnik 71 E4
Trayas, le 31 E4
Trbovlje 70 B2
Trbuk 71 F3
Trbušani 73 D4
Trdinov Vrh 70 C2
Trebbia 60 B2
Trebbin 49 D4
Trébeurden 22 B2
Trebević nac park . . 76 A1
Třebíč 57 E1
Trebinje 76 A2
Trebisacce 67 F2
Trebišnjica 75 F2
Trebišov 112 C3
Trebnje 70 B2
Třeboň 57 D1
Tréboul 22 A3
Trebsen 53 D2
Trebujena 43 D3
Trecastagni 69 D3
Trecate 60 A1
Tre Croci, Pso 59 D2
Tredegar 9 D2
Tredozio 61 D3
Treene 48 A1
Treffort 26 C4
Treffurt 52 B3
Trefynwy 9 D2
Tregaron 8 C1
Trégastel 22 B2
Tregnago 60 C1
Tregony 8 B4
Tréguier 22 C2
Trehörningsjö 102 A1
Treia (D) 47 F1
Treia (I) 61 F4
Treignac 29 D1
Trelleborg (S) 108 C4
Trelleborg (SF) 108 B3
Trélon 20 B2
Tremblade, la 28 A1
Tremestieri 69 D2
Tremezzo 58 B4
Tremiti, I 64 C2
Tremp 37 F3
Trenčín 112 B3
Trendelburg 52 A2
Trentino-Alto
Adige 58 C3
Trento 59 D3
Trent, R 7 D2
Trepča (Crna Gora) . 76 C2
Trepča (Kosovo) . . . 77 D1
Tréport, le 19 E2
Trepuzzi 65 F4
Tresco 8 A4
Trescore
Balneario 60 B1
Tresenda 58 B3
Tresfjord 100 B2
Tresjuncos 40 B3
Treska 77 D3
Treskavica 75 F1
Tres Mares, Pico
de 35 F2
Trešnjevica 73 E4
Trešnjevik 76 B2
Trespaderne 36 A2
Třešť 57 E1
Trets 30 C4
Tretten 104 C1

Treuchtlingen 55 E2
Treuen 53 D3
Treuenbrietzen 53 D1
Treungen 104 B4
Trevélez 44 A3
Trevi 63 E1
Trévières 18 C3
Trevignario
Romano 63 E2
Treviño 36 B2
Treviso 59 E4
Trévoux 26 C4
Trezzo sull' Adda . . 60 A1
Trgovište 77 E2
Trhové Sviny 57 D2
Triánda 93 F1
Tría Nissiá 92 C1
Triaucourt 20 C3
Tribanj Krušćica . . . 70 C4
Triberg 54 C3
Tribsees 49 D2
Tricarico 65 D4
Tricase 65 F4
Tricesimo 59 F3
Trichiana 59 E3
Trie 37 E1
Trieben 57 D4
Trier 54 A1
Trieste 59 F4
Trieste, G di 59 F4
Trifels 54 C2
Trifili 81 F2
Triglav 70 A2
Trigóna 82 C1
Trigueros 42 C2
Trihonída, L 83 D4
Trijueque 40 C2
Tríkala
(Makedonía) 79 F3
Tríkala (Nomos) . . . 82 C1
Trikala
(Pelopónissos) . . 87 D1
Trikala (Thessalia) . . 83 D1
Trikeri 83 F2
Trilj 75 E1
Trillevallen 101 D2
Trillo 40 C2
Trilofo 83 E3
Trim 13 D3
Trimouille, la 25 D3
Trindade 34 C4
Trinità d'Agultu e
V. 66 B1
Trinitapoli 64 C3
Trinité, la 22 C4
Trinité-
Porhoët, la 22 C3
Trino 31 F1
Triora 31 F3
Tripi 87 D3
Tripití 80 B3
Tripití, Akr 85 D2
Trípoli 87 D2
Triponzo 63 E1
Tripótama 86 C1
Triptis 53 D3
Trisanna 58 C2

Trischen 47 F2
Trittau 48 B3
Trittenheim 54 B1
Trivento 64 B2
Trizina 87 E2
Trlica 76 B1
Trnava 112 A3
Trnovo (BH) 75 F1
Trnovo (SLO) 70 A2
Trnova Poljana 75 D1
Troarn 18 C3
Trofa 34 A4
Trofaiach 57 E4
Trofors 97 E3
Trogir 75 D2
Troglav, V. 75 D1
Tróhalos 83 E1
Troia 64 C3
Tróia, Pen de 38 A4
Troina 68 C3
Troisdorf 51 E3
Trois Epis, les 27 E1
Trois-Moutiers, les . . 24 C3
Trois-Ponts 51 D4
Trojan 115 D2
Trojane 70 B2
Trollhättan 108 C1
Trollheimen 100 C2
Troms 94 C3
Tromsdalen 94 B2
Tromsø 94 B2
Trondheim 100 C2
Trondheimsfjorden
. . . . 100 C1
Trondheimsleia 100 B1
Tronö 101 F4
Tronto 63 F1
Troo 4 C2
Troon 4 C2
Tropea 67 E3
Trópea 86 C2
Tropojë 76 C2
Trosa 106 B4
Trossachs, The 4 C1
Trostan 13 E1
Trostberg 56 B3
Trouville 19 D3
Trowbridge 9 D2
Troyes 26 B1
Trpanj 75 E2
Trpezi 76 C2
Trpinja 71 F2
Trsa 76 B2
Tršić 72 B3
Trstenik (Kosovo) . . 77 D2
Trstenik (Pelješac) . . 75 E2
Trstenik (Srbija) . . . 73 D4
Trsteno 75 F2
Trubčevsk 111 F4
Trubia 35 D1
Trubia, R 35 D1
Trubjela 76 B2
Truchas 34 C3
Truchtersheim 21 E4
Trujillo 39 E3
Trun 19 D4
Truro 8 B4
Trutnov 112 A2
Truyère, Gorges de
la 29 E2
Tryde 109 D3
Trysilelva 100 D3

Tržac 70 C3
Trzcińsko-Zdrój . . . 49 E3
Trzebiatów 49 F1
Trzebież 49 E2
Tržič Golnik 70 A2
Tsamandás 82 B1
Tsambíka 93 F1
Tsangaráda 83 F2
Tsangário 82 B2
Tsaritsani 83 E1
Tsarkassiános 82 B4
Tsotili 79 D4
Tsoukaládes 82 B3
Tuaim 12 B3
Tuam 12 B3
Tua, R 34 B4
Tuath, L 4 B1
Tubilla del Agua . . . 35 F2
Tübingen 55 D3
Tubre 58 C3
Tučepi 75 E2
Tuchan 32 B2
Tudela 36 C3
Tudela de Duero . . . 35 E4
Tuella, R 34 C3
Tuerto, R 35 D2
Tuffé 23 F3
Tuheljske Toplice . . . 70 C2
Tuhkakylä 103 E1
Tui 34 A3
Tuineje 42 C4
Tukums 110 B2
Tulach Mhór 12 C4
Tulare 77 D1
Tulcea 113 E4
Tul'čin 113 E3
Tulla 12 B4
Tullamore 12 C4
Tulle 29 D1
Tullgarn 106 B4
Tullins 30 C1
Tulln 57 E2
Tullow 13 D4
Tulppio 95 F4
Tulsk 12 C3
Tumba 106 B4
Tunbridge Wells,
Royal 10 C3
Tundža 115 E3
Tunnhovdfjorden . . 104 C2
Tunnsjøen 97 E4
Tuohikotti 107 F2
Tuoro sul
Trasimeno 61 D4
Tupalaki 95 E3
Turalići 72 B4
Turballe, la 22 C4
Turbe 71 E4
Turbie, la 31 E3
Turckheim 27 E1
Turda 112 C4
Turégano 40 A1
Turenki 107 E2
Turgutlu 115 F4
Turi 65 E3
Türi 110 C1
Túria, R 41 E3
Turija (BH) 71 F3
Turija (Srbija) 73 E3
Turija (Vojvodina) . . 72 C2
Turinge 106 B4
Turis 41 E4

Turjak 70 B2
Türkheim 55 E3
Turku 107 D2
Turmiel 40 C1
Turnberry 4 C3
Turnhout 50 C3
Türnitz 57 E3
Turnov 112 A2
Turnu Măgurele . . . 115 D2
Turnu Roşu 113 D4
Turracherhöhe 59 F2
Turre 44 C3
Turriff 3 E3
Tursi 65 D4
Turtola 98 C2
Tuscania 63 D2
Tuse 108 C3
Tušilović 70 C3
Tustna 100 B2
Tutin 76 C1
Tutrakan 115 E2
Tuttlingen 55 D3
Turun ja Porin
Lääni 107 D2
Tuturano 65 F3
Tutzing 56 A3
Tuulos 107 E2
Tuupovaara 103 F2
Tuusniemi 103 E2
Tuusula 107 E2
Tuxford 7 D3
Tuzi 76 B3
Tuzla 71 F3
Tvedestrand 104 C4
Tver 111 F2
Tverrfjellet 100 B3
Tvøroyri 96 A4
Tweed, R 5 E2
Twelve Pins, The . . . 12 A3
Twimberg 70 B1
Twist 17 E2
Twistringen 17 F1
Tydal 101 D2
Tyin 104 C1
Tyin L. 100 B3
Týn 57 D1
Tyndrum 4 C1
Tynemouth 5 E3
Tynkä 102 C1
Tynset 100 C3
Tyräjärvi 99 E3
Tyresö 106 B4
Tyrifjorden 104 C3
Tyringe 109 D3
Tyristrand 104 C3
Tyrnävä 99 D4
Tyrone 13 D2
Tysfjorden 97 F1
Tysnesøy 104 A2
Tysse 104 A2
Tyssebotn 104 A2
Tyssedal 104 B2
Tysvær 104 A3
Tywi 8 C2
Tywyn 6 A3

U

Ub 72 C3
Ubaye 31 D2
Úbeda 44 A2
Überlingen 55 D4
Ubl'a 112 C3
Ubli (Crna Gora) . . . 76 B2
Ubli (Lastovo) 75 E3
Ubrique 43 E4
Uchte 17 F2
Učka 70 B3
Uckange 21 D3
Uckfield 10 C3

Uclés 40 B3
Udbina 70 C4
Udbyhøj 108 B2
Uddevalla 108 C1
Uddheden 105 E3
Uddjaure 98 A3
Uden 16 C3
Udine 59 F3
Udovo 77 F3
Udvar 72 A1
Uebigau 53 D2
Uecker 49 E2
Ueckermünde 49 E2
Uelzen 48 B3
Uetersen 48 A2

Uetze 48 B4
Uffenheim 55 E1
Ugao 76 C1
Ugento 65 F4
Ugijar 44 B3
Ugine 27 D4
Uglič 111 F1
Ugljan 74 C1
Ugljan I. 74 C1
Ugljane 75 E1
Ugljevik 72 B3
Ugra 111 F3
Ugrinovci 73 D3
Uherské Hradiště . . 112 A3
Uhingen 55 D2

Úhlava 56 C1
Uhrsleben 52 C1
Uig 2 B3
Uimaharju 103 F2
Uithoorn 16 C2
Uithuizen 47 D3
Ukkola 103 F1
Ukmergė 110 C4
Ukonselkä 95 E3
Ukraina 113 D3
Ukrina 71 E3
Ulcinj 76 B3
Uleåborg 99 D3
Ulefoss 104 C3
Uleila del Campo . . 44 C3

Ulëzë 76 C3
Ulfborg 108 A2
Uljanik 71 D2
Uljanovka 113 E3
Uljma 73 D2
Ullånger 102 A2
Ullapool 2 C2
Ulla, R 34 B2
Ullared 108 C2
Ullava 102 C1
Ulldecona 41 F2
Ullsfjorden 94 C2
Ullswater 5 D4
Ulm 55 E3
Ulmen 51 E4

Ulog 75 F1
Ulricehamn 109 D1
Ulrichsberg 56 C2
Ulsberg 100 C2
Ulsta 3 F1
Ulsteinvik 100 A2
Uludağ 115 F3
Ul'ugai'sa 95 E2
Ulva 4 B1
Ulverston 6 B1
Ulvik 104 B2
Ulvsjö 101 E3
Ulzës, Liq i 76 C3

Uman' 113 E3
Umbertide 61 E4
Umbrail, Pass. 58 C3
Umbria 63 E1
Umbukta 97 E3
Umčari 73 D3
Umeå 102 B1
Umeälven 98 A4
Umhausen 58 C2
Umin Dol 77 D3
Umka 72 C3
Umljanović 75 D1
Una 71 D3
Unac 71 D4
Unari 99 D3

Unari L 99 D1
Uncastillo 37 D2
Unden 105 E4
Undersåker 101 D2
Undredal 104 B2
Uneča 111 F4
Unešić 75 D1
Úněšov 53 E4
Ungen' 113 E3
Ungilde 34 C3
Unhais da Serra ... 38 C2
Unhošt 53 F4
Unije 70 B4
Universales, Mts.... 41 D2
Unna 17 E3
Unnaryd 109 D2
Unnukka 103 E2
Unquera 35 F1
Unst 3 F1
Unstrut 52 C2

Unterach 56 C3
Unterhaching 56 A3
Unter-
Schleissheim ... 55 F3
Unterwalden 27 F3
Unterwasser 58 B2
Unterweißenbach .. 57 D2
Upavon 9 E3
Upinniemi 107 E3
Upper L Erne 13 D2
Uppingham 9 F1
Upplands-Väsby ... 106 B3
Uppsala 106 B3
Uppsala Län 106 B3
Upton 9 E1
Uras 66 B3
Urbania 61 E3
Urbasa, Pto de ... 36 C2
Urbasa, Sa de 36 C2
Urbe 60 A3

Urbino 61 E3
Urbión, Sa de 36 B3
Urdos 37 D2
Ure 6 C1
Uredakke 97 E4
Urepel 36 C1
Urfahr 57 D2
Urfeld 56 A4
Urho Kekkosen
kansallispuisto .. 95 F3
Uri (CH) 58 A3
Uri (I) 66 A2
Uriage 30 C1
Urjala 107 E2
Urk 16 C2
Urla 115 E4
Urlingford 14 C3
Urnäsch 58 B2
Urnes 100 B3
Uroševac 77 D2

Urovica 73 F3
Urquiola, Pto 36 B1
Urshult 109 D3
Ursprungpaß 59 D1
Urtivaara 95 D3
Ururi 64 B2
Ury 25 F1
Urziceni 115 E1
Usagre 43 D1
Uşak 115 F4
Usedom 49 E2
Usedom I. 49 E1
Useras 41 E3
Usingen 51 F4
Usk 9 D2
Usk R. 9 D2
Uskoplje 76 A2
Üsküdar 115 F3
Uslar 52 B2

Ussat-les-Bains ... 32 A2
Ussé 25 D2
Usseglio 31 E1
Ussel 29 E1
Usseln 17 F4
Ustaoset 104 B2
Ustaritz 28 A4
Uster 58 A2
Ustevatn 104 B2
Ustibar 76 B1
Ustica, I di 68 B2
Ustikolina 76 A1
Ústí nad Labem .. 53 F3
Ustiprača 76 B1
Ustka 110 A4
Ustronie Morskie . 49 F1
Ust'užna 111 F1
Utajärvi 99 D4

Utebo 37 D3
Utelle 31 E3
Utena 110 C3
Utiel 41 D3
Utne 104 B2
Utrecht 16 C3
Utrecht (Prov) .. 16 C2
Utrera 43 D3
Utrillas 41 E2
Utsjoki 95 E2
Utsjoki R. 95 E2
Uttendorf
(Oberösterreich) . 56 C3
Uttendorf
(Salzburg) 59 E1
Utting 56 A3
Uttoxeter 6 C3
Uudenmaan
Lääni 107 F2
Uukuniemi 103 F3

Uurainen 103 D2
Uusikaarlepyy ... 102 B2
Uusikaupunki 107 D2
Uvac 76 B1
Uvac R 76 B1
Uvdal 104 C2
Uzdin 72 C2
Uzel 22 C3
Uzerche 29 D1
Uzès 30 B3
Užgorod 112 C3
Uzice 72 C4
Uzin 113 E2
Uzunköprü 115 E3

V

Vä 109 D3
Vaajakoski 103 D3
Vääkiö 99 E3
Vaala 99 E4
Vaalajärvi 95 E4
Vaalimaa 103 F4
Vaals 51 D3
Vaaraslahti 103 D2
Vaasa 102 B2
Vaasan Lääni 102 C2
Vaassen 17 D2
Vabre 32 B1
Våc 112 B4
Vaccarès, Etang
de 30 B4
Vacha 52 B3
Väddö 106 B3
Vadehavet 108 A4
Vadheim 100 A3
Vado Ligure 60 A3
Vadsø 95 F1
Vadstena 109 D1
Vaduz 58 B2
Vadvetjåkka 94 B3
Vaféika 81 D2
Vågaholmen 97 E2
Vågåmo 100 B3
Vågan 97 E1
Vaganj 75 E1
Vaganski vrh ... 70 C4
Vágar 96 A3
Våge 104 A2
Væggerløse 108 C4
Vaggeryd 109 D2
Vágia 83 F4
Vagioniá 91 D4
Vagnhärad 106 B4
Vagos 38 B1
Vågsfjorden ... 94 B3
Vågsøy 100 A3
Vágur 96 A4
Váh 112 B2
Vähäkyrö 102 B2
Vahto 107 D2
Vaï 91 F3
Vaiano 60 C3
Vaiges 23 E3
Vaihingen 55 D2
Vailly (Aisne) .. 20 A3
Vailly (Cher) .. 26 A2
Vainikkala 103 F4
Vaisaluokta ... 94 B4
Vaison-la-
Romaine 30 C3
Vaksdal 104 A2
Vålådalen 101 D2
Valadares 34 A4
Valais 27 E4
Valalta 70 A3
Valamen 103 E2
Valandovo 77 F3
Val-André, le .. 22 C2
Valareña 36 C3
Valašské Meziříčí .. 112 B3

Valax 107 F2
Valberg 31 E3
Vålberg 105 E3
Valbiska 70 B3
Valbo 106 B2
Valbondione 58 B3
Valbonë 76 C2
Valbonnais 31 D2
Val Camonica ... 58 C4
Valcarlos 36 C1
Valdagno 59 D4
Valdahon 27 D2
Valdaj 111 E1
Val-d'Ajol, le .. 27 D1
Valdajskaja
Vozvyšennost' ... 111 E2
Valdavia, R. 35 E3
Valdazogues, R. .. 43 F1
Valdecaballeros .. 39 E4
Valdecabras 40 C3
Valdecañas, Emb
de 39 E3
Valdecarros 39 E1
Valdecebollas ... 35 F2
Valdediós 35 E1
Valdeganga 41 D4
Valdeinfierno, Emb
de 44 C2

Valdelacasa de
Tajo 39 E3
Valdosa 36 A3
Valdelinares ... 41 E2
Valdemarsvik 109 E1
Valdemeca 41 D2
Valdemorillo ... 40 A2
Valdemoro 40 A2
Valdenoceda 36 A2
Valdeobispo, Emb
de 39 D2
Valdepeñas 44 A1
Valdepeñas da
Jaén 44 A2
Valderaduey, R .. 35 D4
Valderas 35 E3
Valderiès 29 E3
Valderøy 100 A2
Valderrepisa, Pto
de 43 F1
Valderrobres ... 41 F2
Valdestillas ... 35 E4
Valdeverdeja ... 39 E3
Valdevimbre 35 D3
Valdezcaray 36 B2
Valdieri 31 E3
Valdihuela 39 F2
Val-d'Isère 31 D1

Valdobbiadene 59 D3
Valdosa 36 A3
Valdres 104 C2
Valdres Flya 100 B3
Vale de Açor 42 B2
Vale de Cambra .. 38 B1
Vale de Estrela . 38 C2
Vale de Prazeres . 38 C2
Vale, Emb de ... 37 F2
Valeggio sul
Mincio 60 C1
Valença do Minho . 34 A3
Valençay 25 E2
Valence-
d'Albigeois 29 E3
Valence (Drôme) . 30 C2
Valence (Gers) .. 28 C3
Valencia 41 E4
Valencia (Prov) . 41 D4
Valencia de
Alcántara 38 C3
Valencia de Don
Juan 35 D3
Valencia de las
Torres 43 D1
Valencia del
Ventoso 43 D1
Valencia I 14 A4

Valenciennes 20 A1
Valensole 31 D3
Valentano 63 D2
Valentigney 27 E2
Valenza 60 A2
Våler (Hedmark).. 105 D3
Våler (Østfold) . 105 D3
Valeria 40 C3
Valevåg 104 A3
Valfabbrica 61 E4
Valga 110 C2
Valgorge 30 B2
Valgrisenche ... 31 E1
Valguarnera
Caropepe 68 C3
Valhelhas 38 C2
Valico della
Forchetta 64 A2
Valira 86 C3
Valjevo 72 C3
Valjok 95 E2
Valjunguera 41 F1
Valkeakoski 107 E2
Valkeala 107 F2
Valkenburg 51 D3
Valkenswaard.... 16 C4

Valko 107 F2
Valladolid 35 E4
Vallata 64 C3
Vallbo 101 D2
Valldal 100 B2
Vall d'Alba 41 E3
Valldemossa 45 E2
Vall de Uxó 41 E3
Valle 104 B3
Valleberga 109 D4
Valle Castellana . 63 F1
Valle d'Aosta .. 27 E4
Valle de Abdalajis . 43 E3
Valle de la Serena . 39 E4
Valle de los Caidos . 40 A2
Valle de
Matamoros 42 C1
Vallehermoso .. 42 A4
Vallejera, Pto de . 39 E2
Valle-Mosso 31 F1
Vallentuna 106 B3
Valleraugue 29 F3
Vallet 24 B2
Valletta 68 B4
Vallgrund 102 B2
Valli di Comacchio . 61 D2
Vallø 108 C3
Vallo della Lucania . 67 D1

Valloire 31 D1
Vallombrosa..... 61 D3
Vallon-en-Sully .. 25 F3
Vallon-Pont-d'arc . 30 B3
Vallorbe 27 D3
Vallorcine 27 E4
Valls 37 F4
Vallsta 101 F4
Valmiera 110 C2
Valmojado 40 A2
Valmont 19 D2
Valmontone 63 F3
Valogne 18 B3
Valongo 34 A4
Valoria la Buena.. 35 E4
Valpaços 34 b4
Valpalmas 37 D3
Valparaiso, Emb de . 35 D3
Val Passiria 59 D2
Valpovo 71 F2
Valprato Soana . 31 E1
Valras-Plage ... 30 A4
Valréas 30 C3
Valsamónero ... 91 D4
Valsavarenche . 31 E1
Valserine 27 D4
Valset 100 C1
Valsjöbyn 101 E1

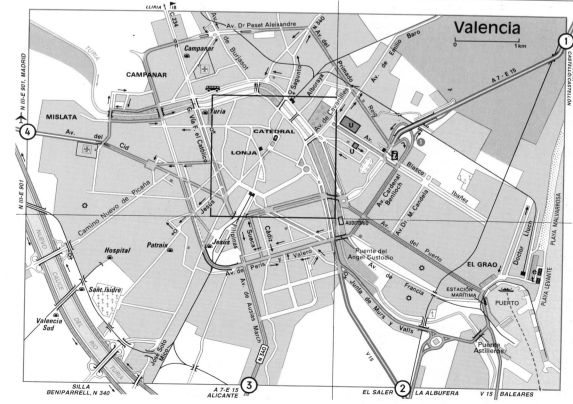

Valencia

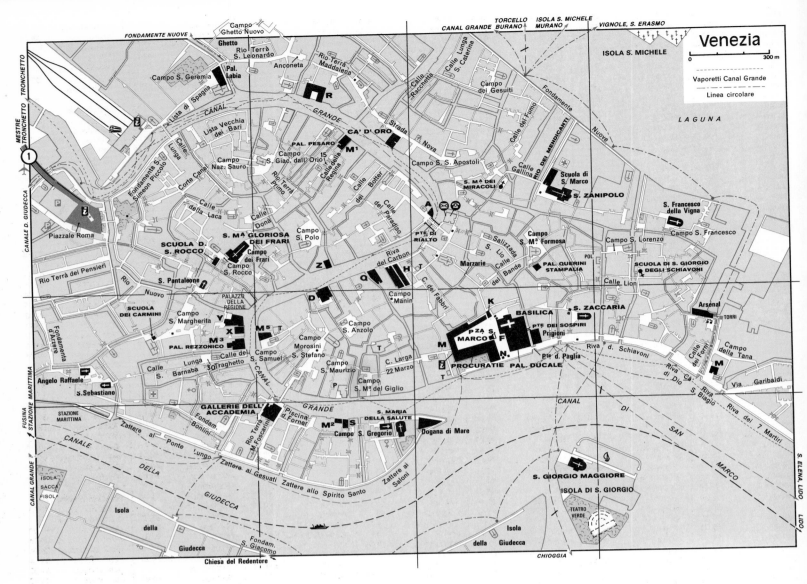

Vals-les-Bains...... 30 B2	Vandellòs............ 41 F1	Varazze............ 60 A3	Värmlands Län 105 E3	Vassiliká (Lésvos) 85 F2	Vathílakos (Kozáni).. 79 E4	Veere 16 B3
Valtellina 58 B3	Vänern............ 105 E4	Varberg............ 108 C2	Varmo............. 59 E3	Vassiliká (Makedonía)....... 80 A3	Vathílakos (Thessaloníki)... 79 F3	Vefsna 97 E3
Valtessiníko........ 86 C2	Vänersborg........ 108 C1	Vărbica............ 115 E2	Varna (BG)........ 115 E2	Vassiliki (Lefkáda) .. 82 B3	Vathípetro 91 D4	Vefsnfjorden........ 97 D3
Val-Thorens 31 D1	Vangshylla........ 101 D1	Varda 72 C4	Varna (Srbija) 72 C3	Vassiliki (Thessalía) .. 83 D1	Vathís 89 F3	Vega 97 D3
Valtierra.......... 36 C3	Vangsnes.......... 104 B1	Várda 86 B1	Várnamo........... 109 D2	Vassilikó 84 B4	Vatin 73 D2	Vega de
Valtimo........... 103 E1	Vangsvik 94 B3	Vardar............ 77 E3	Varnhem........... 109 D1	Vassilikós 86 A2	Vatnajökull 96 B2	Espinareda....... 34 C2
Váltos 81 F1	Vanha Vaasa....... 102 B2	Varde 108 A3	Varnsdorf 53 F2	Vassilís........... 83 E2	Vatne 100 B2	Vegadeo........... 34 C1
Valtotópi 80 B2	Vanna 94 C2	Vardenik.......... 77 E2	Váró 108 C2	Vassilítsa 78 C4	Vatólakos 79 D4	Vega de Valcarce ... 34 C1
Váltou, Óri........ 82 C2	Vännäs 102 A1	Vardø 95 F1	Varoš Selo......... 77 D2	Vassy 18 C4	Vatopediou 80 C4	Vegafjorden........ 97 D3
Valtournenche 27 F4	Vannavålen 94 C2	Vårdö 106 C3	Várpalota 112 B4	Västanbäck 101 E2	Vatra Dornei 113 D4	Vegarienza 35 D2
Valun 70 B4	Vannes 22 C4	Varel 47 F3	Varpaisjärvi 103 E1	Västanfjärd 107 D3	Vågårshei 104 C4	Vegårshei 104 C4
Valvasone 59 E3	Vannsjø 105 D3	Vareleli 84 C4	Värriötunturit 95 F4	Vastenjaure 97 F1	Vättern 109 D1	Vegas 35 E2
Valverde (Is Canarias)....... 42 A4	Vannsundet 94 C2	Varengeville 19 D2	Vars 31 D2	Västerås.......... 106 A3	Vattholma 106 B3	Vegas del Condado 35 E2
Valverde (La Rioja) .. 36 C3	Vanoise, Massif de la 31 D1	Varenna 58 B4	Vars, Col de 31 D2	Västerbottens Län 98 A4	Vaucluse 30 C3	Vegesack 47 F3
Valverde del Camino 42 C2	Vanoise, Parc Nat de la 31 D1	Varennes-en-Argonne 20 C3	Vartdalsfjorden 100 A2	Västerdalälven 101 D4	Vaud 27 D3	Veghel 16 C3
Valverde de Leganés 38 C4	Vansbro 105 E2	Varennes-sur-Allier............ 26 A4	Vartholomió 86 B1	Väster Haninge.... 106 B4	Vau i Dejës 76 C3	Vegoritida, L. 79 E3
Valverde del Fresno 39 D2	Vans, les 30 B3	Varennes-sur-Amance 26 C1	Vartius 99 F4	Västernorrlands Län 101 F2	Vaut të Dejës, Liq i .. 76 C3	Vehkalahti 103 F4
Valverde del Júcar .. 40 C3	Vantaa 107 E2	Vareš 71 F4	Värtsilä 103 F2	Västervik 109 E1	Vauvert 30 B4	Vehmaa 101 D2
Valøya 97 D4	Vanttauskoski 99 D2	Varese 58 A4	Varvára 80 B3	Västmanlands Län 105 F3	Vauvillers 27 D1	Vehmersalmi 103 E2
Våmb 109 D1	Vaour 29 D3	Varese Ligure 60 B3	Varvarin 73 E4	Vasto 64 B2	Vaux-le-Vicomte.... 19 F4	Veidnesklubben 95 E1
Våmhus 101 E4	Vaqueira.......... 37 F2	Vårgårda 108 C1	Varzi 60 A2	Vatan 25 E3	Vávdos 80 A3	Veikkola 107 E2
Vamlingbo 109 F4	Var 31 D4	Vargas 35 F2	Varzy 26 A2	Väte 109 F4	Växjö 109 D2	Veines 95 F1
Vammala 107 D1	Vara 108 C1	Vargsund 95 D1	Vasa............. 102 B2	Vaterá 85 F3	Våxtorp 108 C3	Veinge 108 C2
Vampula 107 D2	Varades 23 E4	Varhaug 104 A4	Vasarapera 99 E2	Vateró 79 D4	Vayrac 29 D2	Veiros 38 C4
Vamvakás, Akr 85 F4	Varallo 58 A4	Vári (Kikládes) 88 B2	Vasárosnamény 112 C3	Váthia 87 D4	V'az'ma 111 F3	Vejen 108 A3
Vamvakoú (Pelopónissos) 87 D3	Varangerbotn 95 F1	Vári (Stereá Eláda) . 87 F1	Vascão, Rib do 42 B2	Vathí (Dodekánissa) 84 B4	Veberöd 109 D3	Vejer de la Frontera 43 D4
Vamvakoú (Thessalía) 83 E2	Varangerfjorden ... 95 F1	Varilhes 32 A2	Vascão, Rib do 42 B2	Vathí (Lefkáda)..... 79 F2	Vecht 17 D2	Vejle 108 A3
Vanajavesi 107 E2	Varangerhalvøya .. 95 F1	Varimbómbi 87 F1	Vasikkaselkä 95 F2	Vathí (Makedonía) .. 92 C1	Vechta 17 F1	Velada 39 F3
Vanån 101 D4	Varano de' Melegari 60 B2	Váris 79 D4	Vasil'kov 113 E2	Vathí (Stereá Eláda) 82 B3	Vechte 17 E2	Velagići........... 71 D4
Vanda............ 107 E2	Varano, L di 64 C2	Varkaus 103 E3	Vaskijärvi 107 D2	Vassarás.......... 87 D3	Vecinos 39 E1	Vela Luka 75 E2
	Varaždin.......... 70 C1	Várkiza 87 F2	Vaskio 107 E2	Vassés 86 C2	Vedelago 59 E4	Velanídia 87 E4
	Varaždinske Toplice........ 71 D1	Varmahlíð 96 B1	Vaskivesi 102 C3	Vassieux 30 C1	Vedrá, I........... 45 D4	Velate, Pto de 36 C1
			Vaslui 113 E4	Vassiliká (Évia) 84 A3	Vedungfjället...... 101 D3	Velayos 39 F2
					Veendam 47 D3	Velbert 17 E3

Velburg 55 F1
Velde 101 D1
Velden (A) 70 A1
Velden (München) 56 B3
Velden (Nürnberg) 55 F1
Veldhoven 16 C4
Velebit 70 C4
Velebitski kanal 70 B4
Velenje 70 B1
Velešta 77 D4
Veleta, Pico 44 A3
Velež 75 F2
Vélez Blanco 44 C2
Vélez de
  Benaudalla 44 A3
Vélez-Málaga 43 F3
Vélez Rubio 44 C2
Velfjorden 97 D3
Veličani 75 F2
Veliés 87 E4
Velika 71 E2
Velika Drenova 73 E4
Velika Gorica 70 B3
Velikaja 111 D2
Velika Jablanica 76 C2
Velika Jamnička 70 C2
Velika Kapela 70 B3
Velika Kladuša 70 C3
Velika Kopanica 71 F3
Velika Kruša 77 D2
Velika Morava 73 D3
Velika Mučna 71 D1
Velika Plana
  (Morava) 73 D3
Velika Plana
  (Prokuplje) 77 D1
Velika Tresta 73 E3
Veliki Alan 70 B4
Veliki Bastaji 71 E2
Veliki Gaj 73 D2
Veliki Grđevac 71 D2
Veliki Izvor 73 F3
Veliki Jastrebac 77 D1
Velikije Luki 111 E2
Veliki kanal 72 B2
Veliki Krš 73 E3
Veliki Popović 73 E3
Veliki Prolog 75 E2
Veliki Radinci 72 C2
Veliki Trnovac 77 E2
Veliki Vitao 76 A2
Veliki Zdenci 71 D2
Veliko Gradište 73 D2
Veliko Lašče 70 B2
Veliko Orašje 73 D3
Veliko Tărnovo 115 D2
Velilla del R
  Carrion 35 E2
Veli Lošinj 70 B4
Velimlje 76 A2
Vélines 28 C2
Velingrad 115 D3
Velino 63 F2
Velino, Mte 63 F2
Veliž 111 E3
Veljun 70 C3
Velká Bíteš 57 E1
Velké Meziříčí 57 E1
Velkua 107 D2
Vellahn 48 B3
Velletri 63 E3
Vellinge 108 C3
Velopoúla 87 F3
Vélos 84 B4
Velpke 48 B4
Velten 49 D4
Velvendós 79 E4
Vemdalen 101 E3
Vemdalsskalet 101 E3
Vemhån 101 E3
Véna 81 E2
Venaco 33 F3
Venafro 64 A3
Venarey-les-
  Laumes 26 B2
Venaria 31 E1
Venčani 73 D3
Vence 31 E3
Venda Nova 34 B4
Vendas Novas 38 B4
Vendée 24 B3
Vendel 106 B3
Vendeuvre 26 B1

Vendôme 25 E2
Vendsyssel 108 B2
Veneheitto 99 D4
Veneta, Laguna 61 D1
Veneto 61 D1
Venezia 61 D1
Vengjaneset 104 A2
Venialbo 35 D4
Venjan 101 E4
Venjansjön 101 E4
Venlo 17 D4
Vennesla 104 B4
Vennesund 97 D3
Venosa 64 C3
Venosta 58 C3
Venray 17 D3
Venta 110 B3
Venta de Cruce 43 D3
Venta de Don
  Quijote 40 B3
Ventana, Pto de 35 D2
Venta Nueva 34 C2
Ventas de Huelma 44 A3
Ventimiglia 31 E3
Ventnor 9 E4
Ventotene, I 63 F4
Ventoux, Mt 30 C3
Ventspils 110 B2
Venturina 62 C1
Vera (E) 44 C3
Vera (N) 101 D1
Vera de Bidasoa 36 C1
Verbania-Pallanza 58 A4
Verberie 19 F3
Verbicaro 67 E2
Verbier 27 E4
Vercelli 31 F1
Vercel-Villedieu 27 D2
Verchnedvinsk 111 D3
Verdalsøra 101 D1
Verde, Col de 33 F3
Verden 48 A4
Verdikoússa 83 D1
Verdon 31 D3
Verdon, le 28 A1
Verdun (Meuse) 20 C3
Verdun (Saône-et-
  Loire) 26 C3
Verdun (Tarn-et-
  Garonne) 29 D3
Verfeil 29 D4
Vergato 60 C3
Vérgi 80 A2
Vergiate 60 A1
Vergína 79 E3
Vergio, Col de 33 F3
Vergt 28 C2
Véria 79 E3
Verin 34 B3
Verl 17 F3
Vermand 20 A2
Vermenton 26 B2
Vérmio, Óros 79 E3
Verna, Pzo di 69 D2
Vernet-les-Bains 32 B2
Verneuil 19 D4
Vernon 19 E3
Vérno, Óros 79 D3
Vernoux-en-
  Vivarais 30 B2
Verny 21 D3
Veroli 63 F3
Verona 60 C1
Verpillière 30 C1
Verran 101 D1
Verrès 27 F4
Versailles 19 F4
Versmold 17 F2
Verteillac 28 C1
Vertiskos, Óros 80 A2
Vertus 20 B4
Verucchio 61 E3
Veruela 36 C3
Verviers 51 D4
Vervins 20 B2
Verzuolo 31 E2
Verzy 20 B3
Vesanto 103 D2
Vescovato 33 F3
Veseli 57 D1
Vesijärvi 107 F2
Vesilahti 107 E1
Vesivehmaa 107 F2
Vesjegonsk 111 F1

Veskoniemi 95 F3
Vesle 20 B3
Véssa 85 E4
Vest-Agder 104 B4
Vestby 105 D3
Vestbygda 104 A4
Vesterålen 94 A3
Vesterø Havn 108 B2
Vestertana 95 E1
Vestfjorden 97 E1
Vestfold 104 C3
Vestmanna 96 A3
Vestmannaeyjar 96 B3
Vestnes 100 B2
Vestone 58 C4
Vestre Jakobselv 95 F1
Vestvågøy 94 A4
Vésubie, Gorges de
  la 31 E3
Vesuvio 64 B4
Veszprém 112 B4
Veteli 102 C2
Veternica 77 E1
Vetlanda 109 E2
Vetralla 63 E2
Vetriolo Terme 59 D3
Vetschau 53 E1
Vettore, M 63 F1
Veules-les-Roses 19 D2
Veulettes 19 D2
Veurne 50 A3
Vevey 27 E3
Vévi 79 D3
Veynes 30 C2
Veyre 29 F1
Veyrier 27 D4
Vezdemarbán 35 D4
Vézelay 26 B2
Vézelise 21 D4
Vézénobres 30 B3
Vézère 29 D2
Vézins-de-
  Lévézou 29 E3
Vezzani 33 F3
Vezzano 58 C3
Via Appia 63 F3
Via Aurelia 60 C4
Via Casilina 63 E2
Via Cassia 63 D1
Viadana 60 C2
Via Emilia 61 D3
Via Flaminia 61 E3
Viana 36 B2
Viana do Bolo 34 C3
Viana do Castelo 34 A3
Vianden 21 D2
Viano do Alentejo 42 B1
Viareggio 60 B3
Viar, R 43 D2
Vias 30 A4
Via Salaria 63 E2
Via Tiburtina
  Valeria 63 F2
Viaur 29 E3
Viborg 108 A2
Vibo Valentia 67 E3
Vibraye 23 F3
Vič 70 B1
Vic (E) 32 A3
Vic (F) 19 F3
Vicálvaro 40 B2
Vicdessos 37 F2
Vic-en-Bigorre 28 B4
Vicenza 59 D4
Vic-Fézensac 28 C4
Vich 32 A3
Vichy 26 A4
Vic-le-Comte 29 F1
Vico 33 E3
Vico del Gargano 64 C2
Vico Equense 64 B4
Vico, Lago di 63 E2
Vic-sur-Cère 29 E2
Victoria 68 B4
Vidá 108 A4
Vidago 34 B4
Viðareidi 96 A3
Vidauban 31 D4
Viddal 100 A3
Videbæk 108 A3
Vidiáki 86 C1
Vidigueira 42 B1
Vidin 114 C2

Vidio, C 35 D1
Viðoy 96 A3
Vidreres 32 B4
Vidrovan 76 B2
Vidsel 98 B3
Viduša 76 A2
Viechtach 56 B2
Viechtwang 56 C3
Vieira 38 A2
Vieira do Minho 34 B4
Viejo, Pto 39 D2
Viekinjärvi 103 F1
Vielha 37 F2
Vielle-Aure 37 E2
Vielmur 32 A1
Vielsalm 51 D4
Vienenburg 52 B1
Vienne 30 B1
Vienne (Dépt) 25 D3
Vienne R 25 D4
Vieremä 103 D1
Viernheim 54 C1
Vierraden 49 E3
Viersen 17 D4
Vierumäki 107 F2
Vierzehnheiligen 52 C4
Vierzon 25 F2
Vieste 64 C2
Vietas 94 B4
Vietri di Potenza 64 C4
Vietri sul Mare 64 B4
Vieux-Boucau 28 A3
Vieux Chaillol 31 D2
Vif 30 C2
Vig 108 C3
Vigan, le 29 F3
Vigeland 104 B4
Vigeois 29 D1
Vigevano 60 A1
Viggiano 65 D4
Vigla 82 C2
Vigla, Akr 91 D1
Vignale 31 F1
Vignanello 63 E2
Vignemale 37 E2
Vignes, les 29 F3
Vigneulles 20 C3
Vignola 60 C2
Vignole Borbera 60 A2
Vignory 26 C1
Vigo 34 A3
Vigo di Fassa 59 D3
Vigone 31 E2
Vigonza 61 D1
Vigrestad 104 A4
Vihanti 99 D3
Vihiers 24 C2
Vihtavuori 103 D3
Vihteljärvi 102 C3
Vihti 107 E2
Viiala 107 E2
Viinijärvi 103 F2
Viipustunturit 95 E3
Viitasaari 103 D2
Vik (Aust-Agder) 104 B4
Vik (IS) 96 B3
Vik (Nordland) 97 D3
Vik (Sogn og
  Fjordane) 104 B1
Vika 105 F2
Vikajärvi 99 D2
Vikanes 104 A2
Vikebukt 100 B2
Vikedal 104 A3
Vikersund 104 C3
Vikeså 104 A4
Vikevåg 104 A3
Vikingstad 106 A4
Vikna 97 D4
Vikoč 76 A1
Vikran 94 B3
Viksdalen 100 A3
Viksjö 101 F2
Viksjøfjell 95 F2
Viksta 106 B3
Vila Boim 38 C4
Vilada 32 A3
Viladamat 32 B3
Vila de Cruces 34 B2
Vila de Rei 38 B3
Vila do Bispo 42 A2
Vila do Conde 34 A4
Viladrau 32 B3
Vila Fernando 38 C4

Vila Flor 34 C4
Vila Franca das
  Naves 38 C1
Vilafranca del
  Penedès 32 A4
Vila Franca de Xira 38 A4
Vila Fresca de
  Azeitão 38 A4
Vilagarcia de
  Arosa 34 A2
Vilaine 22 C4
Vilaller 37 F2
Vilán, C 34 A1
Vilanova 34 C1
Vila Nova da
  Barquinha 38 B3
Vilanova de.
  Arousa 34 A2
Vila Nova de
  Cerveira 34 A2
Vila Nova de
  Famalicão 34 A4
Vila Nova de Foz
  Côa 39 D1
Vila Nova de Gaia 34 A4
Vila Nova de
  Milfontes 42 A2
Vila Nova de
  Ourém 38 B3
Vila Nova de Paiva 38 C1
Vila Nova de
  Poiares 38 B2
Vila Nova de
  Ródão 38 C3
Vila Verde 34 A3
Vila Verde de
  Ficalho 42 C1
Vila Verde de Raia 34 B3
Vila Viçosa 38 C4
Vilches 44 A2
Vilejka 111 D4
Vilhelmina 97 F4
Vília 87 E1
Viljakkala 102 C3
Viljandi 110 C2
Vilkaviškis 110 C4
Vilkovo 113 E4
Villa Adriana 63 E2
Villa Bartolomea 60 C1
Villablanca 42 C2
Villablino 35 D2
Villabona 36 C1
Villabrágima 35 E4
Villabuena del
  Puente 35 D4
Villacãas 40 B3
Villacarriedo 35 F2
Villacarrillo 44 B2
Villacastín 40 A1
Villach 59 F2
Villacidro 66 B4
Villada 35 E3
Villa del Prado 40 A2
Villa del Río 43 F2
Villadiego 35 F3
Villadossola 27 F4
Villaescusa de
  Haro 40 C3
Villafáfila 35 D4
Villafamés 41 E3
Villaflores 39 F1
Villafranca 36 C2
Villafranca del
  Bierzo 34 C2
Villafranca del Cid 41 E2
Villafranca de los
  Barros 43 D1
Villafranca de los
  Caballeros 40 B3
Villafranca di
  Verona 60 C1

Villafranca in
  Lunigiana 60 B3
Villafranca-Montes
  de Oca 36 A2
Villafranca
  Piemonte 31 E2
Villafranca Tirrena 69 D2
Villafranco del
  Guadalquivir 43 D3
Villafrati 68 B3
Villafrechos 35 E4
Villafruela 35 F4
Villafuerte 35 F4
Villagarcía del
  Llano 40 C4
Villager 35 D2
Villaggio
  Mancuso 67 F3
Villagonzalo 39 D4
Villaharta 43 E1
Villahermosa 44 B1
Villahoz 35 F3
Villaines-la-Juhel 23 E3
Villajoyosa 45 E1
Villa, la 59 D2
Villala 103 F3
Villalba 34 B1
Villalba de Guardo 35 E2
Villalba de la Sierra 40 C2
Villalba de los
  Barros 43 D1
Villalba del Rey 40 C2
Villalcampo, Emb
  de 35 D4
Villalcázar de Sirga 35 E3
Villalenga 36 C4
Villaliterno 64 A4
Villalón de
  Campos 35 E3
Villalonga 45 E1
Villalpando 35 E4
Villalpardo 41 D4
Villamañán 35 D3
Villamanrique 44 B1
Villamarchante 41 E3
Villamartín
  (Andalucía) 43 D3
Villamartín (Castilla-
  León) 35 E3
Villamassargia 66 B4
Villamayor 37 D3
Villamayor de
  Campos 35 E3
Villamayor de
  Santiago 40 B3
Villa Minozzo 60 C3
Villandraut 28 B3
Villandry 25 D2
Villanova
  Monteleone 66 A2
Villanubla 35 E4
Villanueva de
  Alcardete 40 B3
Villanueva de
  Alcolea 41 F3
Villanueva de
  Alcorón 40 C2
Villanueva de
  Algaidas 43 F3
Villanueva de
  Argaño 35 F3
Villanueva de
  Arzobispo 44 B2
Villanueva de
  Bogas 40 A3
Villanueva de
  Cameros 36 B3
Villanueva de
  Córdoba 43 F1
Villanueva de
  Franco 40 B4
Villanueva de
  Gállego 37 D3
Villanueva de la
  Concepción 43 F3
Villanueva de la
  Fuente 44 B1
Villanueva de la
  Jara 40 C3
Villanueva de la
  Reina 44 A2
Villanueva de la
  Serena 39 E4

Villanueva de la
  Sierra 39 D2
Villanueva de las
  Torres 44 B2
Villanueva de la
  Vera 39 E2
Villanueva del
  Campo 35 D3
Villanueva del
  Duque 43 E1
Villanueva del
  Fresno 42 C1
Villanueva del
  Huerva 37 D4
Villanueva de los
  Castillejos 42 C2
Villanueva de los
  Infantes 44 B1
Villanueva del Río y
  Minas 43 D2
Villanueva del
  Trabuco 43 F3
Villanueva de San
  Carlos 44 A1
Villa Opicina 59 F3
Villa Potenza 61 F4
Villaquejida 35 D3
Villaquilambre 35 D2
Villarcayo 36 A1
Villard-de-Lans 30 C2
Villar de Cañas 40 C3
Villardeciervos 35 D3
Villar de Domingo
  García 40 C2
Villardefrades 35 E4
Villar del
  Arzobispo 41 E3
Villar del Rey 39 D4
Villar de Peralonso 39 E1
Villarejo de
  Fuentes 40 C3
Villarejo de Orbigo 35 D3
Villarejo de
  Salvanés 40 B2
Villarente 35 E3
Villares de la Reina 39 E1
Villares del Saz 40 C3
Villargordo de
  Cabriel 41 D4
Villaricos 44 C3
Villarín de Campos 35 D4
Villarino 34 C4
Villarquemado 41 D2
Villarramiel 35 E3
Villarrobledo 40 C4
Villarroya 36 C3
Villarroya de la
  Sierra 36 C4
Villarroya de los
  Pinares 41 E2
Villarroya, Pto de 41 E2
Villarrubia de
  Santiago 40 B3
Villars 27 E3
Villars-les-Dombes 26 C4
Villarta de San
  Juan 40 B4
Villarubia de los
  Ojos 40 A4
Villasalto 66 C3
Villasana de Mena 36 A1
Villasandino 35 F3
Villa San Giovanni 67 E4
Villa Santa Maria 64 A2
Villasante 36 A1
Villa Santina 59 E3
Villasarracino 35 E3
Villasayas, Pto de 36 B4
Villaseco de los
  Reyes 39 E1
Villasequilla de
  Yepes 40 A3
Villasimius 66 C4
Villasor 66 B4
Villatobas 40 B3
Villatoro, Pto de 39 F2
Villatoya 41 D4
Villava 36 C2
Villavaara 95 F2
Villaverde del Río 43 D2
Villaviciosa 35 E1
Villaviciosa de
  Córdoba 43 E2

Villaviciosa de Odón 40 A2
Villavieja de Yeltes 39 D1
Villa Vomano 63 F1
Villé 21 E4
Villebois-Lavalette 28 C1
Villedieu, la 25 D3
Villedieu-les-Poêles 18 B4
Ville-en-Tardenois 20 B3
Villefagnan 24 C4
Villefort 29 F3
Villefranche-d'Albigeois 29 E3
Villefranche-de-Lauragais 29 D4
Villefranche-de-Lonchat 28 C2
Villefranche-de-Rouergue 29 E3
Villefranche-du-Périgord 29 D2
Villefranche-sur-Cher 25 E2
Villefranche-sur-Mer 31 E3
Villefranche-sur-Saône 26 C4
Villel 41 D2
Villemur 29 D3
Villena 45 D1
Villenauxe-la-Grande 20 A4
Villeneuve 30 B3
Villeneuve-de-Berg 30 B2
Villeneuve-de-Marsan 28 B3
Villeneuve-l'Archevêque 26 A1
Villeneuve-sur-Lot 28 C3
Villeneuve-sur-Yonne 26 A1
Villeréal 28 C2
Villers 19 D3
Villers-Bocage (Calvados) 18 C3
Villers-Bocage (Somme) 19 F2
Villers-Bretonneux 19 F2
Villers-Cotterêts 19 F3
Villers-devant-Orval 20 C2
Villersexel 27 D2
Villers-Farlay 27 D2
Villers la Ville 50 C4
Villers-le-Lac 27 E2
Villerupt 21 D3
Villerville 19 D3
Ville-sur-Tourbe 20 C3
Villeta Barrea 64 A2
Villiers-St-Georges 20 A4
Villingen-Schwenningen 54 C3
Villoldo 35 E3
Villoria 39 E1
Villotta 59 E3
Villuercas 39 E3
Vilnius 110 C3
Vilppula 102 C3
Vils (Bayern) 55 F1
Vils (Bayern) 56 B2
Vilsbiburg 56 B2

Vilseck 55 F1
Vilshofen 56 C2
Vilusi 76 A2
Vilvoorde 50 B3
Vimercate 60 A1
Vimianzo 34 A1
Vimieiro 38 B4
Vimioso 34 C4
Vimmerby 109 E1
Vimoutiers 19 D4
Vimpeli 102 C2
Vimperk 56 C1
Vinac 71 E4
Vinadio 31 E3
Vinaixa 37 F4
Vinalapó, R 45 D2
Vinaròs 41 F2
Vinay 30 C1
Vinça 32 B2
Vinča 73 D3
Vinchiaturo 64 B3
Vinci 60 C3
Vindafjorden 104 A3
Vindelälven 102 A1
Vindelfjällens N.R. 97 E3
Vindeln 102 A1
Vinderup 108 A2
Vindsvik 104 A3
Vingåker 105 F4
Vingelen 100 C3
Vingeveien 100 C3
Vinhais 34 C3
Vinica (Makedonija) 77 F3
Vinica (SLO) 70 C3
Viničani 77 E3
Vinje 104 B3
Vinkovci 71 F2
Vinnica 113 E2
Vinsternes 100 B2
Vinstra 100 C3
Vinstri 104 C1
Vintilänkaira 95 F4
Viñuelas 40 B2
Vinuesa 36 B3
Viotía 83 F4
Vipava 70 A2
Vipava R 70 A2
Vipiteno 59 D2
Vir (BH) 75 E1
Vir (HRV) 70 C4
Vir I 70 C4
Vira 75 D2
Vire 18 C4
Virgen 59 E2
Virgen de la Cabeza 43 F2
Virginia 13 D3
Virieu 30 C1
Virieu-le-Grand 27 D4
Virihaure 97 F1
Virkby 107 E3
Virkkala 107 E3
Virkkula 99 E2
Virksund 108 A2
Virmasvesi 103 D2
Virmutjoki 103 F3
Virolahti 103 F4
Virónia 80 A2
Virovitica 71 E2
Virpazar 76 B3
Virrat 102 C3
Virsbo 105 F3
Virserum 109 E2

Virsko more 70 C4
Virtasalmi 103 E3
Virton 20 C3
Virtsu 110 B2
Vis 75 D2
Vis I 75 D2
Visaurin 37 D2
Visby 109 F4
Visé 51 D3
Višegrad 72 C4
Višegradska Banja 72 C4
Viserba 61 E3
Viseu 38 C1
Viševica 70 B3
Viskan 108 C2
Viški kan 75 D2
Višnja Gora 70 B2
Višnjica 73 D3
Visočica 75 F1
Visočica R 73 F4
Viso del Marqués 44 A1
Visoki Dečani 76 C2
Visoko 71 F4
Visovac 75 D1
Visp 27 F3
Vissani 78 B4
Visselhövede 48 A3
Vissenbjerg 108 B3
Vissiniá 79 D3
Visso 63 F1
Vistabella del Maestrazgo 41 E2
Vistasväggi 94 B4
Vistheden 98 B3
Vistonída, L 81 D2
Visuvesi 102 C3
Vitaby 109 D3
Vitala 84 B4
Vitanovac 73 D4
Vitebsk 111 E3
Viterbo 63 E2
Vitez 71 E4
Vitigudino 39 D1
Vitina 86 C2
Vitina (BH) 75 E2
Vitina (Kosovo) 77 D2
Vitlycke 105 D4
Vito d'Asio 59 E3
Vitoli 83 D3
Vitolište 77 E4
Vitomirica 76 C2
Vitoria-Gasteiz 36 B2
Vitorog 71 E4
Vitoša 115 D2
Vitovlje 71 E4
Vitré 23 D3
Vitrey 27 D1
Vitry-en-Artois 19 F2
Vitry-le-François 20 B4
Vitsa 78 C4
Vitsand 105 E2
Vittangi 94 C4
Vittangijälven 94 C4
Vitteaux 26 B2
Vittel 27 D1
Vittoria 69 D4
Vittoriosa 68 B4
Vittorio Veneto 59 E3
Vittsjö 109 D3
Vitznau 58 A2
Viù 31 E1
Vivaro 59 E3
Vivel del R Martín 41 E2
Viver 41 E3

Viverio 34 B1
Viverols 29 F1
Viveros 44 B1
Vivier, le 18 B4
Viviers 30 B2
Vivonne 25 D4
Vizille 30 C2
Vižinada 70 A3
Vizítsa 83 F2
Vižnica 113 D3
Vizzavona 33 F3
Vizzavona, Col de 33 F3
Vizzini 69 D4
Vjosë 114 B4
Vlaardingen 16 B3
Vladičin Han 77 E1
Vladievci 77 F3
Vladimirci 72 C3
Vladimirovac 73 D2
Vladimirovo 77 F3
Vladimir-Volynskij 112 C2
Vlagtwedde 17 E1
Vlaháva 83 D1
Vlahérna (Ípiros) 82 C2
Vlahérna (Pelopónnisos) 86 C2
Vlahiótis 87 D3
Vlahokerassiá 87 D2
Vlahomándra 83 D4
Vlahópoulo 86 C3
Vlanen 16 C3
Vlasenica 72 B4
Vlašič (BH) 71 E4
Vlašić (Srbija) 72 C3
Vlasina Okrugla 77 E1
Vlasinsko jez. 77 E1
Vlasotince 77 E1
Vlássio 83 D2
Vlásti 79 D3
Vlieland 16 C1
Vlihó 82 B3
Vlissingen 16 B4
Vlorë 114 B4
Vlotho 17 F2
Vltava 53 F3
Vobbia 60 A2
Vočin 71 E2
Vöcklabruck 56 C3
Vodice (Rijeka) 70 A3
Vodice (Šibenik) 74 C1
Vodna 73 E3
Vodňany 56 C1
Vodnjan 70 A4
Voe 3 F1
Vogatsikó 79 D3
Vogel 70 A2
Vogelsberg 52 A4
Vogelsdorf 49 E4
Voghera 60 A2
Vogošča 72 B4
Vohenstrauß 56 B1
Vöhringen 55 E3
Void 20 C4
Voikoski 107 F1
Vóïo, Óros 78 C4
Voiron 30 C1
Voiteur 26 C3
Voitsberg 57 E4
Vojens 108 A3
Vojka 72 C3
Vojmsjön 97 F4
Vojnić 70 C3
Vojnik 70 B1

Vojska 73 D3
Vojtanov 53 D4
Vojvodina 72 C2
Volary 56 C2
Volchov 111 E1
Volchov R 111 E1
Volda 100 A3
Voldafjorden 100 A2
Volders 59 D2
Volendam 16 C2
Volga 111 F1
Volimes 86 A1
Volissós 85 E4
Volkach 52 B4
Völkermarkt 70 B1
Volkmarsen 52 A2
Volkovija 77 D3
Volkovysk 110 C4
Volmunster 21 E3
Voločisk 113 D2
Volokolamsk 111 F2
Volonne 31 D3
Vólos 83 F2
Voložin 111 D4
Volpiano 31 E1
Volta 60 C1
Volterra 60 C4
Voltri 60 A3
Volturara Appula 64 B3
Volturino, Mte 64 C4
Volturno 64 A3
Volvic 26 A4
Völvi, L 80 B3
Volyn' 113 D2
Volyně 56 C1
Vonitsa 82 C3
Vonnas 26 C4
Voors 17 D2
Voorschoten 16 B3
Voorthuizen 16 C2
Vopnafjörður 96 C1
Vöra 102 B2
Vorarlberg 58 B2
Vóras, Óros 79 E2
Vorchdorf 56 C3
Vordernberg 57 E4
Vorderrhein 58 A3
Vorderriß 56 A4
Vordingborg 108 C4
Vorë 76 C4
Voreppe 30 C1
Vorey 30 A1
Vóri 91 D4
Vória Píndos 78 C4
Vóries Sporádes 84 C2
Vøringfossen 104 B2
Vórios Evoïkós Kólpos 83 F3
Vório Stenó Kerkíras 82 A1
Vorma 105 D3
Vormsi 110 B1
Vorna 99 D4
Voronet 113 D3
Vorsfelde 48 B4
Vorskla 113 F2
Vörtsjärv 110 C2
Võru 110 C2

Votonóssi 82 C1
Voúdia 88 B4
Vouga, R 38 C1
Vouglans, Lac de 27 D3
Vouhorina 79 D4
Vouillé 25 D3
Voukoliés 90 B3
Voúla 87 F1
Voulgára 83 D2
Vouliagméni 87 F1
Voulkariá, L 82 B3
Voúlpi 83 D3
Voulte, la 30 B2
Vouná Goúras 83 E2
Vouraïkós 86 C1
Voúrinos, Óros 79 D4
Vourkári 88 A2
Vourliótes 89 E1
Voúrvoura 87 D2
Vourvouroú 80 B4
Voutás 83 F3
Vouvant 24 C3
Vouvray 25 D2
Voúxa, Akr 90 B3
Voves 25 E1
Vovoússa 78 C4
Voxnan 101 E4
Vöyri 102 B2
Voz 70 B3
Vozarci 77 E3
Voznesensk 113 F3
Vrå 108 B2
Vraháti 87 D1
Vrahiónas, Óros 86 A2
Vrahnéika 86 C1
Vrams-Gunnarstorp 108 C3
Vrana 70 B4
Vrancei, M 113 D4
Vranduk 71 F4
Vranica 71 E4
Vranja 70 A3
Vranjak 75 F2
Vranje 77 E2
Vranjska Banja 77 E2
Vranovská přehr nádrž 57 E1
Vran pl 75 E1
Vransko 70 B2
Vransko jezero 74 C1
Vratama 80 B3
Vratarnica 73 F4
Vratnica 77 D2
Vratnik 70 B3
Vratno 70 C1
Vražogrnac 73 F3
Vrbanja 72 B3
Vrbanja R 71 E3
Vrbas 72 B2
Vrbas R 71 E3
Vrbas klisura 71 E4
Vrbljani 71 D4
Vrbnica 77 D3
Vrbnik 70 B3
Vrboska 75 E2

Vrbovec 71 D2
Vrbovsko 70 B3
Vrčin 73 D3
Vrdnik 72 C2
Vreden 17 E3
Vrela 76 C2
Vrelo (HR) 70 C4
Vrelo (Srbija) 73 E4
Vreoci 72 C3
Vresse 20 C2
Vrésthena 87 D3
Vreta Kloster 106 A4
Vrginmost 70 C3
Vrgorac 75 E2
Vrh Kapele 70 C3
Vrhnika 70 A2
Vrhpolje 71 D4
Vría 79 E4
Vrinena 83 F3
Vríssa 85 F3
Vrísses 90 C3
Vrissiá 83 E2
Vrissoúla 82 B2
Vrlika 75 D1
Vrnjačka Banja 73 D4
Vrnograč 70 C3
Vrondádos 85 F4
Vrondamás 87 D3
Vronderó 78 C4
Vrondissi 91 D4
Vrondoú 79 E4
Vrondoús, Óri 80 B2
Vrossina 82 B1
Vrouhás 91 E3
Vrpolje (Osijek) 71 F2
Vrpolje (Šibenik) 75 D1
Vršac 73 D2
Vršani 72 B3
Vrsar 70 A3
Vrsi 70 C4
Vrška Čuka 73 F4
Vrtac 76 B2
Vrtoče 71 D4
Vrutok 77 D3
Vučitrn 77 D2
Vučjak 77 F3
Vučje 77 E1
Vučkovica 73 D4
Vue des Alpes 27 E2
Vuka 71 F2
Vukovar 72 B2
Vulcano, I 69 D2
Vulture, Mte 64 B3
Vuohijärvi 107 F2
Vuohijärvi L 107 F1
Vuokatti 99 E4
Vuokkijärvi 99 E3
Vuokojaure 94 C3
Vuoksenniska 103 F3
Vuolijoki 99 E4
Vuollerim 98 B2
Vuolvojaure 98 A2
Vuonislahti 103 F2
Vuorji 95 D2
Vuosjärvi 103 D2
Vuoskuvarri 95 D3
Vuostimo 99 E2
Vuotso 95 E3
Vyškov 57 F1
Vyšnij Voločok 111 E2

W

Waal 16 C3
Waalwijk 16 C3
Waasmunster 50 B3
Wabern 52 A3
Wachau 57 E2
Wachow 49 D4
Wächtersbach 52 A4
Waddeneilanden 16 C1
Wadebridge 8 B3
Wädenswil 58 A2

Wagenfeld 17 F2
Wageningen 17 D3
Waging 56 B3
Wagrain 59 E1
Wągrowiec 112 A1
Wahlstedt 48 A2
Waiblingen 55 D2
Waidhaus 56 B1
Waidhofen (Ybbs) 57 D3
Waidhofen (Thaya) 57 E2
Waidring 59 E1
Waischenfeld 52 C4
Waizenkirchen 56 C2

Wakefield 7 D2
Wałbrzych 112 A2
Walchensee 56 A4
Walcheren 16 B3
Walchsee 59 D1
Wałcz 112 A1
Wald 58 A2
Waldbröl 17 E4
Waldeck 52 A2
Waldenbuch 55 D3
Waldenburg 53 D3
Waldfischbach-Burgalben 54 B2

Waldheim 53 E2
Waldkappel 52 B3
Waldkirch 54 C3
Waldkirchen 56 C2
Waldkraiburg 56 B3
Wald-Michelbach 54 C1
Waldmünchen 56 B1
Waldsassen 53 D4
Waldshut 54 C4
Walensee 58 B2
Walenstadt 58 B2
Wales 8 C1
Wallasey 6 B2

Walldorf 54 C2
Walldürn 55 D1
Wallenfels 52 C4
Wallersdorf 56 B2
Wallerstein 55 E2
Wallingford 9 E2
Walls 3 F2
Walsall 9 E1
Walsrode 48 A4
Walsum 17 D3
Waltershausen 52 B3
Walton-on-the-Naze 11 D2

Waltrop 17 E3
Wanderup 48 A1
Wandlitz 49 E3
Wanfried 52 B2
Wangen 55 E4
Wangenbourg 21 E4
Wangerland-Hooksiel 47 E3
Wangerooge 47 E2
Wängi 58 A1
Wanna 47 F2
Wanne-Eickel 17 E3
Wantage 9 E2

Wantzenau, la 21 E4
Wanzleben 52 C1
Warburg 52 A2
Wardenburg 47 F3
Ware 9 F2
Waregem 50 B3
Wareham 9 D3
Waremme 50 C3
Waren 49 D2
Warendorf 17 F3
Warin 48 C2
Warkworth 5 E3
Warmensteinach 53 D4

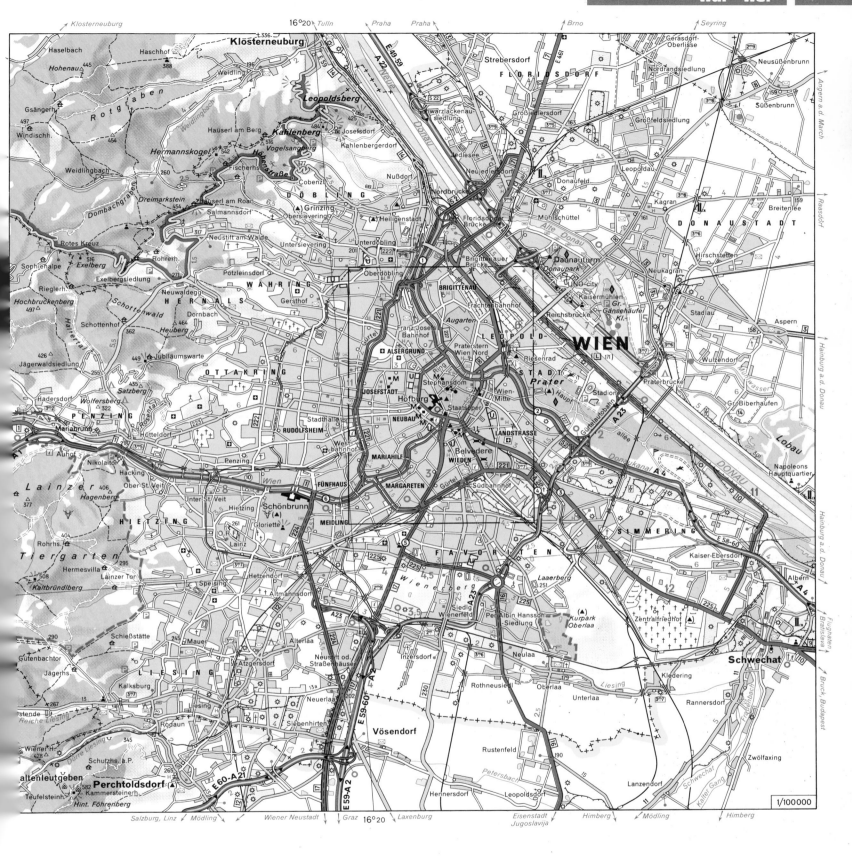

Warminster 9 E3	Warwick 9 E1	Wasser-Kuppe 52 B3	Waterloo 50 B3	Waxweiler 51 D4	Weggis 27 F2	Weil der Stadt 55 D2
Warnemunde 48 C2	Warwickshire 9 E1	Wassertrüdingen .. 55 E2	Waternish Pt. 2 B1	Wear 5 E4	Węgorzewo 110 B4	Weilheim (Baden-
Warnow 48 C2	Washington 5 E4	Wassigny 20 A2	Waterville 14 A4	Wechsel 57 E3	Węgorzyno 49 F2	Württemberg) ... 55 D3
Warrenpoint 13 E3	Wash, The 7 E3	Wassy 20 C4	Watford 9 F2	Wedel 48 A3	Wegscheid 56 C2	Weilheim (Bayern) .. 56 A3
Warrington 6 B2	Wasselonne 21 E4	Wasungen 52 B3	Wattens 59 D2	Wedemark-| Wegberg 17 D4	Weimar 52 C3
Warstein 17 F3	Wassen 58 A3	Watchet 8 C3	Watton 11 D1	Mellendorf 48 A4	Weferlingen 48 C4	Weinfelden 58 A1
Warszawa 112 B1	Wassenaar 16 B3	Waterfoot 13 E1	Wattwil 58 A2	Weener 47 E3	Wegeleben 52 C1	Weingarten 55 D4
Warszów 49 E2	Wassenberg 17 D4	Waterford 15 D4	Watzmann 56 C4	Weert 17 D4	Weichshofen 56 B2	Weinheim 54 C1
Warta 49 F3	Wasseralfingen ... 55 E2	Waterford (Co) 14 C4	Waulsort 50 C4	Weferlingen 48 C4	Weida 53 D3	Weinsberg 55 D2
Warth 58 B2	Wasserbillig 21 D2	Waterford	Waveney 11 D1	Weiden 56 A1	Weikersheim 55 D1	Weismain 52 C4
Wartha 52 B3	Wasserburg 56 B3	Harbour 15 D4	Wavre 50 C3	Weikersheim 55 D1	Weilburg 51 F4	Weißbriach 59 F2

Weiße Elster 53 D3
Weißenbach 58 C1
Weißenberg 53 F2
Weißenburg 55 F2
Weißenfels 53 D2
Weißenhorn 55 E3
Weißenkirchen 57 E2
Weißensee 52 C2
Weißensee (L) 59 F2
Weissenstadt 53 D4
Weissenstein 27 E2
Weissfluhgipfel 58 B2
Weißkirchen 57 D4
Weißkugel 58 C2
Weißwasser 53 F1
Weitra 57 D2
Weiz 57 E4
Wejherowo 110 A4
Weldon 9 F1
Welgetschlag 57 D2
Welland 9 F1
Wellin 20 C2
Wellingborough 9 F1
Wellington 9 D3
Wellington Bridge . . 15 D4
Wells 9 D3
Wells-next-the-Sea . . 7 E3
Wels 56 C3
Welsberg 59 D2
Welschnofen 59 D3
Welshpool 9 D1
Weltenburg 55 F2
Welwyn Garden City . 9 F2
Welzheim 55 D2
Wem 6 B3
Wemding 55 E2
Wemyss Bay 4 C2
Wendelstein 56 B4
Wenden 52 B1
Wengen 27 F3
Wenns 58 C2
Werbellinsee 49 E3
Werben 48 C3
Werdau 53 D3
Werder 49 D4
Werdohl 17 E4
Werfen 59 E1
Werl 17 F3
Werlte 17 E1
Wermelskirchen 17 E4

Wermsdorf 53 E2
Wernberg 56 B1
Werne 17 E3
Werneck 52 B4
Werneuchen 49 E4
Wernigerode 52 C1
Werra 52 B3
Wertach 55 E4
Wertach (R) 55 E3
Wertheim 55 D1
Werther 17 F2
Wertingen 55 E3
Wervik 50 A3
Wesel 17 D3
Wesenberg 49 D3
Wesendorf 48 B4
Weser 47 F3
Weser-Elbe-Kanal . . 48 C4
Wesselburen 47 F2
Wessobrunn 56 A3
West Auckland 5 E4
West Bridgford . . . 7 D3
Westbury 9 D3
Westendorf 59 D1
Westenholz 48 A4
Westerburg 51 F4
Westerholt 47 E3
Westerland 47 F1
Westerlo 50 C3
Westernbödefeld . . 17 F4
Western Isles 2 B2
Wester Ross 2 C3
Westerstede 47 E3
Westerwald 51 E3
Westhofen 54 C1
West Kilbride 4 C2
West Linton 5 D2
West Loch Tarbert . . 2 A2
Westmeath 12 C3
West Mersea 11 D2
Weston-super-
Mare 9 D2
Westport 12 B3
Westray 3 E1
Westray Firth 3 E1
West Sussex 9 F3
West-Terschelling . . 16 C1
West-Vlaanderen . . 50 A3
Wetherby 7 D2
Wetter 17 E3

Wetteren 50 B3
Wettin 52 C2
Wettringen 17 E2
Wetwang 7 D1
Wetzikon 58 A2
Wetzlar 51 F3
Wexford (Co) 15 D3
Wexford 15 D3
Weyer-Markt 57 D3
Weyhausen 48 B4
Weyhill 9 E3
Weymouth 9 D3
Weyregg 56 C3
Whaley Bridge 6 C2
Whalsay 3 F1
Wharfe 6 C1
Whernside 6 C1
Whitburn 5 D2
Whitby 5 F4
Whitchurch 6 B3
Whitebridge 2 C4
Whitehaven 5 D4
Whitehead 13 E2
Whiteness 3 F2
Whiten Head 2 C2
Whithorn 4 C4
Whitland 8 B2
Whitley Bay 5 E3
Whitstable 11 D3
Whittlesey 9 F1
Wick 3 D2
Wickford 11 D2
Wicklow 13 E4
Wicklow (Co) 13 D4
Wicklow Head 13 E4
Wicklow Mts 13 D4
Widnes 6 B2
Wiehe 52 C2
Wiek 49 D1
Wieliczka 112 B3
Wieluń 112 B2
Wien 57 F2
Wiener-Neudorf 57 F2
Wiener Neustadt . . 57 F3
Wienerwald 57 E3
Wies (A) 70 B1
Wies (D) 56 A4
Wiesau 53 D4
Wiesbaden 51 F4
Wieselburg 57 E3

Wiesenburg 53 D1
Wiesensteig 55 D3
Wiesentheid 55 E1
Wiesenttal 52 C4
Wiesing 59 D1
Wiesloch 54 C2
Wiesmath 57 F3
Wiesmoor 47 E3
Wigan 6 C2
Wight, I of 9 E4
Wigton 5 D4
Wigtown 4 C3
Wigtown B 4 C4
Wijhe 17 D2
Wil 58 A2
Wildalpen 57 D3
Wildbad 54 C2
Wildeck 52 B3
Wildeshausen 17 F1
Wildon 57 E4
Wildspitze 58 C2
Wildstrubel 27 E3
Wilfersdorf 57 F2
Wilhelmina kan 16 C3
Wilhelm Pieck-
Stadt 53 F1
Wilhelmsburg (A) . . 57 E3
Wilhelmsburg (D) . . 48 A3
Wilhelmshaven 47 F3
Wilhering 57 D2
Wilkau-Haßlau 53 D3
Willebroek 50 B3
Willemstad 16 B3
Willingen 17 F4
Williton 8 C3
Wilmslow 6 C2
Wilnsdorf 17 F4
Wilsdruff 53 E2
Wilseder Berg 48 A3
Wilster 48 A2
Wilton 9 E3
Wiltshire 9 E3
Wiltz 21 D2
Wimborne Minster . . 9 E3
Wimereux 19 E1
Wincanton 9 D3
Winchcombe 9 E2
Winchelsea 11 D3
Winchester 9 E3
Windeck 51 E3

Windermere 5 D4
Windischeschenbach
. . . . 53 D4
Windischgarsten . . 57 D3
Windsbach 55 E1
Windsor 9 F2
Winkleigh 8 C3
Winklern 59 E2
Winnenden 55 D2
Winnigstedt 52 B1
Winnweiler 54 B1
Winschoten 47 E3
Winsen (Celle) 48 A4
Winsen
(Lüneburg) 48 B3
Winsford 6 C3
Winsum 47 D3
Winterberg 17 F4
Winterswijk 17 D3
Winterthur 58 A2
Wintzenheim 27 E1
Wipper 52 C2
Wipperfürth 17 E4
Wisbech 10 C1
Wischhafen 48 A2
Wisełka 49 E2
Wishaw 4 C2
Wisła 110 B4
Wismar 48 C2
Wissant 19 E1
Wissembourg 21 F3
Wissen 51 E3
Witham R 7 D3
Witham 11 D2
Withernsea 7 E2
Witney 9 E2
Witnica 49 F3
Wittdün 47 F1
Witte 49 D1
Witten 17 E3
Wittenberg 53 D1
Wittenberge 48 C3
Wittenburg 48 B3
Wittichenau 53 F2
Wittingen 48 B4
Wittlich 51 E4
Wittmund 47 E3
Wittow 49 D1
Wittstock 49 D3
Witzenhausen 52 B2

Władysławowo 110 A4
Włocławek 112 B1
Włodawa 112 C2
Wöbbelin 48 C3
Woburn 9 F2
Woburn Abbey 9 F2
Woensdrecht 16 B4
Woerden 16 C3
Wohlen 27 F2
Woippy 21 D3
Woking 9 F3
Wokingham 9 F2
Wołczenica 49 F2
Woldegk 49 E2
Wolfach 54 C3
Wolfegg 55 E4
Wolfen 53 D2
Wolfenbüttel 52 B1
Wolfhagen 52 A2
Wolfratshausen 56 A3
Wolfsberg 70 B1
Wolfsburg 48 B4
Wolgast 49 E2
Wolin 49 E2
Wolin (Reg) 49 E2
Woliński Park
Narodowy 49 E2
Wolkenstein 59 D3
Wolkersdorf 57 F2
Wöllersdorf 57 F3
Wollersheim 51 D3
Wollin 49 D4
Wolmirstedt 48 C4
Wolsingham 5 E4
Wolsztyn 112 A2
Wolvega 17 D1
Wolverhampton 9 E1
Wolverton 9 F1
Wolznach 55 F2
Woodbridge 11 D1
Woodhall Spa 7 E3
Woodstock 9 E2
Wooler 5 E3
Worb 27 E2
Worbis 52 B2
Worcester 9 D1
Wörgl 59 D1
Workington 5 D4
Worksop 7 D2
Workum 16 C1

Wörlitz 53 D1
Wormerveer 16 C2
Wormhout 19 F1
Worms 54 C1
Worms Head 8 C2
Wörnitz 55 E2
Wörrstadt 54 C1
Wörth (Donau) 56 B2
Wörth (Main) 55 D1
Wörth (Rheinland-
Pfalz) 54 C2
Worther See 70 A1
Worthing 10 C3
Woświn, Jez 49 F2
Wragby 7 D3
Wrath, Cape 2 C2
Wrecsam 6 B3
Wrexham 6 B3
Wriezen 49 E3
Wrocław 112 A2
Wroughton 9 E2
Września 112 A1
Wulfen 17 E3
Wullowitz 57 D2
Wümme 48 A3
Wümme R 48 A3
Wünnenberg 17 F3
Wünsdorf 49 E4
Wunsiedel 53 D4
Wunstorf 48 A4
Wuppertal 17 E4
Würzburg 55 D1
Wurzen 53 D2
Wurzen-Paß 59 D2
Wusterhausen 49 D3
Wustrow
(Rostock) 48 C1
Wustrow
(Wismar) 48 C2
Wuustwezel 50 C2
Wye, R 9 D2
Wyk 47 F1
Wymondham 11 D1

X

Xallas, R 34 A2
Xanten 17 D3

Xánthi 81 D2
Xánthi (Nomos) 81 D2
Xarrama, R 42 B1
Xàtiva 41 E4
Xeresa 41 E4

Xerovoúni 82 C2
Xerta 41 F2
Xertigny 27 D1
Xesta, Pto de la . . 34 C1
Xifianí 79 E2

Xilaganí 81 E2
Xilikí 83 E3
Xilis, Akr 87 D4
Xilókastro 87 D1
Xilopáriko 83 D2

Xilópoli 80 A2
Xilóskalo 90 B3
Xiniáda 83 E3
Xinó Neró 79 D3
Xinzo de Limia 34 B3

Xiró 83 F3
Xirokámbi 87 D3
Xirókambos 89 E3
Xirolimni 79 D3
Xistral 34 B1

Xódoto, Akr 89 D3
Xubia 34 B1
Xunqueira de
Ambia 34 B3

Y

Yaiza 42 C4
Yalova 115 F3
Yanguas 36 B3
Yare 7 F4
Yarmouth 9 E3
Yarmouth, Great 7 F4
Ybbs 57 D2
Ybbs R 57 D3

Yebra 40 B2
Yecla 45 D1
Yeguas, Emb de . . 43 F2
Yeguas, R de las . . 43 F1
Yell 3 F1
Yell Sd 3 F1
Yelmo 44 B2
Yeltes, R. 39 D1
Yenne 27 D4
Yeovil 9 D3
Yepes 40 B3

Yerville 19 D3
Yesa 36 C2
Yesa, Emb de 37 D2
Yeşilova 115 F4
Yeste 44 C1
Yeu, I d' 24 A3
Yèvre 26 A2
Y-Fenni 9 D2
Yıldız Dağları 115 E3
Ylämaa 103 F4
Ylämylly 103 F2

Yläne 107 D2
Ylihärmä 102 C2
Yli-Kärppä 99 D3
Ylikiiminki 99 D3
Yli-Kitka 99 E2
Yli-Ii 99 D3
Yli-Muonio 95 D4
Yli-Nampa 99 D2
Yli-Olhava 99 D3
Ylistaro 102 B2
Ylitornio 98 C2

Ylivieska 102 C1
Ylläs 95 D4
Ylläsjärvi 95 D4
Ylöjärvi 102 C3
Yngaren 106 A4
Yonne 20 A4
Yonne (Dépt) 26 A1
York 7 D2
Yorkshire Dales
Nat Pk 6 C1
Youghal 14 C4

Youghal B 14 C4
Yoxford 11 E1
Ypäjä 107 E2
Yport 19 D2
Yppäri 99 D4
Ypres 50 A3
Yr Wyddgrug 6 B3
Yser 19 F1
Yssingeaux 30 B1
Ystad 109 D4
Y Trallwng 9 D1

Ytterhogdal 101 E3
Yttermalung 105 E2
Yuncos 40 A2
Yunquera 43 E4
Yunquera de
Henares 40 B2
Yuste 39 E2
Yverdon 27 E3
Yvetot 19 D3
Yvoir 50 C4
Yvoire 27 D3

z

Zaandam 16 C2
Žabali 72 C2
Žabari 73 D3
Zablaće 75 D1
Žabljak (Durmitor) . 76 B1
Žabljak (Podgorica) . 76 B3
Žabno 71 D2
Zabok 70 C2
Zabrddđe 72 B3
Zadar 74 C1
Zadarski kanal 70 B4
Zadvarje 75 E2
Zafarraya 43 F3
Zafóra, Ni 92 C2
Zafra 43 D1
Žaga 70 A2
Žagań 112 A2
Zaglavak 72 C4
Zagora 83 F2
Zagória 82 C1
Zagorje 70 B2
Zagreb 70 C2
Žagubica 73 E3
Zagvozd 75 E2
Zahara de los
   Atunes 43 D4
Zahara, Emb de . . . 43 E3
Zaháro 86 B2
Zahinos 42 C1
Zahna 53 D1
Záhony 112 C1
Zaidín 37 E4
Zajas 77 D3
Zaječar 73 F3
Zákinthos 86 A1
Zákinthos, N 86 A1
Zakopane 112 B3
Zákros 91 F4
Zala 112 A4
Zalaegerszeg 112 A4
Zalamea de la
   Serena 43 E1
Zalamea la Real 42 C2
Zalău 112 C4
Žalec 70 B2
Zaleščiki 113 D3
Zalew Wiślany 110 B4
Zalla 36 A1
Zálongo 82 B2
Zaltbommel 16 C3
Zalužnica 70 C4
Zambrana 36 B2
Zamora 35 D4
Zamość 112 C2
Záncara, R 40 B4
Zándvoort 16 B2
Zángano, Pto del . . 39 D4
Zanglivéri 80 A3
Zannone, I 63 F4
Zaorejas 40 C2
Zaostrog 75 E2
Zaovine Vežanja . . . 72 C4
Zapadnaja Dvina . . . 111 E2
Zapadnaja Dvina
   R 111 E2
Zapadna Morava . . . 73 D4
Zapardiel, R 39 F1
Zapatón, R 39 D3
Zápio 83 E2
Zapponeta 64 C3
Zaprešić 70 C2
Zaragoza 37 D3
Zárakes 84 B4
Zaratán 35 E4

Zarautz 36 C1
Zarcilla de Ramos . . 44 C2
Zárkos 83 E1
Zarós 91 D4
Zaroúhla 87 D1
Zarrentin 48 B3
Žary 112 A2
Zarza la Mayor 39 D2
Zasieki 53 F1
Žaškov 113 E2
Žatec 53 E3
Zatoka Gdańska . . . 110 B4
Zaton 75 F2
Zavala 75 F2
Zavattarello 60 A2
Zavidovići 71 F4
Zavlaka 72 C3
Zavratnica 70 B4
Zawiercie 112 B2
Žažina 71 D2
Zbaraž 113 D2
Zbraslav 53 F4
Žďár nad
   Sázavou 112 A3
Zdenac 70 C3
Zdice 53 F4
Ždrelac 74 C1
Ždrelo 73 E3
Zdunje 77 D3
Zduńska Wola 112 B2
Zebë, Maj'e 76 C3
Zebreira 38 C2
Žednik 72 B1
Zeebrugge 50 A3
Zeeland 16 B3
Zefiría 88 A4
Žegovac 77 D2
Žegra 77 D2
Žegulja 75 F2
Zehdenick 49 D3
Zeist 16 C3
Zeitz 53 D2
Zejtun 68 B4
Žekovec 70 B1
Zele 50 B3
Zelengora 76 A1
Zelengora (Reg) . . . 76 A1
Zelenika 76 A3
Zelenogorsk 111 D1
Železná Ruda 56 C1
Železnik 72 C3
Železniki 70 A2
Železnogorsk 111 F4
Zelina 70 C2
Zélio 83 F3
Željezno Polje 71 F4
Željin 73 D4
Zell (D) 54 B1
Zell
   (Oberösterreich) . . 56 C2
Zell (Tirol) 59 D2
Zella-Mehlis 52 C3
Zell am See 59 E1
Zellerrain 57 E3
Zeltweg 57 D4
Zelzate 50 B3
Zemun 72 C3
Zenica 71 F4
Zen'kov 113 F2
Žep 72 B4
Žepče 71 F4
Zerbst 53 D1
Zeri 60 B3
Zermatt 27 F4
Zernez 58 B3
Zerqan 77 D4
Zestoa 36 B1

Zeta 76 B2
Zetel 47 E3
Zeulenroda 53 D3
Zeven 48 A3
Zevenaar 17 D3
Zevgaráki 82 C4
Zevgolatió 86 C3
Zevio 60 C1
Zêzere, R 38 C2
Žiča 73 D4
Židlochovice 57 F1
Ziefsdorf 57 F2
Ziegenrück 52 C3
Zielona Góra 112 A2
Zierikzee 16 B3
Zierzow 48 C3
Ziesar 49 D4
Zi, Guri i 77 D4
Zijemlje 75 F1
Žilina 112 B3
Žilindar 76 C1
Ziller 59 D2
Zillertal 59 D1
Zimnicea 115 D2
Zinal 27 F4
Zingst 49 D1
Zinnowitz 49 E1
Zinnwald 53 E3
Zirbitzkogel 57 D4
Zirchow 49 E2
Žiri 70 A2
Žirje 74 C1
Zirl 58 C2
Zirndorf 55 E1
Žiros 91 F4
Zistersdorf 57 F2
Žitište 72 C2
Žitkovac 73 E4
Žitkoviči 113 D1
Žitomir 113 E2
Žitomislići 75 F1
Žitoradđa 77 D1
Zittau 53 F2
Živinice 71 F3
Živogošće 75 E2
Žizdra 111 F3
Zjum 77 D2
Zlarin 75 D1
Zlarin I 75 D1
Zlata 77 D1
Zlatar 76 B1
Zlatar Bistrica 70 C2
Zlatarevo 77 F3
Zlatari 77 D1
Zlatarsko jez 76 B1
Zlatibor 72 C4
Zlatica 72 C4
Zlatni Pjasáci 115 E2
Zlatokop 77 E2
Zletovo 77 E2
Zlín 112 A3
Žljebovi 72 B4
Žlobin 111 E4
Zlot 73 E3
Žlutice 53 E4
Žman 74 C1
Žmerinka 113 E3
Žminj 70 A3
Znamenka 113 F2
Znojmo 57 E1
Zöblitz 53 E3
Zoetermeer 16 B3
Zogaj 76 C2
Zollikofen 27 E2
Zoločev 113 D2

Zolotonoša 113 F2
Žoltyje Vody 113 F2
Zonári, Akr 93 F1
Zóni 81 F1
Zonianá 91 D3
Zonza 33 F4
Zoodóhos Pigí
   (Makedonía) 79 E3
Zoodóhos Pigíí
   (Pelopónissos) 87 F2
Zörbig 53 D2
Zorita 39 E3
Zossen 49 E4
Zoúrvas, Akr 87 F2
Zoutkamp 47 D3
Zoutleeuw 50 C3
Zoúzouli 78 C4
Zrenjanin 72 C2
Zrin 71 D3
Zrinska gora 71 D3
Zrmanja R 74 C1
Zrmanja 75 D1
Žrnovnica 75 D2
Zrze 77 D2
Zschopau 53 E3
Zschopau R 53 E3

Zubcov 111 F2
Zubin Potoku 76 C2
Žuč 77 D1
Zucaina 41 E3
Zuckerhütl 58 C2
Zudar 49 D1
Zuera 37 D3
Zufre 43 D2
Zufre, Emb de 43 D2
Zug 58 A2
Zugspitze 55 F4
Zuid Beveland 16 B4
Zuidelijk-
   Flevoland 16 C2
Zuid Holland 16 B3
Zuidlaren 17 D1
Zújar 44 A3
Zújar, Emb del 39 E4
Zújar, R 43 E1
Žukovka 111 F3
Zuljana 75 E2
Zülpich 51 D3
Zumaia 36 B1
Zumárraga 36 B1
Zundert 16 C3
Zuoz 58 B3

Županja 71 F3
Žur 77 D3
Zürich 58 A2
Zurrieq 68 B4
Zürs 58 B2
Zurzach 58 A1
Zusmarshausen 55 E3
Žut 74 C1
Žuta Lokva 70 C3
Zutphen 17 D2
Žužemberk 70 B2
Zvečan 77 D1
Zvenigorodka 113 E2
Zvijezda nac park . . 72 C4
Zvikovec 53 E4
Zvolen 112 B3
Zvonce 77 E1
Zvorničko jez 72 B4
Zvornik 72 B4
Zweibrücken 54 B2
Zweisimmen 27 E3
Zwenkau 53 D2
Zwettl (Nieder-
   österreich) 57 D2
Zwettl
   (Oberösterreich) . . . 57 D2

Zwickau 53 D3
Zwickauer Mulde . . . 53 D3
Zwiefalten 55 D3
Zwiesel 56 C2
Zwijndrecht 16 C3
Zwolle 17 D2
Żyrardów 112 B1
Żywiec 112 B3

Þ

Þingeyri 96 A1
Þingvallavatn 96 A2
Þingvellir 96 A2
Þistilfjörður 96 C1
Þjórsá 96 B2
Þórlákshöfn 96 A2
Þórshöfn 96 C1
Þórsmörk 96 B3

Map of Zürich, scale 1/80 000